✦ ✦ ✦

COMING OF AGE

COMING OF AGE

America in the Twentieth Century

Michael Schaller
University of Arizona

Virginia Scharff
University of New Mexico

Robert D. Schulzinger
University of Colorado, Boulder

HOUGHTON MIFFLIN COMPANY
Boston New York

We dedicate this book to our children:
Nicholas, Gabriel, and Daniel Schaller
Sam and Ann Swift
Elizabeth Anne Schulzinger

Editor-in-Chief: Jean Woy
Senior Associate Editor: Fran Gay
Senior Project Editor: Carol Newman
Associate Production/Design Coordinator: Jodi O'Rourke
Manufacturing Coordinator: Andrea Wagner
Marketing Manager: Sandra McGuire

Cover design: Sarah Melhado
Cover image: Richard Estes, Untitled (Columbus Circle), Allan Stone Gallery.

Chapter opening photos: p. 1 Library of Congress; p. 39 Picture Research Consultants; p. 76 Imperial War Museum; p. 115 George Rinhart/Corbis-Bettmann; p. 155 Franklin D. Roosevelt Library; p. 194 Franklin D. Roosevelt Library; p. 232 National Archives; p. 269 Loomis Dean, *Life* magazine © Time Warner, Inc.; p. 316 Joe Scherschel, *Life* magazine; p. 353 Art and Artifact Division, Schomberg Center for Research in Black Culture, the New York Public Library, Astor, Lenox, and Tilden foundations; p. 391 Wide World Photos; p. 430 Lisa Law/The Image Works; p. 467 Corbis-Bettmann; p. 518 R. Bossu/Sygma; p. 561 Bob Daemmrich/The Image Works.

Biographical profiles: p. 10 Collection of Greg Martin; p. 63 Library of Congress; p. 96 National Archives; p. 123 Henry Ford and Greenfield Villages Museums; p. 166 Library of Congress; p. 216 National Portrait Gallery, Smithsonian Institution, Washington, D.C.; p. 249 a: Wide World Photos; b: Corbis-Bettmann; p. 290 Robert Phillips, *Life* magazine © Time Warner, Inc.; p. 346 F. DeWitt; p. 370 Burt Glinn/Magnum; p. 414 Claus C. Meyer/Black Star; p. 461 Alfred Eisenstadt, *Life* magazine © Time Warner, Inc.; p. 478 Corbis-Bettmann; p. 550 a: Corbis-Bettmann; b: Corbis-Bettmann; p. 568 Corbis-Bettmann.

Printed in the U.S.A.

Library of Congress Catalog Card Number: 97-72545

ISBN: 0-395-67309-7

123456789-DH-02 01 00 99 98

CONTENTS

11

Thc Victnam Quagmire, 1961–1968 *391*

12

Cultural Revolutions, 1960–1980 *429*

13

A Crisis of Confidence and Some New Opportunities, 1969–1980 *467*

14

Illusion and Renewal: Conservatism Ascendant, 1980–1992 *517*

MAPS

CHARTS

PREFACE

The eve of the twenty-first century offers a unique opportunity to take a fresh look at the last hundred years. Students often enroll in courses on the history of the United States from the 1890s to the present to try to understand the forces that have shaped the world in which they live. We call this book *Coming of Age* because we believe that the United States in the turbulent twentieth century became a modern society with a developed economy, a nation ever more deeply involved in events outside its borders.

We wrote this book after the Cold War ended. The passing of that nearly fifty-year-long conflict between the United States and the Soviet Union allows historians to see many previously obscured continuities between our own day and earlier eras in American history. As we look forward to the next hundred years, we are struck by how many of the contentious issues of the transition from the nineteenth to the twentieth century have endured. We try to point out these continuities in *Coming of Age*. Then, as now, the United States economy was in the midst of a profound economic transition. At the end of the nineteenth century the United States became less agricultural and more industrial. One hundred years later industry and manufacturing have given way to information and services. In both periods, immigration into the United States and migration within it shaped the way Americans lived and thought about their society. The United States has also been a land of many cultures, and we seek to show the impact of these different cultures in forming the social, cultural, and political life of the past hundred years. *Coming of Age* explains how members of sometimes excluded groups—racial or ethnic minorities and women—have asserted their rights over the course of the twentieth century.

Coming of Age presents a balanced account of domestic and foreign affairs and the social, political, and economic developments of the United States in the twentieth century. Each chapter opens with a brief anecdote or vignette of the period, illustrating the major themes to follow. Chapters also begin with time lines of major events to help students follow chronology. We include biographical profiles of such major figures as Henry Ford, Charles Lindbergh, Eleanor Roosevelt, and Bill Gates, to name a few. To provide students with a flavor of the era, each biography includes an original quotation from the individual profiled. All chapters contain concluding summaries and suggestions for further reading as well as maps, charts, and photographs to enrich students' appreciation of the content.

Our friends, colleagues, and students at the University of Arizona, University of New Mexico, and University of Colorado have helped us shape this book. They have provided literally hundreds of suggestions for details, given us leads on readings, and helped us clarify our presentation of complicated events. We also thank the reviewers who commented on earlier drafts of this book:

H. Roger Grant, Clemson University
Melanie Gustafson, University of Vermont
Diane B. Kunz, Yale University
Joseph A. McCartin, State University of New York—Geneseo
Robert Westbrook, University of Rochester

We extend our deepest appreciation to all of them.

M. S., V. S., R. D. S.

✦ ✦ ✦

COMING OF AGE

✦✦✦
CHAPTER 1

On Edge: America Approaches the Twentieth Century

✦ **John Gast "Columbia Brings Daylight to North America," 1872.**

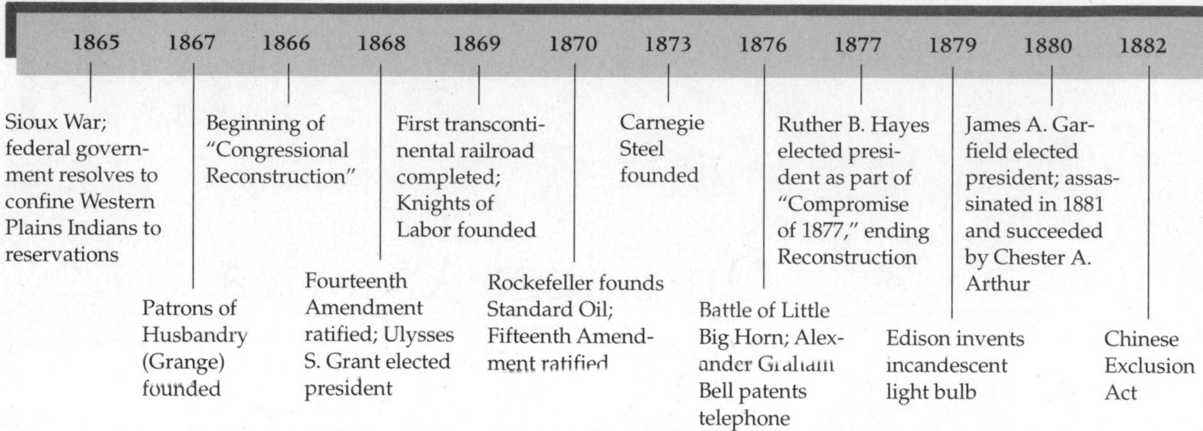

AMERICANS OF THE 1890s approached the coming century with a sense of anticipation and regret not unlike that felt by their descendants one hundred years later. As technology accelerated the pace of change, those who enjoyed the luxury to reflect on events realized how little time separated them from the earliest citizens of the Republic. At least a few elderly Americans had been children when President Thomas Jefferson purchased the vast Louisiana Territory from Napoleon. In their twilight years these individuals could ride a railroad in a Pullman car along the route to the Pacific first explored by Lewis and Clark. Those early intrepid explorers had spent the better part of two years traversing the continent; their descendants could make the trip from the Atlantic to the Pacific coast in less than a week.

Oliver Wendell Holmes, a prominent physician, was born around the time James Madison succeeded Jefferson, and he lived until 1894. His son, Oliver Wendell Holmes, Jr. (1841–1935) fought in the Civil War, sat on the Massachusetts Supreme Court during the 1890s, and was appointed to the U.S. Supreme Court in 1902 by President Theodore ("Teddy") Roosevelt. He served there with distinction until he retired in 1932, shortly before the election to the presidency of Teddy's cousin, Franklin D. Roosevelt. One of Holmes's law clerks, Alger Hiss—who became notorious as an accused spy during the Cold War—lived until 1996. In effect, a single individual on either side of Justice

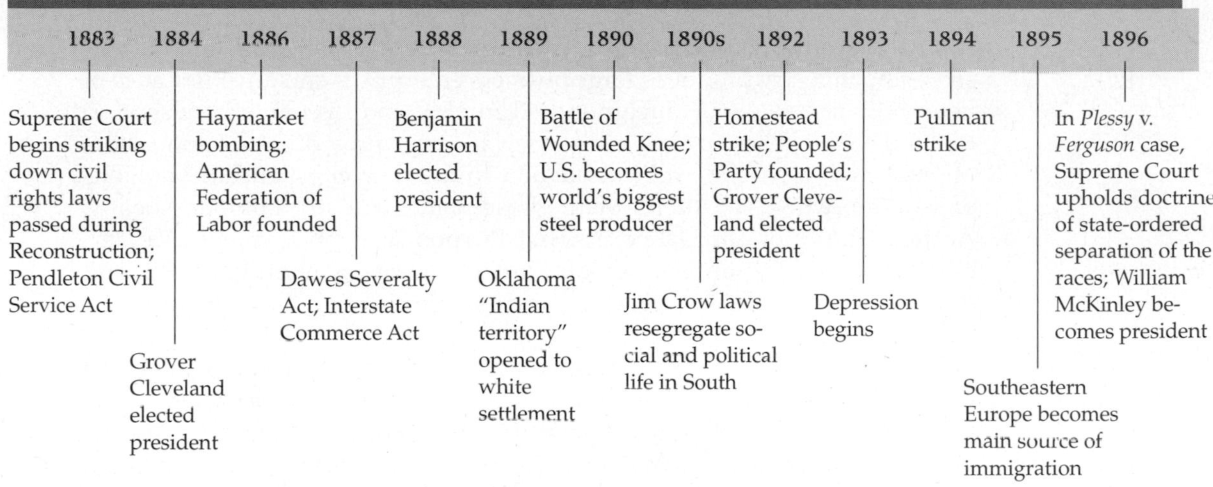

Holmes has spanned the whole of American history, from the era of the Founding Fathers to the threshold of the twenty-first century.

Of course, few Americans have lived so long or prominent a life as Holmes. But millions experienced many of the same technological, economic, political, social, and cultural transformations as he did. They survived a bloody civil war; saw the slaves freed, the Plains Indians conquered, and the West developed; and witnessed the rise of giant new cities, to which millions of Europeans flocked. During their lifetimes the United States experienced agricultural and industrial revolutions that produced great wealth for some and great hardship for others. In short, America changed in ways no one could have imagined.

Like all such transformations, the economic and social changes of the late nineteenth century created both winners and losers—although some of the results of those changes were not apparent for many years. The most extreme changes seem easiest to categorize. The roughly three hundred thousand Native Americans living west of the Missouri River, stripped of most of their land, livelihood, culture, and independence, were obvious casualties of American progress. Nearly 4 million former slaves—most of whom remained in the South—were freed from bondage but not from grinding poverty and oppression.

At the other extreme, the technological and managerial revolutions sweeping industry produced large business enterprises and an abundance of new millionaires (about three hundred in 1860 and over four thousand in the mid-1890s). These people made their fortunes providing transportation, minerals, food, energy, and information to the new cities and the millions of workers who lived there. Men whose names are still familiar, such as Andrew Carnegie, John D. Rockefeller, J. Pierpont Morgan, Cornelius Vanderbilt, Thomas A. Edison, and Joseph Pulitzer became symbols of wealth and power (or, alternatively, greed and exploitation) for millions of ordinary citizens.

A larger group of Americans, consisting of unskilled and semiskilled workers, small farmers, recent immigrants, urban middle-class professionals, and small retailers, existed between these extremes. For them, life in the decades between the Civil War and 1900 was a mixture of hope and frustration as they struggled to influence or simply adjust to the rapidly changing patterns of their daily world.

Many of the issues debated in the 1890s have a familiar sound to us today. Should nearly unrestricted immigration to the United States be permitted to continue? Did the arrival of Slavs, Jews, Italians, and other eastern and southern Europeans enrich society or burden it with inassimilable "castoffs"? How would the nation's dominant (that is, white, Anglo-Saxon, Protestant) religious and social values fare in an increasingly diverse America? What obligation did the federal government have to ensure legal, economic, and social equality for African-Americans?

The explosive growth of cities in the Northeast and around the Great Lakes spawned other questions. Some Americans saw the new urban-industrial centers as powerful engines of economic mobility and cultural creativity. Others condemned them as moral cesspools. Farmers, beneficiaries of cheap land, technology, and a voracious urban market at home and abroad, complained that bankers and commodity brokers were cheating them by manipulating agricultural prices, the money supply, and transportation rates. Workers in the steel, coal, and railroad industries accused corporations of exploiting them mercilessly and discarding them as soon as new labor-saving technologies became available. Like many farmers, they felt squeezed by giant economic forces. When workers tried to redress the balance of power by organizing labor unions, business interests attacked them for interfering with the free market and undermining efficiency. A severe depression from 1893 to 1896 increased these tensions.

Although the United States exported huge amounts of food and minerals to Europe, the nation's labor, business, and political leaders worried about foreign competition, and the Congress imposed high tariffs to limit imports. About 80 percent of adult white males regularly voted (compared to just under 50 percent of all adults today), but nearly everyone considered the government at all levels corrupt and incompetent.

In the decades that stretched from the end of the Civil War to the dawn of the twentieth century, a process of rapid change dominated American life.

Western expansion, reconstruction of Southern politics and life, the growth of big cities and large-scale industry, unprecedented waves of immigration, the emergence of an industrial working class, and the rapid growth of farm production all occurred during this period.

✦ The West of the Imagination and of Reality

The American West, with its vast distances, dramatic landscapes, and clashing civilizations, has long been a powerful symbol for the rest of the nation and even the world. The images of stoic cowboys tall in the saddle, fierce Indians circling wagon trains, the gallant federal cavalry riding to the rescue, sturdy farmers tilling the soil, and sheriffs meting out stern justice with a six-shooter are all indelibly imprinted on our national consciousness.

The realities of the West have always been more complex. In 1900 only 11 million of America's 76 million people lived west of the Missouri River, with most of these clustered in California or on the eastern fringe of the West. Of the 300,000 Indians who lived in the region in 1865, a third had perished by 1890. About forty thousand cowboys (African-Americans, Mexican-Americans, and ex-Confederate soldiers prominent among them) worked the range in the late nineteenth century. But, ironically, the West developed largely as an adjunct to a growing industrial economy in the eastern states and Europe, and with the active assistance of the federal government and the army. Nearly everything produced in the West, from wheat to gold, had value because of industrial demand back in the East. Nearly everything needed to produce and transport western products—rails, plows, barbed wire, dynamite, and power drills—came from eastern factories. Periodic mineral rushes, a cattle boom, and grants of public land stimulated westward migrations as much as the desire for adventure. The emergent agricultural, ranching, and mining economy of the West depended on innovative technology, imported capital, and the forced removal of the original inhabitants.

Before the Civil War, North-South conflict over the extension of slavery had limited federal efforts to promote western development. After secession, the Republicans in control of Congress and the White House pushed a pro-growth agenda for the West. In 1862 Congress passed the Homestead Act, the Pacific Railroad Act, and the Morrill Land Grant College Act. These, together with similar laws passed in the 1870s, provided free or low-cost public land to promote farming, mining, railroad building, and public higher education. Individual homesteaders received a minimum of 160 acres of farmland (more in arid areas), and railroad companies gained title to between ten and twenty miles of land on either side of each mile of track they laid.

This incentive prompted a rush by the Union Pacific and Central Pacific railroad companies to complete the first transcontinental rail line. In May 1869 the two lines met at Promontory Summit in Utah. Railroads proved vital for western economic development. They carried supplies and settlers into the region and cattle, grain, and minerals out. They also became a constant source

Traditional Sioux village before expansion into the West. *Library of Congress*

of tension among westerners, who resented the power, influence, and rate-setting authority of the railroads.

Although it was sparsely populated, the West was not unpopulated. In the 1860s a few more than three hundred thousand Indians lived on the northern and southern plains; tens of thousands of Hispanics of Mexican descent lived in Texas, the Southwest, and southern California; and many of the one hundred thousand whites and eighty thousand Chinese who had trekked to the West Coast after the 1849 Gold Rush remained in the region. (The estimated one hundred thousand Indians native to California in the early 1800s had practically vanished by the 1860s, victims of disease, warfare, violent dispossession, and hunger.) Several thousand Mormons had settled around Salt Lake City beginning in 1847.

European influences transformed the lives of the Plains Indians even before large numbers of whites arrived. During the previous two hundred years the introduction of horses by the Spanish and guns by all Europeans changed Indian culture. Some tribes abandoned agriculture and became full-time hunters of the vast buffalo herds that wandered freely. Heavy hunting, prolonged drought, and the arrival on the plains of new tribes pushed westward by European migration to the eastern United States and northward by Spanish settlement in Mexico had already placed ecological strains on the West (see map).

Disease also devastated the native populations of the New World. Ailments such as measles and smallpox were common in Europe but not in the Americas. Europeans were typically exposed to these diseases as children. Well cared for by adults who had developed immunity, they usually recovered and became immune themselves. When these diseases struck Indians, however, they afflicted whole populations, regardless of age. With few healthy caregivers and with complications from various secondary infections also spread by European contact, death rates among the various Indian tribes soared to between 15 and 90 percent during epidemics.

Over time waves of epidemics contributed to demographic collapse among many Native American peoples, killing far more than ever died in battle. Policies adopted by the federal government made a bad situation even worse. Following the Civil War, court rulings stripped Indian tribes of their earlier status as sovereign nations empowered to deal with Washington on an equal basis. They were redefined as "wards," much like children in relation to their parents, over whom the government had complete authority.

After 1865 federal Indian policy focused on confining Indians to reservations, with the stated goal of offering them physical protection, education, and assistance in becoming farmers. Not incidentally, the land cleared of migratory tribes was then opened to white farmers, ranchers, and miners. Forcing Indians to abandon their culture, religion, and livelihood—in short, their whole way of life—did not strike most other Americans as a misfortune. Nor did they care that much of the land allotted to the Indians in the arid West was not fit for farming.

Meanwhile, well-meaning whites were in a quandary. In 1869 a national commission reported to the Commissioner of Indian Affairs and to President Ulysses S. Grant that although the government claimed to pursue policies that were in the best interests of native peoples, "the actual treatment they have received has been unjust and iniquitous beyond the power of words to express." The commission characterized the history of relations with the Indians as a "shameful record of broken treaties and unfulfilled promises . . . a sickening record of murder, outrage, robbery and wrongs." The report averred that greedy white settlers desiring land, ambitious army officers seeking fame and promotions, and government agents embezzling funds designated for Indian welfare had provoked desperate Indians to lash out against their oppressors. Even Indians who had tried to assimilate into white society by becoming farmers were in peril.

The commission suggested placing Indians on well-run reservations and making them wards of the government. The government, in turn, would protect Indians, "educate them in industry, the arts of civilization, and the principles of Christianity." Boarding schools staffed by Christian missionaries

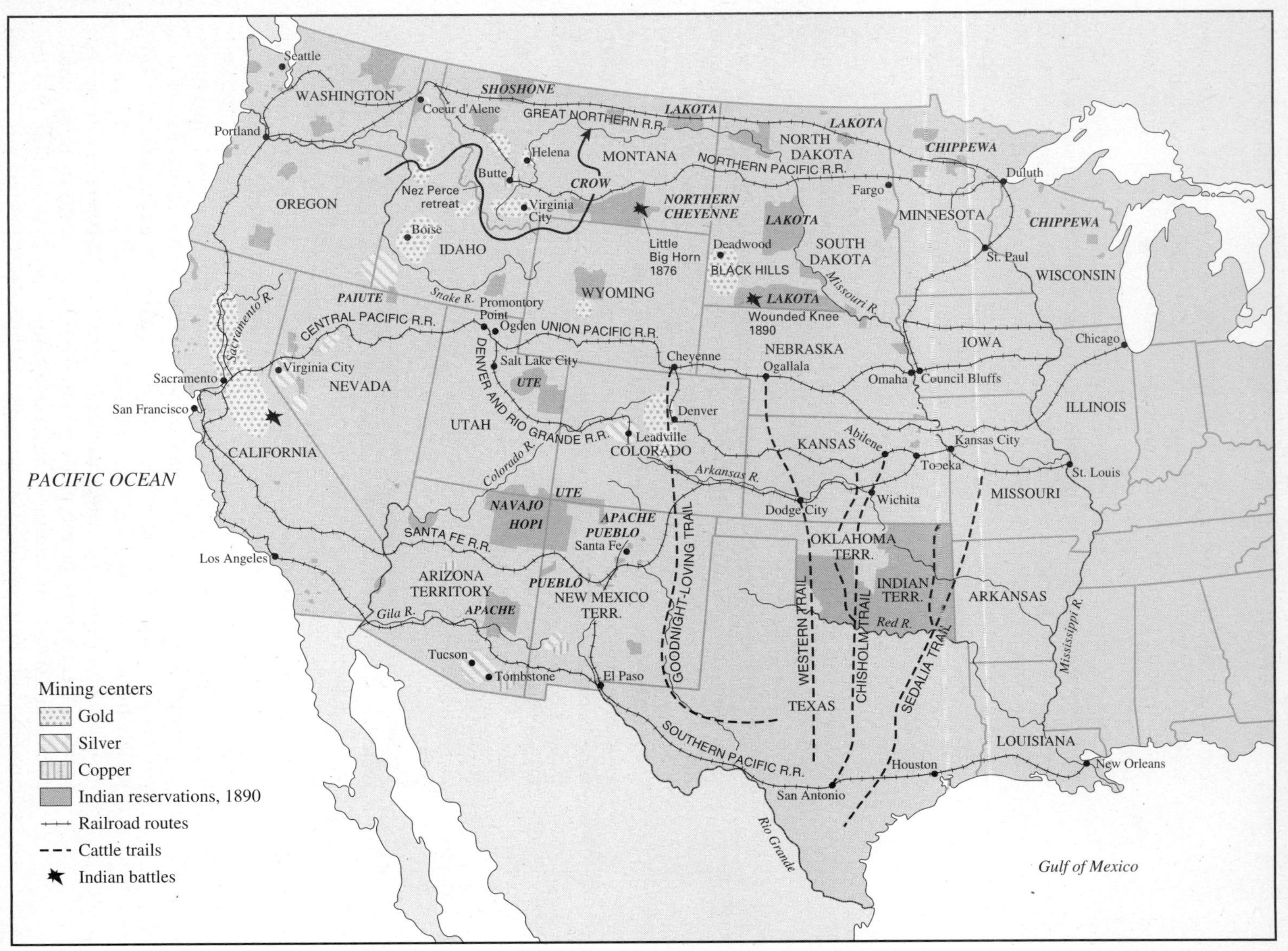

The American West, 1860–1890 Following the Civil War, farmers, ranchers, and miners relentlessly moved west.

would be established to teach Indian children English. The reformers believed that an emphasis on "the religion of our blessed Savior" was probably the "most effective agent for the civilization" and ultimate salvation of the Indian. If the Indians "cannot bear civilization," the liberal *Nation* magazine lamented, reservation life "will at least kill them decently."

To enforce this policy and protect white settlers from the wrath of angry or desperate Indians who rejected reservation life, about twenty thousand of the U.S Army's twenty-five thousand soldiers were stationed in the West. (Most of the rest were in the South.) During the 1870s and 1880s the army, half of whose ranks were filled by the foreign born and by several regiments of black "Buffalo Soldiers," conducted a series of brutal military campaigns to force Indians onto reservations.

Besides the toll brought on by disease and warfare, the systematic slaughter of at least 15 million buffalo by commercial hunters and for sport during the 1870s deprived Indians of their basic source of food, clothing, and shelter. The hides, bones, and meat of the lumbering beasts became leather for clothing, fertilizer for crops, and food for the construction workers pushing the railroads westward. Buffalo Bill became a legend—and a wealthy man—supplying meat to the Union Pacific, killing over four thousand of the animals in a single year. By 1883 only a few hundred of the beasts survived. A few years later, when Congress commissioned the buffalo nickel, the engraver had go to New York's Bronx Zoo to find a model.

Although Indians, who generally fought in small bands, did savor a few victories, such as the Sioux triumph over the 264 soldiers in Lieutenant Colonel George A. Custer's Seventh Cavalry at the Little Big Horn River in Montana in 1876, they were almost always overwhelmed by white firepower, mobility, and numbers. Starvation and disease forced nearly all of the Plains Indians to accept reservation life during the 1880s. The last major anti-Indian military operation by the army occurred in 1890, when several hundred Indians from various tribes gathered at Wounded Knee Creek in South Dakota to participate in a ghost dance, a religious ceremony designed to bring back the buffalo, revive the spirits of dead ancestors, and restore the world as it was before the white onslaught. Indian police sent to detain the Sioux leader Sitting Bull (Buffalo Bill's sometime costar), lest he join the dancers, ended up killing him. When the cavalry finally surrounded a band of several hundred freezing, starving ghost dancers at Wounded Knee, a frightened soldier or Indian shot a gun. In the ensuing slaughter some sixty soldiers and two hundred Indians, mostly women and children, died.

In 1887 the Dawes Severalty Act, intended as a reform, did almost as much harm to the Indians as the cavalry. This law redrew reservation boundaries and divided the land into individual plots of about 160 acres per Indian family. Reformers intended this to spur self-improvement by turning dependent Indians into self-sufficient farmers—a physical impossibility on such small plots in the arid West. Instead the new system destroyed tribal kinship systems and left Indians vulnerable to unscrupulous schemes.

✦✦✦

Biographical Profile

William F. "Buffalo Bill" Cody, 1846–1917

Some of the most enduring symbols of the American West had roots in show business. Beginning in 1883 and continuing for more than twenty years, many Easterners and Europeans discovered the West through William F. "Buffalo Bill" Cody's Wild West Show. Born on an Iowa farm in 1846, Cody rode for the Pony Express and fought with the cavalry before securing in 1867 a contract supplying buffalo meat to workers laying tracks for the Union Pacific Railroad. In one year he shot 4,280 of the lumbering beats, earning a small fortune and niche in history.

Beginning in 1869, writer Ned Buntline popularized these exploits in *Buffalo Bill, The King of the Border Men,* the first of nearly two thousand so-called dime novels written by a variety of authors. Cody organized buffalo hunts for wealthy Americans and European royalty and began appearing in stage plays based loosely on his life. During the Sioux War (1875–1876), he re-einlisted as an army scout and with photographers and journalists in tow often galloped into battle dressed in stage cos-

---

Land speculators embraced the Dawes Act. After the 160-acre parcels of reservation land had been distributed, the substantial unclaimed remainder was declared "surplus" and up for grabs. Even the family plots given to Indians were in jeopardy. The government was supposed to hold the titles on these plots in trust for twenty-five years to prevent land speculation, but scoundrels quickly discovered or punched loopholes in the law. In 1887 Indians received title to about 139 million acres of land. Fifty years later they owned only 48 million acres.

Worse was to come. At first Congress exempted the so-called five civilized tribes (Cherokee, Choctaw, Seminole, Creek, and Chickasaw) from the Dawes Act. These tribes farmed, grazed, and leased out the relatively good land they still held in what comprised most of present-day Oklahoma. But starting in 1889 Congress stripped away this protection. In a series of giveaways to white settlers, Indian territory was transformed into the Oklahoma Territory. On a single September 1893 day, 6 million acres of former Indian land was claimed tume. The Wild West Show, begun in 1883, included racing horses and stage coaches, shooting displays by Phoebe Anne Moses (better known as Annie Oakley), and fake gunfights between cowboys, "outlaws" and Indians—all dressed in costumes that appeared authentic to audiences. Cody even persuaded Sioux Chief Sitting Bull to perform one season. Each year the show traveled to as many as one hundred American and European cities. By the time Cody died in 1917, most Americans envisioned the West through Cody's eyes, a place of wide open spaces where self-reliant men and women tamed nature, subdued savage Indians, and reaped the bounty of the land.

Wild West Program (Selections from 1893 program)
Overture, "Star Spangled Banner"
Grand Review: Introducing the rough riders of the world
Miss Annie Oakley, celebrated shot
Horse race between a cowboy, a Cossack, a Mexican, an Indian
Pony Express Rider will show how the letters and telegrams of the Republic were delivered across the immense continent
Illustrating a prairie immigrant crossing the plains
A group of Mexicans from Old Mexico
Cowboy fun
Capture of the Deadwood Mail Coach by the Indians
Racing between Indian boys on horseback
Life customs of the Indians
Buffalo hunt
Colonel W. F. Cody (Buffalo Bill) unique sharpshooting
The Battle of the Little Big Horn

---

by forty thousand white families who rushed into the Cherokee Strip at a starting signal. In six hours the town of Wharton grew from zero to ten thousand people.

The Cherokee, who received some payment for their land, fared better than many tribes. However, after World War I, when oil was discovered on the remaining Indian-owned land in Oklahoma, they faced a new threat. Oil speculators sometimes got courts to declare Indians "incompetent" as a ruse to seize valuable land. In other cases white men married Indian women, had them murdered, and assumed title to their property. For most tribes cultural and social decline continued until the 1930s, when the so-called Indian New Deal revived their cultural and religious traditions and gave Indians more political autonomy.

The subjugation of the Indian eased the way for commercial development. Spurred by federal and state land grants of over 200 million acres, five transcontinental railroads were built between 1869 and 1893. Railroads west

A Montana "Boomtown" in the 1880s. Eastern cities and industry created a vast market for Western products. *Montana Historical Society*

of the Mississippi River increased from about three thousand miles of track in 1865 to almost seventy-three thousand miles in 1890. During these twenty-five years homesteaders, farmers who bought acreage from the railroads, and ranchers placed more land under cultivation than during the entire previous two centuries of American history. Between the end of the Civil War and 1900 the number of farms in the United States nearly tripled, from 2.5 to 6 million. Railroads made possible the expansion of mining, cattle ranching, and farming, while the growth of these industries made the railroads viable in turn.

The western mining boom began with the California gold rush of 1849 and continued as small prospectors and then large, Eastern-based corporations developed silver, gold, copper, quartz, iron, lead, and zinc mines throughout the region. Cattle ranching also expanded rapidly as Eastern cities developed a taste for beef and railroads provided a fast and inexpensive means to carry the beasts to slaughter and the dinner table.

Western agriculture was shaped and limited by water supplies, especially west of the one hundredth meridian. Over time farmers, ranchers, miners, and cities would battle for control of this scarce resource. Building on a technique developed by Indians and the Spanish, Mormon settlers in Utah relied on irrigation to grow crops in arid regions. Most western states adopted water laws that encouraged farmers to damn rivers, build canals, and appropriate ground water for agriculture. Mechanization (mechanical planters, harvesters, and bailers; barbed wire; wind-driven pumps) allowed family farmers to cultivate large fields of grain, whose output the railroads carried eastward and steamships ferried across the Atlantic.

All three of the West's main economic pillars—farming, ranching, and mining—experienced cycles of boom and bust. Sometimes severe drought or cold killed crops and cattle. Rapidly changing market conditions, affected by competition from South America, Canada, and Russia, could also play havoc when supply and demand varied too widely. Sometimes single families failed and abandoned their farms; other times whole communities moved on, leaving behind ghost towns.

Although the area west of the Mississippi still accounted for a small fraction of the nation's population, Congress moved quickly to integrate the region politically. From 1889 to 1890, North and South Dakota, Washington, Montana, Wyoming, and Idaho were admitted as states. Uneasy with the Mormon's practice of polygamy, Congress delayed Utah's statehood until 1896 (see map).

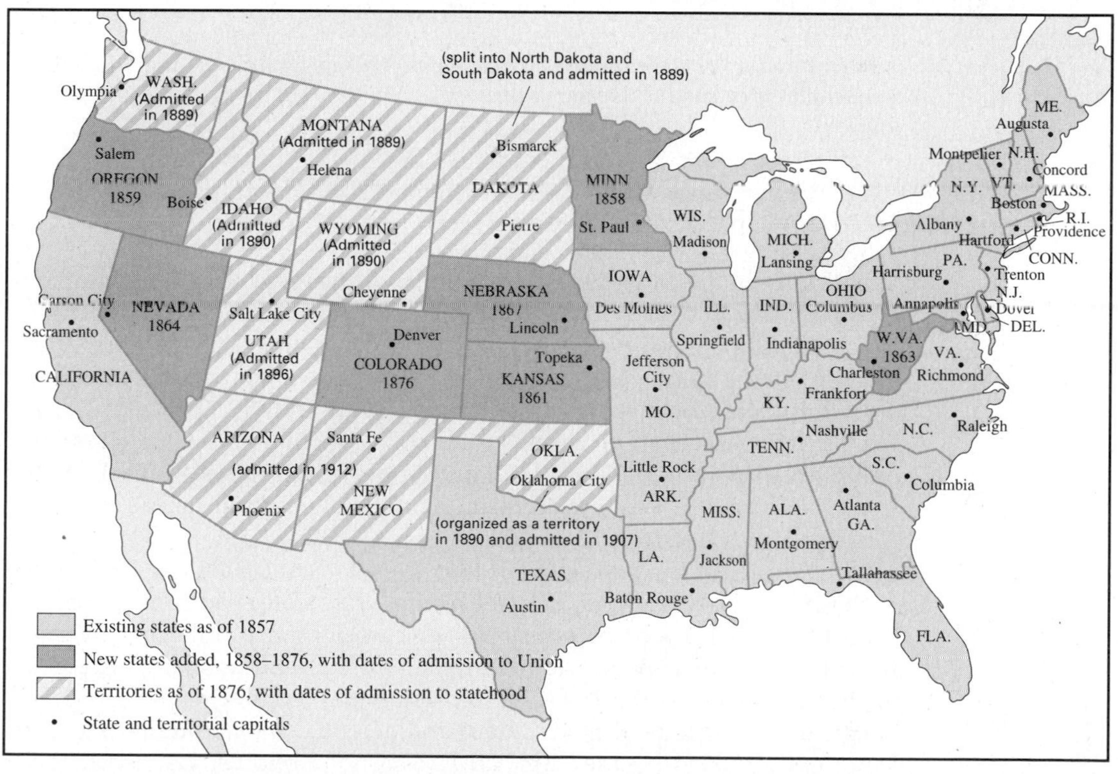

The United States, 1876–1912 As their population increased, Western territories became new states.

A school for former slaves established by the Freedman's Bureau. Hungry for education, children and adults flocked to these schools after 1865. *Collection of William Gladstone*

✦ Reconstruction and Race

Writing in the early 1900s, the brilliant African-American historian and social critic W. E. B. DuBois observed that the "problem of the 20th century is the problem of the color line." In fact, ever since colonial times race, especially black-white relations, has marked one of America's most visible fault lines. The Thirteenth Amendment, ratified by the states in 1865, ended slavery but left 4 million blacks in political, social, and economic limbo. Congressional efforts to reorder Southern politics and improve the status of blacks lasted from 1865 until 1877, but the problems of regional power struggles and rocky race relations lasted far longer.

At the time of his death in April 1865, President Abraham Lincoln differed with Congress over how to bring the Confederate states back into the Union. Lincoln favored a lenient policy by which temporary military governors would cede power to new state governments in the South as soon as 10 percent of those who had voted in the 1860 presidential election pledged renewed allegiance to the federal government and accepted the abolition of slavery. Congress, prodded by the so-called Radical Republicans, insisted that the federal government had a duty to secure not only emancipation for African-

Americans, but also some degree of legal rights and economic well-being for them as well. Yet even the Radicals hesitated to distribute plantation land to ex-slaves, an obvious solution to the problem.

Lincoln's successor, Andrew Johnson, infuriated both Radical Republicans and blacks. A politician from Tennessee who opposed Secession, Johnson favored the recognition of the Southern state governments as soon as they ratified the Thirteenth Amendment, banning slavery. Unlike Lincoln and most Republicans in Congress he cared little about black voting and civil rights.

The former slaves proved eager to make new lives for themselves, preferably as independent farmers. Many flocked to schools created by the Freedman's Bureau (a federal agency that assisted ex-slaves) or Northern churches to teach basic literacy to former slaves. However, their lack of money, land, mules, or implements forced most freedmen (and many poor whites) to work as tenants for large landowners. These sharecroppers borrowed money, horses, and seed to grow crops like cotton or tobacco on land often owned by former slaveholders. The share of the crop due the landlord varied from as little as one-quarter to as much as two-thirds, depending on what had been loaned to the tenant. The system left many sharecroppers in perpetual debt and, along with the region's dependence on one or two crops, contributed to the South's chronic poverty.

The Republican-dominated Congress worried that continued intimidation of the former slaves not only mocked the Thirteenth Amendment but also would soon restore to power in the South those who had caused the Civil War. Defending black voting and civil rights became for many Republicans both a moral imperative and a political necessity if the creation of a solidly white, Democratic South was to be avoided. In April 1866 Congress passed, over President Johnson's veto, a civil rights act that declared all people (except Indians) born in the United States to be citizens entitled to a broad range of civil, legal, and economic rights enforceable by the federal courts. To bar discrimination against blacks by state governments, Congress sent to the states for ratification the Fourteenth Amendment, which established the equal protection of the law for all men (while ignoring women's right to vote) and forbade the states to deprive anyone of life, liberty, or property without "due process of law." States that denied black males the vote risked losing congressional seats and electoral votes. When most of the Southern states balked at ratifying this amendment, the Republicans made the issue the heart of their successful 1866 campaign.

In 1867 a Congress with a lopsided Republican majority fell one vote short in the Senate of impeaching Johnson for violating recently enacted laws. Despite this setback Congress passed the Military Reconstruction Act of 1867, dividing the South into five military districts under army command. Only state governments that allowed blacks to vote and ratified the Fourteenth Amendment would qualify for readmission to the Union. By July 1868 the amendment had been adopted. In February 1869 Congress sent the Fifteenth

Amendment to the states, specifying that the states could not deny any citizen the right to vote based on his race, color, or previous condition of servitude. This won ratification early in 1870, but only at the tip of federal bayonets.

Even at the height of Reconstruction, blacks never dominated Southern politics. They never held more than 15 to 20 percent of elective offices in the South during this period. Nevertheless, powerful whites played on the racial fears of poor whites to convince them that rights for blacks threatened to reduce their own status. By the mid-1870s state Democratic parties in the South, often led by the former planter elite called Redeemers and assisted by terrorist groups like the Ku Klux Klan, resumed efforts to intimidate black voters. In 1875 Mississippi led the way in using legal ruses and threats to scare away black voters and ensure the defeat of Republican candidates for office. When President Ulysses S. Grant declined to use the small number of troops remaining in the South to enforce black voting rights, the trend became clear. Despite last-ditch civil rights legislation passed in 1874, Northern whites and Republican politicians gradually lost interest in enforcing equal rights in the face of strident opposition. In 1875 the Democrats won a majority in the House of Representatives for the first time since the Civil War began.

Reconstruction ended with the presidential election of 1876. The Republican and Democratic presidential candidates were deadlocked over a number of disputed electoral votes, mostly from the South and favoring Democrat Samuel Tilden of New York. In a series of deals that allowed Republican Rutherford B. Hayes to assume office, party leaders agreed to compensate the Democrats by pulling troops out of the South and ceasing enforcement of laws protecting blacks. The Supreme Court hastened the process by ruling in 1876 that most of the guarantees contained in the Fourteenth and Fifteenth Amendments could be enforced only by state, not federal, courts. In 1883 the High Court ruled in a series of civil rights cases that past guarantees of equal rights and nondiscrimination applied only to actions of the state and federal governments. Private citizens and business were free to discriminate in such things as employment, housing, and entertainment.

In the late 1880s and 1890s, the southern states adopted new constitutions or laws that effectively relegated blacks to second-class status. Codifying what had already become common practice, "Jim Crow" laws mandated racial segregation in public accommodations, theaters, schools, housing, and transportation. To get around constitutional requirements, most Jim Crow laws did not single out blacks for segregation or ill treatment. They merely required that "separate but equal" facilities be provided for members of different races. In practice this meant separate and unequal.

Although the Supreme Court ruled in 1883 that private businesses were free to discriminate on the basis of race, government-enforced segregation remained constitutionally dubious. Many of the first Jim Crow laws pertained to railroad transportation, because it involved close contact among passengers—including purportedly "delicate" white women—for many hours, and trains could easily pull two cars, one for each race.

In 1890 the Louisiana legislature enacted a law that required railroads operating in the state to provide "equal but separate accommodations for the white and colored races" by means of separate passenger coaches. Recognizing this threat to their broader status, African-Americans organized the "Citizens Committee to Test the Constitutionality of the Separate Car Law." After some false starts the committee arranged in 1892 for Homer Plessy, a light-skinned, mixed-heritage man who was black according to Louisiana's racial law (all persons who were one-eighth black were considered black), to purchase a ticket for travel within Louisiana. When ordered to move from the "white" to the "colored" car, he refused. State courts upheld his arrest on the grounds that the law applied equally to both races and thus imposed no government-ordered inequality. Louisiana courts even cited northern laws that mandated racial separation in many settings.

When the case (now called *Plessy* v. *Ferguson*, for the defendant and the New Orleans judge who first ruled on the law) reached the U.S. Supreme Court in 1896, Plessy's attorneys argued that state-ordered separation of races on trains (and, by extension, in most other services) represented a perpetuation of aspects of slavery banned by the Thirteenth Amendment. The law, they noted, provided no criteria for defining who was black or white and failed to guarantee equality of service. A provision that exempted black servants and nannies so that they might assist their employers in the all-white cars proved the discriminatory intent of the law. The state, the complaint charged, had illegally drawn a distinction between citizens on the basis of race.

Lawyers for Louisiana retorted that the law was colorblind; it did not discriminate but simply barred people of different races from sharing the same facility. If a passenger's reputation or status were injured by being assigned to the wrong car, he or she could sue for damages. As to how racial assignment would be made, the lawyers for the state insisted that any rational person could tell by eyeballing who was black and who was not. (And, like Louisiana, most of the other southern states had elaborate laws codifying how much "black blood" rendered a person black.)

On May 18, 1896, the Supreme Court ruled 7-1 in favor of Louisiana's right to mandate racial separation. Requiring separate rail cars, the majority declared, had nothing to do with slavery, discrimination, or inequality. Although the Fourteenth Amendment required absolute legal equality among the races, the Court insisted that this did not prevent state governments or private parties from acknowledging racial differences and acting accordingly. This left school boards, hotels, theaters, and railroads essentially free to separate individuals on the basis of race. Although enforced separation, the justices explained, did not "stamp the colored race with a badge of inferiority," the majority opinion stated that "if one race be inferior to the other socially, the Constitution of the United States cannot put them upon the same plane."

In a ringing dissent, Associate Justice John Marshall Harlan ridiculed the decision, writing that the separate-car law clearly violated the spirit and wording of the Thirteenth and Fourteenth Amendments. Harlan condemned his fellow justices for saying that segregation treated both races equally; Jim Crow laws existed to control blacks, not whites. The *Plessy* ruling, he warned, would spur new forms of segregation by state and local governments. Despite this dissent, the Court's decision was so unremarkable in 1896 that newspapers like the *New York Times* reported it under "railway news."

Over the next several years state and local governments formalized the already common practice of segregating public education and accommodations. Southern and western states banned marriages among blacks, whites, Hispanics, and Indians. Poll taxes, literacy tests, and "grandfather clauses" effectively barred blacks, and in some cases poor whites, from voting. State-enforced segregation in most aspects of life remained the norm in the American South and much of the West until the 1950s.

Confronted by a hostile government and assisted by few white allies, black leaders agonized over their response to renewed subordination. Some, like educator Booker T. Washington, urged accommodation. During the 1880s and 1890s, as head of the Tuskegee Institute in Alabama, Washington developed a philosophy of self-reliance that emphasized industrial and agricultural education as the key to survival for blacks. In a widely circulated speech he delivered to a mixed-race audience in Atlanta in 1895, Washington declared that "in all things that are purely social, we can be separate as the fingers, yet one as the hand in all things essential to mutual progress." Other blacks, such as Harvard-educated sociologist W. E. B. DuBois, condemned this approach for consigning blacks to menial careers and ensuring perpetual impoverishment for most of the nation's 10 million blacks, two-thirds of whom, in 1900, still lived in the South. Early in the twentieth century, DuBois joined other black and white critics of segregation in founding the National Organization for the Advancement of Colored People (NAACP), which demanded legal, political, social, and educational equality for blacks.

✦ Forces of Change: Industrialization, Immigration, and Urbanization

By 1900 the process of industrialization had transformed American life in ways no one alive in 1800 could have anticipated. The basics of life—food, clothing, and shelter—were no longer produced at home but now issued forth from industrial production sites: Chicago's meat-packing plants and Minneapolis's flour mills, textile factories in the Piedmont South and shoe manufacturing concerns in Massachusetts, steel mills in Pennsylvania and massive logging and lumber firms in the Pacific Northwest. A burgeoning nationwide system of engineered waterways, railroads, telegraph wires, electric power lines, and even telephone lines etched a national grid of power across a continent only lately brought under the uncontested control of the U.S. government. The nation's communication and transportation network linked the mills and the factories with the raw materials they needed—wheat from the Great Plains, coal from Appalachia, iron ore from Minnesota, petroleum from Pennsylvania—and brought mass-produced goods to consumers on remote farmsteads and in faraway cities. Grand-scale technological systems made possible a national, even international, market. Moreover, high, protective tariffs sheltered American businesses from foreign competition, while cutthroat practices at home drove smaller firms into bankruptcy and led larger firms to merge their assets into trusts and holding companies. Meanwhile, bankers like the celebrated and hated J. P. Morgan developed a whole new range of ways to finance, combine, and control businesses. Corporate capitalism reached deeper and deeper into the lives of ordinary Americans.

The Expansion of Business

The growth in the scale of business and the expansion of markets made for greater productivity and, often, greater efficiency. As firms manufactured larger and larger quantities of the things they made, the cost of making each item went down, creating economies of scale. John D. Rockefeller's success in the oil business exemplified how novel technology, new products, and innovative organization and management shaped the economy.

At the age of twenty, just as the Civil War began, John D. Rockefeller started a commodity trading firm in Cleveland. He recognized that the trains and machinery vital to the Union army required large amounts of lubricating oil, a petroleum product that had formerly been sold as an over-the-counter medicine. Rockefeller acquired an interest in recently discovered oil fields in western Pennsylvania and in refineries that processed petroleum. In the aftermath of the Civil War, new rail lines and factories generated an ever-increasing demand for lubricating oil. Kerosene, another petroleum derivative, became widely used as a fuel for illuminating lamps.

To keep up with demand, Rockefeller invested in new drilling ventures, pipelines, transportation technologies, refineries, and a marketing network. An organizational wizard determined to increase efficiency and lower costs (by reducing the number of drops of solder needed to seal five-gallon cans of kerosene, for example), Rockefeller found uses for nearly all of the by-products from his refineries. To finance the expansion of his business, he incorporated the Standard Oil Company in 1870, selling shares to the public.

As his business increased, Rockefeller pressed the railroads to secretly reduce the rates they charged Standard Oil, to give him a cost advantage over his competitors. Standard Oil used aggressive price wars to drive out or buy out other oil companies, often paying off the losers with Standard Oil stock. Most who accepted Rockefeller's offer became wealthy themselves; those who resisted usually went broke.

Over time Rockefeller expanded his empire from a primary concentration on refining and marketing oil to include drilling and transporting it as well. This "vertical integration"—controlling all aspects of an industry, from gathering raw materials to manufacturing and retailing the finished product—achieved further cost savings and allowed him to significantly reduce the retail price of petroleum products. Increased sales made up for smaller margins. In 1882 Standard Oil lawyer S. C. T. Dodd conceived of the idea of creating a *trust*, an alliance of corporations that would control the pricing and other economic policies of an entire industry. Some consumers and business rivals complained that the 80 percent or greater industry share achieved by Standard Oil (and other corporations in other industries) violated free competition. The outcry contributed to the passage in 1890 of the Sherman Anti-Trust Act. This federal law, and its offspring in several states, declared it illegal to engage in any "conspiracy in restraint of trade." In practice the law had little impact. Rather, judges used the restraint-of-trade provision to issue injunctions against labor unions that called strikes.

Rockefeller got around the slight inconvenience of the Sherman Act by creating, in 1892, the modern *holding company*. This device allowed one corporation to acquire control of any number of other corporations by purchasing a majority of their stock. Thus, instead of being forced to buy 100 percent of a company to gain control of it, the holding company could purchase as little as 51 percent of a rival's shares to assume ownership. By buying a controlling interest in a company, the acquiring company did not need the approval of the acquired company's board of directors. Rockefeller's masterpiece, Standard Oil of New Jersey, was chartered in 1899 and soon controlled nearly all aspects of the nation's oil industry, from drilling to retail marketing.

Andrew Carnegie, a Scottish immigrant who lived one of the relatively rare "rags to riches" stories commonly associated with the United States, brought to the steel industry the same sort of organizational genius and quest for efficiency that Rockefeller brought to the oil industry. After working his way up in the telegraph business, Carnegie became interested in steel during the 1870s. In order to cut costs and maximize profits, he focused his attention on the efficient management of every stage of manufacturing. During the 1880s, as the railroad boom peaked and the demand for rails declined, Carnegie turned toward manufacturing structural steel for use in the high-rise buildings being built in America's growing cities. He invested heavily in new technology and labor-saving procedures, cutting his company's production costs from $40 per ton to $20. Because of the success of Carnegie and others, steel production in the United States increased from 3 million tons to 30 million tons annually between 1870 and 1900. Like Rockefeller, Carnegie amassed immense wealth, often earning a personal profit of over $20 million annually.

Financing corporate expansion was often arranged by a new type of investment banker, epitomized by J. Pierpont Morgan. Like Rockefeller, Morgan made a fortune during the Civil War procurement boom, and by the 1880s he was devoting his energy to straightening out the finances of the often chaotic railroad industry. Accustomed to managing great sums of other people's money, Morgan arranged the sale of bonds to finance gold purchases for the U.S. Treasury in 1895 when a run on the metal threatened to leave the

Bethlehem steel workers in 1885 with Bessemer converter. Abundant labor and investment in new technology made the U.S. steel industry a modern marvel. *Hagley Museum & Library*

government insolvent. In 1901 he purchased Carnegie's steel companies for $480 million and folded them into a new giant, the U.S. Steel Corporation.

Some prominent entrepreneurs and investors became national heroes. Thomas A. Edison, for example, who harnessed electricity for household and entertainment uses (for the light bulb and phonograph), was immensely popular. The self-educated Edison epitomized the inspired tinkerer, whose hands-on approach to technology appealed to Americans. In contrast, men whose abilities lay in the direction of organizing more efficient ways of making steel or mobilizing investors' dollars were often derided as "robber barons" who contributed little to society. But without the modern corporation and the financiers who raised the capital they required there would have been no mass production and distribution of Edison's inventions or installation of the electric power grids needed to make them work. Moreover, business expansion often resulted in lower prices and greater options for consumers, as well as increased profits for corporations.

But corporate consolidation also brought greater dependency and insecurity for many people. Farmers wishing to enlarge their operations and produce cash crops for a mass market were increasingly at the mercy of the banks that controlled their credit, the railroads that shipped their goods to market, and the middlemen who mediated between them and the consumers. The workers who mined the country's coal, poured its steel, packed its meats, ran its railroads, and sewed its clothes were less and less able to bargain with their employers, with whom they had no personal relations and who expected their human laborers to match the pace set by their machines. Long hours, low wages, unsafe conditions, and the absence of job security beset the men, women, and children who kept American industry running.

Workers and Labor Relations

Between 1860 and 1900 the size of the industrial work force in the United States grew from under 3 million to almost 16 million workers (out of a total of 28.5 million workers). During this time the average per capita income of all Americans grew by about 35 percent, with real wages increasing 20 percent. However, the distribution of economic rewards varied widely according to gender, race, region, and skill level. Lower-skilled workers could not support a family on a single income. Often two or three family members worked to support one another. In 1900, when Andrew Carnegie took home a tax-free profit of $23 million, a steelworker had to pull a twelve-hour shift six days a week to earn about $450 per year. Female garment workers earned about $5 per week, or $260 annually. Children under fifteen years old, who made up almost 20 percent of the work force in the 1890s, made even less. Most factory workers were males. Only about 17 percent of women worked for wages, mostly as domestics, in textile or garment manufacturing, or, increasingly, as secretaries.

Workers in America's cities often lived on the edge of destitution, even when whole families worked for pay. It was generally assumed that women workers were worth roughly half as much as men, and children sometimes had to toil for nothing as "learners" so that they could eventually get paying work. For mothers of very small children, "outwork" was one precarious way to combine housekeeping with wage earning. Outworkers took piecework from contractors, who provided the materials and sold the finished products. Most outworkers had to live in extremely crowded and unsanitary conditions and take care of children while doing their work. Small children employed by their mothers as helpers could ruin as much material as they produced. Since the contractors charged the cost of materials against the return on finished pieces, outworkers often found that unscrupulous contractors would refuse to pay for any work, insisting that their materials had been spoiled. Outworkers tried to make the work pay by finishing huge quantities of pieces, but the system was so insecure and exploitative that anyone in a position to take a factory job instead of doing piecework at home did so.

Factory workers, meanwhile, had less and less leverage in dealing with their employers. Because of natural population growth, migration from the countryside to the cities, and burgeoning immigration from Europe, the American industrial work force was expanding rapidly. In order to take advantage of the growing pool of unskilled labor, managers invested in machines that broke work down into simpler and more repetitive tasks. This *deskilling* of work consequently led to lower and lower wages for laborers, who could be replaced far more easily than workers with scarce skills.

These circumstances provoked several major and many minor confrontations. Efforts to organize workers accelerated during the 1880s, spurred by Terence V. Powderly, who headed the Knights of Labor. Powderly, like many workers, did not object to wealth per se but bitterly resented the loss of dignity and autonomy workers had experienced at the hands of the new industrial corporations. The new system, Powderly complained, crushed "the manhood out of sovereign citizens."

The Knights broadly appealed to industrial and many white-collar workers, calling for the creation of public utilities and government regulation of monopolies. Membership grew to 750,000 by 1886, shortly before the organization collapsed. Powderly and the Knights' national leaders opposed a wave of strikes and direct action by workers in 1886 to raise wages and improve working conditions, insisting that gradual reform and cooperation with business were preferable. By 1888 the organization had collapsed.

Several dramatic examples of labor-business conflict occurred after the mid-1880s. In May 1886, for example, several thousand workers rallied in Chicago's Haymarket Square in support of striking workers at Cyrus H. McCormick's reaper factory. At the close of a peaceful rally, police attacked the few hundred workers still in attendance. An unknown person threw a bomb at the police, killing and wounding several. Shooting wildly, the police then killed a half dozen workers and wounded dozens more.

Unable to identify the actual bomb thrower, Chicago officials arbitrarily arrested eight leading anarchists and tried them for murder, claiming that their ideas and speeches had inspired the bomb thrower. The jury, packed by the prosecution with probusiness individuals, convicted all of them of murder. Seven were sentenced to death; two of these sentences were later commuted to life in prison.

More violence occurred at the Homestead steel complex near Pittsburgh in July 1892. There unionized steelworkers resisted efforts by Carnegie and his deputy, Henry Clay Frick, to lower wages and break the union's ability to bargain on behalf of employees. When the company brought in nonunion workers and armed guards to protect them, union members fought pitched battles with the strikebreakers. Eventually the governor sent in eight thousand members of the state militia to keep the plant operating.

In 1894 members of the American Railway Union, led by Eugene V. Debs, staged a strike in support of the workers who built Pullman railroad cars.

Steel workers at Carriegie Steel, 1892, Homestead, Pennsylvania, 1892. Labor violence flared when workers and owners battled for control of industry. *Library of Congress*

(Pullman workers lived in company-owned housing. The depression that began in 1893 led the company to cut wages but not rents, provoking the strike.) Both railway managers and Attorney General Richard Olney saw the strike as an opportunity to cripple Debs's efforts to build a broad-based industrial union movement. A federal court issued an injunction declaring the strike illegal, and federal authorities used U.S. troops to keep the trains running. Ultimately Debs spent six months in prison for violating the injunction, and his union collapsed.

Efforts by workers and labor unions to counter the power of big business during the 1890s failed for several reasons. The use of militias and private police to protect strikebreakers eliminated labor's most effective tool. The influx of immigrants from Europe and rural America created a large labor pool that was desperate for work and suspicious of union aims. Only organizations such as the American Federation of Labor (AFL) that limited their membership to skilled craftsmen achieved modest success in the 1890s.

Furthermore, mechanization meant that machines, not humans, set the pace at which people worked. The monotony of industrial jobs often led workers to pay less attention to what they were doing than they had when they performed a variety of tasks. Since the machines were designed, and timed, with productivity rather than safety in mind, on-the-job injuries abounded. Little time or money was invested in making work pleasant, humane, or even safe, and as a result the industrial workplace was notoriously dirty, crowded, and hazardous.

Some workplace dangers grew out of ignorance. Textile manufacturers were unaware that the dust in factory air caused the "brown lung" disease that killed many workers far too early. But in other instances employees suffered from callous neglect on the part of those who paid their wages. Underground mines collapsed because managers tried to save money on timber for reinforcing shafts. When textile mill managers secretly sped up their machines, unsuspecting children were mutilated. Industrial employers were under absolutely no obligation to help injured or disabled workers. For most workers an accident on the job meant not only physical misery but also automatic unemployment.

Long hours compounded the risks. Most industrial laborers worked at least ten hours each day, six days a week. Some had it worse. In Andrew Carnegie's steel mills, workers pulled twelve-hour shifts, six days a week, changing shifts every other week. Thus once every two weeks they would work twenty-four hours straight.

As corporations grew, multiple layers of supervisors stood between employers and rank-and-file employees. To ensure discipline and efficiency down the line, many firms adopted the scientific-management principles elaborated by Frederick Winslow Taylor. When Taylor, the son of a prominent Philadelphia family, had suffered a nervous breakdown at private school, the family doctor had prescribed manual labor. He took a job in a steel mill and worked his way up to the post of company engineer on the strength of his obsession with efficiency. Taylor believed that most workers slacked off when they thought they could get away with it, and he insisted that most of the stalling "is done by men with the deliberate object of keeping their employers ignorant of how fast work can be done." His philosophy of scientific management, often called simply Taylorism, emphasized central planning and detailed instructions to all employees. Taylor pioneered the use of time-and-motion studies, in which workers are observed at their tasks and each job is broken down into the specific motions required, to eliminate wasted movement and speed up production.

Taylorism revolutionized corporate management as firms worked to maximize profits by controlling everything workers did on the job. Managers installed time clocks, restricted or eliminated breaks, and even prohibited talking and laughing among workers. Such practices increased productivity, but workers chafed at the regimentation and their loss of control. As Samuel Gompers, leader of the AFL, told union members, "So, there you are, wage-workers in general, mere machines—considered industrially, of course.... Not only your length, breadth, and thickness as a machine, but your grade of hardness, malleability, and general serviceability, can be ascertained, registered, and then employed as desirable. Science would thus get the most out of you before you are sent to the junkpile."

Business leaders and other champions of unfettered private enterprise defended the practices of corporations as vigorously as Gompers criticized them. Distorting the concept of evolution pioneered by Charles Darwin, English philosopher Herbert Spencer and Yale University professor William Graham Sumner insisted that by removing the dead weight of government regulation and charity, power and wealth would flow naturally into the hands of those most talented, capable, and deserving. So-called Social Darwinists celebrated the acquisition of great wealth as a natural result of a law of nature, an indication of what they called the "survival of the fittest." Interfering with this law, Sumner warned, would lead to "survival of the unfittest" and the degradation of society.

Andrew Carnegie, championing his right as an industrialist to squeeze as much profit as possible from his workers, noted that although at times the "price which society paid for the law of competition" appeared "hard for the individual, it is best for the race." He softened the harsh rules of the market a wee bit, however, by advocating what he called the "Gospel of Wealth": millionaires should act as "trustees for the poor," using some of their great fortunes to "help those who will help themselves." In his old age Carnegie donated about $350 million to public libraries, educational institutions, museums, a pension plan for teachers, and other philanthropic causes.

Many employers considered Social Darwinism more than enough justification for them to police their employees' behavior, even when they were away from work. Companies hired ministers to preach temperance sermons and in some cases sent investigators into workers' homes to discourage them from taking boarders, drinking, or spending their money recklessly. Encouraging sobriety, punctuality, and thrift among workers raised industrial productivity, but corporate attempts to control employees' behavior often conflicted directly with workers' own traditions. For example, on the Great Lakes, dockworkers customarily consumed four or five kegs of beer before they would unload a vessel; naturally, scientific managers disagreed with this practice. Polish steelworkers were accustomed to celebrating weddings for three to five days. How could workers observe such customs and still conform to the corporate regime?

In some cases managers substituted new, productivity-enhancing treats or rewards for activities that took workers away from their tasks. In Southern textile mills managers wanted to increase cloth output from workers accustomed to going home for lunch, taking breaks as they chose, or drinking whiskey on the job. Thus management decided to speed up the pace of work and to require workers to tend their machines for long stretches of time without breaks. To give the workers a treat that would also keep them alert, the company permitted a vendor to come into the factory and sell Coca-Cola from a cart. Workers referred to the cart as the "dope wagon"—an appropriate name, since in that era one of the ingredients in "the real thing" was real cocaine.

Some industrialists cared about their workers' welfare; others thought of their employees simply as human machines, to be replaced when they created friction or wore out. The most paternalistic employers considered their workers part of a family, with themselves as benevolent fathers teaching their children discipline and providing them the protection of a job. Others, indifferent to their workers' welfare, insulated themselves from the rank and file with layers of middle managers.

When conflict erupted between the capitalists and labor, or when the state and federal governments occasionally tried to regulate business, court rulings nearly always favored the wealthy and powerful over the workers or the public interest. Most judges in the 1890s applied the doctrine of *laissez-faire* capitalism and Social Darwinism, which held that the greatest economic and social good would come when owner and worker were free to set their own terms of employment, without interference from labor unions or the government.

Supreme Court decisions limited the rights of the state and federal governments to regulate business, to levy income taxes, and to restrict business monopolies. The justices based many of their rulings on a creative reading of the Fourteenth Amendment, which prohibits state action abridging the "privileges and immunities" of citizens or denying "any person of life, liberty, or property" without due process of law. Lawyers persuaded the courts that corporations were, legally speaking, persons, whose economic freedom could not be limited or regulated. Previously, "due process" had meant following certain legal procedures for a given circumstance, such as holding a trial for a person accused of a crime. Now the courts ruled that "substantive due process of law and liberty to contract" meant that persons—or corporations—possessed certain irreducible rights that the government could not regulate. This doctrine held that men and women must be left free to sell their labor to any employer, without interference from a union or government seeking to set a minimum wage, limit working hours, or enforce safety standards.

During the 1890s the Supreme Court undermined antitrust laws by ruling that even a company that controlled 90 percent of the sugar industry did not constitute a monopoly (*United States* v. *E. C. Knight,* 1895). In a series of cases (*Ritchie* v. *The People,* 1895; *Allgeyer* v. *Louisiana,* 1897; *Holden* v. *Hardy,* 1898; *Lochner* v. *New York,* 1905), the High Court struck down nearly all state and federal efforts to regulate business practices and working conditions.

As the marketplace expanded, Americans all across the nation had a far greater range of things to buy than they had ever had before. The arrival of the Montgomery Ward catalogue in rural mailboxes heralded the availability of a cornucopia of goods to anyone, anywhere. Although prices for goods were increasingly standardized across the country, consumers who had once known intimately the sources and value of what they ate, lived in, worked with, and wore knew less and less about the origins and quality of what they bought. Purchased food, at first a convenience, became a necessity. American householders had long fed themselves by keeping pigs and chickens and tending gardens. But as farmland grew more expensive and farming became more mechanized and corporate, the sons and daughters of rural towns moved to cities in search of higher-paying work. The Pennsylvania farm girl who moved to Pittsburgh or Philadelphia to seek a living might once have made her own sausage. But as a city dweller working in a factory or office and living in an apartment, she would instead purchase bologna manufactured at one of Gustavus F. Swift's faraway packing plants. Who knew who had made it, how it had been made, or what was in it? The persons who knew most about that bologna were, of course, those who worked for Swift or Philip D. Armour in the packing houses that led the poet Carl Sandburg to call Chicago "hog butcher to the world."

✦ The New Immigration and the New City

Many workers were newcomers to the nation. Some 11 million immigrants came to the United States between 1870 and 1900. (Ten million more arrived by 1914.) Although many continued to come from Germany, Ireland, Scandinavia, and the British Isles, most new arrivals hailed from southern and eastern Europe. Jews fleeing persecution in Czarist Russia, Slavs seeking shelter from nationalist upheavals in Eastern Europe, and Catholics escaping population pressures in southern Italy were especially numerous. In addition to overcrowding and ethnic turmoil in Europe, the export of inexpensive American grain made farming unprofitable for many peasants in Europe, forcing them off the land and into European and American cities.

Regular steamship schedules made trans-Atlantic travel easier and cheaper in the 1890s than ever before. It took about ten days to travel from Europe to the port of New York. The relative ease of travel made it possible for many immigrants to return to Europe for brief visits or, in their old age, permanently (see figure).

The immigrants' limited financial resources, lack of familiarity with English, and rural backgrounds offered them little preparation for life in American cities. They competed for jobs in industry, for places to live in increasingly crowded urban neighborhoods, and for the chance to rise into the middle class. American cities grew at an astounding pace after the Civil War. The development of electric streetcars, cheap structural steel, elevators, and water and sewer systems allowed U.S. cities to expand both vertically and horizontally. In 1870 fewer than 10 million of the nation's 40 million inhabitants lived in urban areas. By 1900 about 30 million out of 76 million Americans did so. Looked at another way, in 1870 there were twenty-five U.S. cities with a population above fifty thousand but by 1895 some sixty U.S. cities surpassed this size. Most were located in the Northeast or near the Great Lakes.

Immigrant groups congregated in neighborhoods like Manhattan's Lower East Side, dominated by eastern European Jews, and St. Louis's Hill, an Italian

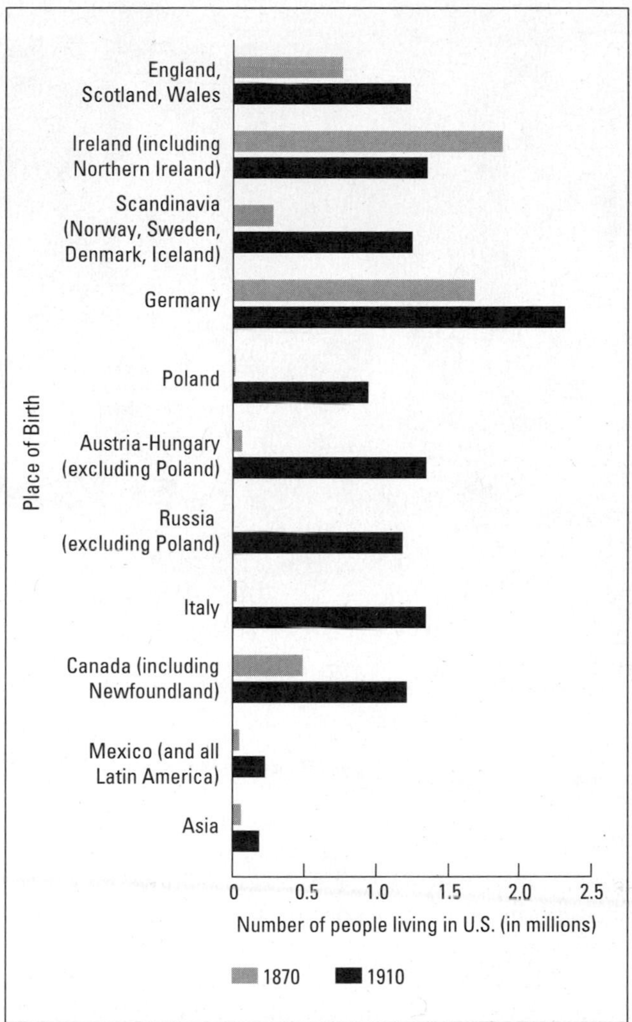

Immigration, 1870 to 1924 Note the shift in origins.

enclave, bringing a proliferation of languages, customs, and goods into American life. Immigrant neighborhoods played host to a lively street culture, with vendors hawking their wares, people hanging laundry out their windows and gossiping on front stoops, and children playing everywhere. Immigrant families clustered together to help one another adjust to life in the new world and to combat the suspicions of native-born Americans. They paid high rents to live in increasingly crowded, filthy tenements. Landlords seeking to increase their profits subdivided buildings again and again, with little regard

Immigrants making a living in a typical American city, ca. 1890. *Library of Congress*

for their tenants' needs for light, air, water, or sanitation. Thus immigrants inhabited some of the most notorious slums in American cities, and the horrible conditions of their domiciles and neighborhoods became targets of reformers' zeal.

In the West, immigrants from Japan and Mexico continued to arrive. More than eighty thousand Japanese entered the United States between 1898 and 1907, most of them young men who worked as agricultural laborers or on railroads. Prohibited by federal law from becoming citizens, and often prevented by real estate covenants from living among whites, Japanese immigrants worked around local racism and created successful farming communities in southern California. Filipinos also migrated to the United States in the wake of the Spanish-American war of 1898, looking for the uplifting freedom and opportunities the U.S. government had insisted it represented when American troops occupied the Philippines. Mexican immigrants worked as agricultural and railroad laborers and took jobs in mining. By 1914 nearly three hundred thousand people of Mexican descent lived in the United States, many of them refugees from the revolution that swept through their homeland for a decade beginning in 1910. They created permanent communities in growing U.S. cities like San Antonio, El Paso, and Los Angeles.

During the 1880s and 1890s Josiah Strong, general secretary of the American Evangelical Alliance and a popular lecturer, articulated a common view of immigration. Fearing the influx of Catholic and Jewish immigrants, Strong warned that "the city is the nerve center of our civilization; it is also the storm center. . . . The city has become a serious menace to our civilization." Between 1887 and 1896 the American Protective Association grew to almost 1 million members through its appeals to Protestants concerning the danger of Catholic immigration.

When the Statue of Liberty was completed in New York Harbor in 1886, Emma Lazarus, only six weeks in America, wrote a poem whose final words were inscribed on the monument:

> Give me your tired, your poor,
> Your huddled masses yearning to breathe free,
> The wretched refuse of your teeming shore;
> Send the homeless, tempest-tost to me,
> I lift my lamp beside the golden door.

But in response to growing immigration, other poetic voices, such as that of Thomas Bailey Aldrich, challenged Lazarus:

> Wide open and unguarded stand our gates,
> And through them presses a wild, motley throng—
> Men from the Volga and the Tartar steppes,
> Featureless figures of the Hoang-Ho,
> Malayan, Scythian, Teuton, Kelt and Slav . . .
> These bringing with them unknown gods and rites
> Those tiger passions here to stretch their claws . . .
> Oh Liberty, white Goddess!
> Is it well to leave the gates unguarded?

In the 1890s, like a century later, Americans expressed mixed feelings about immigrants. Industrialists favored the cheap labor pool they provided, and many observers believed the new arrivals enriched American life. Except for a congressional action in 1882 that suspended Chinese immigration, business interests blocked most serious efforts to limit entry into the United States before World War I. Nevertheless, many Americans worried that ethnic diversity weakened the national spirit and made America a dump for the world's "undesirable" population. Many Protestant opponents of immigration objected most strongly to the influence of ethnic (typically Irish) "urban bosses" who were building a political following among the new immigrants.

Those who came to the United States at the turn of the century—whether from Europe, Asia, or Mexico—came face to face with the often vicious nativism of white Protestant Americans. Aside from a few charitable institutions such as Hull House in Chicago, Henry Street Settlement in New York, and Robert Woods Settlement in Boston, the lack of social services or welfare programs forced new arrivals to rely on those who had come earlier to find work, food, and housing. Help often came in the form of favors from labor contractors and city politicians, who expected return favors in the form of votes and, sometimes, bribes or kickbacks. Urban political machines thrived on the desperation of newly arrived Americans (and, it should be noted, offered not only immediate relief from destitution but also an avenue of social mobility for ambitious young men looking to get ahead).

Tammany Hall, the Democratic Party organization in New York City, epitomized the urban political machine of the 1890s. Led by talented and colorful first- and second-generation Irish-Americans such as Richard Croker and George Washington Plunkitt, Tammany provided a variety of social, employment, and personal services to those who voted the "party line." Tammany representatives greeted new immigrants as they stepped off steamships, steered them to a cheap hotel, put in a word for them with construction companies, and sent gifts when a baby was born, a couple was wed, or a grandparent died. Poor but grateful constituents gladly traded their votes for such favors. As Plunkitt proudly observed, the "machine" leaders made their money through "honest graft": they didn't steal directly from city coffers; they merely "seen their opportunities and they took 'em." For example, knowledge of where a rapidly growing city would build new roads, sewers, or other improvements allowed politicians and their friends to buy undeveloped land cheaply and resell it for a huge profit after the new infrastructure was in place.

But when municipal authorities ran the government as if it were their private business, they did little to serve the public interest at large. The most corrupt politicians raided the public till or larded government contracts with huge profits for themselves. Firetrap tenements went unregulated; garbage piled up in the streets. Those who bucked the power of the machine faced neglect at best and economic or physical reprisals at worst. Critics of this plunder, especially among the middle class, demanded that city governments be restructured to reduce the power of the bosses and that civil service exams be required for municipal employment. But the hard-pressed urban poor resented these ideas, fearing that such reforms were designed to cut government costs and patronage, depriving them of the few services and jobs available to them.

The inequalities in American life showed themselves in the nation's cities. Gleaming skyscrapers vied with teeming tenements for the honor of representing modern America. Corporate consolidation and the proliferation of new technologies and products were making a few people fabulously rich. Newly arrived immigrants shared with some groups born in the United States—notably, African-Americans and Indians—the backbreaking burdens of poverty. And these groups were not far behind most of the descendants of earlier immigrants. In 1900 perhaps as many as 80 percent of Americans lived near the subsistence level. Late-nineteenth-century reformers called attention to the vast gulf between the wealthy few and the miserable many. In the new century the cries for reform would take on renewed urgency as Americans confronted the economic, political, and environmental perils of urban modernity.

✦ National Politics

By any reckoning the quality of national politics in the last decades of the nineteenth century set a low standard. In the wake of Reconstruction, Congress dominated the national government and presidents followed in its wake. Americans enjoyed politics and voted in large numbers, but U.S. campaigns, though spirited, often seemed more a form of entertainment than an effort to address serious problems.

Between 1876 and 1900, even though the Democrats held the presidency for only eight years, the two major parties attracted roughly the same number of voters and often traded control of Congress. Generally speaking the Republicans supported high tariffs, pensions for Civil War veterans and their widows, and a tight money supply. Democrats favored lower tariffs and a more flexible money supply, and they opposed nearly all government economic support for business or labor. Personalities and the desire for spoils drove the political process as much as policy. One powerful politician of the era, Simon Cameron, defined an honest man as one who "when bought, stayed bought."

Most of the time Congress rewarded rather than regulated business. Land grants to railroads, loggers, and mining companies, high tariffs to protect domestic manufacturers, and other forms of aid to business were common. And when Congress or state governments did attempt to regulate railroad rates or interstate commerce, the Supreme Court often struck down the regulations as an abuse of power.

Although workers had little success in organizing unions or getting the government to address their grievances, farmers pushed hard for reform during the 1880s and 1890s. The declining prices they received for their products especially vexed them. For example, in 1870 wheat sold for $1.06 per bushel. By the mid-1890s, however, the price had fallen to sixty-five cents. During the same period the price of a bushel of corn shrank from forty-three cents to thirty cents and the price of cotton from fifteen to only six cents per pound.

Farm prices fell in large part because of increased production in the United States, Argentina, Canada, and Russia. Falling prices forced hard-pressed and heavily indebted farmers to produce even more, further glutting the market. The cost of manufactured goods also declined during this period, partly offsetting the loss in farmers' purchasing power. However, because farmers carried a high level of debt, they had to pay back interest and principal on loans at a relatively high, fixed cost, despite their declining income. Farmers resented their lack of control over the interest rates charged by banks, the freight charges set by railroads, and the storage costs demanded by grain elevators. Many believed that only currency inflation (that is, the creation of more and cheaper money) would raise crop prices and lower the cost of debt. Agitator Mary E. Lease hit a nerve when she told aroused farmers that "Wall Street owns the country. . . . It is no longer a government for the people . . . but a government of Wall Street, by Wall Street and for Wall Street." The West and South, she complained, were "slaves" to the business monopolies of the "manufacturing East." Farmers, she argued, should "raise less corn and more Hell."

During the 1870s and 1880s farmers created several organizations, such as the Grange and the Farmers Alliance, that supported a variety of reforms, from establishing purchasing and marketing cooperatives to women's suffrage and railroad regulation. In 1891 activists organized the People's Party, or Populists, and the next year they ran James Weaver for president. Populists tended to see "the people" as victims of a conspiracy among East Coast and European plutocrats. The preamble to the party campaign platform declared that "a vast conspiracy against mankind has been organized on two continents, and it is rapidly taking possession of the world." Populists demanded a range of reforms, from the fanciful to the practical, including the unlimited, or free, coinage of silver, a graduated income tax, government-run postal savings banks, public ownership of railroads, direct election of U.S. senators, and creation of a so-called subtreasury system that would permit farmers to receive loans against the value of their land or of surplus crops stored in government warehouses. (In effect this would have represented a government price support program for agriculture.) To widen their appeal among urban laborers, the Populists called for an eight-hour workday, immigration restrictions, and the right to strike.

Although these ideas spoke to many real grievances, some Populist leaders revealed a mean, xenophobic streak. Many identified British bankers and rich Jews (of whom there were precious few, in America or elsewhere, in 1892) as the farmers' enemies. In response to rising immigration, Georgia Populist Tom Watson complained that the "scum of creation" was being dumped on America. Dismissing evidence that impersonal forces such as overproduction and a competitive world market accounted for agricultural price fluctuations, Populists saw conspiracies behind U.S. farmers' problems. They were especially incensed at the Coinage Act of 1873, which stopped the production of silver coins.

During most of the nineteenth century the Treasury had minted both gold and silver coins. Typically a silver dollar contained (by weight) sixteen times more silver than the amount of gold in a $1 gold coin. Fluctuations in the relative supply and value of the two metals periodically drove one or the other out of circulation. Until the 1840s gold shortages resulted in the virtual disappearance of gold currency, since the metal was worth more by weight than the face value of the coins. With the influx of gold from California after 1848, however, gold became cheaper and silver more valuable. Those who had silver sold it on the open market rather than to the Treasury, where it fetched less. By 1873 almost no silver coins were in circulation, and Congress temporarily abandoned the minting of silver dollars. During the next twenty years most of Europe also stopped using silver coins.

Beginning in the late 1870s, however, new discoveries in the American West drove down the price of silver relative to gold. Soon silver producers, debtors, and others who favored currency inflation demanded that Congress resume minting silver dollars (at the old weight ratio, relative to gold currency, of sixteen to one) so that they could pay off their debts in less valuable silver currency. Those devoted to silver sometimes justified their position by citing spiritual or religious reasons. Even though Congress agreed to mint small amounts of silver coins after 1878, the metal's advocates were not appeased.

Discontent increased after a severe depression began in 1893. At that time it was the steepest fall ever in the American economy, and it lasted through 1896. Within the first year of the slump nearly six hundred banks, 160,000 businesses, and many transcontinental railroads went bankrupt. Nationally, 20 percent of the work force was idle, with the number rising to 25 percent in industrial states. Populists floated many of their most extreme demands for government action to solve this crisis.

As a political party, the Populists had difficulty bridging the difference between northern and southern as well as black and white farmers. Some Populist farmers saw themselves as workers, others as small businessmen. Some believed their problems stemmed from the capitalist system, while others believed that coining mountains of silver would set everything right. After a poor showing in state and congressional elections in 1894, the Populist Party dropped most of its other tenets and promoted the free coinage of silver as the solution to most of the country's problems. In 1894 William H. ("Coin") Harvey, one of the party's most successful publicists, wrote a book called *Coin's Financial School*, which claimed to explain how silver's enemies had ruined America and how its expanded use as money would save the nation. The book sold over a million copies within two years. With his profits Harvey constructed a 130-foot high pyramid to enshrine his book as well as other "classics."

By 1896 the Democratic Party was desperately seeking an attractive candidate to replace the retiring and unpopular President Grover Cleveland. At a boisterous convention the party nominated a thirty-six-year-old lawyer, newspaper editor, and former Nebraska congressman named William Jennings Bryan. A true believer in the virtues of silver, Bryan electrified the convention delegates with a speech that concluded with the words, "You shall not press down upon the brow of labor this crown of thorns! You shall not crucify mankind upon a cross of gold!"

The Republican Party nominated a stolid defender of sound money and friend of big business as their candidate. Former Ohio governor and congressman William McKinley was best known for the high tariff of 1890 that bore his name. McKinley campaigned exclusively from his front porch in Canton,

Ohio, while his manager, Mark Hanna, scared Wall Street, bankers, insurance companies, and manufacturers into contributing at least $4 million to McKinley's war chest, at that time the largest amount ever collected in a presidential campaign.

Bryan campaigned virtually nonstop around the country, touting free silver as a cure-all. Hanna bought advertisements in newspapers and printed millions of pamphlets in many languages, ridiculing Bryan's notions. He also urged employers to inform their workers that in case of a Bryan victory, factories would close. In the end a combination of intimidation and genuine concern among urban workers that higher food prices and anti-immigrant attitudes might not be in their best interests undermined Bryan's appeal in the East and in most cities. In November, with signs of an economic recovery weakening the appeal for silver coinage, McKinley defeated Bryan by a wide margin. The loser won the South and most of the far West, while the victor triumphed in the more populous Northeast and upper Midwest. The election proved to be the death knell of the Populist Party (which had joined the Democrats in nominating Bryan) although Bryan ran twice more, unsuccessfully, as a Democrat.

Americans often complained that the national parties and candidates stood for little. Yet when the Populist and, to a lesser extent, Democratic Parties did challenge the status quo and offer a different vision of government, the voters shunned them. In 1896 the Republicans, with a probusiness message, emerged as the clear majority party, which they remained for much of the next thirty-five years.

After 1897 gold discoveries in Alaska, Australia, and South Africa rendered moot most of the arguments over silver. The increased supply of gold drove down its cost and led to an expansion of the gold currency in circulation, without reliance on silver.

✦ Conclusion

In 1900 the United States barely resembled the country that had fought the Civil War. Modern industrial corporations produced most of the nation's goods. The new farms and ranches of the trans-Mississippi West relied on railroads to serve national and international markets. Giant cities like New York, Chicago, and San Francisco and smaller urban areas were home to nearly 40 percent of Americans, including millions of immigrants. Consumer goods had improved the quality of life for many, and at least four thousand Americans enjoyed the status of millionaire. But about 80 percent of the population still lived near the subsistence level. The 250,000 Indians who remained alive lived in legal limbo, denied in most cases even the basic status of citizenship. Nearly 10 million blacks—ex-slaves and their descendants—existed in a rigidly segregated world. Many blacks in the North, and nearly all 7 million in the South, were confined by law and custom to separate and inferior schools, housing, and jobs.

The 1890s brought a series of new challenges to American life. The terrible depression that began in 1893 lasted almost four years before recovery began. National leaders worried that economic decline, political protests, and social violence were symptoms of a deeper national problem caused by immigration, the "filling up" of the continent, and foreign competition. Some looked toward the promise of foreign expansion and restrictions on immigration, and others toward domestic reform, as solutions to the crisis.

✦ Further Reading

For an overview of the late nineteenth century, see: Mark Wahlgren Summers, *The Gilded Age, Or the Hazard of New Functions* (1997); H. W. Brands, *The Reckless Decade: America in the 1890s* (1995); Robert H. Wiebe, *The Search for Order* (1977); Nell Irvin Painter, *Standing at Armageddon: The United States, 1877–1919* (1987). On the West, see: Patricia Nelson Limerick, *The Legacy of Conquest: The Unbroken Past of the American West* (1987); Richard White, *"It's Your Misfortune and None of My Own": A History of the American West* (1991); Peggy Pascoe, *Relations of Rescue: The Search for Female Moral Authority in the American West, 1874–1939* (1990); Ronald Takaki, *Strangers from a Different Shore: A History of Asian Americans* (1989); Robert F. Berkhofer, Jr., *The White Man's Indian* (1978); Richard Drinnon, *Facing West: The Metaphysics of Indian-Hating and Empire Building* (1980); Frederick E. Hoxie, *A Final Promise: The Campaign to Assimilate the Indians, 1880–1920* (1984); Joseph G. Rosa and Robin May, *Buffalo Bill and His Wild West* (1989); William Cronon, *Nature's Metropolis: Chicago and the Great West* (1991); Richard Slotkin, *The Fatal Environment: The Myth of the Frontier in the Age of Industrialization* (1985) and *Gunfighter Nation* (1992); Daniel Worster, *Under Western Skies: Nature and History in the American West* (1992) and *Rivers of Empire* (1985). On Reconstruction and race in the New South, see: Eric Foner, *Reconstruction: America's Unfinished Revolution, 1863–1877* (1988); Dan Carter, *When the War Was Over: The Failure of Self-Reconstruction in the South, 1865–1867* (1985); Eric Foner, *Nothing but Freedom: Emancipation and Its Legacy* (1983); Leon Litwack, *Been in the Storm So Long: The Aftermath of Slavery* (1979); Michael Perman, *The Road to Redemption: Southern Politics, 1869–1879* (1984); Edward L. Ayers, *The Promise of the New South: Life After Reconstruction* (1992); and Joel Williamson, *The Crucible of Race: Black-White Relations in the South Since Emancipation* (1985); Charles A. Lofgren, *The Plessy Case: A Legal-Historical Interpretation* (1987). On Gilded Age politics and policy, see: Margaret S. Thompson, *The Spider Web: Congress and Lobbying in the Age of Grant* (1985); Irwin Unger, *The Greenback Era* (1964); Mark W. Summers, *The Era of Good Stealings* (1992); R. Hal Williams, *Years of Decision: American Politics in the 1890s* (1978); Martin J. Sklar, *The Corporate Reconstruction of American Capitalism, 1890–1916* (1988); Theda Skocpol, *Protecting Soldiers and Mothers: The Political Origins of Social Policy in the United States* (1992). On the rise of industry, see: Carl Degler, *The Age of the Economic Revolution* (1977); Robert L. Heilbroner, *The Economic*

Transformation of America (1977); Alan Trachtenberg, *The Incorporation of America: Culture and Society in the Gilded Age* (1982); David F. Noble, *America by Design: Science, Technology and the Rise of Corporate Capitalism* (1977); Alfred D. Chandler, Jr., *Strategy and Structure: Chapters in the History of American Industrial Enterprise* (1962), *The Visible Hand: The Managerial Revolution in American Business* (1977), and *Scale and Scope: The Dynamics of Industrial Capitalism* (1990); Olivier Zunz, *Making America Corporate, 1870–1920* (1990); Sidney Fine, *Laissez Faire and the General Welfare State: A Study of Conflict in American Thought, 1865–1901* (1956); Richard Hofstadter, *Social Darwinism and American Thought* (1955). On labor, see: Paul Avrich, *The Haymarket Tragedy* (1984); Melvyn Dubofsky, *Industrialism and the American Worker, 1865–1920* (1975); Leon Fink, *Workingmen's Democracy: The Knights of Labor and American Politics* (1983); David Montgomery, *The Fall of the House of Labor: The Workplace, the State, and American Labor Activism, 1865–1925* (1987); Roy Rosenzweig, *"Eight Hours for What We Will": Workers and Leisure in an Industrial City, 1870–1920* (1983); Leon Wolff, *Lockout: The Story of the Homestead Strike of 1892* (1965); Nick Salvatore, *Eugene V. Debs: Citizen and Socialist* (1982); Elizabeth Anne Payne, *Reform, Labor and Feminism* (1988). On cities and immigrants, see: Charles N. Glabb and Andrew T. Brown, *A History of Urban America* (1967); Sam Bass Warner, *The Urban Wilderness* (1972) and *Streetcar Suburbs* (1962); Robert A. Mohl, *The New City: Urban America in the Industrial Age, 1860–1920* (1985); Steven Thernstrom, *Poverty and Progress* (1964); Thomas J. Archdeacon, *Becoming American: An Ethnic History* (1983); John Bodnar, *The Transplanted: A History of Immigration in America* (1985); Leonard Dinnerstein and David Reimers, *Ethnic Americans: A History of Immigration and Assimilation* (1975); John Higham, *Strangers in the Land* (1955); Bill Ong Hing, *Making and Remaking Asian America Through Immigration Policy* (1993); Alan M. Kraut, *The Huddled Masses: The Immigrant in American Society, 1880–1921* (1982) and *Silent Travellers: Germs, Genes, and the "Immigrant Menace"* (1994); Matt S. Maier and Feliciano Rivera, *The Chicanos: A History of Mexican-Americans* (1972); Jacob Riis, *How the Other Half Lives* (1890); John M. Allswang, *Bosses, Machines, and Urban Voters* (1977); John Sproat, *The Best Men: Liberal Reformers in the Gilded Age* (1968); James D. Norris, *Advertising and the Transformation of American Culture, 1865–1920* (1990); William Leach, *Land of Desire: Merchants, Power, and the Rise of a New American Culture* (1993). On the depression of the 1890s and Populism, see: Ray Ginger, *Altgeld's America* (1958); Samuel McSeveney, *The Politics of Depression* (1972); John Hicks, *The Populist Revolt* (1931); Steven Hahn, *The Roots of Southern Populism* (1983); Robert C. McMath, Jr., *American Populism: A Social History, 1877–1898* (1993); Norman Pollack, *The Populist Response to Industrial America* (1962); Robert F. Durden, *The Climax of Populism: The Election of 1896* (1965); Paul Glad, *McKinley, Bryan, and the People* (1964).

✦✦✦
CHAPTER **2**

Progressivism and the Search for Order, 1900–1917

✦ **College graduates rally for suffrage.**

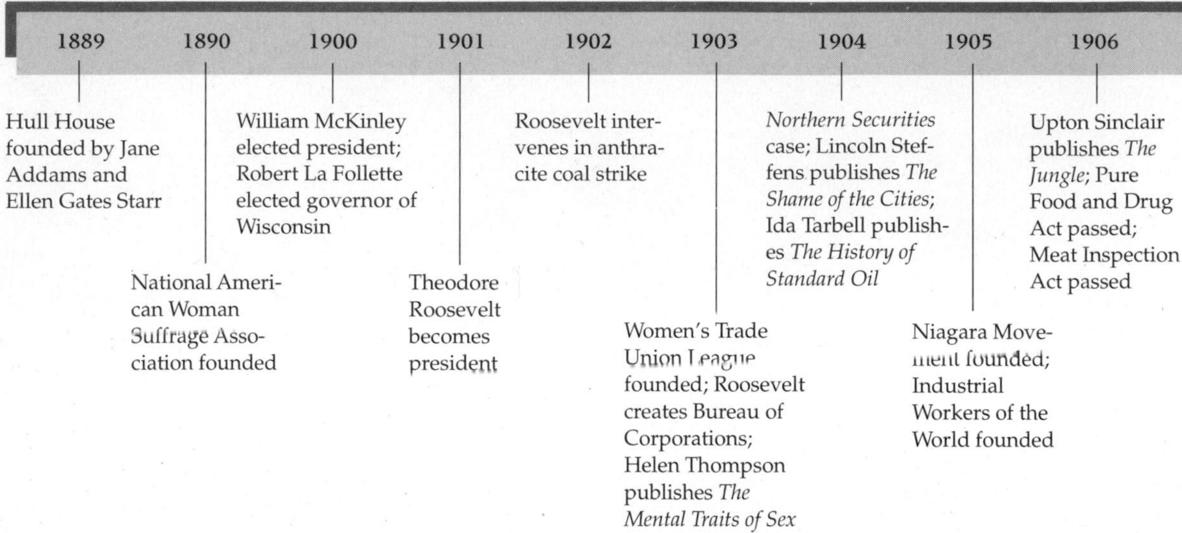

ONE FRIGID MORNING at the end of 1891, a woman made her way with difficulty through the congested streets of Chicago. Soot-blackened snow, mounded high from curb to streetcar track, blocked traffic. So did the horses who had faltered and fallen to the icy streets, sometimes to be shot and laid on top of snowbanks until they could be hauled away. Florence Kelley, newly arrived in the city, had fled an abusive husband back in New York, borrowing the train fare for herself and her three small children. On arriving in Chicago she had left her children in a nursery run by the Women's Christian Temperance Union and set out to seek work and refuge at Hull House, a settlement house established two years earlier by Jane Addams and Ellen Gates Starr. For the next seven years Kelley and her children lived at Hull House, taking up the pressing work of bettering conditions for immigrant workers in the surrounding neighborhood and, eventually, the city, the state, and the nation.

The women of Hull House both addressed and embodied new forces in American life. Many had been raised in comfortable circumstances, and as women of the "leisure class" they had been expected to take their place in society as hostesses and housewives. But Florence Kelley and those like her were unwilling to settle for that kind of life, no matter how luxurious. Mem-

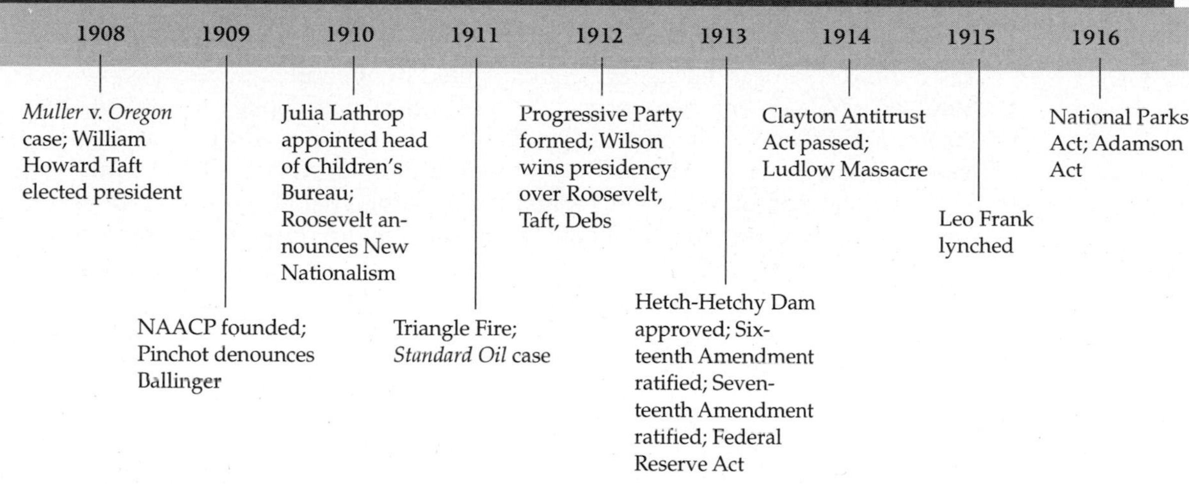

bers of the first generation of college-educated American women, they had studied the social problems and possibilities created by industrialization, immigration, and urbanization. The solutions they suggested ranged from "Americanization" programs and child labor laws to state-mandated garbage collection. They were determined to bring about a more just and humane social, political, and economic order by taking personal responsibility, collecting information, making political alliances, pressing for legislation, and, ultimately, holding government office. Their mothers and grandmothers had created a public-service culture for women by organizing volunteer associations such as literary clubs, moral reform societies, abolitionist groups, and women's rights organizations. Their fathers had taken part in the process, accelerated by the Civil War, of creating a greater role for the government in Americans' lives. Now Kelley's generation would confront the changes brought on by modernization, and they turned to the state to be the chief agent of social progress.

The women and men who came together at the beginning of the twentieth century to pressure local, state, and federal leaders to solve the nation's problems had faith in human expertise and in the positive potential of government. Some assailed the corruption of public life. Others, worried that traditional American virtues were endangered by the influx of new people, new technologies, and new forms of power into society, looked for ways to manage social and economic change efficiently. Some referred to themselves as progressives, and historians have come to call their diverse, often contradictory collection of ideas and programs for change the Progressive Movement. This movement transformed American politics, tapping the radical vision of socialists like labor leader Eugene V. Debs, producing influential political leaders at the state level like Wisconsin's Robert M. La Follette and California's Hiram W. Johnson, and reaching its zenith with the occupation of the White House by Theodore Roosevelt, William Howard Taft, and Woodrow Wilson between 1901 and 1920. As with all reform efforts, the progressives' many projects sprang from assumptions and circumstances of which they were sometimes unaware and had consequences that their proponents never intended or predicted.

✦ Reformers' Search for Justice and Order

By 1900, thousands of Americans believed themselves ready to solve the problems of urbanization, industrialization, rapid technological change, and immigration. Most such reformers lived in metropolitan areas, even if they had been born in small towns or on farms. Most had been raised in at least modest comfort. They were accustomed to the luxuries available to affluent Americans of that time—lavish parties, handsome carriages and monumental houses, elegant furniture, extensive travel. But their affluence did not blind them to others' poverty. Ranging from moderate liberals to socialists, they blamed big business and machine politics for injustice and corruption, for distorting America's promise of liberty and equality. Some, especially labor activists and urban reformers, believed that societal problems demanded public solutions. Many believed in using the state to restore individual freedom and competition. Often themselves the products of the nation's expanding higher education system, progressive reformers believed that "experts"—professionally trained, college educated people like social workers, economists, and city planners—could identify and solve social problems better than laypeople.

Reform in Education

Progressivism was founded on the enlargement of the American educational system. Most Americans believed that the government should provide free schooling for all children (or at least all white children) through the primary grades. More and more people, especially in urban areas, believed in the benefits of a high school education, and by 1900 there were some six thousand high schools in the country. At the same time, colleges and universities proliferated. The Morrill Land Grant College Act of 1862 had provided the basis for funding state agricultural and technical colleges and universities, which were critical to developing the newly established states in the West. In 1890 the government initiated a land grant program directed at African-American agricultural education. Corporate wealth flowed into private universities as well, as entrepreneurs like John D. Rockefeller and Andrew Carnegie gave money to private colleges (including Harvard, Yale, Princeton, and Columbia) and almost single-handedly bankrolled new institutions such as Vanderbilt, Stanford, and Rockefeller's University of Chicago.

Reacting against Social Darwinism and other nineteenth-century ideas that had tended to make people feel they had no capacity to direct their fate, prominent intellectuals insisted that abstract theories could not substitute for empirical investigation. In *Dynamic Sociology* (1883), Lester Frank Ward argued that it was wrong to confuse biological evolution with social evolution. The former, said Ward, operated according to biological rather than conscious processes. By contrast, people built civilizations by intervening in natural processes, in rational, voluntary, and responsive ways. Ward later became the first president of the American Sociological Society, in 1905. Harvard philosopher William James, a leader in the development of psychology, rejected any notion that history revealed innate "laws." He instead insisted that people "carve out" their world from "the jointless continuity of space." James argued that ideas were to be judged by their consequences, as guides to practical actions. The University of Chicago's John Dewey applied James's *pragmatism* to the problem of education, with far-reaching results. The legions of "progressive educators" who adopted Dewey's programs believed that the schools were the incubators of citizenship in a democracy. Under Dewey's direction, the University of Chicago's Laboratory School stressed openness to experience, creativity, problem solving, and practical activities rather than a rigid curriculum. Progressives had high hopes that children educated according to their methods would improve their communities.

As higher education expanded, some institutions began to move beyond an undergraduate curriculum to emphasize advanced professional degrees in new fields. The emerging social sciences—sociology, economics, political science, psychology, and anthropology—reflected a new commitment to using higher education to articulate and solve social problems and to further progressive political agendas. At the University of Wisconsin, for example, economists John R. Commons and Richard T. Ely worked closely with progressive politicians, including Robert M. La Follette, to reform labor laws and regulate public utilities.

Although many social scientists resisted attempts by women and people of color to gain positions in the field, a significant minority of prominent professors provided them not only opportunities for personal advancement but also support research funding to combat negative stereotypes formerly passed off as science. At the University of Chicago, sociologist Robert E. Park challenged Social Darwinists' belief that those with the most money and power represented the "survival of the fittest" in human society. To the contrary, Park insisted that the person barred by virtue of race or sex from social power "inevitably becomes, relative to his cultural milieu, the individual with the wider horizon, the keener intelligence, the more detached and rational viewpoint. The marginal man," said Park, "is always relatively the more civilized human being."

Also at Chicago, John Dewey and James B. Angell mentored women graduate students like Helen Thompson, whose experiments demonstrated that differences between men and women in psychological traits had been vastly exaggerated. Thompson did acknowledge persistent differences between male and female behavior, but she attributed those divergences to society rather than biology. "If it were really a fundamental difference of instincts and characteristics which determined [sex differences]," she wrote in *The Mental Traits of Sex: An Experimental Investigation of the Normal Mind in Men and Women* (1903), "it would not be necessary to spend so much effort in making boys and girls follow the lines of conduct proper to their sex."

Still, Thompson and other researchers dedicated to discrediting "scientific" evidence of the innate inferiority of certain groups had to overcome formidable resistance. Scientific racism persisted long after Social Darwinism had faded from favor. Social scientists like Madison Grant, author of *The Passing of the Great Race,* insisted that the influx of persons of "inferior racial stock" from countries like Hungary, Italy, Russia, and Poland threatened to dilute and eventually overwhelm the purportedly superior "old stock" of Anglo-Americans. Such ideas had political implications. H. H. Goddard, director of research at New Jersey's Vineland Institute for Feebleminded Girls and Boys, invented the term *moron* to describe persons incapable of progressing beyond the mental age of twelve. Using a version of the Stanford-Binet test that would become the standard for IQ tests, in 1913 Goddard accepted a U.S. Public Health Service invitation to test immigrants arriving at Ellis Island. For men and women just disembarking after a grueling passage, mostly illiterate and without any knowledge of English, the experience of being accosted by Goddard's assistants and made to answer a rapid-fire succession of mystifying questions must have been terrifying. When Goddard tabulated the results of his tests, he found that fully 83 percent of the Jews, 87 percent of the Russians, 80 percent of the Hungarians, and 79 percent of the Italians were "morons." To scientific racists like Goddard, such "research" proved the need for immigration restrictions rather than the existence of flaws in their experimental designs.

African-Americans' Continuing Struggle

No group of Americans faced greater prejudice, scientific or otherwise, at the beginning of the twentieth century than African-Americans. The Progressive Era was for them not a time of great strides forward but instead a historical nadir, or low point. Throughout the South, where four-fifths of the nation's 10 million blacks struggled to survive in an economy based on sharecropping, African-Americans faced tightening social and economic restrictions, legalized discrimination, and disfranchisement. Not only was racial segregation legally sanctioned in the South by Jim Crow laws, but racial intimidation, in the form of lynchings and other terrorist acts, silenced any who dared to resist. And the two hundred thousand African-Americans who migrated to northern cities in search of economic opportunity and relief from racial oppression in the first decade of the twentieth century met with hatred and resistance there as well. Although the color line was not as harsh in much of the North as it was in the South, segregation and intimidation remained facts of life for blacks. Whites assaulted blacks on any pretense, and bloody race riots broke out in cities like East St. Louis, Chicago, and Springfield, Illinois.

Thus black intellectuals and political activists labored under the multiple burdens of combating violence, refuting racist ideology, and rolling back segregationist laws and customs. At the end of the nineteenth century the nation's most influential African-American leader was Booker T. Washington, a son of slaves and the founder of Alabama's Tuskegee Institute, a vocational school for blacks. Washington insisted that "agitation of questions of racial equality is the extremest folly." He counseled blacks to strive, instead, for economic self-sufficiency and self-respect. His influential autobiography, *Up from Slavery,* was widely read and much admired. Washington's accomodationist views infuriated some blacks in the North, however. Many northern blacks were well educated and relatively well off and were unwilling to accept second-class citizenship. In 1905 a group including William Monroe Trotter, editor of the *Boston Guardian,* and social scientist T. Thomas Fortune decided to meet near Niagara Falls, New York, in an effort to formulate a less conciliatory program for change. They promised to work for voting rights, integration, equal economic opportunity, and legal equity. The man who emerged as spokesman for the Niagara Movement was the Massachusetts-born sociologist W. E. B. Du Bois. A graduate of Fisk University, Du Bois was the first African-American to have earned a Ph.D. at Harvard, in 1895. As a professor at the all-black Atlanta University, he produced state-of-the-art sociological studies of African-Americans that refuted racial stereotypes and documented black history. "The way for a people to gain their reasonable rights," Du Bois insisted, "is not by throwing them away." Instead, said Du Bois, blacks must militantly pursue their rights and insist on complete political and economic equality for an intellectual elite, or "Talented Tenth," of African-Americans.

Although the Niagara Movement failed to generate much momentum, Du Bois and his colleagues had set out an agenda. By 1909 black leaders had joined with liberal white allies like Hull House founder Jane Addams to found the National Association for the Advancement of Colored People (NAACP). Although Du Bois was the only black officer of this white-dominated organization, he would become its most prominent and eloquent voice as editor of its journal, the *Crisis.*

Publications like the *Crisis* and the *Guardian* provided forums for African-Americans crusading against injustice. When Memphis editor Ida B. Wells denounced the lynching of three black businessmen in 1892, angry whites wrecked her newspaper office and forced her to flee the city. But instead of keeping quiet, Wells embarked on a nationwide crusade against lynching, publicizing how whites used lynching to prevent blacks from achieving social and economic equity. In response to the segregationist membership policy of the white General Federation of Women's Clubs, Wells spearheaded a national black women's club movement, which led to the founding of the National Association of Colored Women in 1896.

Muckrakers Raise the Nation's Awareness

The growth of the popular press gave progressives the chance to investigate social problems and awaken public opinion. When Danish immigrant Jacob A. Riis went to work as a police reporter in New York, he saw firsthand the horrible conditions in the city's sweatshops, tenements, and saloons. In 1890 Riis published *How the Other Half Lives,* using dramatic photographs and sobering statistics to produce a shocking exposé of urban conditions. Riis's work influenced a generation of reformers, including investigative reporters at the newly proliferating mass magazines, including *McClure's, Cosmopolitan, Munsey's,* and *Collier's. McClure's* published Lincoln Steffens's "Tweed Days in St. Louis," an exposé of machine politics in St. Louis, in 1902. "Everything the city owned," Steffens reported, "was for sale by the officers elected by the people." This landmark article led Steffens to write a series of pieces on urban corruption, later collected in the volume *The Shame of the Cities* (1904). Other writers hoped to shock the public into action by writing about shoddy or immoral practices in big business, and even corruption in the federal government. Ida M. Tarbell's *History of the Standard Oil Company* (1904) chronicled John D. Rockefeller's ruthless and duplicitous campaign (described in Chapter 1) to develop a massive monopoly in the oil business. In his 1906 novel *The Jungle,* the socialist novelist Upton Sinclair described the brutal working conditions and horrid sanitation in Chicago's stockyards and packing houses. When the book became a best-seller and prompted calls for reform, Sinclair feared that he had "aimed at the public's heart and hit its stomach." Nonetheless, Sinclair's book helped galvanize public support for consumer protection, and it gave impetus to progressive politicians' successful campaigns for the Meat Inspection Act and Pure Food and Drug Act of 1906. The new laws empowered the Agriculture Department to enforce sanitation in packing houses and to inspect meat, and it established the Food and Drug Administration (FDA). The workers in the packing houses, unfortunately, were left to fend for themselves.

Though such exposés fed the public's appetite for scandal and garnered publishers an expanding readership and profits, crusading writers and editors ran the risk of alienating the powerful people they reported about. When

David Graham Phillips argued in *The Treason of the Senate* (1906) that many prominent U.S. senators were simply errand boys for corporate interests, Theodore Roosevelt condemned investigative reporters as a group. He called them *muckrakers,* after the character in John Bunyan's *Pilgrim's Progress* who was too busy digging up dirt to accept a heavenly crown. Although Roosevelt's outburst did temporarily chill their fervor, muckrakers nevertheless set the standard for twentieth-century journalism, with their penchant for fact collecting, for straying beyond the bounds of discretion and politeness, and for scandalous subjects and sensational prose.

Social Welfare and Labor Reform

While muckraking reporters exposed the excesses and dirty secrets of urban American industry and politics, other progressives dedicated themselves to helping society's casualties—to reforming or, in some instances, revolutionizing the economic and political order. Some believed that the best way to improve American life was to reform politics at the local level. Municipal reformers were often native-born middle-class city dwellers who believed that machine politicians cared more about their own power and profits than about addressing urban problems. Many endeavored to publicize public health problems, from the diseases borne by impure municipal water supplies to the perils of dirty streets, uncollected garbage, and overcrowded housing.

Some reformers agitating to clean up the cities had experienced the hazards of urban slums as workers in settlement houses. The settlement house movement grew out of "Social Gospel" charity work among American and British religious reformers of the late nineteenth century and took root as college-educated women looked for a way to use their learning, talent, and energy to improve American society. The nation's two most famous settlement houses were Chicago's Hull House, founded by Jane Addams and Ellen Gates Starr in 1889, and New York's Henry Street, established by Lillian D. Wald in 1895. These settlement houses attracted a growing community of skilled and energetic women, including physician Alice Hamilton, social investigator Grace Abbott, lawyer Sophonisba P. Breckenridge, child advocate Edith Abbott, and sociologist Florence Kelley. Investigating how poor city people lived and worked, women such as these developed new programs for social improvement and a whole new profession: social work.

Organizations like Hull House and Henry Street also constituted cultural centers for their surrounding neighborhoods. They sponsored educational and vocational programs, including English classes, and hosted musical and cultural events. Moreover, the settlements were strongholds of intellectual and political ferment. Progressive politicians like La Follette and academics like Dewey and James were frequent guests.

Some settlement workers pressed for public education programs in "social hygiene," whereas others lobbied to make local, state, and federal authorities responsible for investigating, regulating, and standardizing public health

Jane Addams, founder of Hull House, in 1889. *University of Illinois at Chicago, Jane Addams Memorial Collection*

practices. Jane Addams became the garbage inspector for her Chicago precinct. Florence Kelley focused on the pitiful wages and horrible working conditions forced on the urban poor. In 1899 Kelley left Hull House to return to New York, live at Henry Street, and take the position of general secretary of the newly formed National Consumers' League (NCL), an organization dedicated to forging an alliance between exploited workers in factories and sweatshops and the middle-class people who bought the goods they produced.

Like many reformers and labor leaders, Kelley insisted that the government had the responsibility to protect workers, especially women and children, from hazardous conditions. Kelley and others worked tirelessly for protective laws, safe working conditions, minimum wages, and maximum hours for women and children. The state of Massachusetts had led the way for such laws in 1887, limiting women's working day to ten hours. By 1914, twenty-seven states regulated the hours workers could be compelled to toil, and many states also passed laws excluding women and children from certain kinds of work deemed harmful to them.

The U.S. Supreme Court was hostile to protective legislation, however, and to most government efforts to assist workers. In 1905 the Court struck down a New York law limiting bakers' hours in *Lochner* v. *New York,* holding that the law violated the Fourteenth Amendment, which guaranteed individuals the freedom to contract for themselves. Justice Oliver Wendell Holmes's

Pittsburgh children, at home in the streets, introduced this settlement worker to the alleyways of their tenement neighborhoods. *Carpenter Center, Harvard University*

strong dissent in the case, however, augured a shifting tide in legal thinking. Progressives insisted that laws, like other ideas, should be judged according to their practical effects and their relevance to social conditions rather than their conformity to theoretical abstractions. By 1908 the Court was ready to affirm Holmes's ideas when it upheld an Oregon law limiting working hours for women. Along with NCL activist Josephine Goldmark, Kelley was instrumental in putting together the data for the brief that Goldmark's brother-in-law, the brilliant lawyer Louis Brandeis, would present in *Muller* v. *Oregon*. Rather than emphasizing legal precedents, Brandeis's brief used extensive sociological and medical information regarding women's health to argue that the social costs of long hours for women might outweigh the advantages of affirming legal principles. The government, Brandeis argued, needed to limit women's working hours in order to protect society's interest in women's ability to deliver healthy babies. Soon much of American justice would be administered according to this kind of *sociological jurisprudence*. But there were hidden costs to this protective strategy: insisting that the state had an interest in limiting women's work options on the grounds that all women were actual or potential mothers did, in fact, restrict some women's opportunities.

Municipal Reform

Other reformers focused on cleaning up the emerging alliance between business and government. Responding to the widespread public belief that corporate monopolies exploited both workers and consumers, they campaigned for public ownership of utilities. The five-cent streetcar fare became a moral touchstone for urban reformers from Los Angeles to Boston and a focus of political struggle between transit companies determined to turn a profit and the riding public, which was outraged at packed cars, haphazard and rude service, and threats of rate increases.

At the same time, some municipal reformers (often local businessmen) concentrated on changing the structure of local government. They insisted that party politics, in the hands of the machine, led to waste and fraud in government. They argued that government should be run as efficiently as any private business, without regard to partisan agendas. Not surprisingly, they felt that the persons best qualified to bring efficiency to government were managers like themselves rather than patronage politicians who had risen through the machines.

When Galveston, Texas, was devastated in 1900 by a hurricane and tidal wave that killed one out of every six residents, local businessmen asserted that the city's political structure was inadequate to meet the emergency. They pressured the state legislature to replace the existing government with a board of five commissioners, each responsible for a particular city department, to be elected at large and accountable to the voters. Cities around the nation adopted this form of government. Some municipalities chose to divide power by giving the commission or council power to legislate but putting administrative tasks in the hands of a nonpartisan city manager, appointed by the council and charged with ensuring businesslike government.

Municipal reforms did streamline government operations, and they did acknowledge that some urban problems were better understood as regional, rather than neighborhood, concerns. However, replacing patronage politicians with professional, nonpartisan leaders shifted political power from the working class to the middle class. For many progressives, the assault on the city political machine was a way of pushing for government by elites. For immigrant workers, "reform" was tantamount to disempowerment.

Other municipal reformers, however, hoped to root out corruption while retaining democratic participation. In Detroit, Republican mayor Hazen S. Pingree, a wealthy shoe manufacturer, won four terms and went on to become governor of Michigan by stressing issues that united the concerns of the business class with the interests of working people. Pingree campaigned against long-term franchises for utilities, alienating some in the business community, and rising streetcar fares, winning the gratitude of the commuting public. The Welsh immigrant Samuel M. "Golden Rule" Jones rose from working in the Pennsylvania oil fields to running an oil equipment factory in Toledo. While other corporate managers adopted the methods of Taylorism to discipline workers, Jones insisted that "I don't want to rule anybody. Each individual must rule himself." He instituted profit sharing, an eight-hour day, a minimum wage, and paid vacations. Jones even abolished the time clock and permitted workers to keep track of their own hours. Elected mayor of Toledo in 1897, he took clubs away from the police, established free shelters for vagrants, built free kindergartens and playgrounds, and established a minimum daily wage of $1.50 for city workers when the prevailing wage was $1 or less. As Jones moved further to the left, insisting that "private ownership is a high crime against democracy," he lost the support of both regular parties. Nonetheless, he was elected four times.

Reform at the State Level

While these men concentrated on local politics, some progressives took the crusade for political reform to the state level. As early as 1892, Illinois farmers and urban workers had come together to elect the remarkable John Peter Altgeld, who combined devotion to the regulatory reforms so dear to Populists' hearts with determination to further the interests of labor. Altgeld anticipated later progressive governors by bringing professional experts and social activists into government. (For example, in 1893 he appointed the sociologist Florence Kelley to the position of chief factory inspector for the state.)

The election of Robert M. La Follette to the governorship of Wisconsin in 1900 marked the arrival of progressive politicians as powers at the state level. The short, pugnacious La Follette had already served three terms in Congress, but he had alienated Republican powers in the state. Ambitious, energetic, and opinionated, La Follette once remarked that he could no more compromise than he could add twenty years to his life simply by wishing it. He won the governorship with fiery speeches, attacking railroads and big business, that appealed to farmers and workers. As governor he pushed the state legislature to approve a direct primary, higher tax rates for railroads and corporations, a civil service act, an anti-lobbying law, and conservation measures. When he left the state house for the U.S. Senate in 1906, Wisconsin was poised to pass the nation's first state income tax law. Like Altgeld, La Follette frequently consulted academics and sociologists, forging alliances between government, the universities, and social services workers.

Most progressive politicians advocated regulating railroads and other large businesses, returning more power to ordinary citizens, and employing experts in an effort to make government more just and efficient. Still, their emphases varied from one part of the country to another. In the West, many states followed the lead of Oregon, where voters passed constitutional amendments instituting measures designed to increase democratic participation in government. The "Oregon System" included the *initiative,* which permitted citizens to petition to put measures on the ballot; the *referendum,* which allowed voters to directly approve or reject legislative measures; and the *recall,* which gave citizens the power to remove elected officials by popular vote. Hiram W. Johnson rode public anger at the Southern Pacific Railroad into the California state house in 1910 and was ultimately elected to five terms in the U.S. Senate. In the Great Plains and Midwest, voters elected anticorporation governors like Iowa's Albert B. Cummins, Missouri's Joseph Folk, and South Dakota's Coe Crawford.

In the agricultural South, politicians who appealed to poor white voters mustered the remnants of Populist anger at corporate interests to overturn elite-run state governments. Arkansas's Jeff Davis, Mississippi's James K. Vardaman, and Georgia's Hoke Smith all profited from the institution of direct primaries, and all appealed to class resentment. They also capitalized heavily on white racism, pitching progressivism as a way for whites to counter the threat of blacks' economic competition and political power. Vardaman, in one of his many anti-black tirades, even claimed divine authority for his views, screaming that "God Almighty had created the Negro for a menial." Whatever the Almighty's political affiliation, white southern progressives proved adept at using "whites-only" primaries and devices like poll taxes and grandfather clauses to simultaneously overturn elite white control and disfranchise southern blacks.

✦ Contradictions and Schisms

As the "whites-only" primary demonstrated, progressive schemes for political reform did not guarantee the expansion of justice and democracy. The initiative, the referendum, and the recall could also be used by special interests that had the money, the organization, and the commitment to staff petition drives and lobby for ballot measures.

The Women's Suffrage Movement

The campaign for women's suffrage embodied, in particularly stark terms, the mingling of democratization with social control. The organized campaign to win the vote for women originated in 1848 with the landmark Seneca Falls convention for women's rights. At that time all American women suffered under severe legal disabilities. Married women could not testify in court, make contracts, exercise control over property, or gain custody of their children in the event of divorce. In such a society, the right to vote was a remote dream for women. During the Civil War, activists like Elizabeth Cady Stanton, Susan B. Anthony, and Lucy Stone had concentrated on assisting the Union cause and agitating for the abolition of slavery. But after the war they resumed their efforts to gain property rights, equal legal standing, and suffrage for women. In 1869 Anthony and Stanton founded the National Woman Suffrage Association (NWSA), an organization focused on gaining a federal constitutional amendment granting women the right to vote. That same year, Stone and others established the American Woman Suffrage Organization (AWSO), which concentrated on state-by-state efforts.

Postwar politics created inconsistencies and even contradictions in suffragists' advocacy of expanded democracy, however. Anthony and Stanton, who had both worked hard to end slavery and win rights for African-Americans, were enraged when Radical Republican men repudiated the cause of women's rights during Reconstruction. They decided to try to raise money and recruit allies by appealing to white opponents of black rights with the argument that "superior" white women deserved the vote more than "inferior" black men. In 1890 the NWSA and AWSA merged to form the National American Woman Suffrage Association (NAWSA). Anthony, the organization's first president, and her successor, Anna Howard Shaw, courted the participation of white southern women with the contention that enfranchising white women would help keep the black man down.

Yet even as some southerners invoked women's suffrage as a means of disfranchising blacks, others in the movement insisted that women deserved to vote in the name of justice and social progress. Black women in particular continued to work for suffrage through their own political organizations, women's clubs, and church groups. In the West, women's suffrage had long-established roots. When Carrie Chapman Catt, a veteran of state suffrage campaigns, took over the presidency of NAWSA in 1915, women enjoyed full suffrage in only eleven states, all of them west of the Mississippi (see map). Catt orchestrated a "Winning Campaign," mobilizing dedicated workers in every state to publicize the cause at the grassroots and national levels and to lobby Congress, as well as state legislatures, to pass laws giving women the vote. Catt and her legions employed tactics ranging from polite calls to congressmen's offices to letter writing and petitioning campaigns, open-air automobile parades, and even cross-country car treks. Under Catt's direction, the women's suffrage movement became a prototype for modern political campaigns, deploying new technologies and mass media on behalf of political aims.

But as is true of all movements that grow to mass proportions, keeping peace among the adherents proved nearly impossible. Some younger NAWSA workers grew impatient with politicians' intransigence and vowed to pursue more militant tactics pioneered by the English women's rights advocates who called themselves suffragettes. Inspired by the British example, Alice Paul and Lucy Burns left NAWSA to found the Congressional Union, an organization dedicated to holding the party in power responsible for its failure to enfranchise women; employing militant tactics, including picketing the White House and engaging in hunger strikes; and focusing exclusively on the effort to win a federal constitutional amendment. By 1916 Paul and Burns had rejected male

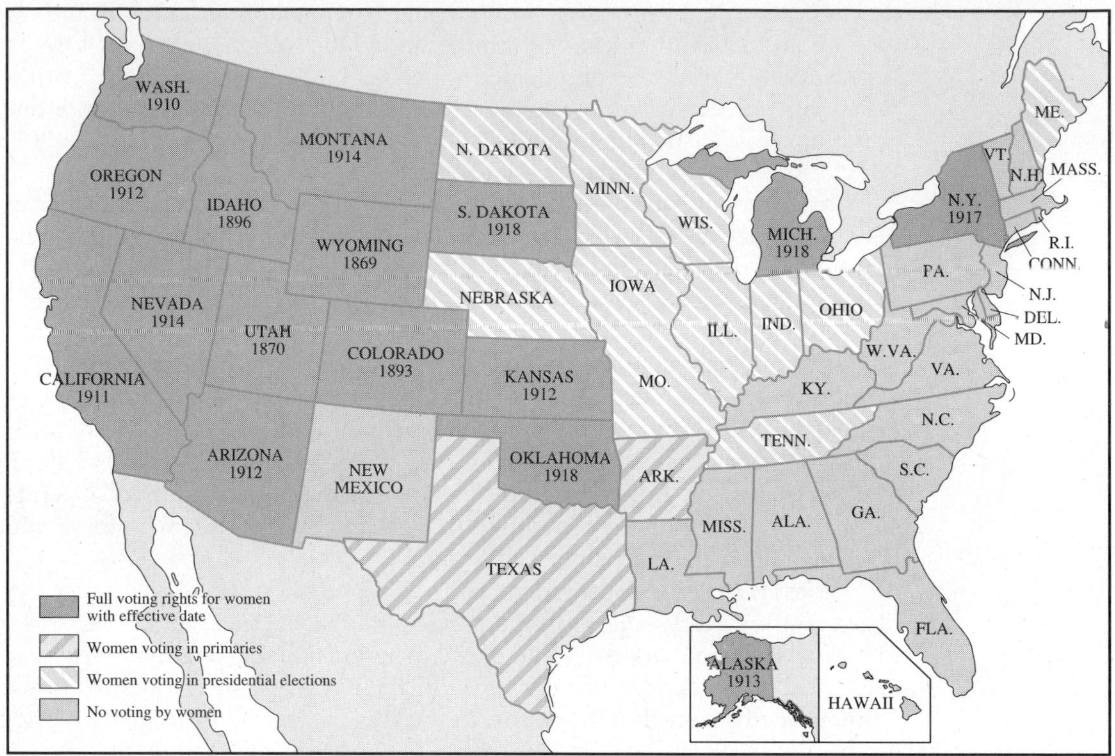

The West Leads the Way Although the most prominent leaders of the woman suffrage movement lived in Chicago and New York, the movement had its early successes in the West. Before the passage of the 19th Amendment, nearly all the states in which women had full voting rights were west of the Mississippi River.

party politics altogether and founded the National Woman's Party. The coming of World War I would nearly tear the women's suffrage movement apart, as advocates of peace like Jane Addams parted company with Catt and others who supported U.S. entry into the war in the hopes that a grateful government would reward supportive women with the vote. Despite this internal conflict, each faction played a role in reaching the movement's ultimate goal, ratification of the Nineteenth Amendment in 1920.

Organizing Labor

For many women reformers, the women's suffrage movement represented only one, fairly narrow dimension of a much larger struggle for social justice. Working-class labor leaders like Mary Kenney, Rose Schneiderman and Leonora O'Reilly, and their middle-class allies, including Florence Kelley and Harriot Stanton Blatch, insisted that the vote was only one weapon in women's struggle for economic equality. For working-class women activists, it was impossible to separate questions of women's rights from the problems of economic exploitation and insecurity. They hoped to turn to labor unions for relief.

American workers had begun to organize on a national scale in the late nineteenth century, despite heavy opposition from corporate management and the federal government. By 1900 unions had organized workers in the steel, coal mining, railroad, garment, and other industries. The nation's most powerful labor organization was the American Federation of Labor (AFL), an alliance of craft unions led by Samuel Gompers. The AFL withstood government and corporate hostility by restricting its membership to skilled workers, focusing on wage and workweek issues, excluding the vast majority of workers, and opposing immigration. Moreover, the union's male leadership insisted that its main goal was to gain "a family wage" for its members that would be sufficient to support a wife and children. The union thus supported immigration restriction to minimize competition for jobs and insisted that women should stay out of the labor force because working women undermined both male wages and the sanctity of the family.

Thus male-dominated unions ignored the millions of women working long, exhausting hours and earning pitiful wages in the nation's grim, dangerous factories. In 1903 Mary Kenney, one of four women unionists at the AFL's annual convention, founded the Women's Trade Union League (WTUL), a group intended to bring together sympathetic middle-class allies like Jane Addams with working-class labor activists on behalf of the working women's struggle. The WTUL soon established chapters in the nation's largest cities and drew its support not only from middle-class reformers but also from such fabulously wealthy women as Anne Morgan, daughter of the nation's wealthiest banker J. P. Morgan, and Alva Belmont, ex-wife of railroad heir William Vanderbilt and widow of banker Oliver Belmont. "When you hear of a woman who presses forty dozen skirts for eight dollars a week," Anne Morgan told the *New York Times,* "something must be wrong."

In some industries, organizing workers was hampered by ethnic diversity as well as gender barriers. New York's garment industry, for example, employed black, Italian, and Russian Jewish workers, among whom different cultural traditions and simmering tensions hampered solidarity, despite their low wages and hazardous working conditions. Employers routinely charged workers for needles, thread, electricity, chairs, and lockers, and many male supervisors assumed they had the right to pressure women workers for sexual favors.

AFL organizers, backed by WTUL activists, urged garment workers to organize and protest, and between 1909 and 1911 thousands did so in New York alone. And in 1911 a tragic event riveted the nation's attention on the plight of working women. At the Triangle Shirtwaist Factory in New York, a shop on the top three floors of a ten-story building, managers locked the doors to stairways to prevent employee theft of materials. A cigarette dropped in a remnant drawer ignited a fire that spread almost instantly throughout the shop. The doors were locked from the outside, so workers threw themselves from the windows, falling eight to ten stories to their deaths. Some were impaled on the iron spikes of the fence surrounding the building. A total of 146 workers died.

"I know from my experience it is up to the working people to save themselves . . . by a strong working-class movement," said Rose Schneiderman. Many others agreed, and as workers began to band together, progressive leaders like Florence Kelley and Frances Perkins of the NCL joined with Tammany Hall politicians like Al Smith and Robert Wagner to mobilize the government on workers' behalf. Responding to the outcry over the Triangle Fire, New York State created a factory inspection commission; the federal government instituted industrial commissions soon afterward on a national scale.

Reformers' efforts notwithstanding, confrontations between labor and management increased, and dangerous working conditions, low wages, and long hours persisted. Frustrated with the slow pace of change, intellectuals like Florence Kelley and Crystal Eastman, journalists like Lincoln Steffens and John Reed, and labor organizers like Eugene V. Debs concluded that the only answer to the abuses of capitalism was socialism. As owners resisted demands for better wages and hours and safer conditions, a new spirit of militancy galvanized workers across the country. Labor radicalism, embraced by some immigrant intellectuals and workers in the industrial East and Midwest, also swept out of the West, where strikes, particularly by miners and loggers, had led to violent confrontations with owners and the government. The Western Federation of Miners (WFM) became a stronghold of radical ideas and a home base for the charismatic, one-eyed organizer and agitator William "Big Bill" Haywood. In 1905 WFM leaders met with Socialist Party leaders and other radicals to form the Industrial Workers of the World (IWW)—better known as "the Wobblies"—which would be the "one big union" that would unite all workers in the struggle to overthrow capitalism and give those who toiled control over the means, and fruits, of their labor.

While the AFL had pursued *craft unionism,* the strategy of organizing skilled workers by trade and relying on the scarcity of their skills and the commonality of their interests, the IWW advocated *industrial unionism:* organizing workers by industry, regardless of their skills, sex, race, or ethnicity. IWW organizers like Haywood, Mary "Mother" Jones, and Elizabeth Gurley Flynn used fiery language and potent images to win adherents, declaring that workers and owners had nothing in common. In stories and songs, Wobbly agitators like the miner and labor martyr Joe Hill ridiculed middle-class sensibilities and glorified the "working stiffs" fighting for their dignity. Wobblies rode the rails to talk to migrant harvest workers, conversing with them in the many languages of their homelands.

The IWW gained a foothold among western miners, lumberjacks, and maritime workers and succeeded, for a time, in organizing some eastern industries as well. In 1911 twenty thousand workers in the textile mills of Lawrence, Massachusetts, staged a walkout to protest pay cuts of thirty cents a week (the price of five loaves of bread). "Better to starve fighting than starve working," one worker cried. The governor called in the National Guard to control the strikers, but the workers remained steadfast.

Divided by heritage (they came from twenty-five different countries) but united by their common experience on the factory floor, Lawrence workers drew support from the AFL, the WTUL, and the IWW. Although the workers carried the day when management recognized their right to unionize, the victory was partial and, for many, disillusioning. The owners' agreement to settle separately with the AFL left women and children workers, who made up half the labor force, unrepresented and unprotected.

Intellectual Ferment and Social Insecurity

The IWW's class-warfare rhetoric and advocacy of sabotage terrified big business and frightened many middle-class reformers away, but others found its radical ideas exhilarating. Many began to criticize not only the economic status quo but also the unequal commerce between men and women, the horror of racist oppression of African-Americans, and the general repressiveness of American society. Such ideas found their way into the bohemian subculture emerging in places like Carmel, California; Provincetown, Massachusetts; and, most importantly, Manhattan's Greenwich Village. In the Village, progressives and radicals sought freedom from moral and ideological restrictions, room for artistic expression, a place for political emancipation, and cheap rent. At her weekly salons, the art patron and writer Mabel Dodge provided a gathering place where IWW leaders like Haywood mingled with intellectuals like socialist birth-control advocate Margaret Sanger, anarchist writer and activist Emma Goldman, political analyst Walter Lippmann, muckraker Lincoln Steffens, and psychiatrist A. A. Brill. Talk of Freud's new theories about sexuality mixed with discussions of the coming revolution of the proletariat, the new and more encompassing women's movement called feminism, and the latest in abstract art.

Most progressives, however, were ambivalent at best about challenges to moral, sexual, political, and racial mores. Indeed, not all of those who were determined to use the state as a mechanism of social control were in any sense progressives. Many people opposed the new manners and morals brought about by urbanization, industrialization, and immigration and sought a political way to counter the disruptive forces of modernization.

Some reformers, ignoring the fact that the United States had been from its birth an ethnically heterogeneous nation, believed that immigrants represented a threat to the "traditional" American way of life based on a common English legal and social heritage. They determined to work to assimilate, or "Americanize," immigrants from Europe, Asia, and Latin America, as well as U.S.-born Hispanics and American Indians. These groups seized the advan-

Mott Street Industrial School students salute the American flag. Photo by Jacob Riis, ca. 1889. *Museum of the City of New York*

tages "Americanization" projects offered, from English classes to health, recreational, and occupational programs—often on their own terms. At the Methodist Houchen Settlement in El Paso, Texas, for example, Mexican-American mothers made use of the clinic and hospital and let their children romp on the playground, but they resisted settlement workers' attempts to convert them to Protestantism. But when the government put its weight behind assimilation schemes, "Americanization" became a force for repression. The Bureau of Indian Affairs, for instance, stepped up its long-standing policy of assimilation, embarking on a campaign to police Indian cultures, suppress traditional religious practices, and wipe out vestiges of communal property holding.

Some progressive Americanizers, affirming the nation's established ideology of white supremacy, insisted that some immigrants simply were not assimilable. Citing their own "expert" social scientists, including the University of Wisconsin's influential E. A. Ross, they held that Asians and southern and eastern Europeans were biologically and culturally incapable of being productive citizens in an Anglo-American democracy. Some became advocates of immigration restrictions; others, from birth-control advocate Margaret Sanger to President Theodore Roosevelt, embraced the new pseudoscience of eugenics. In a widely published letter, Roosevelt argued that American descendants of Anglo-Saxons were committing "race suicide" because Anglo-American women failed to bear as many children as women of "inferior racial stock," who should be discouraged from breeding. Of course, not all progressives shared Roosevelt's enthusiasm for scientific racism. His daughter Alice was so embarrassed by this "absolutely outrageous" letter that she and her friends formed a secret "Race Suicide" club: "We were making the rudest game of my father, and he would not have been at all amused if he had known."

Alice Roosevelt, who smoked cigarettes publicly and insisted on driving an automobile unchaperoned, represented precisely the sort of "New Woman" that many Americans feared would undermine the nation's morality. The dangers of alcohol and sex particularly preoccupied some, who hoped to use the government to ensure social purity, often in the name of protecting innocent women and children. At the dawn of the twentieth century, the long-standing American temperance movement took a new tack. The Women's Christian Temperance Union (WCTU), founded in 1873, had opposed drunkenness as a cause and a symptom of other social evils, including the oppression of women. The WCTU, led by Frances Willard, advocated self-restraint rather than legal prohibition, investigated social problems, and worked for reforms ranging from women's suffrage to economic regulation. But in 1893 a new organization, the Anti-Saloon League, caused a shift in temperance politics with its advocacy of prohibition, a legal ban on the manufacture and sale of alcoholic beverages. As prohibitionists organized to crusade for their cause, individual towns, cities, counties, and states began to pass ordinances outlawing liquor sales within their jurisdiction. By 1900 nearly a quarter of all Americans lived in "dry" places. Soon prohibitionists would insist that only a federal constitutional amendment barring the sale and transportation of alcoholic beverages could effectively combat the manifold evils of drink. With the ratification of the Eighteenth Amendment in 1919, the prohibitionists triumphed. Many progressives opposed prohibition, and most prohibitionists were one-issue activists, but there is no doubt that prohibitionists drew on the progressive urge to use government to improve society.

While prohibitionists campaigned to ban the bottle, other moral reformers worried about the sexual dangers of life in modern America. Many feared that transportation innovations like the streetcar and automobile and new social gathering places like the dance hall and movie theater provided all kinds of new opportunities for men to lead young women astray. Social workers, aided by crusading journalists, exposed the evils of the "white slave trade," in which innocent girls were lured into a life of prostitution by evil men and already corrupt women. Alarms rang out from big cities like Chicago, where the vice commission lay the blame at the door of "lust in the hearts of men." In smaller towns like Kansas City, Kansas, foolish young girls were reported to be taking the streetcar over into Missouri to drink and carouse. In the growing city of Los Angeles, male "mashers" were said to be abducting women off the streets and dragging them off in their autos. In 1910 Congress responded to moral reformers by passing the Mann Act, which forbade men from transporting women across state lines for immoral purposes. As a consequence, any woman who crossed a state line with a man not her husband was presumed to be doing so against her will, and any man who took a woman for a ride across the line was vulnerable to a charge of statutory rape.

Conservation and Preservation

For some reformers cities themselves were the problem, and nature was the solution. Increasing urbanization and mushrooming demand for natural resources convinced many that the country's wild and beautiful places were endangered. At the very least, some experts pointed out, resources that were once considered inexhaustible—from timber and coal to water and air—needed to be treated as finite and fragile and managed efficiently. In the West, growing demand for water, increased grazing on rangeland, and heavy logging spurred a movement to preserve watersheds, build dams, plant trees, and reseed grasslands.

Progressives working in the new sciences of civil engineering, forestry, and range management sought to put new technologies and the power of the state to work in the name of conservation. At the same time, grassroots conservation activists carried on campaigns to preserve local woodlands, clean up towns, and save endangered birds. The conservation movement encompassed a wide variety of individuals and organizations, ranging from the Audubon Society (founded in 1886), which advocated the protection of birds, and the Sierra Club, a group of mountaineering enthusiasts who fought to preserve scenic places, to the General Federation of Women's Clubs, whose eight hundred thousand members were urged to support a variety of conservation causes.

When Theodore Roosevelt entered the White House in 1901, he became the nation's first avowed conservationist president. Roosevelt's attachment to the movement included personal relationships with its two leading lights, Gifford Pinchot and John Muir. Pinchot, a Yale-educated son of the eastern elite, studied forestry and forest management in Germany before becoming head of the U.S. Forest Service in 1898. As chief forester of the United States, Pinchot found himself dealing with questions involving not only trees but also "public lands, mining, agriculture, irrigation, stream flow, soil erosion, fish, game, animal industry, and a host of other matters." He argued that natural resources should be managed, by experts, with the utilitarian goal of creating "the greatest good for the greatest number for the longest time." Pinchot became convinced that private, corporate control of natural resources posed a danger to the public interest. He advocated taking resource-rich federal lands off the market, to be set aside and managed according to a logic of "multiple use." Pinchot became the architect of Roosevelt's conservation policy, and he was largely responsible for setting aside 172 million acres of public land during the Roosevelt administration.

Muir was a Wisconsin-bred Calvinist who became a successful inventor and entrepreneur. When he was temporarily blinded in an industrial accident,

Theodore Roosevelt and John Muir enjoying the strenuous life on a camping trip in Yosemite Valley, 1903. *Yosemite Museum*

he swore that he would dedicate his life to beauty if his sight were restored. He later became the founding president of the Sierra Club and a leading force for the protection of Yosemite National Park, whose splendors he revealed to Theodore Roosevelt on a camping trip. A brilliant writer, Muir also became the guiding spirit of the "preservationist" wing of the conservation movement, which argued that wilderness had value for its own sake, beyond human desires and needs. For Muir and his fellow preservationists, wild country was "a window opening into heaven, a mirror reflecting the Creator," and any encroachments on wilderness amounted to intolerable sacrilege. While conservationists like Pinchot insisted that forests should be managed to produce "maximum sustained yield" and that hunters, miners, loggers, and nature lovers might compatibly use the same piece of land for very different purposes, preservationists like Muir believed that economic development of any sort was a sin against wild places.

Despite their differences, activists like Muir and Pinchot shared a concern for nature and for the careful use of resources. Nevertheless, tensions between multiple-use conservationists and preservationists erupted into an open break over the 1909 proposal to build a dam that would flood the Hetch-Hetchy

Valley, inside Yosemite, to create a water supply for San Francisco. "That anyone would try to destroy such a place seems incredible," Muir wrote. "These temple destroyers, devotees of ravaging commercialism, seem to have a perfect contempt for Nature, and, instead of lifting their eyes to the God of the mountains, lift them to the Almighty Dollar."

Pinchot and, ultimately, Roosevelt sided with the water developers, who carried the day in 1913. Preservationists were devastated, but the Hetch-Hetchy controversy had drawn attention to their cause and won converts across the nation. When Congress passed the National Parks Act in 1916, establishing an agency to administer the national parks created since 1862, the federal government gave its stamp of legitimacy to preservationist ideas.

Progressivism had many faces and many, often contradictory, consequences. Those contradictions were embodied in the movement's most visible individual figures, the three very different men who occupied the White House at the beginning of the twentieth century: Theodore Roosevelt, William Howard Taft, and Woodrow Wilson.

✦ Progressivism and National Politics

When the nation reelected William McKinley to the presidency in 1900, businessmen and conventional politicians assumed that their interests were secure for at least four more years. Solid Republican majorities in both houses of Congress promised continued conservative rule, especially in the hands of the unofficial "boss of the Senate," Nelson W. Aldrich of Rhode Island. Only Mark Hanna, the Ohio Republican power broker most responsible for McKinley's success, seemed concerned that his party might have made a mistake by nominating for vice president the blustering, reformist New York governor Theodore Roosevelt. Hanna reminded his colleagues after the nominating convention that "there's only one life between that madman and the Presidency." His warning proved prophetic. On September 6, 1901, while attending the Pan American Exhibition in Buffalo, New York, McKinley was shot by anarchist Leon Czolgosz. He died soon after, and in Hanna's words, now "that damned cowboy" was president.

Theodore Roosevelt

Upon McKinley's death, the new president assured nervous Republicans that he would carry on his predecessor's programs. While Senator Aldrich and his compatriots maneuvered to limit the president's power, Roosevelt moved cautiously, unsure how the federal government ought to be involved in the process of reform. His temperament did not long permit him to play the role of caretaker, however. After all, quipped his daughter Alice, her father was the kind of person who wanted to be the bride at every wedding and the corpse

✦✦✦
Biographical Profile

Theodore Roosevelt, 1859–1919

The son of an aristocratic old New York Dutch family, Theodore Roosevelt had been sickly and nearsighted as a child. He determined at an early age to overcome his infirmities and turned a room of his parents' house into a gymnasium, where he practiced boxing and wrestling. At the same time, he devoted himself to the study of history and the appreciation of nature, becoming an avid hunter, bird watcher, and naturalist as well as an accomplished historian. Roosevelt cultivated an aggressive "manliness" in all his endeavors, from hunting big game to regulating big business.

Upon graduating from Harvard, Roosevelt hurled himself into the rough world of New York politics, entering the state assembly in 1882. In 1884, anguished by the death of his first wife, he fled west to a friend's ranch in North Dakota, where he rode and roped and roughhoused with real cowboys. Returning invigorated to the East, Roosevelt re-entered politics. In 1886 he ran for mayor of New York, finishing a devastating third. But as police commissioner of New York City he enhanced his reputation as a reformer, and he brought his expertise in naval history to the job of assistant secretary of the navy. One day during the Spanish-American War, when his boss was out of town, he ordered Admiral Dewey's fleet to sail into Manila Harbor and seize the Philippines.

Roosevelt was not, however, the type to settle for a desk job while others were on the battlefield. He resigned from the Navy Department to organize a volunteer regiment he called the Rough Riders, a motley assortment of Harvard boys and Dakota cowpunchers, to fight in Cuba. Returning a hero, he was elected to the governorship of New York and then nominated to the vice presidency. By 1901, at the age of forty-two, he was raring to take the nation's helm.

> *"There are no words that can tell of the hidden spirit of the wilderness, that can reveal its mystery, its melancholy and its charm. There is delight in the hardy life of the open, in long rides, rifle in hand, in the thrill of the fight with dangerous game . . . the silent places . . . the wild waste places of the earth, unworn of man, and changed only by the slow change of the ages through time everlasting."*
>
> —from *African Game Trails*

at every funeral. In time, then, Roosevelt began to outline his own agenda for change and to pursue it with his customary energy. He was ready to preach reform to the nation, and the White House, he believed, would be a wonderful (or "bully") pulpit.

By the time Roosevelt took office, consolidation of business interests had led to the domination of crucial enterprises like the railroad, steel, oil, tobacco, and chemical industries by a few huge trusts. These trusts had been assembled with the assistance of Wall Street financiers, among whom J. Pierpont Morgan was by far the most powerful. Roosevelt was not opposed to big business on principle. He believed that consolidation was a natural outcome of modernization and free-market competition, and he understood the advantages of economies of scale. He was aware, moreover, that there was substantial support for government regulation of business within the business community itself. But he did believe that some trusts operated counter to the public interest, and he held that the federal government had the obligation to distinguish between "bad" and "good" trusts and discipline the former.

The movement to regulate trusts had gathered momentum in the late nineteenth century, spearheaded by Populist reformers eager to enlist the government in the drive to limit the power of great corporations. In 1890 Congress responded to pressures for economic reform by passing the Sherman Anti-Trust Act. But prior to 1900 the Cleveland and McKinley administrations used the Sherman Act as a weapon against labor unions as much as against big business. Of eighteen antitrust suits filed by the Justice Department before Roosevelt took office, half were against unions. In the most notorious of these, Attorney General Richard Olney used the Sherman Act to secure an injunction against the American Railway Union (ARU), which was on strike against the Pullman Company. This move ultimately led to a violent confrontation between federal troops and strikers in 1894 and to the arrest of ARU leader Eugene V. Debs. Debs would emerge from jail a committed socialist, ready to lead American workers away from exploitation and toward economic justice.

As president, Roosevelt worried that the government's failure to regulate the excesses of the marketplace might indeed drive an angry American public toward socialism. He determined to use the power of regulatory agencies, along with the Sherman Act, to discipline and, eventually, bust the trusts. In 1903, over the protests of congressional opponents but backed by businessmen who believed that regulatory agencies could be manipulated by the very businesses they were supposed to be policing, Roosevelt created the Bureau of Corporations within the Department of Commerce and Labor, charging it with collecting data the Justice Department could use to bring antitrust suits. The Justice Department had brought one such suit the previous year, against the giant Morgan-controlled Northern Securities railroad trust. The suit infuriated Morgan, who told Roosevelt to "send your man to my man and they can fix it up." Instead the Northern Securities case won Roosevelt the title "trustbuster," when the Supreme Court ruled in 1904 that the company was in violation of the Sherman Act and had to be broken up.

Once Roosevelt was elected in his own right in 1904, with the help of reformers and businessmen alike (Morgan was one of his largest contributors), he began ratcheting up his antitrust rhetoric and initiating more antitrust suits. During his administration the Justice Department brought more than forty such actions. But Roosevelt believed that business and government should ideally be partners rather than adversaries. He pushed for legislation to give more power to regulatory agencies, with the support of most progressive businessmen. He championed the Elkins Act of 1903, which gave the Interstate Commerce Commission (ICC) the power to prevent railroads from offering reduced rates, or rebates, to preferred customers (such as Standard Oil), a measure highly popular with more humble railroad users. He also pressed for passage of the Hepburn Act of 1906, which made the ICC responsible for setting maximum freight rates and for oversight of railroad business practices. This measure was popular not only with the public but also with corporate shippers, who were happy to have the government tell the railroads how much they could charge. Progressive senators like Robert La Follette complained that the Hepburn Act was a sellout to big business, but Roosevelt insisted that it was a victory for the government and expanded its power to regulate the economy.

Roosevelt also departed from the harsh anti-labor stance of his presidential predecessors. When the United Mine Workers (UMW) struck against the anthracite coal industry in 1902, demanding higher pay and an eight-hour workday, owners took a hard-line position, refusing to recognize the union or negotiate terms. Roosevelt intervened in the strike, insisting that the owners and UMW leader John Mitchell agree to government arbitration of the dispute. When the owners balked, Roosevelt threatened to send in federal troops to run the mines. The arbitration commission split the difference between labor and management, affirming the union's goal of higher wages and shorter hours but also conceding to management the right to negotiate not with the union but with grievance committees elected by the miners. Roosevelt heralded the settlement as a "square deal" for all, sounding what was to become the keynote of his presidency. He would win further support from labor by advocating laws regulating the wages and hours of women and child workers, instituting the eight-hour workday, making employers liable for accidents, and limiting the use of injunctions against strikers.

Roosevelt would make his progressive mark in two other areas, the campaign for consumer protection and the crusade for conservation. He provided crucial and vocal support for the Pure Food and Drug Act and Meat Inspection Act of 1906, on the heels of exposes like *The Jungle.* He also supported Pinchot's plan to put the management of federally controlled resources in the hands of expert regulators, and he pushed hard for the Newlands Reclamation Act of 1902, which earmarked the proceeds from public land sales for the building of dams and for reclamation work. Although Roosevelt's insistence on putting government officials in charge of natural resources did have the effect of reducing the general public's power and oversight over the disposition of the public domain, he left a lasting legacy of fifty-one wildlife reserves, thirteen national monuments, and hundreds of millions of acres of national forests.

Theodore Roosevelt's pugnacious personality and charismatic popular appeal helped him put the power of the federal government behind the wheel of the progressive crusade. But his truculent image belied his deep-seated belief in the necessity of compromise. He liked dramatic gestures, like inviting Booker T. Washington to the White House (which infuriated southern white segregationists), but he was often quietly on the side of conservatives (who applauded his 1906 attempt to woo southern reactionaries by blaming blacks for a white rampage through black neighborhoods in Atlanta.) When he departed office in 1909 with the inauguration of his hand-picked Republican successor, William Howard Taft, he had laid the necessary groundwork for continued compromise, firm in the belief that government would play an expanding role in the economy of the future. As he headed for a year-long safari to hunt big game in Africa, he felt confident that Taft would simply carry on his work.

William Howard Taft

William Howard Taft was a talented and honorable man who had a distinguished record of political service as governor general of the Philippines and the U.S. secretary of war. He had a similar class and educational background as Roosevelt, born into a prominent Cincinnati family and educated at Yale. Taft also shared Roosevelt's progressive political leanings. But whereas Roosevelt's gift for politics made him an ideal person to carry the progressive crusade to the national level, Taft was awkward in public and legalistic in his philosophy, and he was destined to govern at a time when conservatives were digging in their heels and radicals were growing increasingly impatient with the slow pace of change.

In 1908 Taft defeated Democratic candidate William Jennings Bryan in his third and last run for the presidency. Although he lost, Bryan's campaign defined the issues that would move the Democratic Party into the progressive camp. Calling for lower tariffs, stronger antitrust laws, stricter railroad regulation, and a host of reforms benefiting labor unions, Bryan shifted the center of political debate toward the left. His appeals to laborites and discontented farmers probably cut into the support of Socialist Party candidate Eugene V. Debs, who garnered nearly half a million votes, indicating growing support among American voters for leftist ideas.

Taft campaigned as an advocate of party unity, but by the time he took office Republican insurgents like La Follette were at odds with the "stand-pat" conservatives, represented by Senator Aldrich and Speaker of the House Joseph Cannon of Illinois. The new president faced his first test when discontented House Republicans, led by Congressman George W. Norris of Nebraska, tried to loosen Speaker Cannon's iron grip on power. Taft at first supported the dissidents but later decided, on Roosevelt's advice, to cooperate with Cannon and Senate leaders in return for their support of his legislative proposals. The insurgents were furious, and the political gains, Taft learned, were meager.

Among the initiatives Taft hoped to further was a reduction in protective tariffs. Progressives had long campaigned to reduce tariffs, which they saw as nothing more than government subsidies to big business. When the House passed a lower tariff rate, Taft pledged his support. In the Senate, however, protectionists restored high rates. When the Payne-Aldrich tariff arrived on Taft's desk, the president opted to sign the measure. He did so in part because he disliked the insurgents, particularly La Follette, but also because the bill granted the executive branch new powers to revise tariff rates. Thus, Taft thought, he might be able to lower rates, through executive action, later. La Follette was furious, and Taft made matters worse by proclaiming the new tariff "the best bill the Republican party ever passed."

Taft did try to follow in Roosevelt's progressive footsteps in certain regards, and he even surpassed his mentor in some areas. He was the first president to appoint a woman to head a federal agency, naming Hull House's Julia Lathrop as director of the newly established Children's Bureau in 1910. During Taft's presidency Congress initiated two amendments to the Constitution, the Sixteenth Amendment, providing for a federal income tax, and the Seventeenth Amendment, allowing for the direct election of senators (both were ratified in 1913). During his single term the Justice Department brought some ninety antitrust actions, compared to fifty-seven during Roosevelt's nearly eight years in office. In 1911, in two of the most celebrated of those cases, the Supreme Court ruled that the Standard Oil Company and the American Tobacco Company had violated the Sherman Act and must be broken up into smaller entities. Although these cases were seemingly great victories for antitrust advocates, in the Standard Oil case the Court provided what would become the trusts' greatest tool to thwart government regulation. Chief Justice Edward Douglass White wrote that the Sherman Act must be interpreted according to a "rule of reason," by which only "unreasonable" restraints of trade should be seen as unlawful.

One of Taft's antitrust actions, however, not only proved to be a departure from Roosevelt's course but also led, ironically, to a direct confrontation with his predecessor. In October 1911 Taft approved a Justice Department plan to sue United States Steel, a corporation dominated by Morgan's interests and notorious for its exploitative labor and business practices. One quarter of the industry's workers, some twenty thousand people, were putting in twelve-hour shifts, and nearly forty thousand steelworkers earned less than eighteen cents an hour. Moreover, the Justice Department's suit contended, U.S. Steel's 1907 acquisition of the Tennessee Coal and Iron Company violated the Sherman Act. Unbeknownst to Taft, Roosevelt had personally approved the acquisition, which J. P. Morgan had argued was necessary in order for Morgan to help the country stem a spreading financial panic. This foray into trustbusting thus earned the supposedly conservative Taft the fury of the great trustbuster himself, who considered the suit a personal insult.

The split between Roosevelt and Taft publicly erupted over another matter, however: a controversy within the Interior Department. Taft's secretary of the interior, R. A. Ballinger, was a long-time foe of Roosevelt's friend and protégé Gifford Pinchot. In the summer of 1909 Pinchot began to make speeches around the country, suggesting that Ballinger was subverting Roosevelt's conservation policies. When Pinchot learned that Ballinger was being investigated for allegedly corrupt practices, he leaked the information to *Collier's* magazine. Taft reviewed the case but found the charges groundless and ordered Pinchot to cease making allegations against his boss. When Pinchot persisted in bandying the charges about in public, Taft fired him for insubordination.

The Ballinger-Pinchot affair, as it was called, quickly turned into a fight for public approval. Taft insisted that he had done what he thought was right. *Collier's,* fearing a libel suit, hired Louis Brandeis, who worked to see that the public saw Pinchot as a wronged hero. Taft and his opponents wrote letters courting support from Roosevelt, still in Africa and shooting everything his guides could find. Pinchot, however, took the direct approach, going to Italy to meet with Roosevelt in April 1910. By the time Roosevelt returned to the United States two months later, shipping a cargo of some three thousand recently dispatched African game animals, he was convinced that Taft had failed the test of leadership.

When the 1910 elections rolled around, Taft campaigned for conservatives as Roosevelt straddled the growing schism within the party, backing some insurgents as well as conservatives like his good friend from Massachusetts Senator Henry Cabot Lodge. In stump speeches Roosevelt invoked "The New Nationalism," a set of ideas borrowed from Herbert Croly, author of *The Promise of American Life*. Explaining that corporate consolidation was a fact of economic evolution, the pragmatic Roosevelt insisted that the government must step in to act for the national good rather than protecting sectional or private interests. This "New Nationalism," Croly had explained, would use the power of big government to restore the benefits of democracy, achieving "Jeffersonian ends by Hamiltonian means."

In January 1911 Republican dissidents formed a new group, the Progressive Republican League, which opposed Taft's renomination in 1912. They courted Roosevelt's support, but the ex-president remained cagey and publicly affirmed his support for more political reforms. La Follette, meanwhile, began to campaign against Taft in the spring of 1911.

Republican disarray contributed to increasing strength and unity among the Democrats. The new Speaker of the House, Missouri's Champ Clark, and House Majority Leader Oscar Underwood of Alabama moved quickly to assert themselves. While Republicans had long made political capital portraying themselves as competent, careful custodians of the nation's interest (in contrast to the radical, risky Democrats), they were by 1912 saddled with the double difficulty of distancing themselves from corporate corruption on the one hand and La Follette's brand of protest on the other.

The Election of 1912

The Democrats had the opportunity to capture the White House in 1912 by capitalizing on the Republican split and nominating a standard-bearer who would appear thoughtful and dignified yet also embrace progressive politics. One such person was the recently elected governor of New Jersey, Woodrow Wilson. A Virginian by birth and breeding, Wilson was the son and grandson of Presbyterian ministers. A professor of government and writer of scholarly books and popular magazine articles, Wilson had combined his aspirations toward scholarship and politics and established himself as a leader in the new field of political science. In 1902 he became president of Princeton University, an institution he transformed from a small, genteel college into a research university.

Before he entered the New Jersey gubernatorial race in 1910 Wilson had never run for office, but he had long prepared for a political career. As governor he initiated reforms ranging from setting strict limits on campaign spending to outlawing unsafe working conditions. He was savvy with power brokers and popular with voters. Despite his appeal, however, it took him forty-six ballots to win the Democratic presidential nomination in June 1912.

Meanwhile, Theodore Roosevelt challenged Taft for the Republican nomination. Many of La Follette's supporters jumped on Roosevelt's bandwagon when their candidate became ill early in 1912. When conservative Republicans, including Roosevelt's old friend Lodge, seized control of the party's Chicago convention and prepared to nominate Taft, Roosevelt's supporters walked out and regrouped at a nearby auditorium. There Roosevelt told them they must stand against a "corrupt alliance between crooked business and crooked politics. . . . We stand at Armageddon and we battle for the Lord." Two months later the insurgents reconvened to found the new Progressive Party. The Progressives affirmed their support for stronger regulation of business, maximum workweek and minimum wage laws for workers, the abolition of child labor, presidential primaries, and even women's suffrage. Their platform reflected their deep support among women reformers. Jane Addams gave an impassioned speech seconding Roosevelt's nomination, and the newspapers declared her "one of the ten greatest citizens of the Republic." When asked how he felt about running again, Roosevelt told reporters, "I feel as fit as a bull moose!"

From the first, observers believed that in the four-way contest the real race was between Roosevelt and Wilson. To many voters Taft seemed the tool of ultraconservatives, and Socialist Party candidate Debs appealed chiefly to radical workers and dissident farmers. Since Roosevelt and Wilson advocated many of the same progressive goals, each tried to keep his own supporters loyal while courting the other's constituents. Wilson took the tactic of praising the Progressives for their stands on labor rights and the need for social welfare programs but criticizing Roosevelt's ties to the trusts. He announced that his campaign stood for a "New Freedom" permitting corporate consolidation that arose from "conquering in the field of intelligence and economy" but opposing businesses that "pass the point of efficiency."

Roosevelt, who proclaimed his program the "New Nationalism," argued that the government's most important job was not to regulate the marketplace but to ensure that workers and consumers alike were not vulnerable to abuse from big business. He believed that the best way to shape the future of big business was not to break it up but to counterbalance the power of trusts with that of big government. Wilson, by contrast, insisted government's job was to preserve economic competition.

There were therefore philosophical distinctions between the two candidates. At the same time, they agreed that the government should take an active role in American social and economic life, advocated many of the same measures, and, in truth, demurred on many of the same questions. While Roosevelt was on record as favoring women's suffrage, he admitted that his support for the cause was "very tepid." Wilson, who had two suffragist daughters, insisted that women's suffrage was a matter best left to the states. And both candidates maintained silence on the issue of black rights. The Progressive Party capitalized on its split with the Republicans by seeking white southerners' support, fielding "lily white" slates in the South. Wilson was willing to accept black support organized by W. E. B. Du Bois, but he made no public statements about racial issues and declined to appear before black audiences.

When the votes were counted, the Republican split proved decisive. Wilson won nearly 6.3 million popular votes, winning forty states and 435 electoral votes. Roosevelt gained 4.1 million popular votes but won only six states and 88 electoral votes. Taft, finishing close behind Roosevelt, won 3.5 million popular votes but only two states and 8 electoral votes (see map). Many political experts expressed surprise at the strong showing of the Socialist Party and Eugene V. Debs, who won nearly nine hundred thousand popular votes, the best showing by a Socialist candidate before or since.

Woodrow Wilson

As president the former professor sought to apply the new discipline of political science to the practice of modern government. He courted the press, appeared personally before Congress (breaking with the customary distance established by Thomas Jefferson), and made more public speeches than any of his predecessors, including Roosevelt. At the same time, his regional and partisan loyalties influenced his policies and appointments, as he brought Democratic Party loyalists, including many southerners, to the center of national politics for the first time since the Civil War.

Immediately upon taking office, Wilson laid out a legislative program that included tariff reduction, an income tax, a new banking reserve system,

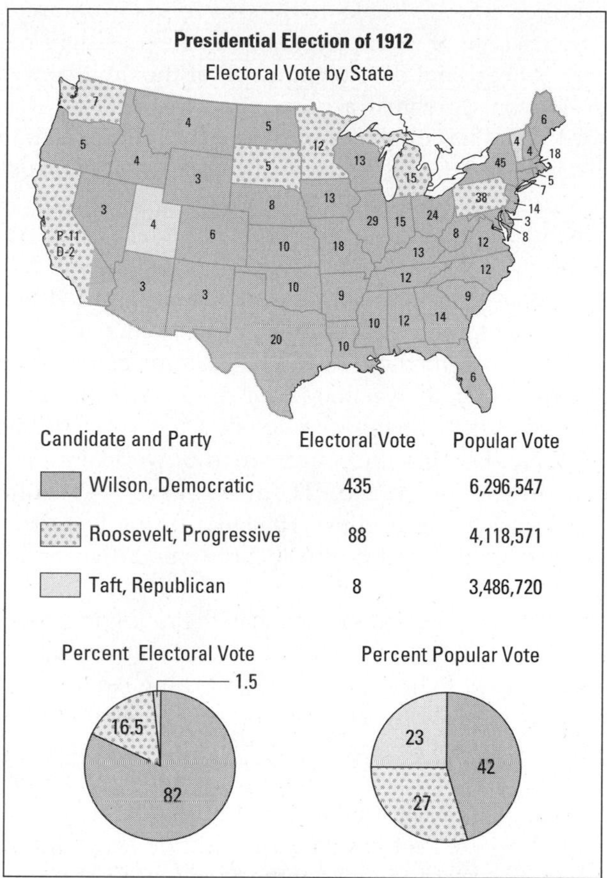

1912 Presidential Election Woodrow Wilson won only a minority of popular votes. Nonetheless, he carried the electoral college by an overwhelming majority.

antitrust laws, and regulation of business. Congress passed the Underwood tariff, which attached a graduated income tax (made constitutional by the ratification of the Sixteenth Amendment) to the new, far lower duties. This first, and highly controversial, federal income tax, which affected mainly the wealthy, seems mild by late-twentieth-century standards. It set a tax rate of 1 percent for those earning more than $20,000 a year, rising to 6 percent for the few who made more than $50,000 annually.

In an effort to stem bank failures and to contend with the shortage of credit and banking facilities in the South and West, Wilson also pushed through a new banking system. In 1913 Congress passed the Federal Reserve Act, creating a system of regional reserve banks under the control of the central, supervisory Federal Reserve Board in Washington. The Federal Reserve System permitted private banks to deposit funds in the regional reserve banks and to name some of their directors, but the president retained the power to appoint most regional directors and all of the members of the central board. Perhaps Wilson's greatest achievement, the Federal Reserve System introduced order and national oversight into the American banking system.

Wilson also enjoyed success in the area of antitrust law. The Clayton Antitrust Act, passed in October 1914, gave labor leaders reason to cheer. It declared that unions should not be considered illegal combinations in restraint of trade, and it forbade federal courts from issuing injunctions against strikers in most cases. Much more detailed and tightly drafted than the Sherman Act, the Clayton Act remains the nation's fundamental antitrust law. Wilson had a rather harder time pushing through legislation establishing the Federal Trade Commission (FTC), the agency established to regulate business. Conservative senators forced the president to accept a law enabling businesses to appeal FTC rulings and giving the courts broad powers of review in such cases. But Wilson's concessions on the FTC in August 1914 resulted from more than simple political horse trading. That month his beloved wife died, and the outbreak of World War I began to draw his attention away from domestic reform.

Wilson's domestic achievements in the following two years of his administration would continue but would not match the major accomplishments of his first two years. When Congress passed the Adamson Act in August 1916, mandating an eight-hour workday for interstate railroad workers, the government gave organized labor a victory that unionists had been working for since the 1880s. Also, despite opposition from the legal community, Wilson managed to secure the appointment to the Supreme Court of his friend and advisor Louis Brandeis, the first Jew to earn a seat on the Court. But by 1916 foreign affairs claimed more and more of the president's attention. The war in Europe and the Mexican Revolution moved to the center of the White House agenda. A president who had campaigned the first time almost without mentioning international questions would, in his run for reelection, speak of little else.

✦ Conclusion

Between 1900 and 1916, a movement for reform that began in scores of American localities swept into the nation's state houses, Congress, and the White House. Those who affirmed the principles of progressivism insisted that the time had come to face, and solve, the problems modern society created for those who stoked its industrial engines; thronged its cities; invested their minds, money, and muscles in its institutions; and raised, made, and used its products. More and more Americans came to believe that the government must seize the power to regulate corporate capitalism, protect workers and consumers, and bring order and democracy to social and political life. By 1916 many Americans had reason to feel optimistic about their nation's future and their own ability to participate in shaping it.

Those who believed that capitalism, properly regulated, promised the greatest possibility of providing a good life for all Americans had most reason to cheer. Progressive businessmen like former Morgan partner and Roosevelt ally George Perkins felt they had effectively shaped the way government and business would interact, as partners, for years to come. Progressive economic reforms curbed some of the worst excesses of the marketplace and offered some protection to workers and consumers, but they came nowhere near to revolutionizing the economic order.

In politics, the progressives had pledged to make government more efficient and accessible. The reforms they championed, from the city manager system to the initiative, referendum, and recall, bore mixed fruit. Appointed experts and citizen interest groups might well be more protective of the public interest and less subject to political pressure; but then again they might not. New governing mechanisms spawned, in time, new techniques for controlling them and, ultimately, new efforts for reform.

For all their sterling achievements, progressives also embraced repressive ideas and policies. In an effort to legislate morality, they legitimated the drive to outlaw the manufacture, sale, and transportation of alcoholic beverages and gave credence to those who pointed their finger at "depraved immigrants" profiting from spirituous poisons inflicted on upstanding native-born Americans. Once the United States entered World War I, nativism, xenophobia, and support for immigration restrictions mushroomed.

Black Americans, neglected by Roosevelt and Wilson, soon found cause to rue the day that they had supported white progressive politicians. The Wilson administration took away federal jobs held by blacks and gave them to white appointees. When southerners in Wilson's cabinet announced plans to institute Jim Crow rules, segregating facilities in their departments and, particularly, ensuring that no blacks supervised whites, Wilson appeared to acquiesce, until a storm of protest from the NAACP and the opposition of Senator La Follette pushed him to rescind the segregation orders. Nonetheless, violence against blacks escalated during Wilson's tenure, reaching a peak in 1915, when seventy-nine African Americans were lynched in the United States.

That same year, Hollywood film director D. W. Griffith made an enormously popular epic movie, *The Birth of a Nation*, glorifying the "heroism" of the nineteenth-century Ku Klux Klan. The movie immediately inspired a revival of the Klan, which expanded its terrorist activities to target Jews, Catholics, immigrants, and "modernists" as well as blacks. U.S. Anti-Semitism reached a violent climax with the lynching of Atlanta factory owner Leo Frank in 1915. Accused of the rape and murder of a white female employee named Mary Phagan, Frank was tried in a courtroom echoing with the screams of a mob outside calling for Frank's blood. When the governor of Georgia commuted Frank's death sentence in 1915, the former Populist leader and veteran racist agitator Tom Watson insisted that right-thinking Georgians give Frank "the same thing that we give to negro rapists." Two months later a band of armed men took Frank from the state penitentiary and lynched him. More than fifteen thousand people swarmed to view the corpse.

Violence also erupted in labor struggles, and workers were often the casualties. In Ludlow, Colorado, in April 1914, private police raided a tent colony housing the families of IWW strikers, killing thirteen women and children. Federal troops had to be called in to restore order. Dozens of white labor activists, most of them IWW organizers in the West, were also lynched in 1915. Wobbly militants contributed their share of dynamiting and shooting to the violence as well, but unlike their opponents they could not expect lenient treatment in the courts.

As the United States watched from afar the escalating horror of the European war, many Americans still believed, along with their president, that their nation might stand as a beacon of peaceful, moral democracy, an enlightened state among corrupt, venal, and secretive nations. Progressives' domestic accomplishments were immense. They had expanded the power of the voting public, put the government in the business of protecting the public health and regulating the power of business, and developed whole new fields of knowledge and expertise with which to meet the challenges of the new century. Progressives did their work conscious of the excesses of American entrepreneurship but believing in the promise of American freedom and initiative. They thought the whole world could benefit from the American example. Soon enough, their hopes and faith would be tragically tested.

✦ Further Reading

For an overview of the early twentieth century, see: John D. Buenker, John C. Burnham, and Robert M. Crunden, eds., *Progressivism* (1977); John Milton Cooper, Jr., *Pivotal Decades: The United States, 1900–1920* (1990); Samuel P. Hays, *The Response to Industrialism: 1885–1914* (1957); George E. Mowry, *The Era of Theodore Roosevelt and the Birth of Modern America* (1958); Nell Irvin Painter, *Standing at Armageddon: The United States, 1877–1919* (1987); Robert Wiebe, *The Search for Order, 1877–1920* (1967). On social and educational reform, see: Rosalind Rosenberg, *Beyond Separate Spheres: The Intellectual Roots of Modern Feminism* (1982); Stephen Jay Gould, *The Mismeasure of Man* (1996); Allen F. Davis, *Spearheads of Reform: The Social Settlements and the Progressive Movement, 1890–1914* (1967); Kathryn Kish Sklar, *Florence Kelley and the Nation's Work* (1995); Glenda Gilmore, *Gender and Jim Crow* (1996). On the conservation and preservation movements, see: Samuel P. Hays, *Conservation and the Gospel of Efficiency: The Progressive Conservation Movement, 1890–1920* (1959); Roderick Nash, *Wilderness and the American Mind* (1967). On the social-control dimensions of progressivism, see: Paul Boyer, *Urban Masses and Moral Order in America, 1820–1920* (1978). For a critique of progressivism, see: Gabriel Kolko, *The Triumph of Conservatism* (1963). On the progressive presidents, see: Lewis L. Gould, *The Presidency of Theodore Roosevelt* (1991); Paolo E. Coletta, *The Presidency of William Howard Taft* (1973); Kendrick A. Clements, *The Presidency of Woodrow Wilson* (1992).

✦✦✦

CHAPTER 3

World Power and World War, 1898–1920

✦ **Wounded soldiers in France, 1918.**

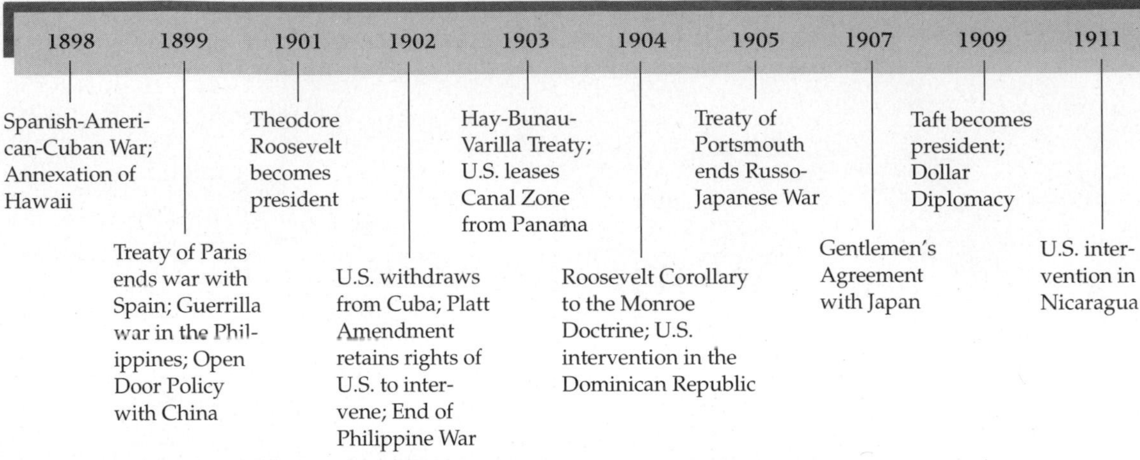

ARTHUR MACARTHUR WON the Congressional Medal of Honor during the Civil War and was promoted to the rank of colonel at the tender age of twenty. After 1865 he spent a quarter of a century in remote western outposts, fighting Indians. In 1900 he became the U.S. military governor of the Philippines, a territory recently taken by the United States in a brief war with Spain. MacArthur commanded seventy thousand U.S. troops, against a Filipino army fighting for independence that numbered as high as one hundred thousand. MacArthur said that the United States' "wonderful" occupation of the Philippines had begun "a stage of progressive social evolution that would result in the unity of the race and the brotherhood of man."

But the fighting was fierce and brutal. "No more prisoners," an American soldier wrote home. To the Americans, all Filipino villagers, no matter how friendly they appeared to be, might be guerrillas. A soldier complained that "the people all greet you with kindly expressions while the same men slip into

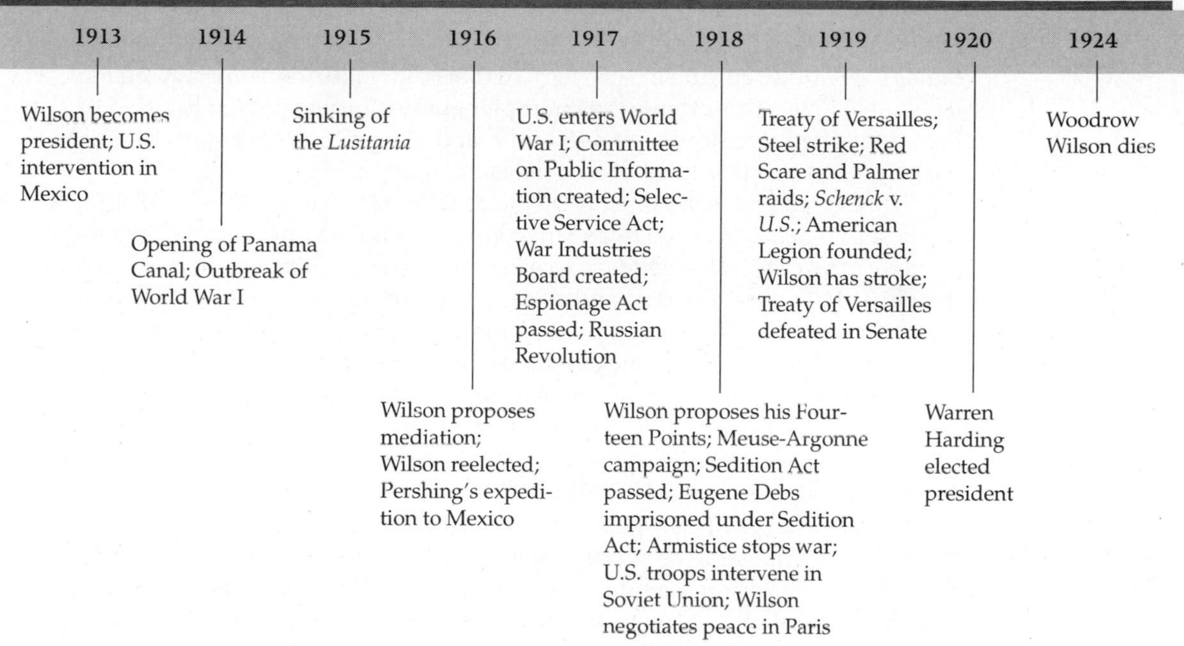

the bushes, get their rifles and waylay you down the road." After fifty American soldiers were killed on the rugged island of Samar in September 1901, the American commander told a Marine major, "I want no prisoners. I wish you to kill and burn; the more you can kill and burn, the better it will please me." American newspapers wrote grisly stories about the carnage in the Philippines, prompting Congress to open hearings on the behavior of the American soldiers suppressing the insurrection. They heard an artilleryman reflect on how U.S. troops had responded when several of their comrades-in-arms were killed by Filipino guerrillas. "We got orders to spare no one," he said. "We went in and killed every native we met; men, women, and children. It was a dreadful sight, the killing of the poor creatures."

The Senate committee finished its work in the spring, and several American officers and soldiers were court-martialed or forced to retire in disgrace. The revelations of brutality sobered some of the more ardent advocates of

American imperial expansion. Imperialists who had once called for the United States to create an empire in Asia to rival that of Great Britain now agreed that the United States should rule the Philippines only temporarily. On July 4, 1902, President Theodore Roosevelt declared that the war was over and the United States was completely in control of the island nation.

The United States became one of the premier powers in the world during the first two decades of the twentieth century. At the beginning of the era the United States played a secondary role in world affairs. European nations were the Great Powers of the day, and Americans remained largely indifferent to European politics. The United States concentrated its foreign interests closer to home and across the Pacific Ocean. It dominated the affairs of the Western Hemisphere, and both private citizens and government officials in America helped alter the political and economic landscape of Asia.

On the eve of the unexpected catastrophe Europeans first called the Great War and later World War I (1914–1918), few people on either side of the Atlantic forecast that the era of European dominance over the world would soon fade. World War I changed the global balance of power. Once the United States entered the fighting on the side of the Allied Powers (Britain, France, Italy, and Russia) in April 1917, American soldiers and equipment ensured an Allied triumph over the Central Powers (Germany, Austria-Hungary, and Turkey). American proposals became the basis for the peace that followed the war. By the time peace was achieved, however, Americans had lost much of their earlier enthusiasm for the international reforms championed by President Woodrow Wilson to prevent future wars.

This rise to international pre-eminence represented a profound change for a traditionally weak republic that had previously displayed little interest in international affairs. World power generated controversies both at home and abroad. Some claimed that unless the United States took a part in the brutal competition among the major powers, the country would suffer economically and maybe militarily. Others offered altruistic reasons for foreign involvement. They claimed that the country's abundance made the United States the only power capable of intervening in European quarrels in a way that would create a safer and more just world order. Still others decried the whole enterprise, fearing a more regimented society should the United States become like the Great Powers of Europe. Critics of efforts to enter the race for pre-eminence believed that powerful and wealthy people wanted the United States to become deeply engaged abroad to enhance America's economy. This engagement would come at the expense of less fortunate citizens.

Meanwhile, people in other countries watched the growth of American power with mixed emotions. Before the outbreak of the World War I, many people in Europe, Asia, and the Western Hemisphere considered the United States a potentially threatening rival. That view changed during the war as the European allies relied on American assistance to win. The stirring rhetoric of President Wilson, promising that American participation in the European conflagration would "make the world safe for democracy," inspired millions of people throughout the world. But the enthusiasm for Wilson's agenda of international reform faded after World War I, leaving a bitter legacy of disillusionment.

✦ A Great Power

The United States began the 1890s as a regional power of relatively little consequence in world affairs. By 1900 it possessed a string of island colonies girdling the Pacific, had humbled Spain in battle, and felt emboldened enough to tell the Europeans and Japanese how to behave in China and elsewhere. Of course, America had never been truly isolated from world affairs. Since its independence it had exported products globally, taken in immigrants from everywhere, and used diplomacy, threats, and war to expand westward to the Pacific. By the 1890s a variety of influential Americans were arguing for a more active foreign policy, one that would promote trade as well as spread American influence into the far-flung corners of the globe. Writers, lecturers, politicians, and historians such as John Fiske, Josiah Strong, Theodore Roosevelt, Captain Alfred Thayer Mahan, Brooks Adams, Frederick Jackson Turner, and Senators Henry Cabot Lodge of Massachusetts and Albert Beveridge of Indiana, to name a few, asserted that the country had reached a turning point and must expand overseas or risk internal collapse. Nearly all of these men argued that America had become rich and powerful because of the racial superiority of Anglo-Saxons, the spiritual benefits of Protestant Christianity, the political virtues of republican values, and the availability of new land. As America "filled up," especially with immigrants of dubious bloodlines, these past accomplishments appeared in jeopardy. The country needed new challenges to test its "manhood," expanded markets for its exports, and a powerful navy to project its power outward.

McKinley and the "Splendid Little War"

The opportunity to implement this program came from a rebellion in Cuba against Spanish rule. Beginning in 1895, rebels waged a guerrilla campaign on the island, which Spain saw as the last real jewel in its once formidable New World crown. Spanish troops fought the guerrillas by implementing the policy of *reconcentrado:* rural civilians were herded into guarded villages by night and allowed to farm, under guard, in daylight (an arrangement somewhat like the strategic hamlets American forces promoted during the Vietnam War). By definition, those outside the perimeter were enemies to be killed. Poor planning, indifference, and disease turned the fortified compounds into disaster zones where as many as two hundred thousand civilians died. The American government and public, prodded by sensational accounts from the newspapers of William Randolph Hearst and Joseph Pulitzer (which went beyond the already dreadful truth), demanded that Spain fight the war humanely or abandon Cuba altogether. Hearst's newspapers characterized the Spanish commander, General Weyler, as "Weyler the brute, the devastator of haciendas, the destroyer of families, and the outrager of women." His "carnal animal brain" delighted in "inventing tortures and infamies of bloody debauchery."

By 1898 the McKinley administration had had enough. In April, after a series of incidents (including the stealing and printing in Pulitzer's papers of a letter by the Spanish ambassador that ridiculed McKinley as "weak and a bidder for the admiration of the crowd," followed by the mysterious sinking of the U.S. cruiser *Maine*, causing the death of 266 sailors, while it was on a port visit to Havana), the United States declared war on Spain with the goal of liberating Cuba.

To prevent the decrepit Spanish fleet in the Philippine Islands from sailing around the world to Cuba, Assistant Secretary of the Navy Theodore Roosevelt arranged for the U.S. Navy's small Pacific squadron to intercept the enemy in Manila. In a brief battle, Commodore George Dewey's ships sent the Spanish fleet to the bottom of Manila Bay.

This "splendid little war," as Secretary of State John Hay characterized it, elicited great enthusiasm. Roosevelt resigned from the Navy Department to lead the Rough Riders in Cuba. William Jennings Bryan organized a group of Nebraska volunteers known, inevitably, as the Silver Battalion. Wall Street financiers donated money and private yachts for naval operations.

Despite chaotic American mismanagement of the war (about five thousand U.S. soldiers died from food poisoning and disease and fewer than four hundred from enemy bullets), Spanish forces in Cuba folded after a few weeks of combat. By August Madrid was begging for an armistice. At a peace conference held in Paris in December 1898, Spain agreed to free Cuba and to sell Guam, Puerto Rico, and the Philippines to the United States for $20 million. At about the same time, the Senate voted to annex Hawaii, something it had deferred doing since 1893, when American plantation owners overthrew Polynesian ruler Queen Liliuokalani with the assistance of the U.S. Navy and American diplomats.

The treaty ending the war in Cuba marked the transformation of the United States into a colonial power. Under the terms of an amendment to the treaty introduced by Colorado Republican senator Henry Teller, the United States renounced any intention of annexing Cuba, but no such restrictions applied to the other territories. Although the United States had acquired new territories, it did not promise U.S. citizenship for the people living in them. The annexation of Guam and Puerto Rico produced little controversy, but the proposal to annex the Philippines sparked a debate among Americans and the senators who had to ratify the treaty with Spain. Nearly everyone had supported the war to free Cuba, but why, many asked, would the United States fight to free one colony from Spain only to take another for itself? Other critics opposed annexing the Philippines because of its large Asian population. America had enough race problems, they asserted, without acquiring more. To complicate matters, Filipinos bitterly resented the prospect of annexation

After the Spanish-American War, the United States sent an army of seventy thousand soldiers to the Philippines to fight a brutal guerrilla war against Filipino nationalists. *California Museum of Photography*

and felt betrayed by Washington, which had won their cooperation against the Spanish with the promise of independence. Proponents insisted that taking the Philippines would make America a respected world power and give it a real advantage in entering the nearby but ever-elusive Chinese market. McKinley's reasons for taking the colony, as he explained to a group of visiting clergymen, were that giving up the Philippines to Japan, Germany, or England would be bad business; that the natives were unfit for self-rule; and that "there was nothing left to do" but "take them all, and educate the Filipinos, and uplift and civilize and Christianize them, and by God's grace do the very best we [can] by them, as our fellow men for whom Christ also died."

The Senate approved annexation in February 1899. As it voted, Filipino nationalists led by Emilio Aguinaldo attacked American forces near Manila. Over the next three years the U.S. Army waged an often brutal war against Filipino guerrillas, employing many of the same tactics made infamous by General Weyler in Cuba. An estimated two hundred thousand Filipinos died from wounds, hunger, and disease, along with five thousand American combat deaths. In the end the Philippines proved both an economic and strategic burden to the United States. Local taxes never paid the cost of the civil service and American military operations stationed on the islands, and the American presence in the western Pacific eventually led to conflict with Japan.

McKinley's reelection victory over Democratic Party candidate William Jennings Bryan in 1900 solidified America's status as an imperial nation. Bryan made little headway with his denunciations of U.S. annexation of noncontiguous territories inhabited by people never likely to become U.S. citizens. McKinley's campaign also benefited from the presence on the ticket of the young governor of New York, Theodore Roosevelt. The Republican candidates embraced overseas expansion as the best way for the United States to compete commercially with the great powers of Europe.

McKinley lived barely six months into his second term before he was felled by an assassin's bullet. Roosevelt, his successor, continued McKinley's efforts to consolidate American control over its new island dependencies. The U.S. Army occupied Cuba under the Platt amendment placing the island nation under U.S. protection. Although Cubans did hold elections and draft a constitution, the United States insisted that Cuban authorities grant the United States the right to intervene militarily to preserve Cuban independence and maintain order. Cuba also agreed to lease territory for naval bases to the United States.

The United States also established tighter control over Puerto Rico. In 1900 Congress passed the Foraker Act, making residents of the island citizens of Puerto Rico but not of the United States. Puerto Ricans could elect a legislature, but final legislative authority would rest with a governor appointed by the president of the United States. In 1901 several Supreme Court decisions upheld the government's claim that Puerto Ricans—and by implication the residents of the other territories gained from Spain—were not entitled to U.S. citizenship.

The United States joined the race among the Great Powers for prestige and commercial advantages in Asia (see map). During 1899 the tottering Chinese empire, only a few hundred miles north of the Philippines, appeared on the brink of collapse. Americans had long savored thoughts of a limitless market in China, and some envisioned the Philippines as a steppingstone to this trade. But if the Chinese government fell apart and the Europeans and Japanese divided the country, the United States would be left holding the Philippines but barred from China. To counter this threat, in September 1899 Secretary of State John Hay sent notes to the European imperial powers calling on them to keep the door to the Chinese market open on an equal basis (the so-called Open Door Notes). He renewed the call a year later when all the powers—including the United States—sent troops to China to rescue missionaries and diplomats under siege in Peking during an antiforeigner uprising led by a group known as the Boxers. Once the foreign diplomats were freed, the European states demanded that China pay an indemnity. The U.S. government returned its share of the indemnity to China after deducting the actual losses suffered by American citizens. China then used the returned funds for scholarships for

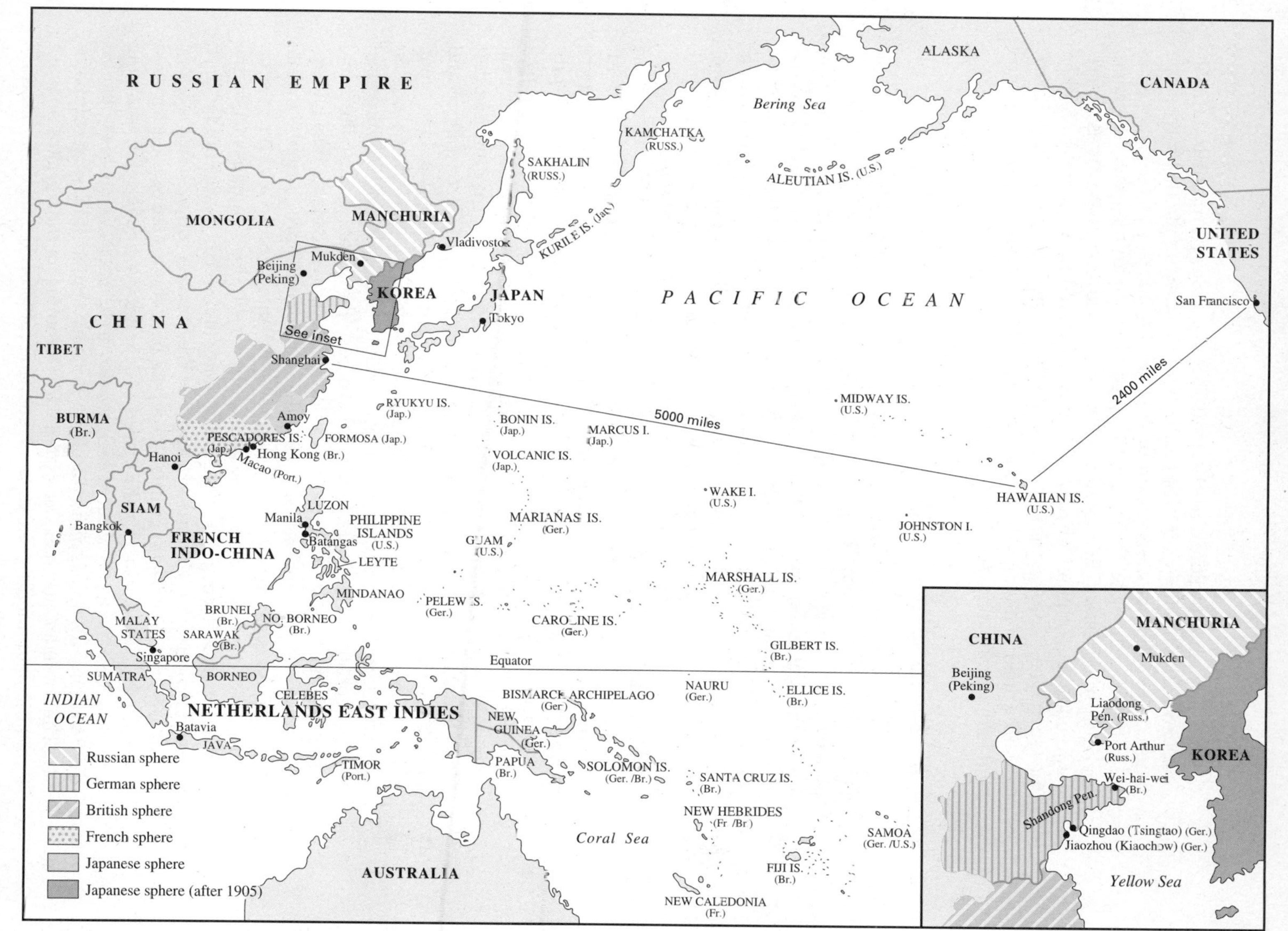

Imperialism in Asia: Turn of the Century The United States joined the European powers and Japan in a race for territory and influence in East Asia and the Pacific at the turn of the century.

Chinese students to study in the United States. Many American officials believed that what the United States had done following the Boxer rebellion marked the nation as more generous than the European powers. Many Chinese, however, lumped the Americans together with all the other foreigners seeking privileges, and European diplomats resented what they saw as American meddling. Although rivalry among the imperial powers did more than the Open Door Notes to preserve access to the Chinese market, many Americans imagined that Hay's diplomatic notes had been designed to help China and had actually done so.

Theodore Roosevelt's Foreign Policy

Theodore Roosevelt pursued an active foreign policy during his seven and a half years as president. As assistant secretary of the navy in 1898, Roosevelt had been one of the most ardent advocates of war with Spain. He belonged to an influential group of writers and strategists—men like Admiral Alfred Thayer Mahan and senators Henry Cabot Lodge and Albert Beveridge—who supported the development of a modern navy and the construction of a canal across the Isthmus of Panama to make the United States into a great power equal to the imperial states of Europe. He said that the "increasing interdependence and complexity of international political and economic relations" required the United States to adopt an assertive foreign policy. He divided the world into "civilized" states, whom the United States would respect and treat as equals, and "backward" lands, whom the United States and the other great powers would dominate for their own good. He explained that "it is our duty to the people living in barbarism to see that they are freed from their chains."

Roosevelt pushed forward plans for a canal across the Isthmus of Panama, to be built and owned by the United States (see map). He first insisted that Great Britain invalidate an agreement made with the United States in 1850 and permit the United States the exclusive right to build and fortify such a canal. Britain, feeling isolated in Europe and eager to cement a growing friendship with the United States, agreed in the Hay-Pauncefote Treaty of 1901. But even though construction rights had been secured, the actual site of the canal remained unclear. There were two options—a sea-level canal across Nicaragua, or a lock-type canal across the northern Colombian province of Panama. A French company had a concession for the Panama route and had begun construction, but it now was near bankruptcy. Philippe Bunau-Varilla, the former chief engineer of the French company and a major stockholder in it, lobbied furiously for Congress to approve the Panama route. Nature helped his cause when a volcano erupted in a lake near the center of the proposed Nicaraguan route. Bunau-Varilla placed a Nicaraguan postage stamp showing a flaming volcano on the desk of each senator. In July 1902 Congress voted for the Panama route and approved a $40 million payment to the French company.

The United States then negotiated with Colombia for the right to construct a canal. Negotiations broke down when Colombia balked at the limitations

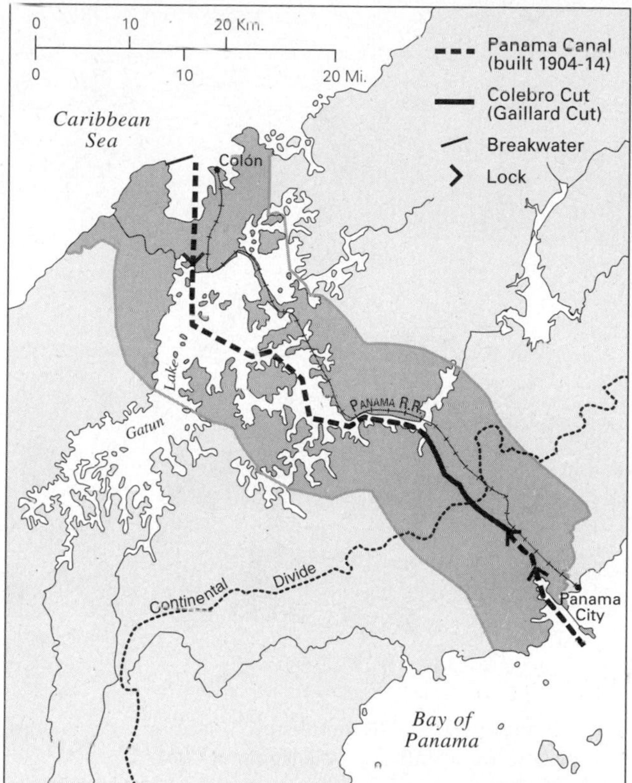

The Panama Canal A massive engineering project, the Panama Canal moved ships between the Atlantic and Pacific Oceans by cutting through mountains and constructing an elaborate series of locks.

the United States wanted to place on its sovereignty. A frantic Bunau-Varilla, fearful that the entire project might collapse, arranged for some Panamanian businessmen to support a group of Panamanian nationalists who had long wanted independence from Colombia. As Panamanian revolutionaries proclaimed their independence in Panama City, Bunau-Varilla traveled to Washington to gain U.S. support for the uprising. Roosevelt obliged by sending a fleet of warships to stand off the coast and prevent Colombian forces from landing and putting down the secession.

Although Bunau-Varilla held French citizenship and had not seen Panama in seventeen years, he named himself the foreign minister of Panama and quickly negotiated an arrangement for the United States to construct a canal. Under the terms of the Hay-Bunau-Varilla Treaty the United States received a permanent lease on a ten-mile-wide zone across Panama in which to build,

President Theodore Roosevelt, determined to build a canal across the Ithmus of Panama, paid scant attention to the rights of Colombia. The cartoon shows TR shoveling dirt dug from the canal onto Bogota, Colombia's capital. *Theodore Roosevelt Collection, Harvard College Library*

operate, and defend a canal. The United States would act in the Canal Zone "as if it were sovereign." For these rights Congress agreed to an initial payment of $10 million and yearly payments of $250,000 thereafter. In 1904 the United States began work on the canal, finishing the job ten years later at a cost of $400 million. During construction thousands of West Indian laborers died from fatigue and bad food. But the canal proved enormously popular in the United States. In the midst of his successful 1904 presidential election campaign, Roosevelt asked his campaign manager, "Can you tell our speakers to dwell more on the Panama Canal? We have not a stronger card" (see map).

As work progressed on the canal, policymakers in Washington developed ways to protect access to it. Roosevelt's way was to establish the United States as the policeman of the Caribbean. Many states in the region had borrowed large amounts from European bankers, and they sometimes threatened to default. In 1904 several European nations threatened to use force to recover debts owed by the Dominican Republic. Roosevelt responded with a message to Congress blasting the Dominican Republic for mismanagement of its finances as "chronic wrongdoing . . . which results in a general loosening of ties

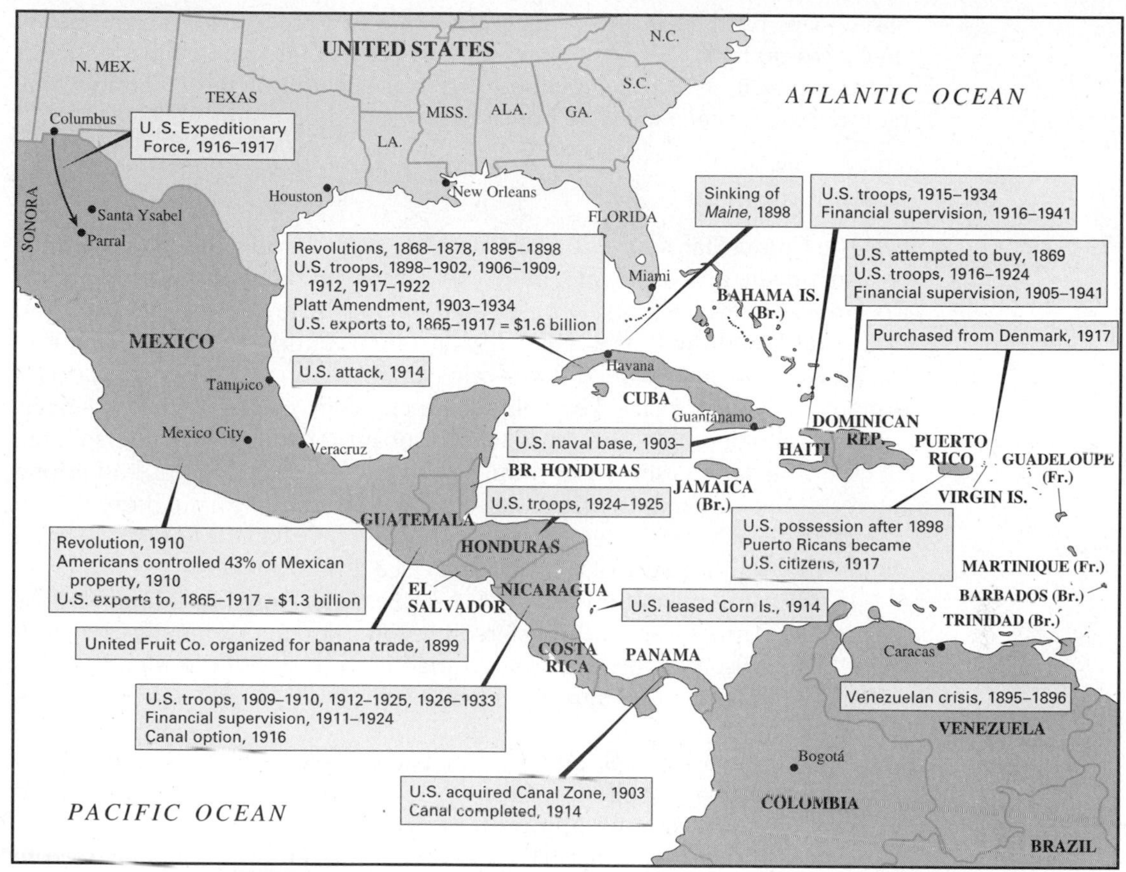

U.S. Hegemony in the Caribbean and Latin America In the first two decades of the twentieth century the United States used a variety of military interventions and economic expansion to become the dominant power in the Western Hemisphere.

of Western societies." But he could not permit the Europeans to collect the money they were owed. Instead he invoked the Monroe Doctrine, the 1823 declaration by President James Monroe that the United States would not permit the establishment of new colonial dependencies in the Western Hemisphere, to justify U.S. intervention in the matter.

The United States implemented this "Roosevelt Corollary" to the Monroe Doctrine by seizing control of the Dominican Republic's finances. In 1905 the government of the Dominican Republic readily agreed to U.S. supervision, but until 1907 Democrats in the U.S. Senate blocked ratification of a treaty providing for U.S. financial administration. In the meantime Roosevelt appointed an American comptroller for Dominican customs houses, granting him the power to use the money collected to repay European lenders. He also stationed U.S.

Navy ships off the coast to prevent the European powers from establishing their own protectorates. When Secretary of State Elihu Root testified in favor of the treaty in 1907, he explained that construction of the Panama Canal required the United States to "police the surrounding premises."

Dollar Diplomacy

The United States continued to dominate the political and financial affairs of Caribbean and Central American states in the administrations of Roosevelt's two successors, Republican William Howard Taft (1909–1913) and Democrat Woodrow Wilson (1913–1921). Taft and his secretary of state, Philander C. Knox, transformed Roosevelt's assertive foreign policy into "dollar diplomacy," which focused on helping American investors and lenders overseas. The aim of dollar diplomacy was to substitute dollars for bullets and to block European investment in countries where the United States had strong interests. Knox hoped that these countries would then become more tightly bound to the United States. In reality, however, dollar diplomacy did not reduce the American use of military force (see figure).

The Taft administration used U.S. Marines to occupy Nicaragua and the Dominican Republic and administered tax collection in Guatemala and Honduras. The Wilson administration occupied both halves of the island of Hispaniola—containing the Dominican Republic and Haiti—and nearly fought a war with Mexico.

In Nicaragua the U.S. government backed American landholders and miners supporting a rebellion against President José Zaleya, who had financed his country's debt through European banks; the triumphant rebels installed Adolf Diaz as president. In 1911 the United States and Nicaragua agreed to refinance Nicaragua's debt through a loan from American banks, with security

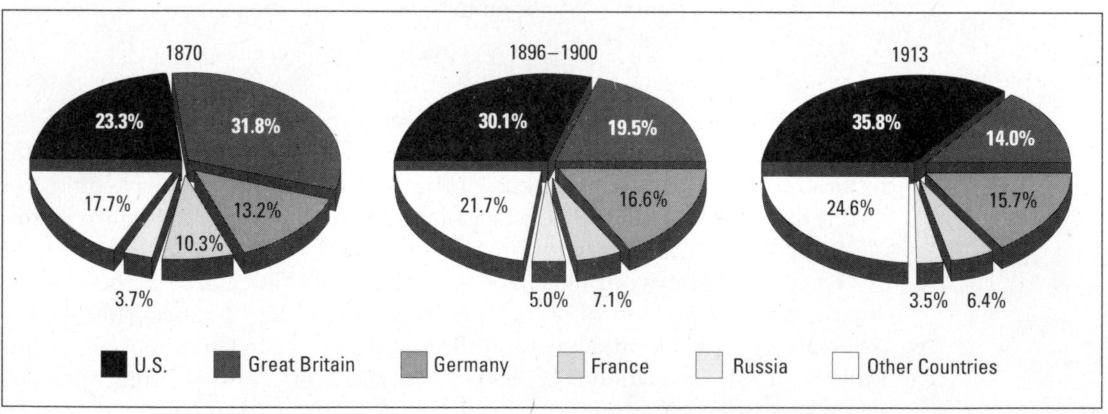

Rise of U.S. Manufacturing Power In the first decades of the twentieth century the United States became the premier manufacturing power in the world.

on the loan to be provided by Nicaraguan customs receipts. The United States would approve the commissioner of Nicaraguan customs. In 1912 the United States sent Marines to put down a rebellion against Diaz by former president Zaleya. American troops remained in Nicaragua until 1916, and U.S. banks put Nicaraguan customs into receivership.

U.S. troops also took charge in the Dominican Republic and Haiti. Taft sent Marines to the Dominican Republic in 1912 to supervise elections. The soldiers came home in December 1912, but by September 1913 the Wilson administration had placed a new squadron off the coast to suppress another rebellion. Marines landed again in 1916, and the United States exercised complete control over the Dominican Republic until the troops finally came home in 1922. In 1915 Wilson also dispatched two thousand Marines to Haiti to establish martial law. Wilson believed the Haitians were "in the childhood of political development," but the presence of U.S. troops did little to improve their lot. The Americans remained in Haiti until 1934.

The greatest U.S. intervention in the political affairs of other Western Hemisphere countries occurred in Mexico from 1911 until 1917. The United States struggled to mount an effective response to the profound social and political revolution that had begun in Mexico in 1910. In 1911 a movement by constitutionalist reformers succeeded in ousting President Porfirio Diaz, a favorite of foreign investors, and installing Francisco Madero as his successor. Madero quickly incurred the wrath of American and British mining and petroleum executives, who worked with the U.S. ambassador to Mexico to oust Madero. In February 1913, a few weeks before Woodrow Wilson was scheduled to assume the presidency in Washington, the plotters murdered Madero and installed General Victoriano Huerta in his place.

Wilson detested Huerta's coup d'état and refused to extend U.S. diplomatic recognition to the new government. Instead the United States engaged in a futile effort over the next four years to force Mexico to create a democratic government. On the surface it appeared that Wilson had the best interests of the Mexican people at heart. Yet he wanted any Mexican government to restrain its nationalistic, anti–United States impulses and welcome some foreign investment. Moreover, Wilson often seemed condescending. He explained that U.S. policy in the Western Hemisphere was to "teach the South American republics to elect good men."

The fiercely nationalistic Mexican constitutionalists resisted Wilson's entreaties to join forces against Huerta. As talks bogged down in late 1913 between Venustiano Carranza, the constitutionalists "first chief," and a U.S. diplomat, the American denounced Carranza's representative for "preventing their friends from helping them." In April 1914 the United States attempted to oust Huerta directly by attacking a poorly armed Mexican force on the Gulf Coast city of Vera Cruz. The occupation of Vera Cruz accomplished the seemingly impossible task of temporarily uniting Huerta and the constitutionalists against U.S. intervention. American action against Vera Cruz also proved widely unpopular throughout Latin America, where street protests against

Yankee heavy-handedness erupted in Chile, Costa Rico, Guatemala, and Uruguay.

The civil war continued in Mexico, with Carranza evicting Huerta from Mexico City in July 1914. It appeared as if Wilson had achieved his diplomatic aims, but the American president now had as little use for Carranza as he had earlier expressed for Huerta. The United States looked for a Mexican leader more likely to accept guidance from Washington. For a few months in late 1914 the United States supported the claims of Pancho Villa, another constitutionalist general. Carranza gained the upper hand over Villa, and in October 1915 Wilson bowed to the inevitable and recognized Carranza's government. Now it was Villa's turn to feel betrayed by Washington. Carranza's forces chased Villa's army northward. In March 1916 Villa crossed the U.S. border and attacked the town of Columbus, New Mexico, killing nineteen Americans. Wilson then succumbed to heavy pressure to send the U.S. Army into Mexico. He dispatched eleven thousand troops under the command of General John J. "Black Jack" Pershing into northern Mexico to arrest Villa.

Once more the Americans became deeply involved in tangled Mexican politics. Carranza initially welcomed the arrival of the Americans, but he did not expect to see such a large force spend four months in his country. Pershing could not find Villa, who tormented his pursuers by again crossing the border and attacking Glen Spring, Texas, fifteen miles north of the Rio Grande. Carranza's troops also fought several battles with the Americans. Carranza and Wilson sent negotiators to resolve their disputes, but they made little progress. American troops left Mexico in January 1917. In the remainder of that year Mexico drafted a constitution providing for land reform and local control over the nation's mineral wealth. American businesses opposed these provisions, but U.S. involvement in World War I precluded the possibility of further military intervention in Mexico. In March 1918 Mexico's congress confirmed Carranza as president, and the United States reluctantly opened full diplomatic relations.

The United States and East Asia

During the first decades of the twentieth century the United States also extended its influence in East Asia. Theodore Roosevelt feared Russian power would undermine America's position in China, so he encouraged American bankers and railroad owners to invest in Chinese lines to ensure an American presence there. When war broke out between China and Japan in February 1904, Roosevelt initially backed Japan. He praised Japan's "perfect preparation and willingness to take action" against the Russian fleet. After a year of fighting, however, Roosevelt adopted a more evenhanded approach. He feared that the revolution that had erupted in St. Petersburg, Russia, might take a radical turn unless the war ended quickly. In the summer of 1905 Japanese and Russian envoys joined Roosevelt in Portsmouth, New Hampshire. Both powers agreed to the Treaty of Portsmouth, which recognized

Japanese dominance of Korea and gave Japan the southern half of Sakhalin Island (between Japan and Russia) and the Russian concessions in southern Manchuria. Roosevelt was awarded the Nobel Peace Prize in 1906 in honor of his mediation efforts.

Roosevelt also mediated a domestic dispute with significant repercussions for U.S. relations with Japan. In October 1906 the San Francisco school board created segregated schools for Japanese children. Roosevelt characterized the order as a "wicked absurdity." He worked out a "Gentleman's Agreement" between Japan and the San Francisco authorities, under which San Francisco agreed to end the segregation in return for a Japanese pledge to stop further immigration to the United States. The agreement permitted the Japanese to claim an advantage over China, whose citizens were excluded by American law from immigrating to the United States.

The Taft administration used dollar diplomacy to maintain an open door for U.S. commercial and banking interests in China. The State Department proposed the internationalization and neutralization of all foreign-owned railroads in China, a direct attempt to reverse the pre-eminent position Japan had achieved via the Treaty of Portsmouth. The other powers rebuffed this American effort. Theodore Roosevelt also thought that Taft believed the United States could do more than its power warranted in China. Roosevelt told his successor that Korea and Manchuria were vital to Japan. He wrote that "we cannot interfere in those areas unless we have an army as good as Germany's or a navy as good as Britain's."

The Taft administration had greater success in encouraging the New York banking houses of Kuhn Loeb and J. P. Morgan to loan the government of China $2 million to meet its operating expenses. But the Chinese government was so weak that it fell to a republican revolution led by Sun Yat-sen, an American-educated doctor, in 1911. The Taft administration pressed the Wall Street bankers to extend their loan to Sun Yat-sen's government, in the hope that the new republic would favor the United States. By the time an agreement had been struck, however, Woodrow Wilson had been inaugurated. In one of his first acts as president he repudiated the Taft administration's promise to guarantee the loan to China. Wilson, a Democrat, believed that dollar diplomacy forged too tight a connection between Washington and Wall Street, which was traditionally a strong ally of the Republican party. The loan to China collapsed, and Wilson found himself preoccupied with more pressing foreign-policy issues in Europe.

✦ The Great War

World War I transformed American foreign policy and society. During the war and the peace conference that followed, President Woodrow Wilson articulated a sweeping vision of a reformed international system. The scope of his agenda was all the more surprising since he had written little about foreign affairs during his distinguished career as a historian and political scientist. Foreign policy played almost no role in his campaign for the presidency in 1912. Indeed, the presence on the ballot of Theodore Roosevelt, someone who had spoken out often on foreign policy, guaranteed Wilson's victory. When Wilson took office in 1913, his foreign-policy views represented the standard fare of Democratic politicians of the day: support for low tariffs and free trade, opposition to Theodore Roosevelt's militant nationalism, and a reluctance to hold colonies. But Wilson was a progressive and a devout Presbyterian, and both influences contributed to the development of his ideas on the proper role of the United States in world affairs. As a progressive he believed in the ability of knowledgeable experts to devise policies that would promote the common welfare. His religious convictions convinced him that God favored America: the abundance in the United States and the country's relative lack of deep class divisions made it the ideal nation to repair a damaged international system.

The outbreak of World War I in August 1914 shocked both Europeans and Americans. Europe had enjoyed a prolonged peace for decades. The Napoleonic wars, the last continent-wide fighting, had ended in 1815. More restricted conflicts had occurred in the Crimea (southern Russia) in the 1850s and between Prussia and France from 1870 to 1871. By the twentieth century many people believed that the growing interdependence of the European nations made war so costly as to be unthinkable.

But Europeans were living on a knife's edge at the beginning of the century. Nationalism was a potent force across the continent, with popular passions inflamed by readily available, cheap newspapers. European states had invested heavily in their armies and navies, and most governments had adopted some form of military conscription. The Europeans had also sought protection in military alliances. One, the Triple Entente, linked Britain, France, and Russia. Britain had also sought to end its previous isolation through an alliance with Japan and friendship with the United States. The Dual Alliance between Germany and Austria-Hungary opposed the Triple Entente.

While nationalism bound people together in some places, ethnic tensions threatened to tear apart the multinational empires of Russia, Austria-Hungary, and Turkey. These three empires all had territorial ambitions or ethnic allies in the Balkan peninsula. There Turkish rule had gradually declined over the previous forty years. An independent Serbia, made up of ethnic Slavs, aligned with Russia. Austria-Hungary feared that Serbia might try to seize Bosnia-Herzegovina, a southern province of the Austrian-Hungarian empire that was home to many Slavs.

These rivalries reached a flash point on June 28, 1914, when a Serbian gunman killed Archduke Franz Ferdinand, heir to the Austrian throne, and his wife, Sophie, in Sarajevo, the capital of Bosnia-Herzegovina. Austria-Hungary consulted with its ally, Germany, and then sent an ultimatum to Serbia. The Serbs sought the support of their protectors in Russia. Russia obtained support from its ally France and began mobilizing in support of Serbia.

Germany sought to pre-empt Russia's military movements with a mobilization of its own. Germany declared war on Russia on August 1 and on France two days later. Germany attacked France through Belgium, a nation whose neutrality Britain had pledged to defend. Although the Triple Entente did not formally commit London to fight for France, British officials believed that a decade's worth of military talks between the two nation's military staffs had committed them morally to assist Paris. Moreover, Britain perceived Germany as a major commercial and military rival. If Germany prevailed in the war, British leaders feared, it would dominate the continent. Turkey, Russia's traditional rival, also joined the war, on the side of Germany and Austria-Hungary.

American Neutrality

The initial American reaction to the war was bewilderment that it had occurred and a profound desire to stay clear of the fighting. Wilson immediately issued a neutrality proclamation, calling on his fellow citizens to be neutral "in thought as well as deed." Some, especially socialists, who characterized the war as a fight among wealthy people at the expense of workers, perceived little difference between the belligerents. But many Americans quickly took sides. A majority had linguistic, ethnic, and economic ties to Britain. The plight of Belgium, carefully kept before the public eye by skillful British propaganda, aroused sympathy in the United States. Theodore Roosevelt became an early advocate of the Allied (British, French, and Russian) cause. He dismissed Wilson's neutrality proclamation as "cowardly and unworthy." On the other hand, there were 27 million Americans of German or Austrian descent, many of whom resented suggestions that their cousins had raped Belgium or caused the war. There also were about 5 million Irish-Americans, who detested British rule of their homeland and therefore did not sympathize with the British cause in the war. And many of the 2 million Jews who had emigrated from Russia opposed doing anything to help the despotic Czar.

In the first months of the fighting the United States adhered to the traditional view of the rights of neutral states. Wilson affirmed the right of Americans to trade with all belligerents in all goods not directly related to their war effort. He also overruled his secretary of state, William Jennings Bryan, to permit Americans to loan money to belligerent governments. Bryan acknowledged that neutrals had always extended credit and loaned money to belligerents, but he feared that too close commercial connections with the Allies, who borrowed more heavily from Wall Street than did the Central Powers, might lead the United States into the war.

Bryan's concerns about U.S. involvement in the war intensified in 1915. Britain blockaded German-controlled ports in Europe and expanded the definition of contraband to include goods that could be used indirectly for the war. Germany retaliated by declaring its own blockade of Britain, enforced by submarines, or U-boats. Since U-boats needed to remain submerged to be safe from attacks from even lightly armed merchant ships, they enforced the blockade by striking without giving the traditional warning.

In February 1915 Wilson warned Germany that the United States would hold it to "strict accountability" for its actions if American lives or property were lost to U-boat attacks. On May 7, 1915, a U-boat sank the British ocean liner *Lusitania,* killing 1,198, including 128 Americans. Most Americans were horrified by the loss of civilian life, although Secretary of State Bryan pointed out to Wilson that the presence onboard of weapons bound for Britain had hastened the ship's trip to the bottom. Despite Bryan's pleas for restraint, Wilson demanded that Germany end submarine attacks on unarmed merchant ships. Bryan resigned over the protest, arguing that the United States was edging closer to war with Germany. Bryan believed that a more realistic approach for the U.S. government, rather than insisting that Germany guarantee the safety of American citizens and vessels, would be to warn American citizens to stay out of harm's way.

Wilson replaced Bryan with Robert Lansing as secretary of state. Along with Colonel Edward M. House, Wilson's closest personal adviser, Lansing favored the Allied cause. He encouraged Wilson to take a tough stand against future U-boat attacks. In March 1916 a U-boat sank the French ship *Sussex* in the English Channel. Several Americans were injured, and Wilson demanded that unless the Germans stopped their U-boat attacks the United States would break off diplomatic relations with Berlin, one step short of declaring war. Germany then issued the *Sussex* Pledge, a promise to stop unrestricted submarine warfare so long as the United States pressed the Allies to lift what Germany considered to be the illegal aspects of their blockade of German ports.

By the time of the *Sussex* Pledge, however, the United States had grown closer commercially and financially to the Allies. Exports of U.S. goods to the Allies rose from $756 million in 1914 to $2.7 billion in 1916. These were enormous sums, considering that the value of all U.S. exports in 1913 had been only $2.4 billion. Between August 1914 and March 1917 (the month before the United States entered the war) the United States sold $2.2 billion worth of arms to the Allies, mostly financed by loans from U.S. banks.

The short war everyone had predicted in August 1914 seemed to grind on forever. On the 475 miles of the western front, hundreds of thousands of Germans on the one side and British and French troops on the other dug trenches in the mud of the French countryside. Men died by the tens of thousands as machine guns and artillery barrages mowed them down when they tried to cross a few hundred yards of no man's land covered with barbed wire. Terrifying new weapons—poison gas, bombs dropped from the air, tanks—killed thousands more. An equal number died from the diseases that ran rampant in the damp cold trenches. Trench life caused many men who had rallied round their country's flag in the heady early days of the war to succumb to madness and despair.

Naturally most Americans wanted no part of the carnage, but many urged their government to do something to stop the slaughter. A growing peace movement encouraged President Wilson to mediate a peaceful solution. Shocked by the horror of what had happened to Europe, Wilson sent his adviser Edward M. House to the major European capitals in 1915 and again in 1916 to arrange a cease-fire. On his first visit House proposed a restoration of the prewar status quo, but the belligerents had invested too much blood simply to go back to where they started. When House returned to London, Paris, and Berlin in early 1916 he carried a much more elaborate peace proposal, one weighted in favor of the Allies. The United States favored territorial concessions by Germany to France and by Turkey to Russia. House also asked the belligerents to promise to join a new international organization designed to keep the peace after the war. It was hardly surprising that all of the warring parties used House's suggestions to gain advantages over their adversaries. But this reaction was not what Wilson had wanted.

With the failure of mediation, Wilson reluctantly endorsed the movement for military preparedness long advocated by Allied supporters like Theodore Roosevelt, General Leonard Wood, and members of the Army and Navy Leagues. In 1915 wealthy sponsors pledged thousands of dollars each to bring hundreds of undergraduates from the most prestigious colleges on the East Coast to an army camp at Plattsburgh, on the shores of New York's Lake Champlain, where they received training as military officers. In June 1916 Congress passed the National Defense Act, doubling the size of the armed forces to two hundred thousand men. Later that summer Congress increased the size of the navy and the merchant marine.

Wilson's support for preparedness helped him in the election of 1916 against Republican Charles Evans Hughes, a justice of the Supreme Court and a former progressive governor of New York. Both Wilson and Hughes avoided definitive statements about what course they favored regarding the Great War. The president asserted that preparedness made it less likely that the United States would actually fight. Some of his campaigners used the slogan "He kept us out of war" to rally voters who wanted to avoid intervening. Wilson disliked the slogan, as he believed that the United States might indeed have to enter the fray if Germany reversed the *Sussex* Pledge. Hughes tried to appeal both to supporters and opponents of the Allies. He stressed preparedness while at the same time he courted the votes of Irish-Americans and German-Americans. In the end Wilson gained enough support from the solid Democratic South and the progressive West. He won a narrow victory of 49.4 percent, to 46.2 percent for Hughes.

The Decision for War

In the winter of 1916–1917, the German military command convinced Kaiser William II that one final offensive against the Allies would win the war for Germany. For the attack to succeed, Britain and France would have to be

✦✦✦

Biographical Profile

Woodrow Wilson, 1856–1921

Woodrow Wilson (1856–1921), the twenty-eighth president of the United States, both excited and exasperated his fellow citizens with a vision of a world reformed through deep American involvement in international affairs. Wilson came to elective office late in life after a distinguished academic career. He left the presidency of Princeton University in 1910 and was elected governor of New Jersey. Just two years later, he was elected president of the United States as a Democrat.

Wilson reflected little about foreign affairs before 1914, but the catastrophe of the Great War thrust him and his nation into the maelstrom of world politics. When war broke out, Wilson urged his fellow citizens to be "neutral in thought as well as deed." For two years he resisted calls for the United States to retaliate when German submarines sank ships carrying American citizens by proclaiming "there is such a thing as a nation too proud to fight." But Wilson gradually came to believe that the United States, prosperous and impartial, alone could end a bloody conflict which threatened to destroy civilization.

In early 1917, convinced that autocratic states like Germany had a natural tendency to make war, Wilson asked Congress for a declara-

---

cut off from their North American suppliers. Germany's commanders therefore recommended the resumption of unrestricted submarine warfare, fully expecting that this policy would bring the United States into the war. Germany expected to defeat Britain and France before fresh U.S. troops could make a difference.

The German government kept its decision to resume unrestricted submarine warfare secret until February 1917. Meanwhile, in late January Wilson explained to the world what he wanted to see at the end of the war. Over the following two years Wilson articulated his vision of a New Diplomacy, in which the United States would play a major role in making future world wars unlikely. He called for a "peace without victory" and a "peace among equals" to end the horrible bloodshed. He advocated the creation after the war of an tion of war against Germany. Under Wilson's leadership the United States embarked on a crusade to foster a new world order. In January 1918 he laid out his peace proposals, the "Fourteen Points." When the war ended in November 1918, Wilson sailed to Europe personally to forge what he called a "peace without victory."

Wilson negotiated in Paris with the leaders of the other victorious states to produce the Treaty of Versailles—far more punitive toward defeated Germany than Wilson had originally planned. It did, however, include a League of Nations, the centerpiece of his blueprint to reform world politics.

But the U.S. Senate refused to ratify the Treaty of Versailles. Wilson hoped to salvage his brainchild with a grueling cross-country speaking trip designed to produce a popular outpouring of support for ratification, but he suffered a massive stroke on the tour. He never fully recovered, and his disability further reduced the chance that the Senate would approve the Versailles Treaty.

Wilson died, deeply embittered, just three years after leaving the White House. But he left a rich legacy. In later years, the American tendency to participate deeply in foreign affairs, justified by appeals to high moral principles and plans for reform and sometimes appearing to be self-righteous, became identified as Wilsonianism.

Woodrow Wilson to Congress, April 2, 1917: "It is a fearful thing to lead this great peaceful nation into war, into the most terrible and disastrous of all wars, civilization itself seeming to be in the balance. But the right is more precious than peace, and we shall fight for the things which we have always carried nearest our hearts—for democracy, for the right of those who submit to authority to have a voice in their own governments, for the rights and liberties of small nations, for a universal dominion of right by such a concert of free peoples as shall bring peace and safety to all nations and make the world itself at last free."

—Link, *Woodrow Wilson and the Progressive Era, 1910–1917*, 1954, p. 282

---

international organization, to be called the League of Nations, to keep the peace. No longer would nations put their faith in competing military alliances; instead they would rely on "a community of power." He also advocated the expansion of democracy, on the grounds that countries in which the people ruled were unlikely to wage war. He also supported freedom of the seas and a reduction in armaments.

Germany's announcement on February 1 that it would resume unrestricted submarine warfare provoked Wilson to break off diplomatic relations. War was declared two months later. By the end of March, U-boats had sunk six American vessels. That alone was not enough to make either the public or the president demand war with Germany, however. Outrage at Germany's efforts to enlist Mexico into the war and Wilson's vision of a reformed world order pushed the United States over the brink into war. Britain helped turn the tide of American opinion in favor of war with Germany when it provided the United States with an intercepted telegram sent by German Foreign Minister Alfred Zimmermann to the German minister in Mexico. Zimmermann had promised German help in restoring Mexico's lost provinces of Texas, New Mexico, and Arizona in return for Mexico's agreeing to attack the United States in the event of war between America and Germany. Wilson released the text of the Zimmermann telegram on March 1, generating vast public support for his plan to arm merchant vessels.

Over the next few weeks Wilson contemplated what could be done to create a peaceful world order. He concurred with his pro-Allied advisers that the undemocratic nature of German society had made Germany the principal instigator of the war. On April 2 he spoke to Congress, advocating a declaration of war against Germany. He accused Germany of waging "warfare against all mankind" with its resumption of unrestricted submarine warfare. Most of his war message, however, proclaimed the loftier goals of the New Diplomacy. "The world must be made safe for democracy," he said. Once more he proclaimed the need for the creation of a league of nations to "bring peace and safety to all nations and to make the world itself at last free." The Senate approved the declaration of war by a vote of 82 to 6. The House approved by a vote of 373 to 50. The small number of progressives who opposed the war supported Wisconsin's Senator Robert La Follette, who warned that the war would destroy progressive reforms at home, turn public affairs over to the richest and most reactionary people in the country, and unleash a tide of intolerance against pacifists, political radicals, unionists, and dissenters.

Total War at Home

The war vastly altered the relationship between the American people and the federal government as the United States mobilized for total war. The power of the federal government vastly expanded—a phenomenon that profoundly gladdened many progressives. Yet the enhanced range of federal authority carried with it deep threats to civil liberties. Congress created the War Industries Board (WIB) in 1917 to coordinate the production of goods necessary for the fighting. Under the leadership of its second director, Bernard Baruch, a highly successful Wall Street speculator, the WIB set production quotas and subsidized new industries. Industrial production increased 20 percent in 1917 and 1918. The government took over the telephone and telegraph systems, and the navy sponsored research into the development of new radio technologies. The government also controlled the nation's railroads, modernizing their schedules to move freight necessary for the war effort. Congress created daylight-saving time to conserve fuel during the summer months. The Food Administration, headed by Herbert Hoover, encouraged Americans to eat less meat and raise their own vegetables. The government raised half of the

$33 billion it spent on the war through taxes, including the new income tax; the other half came from a series of bond drives, or Liberty Loans.

The government also created the Committee on Public Information (CPI), headed by the former muckraker George Creel, to generate public support for the war. The CPI recruited 150,000 people to deliver brief speeches against everything German. By the end of the war these "Four-Minute Men" had delivered more than 755,000 speeches, heard by approximately 300 million people (many attended numerous meetings) across the country. A wave of anti-German sentiment swept over America. Some towns banned the teaching or use of the German language. Books in German were taken from public libraries and burned. Symphony orchestras no longer played the music of Beethoven and Bach.

Radicals, pacifists, and dissenters from the war effort suffered from the new militant patriotism, confronting a wall of silence and repression when they sought to express their views. Congress passed the Espionage Act in 1917 and the Sedition Act in 1918. These laws made it a crime to criticize the war effort or to interfere with conscription or the armed forces. Eugene V. Debs, leader of the Socialist Party, went to jail for saying at an antidraft rally that "the master class has always declared the wars; the subject class has always fought the battles." Frank Little, an organizer for the Industrial Workers of the World (IWW), was lynched by a mob in Butte, Montana, after speaking out against the draft. A Montana senator blamed the government for Little's death. Had he "been arrested and put in jail for his seditious incendiary talk," the senator said, "he would not have been lynched." Justice Department agents raided IWW headquarters across the country in September 1917, and over one hundred Wobbly leaders were tried and convicted of treason.

Some people spoke out against the suppression of dissent. The Civil Liberties Bureau, the forerunner of the American Civil Liberties Union, was formed to object to the silencing of unpopular opinions. When Columbia University fired an antiwar professor, another faculty member, Charles Beard, who was a famous historian and a supporter of the war, resigned in protest. He said that "if we have to suppress everything we don't like to hear, this country is resting on a pretty wobbly basis." But in 1919 the Supreme Court unanimously upheld the constitutionality of the Espionage Act in *Schenck* v. *U.S.* Justice Oliver Wendell Holmes wrote that the government had the right to limit freedom of speech if the words spoken presented "a clear and present danger that they will bring about substantial evil." Holmes said that "free speech would not protect a man falsely shouting fire in a theater and causing panic." A divided Court also upheld the Sedition Act in *Abrams* v. *U.S.*, also in 1919.

The war also sparked vast changes in the workplace. Conscription brought about 16 percent of the male work force into the armed forces. Immigration all but stopped during the war years. To make up for the labor shortage, employers recruited women and nonwhite workers to fill jobs formerly done by men. The overall proportion of women workers rose only

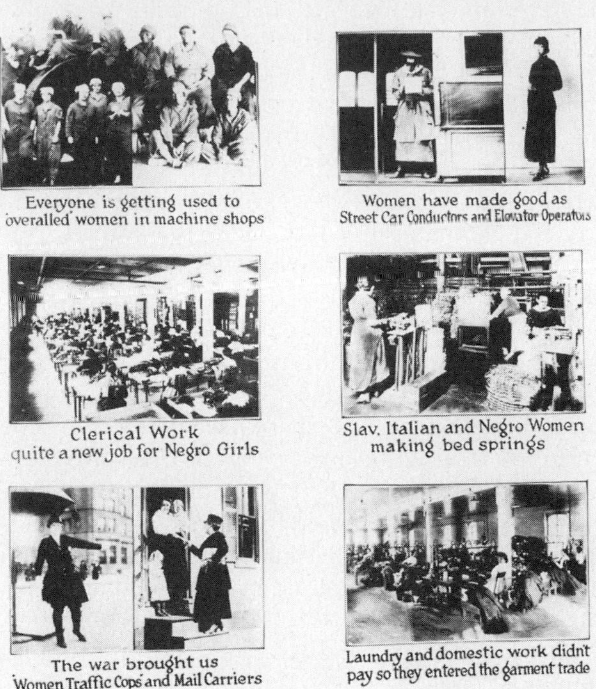

With millions of men in the armed forces, new employment opportunities opened for American women during the First World War, 1917–1918. *National Archives*

slightly, but their presence in formerly all-male occupations shot up drastically. About 20 percent of the workers in electrical and airplane industries were women. As white women took industrial jobs, African-Americans took their places as domestics, textile workers, and sales clerks.

The war fostered a great migration of African-Americans from the South to the North. About five hundred thousand southern blacks moved to northern cities, mostly industrial centers of the Midwest such as Chicago; Gary, Indiana; St. Louis; Detroit; and Cleveland. Industrial jobs in the North paid about $3 a day, compared to the $.50 per day an African-American field worker could earn picking cotton in the South. Lynchings occurred rarely in the North, and African-Americans could vote there. Still, hatred of blacks was common in the North as well as in the South. In 1917 an ugly race riot broke out in East St. Louis, Illinois. Forty African-Americans and nine whites died, and six thousand blacks were made homeless. Even worse violence against blacks occurred in the summer of 1919 in cities across the North. The worst riots took place in Chicago, after an African-American man was stoned for swimming at an all-white beach. In the ensuing six days of rioting, twenty-three African-Americans and fifteen whites lost their lives.

The United States organized a vast armed force to fight the war. Eventually nearly 5 million men served in the U.S. Army, Navy, and Marine Corps (see figure). Congress passed a selective service law, requiring men aged eighteen to forty-five to register with local boards that would determine which men would be conscripted, or drafted, into military service. About 24 million men

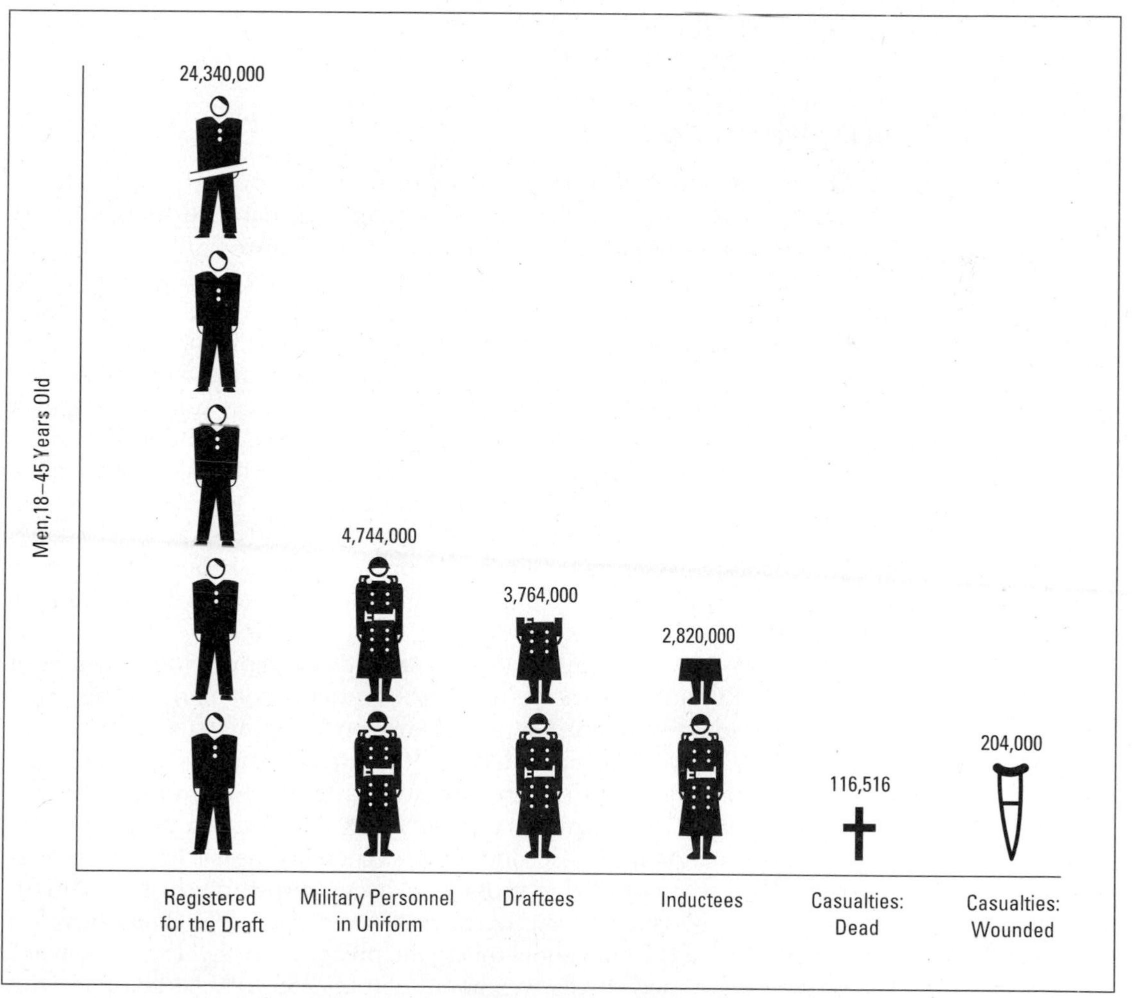

Soldiers in the First World War Nearly five million American men served in the armed forces; most were draftees.

registered, and 2.8 million were drafted. The law permitted conscientious objectors who opposed all war on religious grounds to perform noncombat service within the armed forces. But if they refused to enter the military, they went to jail. General Leonard Wood characterized conscientious objectors as "enemies of the republic."

Most soldiers were white men in their early twenties who had not gone beyond elementary school. About 18 percent were foreign born. About four hundred thousand black Americans served in the armed forces, despite the fears of some segregationist politicians that their participation in the war would fortify their claims to the full rights of citizenship. Approximately two hundred thousand of these African-Americans went overseas, and thirty thousand saw combat. Segregation was strictly enforced within the armed forces, and most of the all-black units served under white officers.

On the Western Front

About 2 million American soldiers arrived in Europe early in 1918 to tip the military balance in the Allies' favor (see map). Germany's armies, fortified by the arrival of hundreds of thousands of men freed from fighting in the east because Russia had sued for peace (see the following section), began an offensive in March. In two months the Germans advanced to within fifty miles of Paris, but in June the fresh American forces helped the French hold the line along the Marne River at Chateau Thierry. In July the Allies won the second battle of the Marne, east of Paris, and began a relentless offensive against the Germans in the Meuse-Argonne Forest. More than 1 million American soldiers took part in a battle lasting three weeks in September and October. When it was over, on October 10, more than twenty-six thousand American soldiers had lost their lives to machine guns, artillery, and diseases in the dank, smelly trenches. But German military power was broken. In late October both Austria-Hungary and Turkey stopped fighting, leaving a virtually defenseless Germany alone.

When they were not fighting, American soldiers enjoyed the pleasures of Paris. Seeing Europe was an eye-opening experience for many young rural Americans. "How You Gonna Keep 'Em Down on the Farm After They've Seen Paree?" became a popular tune. Many formed lifelong friendships with other soldiers and kept up with their army buddies after the war in the American Legion, a veterans' organization formed in 1918. About 15 percent of the American Expeditionary Force contracted a venereal disease. French premier Georges Clemenceau offered to provide inspected prostitutes for the Americans in "special houses." When Secretary of War Newton D. Baker heard of the plan, he warned, "don't show this to the president, or he'll stop the war." The cost to the armed forces was about $50 million to treat soldiers with venereal diseases. Lectures against the dangers of sexually transmitted diseases and threats of courts-martial and imprisonment for soldiers who frequented prostitutes kept the problem from becoming even worse.

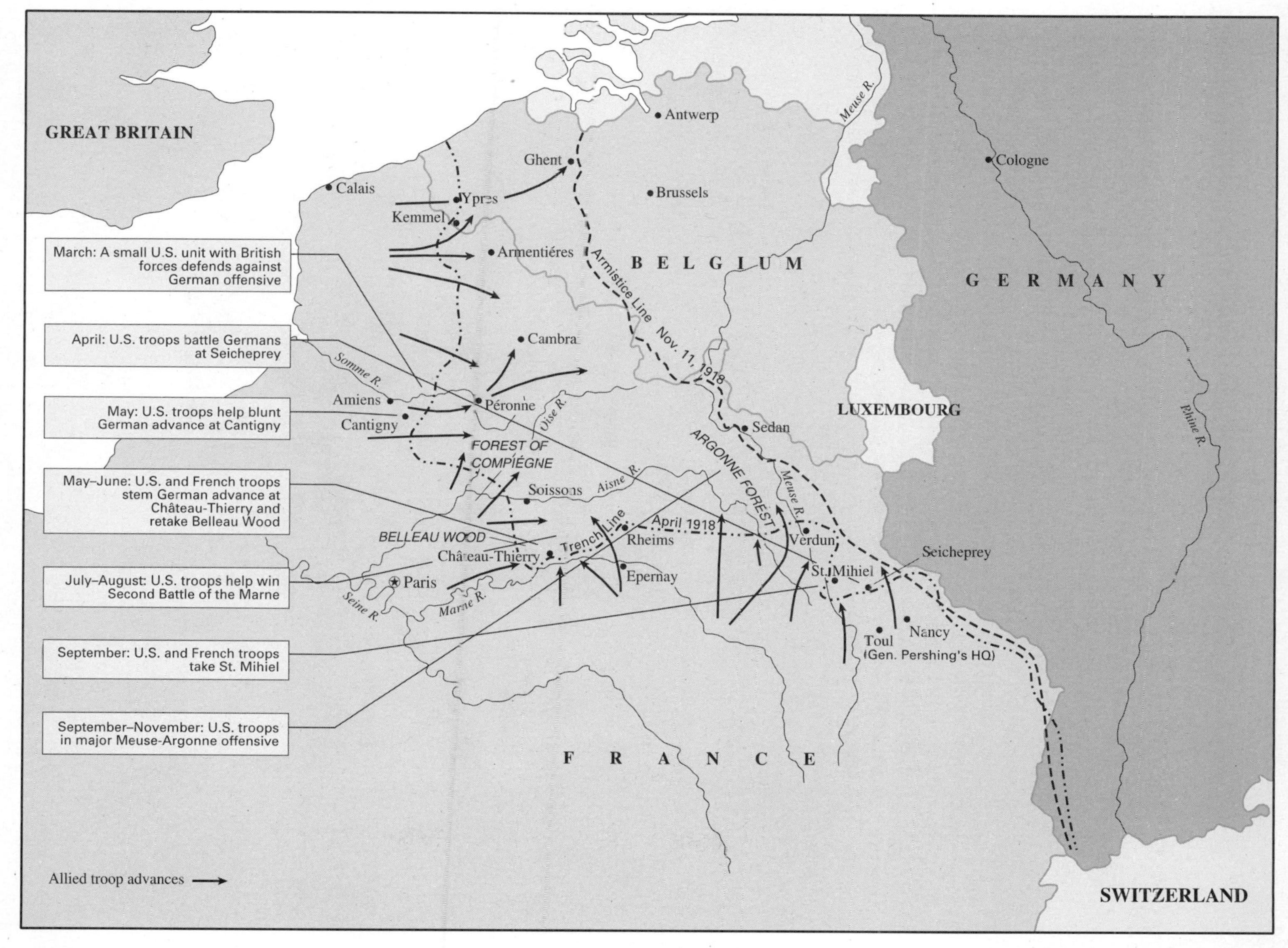

American Troops at the Western Front, 1918 Two million American soldiers in France turned the tide against Germany in 1918.

✦ Wilson's New Diplomacy and the Aftermath of War

During October and November 1918, Germany explored with the United States the possibility of an armistice based on Wilson's Fourteen Points, the plan for peace he had outlined in January of that year. The Fourteen Points summarized Wilson's goal of a New Diplomacy. Wilson had insisted that the United States would fight as an "associated," not an Allied, power. From the beginning he kept the United States aloof from the secret treaties of the Allies. His Fourteen Points were directed toward his fellow U.S. citizens as well as those of the belligerent nations. He wanted to inspire his listeners with an alternative to the far more radical vision of world politics currently being stressed by the Russian Bolshevik leader Vladimir Lenin.

Lenin came to power after a dizzying year of revolution in Russia. In February 1917 war-weary Russians overthrew the government of Czar Nicho-

Russian Communist leader Vladimir Lenin offered a revolutionary challenge to the capitalist countries. To undercut Lenin's appeal, President Woodrow Wilson proclaimed his generous peace program, the Fourteen Points. *Itar-Tass/Sovfoto*

las II. In November Lenin's Bolsheviks overthrew the moderate government of Prime Minister Alexander Kerensky. Lenin's Communists condemned capitalism and claimed that the World War had originated with the sinister plots of rival imperial powers. The Communists encouraged workers throughout the industrial world to start their own revolutions and end the war. The Communists immediately opened peace negotiations with Germany, and in March 1918 they agreed to the harsh terms of the Treaty of Brest-Litovsk. In this agreement Russia surrendered one-third of its population and one-quarter of its European territory to Germany. All this would be worthwhile, Lenin claimed, if it allowed revolutionary Russia to flourish and inspire anticapitalist revolutions elsewhere.

Wilson's Fourteen Points provided an alternative vision for war-weary people everywhere. Points one through five outlined his vision of a reformed world order: no secret treaties, freedom of the seas, lower trade barriers, reductions in armaments, and a re-examination of imperial claims to consider some of the interests of colonized peoples. Points six through thirteen made specific recommendations for territorial and political changes in Europe and the Middle East, most designed to respect the wishes of the people who lived in a given territory. He called for the restoration of the territory lost by France to Germany in 1871, the creation of an independent Czechoslovakia, and the restoration of Polish sovereignty. The fourteenth point called for the creation of a general international organization to guarantee the peace.

Germany considered Wilson's Fourteen Points far less punitive than the Allies' demands for reparations. Facing certain military collapse, the German government offered an armistice on the basis of Wilson's peace plan. Britain and France had little enthusiasm for Wilson's proposals, but they knew they could not continue the war without the United States. The Allies did insist that Kaiser William II abdicate the throne. Wilson readily agreed to this stipulation, because he believed the Kaiser bore a major responsibility for starting the war and hoped that the creation of a German republic would reduce that nation's militarism.

At the eleventh hour of the eleventh day of the eleventh month, November 11, 1918, at 11:00 a.m., the armistice went into effect. The Great War's toll in human lives around the world had been horrendous: over 14 million people dead, 8 million soldiers and 6.6 million civilians. France had lost 1.4 million, including nearly half of its men between the ages of twenty and thirty-two. British dead numbered 908,000. Germany had lost 1.8 million; Russia, 1.7 million; and Austria-Hungary, 1.2 million. American losses were lighter by comparison: 115,000 dead—48,000 in battle, the remainder through disease. Most of the latter had succumbed to the worldwide influenza epidemic of 1918–1919. As many as 40 million people around the world died from the flu in that epidemic. Five to seven hundred thousand of these were in the United States, where the death toll dampened much of the enthusiasm for the end of the war.

The Red Scare at Home

Although the war had ended, the assault on civil liberties in the United States intensified during 1919 and 1920. Fear of the spread of revolution from Russia to the United States unleashed a Red Scare in which local, state, and federal authorities hunted down labor organizers, radicals, and members of the U.S. Communist Party, formed in 1919. A wave of industrial strikes in 1919 set off the Red Scare. A general strike took place in Seattle in January. On May Day, the traditional workers' holiday, prominent Americans received bombs in the mail. In September Calvin Coolidge, the Republican governor of Massachusetts, used national guardsmen to put down a strike by Boston's police officers. Coolidge foolishly characterized the deeply conservative Irish-American cops as radicals, proclaiming that "there is no right to strike against the public interest, by anyone at any time." Radicals did lead a strike by steelworkers in late 1919 and early 1920. The steel companies portrayed the strikers as Bolsheviks, hired strikebreakers, and sent in private militiamen to beat the strikers. The companies broke the strike in 1920.

A. Mitchell Palmer, the Democratic U.S. attorney general, hoped to ride the crest of antiradical fervor into the White House in 1920. He claimed that the "blaze of revolution" could destroy the country. He appointed J. Edgar Hoover to head the newly created Bureau of Investigation within the Department of Justice to track down radicals. Using lists of names compiled by Hoover, the Justice Department summarily deported to the Soviet Union 249 radicals who were not citizens of the United States. In January 1920 "Palmer raids" occurred in thirty-three cities across the country. Breaking into meeting halls and homes without search warrants, Justice Department officials jailed four thousand people. Over the next two years six hundred aliens were deported as political radicals.

The Paris Peace Conference

Although many Americans became disillusioned with Woodrow Wilson at the end of the war, he remained an inspirational figure for millions of people around the world after the November 1918 armistice. Breaking with tradition, he sailed to Europe to direct American negotiators at the peace conference. Before the discussions opened in Paris in January 1919, he made a whirlwind tour of France, Italy, and Britain. Enormous crowds welcomed him and listened enthralled as he outlined his vision of a world restored to harmony and prosperity through American participation in world affairs. He was less popular at home than he had been earlier in his presidency. Voters ignored his pleas to vote for Democrats in the 1918 midterm election, and Republicans gained control of both houses of Congress. Thus any treaty drafted at Paris would have to be ratified by a Republican-controlled Senate. In addition, the chairman of the Foreign Relations Committee was Henry Cabot Lodge, a friend of Theodore Roosevelt and someone who held Wilson in contempt. The proud president made matters worse by resisting advice to name a prominent Republican, or any senator, to the peace delegation going to Paris.

The world seemed broken while the peace negotiators did their work. Communist revolutions broke out and were put down in Germany and Hungary. A savage civil war raged in Russia, where the Red Army of the Communists fought the Whites, an uneasy coalition of monarchists and republicans aligned against Lenin's new dictatorship. Even as the peace talks went forward in Paris, American forces helped the Whites against the Communists. Wilson sent troops in mid-1918 to northern Russia and eastern Siberia to join the British in their support of the Whites. The ostensible reason for the intervention was simply to prevent supplies from falling into German hands, but the Allied forces were clearly helping the Whites. Americans remained in northern Russia until May 1919 and in eastern Siberia until the beginning of 1920. They did not prevent a Communist victory, and their participation in the Russian civil war fueled years of Russian Communist suspicions that the United States wanted to strangle their new state, the Soviet Union.

At the Paris Peace Conference, President Woodrow Wilson (far right), negotiated the terms of the Treaty of Versailles with (left to right) British Prime Minister David Lloyd George, Italian Prime Minister Vittorio Orlando, and French Premier Georges Clemenceau. *Library of Congress*

When the peace conference convened in January 1919, the leaders of the other victorious states—David Lloyd George of Great Britain, Georges Clemenceau of France, and Vittorio Orlando of Italy—who together with Wilson made up the Big Four, made it clear that they did not share the president's vision of a generous peace. They mocked Wilson as a dreamy idealist. "God gave man Ten Commandments," Clemenceau joked. "He broke every one. Wilson has his Fourteen Points. We shall see." The European victors had suffered much during the war, and their citizens demanded vengeance. They had made secret treaties with one another promising to take large amounts of German territory as spoils of war.

From the beginning of the conference Wilson tried to satisfy the Allies, since time seemed precious. He could not linger forever in Europe, and he trusted no one to carry on his domestic work in his absence. Indeed, he stayed in Paris for nearly six months, with only a three-week break in March. All of the participants at the conference feared Communist revolutions in Europe unless a peace treaty restored stability to the continent. Wilson believed that almost any compromise with the other members of the Big Four would be worth it so long as the treaty created a new international organization to preserve order in the postwar world. Wilson therefore agreed that only the victors and not the defeated Germans would have a say in the drafting of the treaty. To speed the proceedings, he accepted Allied proposals that the Big Four meet privately, an apparent violation of his pledge to end secret diplomacy. Liberal hopes that Wilson could carry off his ambitious reform agenda were dashed. John Maynard Keynes, a young member of the British Treasury's delegation to the peace conference, thought that Wilson was simply outwitted by the other members of the Big Four: "There can seldom have been a statesman of the first rank more incompetent than the president in the agilities of the council chamber."

Wilson gave in to Allied demands to exact large reparations from the vanquished. The treaty contained a clause assigning Germany sole responsibility for having started the war and holding it liable for the full cost of it to the victors. A reparations commission later set the amount due at $33 billion. In later years these provisions became rallying cries for German nationalists who believed they had been unfairly punished by the vengeful Allies.

Wilson had some successes and several noteworthy failures in advancing his plans for the breakup of empires and the advancement of subject people's self-determination (see map). The Austrian-Hungarian empire gave rise to the new states of Poland, Czechoslovakia, Austria, Hungary, and Yugoslavia. The collapse of the Russian empire brought the new nations of Latvia, Estonia, Lithuania, and Finland, which the victors transformed into a buffer zone around Communist Russia. The conference also permitted France to occupy the German Rhineland. The treaty stripped Germany and Turkey of many overseas dependencies in the Middle East, Africa, and Asia. France, Britain, and Japan were given mandates by the League of Nations to run the political

Europe Transformed by War and Peace Woodrow Wilson and the other peacemakers at the Paris Peace Conference drafted the Treaty of Versailles which redrew the map of Europe, breaking up old empires and creating new nations.

affairs of these dependencies in the interests of the world community. In Asia the peace conference preferred Japan to China, even though both nations had joined the war against Germany. Germany's lease on the Shandong Peninsula was turned over to Japan as compensation for the victors' refusal to include a declaration of racial equality in the covenant of the League of Nations. Granting Shandong to Japan sparked massive anti-Western and anti-Japanese demonstrations in China.

Wilson believed that whatever compromises he had made on territory and reparations were more than made up for by the agreement to create the League of Nations. All the members of the league would be represented in a general assembly. A smaller council of fifteen states, five of which would have permanent seats, would enforce the league's covenant. Article 10 of the covenant authorized the use of force against nations violating the "territorial integrity and political independence of all members of the league." Wilson considered this provision for collective security the "backbone" of the covenant and the core of his alternative to the discredited rival military alliances of the past generation.

The victors completed the treaty in June and summoned German representatives to the ornate Hall of Mirrors in the Palace of Versailles to sign it. The Germans complained about the harshness of the reparations and territorial concessions, but the Allies would not revise the terms. Having little choice, Germany agreed to all of the terms, and the Treaty of Versailles was signed on June 28, 1919, five years to the day since the assassination of Archduke Franz Ferdinand in Sarajevo. Wilson exulted in the completion of the treaty, which he said, "has come about by no plan of our conceiving, but by the hand of God."

Defeat of the Treaty of Versailles

But the treaty faced an uncertain future at home. Two-thirds of the Senate needed to ratify it for the United States to participate in the League of Nations. Political rivalries, differences of opinion about the proper role of the United States in world affairs, disillusionment with Wilson's deviations from his ambitious agenda of reform, and the president's poor health and political miscalculations doomed the treaty. While the treaty was being drafted, thirty-nine senators—more than the one-third necessary to block ratification—signed a petition demanding that the League of Nations recognize that the Monroe Doctrine gave the United States pre-eminence in the Western Hemisphere. When Wilson formally submitted the treaty for ratification in the summer of 1919, Henry Cabot Lodge, chairman of the Foreign Relations Committee, subjected it to a withering critique. Like his friend Theodore Roosevelt, Lodge despised Wilson as a poor scholar, a hypocrite, and a foolish idealist. The Massachusetts senator believed that Article 10 of the covenant limited U.S. freedom of action and prevented future U.S. expansion. It might also require the United States to engage in military actions the public might prefer to avoid. Lodge began slowly picking the treaty apart in public hearings during the summer of 1919. He introduced revisions to the treaty designed to preserve Congress's war-making power and the country's ability to maintain control over domestic issues with international ramifications, like immigration.

On the other side of the political spectrum, many progressives denounced the treaty as a betrayal of Wilson's high principles. Some, like Idaho Republican senator William E. Borah, claimed that membership in the League of Nations would commit the United States to participate in a club composed of imperialist victors that wanted to stifle any changes in world politics. The anti-Communist elements of the treaty convinced Borah that Wilson would permit the league to embark on a costly anti-Soviet crusade. Other liberals believed that the problem with the treaty was that Wilson had too quickly abandoned some of the loftier principles of the Fourteen Points. He had conducted the negotiations secretly, imposed punitive terms on Germany, offended China, and obtained little for freedom of the seas and nothing for disarmament.

Wilson's response to these criticisms combined a reasonable defense of the give-and-take of negotiations with a haughty disdain for his critics' motives. He explained that he had been forced to accept some of the Allies' punitive terms to gain their consent for the league. Once the new world organization began its work, he claimed, it could change whatever was wrong with the treaty and remedy future international disputes. He opposed revisions to the treaty because the other victors might also demand changes, bringing down the entire agreement.

In September Wilson left Washington for an exhausting eight-thousand-mile speaking tour to generate support for the League of Nations. He delivered thirty-six speeches in twenty-two days before huge, enthusiastic crowds. For a while it seemed that his magical oratorical gifts would carry the day. He brought tears to the eyes of his audience when he told them that without the League of Nations a war would inevitably erupt in the future in which "there would not be a mere seven and a half million slain. The very existence of civilization would be in the balance." He also condemned his critics as "absolute contemptible quitters." Their fear that the United States would be forced to send troops to faraway places were exaggerated, he said: "If you want to put out a fire in Utah you do not send to Oklahoma for the fire engine. If you want to put out a fire in the Balkans you do not send to the United States for troops."

He delivered his last speech in Pueblo, Colorado, on September 26, 1919. He spoke of the mothers of dead soldiers who had grabbed his hand and cried, "God bless you, Mr. President." Why were they so moved? he asked. "Because they believe that their boys died for something that vastly transcends any of the immediate and palpable objectives of the war. They believe, and rightly believe, that their sons saved the liberty of the world." At the end of this speech he collapsed; four days later he suffered a stroke that nearly killed him.

Wilson slowly recovered, but his left side was paralyzed. The stroke also left him depressed, angry, and stubborn. When someone suggested that he compromise with Senator Lodge and permit some revisions to the treaty to pass the Senate, he replied, "Let Lodge compromise." He demanded that Senate Democrats demonstrate their loyalty by voting against all revisions. When the Senate considered the treaty in November 1919, Democrats joined sixteen "Irreconcilables" (senators opposed to any U.S. participation in the league) to defeat the treaty with revisions (39 for and 55 against.) Then Republicans and Irreconcilables defeated the treaty without revisions by a vote of 38 for and 53 against. The treaty came back for another vote in March 1920. Senate Democrats begged the president to release them from their promise to oppose all revisions. He refused, but some broke ranks anyway. The treaty received 49 yea votes and 35 nays, 7 short of the two-thirds majority needed for passage. The president remained undaunted. He expected the Democratic Party to nominate him for an unprecedented third term, and he would turn the election campaign into a "solemn referendum" on American participation in the League of Nations.

Had Wilson been willing to compromise on revisions to the treaty, it would have been approved. Thomas Bailey, a historian writing during World War II, when most Americans believed that the refusal to join the league had been a grave mistake, characterized Wilson's behavior as "the supreme infanticide." Wilson's stubbornness, caused partly by his stroke, had killed his own offspring. But the gulf between Wilson and the opponents of American participation in the league reflected deep divisions over the proper role of the United States in world affairs. For Wilson the lesson of the catastrophic blows the Great War had dealt European civilization was that the United States had to join with other nations to create a stable international environment. To do so meant abandoning the unilateral foreign policy the United States had maintained since George Washington's farewell address, in which the nation's first president warned his fellow citizens to avoid entangling alliances with other nations. Wilson's opponents believed that the United States could best advance its interests by maintaining its freedom of action. They feared that the Great Powers of Europe, however weakened they were by the bloodletting, retained much of their appetite for overseas domination. Critics of the league wanted to avoid a situation in which the United States became an unwitting partner in European imperialism. The division between advocates of Wilsonian collective security and supporters of Lodge and Roosevelt's vision of continuing independent American activism in foreign affairs was too deep for compromise in 1920.

Woodrow Wilson never achieved his dream of seeing the 1920 election become a solemn referendum on the League of Nations. Democratic Party leaders did not seriously consider nominating him for a third term. His stroke left him unable to campaign, and a majority of the public no longer wanted to pursue his reform agenda. (He survived, frail and embittered, until his death in 1924.) The Democrats rejected Attorney General Palmer, whose Red Scare had provoked a backlash. They also refused to nominate Secretary of the Treasury William Gibbs McAdoo, Wilson's son-in-law, whose family ties to the unpopular president, party leaders believed, would alienate voters. Instead they nominated James Cox, governor of Ohio, who had taken no positions on foreign affairs. For vice president they chose Franklin D. Roosevelt, assistant secretary of the navy during the war. They hoped that he could win the votes of some admirers of his famous distant cousin, the former president. The Republicans nominated Ohio senator Warren Harding, who had stayed in the background during most of the discussions of the treaty. For vice president they chose Calvin Coolidge, the Massachusetts governor who had defeated the Boston police strike. Foreign affairs played a subordinate role in the campaign, and Harding won an overwhelming victory with 60 percent of the popular vote, the largest majority gained by a presidential candidate. Voters who chose Harding did so in the expectation that he would provide welcome relief from twenty years of domestic reform and intensive participation in foreign affairs.

✦ Conclusion

America's rise to world power in the first two decades of the twentieth century created vast and unexpected changes in U.S. society. For the first time the United States was one of the Great Powers with interests in the Western Hemisphere, Europe and Asia. The role of government on all levels expanded. The United States was the world's leading economic power in 1920. For the first time in its history it was a creditor, not a debtor nation. Participation in the Great War had also effectively ended progressive reform at home. The war uncovered some of the deep racial, class, and ethnic divisions within American society. During the war immigration into the country stopped, and after 1918 the movement to restrict future immigration intensified. Woodrow Wilson's vision of a harmonious world order led by the United States thrilled millions of people at home and abroad in 1917 and 1918. But the harshness of the war and the cold realities of the Treaty of Versailles created bitter disillusionment in Europe and the United States. In the 1920s and 1930s many people looked back on the Great War as a grand folly, a time of missed opportunities and broken dreams.

✦ Further Reading

For overviews of U.S. foreign relations in the beginning of the twentieth century, see: Walter La Feber, *The American Search for Opportunity, 1865–1913* (1993); Akira Iriye, *The Globalization of America, 1913–1945* (1993). For the cultural impact of the United States abroad, see: Emily S. Rosenberg, *Spreading the American Dream: American Economic and Cultural Expansion, 1890–1945* (1982). For key personalities of the era, see:

John Milton Cooper, Jr., *The Warrior and the Priest: Woodrow Wilson and Theodore Roosevelt* (1983). For the Spanish-American-Cuban war, see: Lewis Gould, *The Spanish-American War and President McKinley* (1980); David F. Trask, *The War with Spain in 1898* (1981). For the American war in the Philippines, see: Stanley Karnow, *In Our Image: America's Empire in the Philippines* (1989); Glenn A. May, *Social Engineering in the Philippines* (1980). For the growth of U.S. power in the Western Hemisphere, see: David McCullough, *The Path Between the Seas: The Building of the Panama Canal* (1976); Lester Langley, *The Banana Wars* (1983). For the Pacific and Asia, see: Michael Schaller, *The United States and China in the Twentieth Century* (1994); Akira Iriye, *Pacific Estrangement: Japanese and American Expansion, 1897–1911* (1972). For Americans' thoughts about changing international institutions, see: Warren Kuehl, *Seeking World Order: The United States and International Organization to 1920* (1969). For an overview of the First World War, see: Ellis W. Hawley, *The Great War and the Search for a Modern Order* (1992). For diplomacy during the war, see: Lloyd Ambrosius, *Wilsonian Statecraft* (1991); Thomas J. Knock, *To End All Wars* (1992). For domestic events during the war, see: Ronald Schaeffer, *America in the Great War: The Rise of the Welfare State* (1991). On the challenges to civil liberties during wartime, see: Richard Polenberg, *Fighting Faiths* (1987). For women in wartime, see: Dorothy Schneider and Carl J. Schneider, *Into the Breach: American Women Overseas in World War I* (1991). For the experience of African-Americans, see: Arthur Barbeau and Florette Henri, *The Unknown Soldiers: Black American Troops in World War I* (1974). For the effects on the war of influenza and venereal disease, see: Alfred Crosby, *Forgotten Pandemic: The Influenza of 1918* (1989); Allan Brandt, *No Magic Bullet* (1985). For the peace conference and the aftermath of war, see: Lloyd Ambrosius, *Woodrow Wilson and the American Diplomatic Tradition* (1987); Arno J. Mayer, *Politics and Diplomacy of Peacemaking* (1967); Klaus Schwabe, *The World War, Revolutionary Germany and Peacemaking* (1985); Arthur Walworth, *Wilson and the Peacemakers* (1987).

✦✦✦
CHAPTER 4

Modern America and Its Discontents: The 1920s

✦ F. Scott and Zelda Fitzgerald.

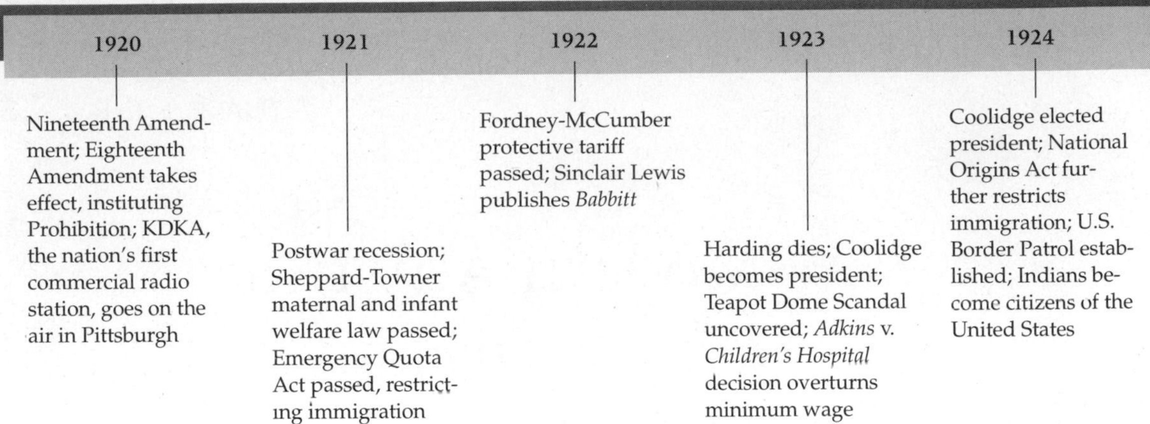

ANTONIO LUHAN LOOKED up at the wide, turquoise sky and thought longingly of rain. The crops and the cattle were parched, but he hoped that the summer storms would soon come to fill the irrigation ditches and turn the Taos Pueblo's fields green. This spring, he knew, in the year 1922, Pueblo farmers faced dangers even more threatening than drought. Officials at the Bureau of Indian Affairs (BIA) had begun a campaign to suppress Indian religious practices, especially ritual dances. BIA commissioner Charles H. Burke regarded the dances as un-Christian, as "excessive performances that promoted idleness, superstitious cruelty, and dangers to health." Burke also believed that the white artists and intellectuals who had begun to flock to the Southwest in search of brilliant light and grand scenery were "stirring up trouble" among the natives. The Indians, Burke thought, did not understand that the BIA had Indians' own best interests in mind in its efforts to stamp out indigenous customs and promote Protestantism. Thus Indians who continued to participate in traditional ceremonies were to be fined or imprisoned for their own good.

In the meantime, Interior Secretary Albert B. Fall, whose name would soon become synonymous with corruption in the Teapot Dome Scandal, had prevailed on New Mexico Republican senator Holm Bursum to introduce a bill into Congress to resolve disputed land claims in the Southwest. If the Bursum Bill became law, virtually all lands claimed simultaneously by Anglos, Mexican-Americans, and Indians would be awarded to the Anglo or Chicano claimants, including cronies of Fall and Bursum. Modern America—with its disillusioned artists, its greedy politicians, its railheads and banks and motor-

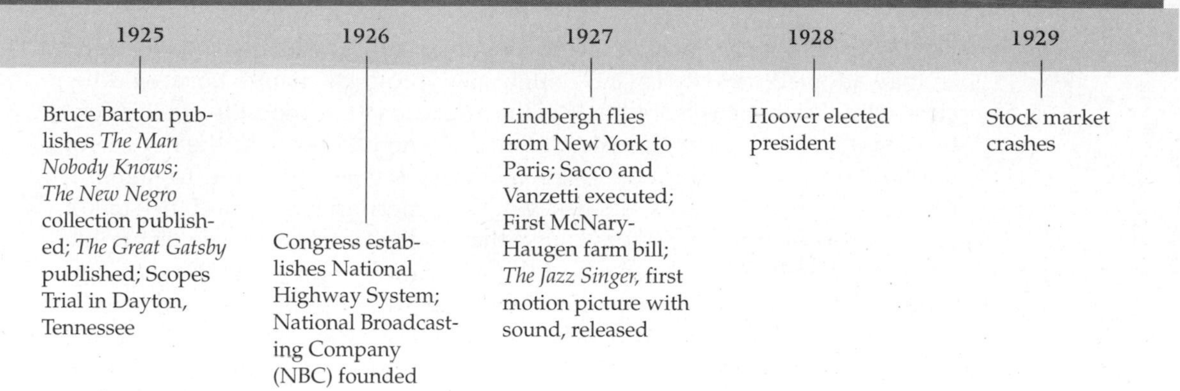

cars—had come to the Pueblos, whose roots in the Rio Grande Valley stretched back thousands of years. People like Antonio Luhan would have to learn new means to preserve old ways. Tony Luhan realized that Pueblo Indians like him had everything to lose, and he was determined to do something about it. He turned the key in the ignition of his Cadillac and prepared to take his passenger, a New York social worker named John Collier, on a tour of the pueblos to sound the alarm.

In the years following the Great War, Americans from Taos to Toledo, from Seattle to Miami, opened up to an expanding, tumultuous array of places, goods, and ideas. American corporations, with plenty of help from a business-friendly government, sold new technologies, products, and services to a public just learning to try and buy. While some, particularly in the working class, were wary of the costs of consumerism, millions of Americans of all classes embraced new mobility, novel forms of entertainment, and more permissive sexual mores. They shortened their skirts and bobbed their hair, drank illegal whiskey, piled into cars for wild joy rides, and sang along with the Tin Pan Alley songwriter's rhetorical question "Ain't We Got Fun?" They celebrated bootlegging gangsters as outlaw heroes. They made the twenties roar.

Still others were determined to confront the new mass culture on their own terms. Many working-class Americans transformed their sense of ethnic identity into a new class-consciousness. For African-Americans, jazz was not simply a pleasurable diversion; it was a cherished means of self-expression. For eastern European and Italian immigrants and their offspring, Prohibition was not simply a restrictive law; it was a violation of time-honored ways of life.

Beyond its immediate allure, the consumer society also bred anxiety. Even as they adopted new styles and bought new products, native-born, middle-class white Americans feared that as they pursued "the good life" they might be overwhelmed by immigrants and others who had been on the bottom of the socioeconomic pyramid. Social openness seemed to some to signal a decline of moral standards, the decay of the American family, and the ruin of American womanhood. Others feared that a secret Catholic (or Jewish) plot, a sinister plan for the subversion of the white race, or an international Communist conspiracy threatened the American free-enterprise system. Some simply felt that their world had become too large and complex, that it had grown inauthentic and out of control. And on dust-choked farms, in grim small towns, and amid big-city chaos all across America, many people wondered why everybody else's plenty and pleasure had passed them by.

To a remarkable degree, Taos's Antonio Luhan embodied the tensions, ironies, and energies of America in the 1920s. In an era that celebrated sex and turned marriage into a problem, and in a country obsessed with defining and controlling race relations, Tony Luhan had left his Pueblo wife to live with a white woman. That woman, the iconoclastic socialite Mabel Dodge, had fled the frenetic confines of Greenwich Village in search of inner peace in the vastness of the West. Her Indian husband was a devoutly religious man, but when he married Mabel he was forced to give up participating in the sacred ceremonies of his own people, who banned interracial marriage. Nevertheless, Tony Luhan was fervently committed to preserving the Pueblos' traditional culture and economy, just as he also enjoyed the trappings of the consumer economy, especially fine automobiles. To help his people protect their way of life, he had to learn the ways of white politics—organizing and petitioning, lobbying and publicizing, and depending on white allies, who were often less than reliable. At the time, this Native American man was not even legally a citizen of the United States.

Tony Luhan was remarkably successful. With help from Mabel and from Collier, the New York social worker, the Pueblos' effort to protect their lands and way of life gained the support of influential Anglos. Prominent writers and artists like Mary Austin, D. H. Lawrence, Willa Cather, and Georgia O'Keeffe, who like Mabel had flocked to New Mexico to seek refuge from the alienating cacophony of modern urban life, lent their money and prestige to the Pueblo cause. In the South and elsewhere in the West, rural white Americans were losing their farms to drought and bankruptcy, and black tenant farmers and sharecroppers were losing their livelihood to machines. But the Pueblos hung on to and expanded their lands by mobilizing political support and harnessing the power of farm machines and scientific agriculture. Tony Luhan owned a threshing machine himself, and it made him a busy and influential man among his people.

Many of the whites who came to know Tony through Mabel celebrated him as a living example of the proverbial "noble savage." Tony navigated, with care and sophistication, the quarrelsome hothouse atmosphere of Mabel's brilliant, troubled circle, not to mention the labyrinth of American politics. As white intellectuals in Taos and Santa Fe were busy turning Indian art and culture into salable commodities for the national market, Pueblos like Tony hoped to protect their traditional communal values from the impacts of materialism and individualism, increasingly huge and powerful corporations, and a vastly expanded postwar federal government. And unlike people from southern and eastern Europe and Asia, who found it increasingly difficult to become U.S. citizens or even to enter the United States, Indians did gain some rights during the 1920s, including the right of citizenship, in 1924.

✦ The Consumer Society

By 1920 the United States was the richest country on earth, its industries augmented and consolidated with the help of a congenial federal government. Businessmen and bureaucrats had built a partnership that would monopolize American politics and culture for more than a decade and survive the cataclysms of global depression and war. The Progressive Era's zeal for reform would be transformed into a drive for productivity, efficiency, and management and into new ways to show off one's wealth, work less, and have fun.

The economic boom induced by the war lasted until 1920, when the government canceled defense contracts, and demobilized veterans flooded the labor market. Unemployment among nonfarm workers reached nearly 20 percent in 1921, and farmers saw prices plummet as overseas demand tailed off. But more significant than the immediate crisis was a shift in the nature of the American economy. Formerly dominated by heavy industries like railroads, mining, and steel, the U.S. economy was rapidly coming under the sway of a new generation of corporate giants, firms that produced consumer goods or provided services.

Producing for the Masses

Mass production, standardization, and transportation and communication networks that spanned the continent made it possible for Americans in widely dispersed places to choose from a vast array of things to buy. From 1910 to 1920 industrial production rose only a modest 12 percent, but between 1920 and 1930 the nation's productivity skyrocketed 64 percent. In large part it was the spread of new technologies that caused the boom: in 1919 only 30 percent of American industry was electrified; by 1929 electrification had been extended to 70 percent of industries. But marketing innovations also powered the consumer revolution. Big national firms used franchising agreements with local retailers, market research, and, increasingly, mass advertising to boost (and even create) demand for their wares, making larger and larger claims on Americans' pocketbooks. Chain stores like the Great Atlantic and Pacific Tea Company (A&P) for groceries, Woolworth's for "variety" goods, and United Cigar Stores for tobacco products began to replace the mom-and-pop operations that had long been familiar fixtures in American towns and cities. By

1930 those chain stores accounted for 20 percent of all retail trade in the nation, up from only 4 percent at the beginning of the decade. They sold everything from toothbrushes to vacuum cleaners, beefsteaks to bicycles.

New infrastructures created demand for a seemingly ever-expanding range of new products, and vice versa. Cities built and extended water and sewer systems, stimulated by progressives' crusades for "municipal housekeeping" and by enterprising plumbing fixture manufacturers like the Kohler company of Milwaukee, which promoted "the fun of being clean" in fifteen national periodicals. As they looked at pictorial advertisements featuring the gleaming white enamel toilets, sinks, and bathtubs of Kohler's "small and simple" modern bathroom, more and more Americans abandoned the discomforts of the pump and outhouse for the benefits of indoor plumbing.

Enterprise and ingenuity would integrate the technological wonders of the day—electric generators, water turbines, aluminum and new metal alloys, synthetic substances like Bakelite, an early plastic. Samuel Insull learned his trade as secretary to Thomas Edison, and by the 1920s he had assembled an electrical empire that encompassed everything from transformers and transmission lines to utility companies and investment banks.

Insull's determination to supply electricity at low cost to a mass market inspired many others to imitate his coordination of technological, economic, and political systems. Gifford Pinchot, once chief forester of the United States and later governor of Pennsylvania, promoted a scheme to erect huge electric power plants in western Pennsylvania's coal fields, string giant power lines hundreds of miles to the eastern part of the state, and build smaller transmission lines to carry electricity to homes in cities, small towns, and even the countryside. Electricity, Pinchot declared in 1925, would bring every worker a higher standard of living, more leisure, and better pay. Electric lights and power would benefit farmers as they went about their round of laborious tasks, from milking to sawing wood. Housewives would find the convenience and ease of use of electric lights and appliances, of irons, washing machines, and other modern devices, little short of miraculous.

Once the economy recovered from the postwar slump and businesses began to hire again, Americans found more and more ways and places to spend their paychecks. Companies like Westinghouse and General Electric offered a host of new domestic technologies, including electric refrigerators, irons, vacuum cleaners, and washing machines, promising American women that these devices would make their housework a breeze. Middle-class families, in particular, bought these new appliances in a new way: on the installment plan. When they made the purchase, they put down only a fraction of the amount listed on the price tag; they then paid a percentage of the cost (plus interest) each month, "on time." Consumers who took advantage of extended payment plans reasoned that as long as the country kept booming, their jobs would be safe and their paychecks would keep coming. And according to the financial experts of the day, as long as workers kept buying (and most imagined that consumer demand might expand endlessly), the economy would keep growing.

Ford and the Automobile

The most prominent advocate of the idea that mass consumerism could pave the way to utopia was the man who brought the nation its emblematic consumer commodity, the automobile.

Henry Ford's Model T—or "flivver" or "Tin Lizzie"—revolutionized American life. In 1908 slightly fewer than six thousand of the cars were sold. By 1927, when Ford ceased production of the model, more than 15 million Tin Lizzies had rolled off the assembly line. The rugged Model T opened new vistas to ordinary people and coped brilliantly with the wretched roads of the American countryside. It brought unprecedented mobility within the reach of ordinary men and women in out-of-the-way places, and even if the Tin Lizzie's shock absorbers were, as wags observed, the passengers, plenty of Americans were more than accustomed to jolting over rutted roads in rickety wagons.

Ford put America on wheels, preaching the gospel of mobility and consumerism. By 1929 over 23 million passenger cars were registered in the United States, up from about 8 million in 1920 (see figure). Americans in larger towns and cities were growing increasingly dependent on their cars to go to work, to shop for necessities, and to connect with the world outside their

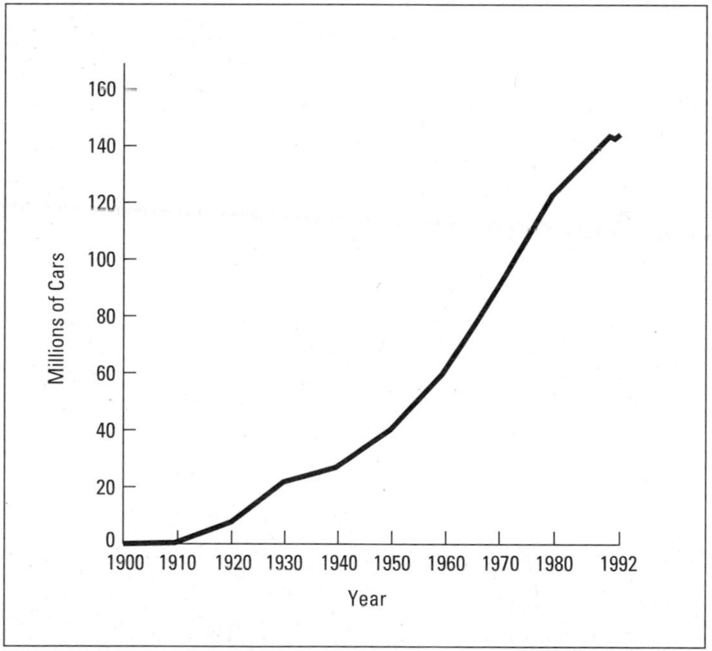

Passenger Car Registration in the United States, 1900–1990 During the 1920s, the automobile cemented its claim to becoming a common part of everyday American life. Auto registration would soar continually through the rest of the century.

✦ ✦ ✦

Biographical Profile

Henry Ford, 1863–1947

Contrary to popular belief, Henry Ford did not invent the gasoline-powered automobile. He was, however, the first giant in the field, the first to introduce modern mass production techniques, and the first to dream of producing a car for the average American family. Most turn-of-the-century American auto manufacturers had followed European carmakers' lead in assuming that automobiles were playthings for the rich. But a small handful of farsighted automakers imagined that automobiles might be made cheaply enough to appeal to the average American man. Henry Ford alone made that vision into a reality.

Everyman's car would have to be strong and durable enough to navigate the nation's miserable rutted back roads and unreliable city streets, and it would have to be cheap enough to fit the budget of even working-class families. In 1908 Ford introduced the Model T, a Spartan machine that sold for an incredibly low $850. During the next few years the price of the Model T declined steadily as Ford's experts streamlined production and distribution. Ford's Highland Park, Michigan, plant featured a new moving assembly line that would become the model for, and symbol of, modern mass production. Workers remained in one place, each performing one task over and over again as overhead pulleys and conveyer belts carried the carcass of each automobile from the start of the line to the finish.

Prospective employees flocked to Detroit to work in Ford's factory, but many found the job unbearably monotonous and quit only months after being hired. Within the year, Ford determined to offer his workers the unheard-of wage of $5 a day. Ford believed that the men who made his machines (at first he exempted female employees from the raise) ought to earn enough to buy them. The auto business, and the American economy, would never be the same. By 1926 customers from coast to coast could purchase a Model T for only $290.

> *One idea at a time is about as much as anyone can handle.*
>
> –from *My Life and Work*

"Everyman's Car" made it possible for American families to enjoy the conveniences of city life and the pleasures of the countryside. *Brown Brothers*

doors. Cities began to spread and sprawl. In places like Los Angeles, real estate developers realized the possibilities for profit in building suburban communities reachable only by motorcar, to house auto-owning middle-class families. By 1925 there was one automobile for every three residents of Los Angeles, twice the national average. As the decade wore on, retail businesses formerly located downtown, notably department stores and banks, followed their clients into the suburbs and established branch outlets. When Bullock's Department Store built a branch on Wilshire Boulevard in 1929, a new suburban era had arrived.

Once behind the wheel, Americans took to the road by the millions. They made motoring vacations a national pastime and spurred a boom in tourism. Municipalities on the way to popular attractions like the Grand Canyon, Yellowstone, and Yosemite National Park established auto camps for touring families, ranging from lots set aside for parking and tents to elaborately landscaped parks with hot showers, concession stands, and even entertainment. The more Americans drove, the more they understood how bad America's roads were. In response to pressure from motorists, Congress established the U.S. highway system in 1926, designating numbers for national thoroughfares, including the famous Route 66. All along proposed routes, citizens levied local taxes to match federal funds, put up garish signs advertising guest cottages and tourist courts and plaster dinosaurs, and waited for the cement mixers and the dollars to roll in.

Just as the auto had created unanticipated consequences for city planners and dwellers, by the mid-20s the consumer revolution Henry Ford had helped to spark passed him by. His share of the market declined precipitously, and his antipathy to union organizing led him to hire Harry Bennett, a vicious thug, to head his company's "Service Department," which consisted of goons hired to spy on and intimidate his employees. Ford had gained his fame and fortune by applying his genius to production problems—by working out a way to produce as many identical cars as possible, as cheaply as possible. During the 1920s, however, other car manufacturers focused instead on marketing and management. No longer interested in simply offering the consumer a car, they now wanted to offer something more: a choice. Ford resisted the idea that automakers ought to consider buyers' aesthetic as well as utilitarian demands. Although Ford owners revealed their desire for comfort and convenience by installing countless accessories on their Tin Lizzies, from windshield wipers and heaters to roofs, Ford offered only one austere design and huffed that he was "not in the millinery [hat-making] business." The Model T's strongest selling point had always been its price, but by the mid-1920s thrifty car buyers had the option of buying a used car for less than a new Ford. To those replacing worn-out cars, General Motors offered innovations ranging from installment financing and used car trade-ins to options like color choices and fixed roofs that appealed to different tastes and made their cars more comfortable. The mid-priced and inexpensive automobiles of the 1920s were notable not so much for their standardization as for their variety—assorted colors, various models, different accesories. Alfred P. Sloan, General Motors' chairman of the board, declared his intention to offer a "car for every person and purpose"—and every pocketbook. Americans who bought GM cars believed that they could stay within their budgets and still ride in comfort and style.

Rise of the Advertising Industry

Americans were eager to make their choices from among the dazzling array of products the nation's factories produced, from motorcars to cosmetics. They admired the corporate businessmen who had turned management into a science—so much so, in fact, that advertising executive Bruce Barton could cash in on that admiration in 1925 with a best-selling book. Barton's *The Man Nobody Knows* depicted Jesus Christ as an organizational genius who preached the gospel of business and service long before Americans perfected management techniques.

But whether or not they were inspired by religious principles, manufacturers took nothing for granted in their zeal to promote their wares and to inculcate in the buying public the values that made their products desirable. They had reason to worry—Americans did not buy everything that was for sale; they made careful choices in light of their own particular wants, needs, and ability to pay. As manufacturers stepped up their attempts to capture consumers' dollars, a vast advertising industry grew up, serving and feeding off the country's burgeoning production. By 1926 the advertising business, once a small-scale and piecemeal affair, had like other enterprises become corporate and consolidated. Advertising in newspapers and magazines and on billboards became larger, more lavishly illustrated, and more carefully researched and crafted. Large agencies like N. W. Ayer and Son, Benton and Bowles, and Batten, Barton, Durstine and Osborne helped their corporate clients "move merchandise" by developing advertising campaigns that appealed to the public's fantasies and aspirations, and also to its fears and anxieties.

"Ad men" sought not only to take advantage of Americans' desire to be glamorous, distinctive, and contemporary but also to cash in on their feelings of insecurity in an ever less personal, more complicated world. As publicists for the modern and the up-to-date, they sought, when they could, to enlist science on the side of capitalism. The Lambert Pharmaceutical Company, makers of Listerine antiseptic, pushed profits on their product from $100,000 in 1921 to more than $4 million in 1927 by creating a campaign so effective that their tactics would shape advertising forever after. Determining to sell Listerine, which had been used as a general antiseptic for years, as a mouthwash, they turned bad breath into a disease—"halitosis"—and made Listerine the cure. Their magazine advertisements featured otherwise attractive young men and women whose one flaw, halitosis, cost them love, happiness, and success. Soon advertising copywriters would speak of "the halitosis style" to refer to a particularly effective way to reach anxious customers, and the advertising business would acknowledge the importance of "the halitosis influence" on the industry. Lambert went on to pitch Listerine as an after-shave, a cold remedy, an astringent, a deodorant, and even a cure for dandruff. Ad agencies invented over a hundred new diseases, including "bromotosis" (sweaty foot odor), "homotosis" (unattractive home furnishings), and "acidosis" (indigestion), not to mention "office hips," "ashtray breath," and "accelerator toe."

The advertising industry employed white people almost exclusively, and men outnumbered women by about ten to one. Though some women managed to rise to positions of power and responsibility, nearly all top executives and design professionals in advertising were male. But ironically, women were the targets of most ads. Industry professionals believed that 85 percent of all retail purchasing was done by women, and thus they imagined a feminine audience for their work. Ad men vacillated between seeing the female public as weak and emotional, and thus easily led, and as strong-willed, fickle, and vexingly shrewd, and thus baffling. "The mighty Ford," home economics writer Christine Frederick warned the ad industry, "was brought to his knees by Mrs. Consumer's power." So if ad men wanted to sell their client's products

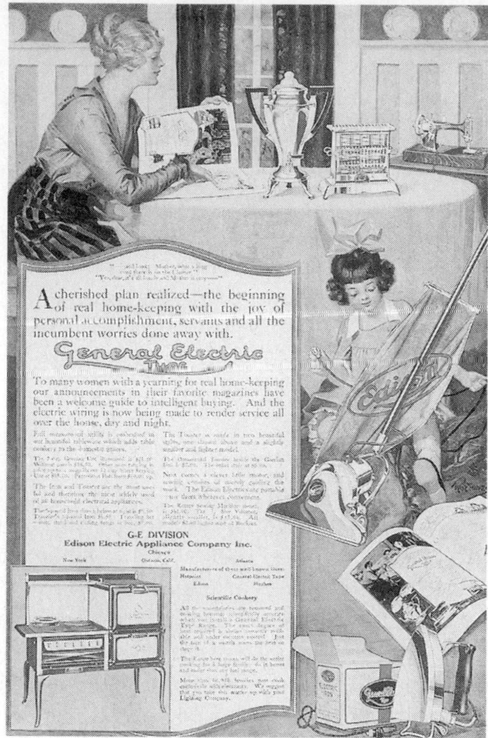

The growing advertising industry targeted women consumers, mixing appeals to practicality with images of glamour and modernity, even in the home. *Strong Museum*

(and keep their never-secure jobs!), they had better pay close attention to women's needs and wants. Never quite sure what pitches would work, advertising copywriters hedged their bets by recognizing housewives' responsibility for family spending and working girls' need to make budget-wise decisions on the one hand but treating American women as lethargic and in need of stimulation on the other. "We must remember," wrote one professional in the ad business trade journal *Printer's Ink*, "that most women lead rather monotonous and humdrum lives. . . . Such women need romance. They crave glamour and color." Advertisements, he said, should be "magic carpets on which they may ride out to love," making housewives and women workers see themselves as "*femmes fatales*, as Cleopatra or Helen of Troy." Retailers took such words to heart, and for newspapers and magazines across the nation, ads appealing to women's hunger for glamour paid the bills. Whether they perused the *New York Times* or the Los Angeles Mexican-American community's immensely popular *La Opinion*, women readers were invited to imagine how glamorous they would be in the latest stylish clothes or after using a scientifically developed face cream.

Advertising clearly reshaped American tastes, values, and habits in the 1920s. Americans learned, from ads, to worry about things that had never crossed their minds and to want things they had never known existed. When they bought motorcars and vacuum cleaners on the installment plan, they exhibited a new willingness to go into debt to make consumer purchases. Believing that prosperity would last and that their jobs were secure, Americans created the modern consumer economy.

✦ The Politics of "Normalcy"

Progressive Era reformers had spoken of making business responsive to the public interest; by the 1920s politicians appeared to believe that the people's interests would be served by giving big business pretty much what it wanted. The presidential election of 1920 ushered in twelve years of devoutly probusiness Republican administrations, with the triumph of the genial, handsome Senator Warren G. Harding over fellow Ohioan James M. Cox. Harding liked poker, good liquor, and, most of all, the company of his friends. Although he was a former newspaper editor, he evidently didn't mind inventing words to suit his purpose, as when he promised voters weary of Wilson's crusades a "return to normalcy."

Harding's "Return to Normalcy"

Harding won the election with 16 million popular votes, to Cox's 9 million. The total number of votes cast was 36 percent higher than the number for 1916, reflecting the participation of newly enfranchised women, who contrary to many suffragists' expectations did not leap to the cause of reform. To his credit, Harding appointed some able men to positions of importance, demonstrated compassion for hard-pressed farmers, and surprised the right wing of his party by pardoning Eugene Debs. But his administration mostly focused on assisting American business. Harding's cabinet was dominated by Commerce Secretary Herbert Hoover, who had gained broad public support as wartime food administrator. It also included such distinguished figures as Agriculture Secretary Henry A. Wallace, formerly editor of *Wallace's Farmer*, an Iowa publication immensely popular among rural Americans. Charles Evans Hughes, the former New York governor and 1916 presidential candidate, proved a creative, deft secretary of state. Andrew W. Mellon, scion of a Pittsburgh banking and financial family, worked closely with the business community as treasury secretary.

As good as some of Harding's appointees were, hundreds of others were so crooked that they made his administration synonymous with political corruption. Harding was not personally in the pay of special interests, but by 1922 he was aware of rumors around Washington of criminal misconduct in high places. He confided to journalist William Allen White, "This is a hell of a job. I have no trouble with my enemies. . . . But my friends, my goddamn friends . . . they're the ones who keep me walking the floor nights." Disillusioned, the president took a trip to Alaska, but he became ill on the way back. He died in San Francisco on August 2, 1923, just as Congress had begun to investigate members of his administration.

By 1924 evidence of massive corruption had come to light. Veterans' Bureau chief Charles Forbes fled the country after he was convicted of looting more than $200 million from his agency. Attorney General Harry Daugherty, suspected of accepting bribes and protecting bootleggers, narrowly escaped conviction. But the emblematic scandal of the Harding years involved the president's former Senate crony, New Mexico's Albert B. Fall, now secretary of the interior. A congressional investigation revealed that Fall had secretly leased government oil reserves in California and Wyoming to private oil companies, receiving in return bribes amounting to some $400,000. The episode, which came to be known as the Teapot Dome Scandal (after the Wyoming oil field involved), cost Fall a jail term and a fine of $100,000. Fall was the first high government official (but hardly the last) to be so discredited.

Whereas Harding had been jovial, easygoing, and gregarious to a fault, his successor, the taciturn Yankee Calvin Coolidge, could not have been more silent and dour. Coolidge was famous for sleeping eleven hours a day and saying nearly nothing, and he was just as reknowned for his stinginess. His thrifty farmer father once observed that "Cal could get more sap out of a maple tree than any other boy I knew." Alice Roosevelt Longworth gleefully observed that Coolidge looked as if he had been weaned on a pickle. But Coolidge's silences were as calculated as they were famous: "If you don't say anything," he once explained in an uncharacteristic burst of speech, "you can't be called on to repeat it."

"Coolidge Prosperity"

Long a staunch advocate of free enterprise and big business, Coolidge carried on his predecessor's policies and presided over a prospering economy. He retained members of Harding's cabinet, including Treasury Secretary Mellon, who balanced the federal budget and persuaded Congress to lower income tax rates, especially for the rich. This contributed to the problem of unequal distribution of wealth, but it satisfied those most influential in national politics. Mellon also spearheaded the push for high protective tariffs, beginning with the Fordney-McCumber tariff of 1922 and culminating in the controversial Smoot-Hawley tariff of 1930.

Coolidge ran for election on his own in 1924. Republicans touted "Coolidge Prosperity," while Democrats warred among themselves. The southern wing of the Democratic Party, mostly Protestant, was committed to white supremacy and dominated by prohibitionists. These Democrats favored former treasury secretary William G. McAdoo. Many midwestern Democrats shared the southerners' views on race, religion, and alcohol, and significant numbers from both regions had ties to a revitalized Ku Klux Klan. The Klan used state-of-the-art advertising techniques to bring its message of hatred for blacks, Catholics, Jews, and immigrants to a nationwide audience. The northeastern wing of the party, however, was composed of precisely the kind of people the Klan reviled, and delegates from that area, along with tenacious Progressives, supported New York governor Alfred E. Smith—a Catholic son of immigrants who favored repealing the Eighteenth Amendment, which had banned the sale of alcoholic beverages.

Deadlocked on the 103d ballot, the Democrats finally turned to compromise candidate John W. Davis, a New York corporate lawyer. But many Democrats who remained suspicious of big business turned to the independent candidacy of Robert M. La Follette of Wisconsin. A coalition of farmers, unionists, socialists, and Progressive Movement veterans nominated La Follette on the Progressive Party ticket. Their platform advocated collective bargaining, political reform, public ownership of utilities, aid to farmers, and a public referendum on matters of war or peace. The La Follette candidacy siphoned off more Democratic than Republican votes, however, practically assuring victory for Coolidge. When the counting was done, Coolidge emerged with nearly 16 million votes (54 percent of the total), while Davis drew only 8 million (29 percent), running strongest in the South. La Follette polled nearly 5 million, but he carried only his home state of Wisconsin.

If voters wanted more of the same, Coolidge did not disappoint them. Production remained high and unemployment low. Union organizing stalled, impeded by a combination of government-sanctioned management resistance and worker indifference. Labor unions like the American Federation of Labor (AFL) disdained to recruit women, blacks, Mexican Americans, and other minorities, who made up the vast pool of unskilled, or at least low-paid, workers. For those in skilled trades real wages rose, and companies introduced "welfare capitalism," offering a host of benefits ranging from insurance, retirement pensions, and paid vacations to company sponsorship of employee baseball teams. Such policies arose both from genuine concern for workers and from management's desire to discourage union organizing.

But "Coolidge Prosperity" did not extend to everyone. Most African-Americans continued to suffer from social segregation and economic discrimination that confined black workers to a narrow range of poor-paying, menial jobs. Mexican-American agricultural workers in the Southwest, many of them new immigrants, faced not only miserable wages, poor living conditions, and discrimination but in many cases the threat of deportation as well.

Farmers in general lagged behind urbanites in reaping the benefits of the expanding economy. The 1920 census marked the first time in the nation's history that city dwellers outnumbered rural residents, and during the next decade many farmers fell victim to low prices for their products, coupled with heavy debt. Declining prices drove farmers to try to make up their losses by producing more, but overproduction pushed prices still lower. Pressed by the American Farm Bureau Federation and a powerful "farm bloc" of representatives and senators, Congress passed the McNary-Haugen bills in 1927 and 1928, mandating government purchasing of and price supports for six basic commodities—cotton, corn, rice, hogs, tobacco, and wheat. Coolidge vetoed both bills, however.

In 1928 Coolidge decided to retire from the presidency, telling his party, "I do not choose to run." Republicans turned to the popular commerce secretary, Herbert Hoover, to be their standard-bearer. Hoover embodied the purported virtues of the free enterprise system. Born to a Quaker family in Iowa, he was left an orphan at an early age. He worked his way through Stanford University and went on to make a fortune as a mining engineer. His tenure as federal food administrator during World War I brought him national prominence as an efficient, innovative manager. "He is certainly a wonder," remarked a young Franklin Roosevelt, "and I wish we could make him president of the United States. There couldn't be a better one."

Hoover and the Election of 1928

As a cabinet member under both Harding and Coolidge, Hoover had worked hard to foster a partnership between business and government, in the tradition of Theodore Roosevelt's New Nationalism. His 1922 book *American Individualism* outlined his belief that the economy ought to operate like a well-oiled machine. Business leaders must strive to cooperate with one another on matters of wages, resource use, and production, he wrote, and they ought to be encouraged to adopt welfare capitalism. Careful planning and voluntary cooperation—not government coercion, which he feared would lead to totalitarianism—would bring ever-increasing prosperity. Under his leadership the commerce department encouraged the formation of trade associations, used new scientific techniques to collect data and issue reports, and sponsored conferences to bring together business leaders.

The Democrats, meanwhile, turned to Al Smith in 1928. As New York's governor, Smith had established an impressive record promoting progressive reforms and civil rights. The first Roman Catholic to run for president, he had deep support among immigrants and eastern urbanites, many of whom shared his opposition to Prohibition. He was a lively campaigner, spicing his speeches with wisecracks and impromptu remarks, whereas Hoover's campaign style was notoriously dull. But the combination of ongoing prosperity and continuing anti-Catholic agitation gave Hoover the edge. Opponents charged that Smith would be unable to choose loyalty to the United States over devotion to the Pope and warned that if Smith were elected, the Vatican would relocate to the United States. While Smith met these accusations head on, he was unable to counter Republican claims that the GOP had brought the nation nearly a decade of wealth and well-being. When candidate Hoover predicted the nearing of "the final triumph over poverty," people believed him.

Hoover won in a landslide, with 58 percent of the popular vote and 444 electoral votes, to only 87 electoral votes for Smith. Although these results marked some critical continuities in American politics, the raw figures masked the beginning of some political shifts. In spite of his urban, Catholic identity, Smith carried six southern states, retaining the South as a Democratic stronghold. In northern cities, Catholics and Jews voted Democratic in record numbers. The nation's twelve largest cities all went for Smith. And in the Midwest, hard-pressed farmers were showing signs of abandoning their traditional Republicanism to vote for the Democrat. The seeds of a new Democratic coalition were germinating.

✦ From Reform to Recreation

The progressive impulse that had dominated American politics in the first two decades of the century did not die in the 1920s, but it did find new channels and new challenges. Although the federal government had backed away from trustbusting, government agencies continued to collect economic data and regulate business practices. Politicians like Gifford Pinchot, alive to the great possibilities industrial systems presented, realized that government had to play some role in fostering, monitoring, and directing those systems for those possibilities to be realized. Graduate university programs in social science continued to train professional city planners and social workers, who devoted their expertise to the cause of improving urban life. Those who had learned reform from the ground up in settlement houses continued to press for justice for the poor, and though they were out of power during the 1920s, they would be sorely needed during the 1930s.

Women's Rights and Feminism

The crusade for women's rights was more and more often identified with the term *feminism.* The movement did have a varied and lasting impact on the nation, even if its newly enfranchised female electorate did not revolutionize the government. After all, American women were as diverse as American men—some were Republicans, some Democrats, some Socialists, some Klanswomen, and some indifferent to politics. African-American women, like black men, remained disenfranchised and continued to press the cause of racial justice, both within and outside women's organizations.

Still, women entered the political arena in striking new ways. In the Northeast, Belle Moskowitz, Frances Perkins, and Eleanor Roosevelt became party activists, building on long-time connections to Progressive Era reform networks. In the West, women ran for, and won, public office. Nellie Tayloe

Ross of Wyoming became the nation's first woman governor in 1924, and Bertha Knight Landis became the country's first woman big-city mayor when Seattle voters elected her.

Deprived of the unifying goal of suffrage, the women's movement fractured, and women activists moved on to support a plethora of other causes. Some, like Jane Addams, a founder of the Women's International League for Peace and Freedom, devoted themselves to the dream of ending war. Others, like Carrie Chapman Catt (also a peace activist), went on to push for "nonpartisan" voter education in the League of Women Voters. Stella Atwood of the General Federation of Women's Clubs, moved by John Collier's descriptions of what he had seen with Antonio Luhan, lent that immense organization's power to the cause of Indian reform. Florence Kelley concentrated on pushing for further protections for women, especially the Sheppard-Towner Act, which was intended to provide states with matching federal funds to set up programs in which public health nurses would teach mothers how to care for babies and doctors would provide prenatal and pediatric care. In a show of female solidarity rare during the 1920s, the push for Sheppard-Towner united women's groups as diverse as the Daughters of the American Revolution and the National Consumers' League. Even though most in Congress probably opposed the bill, the threat of women's vengeance inspired Congress to pass Sheppard-Towner in 1921. As Kelley shrewdly asked legislators, "What answer can be given to the women in a myriad of organizations who are marveling and asking, 'Why does Congress wish women and children to die?'"

Despite this early victory, by the mid-1920s women who had been allies in the suffrage movement found room for bitter disagreement. Alice Paul led the National Woman's Party campaign for an equal rights amendment to the Constitution. But her insistence that women's groups must pursue a "pure feminist" program of reform infuriated Kelley and other labor activists, who believed that such an amendment would endanger protective legislation for working women. Margaret Sanger carried on her crusade for birth control, but Carrie Chapman Catt told her that even though she was "no enemy" of Sanger's, "Your reform is too narrow to appeal to me and too sordid." Jane Addams had been a long-time supporter of racial equality, but other suffragists, particularly in the Midwest and South, moved from work in the women's rights movement to involvement with the Ku Klux Klan.

Meanwhile, the anti-Bolshevik politics unleashed during World War I spilled over into efforts to discredit activist women. General Amos Fries, head of the U.S. Chemical Warfare Service, denounced Catt's National Council for the Prevention of War (NCPW) as a Communist front, prompting two NCPW affiliates, the Parent Teachers Association and the General Federation of Women's Clubs, to withdraw from the council. Fries produced a "spider's web" chart demonstrating connections between women's organizations, charging that these groups favored disarmament as a means to promote a

Bolshevik takeover of the United States. The chart named every major women's organization, from the Women's Trade Union League (WTUL) to the American Home Economics Association, along with leaders such as Catt, Addams, and Kelley.

Given such intense opposition, organized women could not sustain their pressure for reform. A child-labor amendment to the Constitution, backed by a coalition of women's groups, was passed by Congress after heavy lobbying, but it was ratified by only six states. In 1923 the Supreme Court struck down minimum wage laws in *Adkins* v. *Children's Hospital* on the ground that such laws infringed on workers' freedom of contract. And in 1929, after the American Medical Association denounced Sheppard-Towner as "an imported socialist scheme" to take health care out of the hands of private doctors, Congress let the maternal and infant welfare program lapse.

Organized feminism was also, in some regards, a victim of its own success. The concept of women's emancipation proved sufficiently broad, flexible, and vague to encompass everything from the right to vote and earn a living wage to the right to smoke cigarettes and wear short skirts. American corporations moved quickly to cash in on feminism's success, promising housewives that vaccuum cleaners, electric stoves, and washing machines would liberate them from household drudgery. In 1914 Greenwich Village radical Marie Jenny Howe had told a mass meeting that feminism was women's effort to break "into the human race," to enjoy the whole range of activities men took for granted. In the 1920s the suffragists' daughters and sons—and even some of their own generation—explored some new shades on that human spectrum.

The United States had entered World War I with a missionary zeal to spread democracy and freedom, but by 1920 that idealistic spirit had fallen victim to inconceivable battlefield bloodletting and cynical peacemaking. Instead of remaking the world, many Americans reasoned, it was long past time to have some fun.

The Flapper Era

The 1920s were a time in American history when more people enjoyed more leisure and more ways to pursue pleasure than at any time before. For one thing, coming of age in America no longer meant going right to work. Middle-class young people stayed in school longer, developing high school and college peer cultures dedicated to high-spirited fun. Four times as many Americans attended high school in 1929 as in 1910, and among high school graduates, over one-third went on to college. Women's college enrollment increased even faster than men's, so that by 1930 forty percent of bachelor's degrees went to female students. Campus life included not only library and classroom but also "the big game" and "the big dance."

In cities, on college campuses, and even in small towns, young people seized the pleasures of joy-riding in fast cars, dancing to "suggestive" jazz

Race was no barrier to the appeal of the flapper image.
Schomburg Center for Research in Black Culture, New York Public Library

music, drinking illegal (or "bootleg") liquor, and talking more openly about (and evidently engaging more freely in) nonmarital sex. Young women lit cigarettes in public, bobbed their hair, wore rouge and lipstick, and traded heavy corsets and voluminous skirts for the short, body-hugging chemises of the flappers. The term *flapper* was itself an outgrowth of mass culture, coined after a magazine cover depicted an uninhibited girl wearing a short skirt, stockings rolled below the knee, and rubber boots left flapping open. This new model of feminine beauty did, in fact, give women one very concrete new freedom: unencumbered physical movement. But the rage for fashionable slenderness brought with it a new craze for weight loss among women. And the idolization of youth made aging a source of anxiety; as Lorelei Lee, the hilarious flapper heroine of Anita Loos's *Gentlemen Prefer Blondes* (1925) explained, "when a girl is cute for 50 years it really begins to get historical."

Although twenties flappers scandalized their more conservative elders, they were actually joining a leisure culture that had prewar roots. In big cities like New York, respectable middle- and upper-class people had begun to take part in a new "nightlife," patronizing the new restaurants and nightclubs where alcoholic beverages were served and the clientele learned sinuous, intimate tangos and turkey trots from elegant dance instructors like the celebrated Vernon and Irene Castle. Urban working-class people, from African-Americans to new immigrants, found lively company in neighborhood saloons and dance halls and rousing entertainment in vaudeville theaters. The Charleston craze of the mid-20s, inspired by a dance that originated among African-Americans in Charleston, South Carolina, mirrored earlier dance fads. And after 1920 people who wished to imbibe had to patronize shady "speakeasies," those fabled private establishments that required patrons to whisper a password ("Joe sent me") to gain admission, because Prohibition had made drinking liquor a federal offense.

The much talked-about rise in nonmarital sex also predated the Roaring Twenties. Greenwich Village bohemians like Mabel Dodge had long been fascinated with sex, especially after they began to read the work of the Viennese doctor Sigmund Freud. But the heart of the sexual revolution of the 1920s lay not in a rise in nonmarital sexual intercourse but in the rejection of rigid Victorian prescriptions against all sex. The new institution of "dating" gave rise to a range of sexual acts commonly referred to as "necking and petting." In automobiles and on college campuses, particularly coeducational colleges and universities, young middle-class men and women had unchaperoned access to one another as never before. Moralists fretted that any expression of eroticism doomed young women to a life of harlotry. But the so-called "flaming youth" of the twenties preserved the idea of female respectability even as they expanded the boundaries of legitimate sexual expressiveness. The social costs of becoming pregnant without benefit of matrimony were, girls knew, too high to risk. Marriage, after all, remained the object for most middle-class American young people.

Among the vast majority who did marry, birthrates went down. In the late nineteenth century, married American women bore large numbers of children—over half of those who survived to age fifty had five or more. In the 1920s, however, only 20 percent of married women who lived to see their fiftieth birthday had five or more children, and a rising percentage of women chose to remain childless. Greater availability of contraceptive information and devices helped push the birthrate down, and more and more doctors began to lend their support to the cause of birth control by the decade's end.

Smaller families meant changes in family life. More husbands and wives expressed the view that they had married to be companions and equals. More married women worked for wages (29 percent of the female work force in 1930 was married), though their opportunities in business were generally limited to the typing pool. A small but growing number of farm women used the money they earned selling chickens and eggs to pay for indoor plumbing, electric wiring, telephones, household appliances, and the farm wife's favorite diversion, the radio.

Mass Media and Popular Culture

Wireless radio transmissions across long distances had been possible since 1901. During World War I radio was used in ship-to-shore communications, but the commercial possibilities of radio did not begin to be realized until after the war. In 1920 station KDKA of Pittsburgh, Pennsylvania, became the nation's first commercial broadcast station. Within a year, stations in New York and New Jersey had begun broadcasting news and sports, and by 1922 five hundred new stations were operating and airing commercial messages. By 1930 the radio was a familiar fixture in American homes. Midwest farm families were more likely to own a radio than any other type of modern equipment except an automobile or a telephone.

In very short order, radio broadcasting came to be dominated by large corporations. General Electric, Westinghouse, and the Radio Corporation of America jointly founded the National Broadcasting Company (NBC) in 1926. A year later, the Columbia Broadcasting System (CBS) followed. These two networks planned their programming with the help of the new legion of market researchers, and they funded their operations with advertising revenues. By the decade's end, 40 percent of American homes had radios.

As radio brought an increasingly standardized national culture right into Americans' homes, the movies transformed public entertainment. Beginning with Thomas Edison's kinetoscope, a device first marketed to penny arcades in 1893, motion pictures captured an enthusiastic audience. After the 1902 opening in Los Angeles of a shop showing moving pictures, "movie houses" began to open across the country, featuring inexpensively made films that spoke directly to ethnic, working-class viewers. The first movie theater—which charged a nickel for admission and was thus called The Nickelodeon—opened in Pittsburgh in 1905. It was luxuriously furnished and featured a piano to accompany the silent films on the screen. During the 1920s movie theaters left behind their humble origins and audiences to become lavish palaces catering to a wide range of customers. By 1930 movie theaters sold 100 million tickets each week, in a nation of just over 120 million people!

At first most motion pictures were made in the New York City area. But after 1913 Hollywood, California, became the capital of American moviemaking. By this time studios had already established a "star system," signing popular actors like Douglas Fairbanks and Mary Pickford to exclusive contracts. A subsidiary industry composed of agents, publicists, fan magazines, gossip columns, and the like grew up around the studios, promoting their stars as "screen idols." Each star was marketed in a particular way. Darkly handsome romantic heroes like Ronald Colman and Rudolph Valentino supposedly made women swoon, while winsome comedians Charlie Chaplin and Buster Keaton seemed the very spirit of playfulness. Mary Pickford was the soul of innocence, "America's Sweetheart." Douglas Fairbanks promoted a new ideal of the gentleman of leisure, dazzling film audiences with exhibitions of boxing, fencing, and gymnastics and writing articles that reminded his readers, "We read so much of work and success that someone needs to preach the glory of play." Glamorous actresses like Gloria Swanson and Greta Garbo, draped in gorgeous gowns and expensive furs, emerged from block-long limousines at extravagant premieres. The stars' lavish lifestyles mirrored the increasingly elaborate productions of the films themselves, especially after director Cecil B. De Mille began making his immensely popular spectacle films, like *The Ten Commandments* (1923).

Other forms of mass entertainment also produced idols and heroes. Sports moved into the mass market, with baseball tops in popularity. On the radio and in the newspapers, the nation followed the magnificent hitting and base-stealing feats of Ty Cobb of the Detroit Tigers and the awesome home-run blasts of Babe Ruth of the New York Yankees. Other sports likewise produced national celebrities—Jack Dempsey in boxing, Bill Tilden in tennis, Gertrude Ederle in swimming, Bobby Jones in golf. In football, University of Illinois running back Harold Edward "Red" Grange turned his success as an amateur into a golden professional career. Like other sports celebrities, Grange made his money both on the field and off, endorsing products, making personal appearances, even acting in a movie. But Grange pioneered yet another career path for sports heroes. After his playing days were over he became a successful sportscaster, first on radio and later on television.

The electrically transmitted sound of human voices would become a significant factor in the new popular culture. Sound accompanied moving pictures for the first time in 1927, in a musical called *The Jazz Singer*. The movie starred Al Jolson as Jack Robin, the jazz-loving son of an orthodox Jewish cantor who has his big chance to make it on Broadway. At the moment the show is about to open, Jack learns that his father is dying and that, when he dies, there will be no one to sing Kaddish (the prayer for the dead). Jack manages to get to the synagogue in time for the funeral and still be at the theater when the curtain goes up, closing the film with a heart-tugging performance, in blackface, of "Mammy." This landmark film not only established the dominance of "talkies" for all time but also revealed the ethnically diverse origins of the emerging mass culture. From the beginning, Jews of eastern European heritage played a prominent role in the movie industry, as they continue to do to this day. The convention of having white performers appear in blackface, adopted from nineteenth-century minstrel shows, strikes us as racist and exploitative today; but as troubling as blackface performance now seems, it nonetheless demonstrates the impact of African-American performance arts on American popular culture.

The Jazz Singer was, after all, in part about jazz, a musical form developed by African-Americans. Jazz was born of the black experience, evolving from the working songs of slaves into the Chicago blues of singers Bessie Smith and "Ma" Rainey, the ragtime of Scott Joplin, the stride piano of Ferdinand "Jelly Roll" Morton, and the virtuoso trumpet playing of Louis Armstrong. By the 1920s, "Negro" orchestras led by Fletcher Henderson and Edward Kennedy "Duke" Ellington featured full brass and rhythm sections along with pianos and vocalists. Jazz was fast becoming a more varied, sometimes elaborate, art form.

Although millions of white listeners took instantly to jazz, African-American musicians' access to the nationwide market for phonograph records was at first confined to "race" records aimed at a black market and distributed by small labels to a welcoming black audience. White orchestras, like that of Paul Whiting, performed "covers" of African-Americans' compositions on radio and on mass-marketed recordings. Persistent white fans sought out African-Americans' music, however. Black performers were generally glad of the chance to reach a broader, more affluent audience, but they had to cope with the sometimes virulent, nearly always patronizing prejudices of whites, who held that African-Americans were primitives. At places like the famous Cotton Club, whites could watch gorgeous, skimpily dressed African-American chorus girls dance to the "jungle rhythms" of Ellington's band, sipping cocktails brought to them by white-gloved waiters. Some whites who went "slumming" in Harlem surely recognized the brilliance of the performances they witnessed, and a number of influential whites did what they could to assist black artists gain security and success. But many no doubt headed back downtown with their sense of racial superiority intact.

By the mid-1920s Harlem had become the center of a flowering of black art, music, and intellectualism that would come to be known as the Harlem Renaissance. From the time of the outbreak of the war in Europe, rural southern blacks migrated by the thousands to the cities in search of wartime jobs. During the twenties, 1.5 million blacks moved to cities, including Chicago, Detroit, Houston, and New York. In New York, as elsewhere, African-Americans were confined to the poorest, most run-down neighborhoods. But if Harlem was a ghetto, it also offered an exciting community for the artists and intellectuals who flocked there. Writers like Alain Locke, James Weldon Johnson, Claude McKay, Jean Toomer, and Langston Hughes proclaimed the advent of "the New Negro," an individual proud of his African and American heritage, free to create, turning a keen ear to black folk language, and feeling a spiritual yearning for Africa. They broke with the conventions of high art to use words and images in ways that would, they believed, better express the black experience. Artists like painter Aaron Douglas (who illustrated *The New Negro,* the landmark 1925 anthology edited by Locke) and sculptor Augusta Savage, famous for her busts of well-known blacks, found venues for their work. Hughes wrote powerfully about the violence and everyday damage of racism, invoking the rythms of jazz and the blues in his poetry. He also insisted on blacks' right to claim their rightful place in American history and culture—not just African-American history and culture—echoing Walt Whitman when he wrote in 1925, "I, too, sing America." Black artists, said Hughes, must sing their songs and tell their stories proudly, and "if white people are pleased we are glad. If they are not, it doesn't matter. We know we are beautiful."

Heeding such calls for racial pride, thousands of African-American city dwellers went a step further and embraced a movement for black separatism.

In this portrait, painter Winold Rice captured Langston Hughes as a serious symbol of the Jazz Age. *National Portrait Gallery, Smithsonian Institution, Washington, D.C.*

In 1914 the movement's most influential leader, charismatic Jamaican immigrant Marcus Garvey, founded an organization called the Universal Negro Improvement Association (UNIA). The UNIA was dedicated to fostering worldwide black unity and celebrating African culture. Rejecting integration, Garvey urged blacks to develop their own enterprises and institutions. But he believed that in the end blacks would never be allowed to secure their rights where they were a minority, so in speeches and his newspaper, *Negro World*, he exhorted his followers to embrace a movement "back to Africa." At its peak the UNIA attracted at least half a million members and several million more sympathizers. It sponsored a host of commercial ventures, including a hotel, a printing plant, a black-doll factory, chains of groceries, restaurants and laundries, and the Black Star steamship line. But Garvey's separatist position infuriated black leaders who insisted that African-Americans' first task was to achieve integration. The government also harassed the UNIA, arresting ten of the group's leaders on charges of anarchism and prosecuting Garvey for misusing funds raised to promote the Black Star steamship line, which was intended to carry American blacks to Africa.

Garvey went to jail for mail fraud in 1925, and after two years he was deported to Jamaica.

As black writers explored problems centering on black identity and community, mixing social criticism with a celebration of black heritage, the most prominent white writers of the decade turned their sights on the crass materialism, anonymity, and decadence of modern life. Some, like literary experimenter Gertrude Stein, novelists Edith Wharton and Henry James, and poets T. S. Eliot and Ezra Pound, had fled the United States to live in Europe long before the war. In the years after the armistice many other alienated Americans would become expatriates, seeking authentic experiences and refuge from the shallowness of American life in Paris bistros, on the beaches of southern France, and in the bullrings of small Spanish towns. Ernest Hemingway invented a new prose style, terse and lean, and turned a critical eye on his fellow expatriates in brilliant novels like *The Sun Also Rises* (1926).

Hemingway's erstwhile friend F. Scott Fitzgerald was both a critic and an emblem of the Jazz Age culture Hemingway so deplored. With his wife, the brilliant, crazy Zelda, Fitzgerald came to symbolize the madcap, gin-drinking, extravagant, and ultimately disenchanting life of the newly rich in the Roaring Twenties. His masterpiece, *The Great Gatsby* (1925), tells the story of a bootlegger whose American dream of pure love and untold riches is destroyed by the corrupt reality around him. Eager for wealth but wary of greed, sometimes cynical, sometimes naive, and nearly always yearning, Fitzgerald's doomed heroes reflected his own character. "The very rich," he once told Hemingway, "are not like you and me." The acerbic Hemingway replied, "Yes. They have more money."

Other writers and artists chose to escape American society without leaving the country. Many flocked to the bohemian enclaves of Santa Fe and Taos, seeking renewal in the clear light and dry air of the Southwest and refuge from the dirt and noise of the city. Novelist Willa Cather invoked the moral eminence of simpler times in novels like *Death Comes to the Archbishop* (1927). Leaving New York for New Mexico transformed painter Georgia O'Keeffe's palette and subjects from a wash of blacks and blues and buildings to dazzling, sensuous hills, skulls, and flowers.

Still others remained inside urban America, looking on in horror. Dorothy Parker was a poet and short story writer, the central figure among a group of writers who met regularly at New York's Algonquin Hotel. Parker became a legend for her sardonic wit. Among her most famous quips was her response, in 1933, to the news that Calvin Coolidge was dead: "How could they tell?" H. L. Mencken, editor of *The American Mercury*, was even more scathing in his criticism of banal politicians, of the comfortable middle class (which he referred to as the "booboisie"), and of human folly in general. "Man at his best," Mencken wrote, "remains a sort of one-lunged animal, never completely rounded and perfect as a cockroach, say, is perfect." Sinclair Lewis, a native of Minnesota, wrote dead-on satires, taking on small-town America in *Main Street* (1920) and then turning his sights on middle-class conformity in the city in *Babbitt* (1922). As the novel opens, one morning in the city of Zenith, Lewis introduces his protagonist, George F. Babbitt, a forty-six-year-old, balding man. Babbitt is described as "not fat but . . . exceedingly well fed," a man who "made nothing in particular, neither butter nor shoes nor poetry, but he was nimble in the calling of selling houses for more than people could afford."

The country's leading writers revealed the hollowness of the social ethos, based on consumerism, of the day. Yet they reached a wide audience in part because mass circulation made their books and magazines cheap and accessible. And while the American public might admit that compulsive buying could become too much of a good thing, many found hope, meaning, and pleasure in the culture of consumption. Although their work in factories and offices was becoming routinized, monotonous, and impersonal, millions of Americans found self-expression and spontaneity in the things they purchased and in what they did in their free time.

But even though they loved their new possessions and amusements, Americans still admired those who seemed to rise above the culture of acquisitiveness and pleasure. Charles Lindbergh, the decade's greatest hero, seemed to combine the virtue of old-fashioned individualism with the genius of the machine age. Born and reared in the Midwest, Lindbergh dropped out of the University of Wisconsin to study aviation. When in 1927 he became the first person to fly across the Atlantic alone, the mass media propelled him to instant global celebrity as "The Lone Eagle." Up to that time the longest solo flight recorded had been 2,500 miles, between San Diego and New York. When a New York hotel owner offered a $25,000 prize to the first pilot to complete a nonstop run between New York and Paris, some 3,500 miles, Lindbergh determined to make the flight in his monoplane, *The Spirit of St. Louis*. He landed in Paris after a thirty-three-and-a-half-hour flight, and one hundred thousand people jammed the airfield to greet him. Even jaded New York threw a ticker tape parade for him on his return. Popular songs celebrated his heroics, and a dance, the "Lindy Hop," was named for him. In the midst of all the adulation, Lindbergh remained modest and unassuming, seemingly the embodiment of old-fashioned values like hard work, perserverance, and self-denial, qualities that many feared were disappearing in the wake of materialism and debauchery.

✦ Modernism's Discontents

The social, economic, and technological forces that had been transforming American life since the turn of the century picked up speed and power in the 1920s. Americans reacted to those changes in ways that ranged from delight to horror and, nearly always, ambivalence. They welcomed some changes—the convenience of telephones, the companionship of the radio—while worrying about, or deploring, others. Working-class consumers were wary of installment buying, even as they enjoyed tuning in their favorite radio programs. Motorists who loved their cars also knew that automobiles could be dangerous to their health and safety and that traffic and congestion were making life in big cities less than ideal. Flappers who danced and flirted and flaunted their freedoms knew they could not trust every good-looking guy who asked them to go for a ride in his runabout. A Los Angeles newspaper noted that girls had complained that "mashers" lurked at street corners inviting young women to "come and have a good time," and sometimes such men were hard to dissuade. Under pressure from organizations like the California Congress of Mothers and the PTA, the Los Angeles Police Department established a "purity squad," promising to arrest any man caught "ogling, or winking, or [making] obscene remarks."

Prohibition

The automobile was only one of many forces that appeared to imperil Americans' morals. One particularly obvious menace was the widespread prevalence of drinking. The nineteenth-century temperance movement had, by the early twentieth century, shifted its focus from reforming individual drinkers to prohibiting outright the consumption of liquor. Organizations like the Women's Christian Temperance Union and the Anti-Saloon League attracted middle-class, native-born Protestants, who tended to identify drinking with the urban working class in general and immigrants in particular. The prohibition movement rode the reform crest of the Progressive Era and capitalized on a rising nativism that tended to blame political corruption, poverty, and vice on "unassimilable" foreigners from southern and eastern Europe. The movement also cashed in on the xenophobic frenzy generated by the war, targeting beer-brewing Germans in particular. Prohibitionists mobilized grassroots support in Protestant churches for "local option" statutes and, later, state laws banning alcohol. In 1919 these "drys" (as they called themselves) pushed through the Eighteenth Amendment and the Volstead Act, outlawing the manufacture, transportation, and sale of alcoholic beverages nationwide. "The Noble Experiment" would last until 1933.

Many native-born Protestant Americans, whatever their drinking habits, supported prohibition as a means of restoring order to a society seemingly reeling out of control. They believed that what they called American culture was threatened by the arrival of hordes of foreign-born (often Catholic and Jewish) people. And many who favored the abolition of the saloon may not have understood what the law would mean, thinking that beer and wine would still be legal. But immigrants and working-class people, to whom the saloon was a social center and the consumption of beer or wine a family habit, saw Prohibition as an attack on their way of life.

Prohibition did cut alcohol consumption, especially in the early years, perhaps by as much as 30 percent. One big reason Americans were drinking less was that bootleg alcohol was expensive—by one estimate, 1928 prices for beer were up 600 percent over 1916 prices. Prohibition also changed Americans' drinking habits, as many people switched from beer to hard liquor because gin and whiskey were cheaper and easier to produce at home.

The political battle between "wets" and "drys" raged on throughout the twenties, freighted with the overtones of a culture war. When Herbert Hoover beat the avowedly "wet" New Yorker and Catholic Al Smith in 1928, the *St. Paul Pioneer Press* announced that the nation was "not yet dominated by its great cities. . . . Main Street is still the principal thoroughfare of the nation."

But political triumph was one thing and enforcement quite another. People found many ingenious ways to skirt the law, including perfectly legal stockpiling before the ban took effect. The Yale Club of New York, for example, was reputed to have a fourteen-year liquor supply. The law permitted the use of alcohol for medicinal and sacramental purposes, and many people suffered thirteen-year-long bouts of ill health, interspersed with fits of piety. In the countryside, the old tradition of distilling "moonshine" whiskey found new life. On the Canadian border, smugglers made a killing bringing in foreign whiskey. And all over the nation, home distilling made "bathtub gin" a hallmark of the period.

Making and selling booze in quantity became a high-profit, high-risk business, and in time organized crime took on more and more of the risk and garnered more and more of the gain. Although Americans in general feared the violent crime that seemed an inevitable companion to urbanization, Prohibition gave the otherwise law-abiding patron of the speakeasy a common outlaw bond with notorious murderers and extortionists like Chicago's celebrated crime boss Al Capone. Since the criminal syndicates were dominated by immigrants and their sons, especially Italians, Irish, and Jews, millions of Americans shared common cultural ground with the gangsters. Despite well-publicized government efforts to capture and punish crime "kingpins" like Capone (who ultimately went to jail not for his other crimes but for tax evasion), many public officials were themselves on the take. And so, although drys had hoped that Prohibition would help restore moral and social order to the country in ways native-born Protestants could applaud, the measure really helped to spread contempt for law and to promote disorder.

Religion and the Evolution Controversy

For some people chaos and catastrophe could be averted only by embracing religious faith. Within Protestant churches, those who called themselves "fundamentalists" deplored "modernists" and liberals, who held that religion ought to respond to new knowledge and behavior. For fundamentalists there could be no compromise with a sinful world; the Bible was the only guide to truth, and the time had come for Christians of conscience to wage holy war against decadence and depravity.

Fundamentalist Christians varied in their beliefs and even more so in their style. Los Angeles Pentecostal faith healer Aimee Semple McPherson brought show-biz productions into her Angelus Temple of the Foursquare Gospel and, beginning in 1924, to a radio audience numbering into the hundreds of thousands. "Sister Aimee" urged "the old-time religion" on her listeners, telling them to put their hands on the radio and kneel and pray with her. Thousands believed they were miraculously healed. McPherson's brand of Christianity emphasized hope, faith, and good times ahead in heaven. Other fundamentalists had a grimmer view of the reckoning to come, preaching fire and brimstone. Yet fundamentalists agreed on several basic principles: the virgin birth and bodily resurrection of Christ, the necessity of atonement, the possibility of miracles, and the literal truth of the Bible. And since the Bible was to be interpreted literally, many reasoned, modern scientific theories that conflicted with revealed Biblical truth must be false, perhaps even diabolical. From the fundamentalist point of view, Charles Darwin's theory of evolution appeared a particularly fiendish challenge to the true story of creation, as revealed in Genesis.

The controversy over evolution came to a head in a celebrated trial in the small Tennessee town of Dayton in 1925. The Tennessee state legislature, under the sway of fundamentalists, had recently passed a law forbidding the teaching of "any theory that denies the story of the divine creation of man as taught in the Bible, and teaches instead that man has descended from a lower order of animals." With the backing of the American Civil Liberties Union, which regarded the law as an unconstitutional abridgment of the First Amendment right to free speech, a high school biology teacher named John Scopes willfully broke the law and stood as the defendant in a test case.

As hundreds of reporters from all over the nation flocked to Dayton, the Scopes "Monkey Trial" became a media circus. Town boosters, seeing the chance for national publicity, strung telegraph wires to the courthouse, installed radio transmitters and extra telephones, and brought in extra toilets. Sightseers poured in. Famed trial lawyer Clarence Darrow, himself an agnostic and a symbol of the urbane, iconoclastic world fundamentalists deplored, agreed to defend Scopes for no pay. William Jennings Bryan, former candidate for president and former secretary of state, volunteered to take the case for the prosecution. Although Bryan continued to believe in the need for economic and social reform, he also held that irreligion and moral decay, symbolized especially by the teaching of evolution, threatened civilization itself.

The Scopes case raised issues ranging from free speech to parental rights, but Bryan chose to focus his argument entirely on one point: was Genesis correct, or Darwin? Darrow, furious, told Bryan, "You insult every man of science and learning with your fool religion," while Bryan righteously retorted, "I am trying to protect the Word of God against the greatest agnostic in the United States." When Darrow brought in expert witnesses to prove the validity of evolution, the judge allowed them to testify without the jury present but refused to permit testimony in open court. Bereft of his main strategy, Darrow put Bryan on the stand. Under relentless questioning, Bryan revealed his historical and scientific ignorance. Finally Bryan admitted that the "days" of creation described in the Bible might not have been, literally,

Clarence Darrow (left) and William Jennings Bryan (right) at the Scopes Trial, 1925. *Corbis-Bettmann*

twenty-four hours long. Although Scopes was ultimately convicted and fined $100, Bryan was left a broken man, dying within days of the verdict, and the antievolution camp had been made to appear, before a national audience, as a witless gaggle of village hicks. But even though the Scopes Trial was a setback for the fundamentalist movement, antievolutionists continued to be active in local school politics, and as late as 1941 one in three high school teachers admitted to being afraid to teach evolution. The controversy would linger on throughout the century, surfacing from time to time in debates over the place of "creationism" in public school curricula.

The crusades for prohibition and against evolution reflected a larger nativist movement to bring cultural and political homogeneity to an increasingly pluralistic America. The United States had, from its inception, been a nation of immigrants from a variety of places, but in the 1920s nativists mounted an increasingly shrill, paradoxical, and multifaceted campaign to reclaim the nation in the name of the "Anglo-Saxon traditions" of democracy, free enterprise, Protestant Christianity, and moral uprightness. In 1920 Italian immigrants Nicola Sacco and Bartolomeo Vanzetti were arrested in Braintree, Massachusetts, and charged with robbing a shoe factory and murdering the paymaster and guard. Evidence linking the two with the crime was skimpy, and the trial was a travesty, producing guilty verdicts not on the basis of proof but on the defendants' status as immigrants, anarchists, and draft resisters. Their convictions aroused national outrage among liberals and radicals, but in spite of efforts to obtain a new trial, Sacco and Vanzetti were executed in

1927. Whether or not they committed the crimes, the furor over their case reflected bitter conflict over immigration.

The New Nativism

Ever since the late nineteenth century, nativists had questioned the capacity of American culture to assimilate so-called new immigrants—those whose countries of origin were in southern and eastern Europe or Asia. During the Progressive Era "Americanization" programs reflected both a desire to help immigrants succeed in the United States and a belief in the racial superiority of self-styled "Anglo-Saxons." Wartime hysteria had led to concern that "hyphenated Americans" would sell out their new country for the old, prompting clamor to restrict the numbers of people entering the United States from abroad. In 1920, as refugees from a devastated Europe swelled the ranks of immigrants to five thousand a day, the clamor for immigration restrictions reached new heights. Congress passed the Emergency Quota Act of 1921, setting annual quotas for each country at 3 percent of its total U.S. population, based on the 1910 census. Nativists pushed hard for even more stringent quotas, and in 1924 Congress responded with the drastic National Origins Act, reducing the percentage allowed in to only 2 percent of each nation's U.S. population at the time of the census of 1890, not 1910. Effectively shutting out southern and eastern Europeans with this method, the act also expanded outright exclusion of Asians, banning Japanese immigration (in addition to Chinese) in the wave of anti-Japanese agitation on the West Coast (see figure).

California in particular proved fertile ground for anti-Japanese racism, as the population of Japanese immigrants, though small (only 2 percent of the state's population) was remarkably successful economically. Japanese farmers, legally barred from acquiring land by a 1913 California law, nonetheless

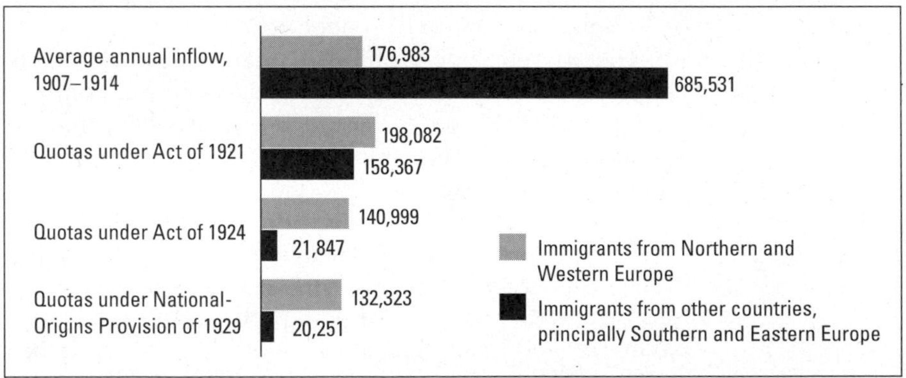

Annual Immigration and Quota Laws, 1860–1994 A long-term view of immigration reveals the changes in the origins of immigrant populations and the importance of American policies toward victims of persecution and poverty, worldwide.

managed to prosper, producing some 10 percent of the total value of California's crops in 1919. Threatened by Japanese immigrants' prosperity, organizations ranging from the California Federation of Labor to the American Legion, with the help of the viciously anti-Japanese Hearst publishing empire, shrieked their warnings about a "Yellow Peril."

Jews were also subjected to particularly furious hate campaigns. Discrimination against Jews in social clubs, hotels, resorts, housing, higher education, and employment proliferated in the 1920s. Henry Ford revealed his dark side by subsidizing *The Dearborn Independent*, the most viciously anti-Semitic propaganda sheet in the nation, and forcing Ford dealers to sell it. Week after week the *Independent* warned of a sinister Jewish conspiracy to overthrow Christian civilization, pointing out that Jews already occupied positions of cultural and economic power. Gullible people, anxious about modern life, found such conspiracy theories handy.

Mexican immigrants were not included in the quota laws (in spite of fervid lobbying by the American Federation of Labor). Nearly half a million Mexicans moved to the United States during the twenties, many fleeing the Mexican Revolution. But when they arrived they were met with fierce discrimination and prejudice. The 1924 establishment of the border patrol reflected anti-Mexican sentiment that would grow in years to come.

Obviously no group endured more racist oppression than African-Americans, whose native-born roots reached back to colonial times. Blacks had long been seen as an exception to the rule of the American "melting pot." Restricted to the worst-paying, most backbreaking jobs and forced into overcrowded ghettos in segregated Northern cities, blacks saw Jim Crow laws extended to a host of public facilities during the 1920s. But with all these burdens, life in the North was far preferable to debt peonage in the South, where lynchings continued apace.

Nothing revealed more starkly the rising tide of nativism in the early twentieth century than the revival of the Ku Klux Klan, the secret society founded in the South after the Civil War to terrorize African-Americans. Sixteen men lit a cross on Stone Mountain, Georgia, in 1915 to mark the coming of a new Klan. But the movement did not really catch fire until 1920, when Atlanta publicity agents Edward Young Clark and Elizabeth Sawyer cut a deal with Klan leader William Simmons, offering to create a new recruitment system for the Klan in return for a share of its profits. Clark and Sawyer combined hucksterism, nativism, and the Klan's long-standing ideology of white supremacy, identifying the Klan as the great protector of "100 percent Americanism," to recruit new members. Between 1920 and 1925 perhaps 5 million people joined up, and the Klan spread out of the South and into the Midwest and even the Far West. During those years the Klan dominated politics in Indiana, Texas, Oklahoma, and Colorado and was influential in numerous other states. The Klan flourished in the cities, including Los Angeles, Chicago, Detroit, Denver, Atlanta, and Dallas, as well as in the countryside. Although the Klan itself was limited to men, the auxiliary group Women of

Klansmen marched proudly, with their faces uncovered, in Washington, D.C. in 1926. *Culver Pictures, Inc.*

the Klan urged newly enfranchised white women to use their votes in defense of 100 percent Americanism and promised that the Klan would uphold pure womanhood and restrain abusive husbands.

For some, joining the Klan was a business decision. Members were expected to trade with one another and to post TWK (Trade with Klan) signs in their windows. Klan connections could also be helpful for aspiring politicians. The Klan promised fundamentalists that it would combat the "weakening of Protestantism's influence," and it offered free membership to ministers (a substantial incentive, given the standard $10 membership fee). Others may have joined simply for the fun of belonging to a secret society steeped in elaborate, clandestine ritual. The hooded regalia of the Klan brought comforting anonymity to those engaged in the thrilling, threatening practices of nighttime intimidation and cross burning.

Whatever its ceremonial allure, the modern Klan was also a sales organization. Salesmen called Kleagles were dispatched throughout the country and instructed to use some local controversy to whip up enthusiasm. They worked on a commission basis, as did their local sales managers (King Kleagles), district sales managers (Grand Goblins), and even the Imperial Wizard himself, William Simmons. As a consequence, the targets of Klan hatred varied somewhat from place to place. In the South Klan Klaverns (local chapters) targeted blacks as the chief threat to Anglo-Saxon Americanism, though Jews and Catholics also came in for harassment and assault. In cities like Chicago, Klansmen promised (ultimately in vain) to restore white Protestant dominance by challenging the powerful ethnic political machines, and in Denver the Klan warned that "the Catholics and Jews were taking over." In other communities, especially in the Southwest, Klaverns attacked bootleggers and public officials perceived as lax in enforcing Prohibition. The anti-Catholic pitch proved so popular that it became a staple of Klan rhetoric. It propelled a Klansman into the governorship of Oregon in 1922 and prompted Oregon voters to pass an initiative making public school attendance mandatory for children between the ages of eight and sixteen, a fairly open attack on the state's Catholic schools.

At the peak of its power in 1924, the Klan was unable to sustain its momentum. Klan leaders vied with one another for profits and influence, and a series of scandals exposed their corruption and hypocrisy. A crippling blow came with the murder conviction of Indiana's Grand Dragon, D. C. Stephenson, who had kidnapped and raped his secretary, Madge Oberholtzer. Denied a pardon, Stephenson released his Klan files, exposing widespread misconduct by Klan politicians. Meanwhile, those who had let the Klan into their communities began to realize that the organization was creating precisely the social and political disorder it claimed to be fighting. As the Klan's strength ebbed, the fight went out of the movement for 100 percent Americanism. Catholics, Jews, Japanese Americans, and African-Americans organized on their own behalf. Ethnic political and social organizations continued to oppose Prohibition, immigration restrictions, and other causes associated with nativist politics.

America's diversity helped stem the tide of nativism and antimodernism. At the same time, Americans got more and more used to the conveniences and pleasures—and even the frantic pace and crowded places—of modern life. Mass society generated anxiety, but this fear was balanced by the smugness that came from widespread prosperity. While the economy continued to be strong, the fruits of the consumer cornucopia remained sweet, and the warnings of cataclysm seemed not much more than sour grapes.

✦ The Boom Unravels

The 1920s was a time when many Americans believed they could make a fortune without working for it. Even middle-class people began to engage in speculative schemes, buying land in Florida and shares of companies listed on the New York Stock Exchange. In the mid-twenties, real estate wheeler-dealers bought up land in Florida, subdivided it into building lots, and offered it for sale with a low 10 percent down payment. In glamorous advertisements they touted Florida as "The American Riviera," possessed of pristine beaches, sparkling waters, and a glorious winter climate. But many who bought lots had no intention of building a dream house in the sun; their purpose was to cash in on mushrooming land values and sell to somebody else. "The Florida boom," wrote economist John Kenneth Galbraith, "was the first indication of the mood of the twenties and the conviction that God intended the American middle class to be rich."

Some learned, to their dismay, that Florida hucksters had very loose definitions of "seashore" property (which might be miles from the nearest beach or, alternatively, under water) and had a tendency to sell lots "convenient to rising cities" that were nothing more than imaginary spots on a map. By the spring of 1926, investors that had been left holding remote patches of scrub, impenetrable swamp plots, and sinkholes in salt bogs had trouble finding buyers.

The following fall nature delivered the coup de grâce to the Florida land boom, in the form of two hurricanes that showed, in the words of Frederick Lewis Allen, "what a Soothing Tropic Wind could do when it got a running start from the West Indies." Winds ripped the roofs from thousands of houses as the storms poured tons of water and no small number of elegant yachts onto Miami streets. Four hundred people were killed, and a call went out for thousands of relief workers, although one real estate booster worried that the bad publicity arising from attempts to raise money for Red Cross relief might do even worse harm to the state. Stuck with unsalable property, those who had borrowed to buy defaulted on loans to people who were themselves in debt. The chain of defaults rippled across the country.

Despite the Florida collapse, the mania for speculation and get-rich-quick schemes persisted. A million and a half fortune-hunting Americans put their money in the stock market during the 1920s. Early in the decade there were sound reasons for people to believe stock prices would rise. Prices were low, yields were high, and corporate earnings were good and growing. At the end of May 1924 the *New York Times* average of twenty-five industrial stocks was 106; by year's end it was 134. But stock prices began heading skyward in 1927. Even Henry Ford's decision to stop producing the Model T and close down his factory to retool to make the Model A had no effect on the market. At the end of that year the *Times* industrials average was 245, up 69 points for the year.

In 1928 the true speculative orgy began, as more and more people bought shares, expecting to make money on endlessly rising prices. General Motors stock rose 75 points in two months; RCA started the year at 85, reached 420 by December, and by September 1929 was selling at 505 points. Buying had reached the point of frenzy, with millions of people making their purchases "on margin"—putting down some small fraction (commonly, 10 percent) of the purchase price and financing the rest by borrowing from their stockbrokers. By late 1929 these loans amounted to some $7 billion. Banks, too, were speculating in the market, using depositors' money, and corporations like Chrysler and Bethlehem Steel got into the picture by backing brokers' loans. As long as the market continued to rise, everyone appeared to make money. But falling prices would mean that debtors could not use their shares to pay off the loans they had taken out for the purchase price.

While many enjoyed unprecedented prosperity during the 1920s, signs of economic trouble appeared even in the midst of plenty. Agriculture remained depressed throughout the decade, and some industries, especially textiles and coal, were in trouble long before the general crisis. An economy dedicated to consumerism required that demand for goods expand faster than supply. But Americans could not consume all they produced, in part because the nation's wealth was so unequally distributed. A mere 5 percent of American families received a third of all the nation's income. Treasury Secretary Mellon's championing of lower income tax rates benefited the wealthy far more than middle- and low-income Americans. The rich were getting richer much faster than the poor were gaining ground. This small proportion of people spent lavishly, but there was a limit to how many washing machines, refrigerators, and even automobiles they would buy. Most workers and farmers did not make enough to buy all the things that rolled off the assembly lines, and even when they took the consumer plunge anyway, most saw no reason to make payments on more than one radio or Tin Lizzie. From the point of view of American manufacturers, the U.S. economy suffered from "underconsumption."

As a consequence America's industries fell victim to the same kind of overproduction that had plagued farmers, and as prices declined, companies reduced their output. As factories cut production, employers began to lay off workers. For the newly jobless, finding a way to feed the family took precedence over making installment payments on the Amana and the Victrola. More and more consumers could not pay their debts, so the companies and banks that had extended credit were left holding mounting piles of bad loans.

But American corporations had additional problems. With the stock craze in full swing, many began to sell more shares of stock, at higher prices, than their companies were worth in terms of real assets. No government agency monitored the market to prevent abuses like this "watering" of stock, and no federal power checked to see if the country's increasingly large holding companies were in sound financial shape. Consequently some of the nation's biggest, most influential enterprises, like Insull Utilities Investment, Inc., were among the shakiest, and they stood to bring many others down when the crash came.

International economic problems contributed to the coming crisis (see Chapter 6). World War I had made the United States the greatest creditor nation in the world, whereas the European nations were in general left with staggering war debts. Germany in particular was saddled with the cost of paying reparations, and France and England in turn depended on German payments to finance their own loans. European nations tried to make money by manufacturing and exporting goods, but high U.S. tariffs made it difficult for Europe to crack the American market. So Europeans resorted to borrowing from American banks to service their debts, and they tried to build domestic markets and cut their international spending. As a result the European demand for American goods dried up, leaving American farmers and manufacturers with even more surplus stock.

All these forces came together on Thursday, October 24, 1929. That morning, prices on the New York Stock Exchange began to sag. Trading reached a feverish pitch, and the ticker lagged further and further behind as prices fell faster and faster. Across the country speculators and corporate executives, unable to find out how much they had lost, gave in to terror. Outside the exchange a crowd gathered, while rumors of wipeouts and suicides swept the trading floor. At twelve o'clock the nation's most powerful financiers convened an emergency meeting in the offices of J. P. Morgan and Company, determined to pool their resources to stop the panic. They told reporters that "there has been a little distress selling on the stock exchange." As the bankers moved in during the afternoon to place strategic orders for shares, selling slowed and prices recovered.

For a couple of days the market seemed to return to calm, but by Monday prices had begun to slide again, and this time there was no recovery. Everyone, it seemed, wanted or had to sell, to pay off debt, to keep from being utterly ruined, and no one wanted to buy. On Tuesday, October 29, the bottom fell out. By the close of business more than 16 million sales had been recorded, more than three times the number for even a fabulous day, and the ticker was two and a half hours behind. The *Times* industrials average was down 43 points, wiping out gains for the entire year.

The stock market crash of 1929 ruined big and small investors alike and rippled throughout the economy (see figure). As the new decade opened, things only got worse. Investors who went to their banks to withdraw the money they needed to pay their margin calls, or simply to see that their deposits were safe, found that the banks themselves were in trouble. In 1930 some sixteen hundred banks failed. Prices and production plummeted, and devastated businesses laid people off. By the beginning of the new decade 5 million Americans were unemployed. By 1932 some 13 million were without work. Although President Hoover insisted that "the fundamental business of the country, that is production and distribution of commodities, is on a sound and prosperous basis," few believed him. Good times had come roaring to a halt; hard times had come.

✦ Conclusion

At no time have the contradictory, volatile energies of modernism been more apparent than during the 1920s. Americans learned to want more, found ways to get more, and imagined how to do more than ever before. At the same

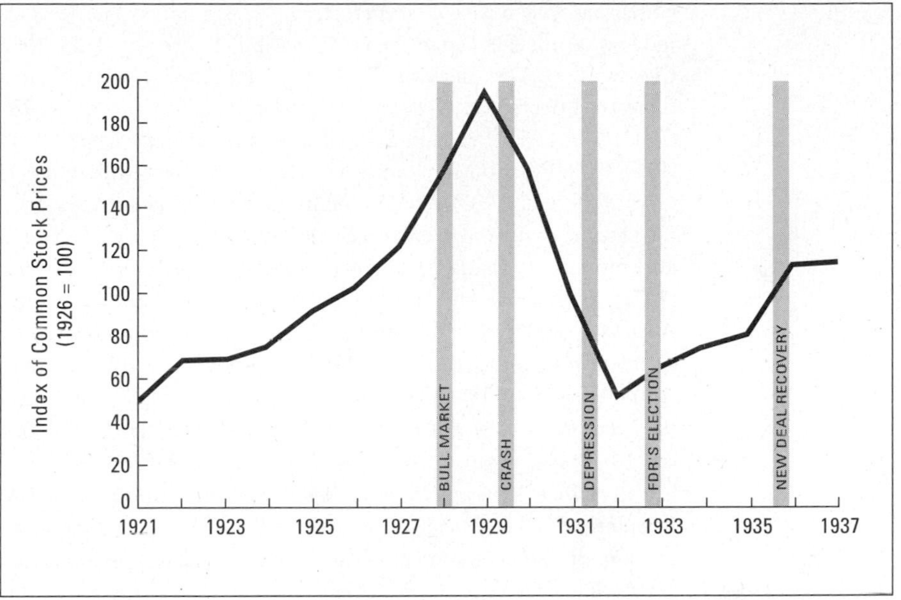

Index of Common Stock Prices, 1821–1937 The steady and spectacular rise of stock prices throughout the 1920s gave way to a drastic drop, and much slower rise, in the following decade.

time, federal authorities, local clergy, and concerned citizens worried that the rage to consume, enjoy, exhibit, and emote would wreck American families and destroy the American character. Immigrants, blacks, and women found new power and new outlets for self-expression, but their efforts often inspired a fierce backlash. Fundamentalist Christians, nativists, and cultural conservatives insisted that the time had come to curb modern excesses.

The federal government, meanwhile, did what it could to help business grow, ignoring signs that corporate expansion, unchecked, could suddenly collapse. And so, while Americans enjoyed the fruits of a seemingly wildly successful consumer economy and their leaders pronounced themselves satisfied with the direction the country was headed, dire troubles lay ahead.

✦ Further Reading

For general overviews of the era, see: William E. Leuchtenberg, *The Perils of Prosperity, 1914–1932* (1970); Lynn Dumenil, *The Modern Temper: America in the 1920s* (1995); Paul Carter, *The Twenties in America* (1968); Paul Carter, *Another Part of the Twenties* (1977). On consumer culture and technological innovation, see: Richard Tedlow, *New and Improved: The Story of Mass Marketing in America* (1990); Lizabeth

Cohen, *Making a New Deal: Industrial Workers in Chicago, 1919–1939* (1991); Katherine Jellison, *Entitled to Power: Farm Women and Technology, 1913–1963* (1993); Suellen Hoy, *Chasing Dirt: The American Pursuit of Cleanliness* (1995); Thomas Hughes, *American Genesis: A Century of Invention and Technological Enthusiasm* (1989); James J. Flink, *The Car Culture* (1975); Virginia Scharff, *Taking the Wheel: Women and the Coming of the Motor Age* (1991); Roland Marchand, *Advertising the American Dream: Making Way for Modernity, 1920–1940* (1985). On women in the years after suffrage, see: Rosalind Rosenberg, *Divided Lives: American Women in the Twentieth Century* (1992). On changes in manners and mores, see: Paula Fass, *The Damned and the Beautiful: American Youth in the 1920s* (1977); Beth L. Bailey, *From Front Porch to Back Seat: Courtship in Twentieth-Century America* (1988); Lewis Erenberg, *Steppin' Out: New York Nightlife and the Transformation of American Culture, 1890–1930* (1981). On sports, see: Elliot Gorn and Warren Goldstein, *A Brief History of American Sports* (1993). On nativism, see: John Higham, *Strangers in the Land: Patterns of American Nativism, 1860–1925* (1955, 1989). On the resurgence of the Klan, see: Kenneth T. Jackson, *The Ku Klux Klan in the City, 1915–1930* (1967); Kathleen Blee, *Women of the Klan: Racism and Gender in the 1920s* (1990); Nancy MacLean, *Behind the Mask of Chivalry: The Making of the Second Ku Klux Klan* (1994). The standard work on the stock market crash and onset of the depression is John Kenneth Galbraith, *The Great Crash 1929* (3d. ed. 1979).

✦✦✦

CHAPTER 5

Depression and the New Deal, 1929–1940

✦ **Breadlines were grim evidence of the economic collapse of the early 1930s.**

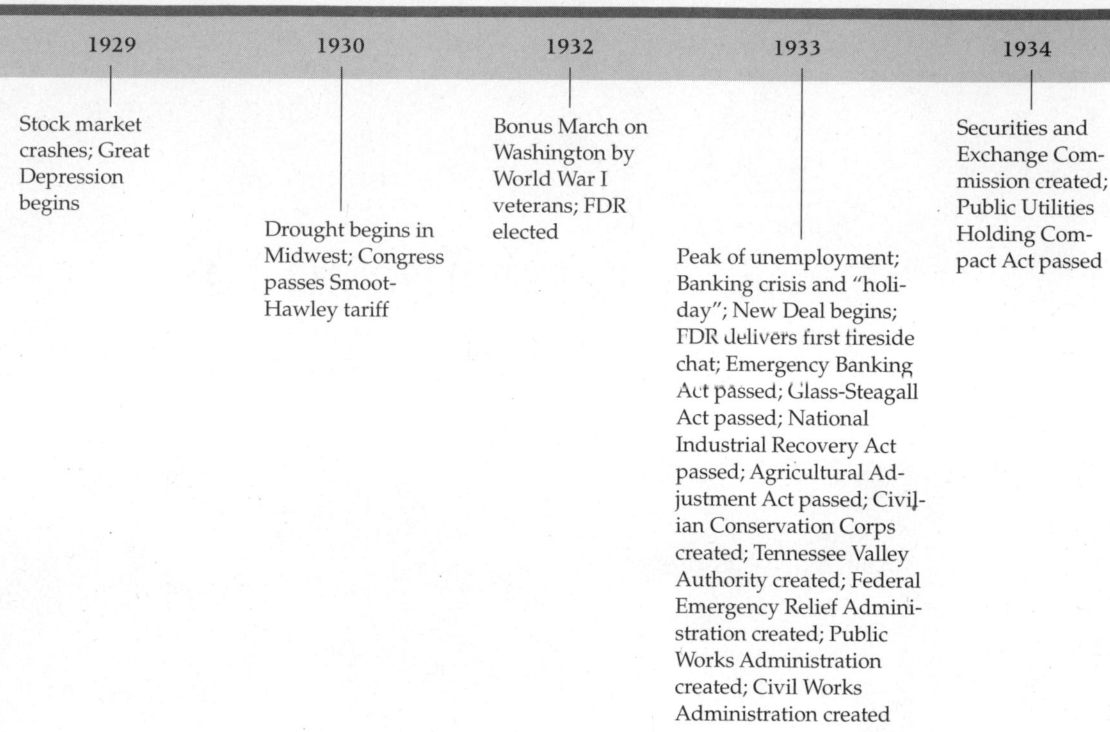

IN JUNE 1932 twenty-two thousand unemployed veterans of World War I—a fraction of the 13 million Americans then out of work—tramped into Washington, D.C. Encamped in shacks and abandoned buildings they derisively called "Hoovervilles," the impoverished veterans urged Congress to pay them immediately a $1,000 pension benefit, or bonus, that had been promised for their retirement. When President Hoover threatened to veto early payment, the Senate defeated a House-passed bonus bill, on June 17. "We were heroes in 1917," one veteran remarked, "but now we're bums." Congress offered to buy the so-called Bonus Marchers train tickets home. Six thousand accepted the offer, and by late July only about ten thousand remained in the capital.

Ignoring pleas from the district police chief to wait until the rest of the veterans drifted away, Hoover and army chief of staff General Douglas Mac-

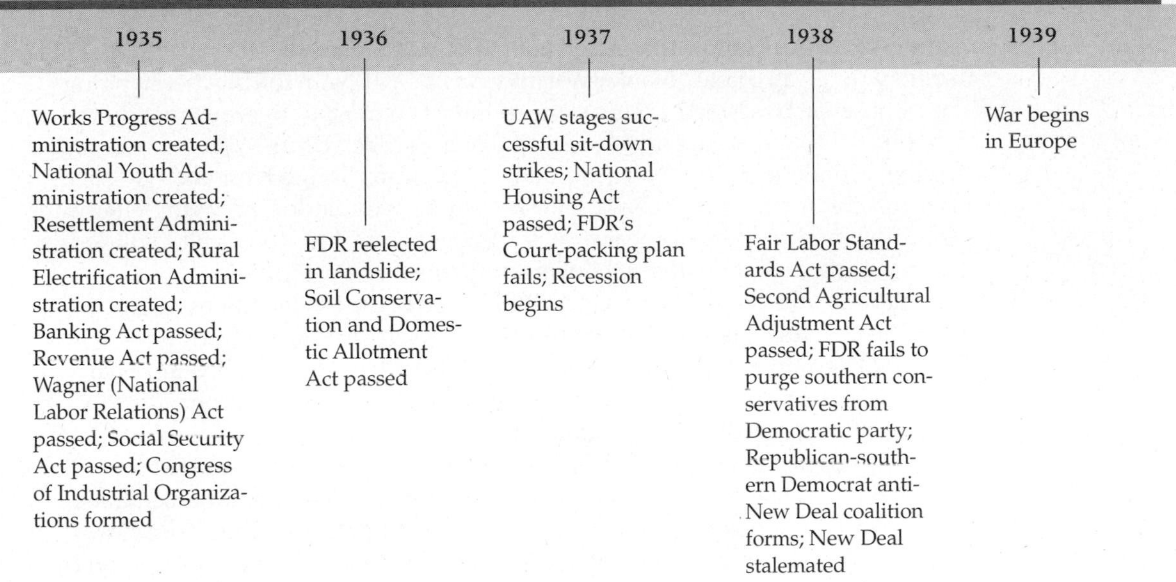

Arthur decided to clear the city. On July 28 police began rousting the peaceful demonstrators out of vacant buildings. During a scuffle a panicked policeman killed two veterans. Warning of "incipient revolution in the air," MacArthur assembled a force of one thousand troops from infantry, cavalry, and mechanized units. Under the command of Major Dwight D. Eisenhower and George S. Patton, they chased the veterans across the Anacostia River toward one of their encampments. The general then ordered the shacks burned, inflicting more casualties. MacArthur told skeptical journalists that the Bonus Marchers were plotting revolution and that in another week the "whole government would have been severely threatened."

Shortly after the so-called battle of Anacostia Flats, Democratic presidential candidate Franklin D. Roosevelt received a telephone call from Senator

Huey P. Long of Louisiana. Long complained that Roosevelt was under the spell of rich Wall Street "blankety blanks" instead of plain folks. After hanging up, Roosevelt described Long as one of the "two most dangerous men in the country." The other, he told aides, was Douglas MacArthur. With the country facing economic ruin, "Nazi-minded" Americans longed for a "symbolic figure—the man on horseback." Few were as well endowed with "charm, tradition, and majestic appearance" as the general. But, Roosevelt confided, he had a plan to "tame these fellows and make them useful to us."

Between October 1929 and March 1933, life in the United States resembled a motion picture played in reverse. The economic progress and optimism of the 1920s crumbled with astonishing speed. In less than four years nearly every measure of economic well-being, from the Gross National Product (GNP) to foreign trade and investment, industrial and agricultural production, and employment, went into a statistical free fall. The stock market lost 90 percent of its value at its lowest point, and over five thousand banks failed, with a loss to depositors of $2.5 billion. By 1932 thirteen million Americans, one of every four working men and women, lacked jobs. Many more labored part-time for reduced wages.

President Herbert Hoover, a celebrated administrator and humanitarian elected amid a wave of optimism in 1928, seemed politically paralyzed and isolated. After his prediction that the economy would correct itself proved false, he shut himself up in the White House.

On the eve of his election in 1928, Herbert Hoover declared, "We in America today are nearer to the final triumph over poverty than ever before in the history of any land." Hoover trumpeted the virtue of "associationalism," a belief that government's proper economic role was promoting voluntary cooperation between business, labor, and consumers to ensure prosperity and a fair division of wealth. A little over a year later, following the collapse of stock prices and a general economic panic, this nostrum sounded absurd. The national mood found expression in a popular song that asked plaintively, "Brother, can you spare a dime?"

✦ Onset of the Depression

The onset of the Depression highlighted the contradictions in the economic progress of the 1920s. Corporate profits had swelled by over 60 percent and real wages had increased by 11 percent. But once these figures were, as economists put it, "disaggregated," the picture was less rosy. For example, farm income failed to grow at all during the 1920s. The income of the top 1 percent of Americans doubled in these years, but the income of the lower one-third increased by only 6 percent. As a result many Americans earned only enough to buy necessities and relied on credit to purchase many of the era's new consumer goods. When credit tightened in 1929 and 1930, consumer purchases declined, inventories mounted, factories laid off workers, and the economy contracted rapidly.

The simultaneous collapse of the stock market and the banking system worsened the downward spiral. Even during the "good" years of the 1920s, nearly five thousand American banks had collapsed. Many of these were small, rural institutions that lacked the reserves to withstand even temporary setbacks. When in late 1929 frightened depositors rushed to retrieve their money, smaller banks were unable to meet the demand for cash. The lack of federal regulation over how banks should protect deposits or any provision for the government to loan banks money to carry them through a panic worsened the crisis.

So did the action of the Federal Reserve, which loosely regulated the nation's banks. Instead of intervening to loan cash to hard-pressed banks to meet short-term demand, the "Fed" mistakenly raised interest rates and shrank the money supply by about one-third. As a result, between 1930 and early 1933, five thousand more banks failed. This spurred terrified depositors to withdraw funds from otherwise solvent banks, threatening them as well. Bankers responded by calling in loans to raise cash and ceasing to extend new credit. These actions placed pressure on small businesses and homeowners and dried up credit, which further weakened retail sales. As the panic spread, governors in thirty-four states ordered the periodic closure of banks, to prevent their collapse.

The stock market boom and bust contributed to banking woes. In 1928 and 1929 the value of shares of corporations listed on the prestigious New York Stock Exchange doubled in value. Much of the cash that flowed into the stock market came from bank and brokerage-house loans. As long as prices rose, this promised a quick path to wealth. But when prices fell, investors had to increase their cash contribution—by withdrawing savings from banks—to satisfy lenders who provided money for stock purchases. By the end of November 1929 even quality stocks on Wall Street had lost over half their value. By 1933 over $85 billion in share values had been wiped out.

None of the economic factors that led to the Great Depression—the stock market crash, bank failures, declining retail sales, falling farm prices, reduced exports, and rising unemployment—would have created a self-sustaining downward spiral by itself. Collectively, however, these events forced the economy into a depression of unprecedented severity.

To get by, working and middle-class families turned first to kinship networks, savings, and cost cutting. Those who could took in lodgers to help pay the rent or the mortgage. Even so, by 1933 one-half of all home mortgages in the United States were in default. Not surprisingly, the birth rate fell sharply during the Depression, as did immigration to the United States, since the country no longer seemed an economic paradise. Churches and ethnic organizations helped many individuals, although much of their assistance went to the aged and the ill rather than to the able-bodied unemployed. Few state or local and virtually no federal welfare programs existed to help the jobless. By 1933 most of the 13 million unemployed and their families were on their own.

Although vilified by those who suffered, President Hoover was not the "do-nothing" that he appeared. He remained an articulate advocate of voluntary measures to cope with the Depression. At first Hoover organized conferences of business leaders to create a voluntary wage, employment, and price stabilization system that would restore order to the marketplace. Confidence-building measures, he argued, would halt the slide of stocks and restore business optimism. The president urged farmers to voluntarily restrict their production to stabilize prices. He promoted fund-raising by private charities to help the unemployed, although he strongly opposed spending federal money directly on relief. As conditions worsened, Hoover pushed Congress to create the Reconstruction Finance Corporation (RFC), with a $2 billion budget to invest in basically sound banks, railroads, and large companies that needed an infusion of cash to stay in business. When these expenditures resulted in the largest peacetime budget deficit the country had ever experienced, of just over $2 billion, both Democrats and Republicans criticized Hoover as a spendthrift. And it soon became clear that even this unprecedented intervention was a case of too little, too late. Hoover had run out of ideas, and the economy spiraled downward.

The Great Depression affected both rural and urban America more than any previous economic decline. In Temple, Texas, in 1932, a farm laborer explained why he was not working: "I picked all week and made 85 cents. I can starve sitting down a lot easier than I can picking cotton." In Detroit in 1931, among families surveyed by the Department of Public Welfare, only one-third of heads of households had full-time work. The weekly median earnings of families had fallen by two-thirds since 1929. In Gary, Indiana, employees of U.S. Steel were limited to working no more than one day per week, for an income of $1.75. The editor of a newspaper in rural Oklahoma, where drought and wind compounded economic troubles, wrote, "not a blade of wheat in Cimmaron County; cattle dying on the range, 90 percent of the poultry dead because of the sandstorms." Chicago journalists described crowds of people gathered at the Roseland garbage dump, "standing in two rows . . . waiting for the load to come down," with rotten food for their supper.

The Depression may have begun on Wall Street, but it soon affected Main Street and every region of the country. Farmers—30 percent of the American work force in the early 1930s—did not expect the stock market crash to affect them. The agricultural sector had fared poorly during the 1920s, hurt by overproduction as much as anything. Better roads and mechanized equipment had boosted yields so much that most farm products were already over-abundant on the market even before massive unemployment in the cities and abroad lowered demand after the crash. Cotton, corn, wheat, beef, and pork prices plummeted. Urban workers needed to eat, but they lacked purchasing power. To make matters worse, many farmers that were *not* stuck with surplus crops during the early thirties were hammered by drought. As a result of all these factors, farm income fell from $6.1 billion in 1929 to $2 billion in 1932. Bankruptcies and foreclosures skyrocketed in rural America. In Mississippi on one day in April 1932, a fourth of all the land in the state was sold at sheriffs' sales.

The prosperity of the 1920s had produced something close to full employment in urban areas. The unemployment rate in the cities stood at a mere 3.2 percent in 1929. In 1930 it rose to 8.7 percent. A year later it hit 16 percent, and by 1933 it peaked at 25 percent. These figures actually understate the problem, since up to one-half of workers who did keep their jobs were placed on reduced hours and wages. By 1932 household income had declined by one-third from 1929 levels. While traditional industries such as coal, textiles, steel, and construction were affected early on, even the technologically advanced automobile and electric appliance sectors suffered a two-thirds decline in sales. In 1929 Ford Motor Company employed 120,000 workers in Detroit; three years later only 37,000 worked in Ford's Detroit plants.

On the eve of the Depression, a respected private "think tank," the Brookings Institution, calculated that a typical family required about $2,000 per year to purchase necessities and $2,500 to enjoy an adequate standard of living. In 1929, *before* the economy collapsed, about 16 million families—consisting of some 70 million people, or 60 percent of the American population—earned $2,000 or less. Only 30 percent of families earned $2,500 or more.

The economic crisis proved especially hard on women and minorities. Women came under great pressure to work to increase family income, and their number in the work force increased from 24.3 percent in 1930 to 35 percent later in the decade. Yet married women faced growing antagonism from those who accused them of taking away men's jobs. One proposal, printed in the *Saturday Evening Post,* called for ending the Depression by firing 10 million working women and employing men in their place: "Presto! No unemployment, no relief roles. No Depression." Many school districts and federal and state agencies adopted informal policies of refusing to hire married women in order to hold jobs for men. As a result, by 1940 only 15 percent of married women worked for wages.

For blacks the Depression erased the modest economic gains achieved since World War I, when around 20 percent of rural blacks moved to cities in the South and North. As jobs disappeared, poor whites moved into many of the domestic-service and unskilled factory jobs previously reserved for blacks. Mexican immigrants, especially in the West, were pressed to leave the United States. As noted later in the chapter, several hundred thousand were deported.

The economic downturn exposed other failures in the nation's social support structures. Benefits for aging Civil War veterans and their widows had been extremely important in previous decades, but they disappeared as these individuals passed away. The lack of any other old-age pension system meant that nearly half of all elderly Americans had to keep working, rely on meager savings, or depend on the good will of relatives. The states provided almost no benefits to the needy. The little they offered went mostly to a small number of widows. For example, in Missouri in 1931 only thirty-four families received Aid to Families with Dependent Children. All were white, and most were headed by widows.

The rural poor, such as the 8.5 million people (including 3 million blacks) who lived as tenant farmers in the South, experienced especially severe hardship as prices for cotton and tobacco collapsed. Indians in the American West remained at the bottom of the economic ladder. Having lost two-thirds of their tribal lands since the Dawes Act of 1887, fully 98 percent had incomes below $500 per year.

✦ Roosevelt and the Origins of the New Deal

Between 1933 and 1941 the veil of despair that hung over American life was at least partially lifted by the New Deal, the program initiated by President Franklin D. Roosevelt to revive industry and agriculture, put people back to work, and provide relief for the unemployed. Although the New Deal's record was uneven, few Americans then or later questioned Roosevelt's success in restoring hope to the nation and his long-term achievement in transforming the federal government and the relationship between citizen and state. As the theme song for his 1932 campaign Roosevelt selected the spirited tune "Happy Days Are Here Again." For a generation of Americans, the song proved both a promise and a reality. The basic agricultural, labor, welfare, banking, and foreign policies established by the New Deal, as well as the structure of national politics Roosevelt forged, lasted for over sixty years.

Through the force of his personality, Franklin D. Roosevelt dominated American political life from 1933 to 1945. The eclectic New Deal program reflected his own style and energy to a remarkable degree. FDR, as most people referred to him, was affable, charming, disarming, and able to convey a sense of reassuring optimism to nearly everyone he encountered. Roosevelt had an unusual ability to relate to people as different as powerful chairmen of congressional committees and poor tenant farmers. Yet beneath the public smile lurked an intensely private, distant man barely known to even his closest associates and family.

Born in 1882 into a wealthy landowning family in New York's Hudson River Valley, Roosevelt had all the advantages that privileged birth conferred. He attended Groton Academy and Harvard University and studied law at Columbia University. Modeling himself on his distant cousin Theodore, FDR won a seat in the New York legislature in 1910, running on a modestly progressive platform that favored conservation and opposed corruption. Most observers considered him a well-meaning dilettante. Like many young men of patrician background, he viewed self-made millionaires as unscrupulous persons lacking taste and conscience.

Although not a deep thinker himself, FDR relished fiery intellects and as president recruited numerous academics and social activists as advisers. His broad but undisciplined mind sought practical solutions to social problems

Franklin Delano Roosevelt, president from 1933–1945, restored America's faith in itself. *Franklin D. Roosevelt Library*

rather than theoretical analyses of them. British economist John Maynard Keynes, whose ideas inspired many New Deal programs, remarked after meeting Roosevelt that he was barely literate concerning economics. No one meeting the young Franklin could have imagined that twenty-five years later this dandy would inspire passionate support among small farmers, minorities, immigrants, and industrial workers. Retiring Supreme Court Justice Oliver Wendell Holmes saw deeper than his peers when in 1932 he described Roosevelt as a "second-class intellect, but a first-class temperament."

Again modeling himself on Theodore, Roosevelt served as President Wilson's assistant secretary of the navy during World War I. He ran, unsuccessfully, as the Democratic nominee for vice president in 1920 on a ticket headed by Ohio governor James C. Cox. The next year Roosevelt suffered a crippling attack of polio. Several years of therapy failed to restore the use of his legs. The experience had two positive effects on his career, however. While convalescing, Roosevelt remained in contact with Democrats throughout the country but managed to avoid the bitter factional strife that divided his party during the Republican-dominated 1920s. Also, his prolonged struggle to overcome paralysis humanized Roosevelt. When he ran for governor of New York in 1928, he related to people intimately.

After his bout with polio Roosevelt could stand only by wearing bulky steel braces. He generally moved about in an office chair with wheels or by holding the arm of an aide. But his emotional vigor so overshadowed his physical handicap that it never emerged as a serious liability, in an age when disabilities often ended public careers. He charmed the press corps so effectively that most journalists voluntarily refrained from writing about or taking pictures of his withered legs. If an uninitiated photographer seemed poised to snap an unguarded picture of Roosevelt, a veteran would quietly block the shot.

At the conclusion of a divisive nominating convention in the summer of 1932 in which conservative Democrats almost blocked his selection as the party's presidential candidate, Roosevelt pledged a "new deal" for the American people. Without specifying exactly what he had in mind—except *reducing* spending—FDR portrayed the election as a "contest between two philosophies of government." He selected a group of academic experts—lawyers and journalists, including Raymond Moley, Rexford Tugwell, and Adolph Berle, Jr.—dubbed the Brains Trust, to advise him. Together they concluded that economic recovery required government action to regulate farm production, distribute wealth more equitably, reform the banking system and stock market, and jump-start industry. The group was by no means anti-capitalist; rather, they advocated a liberal agenda based on government regulation of business. Responding as much to his personality as to his vague program, voters enthusiastically gave Roosevelt almost 23 million votes, to Hoover's 16 million. The November 1932 victory changed little in the short term, however, since the Constitution then specified a four-month delay in seating a newly elected president. In the interim, unemployment increased, production declined, and more banks failed.

In his March 4, 1933, inauguration speech, Roosevelt sought to break the mood of despair that gripped Americans. "The only thing we have to fear," he proclaimed, "is fear itself." He promised to deliver what the nation demanded: "action, and action now." If Congress stalled, he would demand "broad executive power to wage a war against the emergency, as great as the power that would be given to me if we were in fact invaded by a foreign foe."

As Roosevelt's words implied, his New Deal required a federal government that would take a direct and prominent role in the economy and American society. This was a new phenomenon and certainly a dramatic reversal from Hoover's voluntarism. Within a few years the size and scope of federal activity had grown in ways previously unimaginable.

Before 1933 the only routine contact between the federal government and most citizens was mail delivery by the post office. Policies set in Washington rarely affected the daily lives of ordinary Americans. There existed no old-age pension system, no federal unemployment compensation, little aid to dependent children, virtually no regulation of the stock market and banking system, no farm subsidies, no minimum wage, and no protection for labor unions—to name but a few New Deal innovations now taken for granted.

Since the founding of the United States, "good government" had meant minimal government, with most power remaining in the hands of state and local authorities. The country lacked a tradition of a powerful central government committed to solving social and economic problems. Yet it seemed obvious that minimal government had failed to stem the ravages of the Depression. In Roosevelt's view the time had arrived when government must save capitalism from its own faults and ensure every American the "right to make a comfortable living." He warned that a violent revolution "could hardly be avoided if another president failed as Hoover has failed." His fear may have been exaggerated, since most Americans appeared more in the grip of a deep pessimism than seized by revolutionary fervor. Still, it seemed likely that disillusion with democracy and liberal capitalism would spread rapidly—as it already had in Germany, Italy, and Japan—if the government did nothing to combat the Depression.

To a large degree Roosevelt relied on his appeal to what he called the "forgotten man" to stimulate widespread support for New Deal programs. Much of his effectiveness stemmed from his ability to communicate directly to the American people. During his first two terms as president he held an astounding seven hundred press conferences. Journalists adored good-natured banter with the president, and their stories reflected their affection for him, despite the fact that most newspaper owners opposed the New Deal.

Roosevelt found radio an even more direct and effective way to connect with citizens. Within days of his inauguration in 1933 he delivered his first "fireside chat," a live broadcast in which he addressed millions of listeners in their kitchens and living rooms. Americans considered the president a guest in their homes and often planned their evening activities around his talks.

Novelist Saul Bellow recalled the experience of listening to Roosevelt when he was a high school student in Chicago. Because he was working at an after-school job, Bellow feared he would be unable to join his family around the radio to hear the president speak. Walking home on a warm summer evening in the era before air conditioning, he was able to hear every word: cars driving on the street and each house he passed had their radios tuned to the fireside chat, and the president's reassuring words wafted through open windows and screen doors and onto the sidewalk.

Unlike Hitler and Mussolini, who also used the radio effectively, Roosevelt never roused his audience with calls for violence and revenge. His low-key approach included references to American heroes like Lincoln and Washington and ended with an appeal for God's mercy. Without patronizing his audience, Roosevelt discussed the domestic and international problems the country faced and his proposed solutions for them. People who lived in the 1930s and 1940s often recall that FDR gave "hundreds" of such inspirational talks. In fact, in twelve years as president he delivered only thirty. But their dramatic impact forged a sense of community among ordinary citizens and convinced them they had a friend in the White House. This, as much as anything, restored hope to millions of Americans.

✦✦✦

Biographical Profile

Eleanor Roosevelt, 1884–1962

Many Americans found a special friend in First Lady Eleanor Roosevelt. She transformed the role of First Lady from that of hostess to crusader for social justice and was an inspiration to women and minorities.

The child of a mother who did not like her and an alcoholic father, Eleanor Roosevelt was orphaned at ten years old and raised by relatives. When she married her distant cousin, Franklin, his mother objected bitterly and made life miserable for her daughter-in-law, forcing her to stop working at the Rivington Street Settlement House in New York City. The couple had six children, one of whom died in infancy.

Although Eleanor and Franklin admired each other throughout their marriage, as early as 1918 his extramarital affairs created an emotional distance between them. After polio crippled Franklin in 1921, Eleanor became politically active, often serving as her husband's surrogate in Democratic party affairs. During this period, she renewed her close cooperation with social workers, labor activists, and women's reform groups.

As First Lady, Eleanor Roosevelt helped establish much of the New Deal agenda. Her own

Roosevelt's appeal was especially strong among those traditionally outside of mainstream politics. He reached out to recent immigrants, blue-collar workers, and racial and ethnic minorities. They responded by becoming pillars of the Democratic Party, members of the so-called New Deal coalition, which would elect Roosevelt to four terms and contribute to the victory of all his Democratic successors.

✦ The New Deal in Action, 1933–1937

Roosevelt promised the American people action, and even if his programs sometimes failed, he delivered what he promised. In simplest terms, New Dealers hoped to achieve economic well-being through restoration of mass experience working with the poor and minorities provided her husband with an insight into a world he barely knew. Trade unionists, sharecroppers, and women's groups considered her their pipeline into government. She also emerged as the New Deal's leading advocate of civil rights. Beginning in 1937, she wrote a popular newspaper column, "My Day," that appeared in hundreds of papers.

Starting in the early days of the New Deal, she began a series of fact-finding trips to survey the condition of the poorest Americans. On one trip, she trudged across a half mile of mud to visit the shack of a migrant farmer. When she knocked on the door, a laborer opened it and said, "Oh, Mrs. Roosevelt, you've come to see me." Even this most humble of Americans seemed to think it perfectly reasonable that the president's wife would drop in for a chat. In 1933 the *New Yorker* magazine ran a cartoon showing two weary miners glancing as an elevator cage descended. "Oh migosh, here comes Mrs. Roosevelt to check on things," one remarked. A few months later, life imitated art as the First Lady, hard hat and all, descended into a West Virginia coal mine. On average, she traveled two hundred days and as many as forty thousand miles each year to inspect federal projects, rural communities, and poor city neighborhoods. One Washington newspaper ran a humorous headline that proclaimed, "Eleanor Spends Night in White House!"

Reflecting on her relationship with her husband, Mrs. Roosevelt observed that FDR:

> *might have been happier with a wife who was completely uncritical. That I was never able to be, and he had to find it in other people. Nevertheless, I think I sometimes acted as a spur, even though the spurring was not always wanted or welcome. I was one of those who served his purposes.*

---

purchasing power. Neither Roosevelt nor his advisers possessed a master plan. They promoted various, sometimes contradictory approaches to restore industry, stabilize agriculture, boost employment, and help the needy.

During Roosevelt's first day in office the banking crisis threatened to overwhelm the nation's credit system. Five thousand banks had failed since 1929, and runs by nervous depositors threatened to take down the remaining banks (see figure). Roosevelt proclaimed an emergency nationwide "bank holiday," closing all banks for several days while he and Congress enacted legislation to salvage the system. In record time, Congress approved a rescue package that permitted the Treasury Department and the Federal Reserve Board to decide which banks were solvent and allow them to reopen. Government agencies would take over insolvent banks and assist depositors. To provide cash for banking operations, the RFC loaned federal dollars to solvent

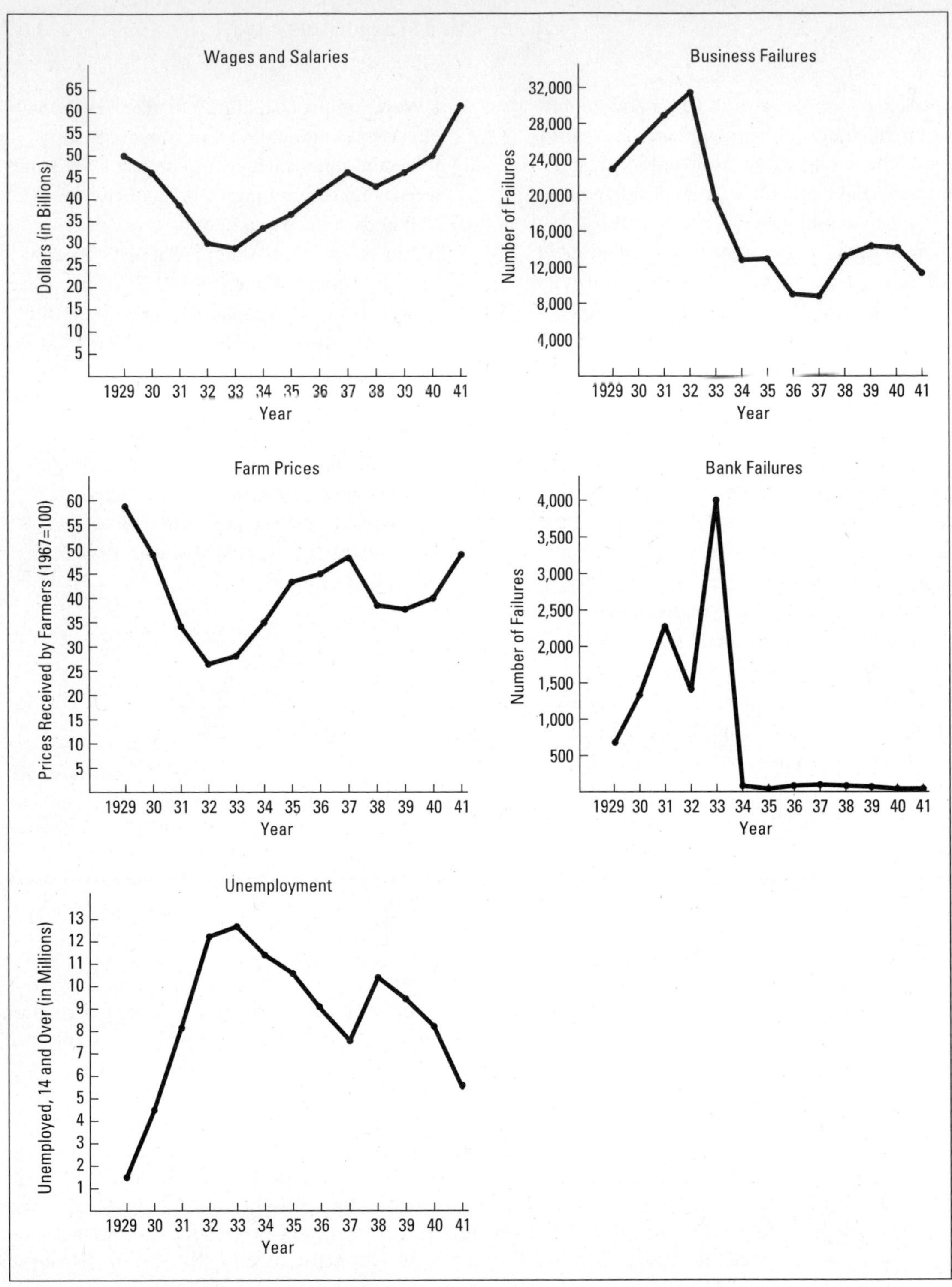

The Economy Before and After the New Deal, 1929–1941 The Federal government played a role in all aspects of the nation's economy.

banks. Three months later Congress sent the Glass-Steagall Act to the White House. It established tighter federal controls over banking practices, ensuring that deposits would not be used for stock speculation or other risky ventures. If a bank did fail, the new Federal Deposit Insurance Corporation (FDIC) guaranteed deposits up to $5,000.

In his first fireside chat of March 12, 1933, Roosevelt explained to a radio audience of 20 million Americans how these safeguards would work. "We had a bad banking system," he admitted. "Some of our bankers had showed themselves either incompetent or dishonest in handling the peoples' funds. . . . And so it became the government's job to straighten out this situation." Now, he assured the public, "it is safer to keep your money in a reopened bank than it is to keep it under the mattress."

In May 1933 Roosevelt prodded Congress to pass the Securities Act, which required corporations selling shares to the public to report on their financial condition. He followed this in 1934 by signing the Securities Exchange Act, which established the Securities and Exchange Commission (SEC), giving it power to oversee the nation's stock markets. These laws, like the banking acts, curbed the worst abuses in the financial markets and restored confidence among depositors and investors.

During the so-called First Hundred Days of the New Deal the president signed fifteen major pieces of legislation designed to stabilize the financial system, promote industrial recovery, raise farm prices, help the unemployed, and allow production of beer and wine. (The Twenty-First Amendment, approved in December 1933, repealed Prohibition.) Ever since then, presidents' success has been gauged by the accomplishments of their first hundred days in office. The twin pillars of the early New Deal program were the National Industrial Recovery Act and the Agricultural Adjustment Act, designed to spur industrial production and stabilize farm prices, respectively.

The National Industrial Recovery Act, passed in June 1933, created the National Recovery Administration (NRA), a federal agency empowered to coordinate business responses to the Depression. NRA chief General Hugh Johnson, inspired in some ways by Hoover's "associationalism," sought to promote recovery through business cooperation. Each industry would be pressed to subscribe to "codes of behavior," which would include pledges to avoid cutthroat competition, wage reductions, and price cutting. Companies were expected to hire additional workers at decent wages. Meanwhile, for the first time the government would officially support labor unions and workers' right to bargain collectively. In exchange, the government would exempt participating businesses from antitrust restrictions. At Roosevelt's prompting, Congress tacked on to the act a $3.3 billion appropriation to create the Public Works Administration (PWA) to stimulate demand by starting large construction projects.

The National Industrial Recovery Act appeared to contain something for everyone. Business received antitrust waivers, workers were promised higher wages and union recognition, and the unemployed expected jobs from PWA projects. Unfortunately, the economic impact of the NRA proved negligible.

Employers liked the opportunity to raise prices but resisted hiring new workers, raising wages, or bargaining with unions. Restoring business confidence through voluntary cooperation was not enough to boost employment, production, and profits. Some new source of mass purchasing power had to be injected into the economy to "prime the pump." In 1933 and 1934, only the government had the resources to do so, but the Roosevelt administration was reluctant to engage in substantial deficit spending. PWA construction projects were slow to start and amounted to only a drop in the bucket.

By the end of 1934 it was apparent that the NRA had failed to spark economic recovery. In 1935 the conservative majority that dominated the Supreme Court (discussed later) killed the NRA by its decision in the *Schecter* case. The Court ruled that processing chickens (Schecter's business) was a local, not interstate, business, over which the federal government had no authority. The Court eventually struck down many New Deal programs on this basis.

In 1933 the plight of America's farmers grabbed the attention of the Roosevelt administration and Congress even more than the hardship of industrial workers and the urban poor. As noted previously, farmers made up 30 percent of the nation's work force during the 1930s (compared to under 2 percent today). The clout wielded by their lobbying organizations and political representatives easily surpassed that of organized labor.

Nearly all sectors of agriculture in the United States suffered from a variety of market and environmental problems. Commodities such as cotton, wheat, tobacco, corn, cattle, pigs, and milk were especially hard hit, with prices diving to a fraction of their pre-Depression levels. As wheat prices fell from $3.00 a bushel in 1929 to 30 cents in 1932, farmers grew desperate. Some tried direct action to raise prices. The Farmer's Holiday Association, organized by Milo Reno in 1932, encouraged farmers to stop marketing their goods or to halt the transport of dairy products and grain to force up prices. When farm property was seized because of unpaid mortgages, neighbors often packed the resulting sheriffs' auctions to ensure that the land was sold for no more than a nickel or a dime and then returned to its owner.

But most farmers responded to falling prices by increasing their production. Since no mechanism existed to enforce general cutbacks, everyone felt compelled to produce as much as possible, which only worsened the problem. Proposals to subsidize farmers foundered on the question of how to control production, to prevent the government from bankrupting itself through unlimited crop support payments.

To deal with this problem Roosevelt appointed one of the country's most knowledgeable farm experts, Henry A. Wallace, as his secretary of agriculture. Wallace was an accomplished plant geneticist, editor of *Wallace's Farmer,* a major agricultural journal, and a broadly learned man. Although critics later portrayed him as a radical who dabbled in spiritualism, he possessed a practical understanding of agriculture's problems. Between 1933 and 1945, as agriculture secretary, vice president, and secretary of commerce, Wallace took the lead among FDR's advisers in promoting the importance of science and technology in solving economic problems. He promoted the rights of labor and argued that deficit spending was needed to create full employment. Farm prosperity, he recognized, depended on industrial recovery.

During the First Hundred Days, Congress passed the Agricultural Adjustment Act. A broad, enabling piece of legislation, it empowered the secretary of agriculture to authorize direct payments to farmers in exchange for their reducing their tilled acreage. It also allowed the government to sponsor deals between farmers and processors to ensure a minimum price for agricultural products. To reduce the farm surplus in 1933, the government paid farmers to plow under crops already planted and to slaughter piglets. With so many Americans going hungry, this one-time measure generated much negative publicity.

If, despite these measures, farmers still produced more than they could sell, the Commodity Credit Corporation would loan them money against crops placed in storage. This scheme resembled the Populist's idea of a subtreasury system (see Chapter 1). For example, farmers might receive 10 cents per pound for unsold cotton placed in storage. If the market price for cotton rose above 10 cents, farmers could reclaim their stored cotton and sell it. If the price remained below 10 cents, the farmer could keep the loan money and abandon the cotton to the government.

The goal of balancing supply and demand was to raise farm income to "parity," which was calculated based on the price ratio between agricultural and manufactured goods in the period 1909–1914. To fund its support programs, the Agricultural Adjustment Act levied a tax on agricultural processing firms, such as grain mills. As it had concerning the NRA's programs, in January 1936 the Supreme Court ruled the act unconstitutional. In the *Hoosac Mills* case the Court held that agriculture was primarily a state and local matter, not a feature of interstate commerce.

Roosevelt and Congress temporarily got around this ruling through legislation that created special "soil conservation" programs, which paid farmers (less than the agriculture act) not to plant wheat and corn, ostensibly to protect fragile soil. In 1938, after a change in the Supreme Court's membership (discussed later in the chapter), Congress passed a new farm act. Like the Agricultural Adjustment Act, it provided for price support payments; but unlike the earlier law it contained weaker provisions for production control. This exposed a dilemma in federal agriculture policy. Farmers wanted as much government financial assistance as possible—and as few controls as they could get away with. The long-term result was a return to surplus production. Demand generated during World War II cushioned the impact of the surplus for some time. By the 1950s the increased use of chemical fertilizers, herbicides, and pesticides, as well as expanded mechanization, led to ever-bigger imbalances. However, the federal price support structure shielded farmers from the market.

The Agricultural Adjustment Act mostly aided larger, relatively prosperous farmers. By 1937 New Deal planners had recognized the special problems faced by farmers on marginal land; by migrant laborers, who were often

Dust Bowl "refugees" streamed out of the Midwest during the 1930s. *Library of Congress*

landless whites and Hispanics; and by southern sharecroppers, many of whom were black. These agricultural workers had little money and less clout. The newly created Farm Security Administration initiated several programs to assist these groups, such as resettling on better land those who worked the poorest soil, building model housing in rural areas, and providing social services to migrants. But even small-scale efforts provoked strong opposition by southern landowners and large California commercial growers. Roosevelt, who needed political support from southern and western Democrats in Congress, hesitated to upset these allies. Ironically, some New Deal programs actually hurt the poorest farmers. For example, price supports paid on cotton enabled landowners to mechanize their farms and dispose of tenants and sharecroppers.

For all their limits, New Deal farm programs proved crucial during the worst years of the Depression, boosting net farm income from $2 billion in 1933 to $4.6 billion in 1939. During those years the federal government spent about $4.5 billion on direct payments to farmers. This set the pattern for agricultural policy for the next half century, with the farm sector becoming the most heavily subsidized part of the economy.

The New Deal also tried to address other problems of western and rural America. During the 1930s, overplowing on the Great Plains, the destruction of native grasses, and prolonged drought created the Dust Bowl, a major ecological disaster. Fierce windstorms blowing from west to east picked up dry topsoil and blocked out the sun, sometimes for days. Oklahoma folk singer Woody Guthrie described these storms in haunting ballads. In his 1939 novel *The Grapes of Wrath,* novelist John Steinbeck immortalized the Joads, a mythical Oklahoma farm family that had been forced to become migrants by hard times and bad weather.

One single dust storm, on May 11, 1934, blew an estimated 300 million tons of topsoil out of states like Oklahoma and Kansas, depositing much of it in eastern cities and the Atlantic Ocean. That year alone, 334 million acres of western farmland suffered wind damage (see map). As a result, by 1935 one million people had left the Plains states. Of these so-called Okies (migrant farm workers, mostly from Oklahoma and nearby states), three hundred thousand traveled west along Route 66 to California in search of jobs.

Roosevelt, long an advocate of conservation, responded vigorously. The Civilian Conservation Corps (CCC), one of the first federal programs to hire

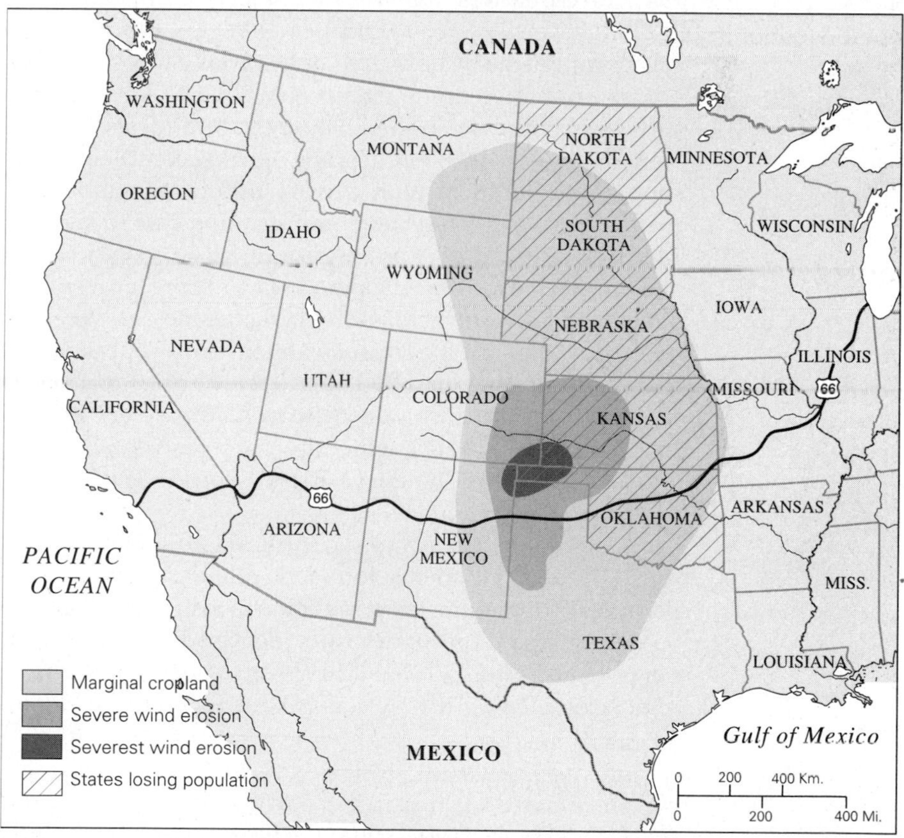

Dust Bowl States This map shows the areas affected by drought and winds of the 1930s.

the unemployed, mobilized over 2 million young urban men between 1933 and 1941 to work on rural conservation projects. Dressed in uniforms and living in military-style camps run by the army, they fought fires, dug irrigation canals, and, at FDR's direction, planted 200 million trees as part of a vast system of windbreaks, or "shelterbelts," in the Midwest. At the time, many experts scoffed at this idea, but in fact, the windbreaks worked as FDR had hoped. Decades later, however, as memories of the Dust Bowl faded, farmers cut down many of the trees to enlarge their fields. To protect the land from overgrazing, the Taylor Grazing Act of 1934 placed stricter limits on the numbers of cattle and sheep that could be grazed on public lands in the West.

Roosevelt also championed the Tennessee Valley Authority (TVA), created in 1933 to stimulate recovery in the Southeast and promote conservation. Its initial project, conceived in the 1920s, was to build a series of dams along the Tennessee River to prevent floods, provide irrigation water, and generate inexpensive electricity in one of the poorest regions of the United States. In 1933 only 2 percent of farms in the TVA area had electric power; by 1945 three-quarters did. The TVA helped spur economic development in the South, especially once World War II began. But it disappointed many of its early proponents by operating basically as a large, government-owned utility, not a regional planning agency sensitive to local needs. Despite the TVA's success, Congress rebuffed Roosevelt's requests in the late 1930s to fund similar projects in other regions. Critics complained that the government should not compete with private utilities or undertake central economic planning. So the Roosevelt administration had to settle for the more modest Rural Electrification Administration (REA) program, which provided loans and tax incentives for cooperatives to bring power to rural America. The benefits to farm households and rural businesses were obvious, since electricity made it possible for rural consumers to buy appliances such as refrigerators and washing machines. By 1945 rural electrification reached about 40 percent of American farms, compared to only 10 percent in 1933. Nearly everyone living on a farm that benefited from the REA recalled the day electric power reached them. In a note to a friend, Roosevelt called REA one of his most important legacies.

As a region, the American West led all other parts of the country in per capita federal payments for work relief, construction projects, and loans. Because of their greater population density, the East, upper Midwest, and South received more money from the New Deal over all, but they received less per person. Between 1933 and 1939, on a per capita basis, the Rocky Mountain region received $716, the Pacific Coast $424, and the Plains states $380.

A New Deal for Labor

As part of its effort to promote recovery, the New Deal assisted the growth of industrial labor unions. Between 1930 and 1940 the proportion of nonfarm workers in labor unions tripled, from under 8 percent to 23 percent. By 1945 they had reached a historic high of 25 percent. Before 1933 union membership was concentrated among railroad, coal, skilled construction, and, to a lesser extent, garment workers. The largest labor organization, the American Federation of Labor (AFL), represented mostly skilled tradesmen, such as electricians, and often took conservative political stands. By 1940 many steel, automotive, rubber, and electrical manufacturing workers belonged to new industrial unions, which became a critical part of Roosevelt's New Deal political coalition, providing both votes and financial support to the Democratic Party.

The federal government and courts had a long history of hostility to labor unions. Before 1933 they sanctioned a variety of antiunion measures, including blacklisting of workers, espionage, court injunctions against strikes, and the aggressive use of police and state militia to break strikes.

Change began with Section 7A of the National Industrial Recovery Act of 1933. It stipulated that industries that received NRA help had to allow their workers to organize unions, and the employers had to negotiate contracts with those unions. Although many companies wiggled out of this requirement, it provided the labor movement with momentum. This momentum culminated in the National Labor Relations Act of 1935, often called the Wagner Act for its sponsor, New York Democratic senator Robert Wagner. The law created the National Labor Relations Board to enforce the right of workers to join unions without retaliation. Activists such as John L. Lewis of the United Mine Workers, Sidney Hillman of the Amalgamated Clothing Workers, and Victor and Walter Reuther of the United Automobile Workers took advantage of the new mood to form a rival to the AFL, the Congress of Industrial Organizations (CIO), in 1935. Over the next three years automobile, steel, rubber, and coal workers in CIO-affiliated unions went on the offensive. For example, in 1937 automobile workers at GM and Ford plants in Flint and Detroit, Michigan, pushed forward by the Reuther brothers, engaged in prolonged sit-down strikes. For several weeks workers occupied the assembly lines, assisted by wives and women supporters who braved a gauntlet of company thugs to bring food to the strikers. Unlike the case in earlier labor conflicts, the Roosevelt administration and New Deal allies such as Michigan governor Frank Murphy refused to send troops or police to evict the workers. These tactics forced the automobile and steel manufacturers to recognize the unions and bargain with them.

Even during the depths of the Depression, most labor activists did not seek to overthrow capitalism. The automobile and steel workers demanded higher wages and benefits, job security, and more influence on the shop floor. Communists often played key roles in organizing campaigns, but most rank-and-file union members rejected anticapitalist doctrines. Rather, out of gratitude for FDR's encouragement, they became fierce supporters of the New Deal. The prosperity brought about by the Second World War enhanced the belief among union members that as long as they had friends in Washington, they could cooperate with corporate America.

Relief, Politics, and Social Security

Given the slow pace of economic recovery during the 1930s, for many Americans the most vivid measure of the New Deal's effectiveness was the creation of welfare programs to help the millions of unemployed. With private charities and local relief agencies overwhelmed, the federal government for the first time provided welfare money directly to states, under the Federal Emergency Relief Administration (FERA), created during the First Hundred Days. Fearing an erosion of personal responsibility and the creation of big government, President Hoover had refused to give federal dollars to state relief programs or directly to the unemployed. Roosevelt gave the Federal Emergency Relief Administration a budget of $500 million; half went directly to the states, and the other half was distributed to them as matching funds. Over the next several years the federal government initiated a variety of programs to assist the needy, hire the unemployed, and provide for the elderly.

To administer the FERA, FDR chose Harry Hopkins, a relief administrator who had worked for him in New York. Born and educated in Iowa, Hopkins was trained as a social worker and had participated in the settlement house movement. He personified the urban, liberal New Deal with its vision that all citizens were entitled to a measure of economic security. Irreverent and hard-drinking, Hopkins became a lightening rod for conservative critics. He quickly emerged as FDR's closest adviser, pushing the president toward more radical social reform initiatives. A battle with cancer removed Hopkins from the center of power in the late 1930s. Although still frail, he rallied during World War II to serve as Roosevelt's most intimate foreign policy adviser and personal emissary to Winston Churchill and Joseph Stalin.

The absence of a federal social welfare bureaucracy in 1933–1934 forced Hopkins to work through local officials and agencies. Following custom in the South and West, these agencies often discriminated against minorities or curtailed relief payments by allocating minimal matching funds. Mississippi, for example, decided that no family should receive more than $3 per week for relief, even though federal authorities believed $12 should be the minimal level. In Phoenix, Arizona, local officials discouraged relief requests by making applicants sit for a day in a room where the temperature exceeded 100 degrees. Those who remained were divided into five categories: Mexican-Americans, Indians, Mexican immigrants, blacks, and whites. Usually relief payments for blacks, Indians and Hispanics were one-third to one-half that provided to whites.

To overcome such impediments, in 1934 Hopkins got Congress to create the Civil Works Administration (CWA). Soon the CWA employed 4 million workers, largely on road construction and public building projects. (The PWA, under the direction of Secretary of the Interior Harold Ickes, concentrated on a few large projects, such as dams, and did not specifically hire the unemployed.) In lobbying for the new agency, Hopkins argued that the poor were not morally inferior deadbeats but fellow citizens who had been victimized by external events. Like many conservatives, he and Roosevelt worried that long term relief would undermine individual responsibility and the work ethic. As a solution to this problem they favored work relief. "Give a man a dole and you save his body and destroy his spirit," Hopkins remarked. "Give a man a job and pay him an assured wage, and you save both the body and the spirit."

In spite of these sentiments, the Roosevelt administration moved cautiously to create a massive federal work relief program and a comprehensive welfare system. During his 1932 campaign and his first three years as president, FDR downplayed appeals to class or regional divisions. He stressed nationalist themes and became a strong supporter of FBI director J. Edgar Hoover's war on crime (even though crime had not increased very much). The president and Hoover recognized that whenever FBI agents, or "G-Men," brought down a notorious gangster such as bank robber John Dillinger, the public felt reassured that its government was working.

This symbolism only went so far, however. By 1935 Roosevelt had come in for criticism from more radical elements, including the American Communist Party, Senator Huey Long of Louisiana, Dr. Francis Townsend (a prominent social reformer), and Father Charles Coughlin (an influential political activist). All accused him of doing too little to help the poor. While these groups and individuals had little use for each other, they shared a common belief that "conspirators"—industrialists, bankers, Jews, or other minorities—were responsible for America's problems. Each mounted a challenge to the New Deal, although none took root.

The Depression generated the first mass appeal for communism in America. The Communist Party had only seven thousand members in 1930, but it expanded quickly as the economy deteriorated. The party championed reforms for the poor, minorities, and the unemployed. By 1939 party membership had risen to one hundred thousand. These numbers must be viewed in historical context, however. As many as two or three hundred thousand Americans flirted with or joined the party during the thirties. Membership rose dramatically in 1935–1936 when the Communist leadership in the United States and abroad encouraged a "united front" of cooperation with liberal leaders such as Roosevelt. But bitter inner-party feuds over the Soviets' decision to end the united front policy, disgust with Stalin's brutal purges in the Soviet Union, and disillusion when Stalin joined Hitler in a nonagression pact in 1939 cut deeply into party support. To their disappointment, Communist leaders in the United States discovered that most Americans—including their own membership—generally supported New Deal reforms and found Roosevelt a great deal more appealing than Stalin.

Father Charles Coughlin, a radio priest from Detroit, posed a challenge from the opposite direction. Coughlin had gained a following before the Depression for attacking communism and birth control. He initially supported the New Deal, but within two years he had turned against it, organizing the

National Union for Social Justice as his alternative. Coughlin blamed bankers, foreigners, and, increasingly, Jews for the nation's economic woes.

Dr. Francis Townsend, a California physician, attacked Roosevelt for not helping the elderly. In 1934 he campaigned for a monthly pension of $200 for every older American, with the provision that they spend it within thirty days, thus benefiting themselves and the economy. Townsend organized a network of several thousand "Townsend Clubs" and published the *Townsend National Weekly*. Especially in the West, Townsend's followers provided vital support to Republican congressional candidates.

Louisiana's flamboyant Democratic political boss, Huey Long, provided the most serious challenge to the New Deal. A Louisiana governor and senator (sometimes both at once), Long won office by appealing to the state's rural poor, attacking the Standard Oil Company, and intimidating his opponents. As governor, beginning in 1929, Long spent lavishly on improving Louisiana's miserable system of education, roads, and public services. He began taxing the powerful oil companies that dominated the state's economy. Entering the Senate in 1931, he blamed the Depression on the maldistribution of wealth in the United States and proposed a "soak the rich" program to give the poor money to buy the good things in life. In 1934 he launched his "Share Our Wealth" campaign, which promised every American a grant of $5,000 to buy a home and an annual income of at least $2,500. To pay for this he would confiscate family fortunes over $5 million and allow no annual incomes over $1.8 million.

Like Coughlin, Long began as a Roosevelt supporter but ended up a bitter opponent. Along with Townsend, they highlighted some real problems—the meagerness of aid to the poor, the maldistribution of wealth, the insecurity of the elderly—but they proposed fantastical solutions. Coughlin, for example, resurrected the old chestnuts of coining silver and nationalizing the banks. These policies would have helped almost no one. Townsend's pensions were to be financed though a regressive federal tax, hitting the poor hardest and yielding only about $50 to $75 per month, not the promised $200. Long's pledge to make "every man a king" was similarly illusory. To grant every family a $5,000 home allowance and a $2,500 annual income would require soaking not just the rich, but everyone.

Long, Townsend, and Coughlin—like the Communists they despised—blamed demons such as Wall Street financiers and the Rockefellers for the nation's troubles. But they failed to lay out any real alternative vision for the economy. Still, many Americans found their promises appealing. By 1935 Long had organized some twenty-seven thousand "Share Our Wealth Clubs," with as many as 8 million members. The senator, who anticipated support from the followers of Coughlin and Townsend, seemed poised to challenge Roosevelt in 1936. Even if he failed to secure the Democratic nomination, by running as an independent Long could tip the race to the Republican candidate.

These challenges help explain why in 1935 FDR launched what his supporters called the Second New Deal. This renewed flurry of reform legislation

WPA workers help control a flood. Millions of Americans were employed in useful labor by this and other New Deal agencies. *Franklin D. Roosevelt Library*

resulted in steeper taxes on great wealth; new controls on large corporations; the Wagner Act, promoting industrial unions; the Rural Electrification Administration; and, above all, the creation of a massive work relief program and the Social Security Administration. These programs undercut the appeals of FDR's critics.

In 1935 Roosevelt asked Congress to appropriate about $5 billion for an expanded work relief program. The bulk of the funds went to a new agency, the Works Progress Administration (WPA), headed by Hopkins. During the next six years—the agency formally closed in 1943, but its activities largely ceased after the United States entered World War II in December 1941—the WPA employed between 1.5 and 3.3 million people per month at wages that varied from $21 to $55. During these years about 8 million Americans, or 20 percent of all adult workers, spent some period of time employed by the WPA. The number of people employed on WPA projects in New York City alone exceeded the size of the U.S. Army. All told, the WPA spent over $10 billion. But even this sum was enough to hire only about a third of the people who sought assistance.

Most WPA workers built roads (650,000 miles), parks (over 8,000), airports (853), public buildings such as schools and hospitals (125,000), and bridges (nearly 125,000 constructed or repaired). But the WPA also employed visual artists, writers, actors, playwrights, and musicians. WPA programs such as the National Youth Administration paid students small stipends to remain in school or to receive technical training. Hallie Flannigan headed the WPA's Federal Theater Project, which provided work for thousands of actors and other theater personnel, who performed plays for free to audiences in parks and public buildings throughout the nation. The Federal Arts Project hired several thousand out-of-work musicians to create thirty-eight symphony orchestras that toured the country. It also hired visual artists to produce paintings, murals, and sculpture for public buildings. Nearly every major American artist active in the 1930s worked at some time for the WPA's art project. In addition, five thousand writers worked for the Federal Writer's Project, assembling such varied publications as guidebooks, local histories, and a collection of slave narratives that chronicled the memories of elderly blacks. The WPA defied the culture of discrimination by establishing, under the leadership of South Carolina educator Mary McLeod Bethune, a special program to assist blacks.

The New Deal moved to close other gaps in the welfare net as well. Until 1935 neither the states nor the federal government provided much assistance to poor single-parent families. Few states offered unemployment benefits for those temporarily out of a job. As for those workers lucky enough to keep their job during the Depression, only about one out of seven had a retirement pension. As they aged, most had to keep working, draw on savings, or seek aid from relatives.

The landmark Social Security Act of 1935, inspired by a measure passed by Wisconsin progressives in the 1920s, committed the federal government to create a retirement system as well as national standards for unemployment insurance, disability payments, survivors' benefits, and aid to families with dependent children. Unemployment insurance and family aid benefits were made primarily state programs, with federal guidelines and financial support. Because of this, assistance levels varied widely from state to state. In the late 1930s the monthly payment in Arkansas for a mother with young children was $8, compared to $61 in Massachusetts. Over the next several decades benefits became more standardized.

Old-age pensions composed the heart of the Social Security Act. Under the law, employers and employees each contributed a small percentage of their weekly salary into a federal pension fund. In effect, younger workers of each generation helped finance the retirements of older workers, and they would benefit similarly when they reached the retirement age of 65. This so-called entitlement went to all who contributed to the system during their working lives, with each person's benefits pegged partly to the amount he or she had paid in. Political resistance from southern and western members of Congress forced the administration to drop coverage for some of those most in need of a pension, including migrant farm workers, waitresses, and household domestics—all occupations in which women and minorities were heavily represented. For covered workers, pension payments in 1940 were only $15 per month. Benefits increased substantially during later decades.

In addition to the humanitarian and political impulses that inspired New Deal relief spending, several of Roosevelt's advisers believed expanded work relief would help the economy. In part because other approaches had failed, New Deal planners gradually concluded that deficit spending might produce economic growth and new jobs. But Roosevelt was dubious about this before 1938, and not until World War II did the impact of deficit spending become clear.

British economist John Maynard Keynes published his *General Theory of Employment, Interest, and Money* in 1936, making the case for deficit spending as a tool to stimulate a sluggish economy by increasing mass purchasing power. As early as 1933 he and others had circulated the idea that in circumstances like those in the Depression, when private investment and orders for goods and services had declined drastically, the government could engage in "compensatory," or "countercyclical," spending to "prime the economic pump." Spending could take the form of building a playground, commissioning a symphony, constructing a dam, and so on. Building a dam, for example, involved placing orders for concrete and steel and creating government-financed jobs for the unemployed. Examples of this were the giant irrigation projects the New Deal initiated in the West. These included the Boulder and Grand Coulee Dams on the Colorado and Columbia Rivers and extensive irrigation canals in California. At the end of the spending chain, workers with money in their pockets would purchase food, pay rent, and buy clothes. Once recovery began, the government could collect additional tax revenues to restore a balanced budget.

Roosevelt had taken office pledging to slash government spending by as much as 25 percent. For humanitarian reasons, he deferred doing so. Hoover, a believer in balanced budgets, had accepted deficits of over $2 billion. Even with the money that went into the FERA, the CCC, and the PWA, New Deal spending only amounted to a paltry 5.9 percent of the gross national product (GNP) in 1936. Deficits during FDR's first three years in office ranged between $3.6 and $4.3 billion.

In evaluating the evolution of federal welfare policy, conservatives today charge the New Deal with having created a culture of dependency. Critics on the left complain that Roosevelt provided only the bare minimum to the poor—and only to stifle dissent. Yet the New Deal had to overcome immense obstacles to accomplish anything at all. During the 1930s over 46 million Americans, a third of the entire population, received some form of public assistance for a period of time. What angered Republicans as much as anything was the fact that for years afterward these benefits secured for the Democratic Party the political loyalty of working-class and minority voters.

The New Deal and Social Change

Along with the revolution in the size and scope of government during the 1930s came a change in the profile of federal workers. Previously most of those at the higher ranks in Washington were white, Anglo-Saxon men with a business background. Breaking tradition, the New Deal reached out to Catholics, Jews, African-Americans, immigrants and their children, and women. Individuals active in universities, labor unions, and social work were sought out. These appointees brought diverse views to policy deliberations and often acted as spokespersons for working-class, minority, and ethnic Americans. A number of Roosevelt's closest advisers, such as Thomas Corcoran, James Farley, Ben Cohen, Sam Rosenman, and Felix Frankfurter, came from Irish or Jewish backgrounds. Harry Hopkins, the first professional social worker to serve a president, became FDR's most trusted adviser on domestic and foreign affairs.

An unprecedented number of women also served in mid-level posts in New Deal agencies. The most important of these was Secretary of Labor Frances Perkins, the first woman to serve in a presidential cabinet. Like Eleanor Roosevelt, Perkins bridged the Progressive and New Deal Eras. After graduating from Mount Holyoke College in 1902, Perkins worked in the settlement house movement, agitated for women's suffrage, and campaigned for health and safety reforms for industrial workers. In 1918 New York Governor Alfred E. Smith appointed her to the State Industrial Board. She served Smith's successor, Governor Franklin D. Roosevelt, as chair of the board. When FDR moved to Washington in 1933 he nominated Perkins as secretary of labor.

As head of the Labor Department, Perkins dedicated herself to legislative efforts to improve the livelihood of American workers. She played a critical role in drafting the Social Security Act of 1935 and the Fair Labor Standards Act of 1938. Perkins was only one of two cabinet secretaries—the other was Interior Department head Harold L. Ickes—who served during all four Roosevelt terms.

The Roosevelt administration addressed only indirectly the social problems faced by ethnic Americans and minority groups. Most recent immigrants and second-generation Americans lived in the cities, and New Dealers believed that general economic recovery as well as work relief programs would assist them. Agencies like the WPA employed many Jews, Catholics, and eastern Europeans as local administrators, and these people made sure that urban areas received their fair share of work relief and construction projects. Ethnic Americans valued this assistance, and after 1933 they became a core constituency of the Democratic Party.

Although Roosevelt appointed Jews to high government posts in unprecedented numbers and counted several among his closest advisers, they were either unable or unwilling to assist Jewish refugees attempting to flee Nazi persecution during the 1930s. In November 1938, after the German government had stripped German Jews of most civil and economic rights, Nazi mobs set upon Jewish businesses, synagogues, and homes, smashing and looting in a destructive orgy known as *Kristallnacht,* or "Night of the Broken Glass." In the wake of this attack German police sent twenty thousand Jews to concentration camps, the forerunners of the mass extermination sites that appeared later. Roosevelt remarked that he could "scarcely believe that such things could occur in a twentieth-century civilization."

Before the outbreak of war in Europe in 1939, German and other European Jews who attempted to flee encountered legal barriers everywhere, including in the United States. The National Origins Act of 1924 restricted most immigration from eastern and southern Europe, even for those fleeing persecution. Even German Jews who theoretically qualified for entry into America under the unfilled German immigration quota faced a maze of red tape placed in their path by anti-Semitic members of the Department of State, led by one of the department's assistant secretaries, Breckinridge Long.

Fear of competition for scarce jobs during the Depression, in addition to latent anti-Semitism, created little sympathy for and much agitation against relaxing the country's strict limits on immigration. Roosevelt was already the target of anti-Semitic smears for his closeness with several Jewish advisers. Bristling at accusations that his name was actually "Rosenfeld" and that he led the "Jew Deal," FDR failed to confront the widespread hostility toward immigrants and refugees of any background and bowed to those demanding continued restrictions on immigration. He allowed the State Department to place impediments in the path of would-be immigrants seeking sanctuary. Only late in World War II, when it was possible to save Jews only in token numbers, did the president create the War Refugee Board, which helped victims fleeing the Holocaust by establishing camps in neutral countries or in territory recaptured from the Nazis.

Roosevelt's actions must be viewed in light of the American public's strong desire to admit fewer, not more, Jewish and other refugees. Even the president's Jewish advisers and the leaders of the American Jewish community feared a domestic backlash if they pressed too forcefully to change immigration policy. Thus, despite his minimal actions on behalf of persecuted European Jews, most American Jews saw Roosevelt as fair-minded and well-intentioned. Like other ethnic groups, they became strong supporters of the New Deal.

African-Americans, who suffered some of the worst ravages of the Depression, continued their postemancipation tradition of voting Republican in 1932. Three-fourths of all U.S. blacks lived in the South in the early 1930s, and few of them were allowed to vote. Among northern blacks, two-thirds voted for Herbert Hoover. Although Roosevelt sympathized with the hardships faced by blacks, he never directly challenged segregation. For political reasons, he declined to antagonize the powerful southern Democrats, whose votes he needed to move New Deal legislation through Congress. For example, the president declined to press Congress to make lynching a federal crime. Instead, Mrs. Roosevelt spoke in support of a new antilynching law.

Organizations like the National Association for the Advancement of Colored People (NAACP), the National Urban League, and the National Negro Congress protested the fact that, especially in the South, local officials denied blacks work relief benefits or paid them only half of what whites received.

Eleanor Roosevelt with Mary McLeod Bethune, Director of Negro Activities, and Aubrey Williams, head of the National Youth Administration. *Corbis-Bettmann*

Gradually the New Deal's civil rights record improved. Several key New Dealers, such as Harry Hopkins and Harold Ickes, insisted that the agencies they administered hire more blacks. Because they had to work through local officials, Hopkins and Ickes never achieved full equality for African-Americans. But in northern cities (where blacks voted), agencies like the WPA attempted to end discrimination in work relief. By 1939 about 1 million black families in the North had a member working for the WPA. These efforts were recognized and appreciated by blacks. As one African-American newspaper remarked, "what administration within the memory of man . . . had done a better job . . . considering the imperfect human material with which it had to work? The answer of course is none."

In spite of the New Deal's limited support for racial equality, blacks recognized that the Roosevelt administration was the best friend they had had in Washington since the Civil War. In 1936 blacks deserted the Republican Party and voted for FDR in overwhelming numbers. At the time, and afterward, some critics charged that FDR deluded African-Americans with hopeful rhetoric but offered only crumbs from the New Deal table. Yet, compared to what had preceded it, the New Deal took major steps in the direction of racial justice.

African-American employment in federal jobs tripled between 1933 and 1945, with many of the gains coming during World War II. Simple acts like Harold Ickes's abolishing segregation in the Department of the Interior's cafeteria attracted headlines. Blacks appointed to second-level administrative and judicial posts, including Mary McLeod Bethune, Robert Weaver, and William Hastie, made up an informal "black cabinet" that conferred with the First Lady and occasionally with the president. In 1939, when the Daughters of the American Revolution refused to allow black opera singer Marion Anderson to perform in its Washington concert hall, Eleanor Roosevelt resigned from the patriotic organization. She and Harold Ickes arranged for Anderson to perform on the steps of the Lincoln Memorial, before an audience of seventy-five thousand, on Easter Sunday. Eventually Roosevelt's eight appointments to the Supreme Court between 1937 and 1944 began to dismantle the legal framework for segregation established in the 1890s.

Mexican nationals and other Hispanics living in the West and Southwest fared poorly throughout the 1930s. Under Hoover the Department of Labor began to deport Mexican citizens to give more jobs to American citizens. Hoover's so-called repatriation campaigns focused on California, the Rocky Mountain states, and the Southwest, where state officials were also anxious to reduce the size of relief rolls. Between 1931 and 1933, for example, the city of Los Angeles chartered fifteen trains to transport over twelve thousand Mexicans across the border. The state of Colorado deported over twenty thousand. Federal authorities expelled over eighty thousand undocumented workers from the West. These efforts continued, with some adjustments, under the New Deal. By 1935 nearly half a million Mexicans—about the same number as had come to work in the United States during the 1920s—were repatriated. After the outbreak of World War II, however, the labor shortage in the United States prompted many of the same federal, state, and local officials to actively recruit Mexican laborers.

Unlike the hostility shown toward Mexicans, the indifference toward Jewish refugees, and the grudging support offered blacks, the New Deal made a sincere effort to improve the treatment of Indians. Since passage of the Dawes Act in 1887, almost two-thirds of reservation lands had been stripped away. The Native American population slowly increased after 1900, but almost half of all Indians who remained on reservations were landless. Meanwhile, pressure to assimilate them continued. During the 1920s the Bureau of Indian Affairs (BIA) banned many traditional religious ceremonies and stepped up efforts to send Indian children to boarding schools.

Secretary of the Interior Harold Ickes found this legacy, as well as the rampant corruption within the BIA, deplorable. He appointed John Collier, a man determined to reverse the policy of forced assimilation, eliminate corruption from the BIA, restore tribal self-government, and defend traditional culture, as Commissioner of Indian Affairs. Like so many New Deal administrators, Collier had been trained as a social worker and had participated in the settlement house movement. He developed an appreciation for cultural pluralism while working among Italian immigrants in New York. During the 1920s he visited his friend Mabel Dodge in Taos, New Mexico. Settling there, he became an advocate for the nearby Pueblo dwellers. Soon Collier emerged as a leading critic of federal Indian policy through his work as executive secretary of the American Indian Defense Association and as editor of the magazine *American Indian Life.*

Collier's good relations with Ickes and FDR helped secure assistance from several other New Deal agencies. The new BIA commissioner persuaded the CCC to create an Indian division, secured employment for Indians on reservation improvement projects as part of the Agricultural Adjustment Act, and lobbied Congress to pass the Pueblo Relief Act (1933), which paid the Pueblo tribe for land taken earlier. The Johnson-O'Malley Act of 1934 encouraged states to provide more educational opportunities and health care to Indians, reimbursing them for expenses. Collier also increased the number of Indians employed by the BIA from a few hundred to over four thousand. Determined to provide Indians with a modern education as well as incentives to preserve their traditions, the BIA began replacing distant boarding schools with community day schools, abolished restrictions on traditional religious ceremonies, and established an Indian Arts and Crafts Board, which promoted native arts and found commercial markets for Indian handicrafts. Collier even encouraged the restoration of buffalo herds.

Getting rid of the Dawes Act emerged as the focus of Collier's program. He proposed an Indian Reorganization Act to reverse the earlier law's land allotment policy, encourage the creation of tribal governments, and establish Indian corporations to control communal lands and manage their resources. For the first time in a century, powerful forces in the federal government were committed to advancing Indian interests.

Collier's proposals elicited strong opposition. Western landowners protested efforts to limit farming, ranching, and mining on or near reservations. Christian missionaries criticized lifting restrictions on traditional worship and depriving Christian religious teaching of its favored status on reservations. Members of Congress objected to losing federal authority over reservation land. Some Indians complained that Collier wanted them to "return to the blanket." As a result, the law passed in 1934 did not grant the reform-minded commissioner all the power he requested.

Besides the outside interests that opposed him, Collier's approach suffered from internal problems as well. He had generalized his view of the Indian experience from his contact with the New Mexico Pueblos, a tribe that had in fact escaped some of the worst injuries suffered by other tribes. The Pueblos retained a fair measure of their cultural traditions, social structure, and religious hierarchy. Many other tribes were more divided over the question of retaining their traditional values. Some tribes had few members and relatively large amounts of land; others had little land but many members. Factionalism—including the vexing question of what amount of "Indian blood" made a person a true Indian—divided some tribes so deeply that effective self-government was nearly impossible.

The Navaho of Arizona and New Mexico, the nation's largest tribe, dealt Collier's plan a severe blow when they narrowly rejected the BIA plan to establish self-government. Some Navaho believed the plan was connected to government efforts to reduce the number of sheep and goats permitted to graze on reservation land. BIA attempts to conserve soil collided with Navaho culture and social structures. Ultimately 77 tribes rejected self-government, whereas 181 others organized themselves under the new law.

In the end, forces outside Collier's control changed Indian life more than his reforms. During World War II as many as half of all Indians left the reservations to serve in the armed forces or work in defense plants. Many never returned. The war effort also promoted an ideology of nationalism, which conflicted with Collier's call for cultural pluralism. Several powerful members of Congress from the West demanded an end to BIA reforms, the abolition of the agency, and the termination of special status for Indians. In effect, they favored restoration of the Dawes Act.

Faced with mounting criticism, Collier resigned as head of the BIA in January 1945. Congress reverted to its former ways and began paying off Indian land claims with small cash settlements. Although most tribes were only marginally better off in 1945 than they had been in 1933, Collier had succeeded in getting the federal courts to recognize that tribal governments possessed at least limited "internal sovereignty" except when expressly limited by Congress. In later years this concept proved extremely important in establishing Indian rights.

The New Deal and Political Realignment

The fact that Franklin D. Roosevelt was the only president to serve four terms—and that in 1951 nervous conservatives secured ratification of the Twenty-second Amendment to prevent anyone else from doing so—speaks volumes about the general popularity of FDR and the New Deal. Huey Long, Roosevelt's most viable rival, fell victim to an assassin's bullet in 1935. Coughlin and Townsend joined Roosevelt-hater and Long disciple Gerald L. K. Smith in supporting the 1936 candidacy of North Dakota congressman William Lemke of the Union Party. As a dispirited Smith later admitted, Lemke had "the charisma of a deserted telephone booth"; he received 1.9 percent of the popular vote.

Like the U.S. Communist Party, populists on the Far Right attracted a core of fanatic adherents and a crowd of "soft" supporters. These sympathizers had gripes with the New Deal and FDR but did not share their leaders' alienation from the system. In 1936 Roosevelt scored an impressive victory over Republican Alf Landon of Kansas, winning forty-six of the then forty-eight states and over 60 percent of the popular vote. In the wake of the election Father Coughlin's church superiors silenced him, Townsend faded from view, and Smith become a marginal purveyor of hate.

When Congress convened in 1937, Democrats held seventy-six Senate seats, compared to the sixteen held by Republicans. In the House the Democratic edge over the Republicans stood at an immense 331 to 89. The results appeared to confirm a strong national consensus in favor of the Democratic

Party and the New Deal. Roosevelt had occasionally spoken of creating a new national "Progressive Party" that would join liberal Democrats and moderate Republicans. In any case, the Democrats' grip on Congress seemed to guarantee that the New Deal would move forcefully in the direction of economic, political, and social reform. Yet by 1938 the New Deal had ground to a halt. The president failed in his attempts to reorganize the Supreme Court. He seemed adrift as the economy slipped back into recession. And he failed in an effort to purge conservative southern Democrats from the party. In the wake of these setbacks, southern Democrats cooperated with revitalized Republicans to block new reform legislation.

Despite FDR's wide base of support in the North, conservative southern Democrats dominated Congress. Seniority rules gave even more power to long-serving southern members. Although as representatives of the country's poorest region they were eager to receive federal emergency relief and benefits, these Democrats had little enthusiasm for the broader goals of the New Deal. They looked with special alarm at programs that aided minorities or set national standards that conflicted with Jim Crow laws.

FDR brought one problem on himself with a bungled attempt to expand (or, as critics charged, "pack") the Supreme Court. Roosevelt's motive was understandable. Between 1934 and 1936 the conservative majority on the Court had repeatedly struck down as unconstitutional key pieces of New Deal legislation, arguing that the federal government—even in an economic emergency— lacked the authority to regulate wages, contracts, and working conditions. The High Court voided so many laws that it threatened the entire New Deal.

Roosevelt insisted that the Constitution gave him authority to meet "extraordinary needs by changes in emphasis." During FDR's first five years in office, none of the elderly conservative judges retired (including one who had been on the Court since 1910). Some administration officials believed they were staying on the bench—refusing to die, even—simply to stifle the New Deal. In 1937 FDR asked Congress for authority to dilute the conservative majority on the Supreme Court by appointing additional justices for each sitting justice over seventy years old. Ostensibly the new members would ease the "burden" borne by elderly incumbents. Although the Constitution allows Congress to change the size of the Supreme Court, since the 1860s it had contained nine justices, a number that had taken on a certain air of inviolability. To Roosevelt's surprise, many moderate and liberal members of Congress joined conservative Republicans in blocking the proposed court reform. This breathed new life into anti–New Deal forces.

Ironically, just as Congress rejected FDR's plan, one of the justices who usually voted with the conservative majority switched sides, and another decided to retire. Soon several other elderly conservatives stepped down. Between 1937 and 1945 Roosevelt appointed a total of eight Supreme Court justices, including Felix Frankfurter, Wiley Rutledge, Frank Murphy, Hugo Black, William O. Douglas, Stanley F. Reed, Robert H. Jackson, and James F.

Byrnes. After 1937 the High Court upheld nearly every New Deal law, ruling that the federal government possessed broad regulatory power over private contracts and commerce at the local, state, and national level.

Ironically, soon after the Supreme Court had affirmed the right of the federal government to intervene deeply in the economy, a severe recession and conservative resurgence shook popular confidence in Roosevelt's leadership and program. Between 1933 and 1937 the GNP had grown about 10 percent annually, industrial output had approached 1929 levels, and the unemployment rate had declined from 25 percent to 14 percent. In 1937 these positive signs convinced Roosevelt, as well as many conservative Democrats, that the government could safely scale back its recovery effort and job creation programs. Congress reduced overall federal spending by 10 percent, from $10.3 billion to $9.6 billion, and sharply cut funding for the WPA. At the same time, the initial collection of Social Security taxes pulled about $2 billion out of circulation. These reductions in purchasing power pushed the economy into a steep recession. Stock prices fell again, and unemployment surged.

Like Hoover before him, Roosevelt seemed trapped between advisers urging further cutbacks and those promoting expanded deficit spending. In the spring of 1938 Hopkins and Interior Secretary Harold Ickes finally persuaded the president to push through Congress $3.75 billion in deficit spending. This new spending restored moderate economic growth but the episode left Roosevelt with a dimmed halo. In 1939 and 1940, after war broke out in Europe, Roosevelt authorized additional military spending. Defense spending quickly accelerated the pace of industrial and job growth, a preview of what would occur during World War II. Between 1941 and 1945 government spending rose to one-third of GNP (compared to about 6 percent in 1933), and the federal budget deficit increased from a 1930s high of $4.3 billion to over $57 billion. The result was the fastest economic growth in American history and an end to the Depression.

The court-packing fiasco of 1937 and the recession of 1937–1938 stymied hopes nourished by the big Democratic victory of 1936. Roosevelt's position was further weakened in 1938 when he tried in vain to purge conservative Democrats from Congress. The president hoped that by breaking the seniority lock held by southern conservatives he could secure additional reform legislation. FDR campaigned on behalf of many liberal insurgents in Democratic primaries in the South, but most of the old guard won renomination and election anyway. Once returned to Congress, these veterans were even less inclined to support Roosevelt's agenda.

The 1938 election brought additional bad news for the president. Without FDR heading the ticket in the midterm contest, fewer Democrats turned out to vote. Republicans picked up eighty-one House and eight Senate seats. This revitalized Republican minority joined forces with southern Democrats to block New Deal proposals. The conservative coalition pressed for balanced budgets, curbs on labor unions, and less help for the unemployed. Southern Democrats adeptly played the race card, demanding a halt to federal efforts to assist blacks and other minorities. Although this coalition of Republicans and conservative Democrats lacked the votes to dismantle the New Deal, it stymied any additional advances. After 1938 the administration failed to secure passage of several priority bills, including tax reform, reorganization of the executive branch, and additional TVA-type regional development projects. Only by twisting arms did Roosevelt win approval for what turned out to be one of the last major pieces of New Deal legislation, the Fair Labor Standards Act of 1938. The law banned child labor, established a federal minimum wage, and set the regular work week at forty hours for many occupations. To secure passage, Roosevelt agreed to exempt from coverage agricultural and domestic workers, whose ranks included a high proportion of women, blacks, and Hispanics.

Conservative Democrats and Republicans joined forces in 1938 to establish the House Committee on Un-American Activities, chaired by Congressman Martin Dies of Texas. The committee investigated allegations of Communist (and, occasionally, fascist) penetration of labor unions and New Deal agencies. Dies and his colleagues were particularly eager to pin the "subversive" label on groups that campaigned for racial justice and on agencies such as the WPA and the Federal Theater Project.

As the threat to the United States from Germany and Japan increased after 1938, Roosevelt felt compelled to backpedal on domestic reform and to repair his tattered relations with business leaders and conservative elements in both the Democratic and Republican Parties. The support of southern Democrats, he reckoned, was vital to the national defense and to securing aid for beleaguered Western Europe and China. The Roosevelt administration downplayed talk of radically restructuring the economy, attacking monopolies, or redistributing wealth. The outbreak of war in Europe in 1939 pushed social reform even further into the background, where it largely remained until the 1960s.

✦ Conclusion

By most statistical measures the New Deal achieved only partial success in restoring the American economy between 1933 and 1940. Although the economy grew at a very respectable 10 percent per year during this period, so much had been lost between 1929 and 1933 that in 1940, after orders for armaments had begun to propel the economy forward, around 9 million workers, 15 percent of the labor force, still lacked regular jobs. Private investment remained 18 percent below 1929 levels. In 1941 the GNP barely surpassed the pre-Depression figure. Try as it did, the Roosevelt administration never developed fully coherent industrial, labor, farm, tax, welfare, or antitrust policies. The president remained reluctant to launch a major deficit spending program until 1938. By then, a coalition of conservative Democrats and resurgent Republicans blocked most New Deal initiatives.

Yet, in the midst of the most severe economic collapse in American history, Franklin Roosevelt accomplished great things. His focus on human needs provided vital relief and temporary work to millions of hungry, desperate individuals and families. His farm and conservation programs saved rural America and mitigated the ravages of nature and past abuse of the land. Millions of workers joined newly respectable labor unions and gained the ability to influence the conditions under which they worked. Blacks, Indians, and the descendants of recent European immigrants were given vital help to carry them through the worst of the Depression. The elderly could finally look forward to retirement with some dignity. In the process of achieving these reforms, the New Deal created a vastly expanded federal government, centered on the presidency, which assumed a growing responsibility for the health and livelihood of the American people. Above all, the New Deal sustained Americans' faith in democracy and liberal capitalism, faith that was lost in Germany and Japan during the 1930s.

In a sense the New Deal provided a holding pattern that sustained the American economy, people, and spirit through the Depression until the catalyst of the Second World War came along. As we will see, that awful conflict, so destructive of human life, had the unintended consequence of finally fulfilling many of Roosevelt's promises.

✦ Further Reading

On the Depression and the New Deal, see: Michael A. Bernstein, *The Great Depression: Delayed Recovery and Economic Change in America, 1929–39* (1988); Broadus Mitchell, *Depression Decade* (1947); Irving Bernstein, *The Lean Years* (1960), *Turbulent Years* (1970), and *A Caring Society: The New Deal, the Worker, and the Great Depression* (1985); Joan Hoff Wilson, *Herbert Hoover: Forgotten Progressive* (1975); Gary Dean Best, *FDR and the Bonus Marchers* (1992); Frank Friedel, *Launching the New Deal* (1973) and *A Rendezvous with Destiny* (1990); Anthony J. Badger, *The New Deal: The Depression Years, 1933–40* (1980); Studs Terkel, *Hard Times: An Oral History of the Depression* (1970); William E. Leuchtenburg, *Franklin D. Roosevelt and the New Deal* (1963) and *The Supreme Court Reborn: The Constitutional Movement in the Age of Roosevelt* (1995); Kenneth S. Davis, *FDR: The New Deal Years, 1933–37* (1986); James MacGregor Burns, *Roosevelt: The Lion and the Fox* (1956); Russel D. Buhite and David W. Levy, *FDR's Fireside Chats* (1992); Blanch Wiesen Cook, *Eleanor Roosevelt* (1992); Ellis Hawley, *The New Deal and the Problem of Monopoly* (1966); Peter Irons, *The New Deal Lawyers* (1982); Jordan Schwarz, *The New Dealers: Power and Politics in the Age of Roosevelt* (1993); George T. McJimsey, *Harry Hopkins: Ally of the Poor and Defender of Democracy* (1987); T. H. Watkins, *Righteous Pilgrim: The Life and Times of Harold Ickes* (1990); Alan Brinkley, *Voices of Protest: Huey Long, Father Coughlin, and the Great Depression* (1982) and *The End of Reform: New Deal Liberalism in Recession and War* (1995); Robert Warren, *Radio Priest: Charles Coughlin, the Father of Hate Radio* (1996); T. Harry Williams, *Huey Long* (1969); Harvey Klehr, *The Heyday of American Communism: The Depression Decade* (1984); Harvard Sitkoff, *A New*

Deal for Blacks (1978); Nancy Weiss, *Farewell to the Party of Lincoln: Black Politics in the Age of FDR* (1983); Richard Lowitt, *The New Deal in the West* (1984); Donald Worster, *Dust Bowl: the Southern Plains in the 1930s* (1979); Kevin Starr, *Endangered Dreams: The Great Depression in California*; Francisco Baldarrama and Raymond Rodriguez, *Decade of Betrayal: Mexican Repatriation in the 1930s* (1995); George Martin, *Madame Secretary* (1976); Lawrence Kelley, *The Assault on Assimilation: John Collier and the Origins of Indian Reform Policy* (1983); Lizabeth Cohen, *Making a New Deal: Industrial Workers in Chicago, 1919–39* (1991); Sidney Fine, *Sit Down: The General Motors Strike of 1936–37* (1969); Jerold Auerbach, *Labor and Liberty* (1966); Nelson Lictenstein, *The Most Dangerous Man in Detroit: Walter Reuther and the Fate of American Labor* (1995); Steven Fraser, *Labor Will Rule: Sidney Hillman and the Rise of American Labor* (1991); Steve Fraser and Gary Gerstle, eds., *The Rise and Fall of the New Deal Order, 1930–1980* (1989); Susan Ware, *Holding Their Own: American Women in the 1930s* (1982) and *Partner and I: Molly Dewson, Feminism, and New Deal Politics* (1987); David Hamilton, *From New Day to New Deal: American Farm Policy from Hoover to Roosevelt* (1991); Richard Kirkendall, *Social Scientists and Farm Politics in the Age of Roosevelt* (1966); Sidney Baldwin, *Poverty and Politics: The Farm Security Administration* (1968); Bruce Shulman, *From Cotton Belt to Sunbelt* (1991); Doris Kearns Goodwin, *No Ordinary Time: Franklin and Eleanor Roosevelt—The Home Front During WWII* (1994); Robert Dallek, *Franklin D. Roosevelt and American Foreign Policy* (1979); David Wyman, *The Abandonment of the Jews: America and the Holocaust, 1941–45* (1984).

✦✦✦
CHAPTER 6

The Restoration and Collapse of World Order, 1921–1941

✦ **FDR and Churchill at the Atlantic Charter Conference, August 1941.**

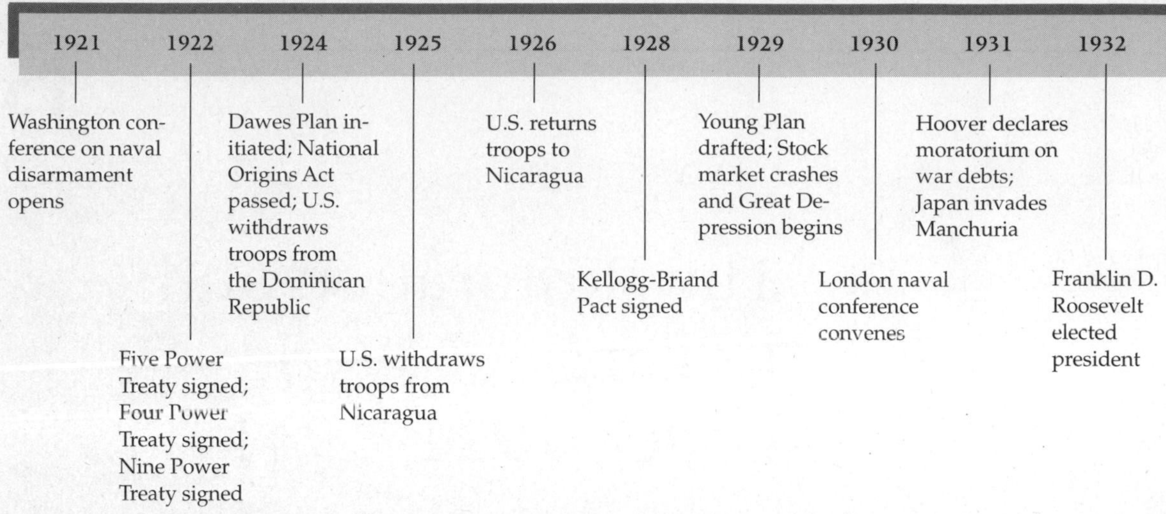

IN EUROPE, AS in America, times got worse and worse after the stock market crash of 1929. Leo Szilard, a young Jewish physics instructor at the University of Berlin, was one of the first to see what was coming. At an international academic meeting in Paris in 1930 he heard the German finance minister say that Germany could not pay any more war reparations unless she got her colonies back. At that point Szilard knew that Germany was about to engage in a frenzy of military expansion. He returned to Berlin, but he took the precaution of sending every penny he owned out of Germany, to Switzerland. Three years later Adolf Hitler, leader of the Nazi party, became chancellor of Germany. Hitler vowed to restore Germany's former glory and rid the country of Jews. Within months Szilard had fled his homeland for England, where he spent the next five years exploring the mysteries of the atom.

In 1938 Szilard came to Columbia University in New York to continue working with the world's most prominent group of nuclear physicists. By the

1933	1934	1935	1936	1937	1938	1939	1940	1941
Adolf Hitler becomes German chancellor; Good Neighbor policy adopted; London economic conference begins; U.S. intervenes in Cuba; U.S. withdraws troops from Nicaragua; U.S. extends diplomatic recognition to Soviet Union	Nye Committee investigates U.S. entry into World War I; U.S. withdraws troops from Haiti	Neutrality Act passed; Italy invades Ethiopia	Italy and Germany sign Axis Pact, Spanish Civil War starts; Neutrality Act revised	Sino-Japanese war begins; Neutrality Act revised again; Roosevelt gives quarantine speech; *Panay* sunk	Munich conference held	Nazi-Soviet nonagression pack signed; World War II begins in Europe; Neutrality Act revised a third time	America First Commitee founded; Committee to Defend America by Aiding the Allies founded; FDR agrees to swap destroyers for use of British bases; Selective Service system created; Roosevelt reelected	Lend-Lease passed; Atlantic Charter issued; Hull-Nomura talks proceed; Japan attacks Pearl Harbor; U.S. enters World War II

fall of that year he was convinced that war would break out in Europe, and he looked for ways to be useful to Hitler's enemies. Applying theories developed by Albert Einstein, another German-Jewish refugee from Nazism, Szilard believed it might be possible to split atoms of the radioactive heavy element uranium in a massive explosion that would unleash astonishing amounts of energy. The next summer, on the eve of the outbreak of war in Europe, Szilard persuaded Einstein to write President Franklin D. Roosevelt and request that the United States embark on an immense research project to develop an atomic bomb before German scientists did so. Roosevelt agreed, and the Manhattan Project was born.

Szilard, Einstein, and a few thousand other refugee intellectuals had a profound impact on American culture in the 1930s. They were among the lucky ones, because the United States was far less hospitable to immigrants after World War I than it had been before. Many thousand more German Jews, lacking special skills, money, or relatives or friends outside their homeland, never did find refuge in the six years between Hitler's ascension to power and the outbreak of World War II.

Between the First and Second World Wars, Americans came slowly to realize that what happened beyond their borders affected them directly. Before World War I, millions more people traveled west across the Atlantic Ocean as immigrants to the United States than went east as tourists or repatriates. That began to change after the 2 million U.S. soldiers who served in France during the Great War experienced Europe firsthand. In the twenty years after the armistice of 1918, Americans learned more than ever before about the rest of the world. The radio and the movies brought Europe and Asia home, and Americans spent billions of dollars abroad. U.S. involvement in international affairs grew during the two decades between the First and Second World Wars, despite early expectations that the United States would turn inward after the unhappy experience of World War I.

At the beginning of the period, many ordinary people and government leaders rejected President Woodrow Wilson's vision of a world order made harmonious by American leadership in the League of Nations. Still, throughout the 1920s the United States remained an active, although independent, world power.

Once the Great Depression had tightened its grip, in the winter of 1929–1930, Americans became preoccupied with finding a way out of the sickening economic slump. The Depression destroyed the limited but real progress that had been made toward restoring world harmony after the Great War. By the mid-1930s violent nationalists were threatening the peace in Europe and Asia. Americans were divided and confused over how the United States should respond to threats made by Germany, Italy, and Japan against other states. Until the actual outbreak of World War II, more Americans favored a policy of nonintervention in European and Asian disputes than advocated active resistance of aggression. Unhappy memories of the suffering brought by the First World War made many people deeply suspicious of claims that the United States had a moral responsibility to help others. Cooperating with other nations risked renewed war, a horrifying prospect.

But internationalism never died. Numerous U.S. opinion leaders, public officials, and ordinary citizens were deeply moved by the plight of the overseas victims of aggression. They urged that the United States do more to contain Nazi Germany, Fascist Italy, and Imperial Japan. From 1935 to 1939 President Franklin D. Roosevelt pursued a cautious policy concerning the collapse of order in Asia and Europe. A veteran of the Wilson administration, Roosevelt shared his old leader's commitment to forming partnerships for peace with other countries. During his unsuccessful run for vice president in 1920, Roosevelt forecast that "we must either shut our eyes . . . and live as a hermit nation, or we must open our eyes and see that modern civilization has become so complex" that it demands international cooperation. Personally Roosevelt detested the aggression of Germany, Italy, and Japan, but he recognized the depth of public opposition to U.S. involvement in another war. A gifted politician, Roosevelt slowly, carefully, and sometimes deceptively prepared the public for just such an eventuality, barely twenty years after the armistice of 1918.

✦ Security, Disarmament, and Economic Expansion in the 1920s

When Warren G. Harding, the handsome, conservative Republican senator from Ohio, won a landslide victory in the presidential election of 1920, his triumph signified in part a repudiation of Woodrow Wilson's blueprint for a new world order. At the center of Wilson's plan was active American participation in the League of Nations. The United States never did join the League of Nations, but the Republican administrations of Harding (1921–1923) and his successor, Calvin Coolidge (1923–1929), involved the United States in numerous international conferences. Secretary of State Charles Evans Hughes (1921–1925), Secretary of the Treasury Andrew Mellon (1921–1933), and Secretary of Commerce Herbert Hoover (1921–1929) moved forcefully to place the United States squarely in the center of efforts to restore stability following the Great War. They understood popular and congressional resistance to the League of Nations—and even shared some of it. They believed that the European powers might limit American freedom of action in the League, so they decided to work outside of it.

A movement toward disarmament was one Wilsonian legacy that did survive during the Republican-dominated 1920s. Wilson had believed that the arms race among the Great Powers had led to the outbreak of war in 1914. During the twenties, support for disarmament crossed party lines. Early in the decade Idaho Republican senator William Borah, one of Wilson's harshest critics on the Treaty of Versailles, agreed that arms spending was a waste of money. Harding administration officials wanted to reduce taxes (including the newly enacted income tax) and government outlays, and construction of naval vessels represented the largest single expenditure of the U.S. government at that time. From 1915 to 1920, the United States spent $1.5 billion on its navy modernization program. By the end of the Great War the U.S. Navy had grown from the fourth-largest fleet in the world to a size rivaling Great Britain's Royal Navy, until then the world's largest. The British, like the other Europeans, had been bled dry by the Great War. Britain could not afford another naval arms race, but the leaders of the Royal Navy wanted to maintain superiority over other navies. Only the British and U.S. navies maintained fleets in both the Atlantic and Pacific Oceans, making their naval construction programs all the more expensive. But both countries wanted to keep an edge over potential rivals such as Japan.

The western Pacific was the most likely place for a new naval arms race to develop. A twenty-year naval alliance between Japan and Great Britain, signed in 1902, would expire shortly. With the elimination of German influence in the western Pacific, Britain no longer felt a need for a naval partner to protect its interests in the waters around China. Australia and New Zealand, two British Commonwealth states, expressed strong racist animosity toward the Japanese. They passed laws barring Japanese immigrants from entering their countries, and they deeply resented the fact that the Paris peace treaty had awarded Japan mandates over former German possessions in the Pacific. Thus Australia and New Zealand encouraged Britain to end its alliance with Japan. In 1920 Britain announced that it would not renew its partnership with Japan when it ran out in 1922.

The end of British-Japanese military cooperation left the political future of East Asia in doubt. Civil war and social upheaval had continued in China ever since the revolution of 1911 ended the Qing dynasty. But despite their many differences, most Chinese nationalists feared and resented Japan's encroachments. Early in the Great War Japan had nearly achieved complete control over China's foreign policy. At the Paris peace conference of 1919, the victors further offended China, a nominal ally, by not returning the German lease on the Shandong peninsula to China but awarding it instead to Japan. Many westerners feared that Japan might take advantage of the United States' and Europe's diminished interest in East Asia to try once more to increase its control over China. Japan's ambitions set off warning bells across the Pacific. American officials worried that U.S. interests in the Philippines, Guam, and Samoa could be threatened by Japan.

In 1921 Secretary of State Hughes saw a connection between naval competition and the future of East Asia. He convinced Harding that the United States could play a major international role outside the League of Nations by convening a conference on naval disarmament and the future of East Asia. In November 1921 representatives of ten nations met in Washington to discuss naval strength and the political situation in China. Hughes advocated a ten-year moratorium on naval construction. He also proposed that in the future the United States and Great Britain maintain a rough parity in the size of their navies, with Japan's fleet set at 60 percent of that size. Since Japan deployed its navy only in the western Pacific, while U.S. and British ships sailed most of the Atlantic and the Pacific, the agreement actually left Japan as the premier naval power in East Asia. Over the next four months naval experts and diplomats worked out the details of Hughes's plan. Politicians loved it because it offered a way to mitigate the crushing burden of naval expenditures.

In February 1922 the Washington conference ended with the signing of three treaties. In the Four Power Treaty the United States, Great Britain, Japan, and France agreed to respect one another's holdings in the Pacific. In the Nine Power Treaty all of the conference participants promised to respect China's territorial integrity.

The Five Power Treaty defined the relative naval strengths of the United States, Great Britain, Japan, France, and Italy. As Hughes had proposed, the United States and Britain would maintain roughly equal fleets, with Japan's navy set at 60 percent of that size. In addition, France and Italy would have

Secretary of State Charles Evans Hughes (fifth from right) opened the Washington Naval Conference with a dramatic call to the major naval powers to scrap a large number of warships. *Brown Brothers*

navies 33.3 percent the size of the American and British fleets. Naval officers who objected to these limits were mollified by various exclusions to the agreement. The parties were free to build as many auxiliary craft—submarines, destroyers, and light cruisers—as they wished. In 1927 the United States convened a meeting at Geneva to set limits on auxiliary ships. It failed, largely because Great Britain wanted more light cruisers to defend its far-flung empire.

Disarmament negotiations represented only a part of a broader movement during the twenties and thirties toward minimizing the danger of war. Nearly everyone favored peace, but talk of peace meant different things to different people at different times. In the 1920s many American veterans of the Paris peace conference wished to continue Wilson's project of discovering and counteracting the root causes of war. Courses in international relations were introduced across the country in prestigious private universities like the University of Chicago, Columbia, Harvard, and Yale and in state institutions like Illinois, Kentucky, and Indiana. Much of the content was devoted to explaining why war had broken out in 1914 and examining ways to avoid

War Is a Crime Against Humanity

Gassed: Near Dun-sur-Meuse, in the Woods, France

To you who are filled with horror at the sufferings of war-ridden mankind;

To you who remember that **ten million men** were slaughtered in the last war;

To you who have the courage to face the reality of **war, stripped of its sentimental "glory";**

We make this appeal:—

> Eight years since the signing of the Armistice! And peace is still hard beset by preparations for war. In another war men, women and children would be more wantonly, more cruelly massacred, by death rays, gas, disease germs, and machines more fiendish than those used in the last war. Those whom you love must share in its universal destruction.

Can You Afford Not To Give Your Utmost To Cleanse The World Of This Black Plague Of Needless Death and Suffering?

Send your contribution to an uncompromising Peace organization

THE WOMEN'S PEACE UNION

39 Pearl Street, New York

We Believe that Violence and Bloodshed Are Always Wrong in Principle and Disastrous in Practice. We Are working to Make War Illegal and to Ensure World Peace.

During the 1920s many peace groups advocated outlawing war. In this flier the Women's Peace Union recalled the suffering of World War I. *Schwimmer Lloyd Collection, Freida Langer Lazarus Papers, New York Public Library*

another such catastrophe. Universities also began offering instruction in the languages, history, and civilization of China, Japan, Russia, and other non-Western countries. In 1921 about sixty of the foremost internationalists from the worlds of banking, journalism, government, and higher education formed the Council on Foreign Relations in New York. The council hosted regular discussion meetings, published books, and published a journal, *Foreign Affairs*. Its activities were designed to foster popular interest in international relations and to combat the influence of those who advocated American withdrawal from active participation in world politics.

Some Wilsonians sought more direct influence on public policy. Columbia University professor James T. Shotwell, who had attended the Paris peace conference as an adviser to the U.S. delegation, campaigned throughout the 1920s to cut the size of the world's armed forces and reduce the danger of renewed conflict. One of his many essays won a prize offered by the *Saturday Evening Post* for the best plan to end war. Shotwell's scheme was simple, if naive: nations could make war less likely by jointly proclaiming it to be illegal. Surprisingly, Shotwell's proposal found a warm reception among high American officials. Secretary of State Frank Kellogg (1925–1929) believed that a variation on Shotwell's proposal might help the United States tactfully refuse a troublesome request from France for a formal military alliance. U.S. officials had resisted French requests for an alliance ever since the Great War. But after the United States refused to join the League of Nations, French demands for a security pact became even more urgent, as Paris feared that an international organization without the United States would be less likely to offer military protection. Kellogg proposed a general agreement to outlaw war, along the lines of Shotwell's plan, in place of the formal security guarantee France had requested. In August 1928 Kellogg and French Foreign Minister Aristide Briand signed a promise not to use war as an instrument of national policy. They invited other nations to join, and most eventually signed the Kellogg-Briand Pact, or Pact of Paris. The agreement was a grand but hollow gesture, as some officials of the time recognized. The U.S. ambassador to France likened the pact to a child's game: "When some child does not want to play any longer, he breaks up the game and that's the end of it." Still, U.S. officials later based some of their resistance to German, Italian, and Japanese aggression on the fact that these nations had violated their promise to renounce war.

During the 1920s many Americans believed that a new era of prosperity had dawned. Politicians and publicists glorified business leaders: "The business of America is business," proclaimed President Calvin Coolidge. Furthermore, many Americans thought that the blessings of American prosperity could be expanded around the globe through increased investment abroad, more international trade, and a resolution of lingering financial issues left over from the Great War. Commerce Secretary Herbert Hoover used the power of his office and a corps of hundreds of foreign commercial attachés to promote American business interests around the world, from Malaya to Iran, China, Russia, and South America. Despite his energetic and imaginative use of government power to pry open foreign markets for U.S. companies, Hoover believed that America's business success depended on private initiative motivated by self-interest and civic spirit, not government action. Henry Ford, the foremost industrialist of the 1920s, believed that the American techniques of mass production and rigid management control (Taylorism) could be exported for the benefit of other nations. Ford wrote in 1929 that "foreign lands are feeling the benefit of American progress, our American right thinking. Both Russia's and China's problems are fundamentally industrial and will be solved by the application of the right methods of thinking, practically applied." Even Reinhold Niebuhr, beginning a career as an influential Protestant theologian alert to the suffering of the poor, hoped that business expansion might replace military power as the focus of American foreign relations. He believed that the 1920s represented a new "economic age" in which "the legates of our empire are not admirals or proconsuls, but bankers."

A river of American money flowed overseas in the 1920s. Spending on foreign imports, cash sent by American residents to relatives living abroad, tourism, direct investments, and overseas lending all contributed to the $12 billion Americans spent outside the United States in the 1920s. Direct investment by American firms overseas (creating foreign subsidiaries or purchasing parts of foreign enterprises) varied from region to region. In the developed countries of Europe and in Canada, Australia, and Argentina, American companies set up local subsidiaries to sell cars, electrical equipment, and processed foods. American oil companies marketed their products wherever automobiles were sold. Elsewhere, mining concerns joined the petroleum giants to find raw materials in Latin America, Asia, and the Middle East.

American products, films, and visitors touched the lives of millions of people abroad. Tens of thousands of Americans went to other lands as tourists, missionaries, or scholars. The Rotary Club, an organization for businessmen, was founded in Chicago in 1905. After the Great War it expanded abroad rapidly, opening hundreds of chapters around the world dedicated to promoting American business values. The spread of American products and visitors deepened other peoples' views of the United States. Everywhere people considered the United States the home of the wonders of modern life—electricity, the movies, radio, and the car. An American sociologist who traveled widely overseas measured the impact of American entertainment on the rest of the world. He thought that the new media of radio and film brought "all the peoples of the earth" into "a common culture and a common historical life." The slide toward war in the 1930s exploded much of this easy optimism. Nevertheless, the global spread of American culture after the Great War did as much as anything to consolidate the position of the United States as a major power.

Although American culture, products, and tourists helped foster good will toward the United States abroad, many Americans remained deeply hostile to foreign influences. The fifty-year-old movement to restrict immigration culminated in the Emergency Quota Act of 1921 and the National Origins Act of 1924 (discussed in Chapter 4). Tens of thousands of prospective immigrants from southern and eastern Europe, mostly Catholics and Jews, were turned away while the quotas for British and German immigrants remained unfilled. American consular officials with the job of granting visas to prospective immigrants often expressed the ethnic prejudices that had led to the quota system. One diplomat working in Poland in the twenties complained that the mostly Jewish crowd applying for entry permits gave his office "a smell no zoo could equal." The American quotas provoked fury abroad. Japanese politicians deeply resented having their nationals placed on the same basis as the despised Chinese. Japan also resented America's abrogation of the Gentlemen's Agreement of 1907, in which Japan had voluntarily restricted emigration to the United States in return for a U.S. promise not to legally ban Japanese entry. The immigration quota system also soured U.S. relations with the new Fascist government of Italy, led by Benito Mussolini. In addition, the restrictions contributed to a great human tragedy in the 1930s by denying shelter to desperate refugees from Nazi persecution.

U.S. government officials and private bankers worked hard to remedy the economic hardships in Europe created by the Great War. Nine million soldiers and civilians had died, and estimates of the war's direct and indirect costs exceeded $400 billion. Allied (mostly British, French, and Italian) war debts to the United States and German reparations obligations slowed recovery in the immediate aftermath of the war. Allied borrowers owed the United States approximately $10 billion, plus interest, for loans made from 1917 to 1920. European debtors delayed their repayment of American loans until they could be assured of receiving reparations payments from Germany. The United States countered that American loans and German reparations were separate issues. Washington would discuss with borrowers the possibility of reducing interest payments, but it would not link repayment of loans to German reparations. Germany considered the reparations bill exorbitant and stopped payment in 1923. France and Belgium responded by occupying the German industrial district of the Ruhr Valley. Sickening inflation followed in Germany. The value of the mark plunged to the point where a loaf of bread sold for over a billion marks. The inflation wiped out the savings of the German middle class and created bitter resentment, to be exploited later by Adolf Hitler and the National Socialist (Nazi) Party.

President Coolidge offered American help to rebuild Europe's shattered financial infrastructure. He invited three American bankers to help reorganize Germany's finances, restart reparations payments, and thereby enable European borrowers to resume repayments of their American loans. The bankers went to Europe and came back with a proposal labeled the Dawes Plan, after Charles Dawes, the chairman of the commission. Germany's reparations obligations were to be scaled back, and the German currency would be stabilized through a $110 million loan raised from private banks in the United States. The Dawes Plan ignited an American investment boom in Europe, enabling most countries there to recover from the devastation of the Great War. In 1929, a few months before the onset of the Great Depression, another American banker, Owen Young, sponsored a new plan to further reduce Germany's reparations obligations. In mid-1929 it appeared that cooperation between the U.S. government and American business had worked to restore Europe's financial health. But this prosperity rested on indefinite American loans to Europe and increased trade across the Atlantic. The Depression halted both and ruined hopes that the Dawes and Young Plans could create long-lasting prosperity.

In the end, U.S. dollar diplomacy failed to foster prosperity and international harmony in the 1920s. Advocates of government involvement in international economic affairs found that U.S. political leaders' commitment to limiting government regulation of business hampered their efforts. Throughout the twenties, the U.S. government shied away from providing guidelines to American bankers for the sort of loans they should make overseas. As a result, American bankers flooded the world with loans for projects that never turned a profit, and therefore they had trouble collecting payment on many loans. The prosperity of the twenties depended partly on the willingness of U.S. bankers to continue to lend. But the onset of the Depression set off a downward spiral of defaults, refusal by bankers to make new loans, collapse of international trade, and worldwide unemployment.

✦ Coping with Nationalism, Instability, and Revolution

In the 1920s the United States modified its policies concerning nationalism, instability, and revolution around the world. The goal remained to promote the interests of the United States as a great power, supreme in the Western Hemisphere and the equal of the European and Asian powers. But the tactics changed. The United States accommodated some revolutions and sought to contain others. Washington often opposed stridently nationalist movements and sought to diminish instability abroad that was likely to threaten American business interests. At the same time, however, the United States began to discard the use of direct military intervention.

Nowhere did the United States change its methods more than in the Western Hemisphere (see map). The three Republican administrations of 1921–1933 gradually pulled back from direct military interventions in Mexico, the Caribbean, and Central America. They did so in response to widespread opposition to U.S. imperialism both at home and among the other nations of the hemisphere. But even though the United States withdrew its troops, it continued to dominate many of its neighbors.

The Republican platform of 1920 criticized the Wilson administration for sending troops to the Dominican Republic, the eastern part of the island of Hispaniola, in 1915. The Harding administration made good on the party's promise to withdraw U.S. soldiers in 1924, after the U.S. Navy trained local National Guard units to enforce order. Although the troops were gone, the United States still retained control over the Dominican Republic's finances, begun in 1907 (see Chapter 3). A few years after the Marines left, Rafael Trujillo, a soldier trained by the National Guard, took power and imposed a brutal dictatorship that lasted until 1961.

The American troops stayed longer in Haiti, the poorest country in the Western Hemisphere, which occupied the western part of Hispaniola. In Haiti too the Marines trained National Guard units to impose rough order. The U.S. forces built roads, bridges, hospitals, and power plants. But they also brutally mistreated the Haitians. The United States introduced racial segregation into

The United States and Latin American Between the Wars In the interwar period the United States continued its political and economic hegemony of the Western hemisphere.

During the 1920s the government recruited young men to join the armed forces which would spread American influence abroad. *Library of Congress*

Haiti, favoring the small, light-skinned mulatto elite over the black majority. In 1919, when the Marines drafted Haitians into chain gangs to build roads, the Haitians rebelled. The Marines responded by killing over two thousand people. Strikes and protests resumed in 1929. The next year a U.S.-sponsored commission reported that the occupation forces had failed to "understand the social problems of Haiti." President Franklin D. Roosevelt withdrew the last of the U.S. forces. After the Americans left, Haiti sunk further into poverty and brutal dictatorship.

An even more complicated political situation arose in Nicaragua. The United States withdrew its forces from that Central American republic in 1925. The next year, however, civil war broke out between supporters of the Catholic Church, the Conservative Party, and the anti-clerical Liberal Party. Washington feared that the fighting could threaten the property of American businesses in Nicaragua, so the Marines returned in 1926. Former secretary of war Henry Stimson, now a prosperous Wall Street lawyer, accompanied the five thousand Marines to Managua, the capital, to arrange a peace agreement. Stimson concluded that the United States could not impose a government on Nicaragua and that the Nicaraguans needed to elect their own leaders. Under the terms of the 1928 Peace of Tititapa, U.S. Marines supervised elections in 1928, 1930, and 1932. By the time of the last election, however, the Liberal Party had split. A Liberal Party general, César Augusto Sandino, denounced the peace as an American effort to impose Yankee rule. Sandino led several thousand guerrillas into the hills. Anastasio Somoza, another Liberal Party general, commanded the U.S.-trained National Guard units. In January 1933 the Hoover administration withdrew the last of the U.S. Marines from Nicaragua. Somoza, supported by the United States, began a forty-year-long family dictatorship. Among his first acts as president was to invite Sandino to Managua for peace talks. When the guerrilla leader arrived, Somoza had him shot.

At the same time that it put down revolutions elsewhere in the hemisphere, the United States accommodated a revolution in Mexico, its next-door neighbor. Many Americans had grown disillusioned with the Wilson administration's military interventions in Mexico. U.S. troops had left Mexico in 1917, but bitterness remained between the two countries. Mexico's new constitution declared that all of Mexico's "land and waters," including its subsoil mineral and petroleum deposits, belonged permanently to the Mexican people. American mining and petroleum firms pressured the Harding administration to demand compensation for Mexico's confiscation of their mining and drilling rights on land previously leased to them. Some American oil executives joined forces with the Catholic Church to demand that the revolutionary Mexican government restore Church properties. In 1923 the United States and Mexico reached an agreement in which Mexico acknowledged the legitimacy of American mining and drilling rights granted before the adoption of the Mexican constitution in 1917.

In 1925, however, a new, more radical Mexican president, Plutarco Calles, took office. He repudiated the 1923 arrangement, complaining that it left over 50 percent of Mexico's petroleum in the hands of U.S. companies. Once more American oil company executives lobbied Washington to threaten Mexico with the possibility of armed intervention, but President Coolidge resisted. He made Dwight Morrow, an old college friend and a partner in J. P. Morgan and Co., the U.S. ambassador to Mexico. Morrow believed that long-term U.S. business interests would be best served byaccommodating Calles. He won the respect of the Mexican leadership by learning a few words of Spanish. A romance between his daughter and Charles Lindbergh, whose solo 1927 transatlantic flight made him the world's most eligible bachelor, humanized Morrow for ordinary Mexicans. In 1928 Morrow worked out a ten-year deal with the Mexican government, allowing U.S. petroleum firms to retain ownership of lands they had developed before 1917 and to lease rights to oil fields activated after that time.

At the end of the 1920s Latin America pressured the United States to renounce the use of military occupation anywhere in the Western Hemisphere. Latin American delegates to the 1928 Pan-American Conference in Havana introduced a resolution opposing the right of any state to "intervene in the internal affairs of another." Only by promising a thorough review of U.S. Latin American policy could the U.S. delegation avoid the adoption of an anti-U.S. resolution. During the Hoover administration J. Reuben Clark, the State Department's legal adviser, studied the basis in international law for unilateral intervention in another country. In 1930 the State Department adopted Clark's memorandum on the Monroe Doctrine, holding that Theodore Roosevelt had gone too far with his Corollary (see Chapter 3). Clark's memorandum affirmed that neither the Monroe Doctrine nor international law authorized unilateral U.S. military action in the Western Hemisphere. The result was a subtle shift in U.S. policy toward its neighbors. The U.S. government has continued to send troops into other Western Hemisphere countries throughout the twentieth century, but after Clark's memorandum it often first obtained the agreement of the other countries in the region before using force.

✦ Depression Diplomacy

Herbert Hoover, inaugurated as president on March 4, 1929, personified the spirit of business-government partnership that characterized the 1920s. When the public elected him in a landslide in 1928 they expected that he would use the skills he had honed as commerce secretary to expand and perpetuate prosperity. Instead, within nine months of taking office he faced the Great Depression, the most serious economic crisis in the nation's history.

The Depression sharply reduced the ability of the United States to influence international events. The first impact of the worldwide slump was to reverse the tide of American goods, loans, and visitors flowing abroad. U.S. bankers slowed lending to foreign governments in 1929. In 1930 Congress raised barriers to foreign imports with the Smoot-Hawley tariff. Hoover signed the bill into law despite warnings from prominent economists that the tariff would lead to a trade war. Their concerns proved prophetic, as other nations raised their tariffs in response. With less money available to purchase imports, international trade spiraled downward from nearly $2.9 billion in 1929 to about $2.3 billion in 1930, $1.6 billion in 1931, and $1.1 billion in 1932. American exports were especially hard hit. In 1929 the United States exported $541 million in automobiles and parts. By 1932 that figure had fallen to $76 million. Steel exports went from $200 million to $29 million. The thousands of American tourists in foreign hotels and spas nearly vanished by 1931, adding to a 68 percent decline in the number of dollars available outside the United States.

The magnitude of the economic slump probably would have overwhelmed most political leaders, but Hoover's response seemed especially feeble. He exhorted Americans to rely on their own resources, and he looked for ways to reduce government expenditures. He was more energetic at seeking international solutions to the Depression than at providing political leadership or inspiring programs to revive the domestic economy. In June 1931 Hoover helped prevent a formal default on World War I debts by joining with other nations to proclaim a twelve-month moratorium on the repayment of war loans. He also pursued naval disarmament as a way to reduce government spending. Hoover called another disarmament conference, to meet in London in January 1930, hoping that further reductions in naval spending would diminish the ballooning budget deficit. He and most economists erroneously believed that balancing the federal budget would alleviate the Depression. Faced with the impending economic crisis, the London Conference succeeded where the Geneva gathering of 1927 had failed. The participants extended the 1922 agreement defining the size of the U.S., British, and Japanese fleets to include auxiliary as well as capital ships, with a slight upward adjustment permitted in some categories for Japan.

The success of the London conference convinced American leaders that relations with Japan would steadily improve. Both Americans and Europeans were therefore surprised when Japan moved against the northern Chinese province of Manchuria in September 1931. The Japanese military leadership, impatient with the civilian government's efforts to peacefully resolve differences with China over Manchuria, took matters into its own hands on the evening of September 18, 1931. Japanese troops exploded a section of track of the Japanese-owned South Manchurian Railway near the town of Mukden. The Japanese blamed China and used the incident to justify invading Manchuria. Governments in Europe and the United States, overwhelmed by the Depression, were unable to respond effectively. In Washington, Secretary of State Henry L. Stimson supported an investigation by the League of Nations and encouraged the Chinese government to wait for a report by a League commission. He reminded Japan of its obligations to avoid war under the Kellogg-Briand Pact, but he made no threats of retaliation. Unmoved, Japan raised the stakes in the winter of 1931–1932. The Japanese cabinet, now dominated by the military, authorized the army to take all of Manchuria and to seize the international port of Shanghai. American supporters of China demanded that the U.S. government impose economic sanctions against Japan.

But with international trade already in a free fall, Hoover opposed any actions likely to dampen it further. Stimson, however, was moved by the plight of Shanghai, a city with a significant American presence. In February 1932 Stimson wrote Senator William Borah, chairman of the Foreign Relations Committee, that the State Department would not recognize any Japanese claims on Chinese territory. The Stimson Non-Recognition Doctrine charged Japan with violating the Nine Power Treaty of 1922 and the Kellogg-Briand Pact of 1928 and implied that as a result the United States was no longer bound by its commitment to limit its fleet in the western Pacific. But Hoover, looking to the upcoming presidential election, believed Stimson had gone too far. He assured the public that the United States would not use force to back Stimson's doctrine. Japan defused the crisis by withdrawing from Shanghai in May 1932. It did, however, turn Manchuria into a puppet state, renaming it Manchukuo.

The Depression was the only issue in the presidential election campaign of 1932. Franklin D. Roosevelt, the Democratic candidate, had served as assistant secretary of the navy during the Great War and had been his party's vice-presidential nominee in the 1920 election. Despite his background as an internationalist, Roosevelt advocated domestic solutions to the Depression. He claimed that Hoover's search for international causes and remedies for the Depression was only an excuse for inaction. The public agreed, and they elected Roosevelt in a landslide.

In his first three years as president, Roosevelt stressed domestic over foreign affairs. His early foreign policies reflected the public's desire to turn inward. And when he did become involved abroad, Roosevelt concentrated on improving the economic position of the United States. Accordingly, during the four-month lame duck period following the 1932 election, Roosevelt resisted Hoover's pleas that he commit to participate in an economic conference in London scheduled for the summer of 1933. Roosevelt also said nothing about the moratorium on war debt repayments, which lapsed in December 1932.

The U.S. government participated in the London economic conference in June and July 1933, but the results were disappointing to internationalists hoping for joint efforts to end the Depression. The United States offered a plan to reduce trade barriers, but the British delegation responded that a revival of international trade would have to wait until each nation agreed to fix the value of its currency relative to that of the other countries' currencies. Roosevelt's more nationalistic advisers opposed efforts to fix the value of the dollar, fearing it would interfere with efforts to raise wages and prices in the United States. The president agreed, and wired the conference that "the sound internal economic system of a nation is a greater factor in its well-being than the price of its currency." Roosevelt's message effectively scuttled the work of the London conference, and only slight progress was made for the remainder of the 1930s on currency stabilization.

The Roosevelt administration made more progress in boosting international trade. Roosevelt appointed Cordell Hull, a sixty-one-year-old former Democratic senator from Tennessee, as his secretary of state. Hull believed that trade rivalries were a major cause of war. In 1934 Congress responded to Hull's concerns by passing the Reciprocal Trade Agreements Act. This law reversed the high tariff policies of the 1920s, permitting the president to slash duties by 50 percent if other nations did so as well. The law did little to revive trade in the 1930s, but U.S. foreign trade policy after the Second World War rested on Hull's commitment to general reductions in barriers.

The Roosevelt administration also hoped to find more foreign markets for U.S. goods. In its first year the Roosevelt administration opened formal diplomatic relations with the Soviet Union, a nation the United States had shunned since 1917. Executives from Ford, General Electric, and other major

U.S. industrial concerns hoped that formal diplomatic ties with the Soviets would help American exporters. In 1933 Joseph Stalin, the Soviet dictator, faced threats from Nazi Germany in the west and Japan in the east. These potential enemies forced Stalin to reverse his previously ultrarevolutionary policy. He agreed to open formal diplomatic relations with the United States in November 1933. The next year the Soviet Union joined the League of Nations and became an ardent champion of collective security arrangements against Germany. American business executives believed that a vast market awaited them in the Soviet Union. American friends of China hoped that the Soviet Union could provide a bulwark against Japanese aggression. Most of these hopes proved futile. U.S.-Soviet trade barely increased in the remainder of the decade, and Japan continued to threaten China and Southeast Asia.

The Roosevelt administration continued the movement away from direct military intervention in Central America and the Caribbean. In one of his few references to foreign affairs in his inaugural address, Roosevelt promised that "in our relations with the Western Hemisphere we shall be guided by the principle of the good neighbor." Over the remainder of the decade the United States used moral persuasion and economic pressure, rather than direct military force, to influence the policies of nearby governments.

The United States had indirectly controlled the government of Cuba since 1900 (see Chapter 3). The price of sugar, Cuba's main cash crop, plunged in late 1929. Gerardo Machado, the U.S.-supported president of Cuba, quelled strikes and demonstrations against his regime by jailing and murdering labor leaders and student activists. When Roosevelt became president he dispatched an envoy to Cuba, who decided that Machado had to go. The United States sent warships to patrol the coast of Cuba but did not land any troops. Machado departed in August 1933, but the new president, Ramón Grau San Martín, proved too independent and nationalistic for American tastes. For a while Washington considered sending troops to oust Grau, but Secretary of State Hull resisted such an obvious departure from the administration's Good Neighbor policy. Instead the U.S. Navy once more sailed off the coast while U.S. officials on the island helped Sergeant Fulgencio Batista lead a successful coup against Grau in January 1934. The United States supported Batista with credit from the Export-Import Bank and by lowering the tariff on Cuban sugar under the Reciprocal Trade Agreement Act. Congress also rescinded the Platt Amendment of 1902, which had given the United States the right to intervene militarily in Cuban affairs. With U.S. support Batista continued to rule, either as president or through puppets, until he was forced to flee by Fidel Castro on December 31, 1958.

During the 1930s the United States again reached an accommodation with Mexican nationalists. In 1938 Lazaro Cardenas, a strongly nationalistic Mexican president, confiscated the property of foreign oil companies. They responded by pressuring the U.S. government to consider sending troops to Mexico to force Cardenas to return their land. Roosevelt wanted Mexican support in the event of a showdown with Nazi Germany, so he followed the advice of Josephus Daniels, the U.S. ambassador to Mexico, to negotiate a settlement. The United States accepted Mexico's right to expropriate foreign oil firms' holdings in return for compensation, and Roosevelt gave Mexico a $30 million trade credit. U.S. oil firms exacted their own revenge, however, by refusing to purchase or refine Mexican oil. Not until the 1970s, when worldwide demand for oil soared, did Mexico become a major petroleum producer.

✦ Neutrality

The Depression fostered a worldwide movement toward dictatorship and away from democracy. Economic desperation created a crisis of confidence. People looked for enemies to blame and questioned old institutions that seemed to have failed them miserably. Millions of Germans, battered by unemployment, rallied behind Adolf Hitler's Nazi Party. The Nazis blamed Jews, Communists, socialists, and liberals for Germany's defeat in the Great War, its humiliation at the Paris peace conference, and the Depression. On January 30, 1933, Hitler became chancellor of Germany, promising to restore Germany's economy and its place in Europe by crushing the Jews and the Nazis' political opponents. In Hitler's first years in power many people outside Germany were aghast at the Nazi concentration camps and the beatings and roundups of Jews and political opponents. But, unfortunately, many more marveled at the way the Nazis were able to put ordinary Germans back to work. Similarly, Joseph Stalin won praise outside the Soviet Union, despite the brutality of his dictatorship, for building an industrial economy in the midst of a worldwide depression.

The economic success of the totalitarian regimes caused some Americans to question their own institutions. A contributor to *Harper's* wrote in 1934 that "to attempt a defense of democracy these days is a little like defending paganism in 313 or the divine right of kings in 1793. It is taken for granted that democracy is bad and that it is dying." Americans also took a hard look at their recent past. The Depression had discredited the very business leaders who had been exalted in the 1920s. When Richard Whitney, vice president of the New York Stock Exchange, went to prison for swindling thousands of small investors, his disgrace seemed to embody the false promises of the consumer culture of the Roaring Twenties. People became angry at what they considered the hypocrisy and selfishness of business leaders. They paid more attention to past claims that greedy bankers and arms dealers had led the United States into war in 1917 to advance their own narrow interests.

These views, labeled revisionism, questioned the worth of American participation in the Great War. Revisionists also challenged the Allies' judgment, reflected in the Treaty of Versailles, that Germany bore sole responsibility for the outbreak of hostilities and therefore should pay heavy reparations. By the time of Roosevelt's New Deal, war debt repayments had effectively stopped. Hitler's Nazi government tore up Germany's agreement to pay reparations. Many Americans believed that the postwar cycle of reparations and debt payments—in which Germany paid the European victors, who used those funds to repay their debts to the U.S. government, which in turn persuaded American bankers to loan money to Germany—had sown the seeds of the Depression by creating a mountain of unstable credit and debt. Americans were not alone in these views. Great War revisionism took hold among the European victors as well. In Britain in the 1930s there was widespread agreement that the arms race and alliance system, not German aggression, had created the conditions leading to war in 1914. Many people also believed that Germany had been mistreated by the Versailles treaty and that the reparations requirements were unfair.

As more and more people came to believe that the Great War had been fought for the benefit of a few rich and powerful people and corporations, new voices gained prominence in the American peace movement. During the 1920s, conservative peace advocates had predominated. They encouraged U.S. participation in world affairs, hoped that the United States would join the League of Nations, and applauded efforts at international disarmament. In the early thirties, however, different peace activists, deeply distrustful of government officials, came to the fore. These people looked for other ways to prevent the United States from becoming involved in foreign wars. In 1933 Dorothy Detzer, head of the Women's International League for Peace and Freedom, an advocacy group created in 1917 to keep the United States out of the Great War, proposed that the Senate investigate the circumstances under which Congress had declared war in 1917. Detzer hoped that the Senate would confirm the claims made in *Merchants of Death,* a highly popular 1934 exposé of the role played by bankers and munitions manufacturers in bringing the United States into the war in 1917. In late 1934 and early 1935 a special committee chaired by Republican Senator Gerald Nye of North Dakota held hearings on the events leading up to U.S. entry into the war. Panels of historians, journalists, business executives, and diplomats testified. The committee concluded that the United States had not truly been neutral for at least two years before entering the war against Germany. Nye's panel decided that private U.S. bank loans to the Allies before 1917 had inexorably drawn the United States to their cause. The only way to remain out of future foreign wars, they decided, was for the United States to limit financial and commercial dealings with belligerents.

The Nye Committee's finding laid the groundwork for a major overhaul of U.S. neutrality legislation in 1935. Congress acted just as Europeans were turning worried eyes to an overseas adventure undertaken by the Fascist government of Italy. Since 1922 Italy had been led by Benito Mussolini, whose Fascist Party program foreshadowed much of the barbarism later practiced by Hitler's Germany. The Fascists promised to restore the glory of the Roman Empire to Italy. For the first dozen years of Mussolini's rule, the regime concentrated on imposing a dictatorship, jailing political opponents, and embarking on an extravagant program of public works. In 1934 and 1935

Mussolini attempted to expand the Italian empire in East Africa. He demanded that Ethiopia, one of only two independent, black-led states on the continent, yield territory to the Italian colony of Somalia. Ethiopia's Emperor Haile Selassie refused Italy's ultimatum. On October 3, 1935, Italian troops slashed into Ethiopia, forcing the emperor to flee into exile. He made a desperate appeal for assistance to the League of Nations at Geneva. The emperor cast a heroic, but forlorn, figure. Most European and American officials wanted to make certain that the Ethiopian crisis did not lead to a new world war. Roosevelt neatly expressed the public mood in a message delivered on Armistice Day (November 11), 1935. He called the Great War the "folly of twenty years ago" and warned that the Ethiopian crisis presented an even greater danger of war than the Balkan crisis of the summer of 1914. A new war, he said, would "drag civilization to a level from which worldwide recovery may be all but impossible."

The 1935 neutrality law banned travel by U.S. citizens into a war zone (to avoid a repetition of the *Lusitania* incident, in which a number of Americans had died). The law also forbade loans by American banks to foreign governments involved in a war. Finally, once the president declared that a state of war existed between foreign governments, no American citizen or company could sell weapons to any belligerent. Initially Roosevelt opposed a blanket embargo on trade with all the combatants, hoping that Congress would authorize him to declare Italy an aggressor and Ethiopia a victim of aggression, entitled to U.S. assistance. But Congress was in no mood to grant much discretion to any president, and certainly not to Roosevelt, who was thought to maintain some of his old Wilsonian ideals. Roosevelt reluctantly signed the 1935 neutrality law, but he warned that its "inflexible provisions might drag us into war instead of keeping us out." Of course, the neutrality law contained a great loophole: it permitted the unrestricted sale of U.S. raw materials to warring nations.

Peace in Europe again seemed threatened when a bloody civil war broke out in Spain in 1936. Fascist Italy and Nazi Germany were now partners in what Mussolini called the Axis Alliance. They backed rebellious Spanish army officers, led by General Francisco Franco, in their attempt to overthrow the elected government of the Spanish republic. A nationalist, strongly backed by the Catholic Church, Franco shared much of the antidemocratic outlook of his German and Italian supporters. German pilots flew bombing raids for the rebel forces against civilian targets. The bombing of one town prompted the Spanish abstract artist Pablo Picasso, an ardent backer of the republican cause, to immortalize the suffering of the victims of war in his famous painting *Guernica,* named after the city destroyed by German bombs. Pictures of the devastation wrought by the bombs were published around the world, creating sympathy for the republican cause. The Soviet Union responded to pleas from the republican government with a small amount of military aid. Britain and France, however, did not want the Spanish civil war to escalate into a general war. They led an international movement to impose an arms embargo, which effectively deprived the republicans of the means of defending themselves. The United States joined the embargo after Congress declared that the Neutrality Act applied even though the fighting in Spain was a civil, not an international, war. Americans were deeply divided over the implications of the Spanish civil war. American liberals and leftists supported the Spanish republic as a bulwark against Fascism and Nazism. But conservatives and the bulk of the hierarchy of the Catholic Church favored the Spanish rebels. Facing an election in which many voters wanted to avoid U.S. involvement in another European war, FDR was happy to downplay events in Spain. As he said shortly after Franco took up arms against the republican government, "I have seen war. . . . I have seen blood running from the wounded. I have seen men coughing out their gassed lungs. . . . I have seen the agony of mothers and wives. I hate war." As a result, the United States and the European democracies stood aside while Franco defeated the elected government of Spain in 1939.

In 1937 Congress passed a permanent extension of the neutrality law. The new version maintained the ban on American citizens' travel in war zones, the prohibition on loans to belligerents, and the arms embargo, enlarging it to cover civil as well as international wars. Senator Nye wanted to expand the embargo to include a complete ban on American commerce with belligerents, a move many businesses opposed. Eventually Congress approved a compromise, under which American ships were barred from war zones but belligerents were able to purchase nonlethal goods from U.S. firms, provided they paid cash and used their own vessels to transport them. Roosevelt supported this "cash-and-carry" provision. He believed it ever so subtly shifted the balance in favor of Britain and against Germany, since Britain possessed a sizable merchant marine and Germany did not.

✦ The Approach of War

War between China and Japan resumed in July 1937 when Japanese troops attacked south of the Great Wall to bring all of China under its control. As Japanese forces advanced, the world saw horrifying photographs of the costs of war to civilians. Friends of China in the United States, led by former secretary of state Stimson, called for condemnation of Japan and a boycott of Japanese goods. But Roosevelt, like Hoover before him, moved cautiously in responding to Japanese attacks on China. In the fall of 1937 Roosevelt spoke out against disruptive states. He condemned Italy for its attack on Ethiopia, Germany for rearming in violation of the terms of the Versailles treaty, and Japan for its attack on China. He called for a "quarantine" of aggressors, including some economic and financial steps against them. Many newspapers backed the aims of the quarantine speech, but Roosevelt never acted on his own suggestion. He considered economic sanctions against Japan unworkable in the midst of the Depression, and he believed that the American public staunchly opposed war.

✦ ✦ ✦

Biographical Profile

Charles A. Lindbergh, 1902–1974

In the two decades between the First and Second World Wars, no American earned greater adulation for his or her accomplishments (or received greater scorn for his or her political opinions) than did Charles A. Lindbergh (1902–1974). In 1927, during a four-day celebration in New York City, 3 to 4 million people jammed into the urban canyons of downtown Manhattan to cheer Lindbergh and his plane, *The Spirit of St. Louis.*

Lindbergh remained a celebrity for nearly fifty years, but the rest of his full life had more than its share of tragedies and blunders. He became wealthy, and he tirelessly promoted the cause of civil aviation. He married Anne Morrow in 1929. Their son, Charles, Jr., was born in 1930. Two years later, the "Crime of the Century" struck the Lindbergh household when the sleeping twenty-month old Charles, Jr., was snatched from his crib and murdered. Bruno Richard Hauptmann was convicted and executed for the crime.

Brokenhearted, Charles and Anne Lindbergh traveled the world in the 1930s. He developed an interest in world politics, a subject he had previously avoided. A visit to Germany in 1936 impressed Lindbergh. Adolf Hitler's air force seemed invincible, and Lind-

---

Domestic reaction to a Japanese attack on an American gunboat, the *Panay,* in the Chang Jiang (Yangtze) River in December 1937 demonstrated the American public's reluctance to confront Japan. Although many Americans condemned Japan's attack on the ship, just as many questioned why the U.S. Navy had been protecting the interests of the Socony-Vacuum (later Mobil) Oil Company on a Chinese river in the first place. When Japan apologized and paid for damages, the crisis abated. In the aftermath of the attack, Louis Ludlow, an Indiana representative, used the *Panay* incident to bring to the House floor a proposed constitutional amendment requiring a national referendum before the United States could declare war. The amendment received more than a simple majority in the House, but it failed to gain the bergh was also smitten by the energy, organization, and sense of purpose he found in the Nazi state. He called Hitler "a great man" who "has done much for the German people."

Worse followed. After war broke out in Europe in 1939, Lindbergh became an outspoken critic of every effort by FDR to aid the Allies. He made overtly racist appeals, declaring that war with Germany would "reduce the strength and destroy the treasures of the white race." Once a hero to millions, Lindbergh began receiving thousands of letters denouncing his views.

Like most noninterventionists, he did support the war after Pearl Harbor. In 1944 he flew combat missions against Japan. His ardent anticommunism made him a staunch supporter of U.S. military policy during the Cold War. But Lindbergh never lived down his reputation as a Nazi sympathizer, and many Americans never forgave him before his death in 1974.

"Instead of agitating for war, the Jewish groups in this country should be opposing it in every possible way, for they will be among the first to feel its consequences. . . . A few Jewish people realize this, and stand opposed to intervention. But the majority still do not. Their greatest danger to this country lies in their large ownership and influence in our motion pictures, our press, our radio, and our government.

I am not attacking either the Jewish or the British people. Both races I admire, but I am saying that the leaders of both the British and the Jewish races, for reasons which are as understandable from their viewpoint as they are inadvisable from ours, for reasons which are not American, wish to involve us in the war."

—Charles Lindbergh at an America First rally, September 11, 1941

---

two-thirds majority necessary for further consideration by the Senate and the states.

In 1938 war seemed likely in Europe. Three years before, Hitler had begun his campaign to tear up the Versailles treaty when he commenced a massive military rearmament program. In 1936 his troops retook the Rhineland, a region occupied by the Allies since the Great War, also in violation of the Versailles treaty. Later that year he sent his flyers to bomb Spanish republican cities. In March 1938 Hitler declared a union between Germany and Austria, yet another violation of the Treaty of Versailles. That summer Hitler promoted the claims of 3.5 million German speakers living in the Sudetenland (the northern part of Czechoslovakia, a republic created at the Paris peace confer-

Adolf Hitler, the leader of Nazi Germany (1933–1945), embarked on a campaign of brutal anti-Semitism and military expansion that culminated in World War II. *Library of Congress*

ence) that they should rightfully be permitted to join the German Reich. Unlike the Austrian government, which had favored unification with the Nazi state, most Czechs resented Hitler's demands as the first step toward the destruction of their democracy. Moreover, Czechoslovakia had security treaties with France and the Soviet Union, designed to prevent an attack by Germany. Officials in Britain and France, however, dreaded the prospect of fighting Germany for what British Prime Minister Neville Chamberlain called "a faraway people of whom we know nothing." Chamberlain hoped that Hitler's ambitions could be appeased or satisfied by ceding some Czech territory to Germany. In September he flew to Munich to discuss directly with Hitler an alternative to war.

The United States looked on as tensions in central Europe escalated. Roosevelt was torn between his publicly expressed desire to see the Munich negotiations avert war and his personal revulsion at Hitler's bullying. He was outraged that Czechoslovakia's fate was to be decided solely by the leaders of Germany, France, Britain, and Italy. No invitation to participate in the talks went to Czechoslovakia, the country most directly affected by Germany's demands. On the eve of the first of three visits by the British prime minister to Hitler, Roosevelt complained privately that "Chamberlain is paying the usual game of the British—peace at any price, if he can get away with it and save face."

The first talks went poorly, with Hitler insisting that Britain and France squeeze Czechoslovakia ever harder. The German dictator set a deadline of October 1, after which he would take what he wanted by force. As talks seemed to break down, Roosevelt publicly repressed his indignation at Hitler's appetite. He encouraged the Europeans to resume negotiations, for "once they are broken off, reason is banished and force asserts itself." When Chamberlain decided to fly one last time to Munich to avert war, Roosevelt cabled him, simply, "Good man!" The Munich conference ended with Britain and France accepting Hitler's terms. The northern part of Czechoslovakia was ceded to Germany. The two western democracies demanded that Czechoslovakia publicly acknowledge Germany's right to its northern province, the loss of which made the rest of the country virtually indefensible. Chamberlain received a hero's welcome when he returned home. A grateful British public believed that his policy of appeasement had worked to avert a war more terrible than the one that ended in 1918. A few dissenters warned that appeasement would not work. Winston Churchill, a member of parliament out of favor with his own Conservative Party, growled that "Britain and France had to choose between war and dishonor. They have chosen dishonor. They shall have war."

Meanwhile, Hitler stepped up his campaign of domestic terror. The status of German Jews became more and more desperate in 1938 and 1939. Since Hitler had come to power in 1933, the Nazi government had imposed ever harsher restrictions on Jews. First came the loss of citizenship and the right to work in public institutions. Then the government enacted laws forbidding Jews to marry or have sexual contact with non-Jews or to be educated in the same schools as other Germans. In November 1938 Hitler unleashed thousands of storm troopers to burn synagogues, loot Jewish-owned stores, and send thousands of Jews to concentration camps. The steady stream of Jews seeking to leave Germany since 1933 became a flood in 1938 and 1939, but U.S. immigration policy remained as restrictive as ever. A ship laden with German-Jewish refugees was forced out of Havana Harbor in 1939 when Cuban authorities would not let it land. Neither the United States nor any other Western Hemisphere country would let these victims of Nazism disembark, so the vessel returned to Germany. Many of the more than one thousand people on board later perished in death camps. In 1938 the United States did convene an international conference on refugees at Evian-sur-les-Bains, a comfortable French resort. The countries of Europe, Latin America, and North America all deplored Germany's treatment of its Jews, but they offered no practical measures for helping them escape. The delegates agreed that fear brought on by the Depression of competition for jobs had intensified the already high resistance within their countries to additional immigration.

The Munich settlement staved off war for less than a year. In March 1939 Hitler tore up the Munich pact and occupied half of what was left of Czechoslovakia. The remaining part of the republic became Slovakia, a small state ruled by Nazi sympathizers. Germany's trampling of the Munich arrangement made a mockery of Chamberlain's hopes that appeasing Hitler would avert a slide toward war. Throughout western Europe and the United States the unthinkable prospect of another major war in Europe became real during the summer of 1939.

This time the crisis erupted over the future of Danzig, a German-speaking "free city" on the Baltic Sea under League of Nations supervision. Although it was not formally a part of Poland, Danzig did give Poland vital access to the sea. The German majority in Danzig sympathized with the Nazis and demanded the right to unite with Germany. Hitler took up their cause, as he had done a year earlier with the German-speaking residents of northern Czechoslovakia. After Hitler's betrayal of the Munich agreement, however, British and French officials had lost their enthusiasm for appeasing him. They resigned themselves to the certainty that war would come over Danzig unless Hitler backed down.

In order to prepare for the inevitable fighting, Britain and France explored the possibility of a formal military alliance with the Soviet Union in the summer of 1939. But most officials in the two western European democracies loathed the prospect of joining with Joseph Stalin and his Communist government. Stalin understood how much he was despised in the West. A deeply suspicious man, he feared that Britain and France only wanted an alliance so that the Soviet Union would bear the brunt of the fighting should war break out with Germany. At the same time that his subordinates were negotiating with Britain and France, he sought protection in the most unlikely quarter—Germany. In August he fired his Jewish foreign minister, Maxim Litvinov, an outspoken advocate of resistance to Nazi aggression through collective security and the League of Nations. Stalin's action signaled his willingness to make a deal with Hitler. On August 23 the German and Soviet foreign ministers stunned the world with the announcement that their two countries had agreed to a nonagression pact: neither would wage war on the other. This Hitler-Stalin pact, as it became known, effectively gave the German dictator a free hand to attack Poland on the pretext of annexing Danzig. In addition to the public nonagression agreement, Germany and the Soviet Union signed a secret agreement dividing Poland between them after it was defeated by the German army.

News of the nonagression pact provoked action in Britain, France, and the United States. Britain signed a formal military alliance with Poland on August 25. (France already had a mutual defense treaty with Poland.) Roosevelt cautioned restraint. He advised the governments of Germany and Poland to avoid war and urged the king of Italy to intercede. But after what had happened to Czechoslovakia, the leaders of Britain and France did not believe Hitler would settle for Danzig in Poland, so they refused to turn the city over to Germany. On September 1 German forces attacked Poland. On September 3 Britain and France retaliated by declaring war on Germany. The Second World War had begun.

✦ American Entry into World War II

Americans were much better informed about European affairs when war broke out in 1939 than they had been in 1914. The radio and weekly newsreels made world events real and immediate to Americans. For six years they had seen pictures and films of Nazi storm troopers beating Jews, Communists, socialists, homosexuals, gypsies, and others the Nazi government despised. They had observed bonfires of books and huge candle-lit Nazi marches and rallies. Such sights sickened many Americans. Still, until the fall of 1941 a majority wanted to make certain that the United States would not become directly involved in the war.

From the time war started in Europe until the United States became directly involved in December 1941, Americans sympathetic to the Allies (self-described internationalists) and those who wanted to preserve American neutrality (who called themselves noninterventionists but were labeled isolationists by their foes) fought a ferocious battle for public support. Internationalists believed that U.S. interests were intimately tied to the fate of the European democracies. They tended to support the New Deal, to live in the Northeast, and to have personal or cultural ties to the victims of Nazi aggression. Isolationist sentiments were strongest in the Midwest, particularly among people of German descent and others distrustful of Great Britain or the Jews. But even some liberals, remembering the disillusionment following the First World War, wanted to avoid involvement in another one. And after the Soviet Union signed its nonagression pact with Nazi Germany in August 1939, members of the American Communist Party abruptly switched from demanding action against Hitler to calling for the United States to stay out of "Europe's war."

In June 1940 internationalists, encouraged by Roosevelt and Secretary of the Interior Harold Ickes, organized the Committee to Defend America by Aiding the Allies. They sponsored speakers and placed articles in leading newspapers and journals of opinion advocating private and government efforts on behalf of the Allies. They also sought to discredit the work of the America First Committee, a group formed by noninterventionists to keep the United States out of the war. America First saw echoes of 1915–1917 in the efforts of the internationalists to support Britain and France. They complained that the reports of German atrocities were exaggerated, and they argued that Britain wanted to draw the United States into the war to preserve its endangered empire.

The battle for public sympathy developed ugly overtones. Isolationists flirted with and occasionally embraced anti-Semitism. Charles Lindbergh, a prominent spokesman for America First, claimed that only Jews and British sympathizers wanted the United States to become involved in the war against Germany. Internationalists engaged in occasional dirty tricks against opponents of American involvement in the war. The president and J. Edgar Hoover, the director of the Federal Bureau of Investigation, encouraged a campaign of disinformation targeting leaders of America First, charging that they took orders directly from the German government. The FBI opened the mail of America First leaders and produced phony letters designed to show that prominent noninterventionists sympathized with the Nazis. Such tactics helped undermine the isolationists' appeal. By the fall of 1941 opinion surveys revealed that 40 percent of the American public was willing to enter the war on behalf of the Allies. The government's campaign against the noninterventionists also set a bad precedent for the future. In the years after the Second World War successive presidents looked back on the way Roosevelt had used both fair and foul tactics to gather support for the internationalist cause. His successors often used similar means to achieve their own, vastly different foreign policy objectives.

Roosevelt shared the revulsion of the internationalists at the barbarity of the Nazis' conduct, but he also dreaded getting too far ahead of public opinion. He wanted to avoid what had happened to Woodrow Wilson—initial public exaltation followed by sharp disillusionment. At every step along the road to war, Roosevelt tried to convince the public that his proposals served U.S. interests and that they were not simply altruistic schemes to relieve the suffering of overseas victims of aggression. When the war began he immediately sympathized with Britain, France, and Poland. In sharp contrast to President Wilson, who had initially exhorted Americans to be neutral in thought as well as deed, Roosevelt advocated revising the neutrality laws to permit the Allies to purchase arms on a cash-and-carry basis. Congress initially rebuffed his efforts, but in the fall of 1939, after Germany had conquered Poland in only six weeks, the law was changed. Roosevelt claimed that the new provision would actually keep the United States out of the war by permitting the Allies to defend themselves. In the winter of 1939–1940 Britain and France bought $50 million in arms from the United States.

The war between Germany and Britain and France paused for six months after Germany defeated Poland. Some people called it a phony war. But another unexpected front opened in December when the Soviet Union, after having taken one-third of Poland and the independent Baltic states of Latvia, Lithuania, and Estonia, attacked neighboring Finland in December 1939. Finland had garnered particular respect among Americans by being the only country to fully repay its World War I debts to the United States. The Roosevelt administration promised arms to the Finns, who put up unexpectedly strong resistance to the Soviet forces. Great Britain contemplated sending a division across Norway to assist the Finns, and the League of Nations responded by evicting the Soviet Union. This was the only time the League had ever expelled a member, since Germany, Italy, and Japan had all left on their own before they could be ousted. These actions all proved ineffectual, however, and the vastly outnumbered Finns sued for peace in early 1940.

Germany turned its forces north and west in April, initiating blitzkrieg, or "lightning war," attacks on Norway, Denmark, and Holland. All were overwhelmed and surrendered within six weeks. In the midst of the debacle Neville Chamberlain resigned as Britain's prime minister. His replacement, Winston Churchill, had waged an often lonely battle against German rearmament during the 1930s. As a Conservative Party backbencher Churchill had been considered a hopelessly old-fashioned romantic and imperialist; as prime minister he proved to be bundle of energy and one of the twentieth century's most moving orators. He took office as the million-man German army attacked France. French resistance proved as weak as that of Hitler's earlier victims. In early June Churchill flew several times across the English Channel to stiffen the spine of the French government, shocked by the ease with which Germany had run over the supposedly invincible Maginot line, a series of concrete antitank fortifications built in the 1920s and 1930s. Churchill could not rally the French ministers, some of whom resented Britain for having evacuated its 220,000-strong British Expeditionary Force from the beaches of Dunkirk in May when it appeared they might all be captured by the onrushing Germans. On June 22, 1940, France surrendered to Germany in the same railroad car, resting on the same spot, in which German generals had surrendered to the Allies on November 11, 1918.

With Britain facing Germany alone in the summer of 1940, the Roosevelt administration took several steps to show its support for the last remaining European democracy. In July the president appointed two prominent internationalist Republicans to his cabinet. Former secretary of state Henry L. Stimson, a leading advocate of American resistance to Japan, became secretary of war. He advocated compulsory military training for able-bodied men and the repeal of the neutrality laws. Roosevelt appointed Frank Knox as secretary of the navy. Knox, the Republican vice-presidential nominee in 1936, made no secret of his support for Great Britain. He wanted the United States to expand its army to 1 million men, build the largest air force in the world, and immediately ship hundreds of warplanes to Britain. By bringing these Republicans into his cabinet, Roosevelt tried to demonstrate bipartisan support for his pro-Allied sympathies on the eve of the 1940 election.

In August Roosevelt evaded the restrictions of the neutrality laws by granting Britain fifty obsolete destroyers in return for the right to use British naval bases in the Caribbean. The same month he announced support for a law creating the Selective Service system to conscript men into the armed forces. In September Congress passed a draft law, limiting its term to just one year and specifying that conscripts would serve only in the Western Hemisphere.

Roosevelt did nothing more to aid Britain overtly before winning reelection over Wendell Willkie, the Republican candidate, in November 1940. Willkie, like Roosevelt, backed Britain, and he supported the destroyers-for-bases arrangement and conscription. Nevertheless, he did appeal to voters' fears. "If you elect me president," he said, "I will never send American boys to fight in any European war." Not to be outdone, Roosevelt assured the mothers of the country, "your boys are not going to be sent into any foreign wars." Neither man meant it, and Roosevelt's experienced foreign policy leadership carried the election. His majority of 55 percent of the vote, while still substantial, was down sharply from his landslide of 1936. A majority of voters told pollsters that they would have voted for Willkie had they not believed that the country needed Roosevelt's stewardship in the midst of a war more and more people began to consider inevitable.

As Americans were electing their president, Britain's financial position deteriorated. In December 1940 Churchill told Roosevelt that his country lacked the cash to purchase American arms. In response the president crafted a plan to get Britain all the weapons it needed without technically violating the neutrality laws. In January he asked Congress to enact a "lend-lease" law, under which the president would be authorized to "lease, lend, or otherwise dispose of" American arms and equipment to any country the president deemed vital to the defense of the United States. Under the Lend-Lease Act, $7 billion, a huge sum for 1941, was made available for the manufacture of ships, planes, and materiel. While arguing for Lend-Lease, Roosevelt likened the situation of Great Britain to that of a family seeing its house on fire and begging its neighbor for a garden hose to douse the blaze. As a good neighbor, Roosevelt said, the United States should be happy to oblige and should not demand payment, only the return of the hose after the fire was out. The imagery was effective, although most people realized that equipment used in wartime might not be in very good shape when returned. Wendell Willkie's support gave a bipartisan cast to Lend-Lease. Congress passed the law over the objections of isolationists, one of whom begged the lawmakers to "preserve one stronghold of order and sanity even against the gates of hell."

Roosevelt took other steps to aid Great Britain in 1941. Representatives of the British and American military chiefs of staff met in Washington to coordinate strategy should the United States become involved in the war. They agreed that in the event the two countries became involved in a war against both Germany and Japan, they would try to defeat Germany first. In April Roosevelt authorized the U.S. Navy to patrol the North Atlantic to make certain that cargo ships carrying Lend-Lease aid made it past German submarines to Great Britain. The United States also signed agreements with Iceland and the Danish government-in-exile extending U.S. naval protection to the islands of Iceland and Greenland, a Danish possession. These actions provoked German submarine retaliation. In September and October German U-boats attacked several American destroyers and merchant ships, sinking two and killing over one hundred seamen and sailors. Roosevelt used the German attacks as justifications for the U.S. Navy to convoy merchant ships as they crossed the Atlantic. By November the United States and Germany were on the brink of a full-scale naval war in the Atlantic.

At the same time, rearmament was in full swing. The United States produced six thousand military aircraft in 1940 and over twenty thousand in 1941. In 1940 and 1941 the government created the National Defense Research Council and the Office of Scientific Research and Development to distribute millions of dollars in federal contracts to mobilize universities and scientific research institutions for the war effort. In July 1941 Roosevelt asked Congress to extend the Selective Service Act, to have draftees serve for the duration of any war that might be declared, and to grant the president the right to send them anywhere in the world. America First complained that extension of the act made war inevitable. Many members of Congress said they had been deceived in 1940 by a president who had promised to keep conscripts close to home. After furious debate Congress extended the draft in September. The measure passed the House of Representatives by only one vote.

By the summer of 1941 a deep political friendship was flourishing between Roosevelt and Churchill. The two men exchanged telegrams nearly every day. "It is fun to be in the same decade as you," Roosevelt once wrote Churchill. They agreed to meet face to face on warships off the coast of Newfoundland in August. By that time the Soviet Union had joined the war after Hitler's armies attacked it in June. In July Roosevelt made Lend-Lease supplies available to the Soviet armed forces. At their Atlantic Summit, Roosevelt and Churchill agreed to continue to aid the Soviet Union, which they hoped would be able to withstand the German blitzkrieg and take some pressure off beleaguered Britain. They issued a public declaration, the Atlantic Charter, outlining their vision of what the world would look like after the defeat of Germany. The new world order would uphold the "four freedoms" Roosevelt had proclaimed vital to civilization in December 1940—freedom of speech, freedom of religion, freedom from want, and freedom from fear. It would also ban aggression, include some sort of new international organization to replace the League of Nations, and commit the nations of the world to reducing trade barriers. The publication of the Atlantic Charter pleased interventionists, who considered its denunciation of aggression and its depiction of a world without Nazi tyranny as a clear indication that Roosevelt had cast his lot with Britain. Noninterventionists were outraged, for just the same reasons. They saw the Atlantic Charter as a declaration of war in everything but name. They did not know it at the time, but Churchill validated their worst nightmares when he addressed the British cabinet upon his return from the summit. He told his colleagues that Roosevelt had assured him the United States would "wage war but not declare it."

The war between Japan and China once more intruded on the American public's consciousness in 1941. Japan had continued its attacks on China since 1937 (see map). By mid-1941 Japan controlled all of the Chinese coast, one-third of China's territory, and 40 percent of China's population. But the government of Jiang Jieshi would not surrender. Jiang and Mao Zedong, the leader of the Chinese Communist Party, which had conducted a civil war against Jiang's Nationalist Party for over a decade, agreed to an uneasy truce

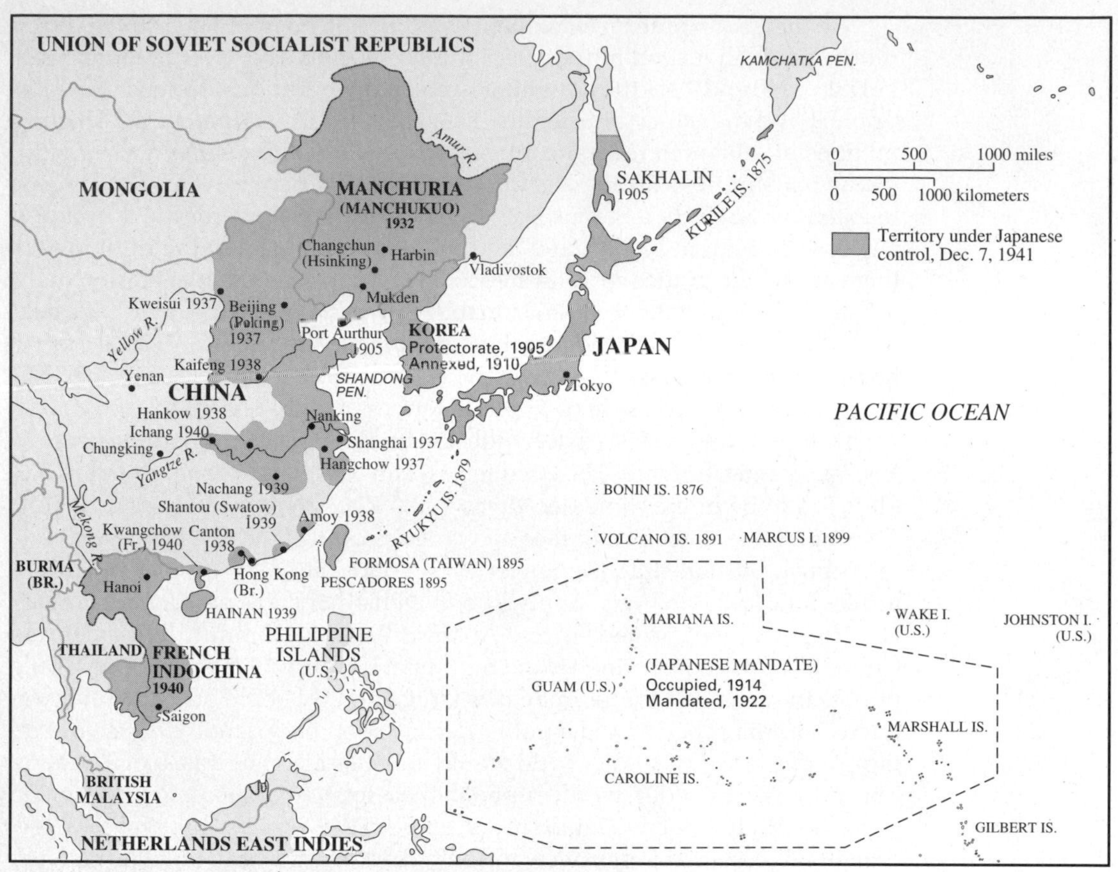

Japanese Expansion Before Pearl Harbor Japan began building an empire in the Pacific early in the twentieth century. In the 1930s Japan began military operations against China. By 1941 Japan directly challenged the position of the United States in the Pacific.

so their forces could jointly confront the Japanese. Facing this continuing Chinese resistance, Japan's military leaders looked for ways to expand the war beyond China. They hoped to secure additional raw materials to supply Japan's armed forces, encircle China, and eventually force Jiang to surrender. Japan considered attacking Soviet Siberia, but the coal supplies of that vast, largely uninhabited territory seemed less alluring than the oil, rubber, and tin available in French Indochina, British Malaya, the Dutch West Indies, and the American-controlled Philippines.

Preoccupied with the war in Europe, the Roosevelt administration had said little about Japanese aggression since the president's quarantine speech in 1937. That reticence began to erode with the appointment of the outspokenly anti-Japanese Henry Stimson as secretary of war in 1940. In July Roosevelt finally endorsed a portion of the pro-Chinese lobby's proposals when he froze Japanese assets in the United States and barred the sale of oil and scrap iron, items necessary for the proper maintenance of a modern navy, to Japan. The United States also increased economic and military aid to China. Roosevelt stopped short of breaking diplomatic relations with Japan, and he assured the Japanese that normal relations could be restored if the two countries reached agreement concerning the future of China. Secretary of the Interior Ickes characterized Roosevelt's Japan policy as slipping "the noose around Japan's neck and giving it a jerk now and then." In effect Roosevelt hoped to keep China fighting Japan while avoiding for as long as possible an American war with Tokyo.

Japan responded to the freezing of its assets with plans for attacks on U.S. territory and possessions in Hawaii, Guam, and the Philippines. The goal was to inflict immediate damage at a time when Japan's armed forces were strong and those of the United States were relatively weak. On September 6 the Japanese cabinet agreed to prepare for war in Asia against Great Britain, the Netherlands, and the United States. The Japanese chief of naval operations likened his country's condition to that of a man facing death who could "find a way to life out of a seemingly fatal situation" only by means of some highly dangerous surgery.

While Japan prepared for war in the Pacific, Secretary of State Cordell Hull continued to discuss a compromise settlement with Japanese negotiators. In late November he told Kichisaburo Nomura, the Japanese ambassador, that the United States would resume oil sales to Japan if the Japanese withdrew from all the territory they had occupied in Asia since 1931. Nomura told his superiors in Tokyo that Hull had in effect delivered an ultimatum and that the United States was plotting a war. The Japanese diplomatic cables were quickly deciphered by American code breakers, who relayed their contents to Stimson and Roosevelt. The president said that "we are likely to be attacked." Stimson wrote in his diary that "the question was how should we maneuver them into firing the first shot without allowing too much danger to ourselves."

As the Hull-Nomura talks stalemated, a carrier force secretly left Japan, destined to attack the American fleet in Hawaii. On Sunday morning, December 7, wave after wave of Japanese planes flew over Oahu, bombing U.S. warships in Pearl Harbor. The two-hour long raid sank seven battleships, destroyed on the ground most of the U.S. warplanes stationed in Hawaii, and killed over 2,400 Americans. The same day, Japanese air, sea, and ground forces attacked the U.S.-controlled Philippines and the British possession of Malaya. News of Pearl Harbor came over the radio on the mainland on a quiet Sunday afternoon. Most people had expected war soon, but they had little idea how badly relations with Japan had deteriorated. Churchill was elated at the news of Pearl Harbor, despite the carnage. "So we have won after all," he recalled as he contemplated having the United States as a full-fledged military ally. In China, Jiang voiced similar enthusiasm.

On Sunday morning, December 7, 1941, hundreds of carrier-based Japanese warplanes bombed the U.S. naval base at Pearl Harbor, bringing the United States into World War II. *National Archives*

The next day Roosevelt asked Congress for a declaration of war, calling December 7, 1941, a date that will "live in infamy." Isolationists were cowed into silence by the devastation wrought by the Japanese at Pearl Harbor. The declaration of war passed Congress immediately, with only one dissenting vote, that of Montana representative Jeannette Rankin, who had also voted against U.S. entry into the First World War in April 1917. Three days later, on December 11, Hitler invoked Germany's alliance with Japan and declared war on the United States. Roosevelt felt relieved that Hitler had acted, since the United States could now, as he and Churchill had hoped, fight Germany as well as Japan.

✦ Conclusion

The events leading to the entry of the United States into the Second World War exposed many flaws in U.S. foreign policy following World War I. Disillusioned by the outcome of the Great War, most Americans had hoped to remain deeply involved in world affairs but at the same time maintain their nation's freedom of action. The strategy worked for a while during the prosperous 1920s, but the Depression brought new constraints. Americans had little time or energy to devote to foreign affairs as the Depression tightened its grip. The later rise of the dictators in Europe alarmed many Americans, but unhappy memories of World War I limited what people were willing to do to counter Nazism and Fascism. Once war broke out in Asia and Europe, more and more Americans came to believe that U.S. interests were aligned with those of the enemies of Japan, Italy, and Germany. President Franklin D. Roosevelt was more alert than most of his fellow citizens to the danger posed by the dictators. He carefully nurtured pro-Allied sentiment. Until the very end, though, most Americans hoped to avoid war while still supporting the Allies. They could not. The Japanese attack on Pearl Harbor left some people who had earlier opposed strong U.S. action feeling guilty over their resistance to U.S. involvement in the war. Americans were furious at Japan and threw their anger behind their political leadership as the country embarked on its second major war effort in less than twenty-five years.

✦ Further Reading

For general overviews of America's foreign relations during the period, see: Warren Cohen, *Empire Without Tears* (1987); Akira Iriye, *The Globalization of America, 1913–1945* (1993); Emily Rosenberg, *Spreading the American Dream: American Economic and Cultural Expansion, 1890–1945* (1982). For U.S. relations with Europe, see: Melvyn P. Leffler, *The Elusive Quest* (1979); Douglas Little, *Malevolent Neutrality* (1985); David Reynolds, *The Creation of the Anglo-American Alliance* (1981) For relations with Asia, see: Roger Dingman, *Power in the Pacific* (1976); Akira Iriye, *After Imperialism* (1965); Dorothy Borg and Shumpei Okamoto, *Pearl Harbor as History* (1973); Warren Cohen and Akira Iriye, *American, Chinese and Japanese Perspectives on Wartime Asia* (1990); Michael Schaller, *The United States and China in the Twentieth Century* (1994); James C. Thomson, *When China Faced West* (1969). On Latin America, see: Lester Langley, *The Banana Wars* (1983); Dana Munro, *The United States and the Caribbean Republics in the 1920s* (1972); Neill McCauley, *The Sandino Affair* (1967); Irwin Gellman, *Roosevelt and Batista* (1973) and *Good Neighbor Diplomacy* (1979). For U.S. economic diplomacy in the twenties, see: Joseph Brandes, *Herbert Hoover and Economic Diplomacy*; Joan Hoff Wilson, *American Business and Foreign Policy, 1920–1933* (1976); Marc Trachtenberg, *Reparations in World Politics* (1980). For discussion of the impact of the Great Depression on U.S. foreign policy, see: Robert Ferrell, *American Diplomacy in the Great Depression* (1957); Charles Kindleberger, *The World in Depression* (1973); Christopher Thorne, *The Limits of Power* (1973); Robert Dallek, *Franklin D. Roosevelt and American Foreign Policy* (1979); Lloyd C. Gardner, *Economic Aspects of New Deal Diplomacy* (1964). For information on the American public's attitudes toward foreign affairs during the period, see: Charles DeBenedetti, *Origins of the Modern American Peace Movement* (1978); Charles Chatfield, *For Peace and Justice* (1971); Warren Cohen, *The American Revisionists* (1967); Robert D. Schulzinger, *The Wise Men of Foreign Affairs: The History of the Council on Foreign Relations* (1984); Robert A. Divine, *The Illusion of Neutrality* (1962) and *The*

Reluctant Belligerent (1986); Wayne S. Cole, *Roosevelt and the Isolationists* (1983); and Walter Hixson, *Lone Eagle* (1996) (a biography of Charles A. Lindbergh). To grasp the complicated story of the outbreak of World War II, see: Akire Iriye, *The Origins of the Second World War in Asia and the Pacific* (1991); D.C. Watt, *How War Came* (1989). For U.S. policy toward the war from its outbreak until Pearl Harbor, see: Saul Friedlander, *Prelude to Downfall* (1967); Waldo H. Heinrichs, Jr., *Threshold of War* (1988); Gordon Prange, *Pearl Harbor* (1986); Roberta Wohlstetter, *Pearl Harbor* (1962).

✦✦✦

CHAPTER 7

The Second World War and the Remaking of America, 1941–1945

✦ **Destruction at Pearl Harbor, December 7, 1941.**

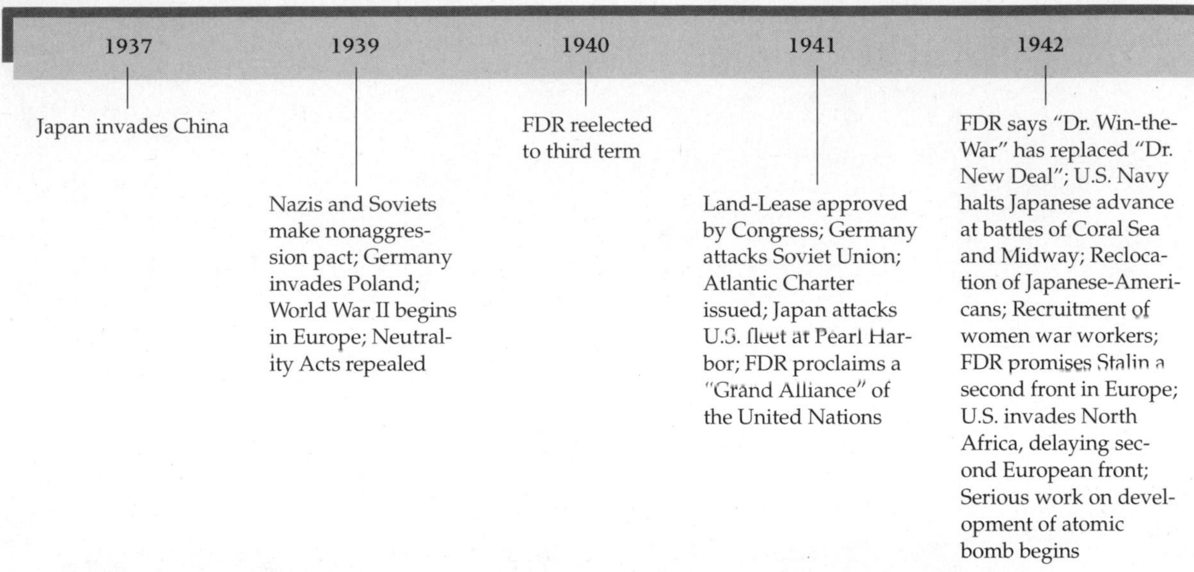

JACK SHORT OF Poughkeepsie, New York, was only twenty years old when his unit landed in France shortly after D-day in June 1944. Over the next several months they raced across western Europe. Shortly before the Nazi surrender, Short and his comrades came across a concentration camp at Nordhausen, Germany, where the bodies of thousands of the dead and dying were "stacked up like cordwood." Decades later he occasionally took out photographs he snapped that day to remind himself of the horror he had encountered.

In spite of the painful memory, Jack Short told interviewer Studs Terkel about the war's positive impact on his life. He had come from a working-class family whose members had all worked in factories, with their hands. High school was as far as any of them had ever gone. After three years in the army, meeting other young men from all over the United States, Jack had developed different aspirations. He didn't want to be a blue-collar worker in his old hometown. Unlike his relatives, after 1945 Jack had the opportunity to change his life. As a veteran he was educated under the GI Bill. "It paid for 99 percent of your college expenses and gave you money each month to live on," Jack

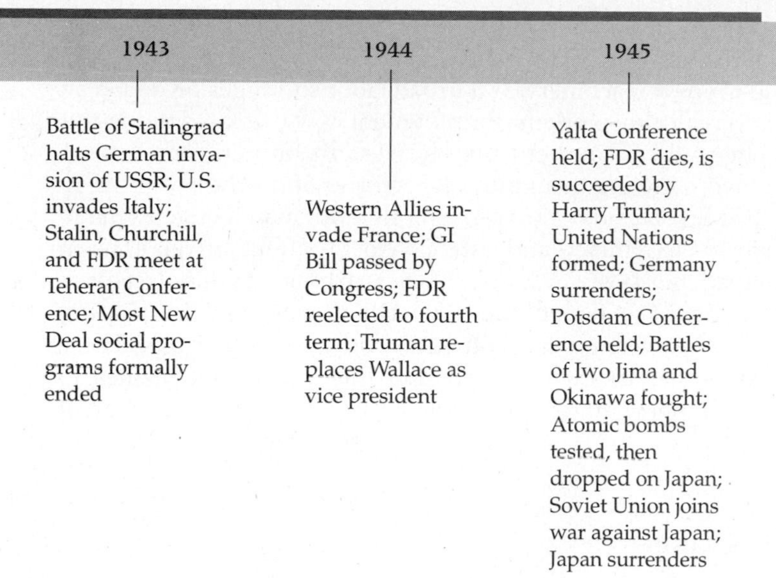

explained. In 1950 he became the first member of his family to graduate from college and went to work for IBM. "Everything in my life since the war," Jack believes, "has been positive."

Not only was the Second World War the most destructive event of the twentieth century, it also transformed the lives of nearly all Americans, whether or not they served in the military. During World War II the United States assumed a new position of chief importance in international affairs. By the time President Franklin Roosevelt died in 1945 the United States had become a superpower—a difficult, uneasy role that has shaped the nation's history ever since. But the war did much more than propel the United States into the position of the world's leading military power. It also brought the New Deal to fulfillment.

The vast government spending that made victory possible also created full employment, mass purchasing power, and, for the first time, the possibility of affluence for a majority of Americans. For business the war created an era of government-ensured profitability and restored the public esteem of large corporations. Good weather during the war years produced bumper harvests, and high demand and farm prices transformed rural America. Rising farm income paid for new machinery, and urban labor shortages provided an outlet for surplus agricultural workers. Employment in war-related industries created a magnetic pull on southern blacks, western farmers, small-town laborers, and women, drawing them into the factories of northern, midwestern, and western cites. During the war, unions and management finally accepted each other's legitimacy and established a pattern of relations in industry that shaped the postwar era. Finally, wartime scientific research created the foundations of such revolutionary technologies as nuclear fission, digital computers, microelectronics, synthetics, and antibiotic drugs. These developments inspired Henry Luce, publisher of *Time* and *Life* magazines, to proclaim the dawn of a new "international moral order" and the "first great American Century."

✦ America and the World Crisis

Until the late 1930s the Great Depression limited the American public's concern with foreign affairs. Many Americans, including a substantial number in Congress, wanted to isolate the nation from conflicts between foreign countries, a desire reflected in the Neutrality Act passed in 1935.

With American attention turned to the crisis in Europe following the outbreak of war there in September 1939, Japan took the opportunity to seize southern French Indochina, demand special access to oil from the Dutch East Indies, and insist that Washington stop military aid to China. In response Roosevelt shifted U.S. naval units to the Pacific and imposed a trade embargo on Japan, leaving Tokyo with only a few months' reserves of petroleum.

When negotiations between Japanese emissaries in Washington and Secretary of State Cordell Hull broke off on November 26, 1941, American officials expected a Japanese attack in Southeast Asia or the Philippines and sent warnings to commanders there and in Hawaii. But American intelligence intercepts of Japanese communications did not reveal that Japan's leaders had designated the Pacific Fleet, based at Pearl Harbor in Hawaii, as the first target.

On December 7, 1941—a date, Roosevelt declared, that would "live in infamy"—Japan mounted a surprise air attack on the military facilities at Pearl Harbor. The assault killed over 2,400 sailors and soldiers, damaged or sank eight American battleships, and destroyed hundreds of planes. By chance the Japanese attackers missed the navy's aircraft carriers, which were out on maneuvers. At Roosevelt's request Congress promptly declared war on Japan. On December 10 Japan's allies, Germany and Italy, joined the war against the United States. As Japanese forces rolled to a string of easy victories in Southeast Asia, the shock and humiliation terrified Americans, who had previously felt immune from war.

To buoy morale in the first terrifying weeks after the attack on Pearl Harbor, when all the news seemed bad, Roosevelt did what he did best: he held a fireside chat. The president asked Americans to buy maps and spread them out on their kitchen tables or living room floors while he spoke. Stores quickly sold out their entire inventory. Eight out of ten adults listened as Roosevelt, referring to the maps, gave a frank account of the losses suffered at Pearl Harbor, described the German and Japanese successes in Europe and the Pacific, and explained what he proposed to do about it. The struggle would be long and difficult, he warned, with many setbacks. Quoting the American revolutionary patriot Tom Paine, Roosevelt declared, "Tyranny, like Hell, is not easily conquered." But, he continued, "the harder the sacrifice, the more glorious the triumph." He reassured a frightened population that Germany and Japan had sown the seeds of their own doom by engaging America's vast military potential.

The Japanese attack ended dissent over participation in the war. On New Year's Day in 1942, the United States, Great Britain, the Soviet Union, and twenty-three other partners issued a "Declaration of the United Nations," a pledge to fight for victory against the Axis alliance of Germany, Japan, and Italy. Roosevelt and his military advisers resolved that the United States would provide additional Lend-Lease aid to Britain, the Soviet Union, and China to help them carry the bulk of the fighting against Germany and Japan. As soon as possible, British and American armies would open a second front by invading western Europe. This would relieve the pressure on the Soviets, who were fighting about two-thirds of all the German forces. This so-called Europe First strategy meant that the war against Japan would take second place until Germany's defeat. Roosevelt hoped that once Germany was crushed the Soviets would join in the final assault on Japan (see map).

The military strategy favored by American planners encountered numerous obstacles. Prime Minister Winston Churchill, who guided Britain until the final months of the war, feared high casualties in an early assault on western Europe. He preferred to wear down the Germans instead by attacking their flanks in North Africa and Italy. American commanders preferred a frontal assault on western Europe as the most efficient way to win the war. Any delay might increase total casualties and risk the collapse of the hard-pressed Soviet Union. Roosevelt knew that Stalin would interpret any delay in opening a second front in Europe as encouraging Germany's devastation of the Soviet Union. Because both the Soviet army and Soviet civilians were suffering enormous casualties, and out of fear that the Soviets might make a separate peace with Germany, Roosevelt promised Stalin a second front in 1942. But supply problems, British resistance, the competing demands of the Pacific war against Japan, and other factors delayed the Allies' entry into France until June 6, 1944. This delay embittered Stalin and ordinary Soviets, who scoffed at British and American explanations. At the same time, however, the air forces and navies of the United States and Great Britain played a critical role in destroying Germany's war-making capacity.

The massive Normandy invasion of June 1944 gave the Anglo-American forces a foothold in western Europe. During 1944 and early 1945 the Soviet

The European War, 1942–1945 Soviet armies did most of the fighting in Europe until D-Day, June 6, 1944, when the Western allies invaded France.

Red Army continued the bulk of the fighting against the German army. At a cost of more than 20 million civilian and military dead, Soviet troops pushed the Germans out of Poland, and as 1945 began they were poised to push on to Berlin. However, the long-delayed Anglo-American invasion of France fueled Stalin's mistrust of his Western allies. Like many Soviets, Stalin believed that FDR and Churchill had intentionally delayed invading France so the Soviet Union would wear itself down doing most of the fighting against Germany. Then, Stalin believed, the Americans and British could move to control Europe themselves.

The behavior of Soviet leaders tended to arouse similar fears in London and Washington. For example, beginning in 1942 Stalin demanded that Roosevelt and Churchill approve the postwar transfer of parts of prewar Poland and southeastern Europe to the Soviet Union. Although Western leaders believed such concessions would violate the rights of Poland and the other nations involved, they also recognized that the Soviets had a legitimate interest in creating a security zone in eastern Europe, the route of two German invasions since 1914. Churchill and Roosevelt eventually accepted the Soviet demands in return for Stalin's promise to respect the political independence of the rest of eastern Europe.

Some American policymakers believed that at times Churchill seemed more interested in safeguarding British interests in the Mediterranean than in defeating Hitler. Like the Soviet Union, Britain also worried about America's power in the postwar world. Roosevelt hoped, however, that wartime cooperation would create support for a new world political order. At a series of summits held between 1941 and 1945, the president sketched plans for a postwar international organization, the United Nations, to be dominated by what he sometimes called the "four policemen"—the United States, the Soviet Union, Great Britain, and China. Each nation would be predominant in the security zone, or sphere of interest, most important to it. At the same time, each would work toward opening world trade, gradual decolonization, and the rehabilitation of Germany and Japan to encourage their forming democratic societies. Roosevelt first pressed these points in August 1941, even before the United States formally entered the war, when he and a skeptical Churchill met at sea near Newfoundland and jointly issued their Atlantic Charter. Plans for the United Nations went forward during the war, and it was chartered in 1945, shortly after Roosevelt's death. By then, however, growing mistrust between the United States and the Soviet Union frustrated efforts to have the UN serve as an international peace keeper.

Although the diplomatic and strategic logic of the war often seemed confused, by 1945 a pattern had emerged. As Stalin remarked, "whoever occupies a territory also imposes on it his own social system." Thus between 1943 and 1945 the British and the Americans, joined by Charles de Gaulle's Free French, eventually occupied and then established pro-Western, anti-Communist regimes in North Africa, Italy, Greece, France, western Germany, Japan, and southern Korea. As American forces advanced across the

Pacific (see map), the United States took possession of hundreds of islands formerly held by Japan, eventually declaring them "strategic trusteeships" (see map).

Some critics faulted Roosevelt as naive, but he usually showed a keen appreciation of the long-term national interests of the United States. For example, during the war he took the lead in making certain that the United States became more involved in the Middle East, an area containing immense petroleum reserves. To make certain that American oil companies gained a firm foothold in the region, Roosevelt met with the ruler of Saudi Arabia, King Ibn Saud, and began a cooperative relationship that secured U.S. access to Saudi oil for the next half century. Reliable and inexpensive supplies of oil proved essential to the postwar recovery of the non-Communist world.

In truth, all the Allies looked after their own interests even while they pursued common goals. For example, the British, French, and Dutch rushed to recolonize Southeast Asia after Japan retreated. As Soviet forces pushed the

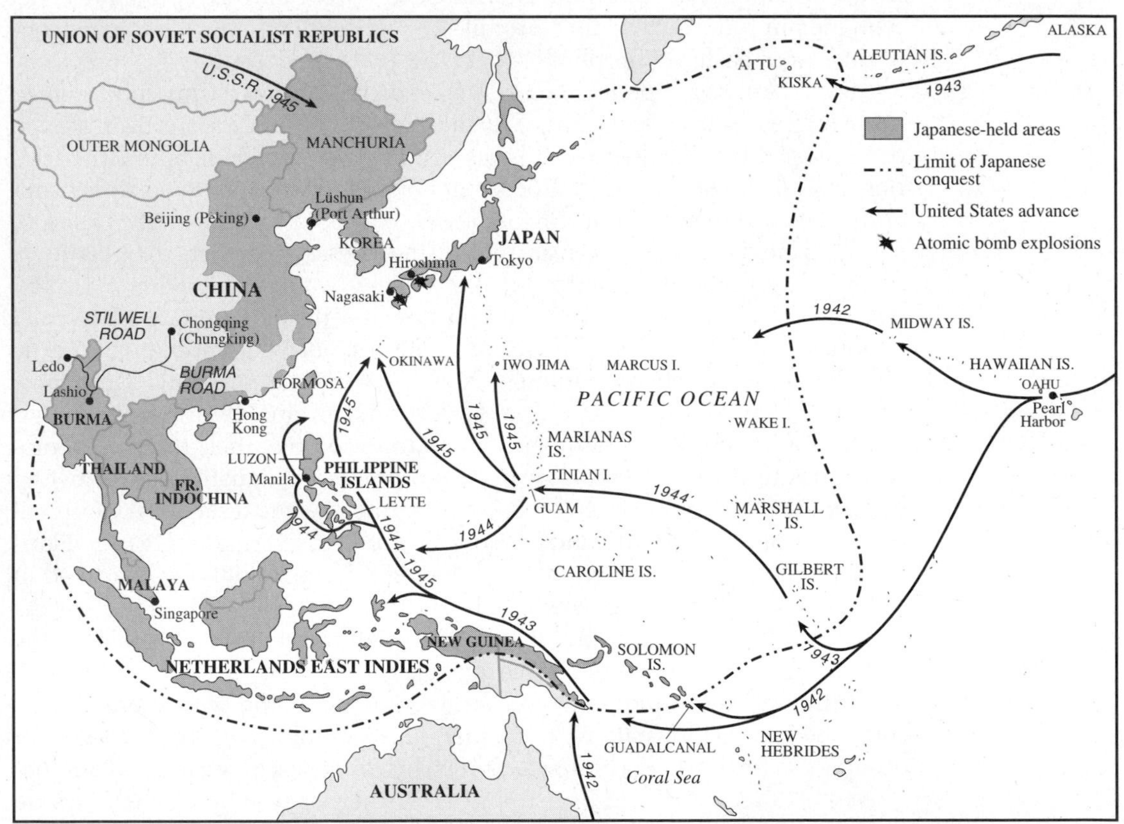

The Pacific War, 1942–1945 The U.S. navy, army, and air force pushed across the Pacific in order to isolate, blockade, and bomb Japan into submission.

Nazis toward Berlin, Stalin similarly imposed pro-Soviet regimes in most of eastern Europe. Roosevelt, who was hardly naive or sympathetic to Soviet brutality, nevertheless preferred delaying most bargaining over spheres of influence until the war's end, when he thought the American position would be stronger. Nor did he favor punitive actions toward the Soviet Union while the war in Europe continued and Washington still needed Stalin's cooperation in the war against Japan. When several of his advisers urged him to confront Moscow, perhaps even to cut off Lend-Lease aid once German troops had been pushed out of Soviet territory, Roosevelt refused to risk a break in the alliance and declared that everything would be negotiable after victory.

But by February 1945, as victory in Europe approached, the Allies could no longer defer discussing postwar issues. Roosevelt and Churchill joined Stalin for a crucial meeting at Yalta, a Soviet city on the Black Sea. There the "Big Three"—Great Britain, the United States, and the Soviet Union—agreed to participate in the new United Nations and to require industrial reparations from Germany. They also agreed that the Soviets would enter the war against Japan three months after Germany's defeat. Critics of the Yalta agreement later charged that Roosevelt had acceded to Stalin's demands out of naiveté, deteriorating health, or perhaps even Communist sympathies. Why else would he sanction a dominant Soviet role in Poland or grant Stalin special economic privileges in Manchuria? "Yalta" became shorthand, especially among Republicans, for appeasement of Soviet territorial demands.

In reality the Yalta agreement mostly recognized what Stalin had already taken. Soviet forces had occupied the Baltic states of Estonia, Latvia, and Lithuania; Poland; and parts of Rumania and Bulgaria. The Soviets were poised to invade Germany and would soon be able to attack Japan through Manchuria. So Roosevelt "gave away" little. Furthermore, American military leaders, who feared high casualties in the final stages of the war against Japan, pressed Roosevelt to make concessions to Stalin to get Soviet forces into the Pacific war.

As part of his price for joining the fight against Japan, Stalin demanded special economic privileges in Manchuria (northeastern China). In return he promised not to assist the Chinese Communists' struggle against the American-backed government of the Chinese Nationalist Party. Stalin also promised to reorganize the Soviet-installed regime in Poland along more democratic lines. A "Declaration of Liberated Europe," signed by the three leaders, pledged cooperation in restoring democratic government in the liberated territories.

Roosevelt's chief of staff complained that the agreement was "so elastic that the Russians can stretch it all the way from Yalta to Washington without technically breaking it." Roosevelt agreed, but he added that it was the best he could do under the circumstances. Without continued Soviet cooperation, Roosevelt knew the Western allies would face a far bloodier road to Berlin and Tokyo. Soviet domination of eastern Europe and northeast Asia—which Stalin could impose with or without American permission—seemed, at the time, a

Allied leaders Winston Churchill, Franklin D. Roosevelt, and Joseph Stalin at Yalta, February 1945. *Franklin D. Roosevelt Library*

reasonable price for saving American lives and shortening the war. Even American hard-liners did not seriously recommend fighting the Soviets to move them out of Poland. Most Americans rejoiced, in fact, when the Soviets captured Berlin and when Germany surrendered on May 8, 1945. On the basis of earlier agreements, the Soviet Union turned over part of the German capital and other territories to its allies.

It is important to note that when the war ended, the United States and its Western allies dominated most of the industrialized world and most of the world's oil reserves, including North America, Great Britain, Western Europe, Japan, and the Middle East. The Soviets occupied much of eastern Europe, a portion of Germany, and parts of China and Korea, but their spoils did little to enhance their industrial or economic power. This fact helped ensure American supremacy after 1945. Among the warring powers, the United States had made the smallest human sacrifice—about four hundred thousand dead, compared to a worldwide total that approached 50 million—and had gained the most from the conflict. Soviet civilian deaths during the three-year siege of just one city—Leningrad (now St. Petersburg)—exceeded the total number of military deaths sustained by the United States. America emerged from the war with the world's strongest economy and most powerful armed forces, as well as a monopoly on atomic power. When the killing stopped, the United States, with only 6 percent of the world's population, produced half of the world's goods. This relative level of power and economic well-being was never surpassed in the half century after the war. As one sensitive observer noted, "while the rest of the world came out bruised and scarred and nearly destroyed, we came out with the most unbelievable machinery, trade, manpower and money."

War on the Home Front

The war years brought to a halt most New Deal social programs. But even if the New Deal was gone, the war itself acted as a catalyst for far-reaching social and economic changes. In 1941 the United States was still largely a rural and small-town society. Of 132 million Americans, about 44 percent, or 58 million, lived in communities with ten thousand or fewer inhabitants. One-third of the nation's dwellings lacked indoor plumbing, and two-thirds lacked central heating. Only 40 percent of U.S. adults had as much as an eighth grade education. One-fourth had graduated from high school, one-tenth had attended college, and only half of those had completed a degree. Ninety percent of white men, the most affluent group, made $2,500 per year or less. Over half of all wage-earning men and three-fourths of wage-earning women earned $1,000 per year or less. In January 1941 the economy still suffered the symptoms of depression. Around 9 million workers, or 15 percent of the labor force, had no job. Private investment stood at 18 percent *below* the 1929 level. The gross national product (GNP) barely surpassed the 1929 figure (see figure).

All of this changed dramatically after the war began. As the war progressed, unemployment virtually disappeared, and ordinary Americans felt the shadow of the Great Depression finally lifting from their lives. Private investment soared to new heights. During the war years the economy created 17 million new jobs, and the GNP swelled from a prewar level of $100 billion per year to over $212 billion in 1945. Universities and private industries vastly expanded their research facilities. Mass population shifts occurred as millions of Americans moved to the cities. By the war's end the United States had taken a giant leap from its lingering small-town past toward its urbanized, high-tech present.

The most obvious economic effect of the war was the surge in federal spending. Defense allocations rose sharply with the passage of Lend-Lease in 1941. The initial Lend-Lease appropriation of $7 billion ballooned to $50 billion over the next 4 years—an enormous sum compared to the total federal budget of $9 billion for 1939. By 1945 the federal government was spending $95 billion per year, more than ten times its annual expenditures before the war. Correspondingly, the size of the federal government's civilian work force more than tripled, rising from 1.1 million workers in 1941 to 3.4 million workers in 1945. The size and scope of the federal government had expanded during earlier wars, especially during the Civil War and World War I. But after

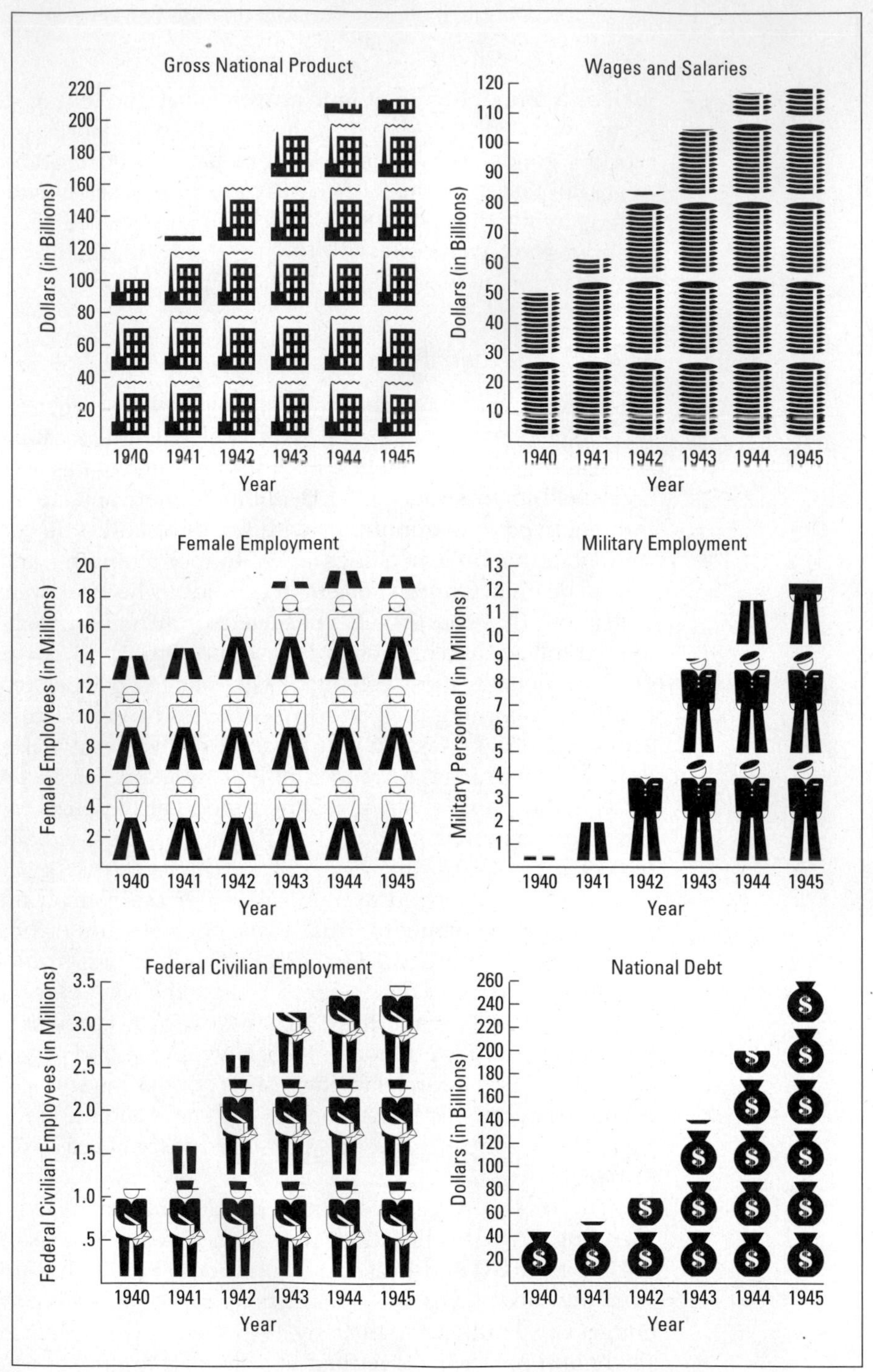

Statistics on U.S. Wartime Industrial Production Between 1941 and 1945, the economy grew at a remarkable pace.

these earlier conflicts it had shrunk. This time the government grew and remained large.

To pay for a war that cost about $250 million per day and over $300 billion by 1945, the United States assumed its first substantial national debt. Although Treasury Secretary Henry Morgenthau, Jr., planned to pay half of the war's costs by raising taxes, the other half had to be financed by the sale of bonds to individuals and banks. With the help of popular film and radio stars, the government promoted Treasury bonds so successfully that bond drives raised $135 billion. By the end of the war the national debt had risen from $40 billion to $260 billion (see figure). Besides raising money, war bond drives served to hold down inflation, by reducing consumer spending, and to involve American civilians in the common war effort.

The government's first mechanism to coordinate defense production, the War Production Board, proved disappointing. Thus at the end of 1942 Roosevelt established the Office of Economic Stabilization to further centralize planning, appointing Supreme Court justice James F. Byrnes to head the agency. In May 1943 Byrnes took over the even more powerful Office of War Mobilization. Roosevelt called Byrnes's job the "assistant president." Relying more on incentives than coercion, Byrnes and his business advisers proved remarkably successful at mobilizing the private sector to produce war goods. Secretary of War Henry Stimson expressed the business community's attitude best: "If you are going to try to go to war in a capitalist country," he observed, "you have to let business make money out of the process, or business won't work."

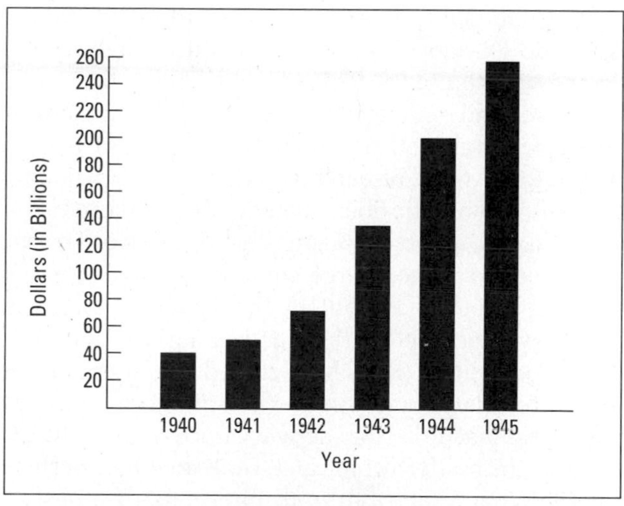

Increase of Federal Spending on Defense, 1940–1945 In borrowing about $260 billion to fight the war, the U.S. government accumulated its first substantial debt.

Corporations were initially reluctant to invest the huge amounts of money needed to convert their facilities from civilian to military production. For example, it would cost General Motors billions of dollars to retool plants to produce tanks and jeeps instead of cars. Who would pay for the conversion, or for reconversion when the war ended? How could profits be assured? Should private businesses be asked to invest in costly, experimental technology that might have no consumer application?

To encourage industrial production, the Justice Department relaxed antitrust enforcement. Washington offered manufacturers the innovative "cost plus a fixed fee" contract, whereby the federal government paid research and production costs and purchased items at a guaranteed markup. With this incentive, conversion to war production accelerated. For example, at Ford's newly built Willow Run plant, outside Detroit, workers on the mile-long assembly line produced 8,564 B-24 bombers at the astounding rate of one every sixty-three minutes.

To meet the immense demands for merchant ships, innovators like Henry J. Kaiser, a West Coast industrialist, used a combination of assembly-line techniques like those used to build automobiles, high wages, and generous benefits to revolutionize production. Kaiser shipyards slashed the time it took to build a cargo ship from three hundred days to only seventeen. The combination of burgeoning military orders and technical innovations boosted the after-tax profits of U.S. corporations from $6.4 billion in 1940 to $10.8 billion in 1944.

Defense mobilization led to other innovations as well. Before 1941 the federal government spent little money on scientific research. Recognizing the contribution science and technology would make toward victory, Roosevelt created the National Defense Research Committee and the Office of Scientific Research and Development (OSRD) to encourage scientists and industry to develop new technologies. By 1945, not counting the $2 billion spent on atomic bomb research and billions more used to construct plants to produce synthetic rubber, steel, aluminum, and aircraft, Washington was funneling $1.5 billion annually into scientific research and development. Radar, electronic computers, jet engines, synthetic fibers, wonder drugs like sulfadiazine and penicillin, nuclear weapons, and ballistic missiles all came out of wartime research. The military's need to process large amounts of data provided a special impetus to the development of computers. Binary digits, the basis of computer logic, had been developed before the war. During the 1930s International Business Machines Corporation (IBM) had worked with the Social Security Administration to process large amounts of information. After 1941 IBM developed code-breaking machines for the war effort, and in 1944 the company built a precursor of the modern computer. By 1946 it had perfected ENIAC, the first large digital computer. Built with hundreds of miles of wire and eighteen thousand vacuum tubes, the behemoth filled an entire room but delivered far less computing power than today's laptop models.

The OSRD, headed by Vannevar Bush of the Massachusetts Institute of Technology, poured $2 billion into the vast, highly secret atomic bomb project. In three new "atomic cities"—Oak Ridge, Tennessee; Hanford, Washington; and Los Alamos, New Mexico—nearly 150,000 people conducted research, refined uranium, and produced weapons. The facilities rivaled the entire U.S. automobile industry in size. Additional government funds helped universities build modern scientific laboratories. Colleges and universities enrolled several hundred thousand officers in army and navy programs for accelerated college degrees.

Research facilities also mushroomed in private industry. By the end of the war almost 2,500 private industrial research laboratories were employing 133,000 people, twice the prewar number. In an influential study called *Science: The Endless Frontier,* published in 1945, Vannevar Bush proposed creating a permanent government agency to fund basic research. Congress finally approved the idea in 1950 when it created the National Science Foundation.

Overall, the administration's policies spurred military production that was little short of miraculous. U.S. aircraft plants, which had produced barely two thousand planes a year before the war, turned out nearly fifty thousand in 1942 and one hundred thousand in 1944. By 1945 American industry had produced over one hundred thousand tanks, eighty-seven thousand ships of all types, 2.5 million trucks, 5 million tons of bombs, and 44 billion rounds of ammunition. As a result American soldiers had a three-to-one advantage in arms over their Axis enemies.

During the war industrial production increased a startling 25 percent annually. The average annual increase in the previous half-century had been 2 percent. The GNP more than doubled, from $100 billion in 1940 to over $200 billion in 1945. Soviet leader Joseph Stalin recognized the importance of this achievement. At the 1943 Teheran Conference with Roosevelt and Churchill, he offered a toast to "American production, without which this war would have been lost."

On the negative side, war production gave birth to what later critics, including President Dwight D. Eisenhower, would call the "military-industrial complex." In 1940 the hundred largest American companies produced 30 percent of all the goods manufactured in the United States. Wartime defense spending disproportionately benefited large firms. By 1945 the "Big 100" American companies received nearly 70 percent of military production dollars, and the ten biggest companies received over 30 percent of the total. The close relationship between the military and large defense contractors would continue after the war, and the economic health of many American communities would come to depend on military appropriations.

As big business prospered during the war years, so did its traditional antagonist, organized labor. For both patriotic and practical reasons, most union leaders supported the effort to maximize production. Shortly after the Pearl Harbor attack, the largest unions issued a "no strike pledge" for the duration of the war. To harmonize labor-management relations, FDR established the National War Labor Board (NWLB) in January 1942. The board's union, business, and public members set criteria for working conditions, wages, and hours. They frequently mediated disputes. The labor board moderated pressure for wage increases by limiting raises to cost-of-living increases. But between the raises allowed and the large amount of overtime work available, many industrial workers saw their income grow by as much as 70 percent by 1945.

To keep workers happy and to get around wage ceilings, union and management often relied on fringe benefits. During the war major employers began providing medical insurance as a benefit. For example, the Kaiser shipyards created a prepaid medical insurance program for its employees that would become Kaiser-Permanente, an early health maintenance organization. Blue Cross and Blue Shield, established before the war, expanded quickly as fringe benefits began to cover health insurance. This had a down side, however. Job-based medical benefits reduced the political pressure for national health insurance. This left the unemployed, the elderly, and those between jobs uncovered.

By and large, the willingness of most labor leaders to cooperate with corporations and the government enhanced their role as part of the economic and political establishment. The major exception was John L. Lewis, head of the United Mine Workers. Mining remained one of the most dangerous and unpleasant jobs in America, war or no war. Lewis demanded larger raises for his membership than the NWLB formula allowed. Periodic strikes in the coal mines caused major disruptions in 1943. Congress responded by passing the Smith-Connally War Labor Disputes Act, which empowered the president to seize any strike-bound company whose output was deemed vital for the war effort.

The effect of rising employment and a friendlier business attitude toward organized labor could be seen in the expansion of union membership. Among factory workers, union membership increased from 10.5 million in 1941 to 15 million in 1945. This figure, equivalent to one-third of the nonfarm work force, marked a historically high percentage. The experience of working closely with managers and government bureaucrats changed the outlook of many union officials, tempering their militancy and making them more disposed to cooperate with their traditional adversaries.

To help pay for the war, the government revised the tax structure and introduced payroll withholding. Before 1941 most lower- and middle-income Americans paid little or no federal income tax. A married worker without dependents earning $2,000 annually paid no federal taxes at all. In 1945 he or she paid just over $200. For individuals earning more, the tax bite increased at a progressive rate. As a result, tax revenues swelled from $5 billion in 1941 to $49 billion by 1945.

At first the combination of defense spending, full employment, and shortages of civilian goods fueled inflation. Agencies like the NWLB and the

Office of Price Administration imposed a variety of wage and price controls, along with rationing. Consumers needed ration coupons and tokens to buy many items, including gasoline, meat, and sugar. Children were encouraged to collect old cans and tires, and cooks to save fat, which could be recycled into war goods. City dwellers cultivated millions of tiny "victory gardens" to supplement their diet.

But even while ordinary people conserved sugar and saved cans, a remarkable process was occurring. The war years brought about the most dramatic redistribution of income for working Americans in the twentieth century. Real factory wages rose from $24 to nearly $37 per week during the war. The share of the national wealth held by the richest 5 percent of Americans declined from 23.7 percent to 16.8 percent. The number of families with an annual income below $2,000 fell by half, while the number with annual incomes over $5,000 increased fourfold.

Because of the high employment rate and the shortage of consumer goods, personal savings jumped from $2.9 billion annually in 1939 to over $29 billion annually in 1945. Purchases of "expendables" (jewelry, cosmetics, books, movie tickets) also grew, from $66 billion in 1939 to just over $100 billion in 1944. Record numbers of people frequented movies, nightclubs, and racetracks. Though wartime shortages continued, people found ways to enjoy their new prosperity. Because of the war's stimulus to the economy, the Great Depression was history at last.

In addition to its economic impact, the war had a dramatic effect on where Americans lived and worked. Most obviously, 16.4 million people (including 350,000 women) entered military service between 1941 and 1945. Almost all eligible men between the ages of eighteen and thirty-five served in the armed forces. All told, over 12 percent of the American population spent time in uniform. Many GIs were sent to parts of the country they had never seen before, and often they liked what they saw. In this way, military conscription helped break down regional barriers.

An upheaval also took place among civilians. Six million rural Americans headed for war work in cities, while as many urban residents moved to jobs in new locations. Many of the migrants were African-Americans who left the South for jobs in the North and West. With shipbuilding, aircraft manufacturing, and other war industries concentrated on the East and West Coasts and in the upper Midwest, these areas grew rapidly. Washington, D.C., the hub of the federal government, doubled in population.

The Sunbelt—the warm states of the South and Southwest—as well as the West in general grew dramatically during the war years. As one observer remarked, "It was as if someone had tilted the country," and "people, money, and soldiers all spilled West." Cities and industry grew at an unprecedented rate in Florida, around the Gulf coast, and up the Pacific coast to Washington State. Rather than mine minerals in the West, ship them east for processing, and then transport war goods back to the Pacific coast, federal planners decided to promote industrialization on the West Coast. Between 1941 and

Lockheed begins mass production in the aircraft industry as part of the military buildup. *Lockheed-California Company*

1945 the government invested $40 billion in western factories and military facilities and spent a total of some $70 billion in the region. Federal agencies worked closely with corporations to develop mines, shipyards, aircraft plants, steel mills, and aluminum smelteries.

All along the West Coast, shipyards, aircraft plants, and staging areas for the Pacific front employed thousands of locals and hundreds of thousands of migrants. California alone received 10 percent of all military production expenditures during World War II. Not only factory workers but also tens of thousands of military personnel migrated to San Diego, Portland, Seattle, Los Angeles, and San Francisco—or returned from overseas to these cities and decided to remain as permanent residents. Many pilots who had trained in Arizona because of the good weather returned to Tucson and Phoenix after the war. California's population grew by over a third during the war years, as 2 million people came from the South and from rural areas to work in the aircraft and shipbuilding industries. The population of Los Angeles alone increased by half a million. All told, the population of the West grew 40 percent between 1940 and 1950, with much of that explosive growth a direct result of the war.

✦✦✦

Biographical Profile

Rosie the Riveter

As labor shortages stressed production schedules, government and industry encouraged more women to enter factories. Artist J. Howard Miller's "WE CAN DO IT!" poster, depicting "Rosie the Riveter," a fictional muscular woman in bulging overalls, enjoyed wide distribution. "Rosie" quickly became a patriotic symbol and the subject of a hit tune sung by Kaye Keyser. When a film crew visited the Willow Run aircraft plant in Michigan to shoot a short movie on female workers, they encountered a woman riveter named Rose Monroe. She proved too good for the film producers to resist.

Rose Monroe became a symbol of the millions of U.S. women who did defense work during the war. A widow with two young children when the war began, she joined the labor force to support her family and her country. Mrs. Monroe enjoyed brief fame as the star of the Rosie the Riveter film, which was shown in theaters between features to encourage the sale of war bonds. After 1945, when good-paying factory jobs for women disappeared, she drove a cab, operated a beauty salon, and later founded Rose Builders, a home construction firm. She died in 1997 at the age of 77.

"They couldn't find a better role model, to be honest. Everything she does, she does well. She makes it very tough for the rest of us to follow in her footsteps."

—Viki Jarvis, daughter of Rose Monroe

Women's roles changed dramatically during the war too, even though gender-based inequality remained deeply ingrained in American society. In 1940, before the United States entered the war, about 27 percent of all women worked outside the home, but only 15 percent of married women did so. Moreover, most women in the labor force held low-paying jobs in light manufacturing, service, and clerical areas.

With the wartime labor shortage came a shift in public policy and private attitudes toward women in the labor force. Women were encouraged to work and to take jobs traditionally held by men—for the time being. A War Department pamphlet put it bluntly: "A woman is a substitute—like plastic instead of metal." The Office of War Information, which produced radio plays, films, and posters to mold public opinion to support the war effort, encouraged women to join the work force. Such appeals swayed public opinion. Before the war 80 percent of surveyed Americans opposed having wives work outside the home; by 1942 the same percentage approved.

By 1945 over 6 million additional women, including 4 million who had been housewives before the war, had entered the industrial work force, accounting for a third of the total. They worked as riveters, welders, assembly-line workers, aircraft builders, and in numerous other positions previously held only by men. Steel mills, shipyards, and aircraft plants employed virtually no women before 1942, but three years later women made up as much as 40 percent of the work force in key defense plants. African-American women contributed to the trend. During the war about four hundred thousand black women left domestic service to enter manufacturing and clerical work, the first time black women had done so in significant numbers.

Women also ran heavy equipment, drove trucks and trains, and took jobs as "cowgirls" and "lumberjills." They surged into growing government bureaucracies as clerical workers, and even professional opportunities for women improved as newspapers, orchestras, radio stations, and financial institutions recruited them. Barred from combat duty, female pilots often shuttled airplanes around the country.

But despite the wartime labor shortage, women still were often assigned to sex-segregated tasks, received lower wages than men for the same work, and found few support services such as day care for young children. Social workers discovered babies sleeping in cars outside defense plants because their working mothers had nowhere else to leave them. At the urging of Eleanor Roosevelt, the federal government spent a small amount of money on day care and extended school programs, but not nearly enough to meet demand. Business and political leaders offered various rationalizations for denying women equal pay and access to day care. Middle-class women were encouraged to think of factory work as a temporary expedient, to keep their sights on the home, and to be prepared to resume the roles of housewife and mother when their husbands returned from the war. Black and Hispanic women faced additional obstacles stemming from racist treatment by management and coworkers.

As men entered military service, women's responsibilities increased in many ways beyond that of wage earner. Women became the center of family life as never before. They also assumed responsibility for critical unpaid work. They served as Red Cross nurses, canteen volunteers, and actresses on tours sponsored by the United Service Organizations, or USO. Max Lerner, a popular columnist, voiced a common male complaint that war work had created a "new Amazon" who could "outdrink, outswear, and outswagger the men." Surveys by the Labor Department found that although many women resented unequal pay and sexual harassment on the job, they found the new opportu-

Women played a critical part in wartime airplane construction.
Lockheed-California Company

nities and responsibilities exciting. Women enjoyed spending and saving their higher earnings, valued the independence and self-confidence that came with earning an income, and liked acquiring new skills. Most employed women hoped to continue working when peace returned—but they did so, as we will see, under changed rules.

Although they were exempt from the draft, women, like men, joined the armed services out of patriotic duty and a sense of adventure. Of the 350,000 women who volunteered, 140,000 served as "Wacs" (for the Women's Army Corps), 100,000 as Navy "Waves" (for Women Accepted for Voluntary Emergency Service), 13,000 as Coast Guard "Spars" (after the Coast Guard motto, *semper paratus*), and about 1,000 as "Wasps" (Women's Airforce Service Pilots), who ferried planes in noncombat zones. In addition, 75,000 female nurses served in the military. Typically women in the military were assigned jobs that resembled "female" jobs in the civilian economy. Usually this meant typing, filing, working switchboards, or serving as medical technicians.

Just as the war transformed women's roles, it also created new chances and challenges in race relations. Before the Second World War over three-fourths of all African-Americans lived in the South, employed mainly as tenant farmers and domestic workers. In the North they were limited to the least desirable industrial jobs. The Great Depression hurt these workers more severely than any other group, and New Deal work relief programs, although appreciated, had only partially lightened their burden.

From 1938 on, Roosevelt's judicial appointments had a lasting impact on civil rights. With the exception of South Carolinian James F. Byrnes, Roosevelt's appointees to the Supreme Court, especially Justices Hugo Black, William O. Douglas, Frank Murphy, and Wiley Rutledge, sympathized with efforts to dismantle legal discrimination. By the late 1940s the Supreme Court had struck down state laws excluding minorities from juries, established the right to picket against discrimination in employment, outlawed racially restrictive covenants in housing, challenged inequality in interstate transportation, forbidden peonage on farms, overturned laws mandating lower pay for African-American teachers, and outlawed the white primary system that barred nonwhites from voting in the all-important southern Democratic primaries. These Supreme Court rulings provided momentum for further legal challenges to segregation and for the civil rights movement of the late 1940s through the 1960s.

The war also brought new dissatisfaction among African-Americans with the slow pace of change. The United States was fighting enemies who proclaimed the right to enslave or exterminate "inferior" races. Presumably, American citizens were united in detesting such hateful ideologies. Yet American minorities at home and in the armed forces still faced discrimination and abuse. Law and tradition segregated African-Americans in schools and workplaces, in numerous aspects of social life, and in the armed services.

In 1941, as defense orders poured in to factories, African-American leaders expressed outrage that employment on military production lines remained largely segregated. A. Philip Randolph, head of the Brotherhood of Sleeping Car Porters, a union composed mostly of African-Americans, challenged racial economic discrimination directly. That spring he announced plans for a mass march on Washington to demand equal employment rights.

To avert an embarrassing protest march Roosevelt issued Executive Order 8802, creating the Fair Employment Practices Committee (FEPC) to investigate complaints of discrimination in the defense industry. In exchange, the march on Washington was called off. Even though the FEPC lacked enforcement power, it pressed segregated industries to hire about six hundred thousand African-American workers by 1945. For example, in 1941 the mass transit system of Philadelphia employed no blacks among its ten thousand workers. When the FEPC ordered that William Barber, a black man, be hired as a motorman, the entire white work force went on strike. When the president let it be known that the strikers would be drafted, they quickly relented, and Barber became the first black motorman in Philadelphia. The lure of new jobs contributed to the migration of about 2 million African-Americans from the South to the North and West during the 1940s.

African-American leaders supported the war effort and sought what they called a "double victory"—a victory over Nazi racism abroad and discrimination at home. After touring units in the Pacific, NAACP official Walter White commented that most African-American GIs would not see the defeat of Germany and Japan as a complete victory because they would have to return to a rigidly segregated America: "[They] believe their fight for democracy will begin when they reach San Francisco on the way home." The NAACP urged its members to "persuade, embarrass, compel, and shame" the federal government into acting against racism. Migration, employment in industry, and military service created a collective demand among African-Americans for the full rights of citizenship long denied them. Nevertheless, segregation and racism remained the norm both in the military and in civilian life during and after the war.

Ironically, the shared experience of the war helped remove old ethnic barriers between white groups. On the battlefields and in the canteens, white Americans from varied ethnic and religious backgrounds mingled and got to know one another. But the black-white barrier was much harder to crack. When the military drafted a million African-Americans, it placed most of them in menial positions such as cook, driver, or construction worker. The Red Cross maintained segregated blood banks. African-American troops were often commanded by southern white officers who treated them harshly. Eleanor Roosevelt sent so many memoranda to Army Chief of Staff George C. Marshall about the mistreatment of blacks in the army that he assigned a general to deal with the First Lady. At the same time, African-American soldiers pressed ceaselessly for greater responsibilities and often challenged the status quo. For example, during the war a young lieutenant named Jackie Robinson—who would later become the first black player in major-league baseball—refused to sit in the segregated section of a military bus. Court-martialed for his defiance, Robinson successfully defended himself, and the charge was dismissed. The rise in the number of black officers in the army was one measure of success: in 1940 the army had five; by 1945 it had seven thousand.

Nevertheless, the achievements and bravery of African-American soldiers in combat were often disparaged. For example, not until more than fifty years after most of them had died in combat were seven black soldiers finally awarded the Congressional Medal of Honor. In 1997 the seven men, only one of whom, Joseph V. Baker, still lived, received the medals from President Bill Clinton in recognition of their actions while fighting in segregated units, protecting freedoms they did not fully share. Congress and the president acted after a special army commission concluded that a pervasive climate of racism had prevented proper recognition of the extraordinary heroism of these soldiers.

African-Americans' anxieties were confirmed by several violent wartime race riots, most notably in Detroit in 1942 and in Harlem in 1943. In Detroit a black-white fight at a park sparked the riot; in Harlem the violence started with the shooting of a black soldier by a policeman. White resentment of blacks seeking homes in segregated neighborhoods and applying for factory jobs previously reserved for whites contributed to the intensity of these conflicts.

In spite of such outbreaks of racial violence, the war years generally aided the struggle for equality and civil rights. Military service, even in a segregated system, brought a certain sense of empowerment. New employment opportunities, exposure to a world outside the rural South, northward migration, and growing membership in civil rights organizations also gave a tremendous boost to African-Americans. The wartime generation was unwilling to suffer silently; its militancy and expectations were both on the rise. These people and their children would play a critical role in the postwar challenge to segregation.

The official attitude toward Mexican nationals working in the United States changed during World War II, but the treatment accorded them and Mexican-Americans remained harsh. In 1942, after a decade of pressing Mexican laborers to leave the United States, state and federal officials reversed course. As large numbers of agricultural workers entered the armed services or sought more lucrative defense work, farm managers experienced severe labor shortages. The federal government then negotiated a contract labor program with Mexican authorities that continued, in various forms, until 1964.

Under this so-called *bracero* ("laborer") program, the American government promised to supervise the recruitment, transportation, and working conditions of large groups of Mexican farm workers. During the war this agreement brought in about 1,750,000 farm and railroad laborers. The promised supervision of working conditions was so lax, however, that *braceros* were paid as little as 35 cents per day, and many lived under miserable conditions.

The country's nearly 2.7 million Mexican-Americans faced additional problems. Living mostly in the Southwest, they were confronted with segregation in schools, housing, and employment. New social tensions flared in communities like Los Angeles, where rapid growth had inflamed traditional racism. Mexican-American youth gangs, whose members dressed in flamboyant outfits called "zoot suits," were frequently harassed by the police and by white servicemen. To many young Mexican-American men, their clothing became an assertion of identity and a way to flout white culture.

In August 1942 a Mexican-American youth attending a party died of unknown causes in the Sleepy Lagoon neighborhood of Los Angeles. Police arrested members of a street gang reported to have fought earlier with the dead youth's friends. Despite the lack of evidence linking the accused to the victim, prosecutors were eager to pin blame within the ethnic group and charged twenty-two Mexican-Americans with murder. After a biased trial, all were found guilty. In 1944 a citizens committee convinced a federal court that there was no basis for the convictions and that the defendants' constitutional rights had been violated. Eventually the convictions were reversed.

Ethnic relations in Los Angeles were worsened by the actions of sailors and Marines on shore leave. In June 1943 hundreds of sailors and Marines went on a several-day rampage, attacking Mexican-Americans, African-Americans, and Filipinos in East Los Angeles. Local police often stood by,

General Eisenhower with American soldiers examining bodies at Bergen-Belsen, 1945. *Yivo Institute for Jewish Research*

doing nothing, and military police had to quell the riot. The *Los Angeles Times* reported the incidents with headlines such as "Zoot Suiters Learn Lesson in Fight with Servicemen." When Eleanor Roosevelt suggested that long-standing discrimination against Mexican-Americans lay behind the riots, the *Times* accused her of promoting racial discord.

But for Mexican-Americans, as for African-Americans, the war years brought some advances. Service in the military gave young Mexican-Americans a feeling of personal worth and power. After the war, Mexican-American veterans took a prominent part in organizing civil rights campaigns against postwar discrimination in the Southwest.

As mentioned earlier, the American government largely ignored the plight of Jewish refugees fleeing Nazi persecution. Public opinion polls and members of Congress made it clear that despite the distaste they felt for Nazi attacks on Jews and other groups in Europe, sentiment ran strong against relaxing restrictive immigration quotas.

Evidence surfaced in 1942 that the Nazis planned to exterminate all of Europe's Jews with poison gas; ultimately the Nazis would succeed in killing 6 million. Yet even after the plans became known, British and American strategists rejected the idea of bombing facilities at the death camps or the rail lines leading into them. Such diversions from more important missions, Allied leaders argued, would delay victory.

In 1944 Roosevelt finally created the War Refugee Board to establish refugee camps in neutral countries or American-occupied territory overseas. Eventually these centers helped save the lives of two hundred thousand refugees. Only one thousand refugees were admitted directly into the United States. As one scholar has written, "Franklin Roosevelt's indifference to so momentous an historical event as the systematic annihilation of European Jewry emerges as the worst failure of his presidency."

Roosevelt's unwillingness to champion the cause of Jewish refugees must be viewed in light of the strong American sentiment favoring less, not more, support for the Jews. Fueled by economic fears and long standing religious bias among Christians, anti-Semitism flourished in the United States as in Europe during the 1920s and 1930s. Opinion polls taken during the war found that many Americans believed the Jews posed nearly as great a threat to national security as Germany and Japan. Leaders of the American Jewish community anguished over the horrors of Nazi persecution, but they feared a backlash among Christian Americans if they spoke out too forcefully. As a result most Jewish organizations refrained from pressing politicians to rescue Holocaust victims. Instead they called for creating a Jewish homeland in Palestine for those lucky enough to survive.

Meanwhile, at home the Japanese-American community was singled out for special persecution. Not only was Japan a wartime enemy, but the United States had also had a century-long tradition of anti-Asian agitation and hysteria. The attack on Pearl Harbor, followed by Japan's quick victories elsewhere in the Pacific, intensified the racial distrust on the West Coast and spurred an exaggerated fear that Japanese-Americans would conspire to aid the enemy.

About 120,000 people of Japanese ancestry lived in the United States in 1941, nearly all in Hawaii and along the West Coast. The forty-seven thousand who had arrived in the United States before Asian immigration was banned in 1924 were barred by law from becoming U.S. citizens. Their seventy thousand children, however, who were born in the United States, were full citizens. Although no members of this community ever attempted to sabotage the war effort, their mere existence in the United States aroused public hysteria.

Journalists such as Westbrook Pegler demanded that every Japanese man, woman, and child be placed under armed guard. Congressman Leland Ford of California insisted that any "patriotic native-born Japanese, if he wants to make his contribution, will submit himself to a concentration camp." General John De Witt, head of the Western Defense Command, declared that all Japanese, regardless of citizenship, were enemies. One popular song chortled "We're Gonna Find a Feller Who Is Yeller and Beat Him Red, White and Blue," while another gloated "Wait Till the Little Yellow Bellies Meet the Cohens and the Kelleys."

In an effort to counter this racial hatred, soon after the Pearl Harbor attack Eleanor Roosevelt went to California and deliberately had her picture taken with a group of Japanese-Americans. When she appealed for tolerance toward these people, the *Los Angeles Times* published an editorial urging that she be "impeached as First Lady" for ignoring the military threat posed by the families she defended.

In February 1942 President Roosevelt—unpersuaded by his wife's pleas for tolerance—issued Executive Order 9066, declaring parts of the country "military areas" from which any or all persons could be barred. Congress quickly backed the measure, and nearly every politician in the West applauded the move. Although the regulations also targeted German and Italian *aliens* (most Italians were later exempted), *all* persons of Japanese ancestry in the western United States, regardless of their citizenship, were affected. In May the War Relocation Authority ordered that 112,000 persons of Japanese descent leave the West Coast in a matter of days. Ironically, in Hawaii—where the danger of a Japanese invasion was much more real—residents of Japanese descent made up such a large portion of the population and were so vital to the economy that only a few individuals were interned.

Nearly all those affected by the forced relocation orders complied without protest, abandoning their homes, farms, and personal property to speculators. Bleak internment camps were hastily established in several western states and Arkansas. Even though these were not Nazi-style death camps, this mass

A grandfather and his grandchildren await transportation to a detention camp in California, 1945.
National Archives

imprisonment marked the greatest violation of civil liberties in wartime America. Families lived in rudimentary dwellings and were compelled to do menial work under armed guard.

In 1942 police arrested Gordon Hirabayashi, a college student and native-born American of Japanese descent, for refusing to report to a control center and for violating curfew. The Supreme Court ruled in *Hirabayashi* v. *United States* (1943) that federal authorities could impose a curfew on racial grounds for military reasons.

In 1944 the Supreme Court finally addressed the policy of forced relocation in a case against Fred Korematsu, a citizen who had refused to leave a designated war zone on the West Coast. The Court's decision in *Korematsu* v. *United States* affirmed the government's authority to exclude individuals from any designated area on the basis of military necessity. The majority ruled that the defendant's race was irrelevant because the government could, if it wished, exclude groups besides those of Japanese ancestry. This reasoning resembled the court's finding in the *Plessy* case of 1896 (see Chapter 1), which had upheld state-mandated segregation on railroads because the law applied nominally to whites as well as blacks. In a powerful dissent, Justice Frank Murphy denounced the *Korematsu* verdict as the "legalization of racism" based on prejudice and unfounded fears.

Despite the relocation orders and the degradation of life in the internment camps, Japanese-Americans contributed significantly to the American war effort. Many male internees volunteered for military duty and served in Europe, achieving recognition for bravery in action. Others worked in the Pacific theater of war as translators and intelligence officers. As the war progressed, some internees were permitted to leave relocation camps if they agreed to settle in eastern states. By the summer of 1945 all could leave. A fortunate few found that friends had protected their homes or businesses; the rest lost the work of a lifetime.

Despite growing recognition that internment had been a grave error, Congress and the courts hesitated to make formal redress. Congress offered a token payment to victims of internment in 1948, but it was not until the 1980s that several Japanese-Americans convicted of wartime offenses successfully reopened their cases. Files from the Justice Department and the Federal Bureau of Investigation revealed that prosecutors had withheld evidence showing that no danger existed to justify relocation. In 1988 Congress finally passed the Japanese-American Redress and Reparations Act, which offered an apology and compensation of about $20,000 for each of the sixty thousand internees still alive.

✦ Domestic Politics in Time of War

As the wartime economic boom gradually erased memories of the Great Depression, many Americans felt that the reform programs of the New Deal no longer mattered. The 1942 congressional elections, in which 22 million fewer people voted than in 1940, proved disastrous for the Democrats. The Republicans gained 9 Senate seats (for a total of 43 out of 96) and 44 House seats (giving them 209 to the Democrats' 222). And of those Democrats who did retain their seats, nearly half came from the party's conservative, southern wing. The new Congress proceeded to kill a number of New Deal agencies, including the Work Projects Administration (successor to the Works Progress Administration) and the Civilian Conservation Corps. In the short run, of course, the wartime boom had eliminated the unemployment problem.

Many business executives entered the government during the war, but only three committed New Dealers remained in the president's inner circle: Vice President Henry Wallace, Harry Hopkins, and Eleanor Roosevelt. Wallace had a weak political base. Hopkins, a physical wreck, devoted all his time and energy to foreign policy. Thus it fell to the First Lady to carry the torch of liberal reform. During the war years she increased the frantic pace of her travel, visiting troops in New Guinea and England and lobbying on behalf of women defense workers, minorities, and the poor. She pushed so hard to hold back the tide of conservatism that her exasperated husband finally offered her a deal: if Eleanor agreed to send him only "three memos a night" rather than "twenty memos a day," he would "read them and initial them by morning."

Although the First Lady had some impact on events, the political tide ran against her. The president's chief of mobilization, James F. Byrnes, gloated that the war had helped elbow the "radical boys out of the way [and] more will go." The 1942 elections seemed to prove his prediction accurate. Nervous Democratic Party leaders blamed their electoral losses on the left-leaning vice president, Henry A. Wallace. Unlike his more cautious boss, Wallace had actively promoted civil rights and called for postwar economic intervention by the government. Witnessing Roosevelt's obvious physical decline, party barons feared that if renominated in 1944, Wallace might assume the presidency upon Roosevelt's death.

Bowing to their complaints, and anxious to keep more conservative Democrats off the ticket, a week before the July 1944 Democratic convention Roosevelt agreed to replace Wallace with Supreme Court Justice William O. Douglas or Senator Harry S Truman, a political moderate from Missouri. Truman was famous for his investigations of profiteering by defense contractors and was favored by party officials.

In 1944 the Republicans nominated moderate New York governor Thomas E. Dewey for president and Governor John Bricker of Ohio, a conservative, as his running mate. Despite Dewey's charge that the Democrats were "soft on communism" and prisoners of organized labor, he confounded conservatives by accepting many of Roosevelt's innovations and his plans for the postwar world.

Roosevelt remained the people's choice, aided in part by Dewey's ineffective campaign style and in part by a big boost from organized labor, which created the first political action committee, or PAC, to raise campaign funds. Roosevelt won a fourth term, though by his smallest majority yet (53.4 percent). The party lines in Congress remained largely unchanged.

Despite the political challenges and his own preoccupation with winning the war, Roosevelt made some effort in his last years to impart a vision of postwar reform. In his January 1944 State of the Union address he called for drafting a "second Bill of Rights under which a new basis of security and prosperity can be established for all." In Roosevelt's vision the federal government would work to ensure every American an education; a decent job, home, and retirement; and adequate medical care.

The only important piece of social legislation approved by Congress during the war had to be camouflaged as a military measure. In 1944 Congress passed the administration sponsored Servicemen's Readjustment Act, or GI Bill. This program had a dramatic, if unintended, impact on postwar America.

In a draft speech dictated on April 11, 1945, as victory in Europe loomed, Roosevelt appealed to the American people to "conquer the fears, the ignorance, and the greed" that made the horror of world war possible. "The only limit to our realization of tomorrow," he declared, "will be our doubts of today. Let us move forward with strong and active faith." But the next day, April 12, while at his retreat in Warm Springs, Georgia, the president died of a cerebral hemorrhage.

Roosevelt's passing on the eve of victory left a void in American life and politics. As one soldier remarked, "America will seem a strange place without his voice talking to the people when great events happen." Poet Carl Lamson Carmer put it this way:

> I never saw him—
> But I knew him. Can you have forgotten
> How, with his voice, he came into our house,
> The President of the United States,
> Calling us friends?

✦ Truman, the Atomic Bomb, and Victory

On April 12, 1945, Harry S Truman sat with several congressional friends in the office of House Speaker Sam Rayburn. After moderating a tedious Senate debate on a water treaty, the vice president savored a stiff bourbon. A phone call from presidential press secretary Steve Early abruptly summoned him to the White House. There, Eleanor Roosevelt delivered the somber news: "Harry, the president is dead." Truman asked if there was anything he could do for her. "Is there anything we can do for you?" she replied; "you are the one in trouble now."

A former haberdasher, regarded by many as a political nobody, the new president was suddenly in charge of concluding the world war and shaping the peace. "Trouble" was indeed an apt, and perhaps too mild, description of what faced him. Although Germany was on the verge of surrender, Truman faced the thorny problem of managing relations with the Soviet Union, a wartime ally that appeared to be emerging as a threatening competitor. Within a few months Truman would also have to decide whether to use the atomic bomb on Japan. Heading the most powerful nation in the postwar world, Truman found his every choice greatly magnified in importance.

Truman came from a modest farming family near Independence, Missouri. As a young man he had worked beside his father in the fields and then as a bank clerk. When the United States entered the First World War in 1917, Truman, then thirty-three, enlisted in the National Guard and commanded an artillery battery in Europe. At the end of his service he returned to Missouri, married Bess Wallace, and opened a clothing store in Kansas City. When the business failed, he turned to politics.

In the 1920s and early 1930s Truman served as an elected judge in Jackson County, on the fringe of the area controlled by "Boss" Tom Pendergast's Kansas City political machine. Working in the shadow of corruption, Truman nevertheless earned a reputation as an honest and efficient administrator. In 1934, aided by Roosevelt's popularity as president, he won election to the U.S. Senate as a Democrat.

Truman's early social outlook reflected the racism prevalent in the midwestern border region. "I think one man is just as good as another," he wrote to his future wife, "so long as he's honest and decent and not a nigger or a Chinaman." As he matured, Truman expressed greater toleration for ethnic minorities. After taking up his Senate seat in Washington, he worked to convince more liberal Democrats that he supported civil rights and liberties.

During the three months in which they served together as president and vice president in 1945, Roosevelt and Truman had scant contact. Truman knew little of what transpired in Roosevelt's meetings with Churchill and Stalin. He was, Roosevelt biographer William Leuchtenburg surmised, "too insignificant a subaltern to be trusted with secrets of state." When Truman became president, Secretary of War Henry Stimson took him aside after the first cabinet meeting to brief him on the Manhattan Project. The new president had known almost nothing about the development of the atomic bomb, now close to the testing stage.

Truman recognized that as vice president he had been kept in the dark on matters vital to national security, and as president he was surrounded by better-informed men who were chary with their information. In consequence he grew distrustful of most of the Roosevelt cabinet he had inherited. There was not a "man on the list who would talk frankly," he later recalled. "The honest ones were afraid and the others wanted to fool me."

Within the first four months of his administration Truman established his own chain of command, firing or easing out nearly all the cabinet members who had been close to Roosevelt. The profile of his appointees differed considerably from that of Roosevelt's advisers. In his first two years in office Truman appointed forty-nine bankers, financiers, and industrialists; thirty-one career military men; and seventeen business lawyers to fill the top 125 federal job vacancies. Among those pushed out of the cabinet were New Deal veterans Harold Ickes, Henry Morgenthau, and Henry Wallace, the last dismissed as secretary of commerce in 1946 after a dispute with Truman about how to deal with the Soviet Union.

Even though in 1945 and 1946 Truman proposed extending several New Deal–style reforms, progressives considered him a lukewarm liberal and never gave him the support Roosevelt had enjoyed. Nor was he accepted by the political Right, which wanted to eliminate all surviving New Deal programs. Politically he wobbled on a tightrope between the Right and the Left, and often it seemed that both sides were shaking the rope to make him tumble.

As British, American, and Soviet armies closed in on Berlin in April 1945, President Truman had to respond almost instantaneously to problems he knew little about. Determined to appear a forceful leader, he sometimes made snap judgments. Hours after taking office he boasted that, unlike his predecessor, he would "stand up to the Russians," implying that Roosevelt had been too easy on Stalin.

The new president's suspicion of Soviet goals was fueled by talks with the American ambassador to the Soviet Union, Averell Harriman; Secretary of the Navy James Forrestal; his chief of staff, Admiral William Leahy; and Undersecretary of State Joseph Grew. All had urged Roosevelt to demand a larger role for non-Communists in the government the Soviets had installed in Poland. Their advice appealed to Truman partly because their recommendations gave him an opportunity to distinguish himself from his predecessor.

Ambassador Harriman flew to Washington from Moscow to explain his fear that Stalin was breaking the agreements made at Yalta. He described Soviet actions, which included installing puppets in power and arresting real and imagined foes, as a "barbarian invasion of Europe" and claimed that, had Roosevelt lived, he would have become tougher with Stalin. Communism, he told Truman, confronted America with "ideological warfare just as vigorous and dangerous as Fascism or Nazism." Truman, who was not a party to the wartime deals, accepted Harriman's claim that Stalin considered compromise a sign of weakness. After all, had not appeasement encouraged Hitler? Truman, like many Americans, looked upon Soviet domination of the liberated countries of eastern Europe as a replay of Nazi aggression and a possible prelude to global expansion.

On April 23, 1945, the president used "words of one syllable" to accuse visiting Soviet foreign minister Vyacheslav M. Molotov of violating promises made at Yalta regarding free elections in Poland. When Molotov disputed this interpretation and complained about Truman's harsh language, the president allegedly retorted, "Carry out your agreements, and you won't get talked to like that." Truman spoke of giving Molotov the "straight one-two to the jaw," but in private he wondered aloud if he had done right.

In fact, Truman's tough words barely affected Soviet policy, in Poland or elsewhere. Responding to the president's charges of treaty violations, Stalin offered a blunt interpretation of the Yalta accords: "Poland borders with the Soviet Union [which] cannot be said of Great Britain or the United States."

Moscow claimed no right to interfere in Belgium or Greece, where the Western allies had imposed governments of their choosing. Stalin made it clear that he cared more about creating a security zone in eastern Europe than maintaining good relations with his wartime allies.

When Churchill conveyed to the Soviet leader in mid-1945 his fears of an "iron fence" (this preceded the term iron curtain) dividing Europe, Stalin angrily dismissed the notion as a fairy tale. But Truman and Churchill were not fooled. Soviet forces had installed puppet regimes in Poland, Rumania, and Bulgaria. They later used local Communists to take control of Hungary in 1947 and Czechoslovakia in 1948. Even if Stalin had no master plan of world conquest, Soviet troops and henchmen behaved brutally in areas that fell under their domination, and this aroused both anger and fear among Americans.

For his part, Stalin feared a revived Germany and capitalist encirclement of the Soviet Union, as had occurred after the First World War. This encouraged his ironclad domination of eastern Europe. In the tradition of the Russian Czars, Stalin measured Soviet security by the weakness of its neighboring states and by the intimidation and control he could exercise over them. Because of long-standing eastern European distrust of Russia, nothing short of total Soviet control could keep the region under Moscow's thumb. The harsh imposition of Communist control and the large number of Soviet troops maintained in eastern Europe appalled and frightened Western leaders. Ironically, Stalin's brutal exercise of power aroused the very hostility he feared from the capitalist West.

When Germany formally surrendered on May 8, 1945, Soviet troops occupied Berlin. The victorious Allies had agreed to partition Germany into occupation zones, but they had not established mechanisms for interzonal cooperation or addressed how they would exact reparations from Germany. The Polish-German border problem sparked additional dissent. The Soviets annexed a swath of Polish territory along their border and compensated Poland by grafting onto it part of eastern Germany. The swap displaced millions of ethnic Germans and moved Soviet power closer to central Europe, a chilling development in the eyes of British and American leaders.

As disputes over the postwar balance of power in Europe raged on, the war continued against Japan. Despite much aid to Chinese Nationalist Party leader Jiang Jieshi, his army remained unable or unwilling to fight the Japanese. Instead, U.S. Army and Navy forces fought their way across the central Pacific, seizing key islands from which to mount a naval blockade and a bombing campaign against Japan. By early 1945 the Japanese homeland was isolated. In March American planes fire-bombed Tokyo, killing about one hundred thousand civilians and destroying sixteen square miles of the city. American Marines, army troops, and naval personnel also suffered tens of thousands of casualties taking islands such as Iwo Jima and Okinawa, which then became bases for assaulting Japan. In the final stages of the war, Japanese *kamikaze* (suicide) plane attacks proved especially damaging to American forces. Still, the bulk of Japan's troops remained in China and Manchuria, far from the American forces. U.S. military planners dreaded the prospect of having to fight them, but there appeared to be few alternatives. The Soviets had pledged to fight Japan after Germany's defeat, but Washington did not fully trust them; and no one could yet tell if the still experimental atomic bomb would work. As a result, soon after he took office Truman approved a plan to invade Japan on November 1, 1945.

Truman, Churchill, and Stalin held a summit in mid-July in Potsdam, a once opulent suburb of bombed-out Berlin. Amid the rubble of what Hitler had boasted would be the Thousand Year Reich, the Big Three spent most of their time arguing over German boundaries, the payment of reparations to Moscow, British and American demands that Stalin loosen his grip on Poland and Rumania, and the timing of the Soviets' entry into the Pacific war. The emergence of a new, postwar political outlook in the West was evidenced by the defeat of Churchill's Conservative Party by the British Labor Party in elections held during the conference. Midway through the summit, Clement Attlee replaced Churchill as prime minister, pledging to improve life for the British working class. On foreign policy matters, however, Attlee was as suspicious as his predecessor of Soviet behavior in eastern Europe.

Although Churchill and Truman accepted the Polish-German boundary changes already made by Stalin, they refused to turn over to the Soviets industrial resources in the British and American occupation zones in western Germany. Stalin charged that this refusal to share resources violated earlier promises and wondered if American and British officials intended to rebuild western Germany as an anti-Soviet state.

Stalin tried to placate his allies by promising that Soviet forces would join the campaign against Japan by mid-August. This pledge did not please all who heard it, however. Although American military planners still believed that Soviet assistance would help reduce American casualties, Truman now worried about the cost of Soviet involvement in the Pacific war. Specifically, he feared that Soviet forces might assist the Chinese Communists and that Stalin would demand a role in the occupation of Japan.

On July 16, 1945, in the course of the inconclusive discussions at Potsdam, Truman received a coded message that an atomic bomb had been tested successfully at the Trinity Site in New Mexico—a remote location chosen both because it was close to the Los Alamos laboratory and because it met the demand of Interior Secretary Harold Ickes to avoid relocating a single Indian. The president's aides described him as excited and cheered by the prospect of having a weapon that might make Soviet help unnecessary in the war against Japan. Like Roosevelt before him, Truman maintained a policy of not telling Stalin about the atomic bomb. Instead he casually mentioned the discovery of a new weapon of great power. Stalin, who knew of the Manhattan Project through espionage and had already ordered Soviet physicists to build a similar weapon, did not press for details, leaving Truman incorrectly thinking that he

The first atomic casualty: Horoshima, August 1945. *National Archives*

had "fooled Mr. Russia." At the end of the conference, without inviting the Soviets to join in, the British and American governments issued the Potsdam Declaration, an ultimatum warning Japan to surrender at once—without conditions—or face utter destruction.

Truman ordered that the two available atomic bombs, code-named Fat Man and Little Boy, be used as soon as possible. On August 6 a B-29 bomber named *Enola Gay,* for the pilot's mother, flying from the island of Tinian, dropped the first bomb on Hiroshima, Japan. Two days later, a bit earlier than the Americans had expected, the Soviets declared war on Japan and sent the Red Army to fight in Japanese-occupied Mongolia and Manchuria. On August 9 a second bomb obliterated the city of Nagasaki. Nearly two hundred thousand Japanese civilians—and many conscripted Korean laborers—died in the two attacks, with radiation sickness later claiming additional lives.

The Japanese government had for some time been divided between a group of civilians favoring surrender and a core of hard-line militarists who urged fighting to the bitter end. On August 10 the Japanese emperor sided with his civilian advisers and informed the United States of Japan's readiness to surrender, provided the emperor was permitted to remain on the throne.

On August 14 Truman accepted Japan's surrender, with the provision that the armed forces and emperor accept occupation by American troops under the command of General Douglas MacArthur.

Publicly Truman never admitted doubts about the decision to use the atomic bomb. He thanked God for giving him a weapon that saved "thousands and thousands of American lives" and "shortened the agony of war." Almost immediately, however, questions arose about Truman's decision. Some scientists had urged that, before using the bomb in combat, the United States demonstrate the bomb's power on unoccupied territory to convince the Japanese to surrender. They questioned the later claim of the president and his top aides that an invasion would have cost the lives of half a million Americans. In fact, U.S. intelligence estimates in 1945 predicted about fifty thousand deaths, not five hundred thousand. Truman later ridiculed "crybaby" scientists who had wanted to give Japan clear warning of the bomb's potential before dropping it on Japanese cities.

American use of the bomb against Japan also raised the question of racism. Would American decision makers have used such a weapon against non-Asians? After all, the president had declared in private, "When you have to deal with a beast, you have to treat him like a beast." Some prominent Americans had called for "gutting the heart of Japan with fire" and "sterilizing every damn one of them so that in a generation there would be no more Japs." As racist as these remarks may sound, historians point out that European cities—Dresden, Germany, in particular—also suffered massive civilian casualties from Allied bombs.

Some critics thought the real motive for the atomic attack on Japan was to force a change in Soviet behavior in Europe and to speed victory in the Pacific to keep Soviet forces out of China and Japan. Within days of Japan's surrender, Soviet leaders complained that Truman had sought to intimidate Moscow through "atomic diplomacy." Remarks by Truman and his staff suggested that they had indeed considered the postwar status of the Soviet Union in deciding to use the bomb. Secretary of State James F. Byrnes felt that a mistake had been made in allowing the Soviets to become so powerful. He stressed the importance of using the bomb not simply to defeat Japan but also to do so in a manner that excluded Moscow from sharing in postwar decisions about Japan.

Clearly Truman and those close to him felt ambivalent about the reasons for using the bomb. They probably hoped both to end the war with the fewest American casualties possible and to limit the Soviets' opportunity to gain a foothold in China and Japan. But even without his growing mistrust of Stalin, Truman might have made the same decision to use the bomb. The United States had spent several billion dollars constructing the weapon. Military and civilian decision makers had always planned to use it as soon as possible, against Germany or Japan. Except for a handful of scientists, few top leaders gave any serious thought to *not* using the bomb. The Japanese had extended peace feelers before the bomb was dropped, but they had been vague at best and had not met even minimal American requirements. Also, by 1945 the utter destruction of cities and indiscriminate slaughter of civilians had become so commonplace that few moral objections were raised in public.

Victory over Japan confirmed the United States' place as the world's leading economic and military power. This position presented both opportunities and risks. Most Americans hoped to maintain their privileged status, but some realized that their continued prosperity depended on the revival of the devastated economies of Europe and, to a lesser extent, those of Asia. Moreover, wealth alone provided no easy way to halt the division of Europe by the "iron fence" or to stabilize Asia. When British, Soviet, and American foreign ministers met in London in September 1945, they argued bitterly about who threatened whom. The Western powers demanded relaxation of Soviet control in eastern Europe, and Moscow responded by blasting "capitalist encirclement" and "atomic blackmail." The Cold War that followed from these mutual suspicions dominated world politics for two generations thereafter.

✦ Conclusion

The Second World War brought vast changes to the nation and to its role in the world arena. The struggle at home and abroad molded the postwar world in fundamental ways that continue to affect us. Accelerating what began during the New Deal, the war prompted rapid growth in the federal government's size and scope of action. For the first time in the nation's history, the U.S. government had a direct and frequent effect on the daily lives of ordinary citizens. With the coming of war, the government managed the economy to an unprecedented degree. To build the weapons required for victory, it funded scientific research that changed the face of American industry and made possible today's high-tech society.

During the war millions of rural or small-town Americans packed their bags and headed to the major industrial cities. African-Americans left the rural South in huge numbers, and many of them made their new homes in the North and West. The *bracero* program contributed to a substantial influx of Mexican farm and railroad workers. The Sunbelt and the West Coast began their rise to prominence.

For women the war meant a chance to take jobs traditionally reserved for men, a first step toward the revolution in women's lives that is still occurring. For ethnic minorities the war years were times of mingled hope, fear, and disappointment. The wartime internment of Japanese-Americans left a blot on the nation's record that no later compensation could remove. The government's failure to help European Jews escape the Holocaust would seem almost incomprehensible to later generations. Yet the Roosevelt era also brought a rising concern for the rights of minorities and new hopes that protest could lead to improvement—crucial ingredients for the civil rights movement of the postwar years.

Like many of his compatriots, President Truman shared the self-satisfied vision articulated by Henry Luce, the publisher of *Time* and *Life,* in 1945. The "American experience," Luce wrote, "is the key to the future. America must be the elder brother of the nations in the brotherhood of man." The idea that the United States had a special mission in the history of the world was not a new one. Now, however, the nation held a uniquely powerful position. To the Soviets—and to other critics of U.S. policy in the postwar years—an attitude of the sort expressed by Luce smacked of dangerous arrogance. In the years to come, America's desire to act as "elder brother" often provoked hostility rather than gratitude.

✦ Further Reading

On American society during the Second World War, see: Doris Kearns Goodwin, *No Ordinary Time: Franklin and Eleanor Roosevelt : The Home Front During WWII* (1994); John Blum, *V Was for Victory: Politics and American Culture During World War II* (1976); Lewis A. Erenberg and Susan E. Hirsch, *The War in American Culture: Society and Consciousness During World War II* (1996); Richard Polenberg, *War and Society* (1972); James MacGregor Burns, *Roosevelt: The Soldier of Freedom* (1970); Nelson Lichtenstein, *Labor's War at Home: The CIO in World War II* (1982); Karen Anderson, *Wartime Women* (1981); Susan Hartman, *The Homefront and Beyond* (1980); Peter Irons, *Justice at War: The Story of the Japanese-American Internment Cases* (1982); Roger Daniel, *Prisoners Without Trial* (1993); Gerald D. Nash, *The American West Transformed: The Impact of the Second World War* (1985); Studs Terkel, *"The Good War": An Oral History of World War II* (1984); Michael C. C. Adams, *The Best War Ever: America and World War II* (1994); William O'Neill, *A Democracy at War: America's Fight at Home and Abroad During W.W. II* (1993); Leisa Meyer, *Creating G. I. Jane: Sexuality and Power in the Women's Army Corp Curing World War II* (1996). On military strategy and foreign policy, see: Robert Dallek, *Franklin D. Roosevelt and American Foreign Policy* (1979); Michael Schaller, *The U.S. Crusade in China, 1938–1945* (1979); Mark Stoler, *The Politics of the Second Front: Planning and Diplomacy in Coalition Warfare, 1941–45* (1977); Warren Kimball, *The Juggler: Franklin Roosevelt as Wartime Statesman* (1991); Russel D. Buhite, *Decision at Yalta* (1986); David Wyman, *The Abandonment of the Jews: America and the Holocaust, 1941–45* (1984); Michael Sherry, *The Rise of American Air Power* (1987); John Dower, *War Without Mercy: Race and Power in the Pacific War* (1986); Ronald Specter, *Eagle Against the Sun: The American War with Japan* (1985); D. Clayton James, *The Years of MacArthur* (3 Vols., 1970–85); Martin J. Sherwin, *A World Destroyed: The Atomic Bomb and the Grand Alliance* (1975); Richard Rhodes, *The Making of the Atomic Bomb* (1987); Michael J. Hogan, ed., *Hiroshima in History and Memory* (1996).

CHAPTER 8

America and the Cold War, 1945–1960

✦ **Atomic dummies at Yucca Flat test site, November 1955.**

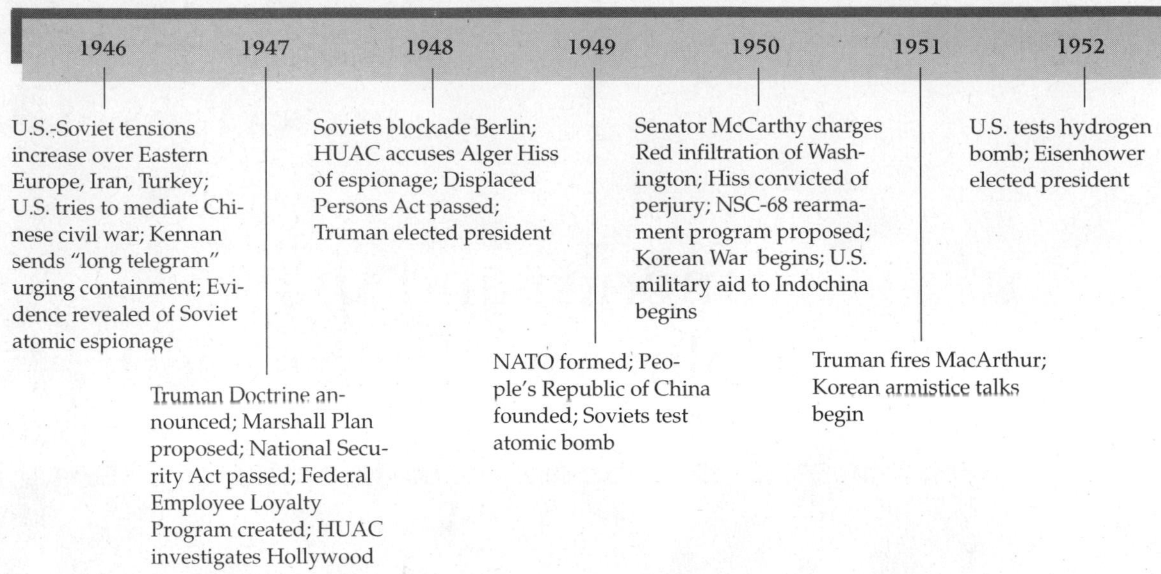

ON SEPTEMBER 12, 1946, Commerce Secretary—and former vice president—Henry A. Wallace addressed a large crowd in New York's Madison Square Garden. The escalating war of words between Washington and Moscow deeply troubled Wallace. He feared President Truman had fallen under the spell of hard-liners such as Secretary of State James F. Byrnes, who thought the only way to handle the Soviets was to "get tough." But "getting tough," Wallace declared, "never brought anything real and lasting—whether for school yard bullies or businessmen or world powers. The tougher we get, the tougher the Russians will get." He urged both nations to re-examine their behavior and to find ways to compromise, perhaps by adopting a spheres-of-influence approach that accepted each other's special interests.

But Wallace sought a middle ground where none existed. The audience, which included many members of the American Communist Party, booed the suggestion that the Soviet Union had any need to change its ways. Truman, equally upset at the suggestion that the United States bore any responsibility for tensions with the Soviets, reacted by firing Wallace from his cabinet. The "Reds, phonies and 'parlor pinks,'" Truman angrily told an aide, "seem to be

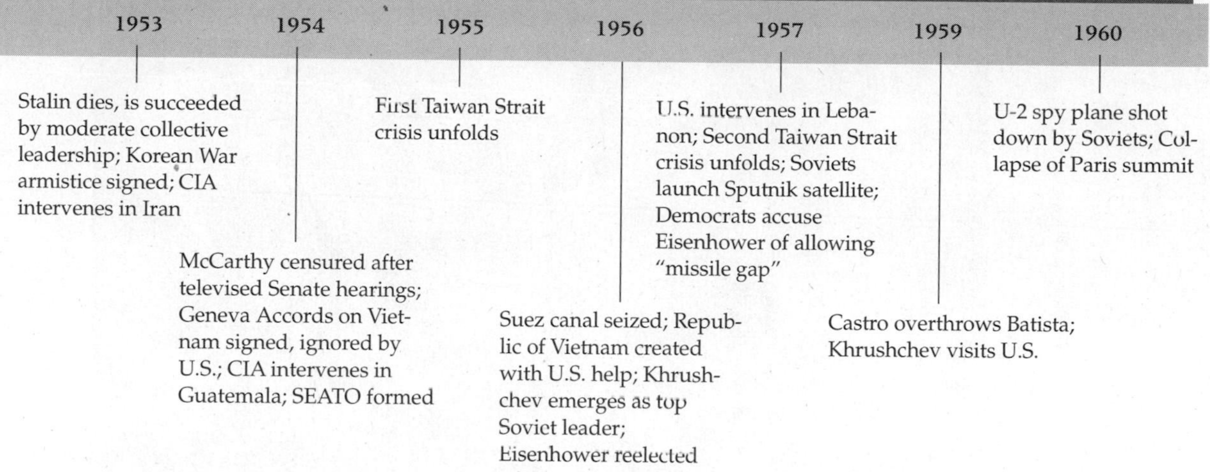

banded together and are becoming a national danger. I am afraid they are a sabotage front for Uncle Joe Stalin." The intensity of Truman's reaction, like his suggestion that criticism was akin to treason, revealed the stark change in both domestic and foreign policy since Roosevelt's death.

By the time the Second World War ended, the national security policies of Washington and Moscow were on a collision course. Joseph Stalin's determination to forge an inviolable security sphere around the Soviet Union led, inevitably, to his policy of dominating Eastern Europe. In doing so he brutally suppressed all local political movements he could not control. Stalin's talk of a coming world revolution understandably frightened Western audiences, even if he did relatively little to assist Communists outside the Soviet Union.

American leaders, for their part, insisted on breaking down international trade barriers and rebuilding the defeated Axis nations, policies that upset the Kremlin. Washington often paid more attention to Soviet rhetoric about spreading communism—and to its harsh suppression of freedom in areas it actually controlled—than to Stalin's actual posture of hiding behind the Iron Curtain he had created. In this atmosphere of distrust, Americans often

Truman and Stalin meet in Potsdam, Germany, July 1945. The smiles soon faded.
Harry Truman Library

blamed the Soviet Union for events over which it had only slight control, including much of the economic and political chaos that swept over the world after 1945.

During the decade following World War II an anti-Communist hysteria erupted onto the national scene. Fueled by legitimate worries about the Soviet Union as well as by political opportunism, the Red Scare distorted national politics from the end of the war well into the 1950s. It frustrated attempts by progressives—including, to some degree, President Truman himself—to expand the social reforms of the New Deal, and it led to widespread political intolerance and suppression of civil liberties.

The outbreak of the Korean War in June 1950, and its bloody and indecisive nature, both expanded the Red Scare and paved the way for the Republican Party's return to national power. Although he had pledged to "win the Cold War," General Dwight D. Eisenhower's election to the presidency in 1952 signified more of a continuation of that global struggle than a bold departure from it.

✦ Origins of the Cold War

Historians who have tried to fathom the causes of the Cold War have often emphasized the differences in perception between U.S. and Soviet leaders after the war. Hostility between the two countries stretched back to the Bolshevik Revolution of 1917, when Vladimir Lenin's followers proclaimed a goal of world revolution and President Woodrow Wilson sent American troops to fight alongside troops from western Europe and Japan to crush the Communist movement. In the subsequent decades, neither side trusted the other much. In 1939, when Stalin and Hitler signed a nonagression pact, American mistrust of Soviet intentions grew stronger. Only the common threat posed by the Nazis after 1941 drew them together.

East-West Disputes

Despite that legacy of suspicion, during the Cold War few American leaders expected the Soviet Union to unleash a sudden military attack against Western Europe or anywhere else. Rather, most officials guessed, the Soviets would try to take advantage of power vacuums created by economic chaos or anticolonial revolts to expand their influence. President Truman probably understood that the Soviet Union was more of a long-term rival than an immediate military threat. Yet early in 1946 he ruminated that he was "tired of babying the Soviets. Unless Russia is faced with an iron fist and strong language, another war is in the making." With much insight, he told his wife and daughter that a "totalitarian state is no different whether you call it Nazi, Fascist, [or] Communist."

Former British prime minister Winston Churchill encouraged anti-Soviet sentiment. Early in 1946 Great Britain faced bankruptcy and required a multibillion dollar emergency loan from the United States. Like many of his compatriots, Churchill felt that he could garner U.S. support by presenting Britain as a partner in a campaign against Soviet expansionism. Speaking in Fulton, Missouri, on March 5, 1946, to an audience that included President Truman, Churchill declared dramatically that "from Stettin [Poland] in the Baltic to Trieste [Italy] in the Adriatic, an Iron Curtain has descended" across Europe. He proposed an alliance of all English-speaking peoples, backed by the atomic bomb that "God has willed to the United States."

Stalin had his own doubts about the possibility of peaceful cooperation between East and West. Fearful of superior American economic and military power, he tried to isolate the Soviet Union and its Eastern European satellite nations from outside contact. Exposure, he feared, would alert the West to Communist weaknesses and make those living under Soviet domination painfully aware of the better life enjoyed by those on the other side of the Iron Curtain. In a widely publicized speech to Soviet citizens delivered in February 1946, Stalin warned that it was in the nature of capitalism to prepare for war. He called on the hard-pressed Russian people to make greater sacrifices to develop heavy industry and safeguard their nation. Stalin used the threat of "capitalist encirclement" to justify the harshness of his regime and to suppress demands for greater liberty and more consumer goods. The next month he described Churchill's Iron Curtain speech as an incitement to war against the Soviet Union.

In the aftermath of these accusations, the Soviet government rejected membership in the newly created World Bank and International Monetary Fund. These institutions were designed to promote trade and economic development by establishing orderly methods for making international loans, setting currency values, and reducing trade barriers among member states. As the most stable medium of exchange, the U.S. dollar—redeemable for gold at $35 per ounce—served as the world's reserve, or benchmark, currency.

As the two sides exchanged recriminations, Washington stopped dismantling German industry and halted reparations to Russia. American officials dropped a prohibition against employing former Nazis. Operation Paper Clip brought over seven hundred German scientists to the United States. Some were physicians who had performed horrible "medical" experiments on concentration camp inmates; others had overseen the death by exhaustion and starvation of slave laborers. Both the Soviets and the Americans recruited German rocket scientists, like Wernher von Braun, who had built the V-1 and V-2 rockets that had so terrified British civilians during the last stages of the war.

In 1946 Soviet-American tensions mounted when disputes arose in Iran and Turkey. During the Second World War the Allies had deposed the pro-Nazi shah of Iran and jointly occupied that country. British and American forces departed in early 1946, but the Soviets lingered, demanding an oil concession like the one held by the British for decades, and supporting a separatist regime in northern Iran. Moscow also revived a long-standing demand that Turkey permit joint Soviet control over the Dardenelles, one of the strategic straits linking the Mediterranean with the Black Sea. Some American diplomats feared a Russian sweep across Turkey into the Mediterranean and across Iran to the Indian Ocean.

Declaring that the United States might as well find out now rather than later whether the Russians were bent on world conquest, Truman issued tough warnings to the Soviets and dispatched naval units to the Mediterranean. Although Stalin was willing to probe, he had no desire for a military showdown with the far more powerful United States. He backed down quickly in both Iran and Turkey. In many ways it appeared that the Soviet Union's goals—to gain resources, security, and influence—were not very different from those of traditional empires.

Suspicion affected nearly all areas of Soviet-American relations, including efforts to control atomic weapons. Estimates of when the Soviets would build an atomic bomb of their own varied from five to twenty years. Nevertheless, American hopes that the U.S. atomic monopoly would compel Stalin to accept American demands faded quickly. Whenever the subject of the bomb entered Soviet-American discussions, Russian negotiators toughened their position. Determined not to allow the Americans to think that he feared the weapon, Stalin told his colleagues that atomic bombs were meant to frighten those with weak nerves. Meanwhile, the Soviet leader pressed his spies to gather more data on American research and commanded Soviet scientists to build him a bomb.

With the goals of preserving at least a modest edge in armaments and, perhaps, avoiding a dangerous arms race, the United States proposed in March

1946 that the Soviets accept a plan for international control of atomic energy. The scheme, named for financier Bernard Baruch, who presented it to the United Nations, called for placing nuclear research, weapons, and facilities under a U.S.-controlled international commission. In the middle of the UN debate, the United States conducted a dramatic series of atomic bomb tests on a Pacific atoll named Bikini (a name later made famous by a new two-piece French bathing suit). The Soviets rejected the Baruch plan as an infringement on their sovereignty. They proposed an immediate ban on existing—that is, American—bombs, but they suggested that a compromise might be possible. Washington responded by ending the dialogue.

The Birth of Containment

Despite the growing international tensions and hostile rhetoric, the Soviet and American governments actually reduced their military expenditures after 1945. The United States built few atomic bombs before 1948. Stalin, despite his fiery rhetoric, backed off in Turkey and Iran, withdrew Soviet troops from Manchuria, and endorsed American mediation efforts in the Chinese civil war. Yet over the next two years the United States began major programs to resist Communist guerrillas in Greece, expand its nuclear arsenal, and forge a Western military alliance—justifying each step as a response to the Soviet threat.

By early 1947 chaos had again engulfed so much of the world that it appeared that vast new riches might simply fall into the lap of the Soviet Union. A nearly bankrupt Britain prepared to abandon India, Palestine, and Greece. Vietnamese and Indonesians rose against their French and Dutch colonial masters. In China a civil war raged. Preventing starvation in occupied Germany and Japan cost the United States nearly $1 billion per year—a huge sum at the time. Even if the Soviets did not cause these problems, Americans feared they stood to benefit from them.

George F. Kennan, second in command at the U.S. embassy in Moscow and the leading State Department expert on Soviet affairs, sent Washington a telegram in early 1946 detailing his conclusions about the deteriorating relations between the United States and the Soviet Union. Kennan argued that Stalin provoked tensions with the West as a means of justifying his harsh oppression of the Soviet people. Although Soviet power was "impervious to the logic of reason," it remained "highly sensitive to the logic of force." Instead of placating the Kremlin, Kennan believed, Washington should respond with "long-term, patient but firm and vigilant containment." Before long the notion of containment, or halting the extension of Soviet influence wherever it might occur, became the operating principle behind American foreign policy.

Truman and his advisers knew that the gravest problem in Europe and Japan was a huge "dollar gap"—the difference between the value of American exports and the amount of dollars foreign customers had available to pay for them—of more than $8 billion. The dollar gap threatened to halt world trade.

Foreign trade could continue only if the U.S. government and private lenders provided credit to overseas customers, and they would risk doing so only if Europe and Japan showed signs of industrial recovery. Once credit disappeared, foreign nations would be unable to trade with the United States, causing the kind of global collapse that had fed the Great Depression. The Soviets might take advantage of such chaos by moving into vulnerable areas in Europe and Asia.

U.S. policymakers agreed that containment depended on the reconstruction of the German and Japanese economies, what Undersecretary of State Dean Acheson called the "great workshops" of Europe and Asia. Yet Congress rejected this approach, because rebuilding Europe and Japan would require a major increase in foreign economic aid, something never before done in peacetime. Only a simple, dramatic issue might mobilize Congress and the public.

Since 1944 a brutal civil war had raged between Greek monarchists, supported by Britain, and the leftist National Liberation Front, or EAM. The EAM included both Communists and non-Communists. On February 21, 1947, the financially hard-pressed British government informed Washington that it could no longer afford to support the Greek regime. Assuming the full British burden would cost hundreds of millions of dollars, Undersecretary of State Acheson took charge of selling the aid program to Congress.

Acheson told the president and others that the United States and the Soviet Union were divided by an "unbridgeable ideological chasm." He depicted the contest as one between democracy and liberty on the one side and dictatorship and absolute conformity on the other. If the United States walked away, then "like apples in a barrel infected by one rotten one," the "corruption of Greece would infect Iran and all to the east."

Republican senator Arthur Vandenberg, chairman of the Foreign Relations Committee, reportedly told Truman that if the president would make this case to Congress, it would lend support for an aid program. (According to another version of the same meeting, Vandenberg declared that if the Democrats wanted to provide a WPA-style welfare program for Greece, Truman needed to "scare the hell out of the American people.") In the end the president stressed the "global struggle between freedom and totalitarianism." When Truman addressed Congress on March 12, 1947, he declared that "it must be the policy of the United States to support free peoples who are resisting attempted subjugation by armed minorities or by outside pressures." Almost immediately this statement was dubbed the Truman Doctrine. Specifically, the president called for a $400 million program of aid to Greece and Turkey. Swayed by Truman's appeal, the Republican-led Congress passed the aid bill quickly. For most of the next forty years, the phrase "supporting free peoples" meant defending practically any regime threatened by communism—or, often, non-Communist rebels—even if, as in the case of Greece, the government in power was not democratic.

As it turned out, Yugoslavia, rather than the Soviet Union, supplied most aid to the Greek Communist rebels. Josip Tito, the Yugoslavian Communist leader, had visions of adding Greece to a Balkan federation dominated by himself. But Stalin resented empire building by his subalterns, and in mid-1948 he denounced Tito as a renegade and tried to topple him. Desperate for Western support, Tito halted aid to the Greek rebels and forced them out of Yugoslavian sanctuaries. This, along with American military aid to the Greek government, soon led to the defeat of the rebels. The greatest impact of the Truman Doctrine came not in Greece, however, but in Western Europe. On June 5, 1947, speaking at Harvard University, Secretary of State George C. Marshall revealed the outlines of an ambitious plan for European recovery, which soon became known as the Marshall Plan. To prevent the Soviets from taking advantage of European economic collapse, the plan envisioned a multiyear, comprehensive program to assist industrial recovery and trade in Western Europe and Japan. Truman asked Congress to back these ideas with a $27 billion appropriation. Stalin feared the Marshall Plan might unite both Western and Eastern Europe in a pro-American, anti-Soviet alliance. To discourage this he encouraged Communist-led strikes in Italy and France and a Soviet-inspired coup in Czechoslovakia. The ultimate effect of these provocations, however, was to convince Congress to fund the Marshall Plan. On February 25, 1948, Czech Communists—supported by a massing of Soviet troops on the Czech border—seized power in Prague and brought their nation into the Soviet bloc. The sense of crisis deepened on March 5, when the commander of the American forces in western Germany warned of a "subtle change" in the Soviets' behavior in the region. He felt that war might come with dramatic suddenness. Truman played up these suspicions in a speech to Congress on March 17, 1948. Pleading for passage of the Marshall Plan and for measures to boost U.S. military preparedness, he argued that recent events proved Moscow's intention of gobbling up Europe.

Congress finally passed a trimmed-down Marshall Plan that also included funds to rebuild the economy of Japan. The United States saw Japan as the Asian anchor of containment, the counterpart to Germany in Europe. Also, as with Germany, the initial occupation policy for Japan, which had stressed economic and political reform, was replaced by one that emphasized aid to big business and a conservative political order. Over the next several years the United States provided more than $15 billion in assistance to Europe and Japan, the equivalent of over $90 billion in 1997 dollars.

The National Security Act of 1947 reformed the long-squabbling military and intelligence arms of the government. It consolidated the separate War and Navy Departments into the Department of Defense, led by a civilian defense secretary. The act named the military head of each service to the Joint Chiefs of Staff and made the Joint Chiefs military advisers to the president. The new law also created the National Security Council (NSC) to advise the president on foreign policy, as well as the Central Intelligence Agency (CIA) to gather and analyze intelligence and carry out covert missions abroad. Congress also revived the peacetime draft. Finally, the administration began rebuilding America's military power, increasing the size of the atomic arsenal from fifteen to more than two hundred bombs by 1950.

In response to these initiatives, Stalin imposed even tighter economic and political controls on his Eastern European satellites and purged Communist Party members he feared might harbor independent tendencies. Most dramatically, in June 1948 the Soviets blockaded land routes into West Berlin, the non-Communist enclave deep inside Soviet-occupied eastern Germany.

Before June 1948 the Western Allies had already agreed in principle to unite their occupation zones into a single unit. Having failed to prevent the restoration of a potentially powerful West German state, Stalin hoped to drive the Western powers out of Berlin, lest that city become an anti-Soviet rallying point within the Soviet Union's sphere of influence. When Washington decreed a currency reform measure for the Western-occupied zones of Germany and Berlin, Moscow declared it a violation of earlier agreements and stopped most road and rail transport into West Berlin. The Soviets did not, however, block air corridors into Berlin, which they had earlier pledged to respect.

Occupation commander General Lucius Clay urged Truman to allow him to shoot his way through the Soviet barriers. If Berlin fell, he warned, "western Germany will be next." Truman opted instead for an airlift to run the blockade. He also bluffed Stalin by sending sixty atomic-capable B-29 bombers—without atomic weapons—to England. As the president had guessed, Stalin did not want a war. Soviet planes never challenged the massive American air-transport lifeline into the besieged city. In May 1949, after a yearlong stand-off, the Soviets lifted the blockade. The Berlin airlift became a symbol of American resolve and Soviet brutality. It hastened the creation of what the Soviets greatly feared, an independent West German state, which was born in May 1949 as the Federal Republic of Germany. In rebuttal the Soviets created the East German state, the German Democratic Republic, the following month.

When Stalin relented and lifted the blockade of Berlin, the United States had, by most measures, won the Cold War in Western Europe and Japan (see map). The Marshall Plan had placed these key allies on the road to economic recovery. Communism had lost its attraction for most Europeans. Stalin's attempt to keep Japan and Europe weak, divided, and isolated from the United States had backfired.

Following Truman's election in November 1948 he appointed Dean Acheson, the former undersecretary of state, as the new secretary of state. Acheson favored creating a Western military alliance, to include a rearmed West Germany, to resist any potential Soviet threat. In April 1949 he oversaw the creation of the North Atlantic Treaty Organization (NATO). NATO committed the United States, Britain, France, Belgium, the Netherlands, Italy, Portugal, Denmark, Iceland, Norway, and Canada to a common defense; Greece, Turkey, Spain, and West Germany joined later. NATO, Acheson told an approving Congress in mid-1949, would go beyond achieving a "balance

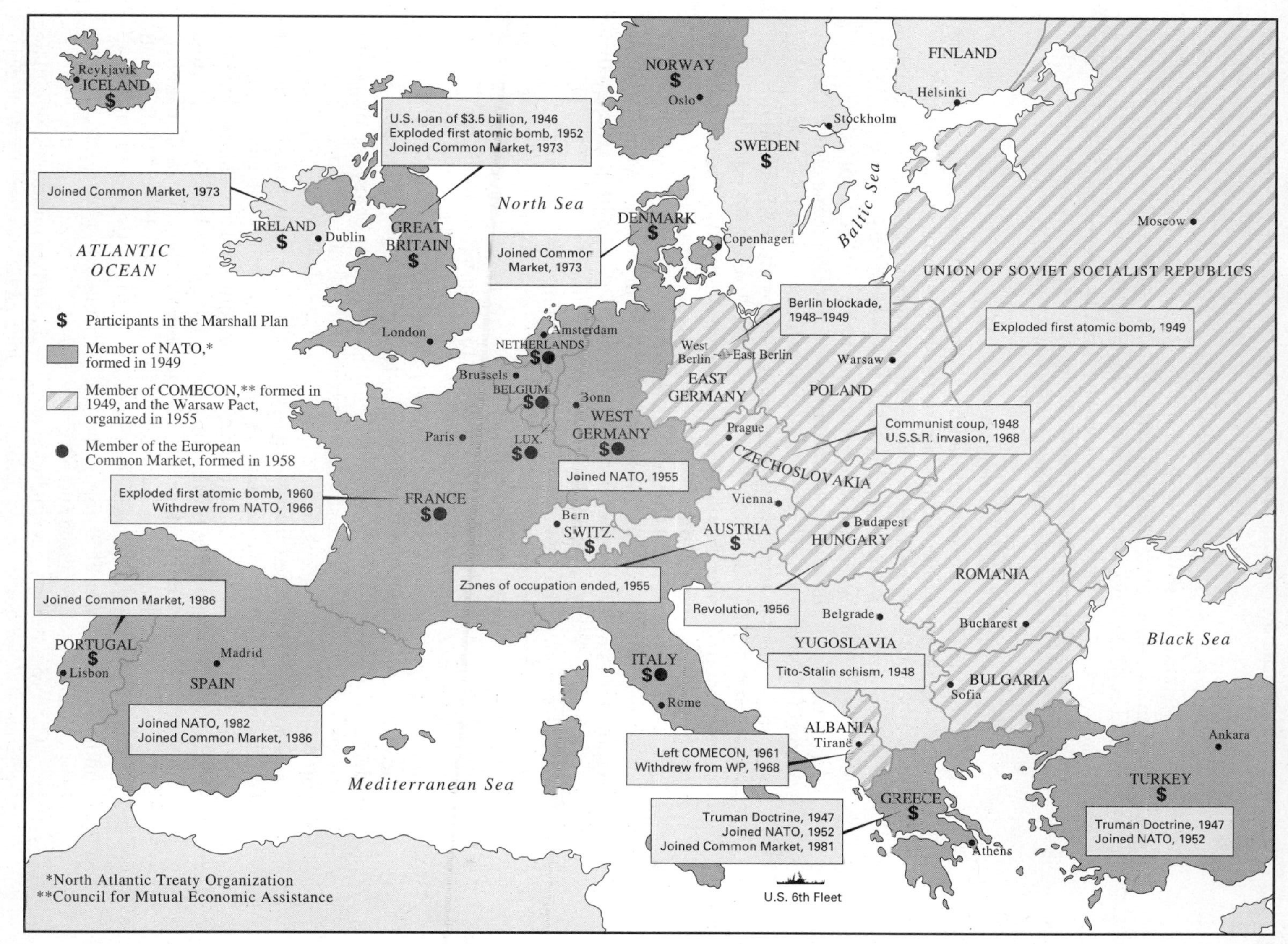

European Divisions By 1948 the continent was split between Soviet- and U.S.-dominated spheres.

of power" to give the West a "preponderance of power" over Moscow. The Soviets countered the Marshall Plan by creating the Council for Mutual Economic Assistance (known as CMEA or COMECON). And after Germany entered NATO, Moscow responded by forming the Warsaw Pact military alliance among its Eastern European satellites. These actions on both sides formally split Europe.

National Politics, 1946–1950

After the Republicans captured both houses of Congress in 1946, they confidently looked forward to winning the White House in 1948. In a way, memory of the late President Roosevelt helped them, for whatever Truman's merits might have been, he inevitably suffered in comparisons with his predecessor. Roosevelt had reshaped the nation's very concept of the presidency, making it difficult for Americans to think of someone else in the job. Moreover, Roosevelt had been a master of coalition politics, establishing an alliance among labor unions, urban ethnic groups, minorities, and farmers. Now that the Depression and the war were over, Truman found it difficult to sustain that coalition and to build support for new initiatives. Even though his political beliefs resembled Roosevelt's, the appeal of Truman's humble background, folksy style, and testy personality never matched that of FDR.

Nevertheless, Clark Clifford, a young Missouri lawyer whom Truman appointed as his special counsel in 1947, developed a political strategy that proved remarkably successful. Clifford urged Truman to attack Republican efforts to unravel the economic and social reforms of the New Deal while pushing a liberal program of his own. Clifford also argued that if former vice president Henry Wallace carried out his threat to run for president as a third-party candidate, Truman should identify him in the public mind with communism.

Following this advice, in 1947 and 1948 Truman vetoed sixty-two Republican-sponsored bills that threatened the New Deal legacy. Often the president's veto messages rang with angry language. Conversely, he proposed programs to increase aid to small farmers, raise the minimum wage, liberalize immigration policies, enhance civil rights, reduce taxes for working people, and increase Social Security benefits. As each measure went down to defeat at the hands of Republicans, Truman's standing rose among elements of the Roosevelt coalition. Then, abandoning his previous antilabor stance, Truman recaptured the support of unions through his stinging veto (which Congress overrode) of the Taft-Hartley Bill. He denounced the law, which limited workers' right to strike, as a "slave-labor act." When Henry Wallace did challenge Truman, running on the Progressive Party ticket, the White House undermined his appeal. Truman announced that he was glad not to have the support of "Henry Wallace and his Communists."

Clifford's strategy also included an appeal to urban minorities, whom he predicted would form a crucial voting bloc in the 1948 election. By endorsing the recommendations of his Committee on Civil Rights, which called for a more forceful federal attack on segregation, Truman solidified his support among African-Americans. At the same time, concerned about alienating moderate whites, he took only modest steps to put those recommendations into practice. The president also reached out to Jews and eastern Europeans by endorsing a liberalized immigration law and by extending diplomatic recognition to Israel immediately after its creation in May 1948.

At the Democratic convention in July 1948, Truman tried to appease all factions by supporting an innocuous civil rights platform. However, a revolt by party liberals, including the young mayor of Minneapolis, Hubert H. Humphrey, forced the adoption of a stronger civil rights agenda. Angry southerners, such as Senator James Eastland of Mississippi, denounced attempts to "mongrelize the nation"; others complained that Truman was "kissing the feet of the minorities."

Some southern Democrats walked out of the convention and organized the States Rights Party. The presidential nominee of these "Dixiecrats," Governor Strom Thurmond of South Carolina (later an eight-term U.S. senator), declared that his party represented the "deepest emotion of the human fabric—racial pride, respect for white womanhood, and superiority of Caucasian blood." He dismissed demands for civil rights as part of a Communist plan promoted by the "radicals, subversives, and Reds" surrounding Truman.

Now that the Democratic Party had split three ways, many observers simply wrote off Truman's political prospects. In fact, the split may have actually helped Truman, as it allowed him to stress his anti-Communist credentials and appeal to black urban voters. Ignoring polls that gave Republican nominee Thomas Dewey nearly a fifteen-point lead during the summer of 1948, Truman crisscrossed the nation by train, delivering hundreds of combative speeches. Virtually ignoring Wallace and Thurmond, he concentrated his fire on the Republican-dominated Eightieth Congress, the "gluttons of privilege" who "stuck a pitchfork on the back of the farmers," tried to "enslave totally the working man," and wanted to do "a real hatchet job on the New Deal." A Republican president would bring back the Depression, Truman insisted. Energized crowds roared "Give 'em hell, Harry."

In fact, Dewey was a moderate and a decent man who did not intend to roll back the New Deal. But his personality was stiff, and his campaign suffered from overconfidence. Dewey devoted more energy to planning his inauguration than to campaigning, failing even to rebut Truman's charges.

Gradually Truman's appeal to labor, farmers, urban ethnic voters, and blacks—the former Roosevelt coalition—took hold. Also, Truman proved relatively immune to Republican charges of softness on communism. He had proven his loyalty to the anti-Communist cause with the Truman Doctrine and by supporting the Marshall Plan and the Berlin airlift, all popular with voters. Compared to either Thurmond or Wallace he was a centrist. Many polling organizations, whose methods were rather crude, lost interest in the seemingly one-sided race and stopped taking surveys three weeks before the November election. When the tally came in, Truman received 24 million votes to Dewey's 22 million—one of the most dramatic upsets in the history of presidential politics. Wallace and Thurmond each received slightly more than 1 million votes, and their parties soon dissolved.

Now president in his own right, Truman tried to emerge from Roosevelt's shadow by proclaiming his own reform program, the Fair Deal. He introduced legislation for national health insurance, public housing, expanded Social Security benefits, a higher minimum wage, a program to build public power systems that resembled the TVA, greater protection for civil rights, an agricultural support program that favored small farmers, and repeal of the Taft-Hartley Act. Although Congress raised the minimum wage from 40 to 75 cents per hour and boosted Social Security benefits, the enduring coalition of Republicans and southern Democrats in Congress bottled up most of the other proposals. The outbreak of the Korean War in June 1950, Republican gains in that November's congressional election, and a series of scandals involving Truman cronies further frustrated Truman's efforts at reform.

Although the Fair Deal remained more a promise than a reality, Truman's proposals set a social agenda for later administrations. In this sense they were more influential than politicians of the time guessed. Regrettably, Truman's own anti-Communist fervor undercut his reforms by inflaming public fear of liberal policies.

✦ Expanding Dimensions of the Cold War

Even as the Marshall Plan and NATO blocked the threat of Soviet expansion into Western Europe, the Cold War brought new concerns. The Soviets' development of an atomic bomb led Washington to re-evaluate American security needs. Communist successes in China and Vietnam prompted demands for deeper American involvement in Asia. Meanwhile, sensational espionage cases raised fears that the Soviets could gain dominance simply by stealing American secrets.

In September 1949 American reconnaissance planes collected air samples that indicated an atomic explosion had recently occurred inside the Soviet Union, years earlier than expected. Many people feared that a Soviet nuclear bomb would place the Soviet Union on an equal military footing with the United States and encourage it to take direct military action against the West. The Soviet bomb triggered a debate in Washington over whether to build a new bomb a thousand times more powerful than the first atomic weapon. Whereas the atomic bombs used in World War II had gained their energy from the splitting, or fission, of uranium atoms, the super, or hydrogen bomb would use the energy released from the fusion of hydrogen atoms. Those who opposed development of the H-bomb, such as physicist J. Robert Oppenheimer and diplomat George Kennan, doubted that Soviet atomic weapons would greatly alter the American military advantage, because the Soviets lacked an effective delivery system. With some modifications, American atomic bombs could be made far more powerful than the early ones. Thus the H-bomb might not give the United States much additional advantage in deterring the Soviets. Others, who favored a slow approach to the exceedingly costly build-up of nuclear weapons, believed that Washington should first try to negotiate an arms control pact with Moscow. If Stalin stalled or raced ahead with his own hydrogen bomb project, the United States would still have the option of matching him.

Neither moral, political, nor technical arguments swayed top policymakers against developing the new weapon. Oppenheimer's opposition to the H-bomb was soon used to drive him from his position as a government consultant on nuclear policy and became the basis for labeling him a "security risk." Kennan, too, was eased out of influence. Acheson selected hard-liner Paul Nitze to replace Kennan as head of policy planning in the State Department and as chair of a committee that urged rapid development of the hydrogen bomb. President Truman needed little convincing. America had to make the bomb, he said later, if "only for bargaining purposes with the Russians." After beginning development in January 1950, American scientists exploded a prototype hydrogen device in November 1952. The Soviets followed suit the next August.

When Truman asked Acheson to undertake a comprehensive study of American security policy, the secretary of state again tapped Nitze for the job. In the resulting top-secret document, known as NSC-68, Nitze and his staff described the risk of a Soviet attack as great and steadily increasing. In a departure from Kennan's description of Soviet policy as cautious and calculating, NSC-68 claimed that Soviet behavior showed a boldness that "borders on the reckless." Nitze advocated a dramatic increase in American defense spending, from $13 billion to $50 billion annually. This increment would be used to fund both increased conventional forces and a new generation of nuclear weapons and delivery systems. Nitze confided to his staff that such huge sums were unlikely to be appropriated except as a result of a scare campaign to shock the public.

NSC-68, given to the president in April 1950, painted a lurid picture of the Kremlin's "fanatical faith" in communism, which motivated it to "impose its authority on the rest of the world." It greatly exaggerated Soviet military strength, claiming that by 1954 Moscow would possess the nuclear capacity to destroy the United States. Abandoning containment's previous focus on Western Europe and Japan, the new report called for an immediate large-scale build-up of U.S. nuclear and conventional weapons to meet new Soviet challenges anywhere in the world. Acheson hoped the report's strategic overkill would "bludgeon the mass mind of government" into action. Other high officials supported the proposed increase in defense spending for a variety of other reasons. For example, members of the president's Council of Economic Advisers argued that large defense expenditures would boost industrial output and employment. Yet Truman remained cautious. He endorsed NSC-68 in principle but worried about its high price tag.

In October 1949, a month after a Soviet atomic test had been confirmed by American intelligence, Americans received more bad news when Communist leader Mao Zedong established the People's Republic of China. After four years of civil war, Nationalist Party leader Jiang Jieshi had fled to the island of Taiwan (or Formosa, as many Westerners called it), off the South China coast. The Communist victory outraged Jiang's American supporters—the so-called China lobby—and disheartened Americans who considered China theirs to "lose." The long civil war between the Communists and Nationalists had resumed as soon as Japan surrendered. During 1946, General George C. Marshall served a year as a mediator in China, trying to arrange a political compromise. Both Nationalists and Communists, however, believed they could win a military showdown and opposed real power sharing. Marshall gave up in January 1947 and returned to Washington to become secretary of state. Although the United States gave Jiang about $2 billion in aid between 1945 and 1949, Nationalist Party corruption and military incompetence nullified its effect. Further U.S. military aid seemed pointless, as the Communists had driven well-armed Nationalist Party troops from positions that American military observers regarded as easily defensible. In private Truman called Jiang a crook, and even many Republican politicians quietly agreed that aid to him was "money down a rat hole."

In August 1949 the State Department issued a massive report, known as the China White Paper, that condemned the Chinese Communists for their subservience to Russia but insisted that Jiang, not the United States, had "lost China" and that he deserved no more help. Most American diplomats expected that the Chinese and Soviet Communists would eventually fall out. Ceasing aid to Jiang on Taiwan, they predicted, would reduce tensions with the Chinese Communists and hasten a break between the Soviet Union and China. Although Truman was not ready to extend diplomatic recognition to the new Chinese regime, he did announce in January 1950 that American forces would not defend Taiwan against an anticipated Communist assault but that the United States would "wait for the dust to settle" and then size up its options.

Truman and Acheson urged Americans to shift their attention in Asia away from China and to the "Great Crescent," the lands that stretched from Japan through Southeast Asia to India. Southeast Asian resources, including oil, rice, rubber, and tin, they stressed, were more vital to European and Japanese economic security—and hence to U.S. security than was anything in China. In a remark little noticed at the time, Acheson described South Korea as being outside the U.S. defense perimeter in Asia.

Whatever they really thought about China, many Republicans (and a few Democrats) in Congress saw the Communist victory there as a handy stick with which to beat the Truman administration. The president might have held the line against a Soviet advance in Europe, but he had done so, they reasoned, at the cost of a defeat in Asia. The so-called China bloc in Congress, which had some allies among journalists and paid lobbyists for Taiwan, labeled the White Paper a whitewash and accused Truman and Acheson of coddling advisers who had sold out America's Chinese allies. Among those who spoke most bitterly about the decision not to intervene in China was a young Democratic congressman from Massachusetts, John F. Kennedy. China, he declared, "whose freedom we once fought to preserve" and "our young men had saved, our diplomats and president have frittered away."

As part of the effort to erect a containment barrier on the periphery of China, in 1950 the United States began to assist French forces fighting a Communist-led uprising in French Indochina (Vietnam, Cambodia, and Laos). Ho Chi Minh, a lifelong Communist and fighter for Vietnam independence who led the Vietminh guerrilla movement, had cooperated with Americans in fighting Japan and appealed for U.S. support in securing independence for Vietnam in 1945. During World War II FDR had urged French leaders to loosen their hold on Vietnam after Japan's defeat. Truman, however, who was more concerned with keeping France a strong and reliable ally in Europe, proved less inclined to support anticolonial movements. Few American diplomats knew much about Southeast Asia, and those who sympathized with Ho and the Vietminh were ignored.

Truman and Acheson condemned the Vietminh guerrillas as Soviet or Chinese Communist stooges whose victory would weaken Western Europe and expose all of Southeast Asia to Communist influence. But because of American unease about directly supporting colonialism, Washington urged Paris to transfer nominal power in Vietnam to Bao Dai, a former emperor. In 1950, under this cloak of phony independence, U.S. aid began flowing to French forces fighting in Vietnam.

The Red Scare

During the decade following victory in the Second World War, a mounting anti-Communist movement dominated American political debate. As mentioned earlier, American anticommunism stretched back to 1917 and the first Red Scare that followed the Bolshevik Revolution. Part of the domestic tension over communism came from disputes dating back to the 1930s, when left-wing factions in the Democratic Party, the labor movement, and American intellectual circles had squared off against centrists and conservatives who abhorred the Soviet Union and any Americans who defended it. Republican politicians who hated New Deal programs but failed to win votes by promising to repeal them found that the public would listen to accusations that Democratic policies contributed to the rise of international communism. This mixture of ideological fervor and opportunism, combined with the disgust many Americans felt about Soviet domination of Eastern Europe, fed a Red Scare that began in 1946 and 1947 and soon grew to a fever pitch. Eventually Joseph McCarthy, a Republican senator from Wisconsin, would give his name to the movement, but it was well under way by the time he emerged as a national figure, and many other public figures contributed to it.

At the end of World War II the Communist Party of the United States, a legal organization, had fewer than one hundred thousand members. During the next decade it sank like a stone, to one-fourth that size. Although party members supported Soviet policies and overlooked Stalin's brutality, American Communists did not advocate violence or plot to overthrow the U.S. government. The FBI had infiltrated the party so thoroughly that it could not organize a picnic in secrecy. After 1945 the Soviet Union was arguably an external danger to the United States, but communism was no threat within its borders.

Nevertheless, certain conservatives linked the New Deal, liberalism, and progressive politics to "the Reds," primarily as a way of discrediting them all. For example, defenders of segregation labeled anyone who campaigned for racial equality a Communist. Conservative union leaders found it possible to oust left-wing opponents in the labor movement by calling them stooges of Moscow. Republican politicians, stymied by the popularity of New Deal programs, encouraged voters to desert the Democratic Party by accusing it of disloyalty and softness on communism.

The House Committee on Un-American Activities (HUAC) played a particularly influential role in stirring up the Red Scare. Between 1944 and 1946 Democrats John S. Wood of Georgia and John Rankin of Mississippi used the committee as a forum to attack liberal causes. Rankin, the most active member of the panel, took pride in bringing to the nation's capital a law modeled on statutes in twenty-two states that banned interracial marriage. He spoke darkly of conspiracies among "alien-minded communistic enemies of Christianity"—his code for Jews—to take over the nation.

In November 1946, to counter charges of Democratic waffling on subversion, President Truman established the Temporary Commission on Employee Loyalty. The following March he created the Federal Employee Loyalty Program to verify the loyalty of government employees. The attorney general compiled a list of eighty-two supposedly subversive organizations in the United States. Congressional committees developed a list of over six hundred such groups. These ran the gamut from the Communist Party to pro-Nazi groups, including many organizations active in the struggles against racial segregation, for disarmament, and for workers' rights. Membership in any of these organizations could, by itself, constitute reasonable doubt of a federal employee's loyalty and justify dismissal. The program required current and prospective federal employees to undergo an investigation. Hearsay, anonymous accusations, and information from wiretaps and illegally opened personal mail could be used to discredit someone.

The FBI conducted most loyalty probes of government employees. Its director, J. Edgar Hoover, had been "chasing Reds," as he put it, since the

Palmer Raids of 1919. Although relations between Truman and Hoover were frosty, the FBI director was on good terms with nearly every other president he served under, from Warren Harding through Richard Nixon. During his long career the FBI mirrored Hoover's contempt for Communists, African-Americans, and nearly every kind of political or social nonconformity. By the early 1950s over 5 million government employees had undergone some form of security check. Several thousand quit in protest. A few hundred were fired for belonging to groups on the attorney general's list.

The Soviet Union of course conducted espionage. It especially sought information on nuclear weapons and other useful technologies. Soviet agents typically recruited disgruntled employees of private companies who nursed grievances or needed cash. Few of their American spies had political motives. Thus loyalty programs and congressional inquiries that focused on exposing leftists or Communist Party members did little to enhance security.

Nearly every case of actual espionage unearthed and prosecuted in the 1940s and 1950s was the product of criminal investigations by the FBI; grandstanding politicians did little but sow confusion and fear. Still, a few high-profile cases of real or alleged treason involving Communist sympathizers and former members of the Roosevelt administration created a false impression among Americans of a nation at risk from internal subversion.

With the cooperation of FBI director Hoover, congressional redbaiters stepped up their activity in 1947. J. Parnell Thomas, a New Jersey Republican named to chair HUAC when his party won control of the House in 1946, announced the discovery of a Red plot, centered in Hollywood, to overthrow the government.

The movie industry made an enticing target for HUAC. Jewish immigrants headed several of the eight major studios. Most had assimilated, Anglicized their names, and made movies celebrating American life. Nevertheless, the anti-Semitic Congressman John Rankin found them an irresistible target. Rankin and J. Parnell Thomas recognized that an investigation of the film industry would generate huge publicity.

A small number of screenwriters, who frequently clashed with studio executives over salaries and creative freedom, had formed a left-leaning union, the Screen Writers Guild. Studio bosses like Jack Warner and Sam Goldwyn hoped that by cooperating with HUAC they could crush the Guild, reassert their control over writers, and demonstrate their own patriotism. HUAC subpoenaed testimony from ten writers and directors whom it considered suspicious, including Dalton Trumbo; Ring Lardner, Jr.; and John Howard Lawson. Several were current or past Communist Party members. All ten refused to testify, citing the First Amendment's protection of free speech and political association. Nevertheless, they were convicted of contempt of Congress and went to jail for terms of up to one year. (HUAC chairman J. Parnell Thomas, convicted of taking salary kickbacks from his staff, joined writer Ring Lardner, Jr., in prison.)

Following the Hollywood hearings, studios pledged not to hire Communists. They and the emerging television industry created a blacklist of actors, writers, and directors who had either refused to cooperate with HUAC or been identified as suspect by someone else's testimony.

As the anti-Communist hysteria mounted, many public schools and universities required teachers to sign loyalty oaths or face summary dismissal. The CIO threw out unions whose officers were accused of Communist affiliations. The Catholic Church called on the faithful to combat the "aggression of enemies within."

In 1948 HUAC began its most famous inquiry. For several years Whittaker Chambers, an editor at *Time,* had been telling various government officials that he had been part of a Soviet espionage ring in the mid-1930s. Chambers claimed that members of the Roosevelt administration had fed him material to pass on to Moscow. After 1937, he said, he lost faith in communism and became a devout Christian. Eventually he confessed his sins to California Republican congressman Richard M. Nixon and other members of HUAC. In August 1948 they presented him to the public.

Initially Chambers claimed that former State Department official Alger Hiss was a secret Communist, though not one of those who had passed information to him. Later, when Hiss filed a libel suit, Chambers counterattacked by naming Hiss as one of the informants. In contrast to the sinister-looking Chambers, Hiss seemed a paragon of charm, eloquence, and professional accomplishment. He had worked for several New Deal agencies, as well as the State Department, and had attended the Yalta conference. After the war Hiss became head of the prestigious Carnegie Endowment for International Peace.

When Hiss denied knowing Chambers, several HUAC members were prepared to drop the case. But Nixon, a freshman who had won election in part by linking his opponent to subversion, refused to stand aside. He arranged a face-to-face meeting between Chambers and Hiss, coaxing an admission from Hiss that he had indeed met Chambers but knew him by a different name.

Republicans pushed the case with renewed vigor after November 1948, when Truman unexpectedly defeated Dewey. "Remembering" new details supplied to him by the FBI, Chambers now charged that Hiss had passed government secrets to him as late as 1938. To prove this claim, he and Nixon brought reporters to Chambers's Maryland farm, where Chambers reached into a hollow pumpkin and extracted several rolls of microfilm. The FBI determined that the films and associated documents (dubbed the Pumpkin Papers) were secret government reports, many of which had been retyped on a machine owned by the Hiss family. Although the statute of limitations on espionage had lapsed, Hiss was indicted for lying to Congress about his Communist affiliations and contact with Chambers.

A trial in 1949 resulted in a hung jury, but in January 1950 a second jury found Hiss guilty of perjury. Hiss went to jail maintaining that the FBI had framed him. Chambers went on to write *Witness,* a best-selling account of his troubled life, and accused many other private citizens and government officials of espionage. Nixon parlayed his fame into a California Senate seat in 1950 and the vice-presidential slot two years later.

The Chambers-Hiss case became a political morality play both for liberals and for conservatives. Republicans felt they had proved a conspiracy, even though Hiss was not shown to have given away any great state secrets. When Truman initially dismissed HUAC's case against Hiss as a red herring, he drove Republicans wild. Adding fuel to this fire, in February 1950 British police arrested Klaus Fuchs, a German scientist émigré, who confessed to being part of a spy ring that had passed secrets to the Soviets from the American nuclear laboratory at Los Alamos, New Mexico, during World War II. By the summer of 1950 evidence from Fuchs led to the arrest of American Communists Julius and Ethel Rosenberg, who were charged with being members of the atomic spy ring. At a highly publicized trial the Rosenbergs denied committing espionage, even though a relative who had worked at Los Alamos confessed to giving Julius information during the Second World War. After sifting the evidence for years and gaining access to some relevant Soviet documents, many historians have concluded that Julius Rosenberg probably did pass a variety of secrets to the Soviets, including information on atomic weapons. The evidence against his wife was less clear. Both Rosenbergs were convicted, and in 1953 they died in the electric chair. Fuchs and several other confederates were sentenced to prison.

While Congress probed for spies, in October 1949 a jury in a federal trial convicted twelve leaders of the American Communist Party of violating the Smith Act, a law that made it a crime to advocate the overthrow of the U.S. government by force or to belong to a group advocating such action. In 1951, in *Dennis v. United States,* the Supreme Court upheld the conviction. Chief Justice Fred Vinson ruled that citizens had no right to pursue violence where the opportunity for peaceful change existed. In the dissent, Justices Hugo Black and William O. Douglas argued that although American Communists disapproved of the U.S. government, they had neither advocated nor worked for its violent overthrow.

By then Congress had passed the Internal Security Act of 1950, also called the McCarran Act, which declared the existence of an international Communist conspiracy that posed an immediate threat to the United States. The law stopped short of outlawing the Communist Party, but it ordered all organizations and individuals labeled Communist-affiliated to register with the newly created Subversive Activities Control Board or face a $10,000 fine and five years in prison. Real and alleged Communists were denied passports and barred from jobs in government or the defense industry. The law permitted the deportation of naturalized citizens and the detention without trial of alleged subversives during periods of emergency.

In the anti-Communist climate of the early Cold War, immigration was often seen as a threat to America. The quota, or national origins, system

✦ ✦ ✦

Biographical Profile

Senator Joseph "Tail Gunner Joe" McCarthy, 1908–1957

Amid worries over espionage and traitors, Republican Joseph R. McCarthy of Wisconsin staked his claim to fame. A relative latecomer to the Red Scare, he so dominated the years from 1950 to 1954 that *McCarthyism* became the catchword for the era.

A former county judge, McCarthy served as a Marine desk officer during the Second World War, flying a few routine missions in the tail gunner's seat. Despite this modest record, in 1946 he campaigned successfully for a Senate seat as "Tail Gunner Joe." During his first four years in office he was considered something of a buffoon by colleagues and journalists. Early in 1950 he pieced together information provided by several friends, including Congressman Richard Nixon. On February 9, at a gathering of Republican women in Wheeling, West Virginia, McCarthy declared that the United States risked defeat in the Cold War because Secretary of State Dean Acheson had turned over American foreign policy plans to hundreds of Communists (see the accompanying quote). In trumpeting his charges of treason, he often changed the number of Reds supposedly selling out their country. Eventually he labeled as spies and traitors the "whole

---

established in the 1920s allowed a small number of people from Western Europe to immigrate to the United States but restricted most others. Shortly after the Second World War, pressures mounted to amend these restrictions. The tragic condition of more than a million "displaced persons" in Europe proved especially problematic. These refugees included some two hundred thousand Jewish survivors of the Holocaust, ethnic Germans pushed out of Eastern Europe, and Latvians, Estonians, and Lithuanians who had fled Soviet control. After intensive lobbying by citizens groups, in June 1948 Congress passed the Displaced Persons Act, which opened two hundred thousand slots for these people. An extension of the law let in an equal number in 1950.

In 1952 Congress passed the Immigration and Nationality Act, also known as the McCarran-Walter Act. Senator Pat McCarran complained that the group of twisted-thinking" New Dealers, who he said had "led America to near ruin at home and abroad."

McCarthy was a cynical opportunist who came to believe his own ravings. His conspiracy theory provided simple answers to complex questions. America did not need a Marshall Plan or NATO to win the Cold War, only a purge of Red sympathizers at home. At Senate hearings he made wild accusations about the loyalty of government officials but changed the subject when challenged to offer proof. Republican leaders encouraged his antics, which undermined public faith in the Democratic Party and liberal bureaucrats. Journalist George Reedy recalled that reporters felt obliged to cover McCarthy even though most knew that "Joe couldn't find a Communist in Red Square. He didn't know Karl Marx from Groucho."

McCarthy's charges paralyzed the State Department and other government agencies. His influence increased after the Republicans captured the White House and a Senate majority in November 1952. In 1954, when he suggested that President Dwight D. Eisenhower and the U.S. Army sheltered Communists, Republicans deserted him. Despite receiving a formal censure, he remained in the Senate until his death in 1957 from alcohol-related illness.

"The reason why we find ourselves in a position of impotency is not because our . . . powerful . . . enemy has sent men to invade our shores, but rather because of the traitorous actions of those who have been treated so well by this nation. When [Dean Acheson] this pompous diplomat in striped pants, with a phony British accent, proclaimed to the American people that Christ on the Mount endorsed communism, high treason, and betrayal of a sacred trust, the blasphemy was so great that it awaked the dormant indignation of the American people."

—From a McCarthy speech at Wheeling, West Virginia

---

country already had too many "indigestible blocs" and did all he could to retain the old restrictions. The new law repealed the virtual ban on Asian immigration but set an absurdly low annual quota of one hundred persons for each Asian-Pacific nation. Western Europeans continued to be favored over all others. The law barred entry of suspected Communists and homosexuals and, like the earlier law, permitted the deportation of naturalized citizens accused of subversive activities. Passed over Truman's veto, it remained the basic immigration law until 1965.

Whatever damage the Rosenbergs and Hiss may have done, it seems clear that domestic subversion never presented much of a threat to the United States. Soviet penetration of atomic projects and government agencies pretty much lapsed after 1945. Yet the general anxiety provoked by the Cold War and, after June 1950, the Korean war heightened the feeling that large numbers of traitors were still giving the Kremlin vital data.

The Korean War and Its Consequences

The North Korean invasion of South Korea on June 25, 1950, transformed the Cold War into a hot one. By the time the fighting stopped in 1953, U.S. defense spending had reached the levels envisioned in NSC-68, and several hundred thousand American troops were stationed permanently in Europe. Moreover, the war created a precedent of great significance: by committing the country to an extensive military effort without a congressional declaration of war, Truman set the pattern for Vietnam and other American military involvements in the following decades.

In August 1945 the United States and the Soviet Union divided Korea, a Japanese colony since 1910, into temporary occupation zones north and south of the thirty-eighth parallel. Proposals to unite and free Korea lapsed as the Cold War intensified. The Soviets sponsored a Communist regime, the Democratic People's Republic of Korea, led by Korean Communist Kim Il Sung, north of the dividing line. In the South, the United States supported a right-wing government, the Republic of Korea, led by Syngman Rhee, a Korean nationalist who had lived in the United States for decades. Most Soviet and American occupation forces departed in 1949, leaving behind rival regimes, each claiming the right to rule an undivided Korea. Violence within and between both states was rampant.

Most American military officials considered Korea an unimportant backwater, but State Department planners worried that abandoning the South Korean government would be interpreted as a betrayal of U.S. friends in Asia. Despite misgivings about the authoritarian government in South Korea, the United States continued to assist the regime. Truman and his advisers perceived the North Korean invasion of the South on June 25, 1950, as a Soviet test of American resolve, not as a civil war in a divided country. Recent evidence suggests that Kim Il Sung pressed Stalin and Mao to approve and aid his army's invasion of the South and that they did so with the understanding it would succeed quickly and not provoke U.S. intervention. Stalin and Mao probably believed a unified Korea would counterbalance their traditional enemy, Japan, which was then being rebuilt and rearmed by the United States. American officials focused on the Soviet threat in the region and largely dismissed the Korean origins of the war. The relationship between the Soviet Union and North Korea, one official remarked, was "the same as that between Walt Disney and Donald Duck."

The United States secured quick UN support for military aid to South Korea. On June 27 Truman ordered American air and naval forces into Korea, and three days later he sent ground forces as well. Congress was not asked to declare war. Truman referred to the armed intervention as a "police action."

When the United Nations gave its approval to a joint force under an American commander, Truman assigned this critical role to General Douglas MacArthur, who headed the occupation forces in Japan. Although a number of countries eventually sent token forces, 90 percent of the UN troops were American, and MacArthur acted as a U.S., not a UN, commander.

After two months of hanging on to a toehold in South Korea, General MacArthur assembled a large force to counterattack. On September 15, 1950, he supervised a daring amphibious assault behind enemy lines on the coastal city of Inchon. Within two weeks American troops had cleared the North Koreans out of the South and achieved the original goal of the war, reestablishing the South Korean regime.

The deceptively easy victory at Inchon and the appearance of infallibility it gave to MacArthur encouraged President Truman to expand American goals. Instead of merely restoring the prewar border, Truman ordered MacArthur to cross north of the thirty-eighth parallel and unify the entire country under Rhee's regime. From the earliest days of the fighting, MacArthur chafed at talk of a limited war and pushed for a crusade to roll back communism in Korea, China, and elsewhere. Worried that such talk might provoke an unwanted war with China or the Soviet Union, Truman several times considered firing MacArthur. But as a potential Republican presidential candidate—he had sought the nomination in 1944 and 1948—MacArthur had to be treated with care. He could not be recalled without provoking a backlash among the many Americans who regarded him as a hero.

Even though he was fearful that MacArthur might provoke a wider war, Truman discounted warnings from China during October 1950 that American forces should not cross the thirty-eighth parallel into North Korea or approach the Yalu River, which separated North Korea from Manchuria, China's industrial heartland. Like Truman, MacArthur dismissed Chinese pledges to defend North Korea as bluff. During an October conference on Wake Island, the general assured the president that the war was practically won. If the Chinese dared to intervene, MacArthur predicted, there would be the "greatest slaughter." The prophecy came partly true, but not exactly as the general had supposed.

In November 1950 Chinese troops stunned MacArthur—and Americans at home—by crossing into North Korea and driving American forces south to the thirty-eighth parallel in a humiliating retreat. MacArthur told the Joint Chiefs of Staff that he faced an entirely new war that could only be won if he received massive reinforcements, troops from Taiwan, and permission to attack China by air and sea. Atomic bombs might be needed as well, he said. Most civilian and military officials in Washington disagreed. In their minds the real danger remained a Soviet threat to Europe and Japan. It made no sense to fight a major war in a backwater like Korea. Officials weighed using the atomic bomb, but few appropriate military targets existed in North Korea. Using it against Chinese cities would be immensely destructive and, diplomats concluded, would almost certainly bring the Soviets into the war.

Once China entered the war and the front line bogged down, the public showed little sympathy with the limited aims of preserving South Korea and building up NATO and Japanese security. Soldiers complained they did not want to "die for a tie." After less than a year of the fighting, nearly two-thirds of the American public expressed dissatisfaction with the administration's handling of the war.

In the spring of 1951 the battle lines in Korea finally stabilized when American forces halted the Chinese army near the thirty-eighth parallel. But when Truman prepared to send China a peace feeler in March 1951, MacArthur sabotaged it. The general followed this with a letter to Republican congressman Joseph Martin, in which he implied that Truman was guilty of the murder of American boys. Calling again for attacks upon China, MacArthur asserted, "There is no substitute for victory."

Outraged, Truman decided to remove MacArthur. On April 11 he sacked the general and replaced him with General Matthew Ridgway, the field commander who had blunted the Chinese drive south. Republican politicians were appalled by this rebuff of a popular general who had voiced the anti-Communist sentiments of many.

On April 19, after arriving home to huge parades in his honor, MacArthur told both houses of Congress that Truman's policy of confining the war to Korea condemned all Asia to Communist rule. He brought the audience to cheers and tears by closing with the lyrics of an old army song, "Old Soldiers Never Die, They Just Fade Away." Obviously hoping *he* would not fade away, the general began a speaking tour, but the public rapidly lost interest in him.

That summer China agreed to peace talks. The talking and fighting continued for two more years, until July 1953. An immediate consequence of the Korean War was the expansion of the American defense budget. By 1953 defense spending had reached $52 billion, up from $17 billion in 1950; the NSC-68 proposals had become reality. The military budget would remain high throughout the 1950s. This had an especially dramatic impact on Sunbelt states such as California, with their heavy concentration of defense plants and military bases. Moreover, America expanded its international defense network during the war. Besides ensuring Japan's security and placing several hundred thousand troops in NATO countries, Washington sent extra aid to the French for their struggle in Vietnam. Additional American arms also went to Taiwan and the Philippines. New American military bases opened in such places as Morocco and Spain.

Mounting public resentment over the stalemate in Korea and the recall of MacArthur was not the only trouble Truman faced in 1951 and 1952. A series of petty scandals put his administration on the defensive. Truman appointees in several government agencies were condemned as bribe takers, "five-percenters" who awarded government contracts in exchange for 5 percent kickbacks. The war issue, combined with charges of Democratic corruption and subversion, doomed the party of the retiring president. In 1952 Dwight D. Eisenhower beat Democrat Adlai Stevenson in a landslide, and Republican congressional candidates rode Eisenhower's coattails into the Capitol, gaining control of both houses of Congress.

By the time Truman left office, the basic outlines of America's Cold War policy were firmly established. To contain the perceived Soviet threat and rebuild world trade, the United States had provided generous aid to Europe and Japan, expanded its military budget, and committed itself to an ongoing nuclear arms race. Most important, it had established the principle that America would intervene—with aid, with airplanes, and, if necessary, with American troops—whenever it appeared that the Soviet Union, China, or any of their clients were trying to extend Communist influence.

✦ A New Look: Eisenhower Takes Command

As a presidential candidate, Eisenhower had pledged he would never rest until he had liberated the "enslaved nations of the world." John Foster Dulles, his newly appointed secretary of state, denounced containment as a "treadmill, which at best might keep us in the same place until we drop exhausted." Both men criticized Truman's foreign policy because it was not designed to win a conclusive victory, and Republican rhetoric castigated the Democrats for "abandoning people to Godless terrorism."

With the campaign behind him, however, Eisenhower pursued a relatively moderate foreign policy through his two terms in office. His approach to foreign affairs was not easy to categorize. Although he declared that America could never rest until the Communist yoke had been lifted from Eastern Europe and China, he resisted calls from the Pentagon and Congress to increase defense spending, fearing that large budget deficits would be as destructive as war in the long run. He was willing to threaten other countries with nuclear weapons, but he avoided full-scale conflict and never employed America's expanded nuclear arsenal. Under Eisenhower's leadership the United States and the Soviet Union gradually learned how to coexist. Yet the two powers displaced much of their direct competition into an often unsavory contest for influence in the Third World.

Eisenhower's secretary of state seemed a marked contrast to the avuncular president. A powerful corporate lawyer active in the Presbyterian church, Dulles often wore a sour expression and delivered lectures on Christian virtue and Communist sin. He was so noted for his toughness against communism, in Asia and elsewhere, that Winston Churchill joked he was the only bull who carried around his own "China shop."

During the Eisenhower administration, Dulles and Vice President Richard Nixon frequently made bellicose and controversial statements, creating a widespread impression that they, not Eisenhower, controlled the administration's foreign policy. In fact, as historians have come to realize, Eisenhower used them to float controversial ideas, warn adversaries, and appease Republican hard-liners. The president remained in charge.

Secretary of State John Foster Dulles and President Dwight Eisenhower. *Dwight D. Eisenhower Library*

Shortly after taking office, Eisenhower endorsed a basic security policy, code-named NSC 162/3, that closely resembled the containment program he had criticized as a presidential candidate. The new plan did, however, place a greater emphasis on the use of nuclear weapons, both as weapons and as bargaining chips in the Cold War. In case of war, Eisenhower's advisers favored using the bombs as weapons of choice.

This strategy had economic as well as military benefits. By relying more on nuclear weapons and the air force, the United States could slash the size of its costly ground forces. Unlike military officials who asked for more troops, ships, and conventional munitions to achieve decisive *superiority* over the Soviet Union, Eisenhower favored *sufficiency*—enough striking power to deter or, if necessary, destroy the Soviet Union, but no more than was needed. Attempting to match the enemy "man for man, gun for gun," he warned, would bankrupt the nation. Eisenhower reduced military spending from about $52 billion annually to about $36 billion at the end of his first term. In his second term military spending increased again because of congressional pressure and renewed competition with the Soviet Union.

Eisenhower and Dulles labeled their strategy the New Look. It depended on what Dulles called the threat of "massive retaliation" against Soviet or Chinese provocation. The administration had inherited a nuclear arsenal of about a thousand atomic bombs. Over the next eight years this stockpile grew to eighteen thousand weapons. An important addition to the military's armaments was the huge, eight-engine B-52 bomber. The B-52, first deployed by the air force in 1955, was so effective a weapon that it remained in service through the 1990s. Meanwhile, small, tactical nuclear weapons as well as intercontinental ballistic missiles (ICBMs) and submarine-launched missiles were under development. When Eisenhower left office in 1961, the United States had enough air-, sea-, and ground-launched nuclear weapons to destroy Soviet targets many times over—far surpassing Eisenhower's goal of sufficiency.

Critics, especially Democratic politicians and some career army officers, argued that the New Look and the doctrine of massive retaliation locked the United States into an all-or-nothing response to foreign threats. To soften the all-or-nothing posture, the administration signed anti-Communist military alliances with numerous countries, promising American material support to local troops fighting in small wars. For situations short of war, the CIA was authorized to carry out covert military operations against unfriendly regimes or groups. Finally, the administration pushed development of tactical atomic weapons for battlefield use. These explosives, small enough to be fired in artillery shells or even carried in a commando's backpack, were intended to counter a conventional attack by Soviet or Chinese forces without escalating to global nuclear war.

The policy of relying more heavily on the nuclear threat received its first test in Korea, where fighting continued near the thirty-eighth parallel. The major unsettled points included China's demand that the United States observe international law by returning all Chinese and North Korean prisoners of war (POWs) held in South Korea, including several thousand who were seeking asylum. Like Truman, Eisenhower feared criticism if he agreed to repatriate POWs to a Communist country against their will.

Eisenhower's advisers determined that the atomic bomb would be of little use in Korea. For bargaining purposes, however, the president decided to bluff about his intention to employ atomic weapons. When a Korean armistice was reached in July 1953, Dulles claimed that the atomic threat forced the Chinese to make peace on American terms, which included voluntary prisoner returns.

In reality, several factors contributed to the settlement. Joseph Stalin's death in March 1953 brought to power Soviet leaders eager to improve relations with the United States. China, too, had grown weary of the costly war. Even before Washington dropped hints about escalation, Chinese and American negotiators made progress on a partial exchange of sick and wounded prisoners. They then agreed that POWs resisting repatriation would be remanded to a neutral commission to determine their ultimate fate. By the time the fighting ended, the war in Korea had claimed the lives of fifty-four thousand Americans, an estimated 3 million Koreans, and 1 million Chinese.

Immediately after Stalin's death, a triumvirate composed of Georgi Malenkov, Nikolai Bulganin, and Nikita Khrushchev assumed power in the Soviet Union. The three new leaders, who had barely survived their boss's bloody purges, resolved to do away with Stalin's terror network, improve life for Soviet citizens, and seek improved relations with the West. Malenkov announced that no dispute, even one with the United States, was so bad that it could not be settled peacefully through negotiations. The Soviet Union resumed diplomatic ties with Yugoslavia and Israel and began providing economic aid to non-Communist developing nations like Egypt.

By 1955 Khrushchev's political skills had allowed him to oust (without killing) his colleagues and emerge as the first among equals. In 1956 he shocked his country and the world by denouncing Stalin's crimes. Khrushchev charged that Stalin's "personality cult" had distorted communism and led to the slaughter of several million loyal Bolsheviks and countless Soviet citizens.

Although both Russian and world opinion cheered this break with the past, the changes within the Soviet Union posed a dilemma for Eisenhower. Should he accept at face value Soviet talk of "peaceful coexistence," or should he increase pressure on Moscow now that a less oppressive regime held power? Did Malenkov and, later, Khrushchev really seek cooperation with the West, or were they merely deceiving him? Should the United States try to break up the Sino-Soviet alliance? If so, should Washington try to woo China by moderating American hostility, or should it continue its efforts to isolate and bring down Mao's government? Some Western leaders, among them Winston Churchill, urged Eisenhower to meet with the new Kremlin bosses and expand trade with both the USSR and China, but restrained by Dulles, Eisenhower reacted cautiously to changes in the Communist camp.

The Ebbing of McCarthyism

The ebb and flow of the domestic Red Scare also influenced Eisenhower's approach to foreign policy. During 1953 and 1954 Senator Joseph McCarthy escalated his attacks on Reds in the U.S. government. Although Eisenhower disliked McCarthy, he had done little during the presidential campaign or after taking office to alert the public to McCarthy's excesses. Even when McCarthy labeled retired general George C. Marshall—the heroic wartime chief of staff, namesake of the Marshall Plan, and mentor to Eisenhower in the army—a traitor who had perpetrated a "conspiracy so immense as to dwarf any previous such venture in the history of man," Eisenhower refused to condemn the senator or defend his old boss. In fact, he made numerous concessions to McCarthy and other extremists during his first two years as president.

But McCarthyism began to wane anyway in 1954. Early in that year, piqued at the army's refusal to give his staff aide David Schine a draft deferment and other special treatment, McCarthy charged the army with coddling Communists. The bizarre allegation focused on an army dentist who had been drafted, promoted, and honorably discharged despite his admitted Communist sympathies. When high army officials, acting on the president's orders, refused to open personnel records to the senator, McCarthy charged them with incompetence and treason. Ignoring White House warnings to back off, the Wisconsin Republican declared that he did not "intend to treat traitors like gentlemen." The "twenty years of treason" allegedly perpetrated by FDR and Truman had, McCarthy charged, become twenty-one under Eisenhower.

Realizing that he might be the senator's real target, Eisenhower urged army officials to countercharge that McCarthy had tried to blackmail them into giving David Schine special treatment. In April 1954 the Senate launched an inquiry into the matter. Meanwhile, TV journalist Edward R. Murrow aired a segment of his popular show *See It Now* spotlighting McCarthy's unsavory actions.

During dramatic televised Senate hearings, known as the Army-McCarthy hearings, 20 million viewers had their first close look at McCarthy's attacks on all who resisted him. Army counsel Joseph Welch, the soul of telegenic respectability, softly parried McCarthy's tirades—even when the senator charged that a member of Welch's firm was a Communist—and refused to be goaded by the slashing attacks of Roy Cohn, the senator's legal aide.

Even though the Army-McCarthy hearings rendered no formal verdict, the senator had failed a critical media test. Opinion polls taken during and after the televised sessions revealed a dramatic slide in McCarthy's approval rating, from nearly 50 percent at the beginning of 1954 to only 30 percent in June. In December 1954 the Senate voted to censure him for "unbecoming conduct." McCarthy never recovered from these defeats. Shunned by old friends, he increased his legendary drinking, lost political influence, and died of alcohol-related illness in 1957.

America and the Challenges of the Third World

In the fifteen years following the end of the Second World War, thirty-seven nations emerged from colonization to gain independence. Most of these new states were nonwhite, poor, nonindustrial, and located in Asia, Africa, or the Middle East. Many had gained independence through armed struggle; in some the violence continued after independence. They had much in common with previously independent but poor nations, especially in Latin America, where political unrest had turned into armed rebellion. During the 1950s there were at least twenty-eight prolonged guerrilla insurgencies around the globe.

Most of these emerging nations, loosely called the Third World, existed outside the bloc of industrialized democracies (the First World) and the Communist nations (the Second World) (see map). Few had democratic governments, but most sought to remain neutral in the Cold War, soliciting aid from both East and West as they pursued economic development. Poor nations both resented America and sought to emulate it. They often employed socialist rhetoric even as they aspired to the material rewards of capitalism.

Under Stalin the Soviet Union had shunned most independent liberation movements. Khrushchev proved more adroit, offering economic and military assistance to emerging nations whether or not they adhered to Moscow's line.

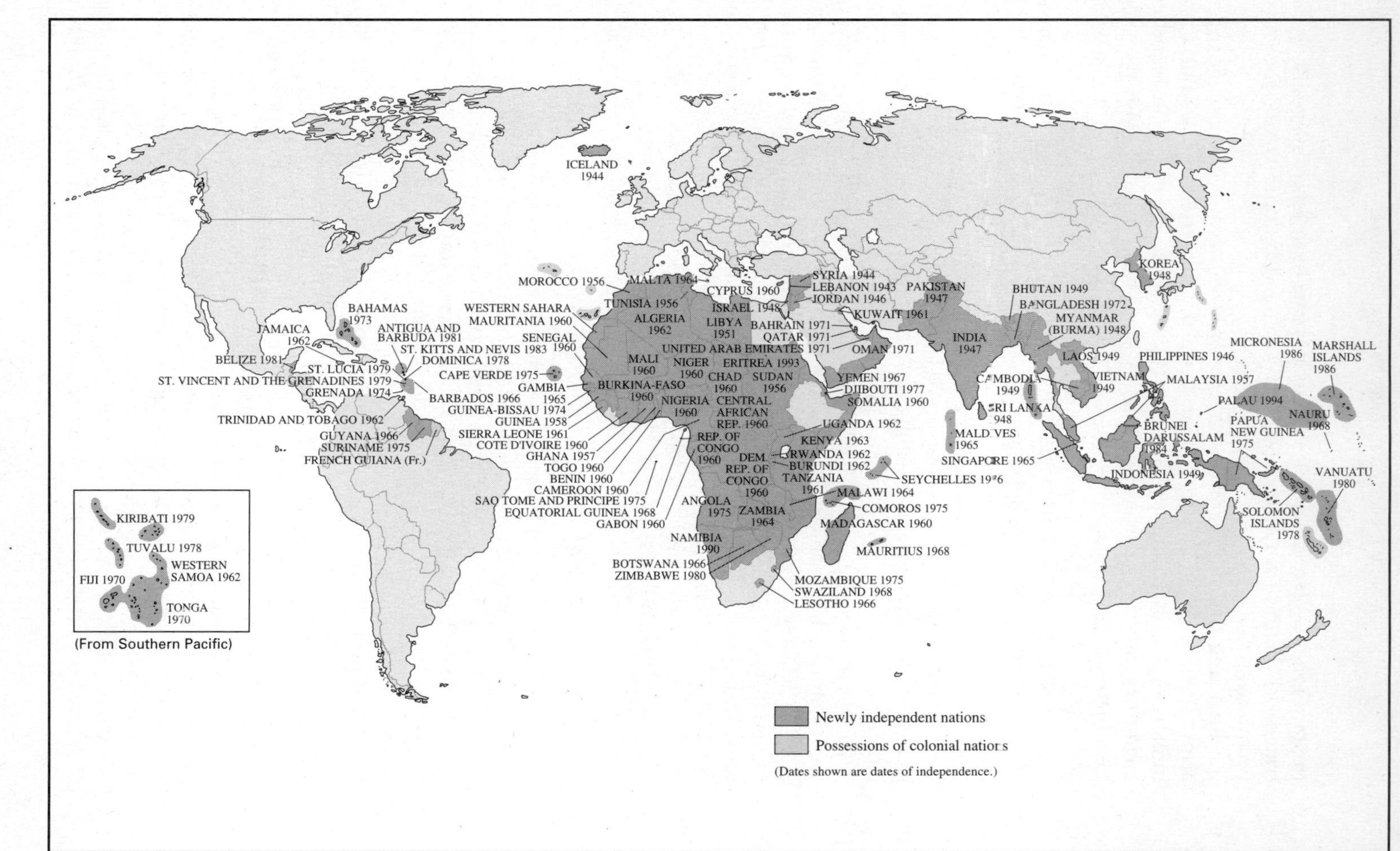

The Rise of the Third World The end of European colonialism during the 1950s and 1960s gave birth to dozens of new nations.

This probably represented a Soviet effort to avoid a direct challenge to the United States while still supporting revolutionary goals.

Washington shared Moscow's concern with the Third World. The emerging nations contained vast raw material wealth and a huge population. Eisenhower and Dulles worried that the Third World's criticism of imperialism and capitalism would provide a wedge for increased Soviet influence. Many Americans also mistrusted any model of national development that deviated from their own.

To counter Soviet overtures, the Eisenhower administration forged numerous military alliances with friendly Third World countries and increased the level of U.S. military and economic aid to Africa, Asia, the Middle East, and Latin America. In addition it supplied military advisers and authorized covert actions by the CIA. By doing so Eisenhower deepened American involvement in conflicts in Vietnam, the Middle East, and Latin America.

Using the CIA to conduct secret operations had a strong appeal to American leaders. Covert actions provided an opportunity to achieve foreign policy goals inexpensively and without facing the scrutiny of public debate. The secrecy of CIA operations also permitted the U.S. government to act in ways the American public found too uncomfortable to discuss, including bribing and assassinating members of foreign governments. The CIA began to play an important role in America's interventions in the Third World.

Eisenhower inherited the war in French Indochina and passed it on to his successors. In the 1950s policymakers worried that if the Communist Vietminh guerrillas won in Vietnam, first Southeast Asia and then resource-starved Japan would "fall like dominoes." After this, Eisenhower predicted, the Pacific Ocean would "become a Communist lake."

Since 1950 the United States had spent over $1 billion in Vietnam, providing about 70 percent of the cost of France's war against the Vietminh and its leader, Ho Chi Minh. Yet, as American analysts admitted, most Vietnamese hated the French forces supposedly protecting them. Eisenhower and Dulles hoped that if the French granted real power to non-Communist Vietnamese other than the puppet emperor Bao Dai, the war would change from a colonial struggle to a battle against communism. Defending the freedom of an independent Vietnam would prove more popular among Americans than saving a colony.

In the spring of 1954 the war in Indochina reached a climax when Vietminh guerrillas trapped twelve thousand French troops at Dienbienphu, a valley in northern Vietnam. Washington again urged the French to grant Vietnam independence as a way of building support for expanded American and British military aid. American officials even considered launching air strikes against the Vietminh or possibly sending in U.S. troops.

Early in May 1954 the French base at Dienbienphu fell. A new French prime minister, Pierre Mendes-France, pledged to negotiate a quick end to the Indochina war. Talks took place at an international conference in Geneva. Most observers predicted a quick French evacuation, followed by Vietminh control of all Vietnam. Eisenhower sent an American observer to Geneva, and Dulles also attended briefly.

China and the Soviet Union actually played a moderating role at the Geneva talks, urging Ho Chi Minh to accept a temporary division of Vietnam rather than immediate control of the whole country. The Geneva Accords, reached in July, drew an armistice line, intended as a temporary military division, along the seventeenth parallel, with French forces moving to the south and Vietminh troops to the north. The key provision called for the departure of all French forces and the holding of national elections in Vietnam by 1956. As the French withdrew from Indochina, they also granted complete independence to Laos and Cambodia, which bordered Vietnam.

American leaders feared that Ho Chi Minh would win the promised election. To prevent this the United States began providing economic and military assistance, as well as military advisers, directly to non-Communist groups in southern Vietnam. As the French departed, American personnel backed Ngo Dinh Diem, a Vietnamese Catholic (in a largely Buddhist nation) who had lived for several years in Europe and the United States. CIA officers helped Diem organize a government and army in the southern city of Saigon. To expand Diem's base of support, the CIA encouraged northern Catholics to move south.

In 1956 Diem won a sham election south of the seventeenth parallel, deposed Emperor Bao Dai, and proclaimed himself president of the Republic of Vietnam. Washington recognized this republic, better known as South Vietnam, as an independent nation and denied that the Democratic Republic of Vietnam (North Vietnam) had any claim on the South. Between 1956 and 1960 the United States spent over $1 billion supporting Diem. Nevertheless, Diem's support of landlords over the peasantry, his favoritism toward the Catholic minority, and his repression of dissent generated a renewed guerrilla movement in the South that won backing from the Communist North.

U.S. concern over Vietnam stemmed from the larger fear of the People's Republic of China (or Red China, as Americans called it during the 1950s). From 1954 to 1955 and again in 1958, the United States and Red China came close to war over the fate of several small islands in the Taiwan (Formosa) Strait. The most important of these, Quemoy and Matsu, lay only a few miles off the China coast. The pro-American Chinese government on Taiwan had stationed troops on these islands and used the outposts to stage commando raids against the Communist regime on the mainland. In retaliation, and in hopes of eventually taking over Taiwan, the Chinese began shelling Quemoy in September 1954. The United States responded by organizing a regional anti–Communist alliance, the Southeast Asian Treaty Organization (SEATO) and by signing a mutual security pact with Taiwan, even though in private Eisenhower and Dulles had little respect for Jiang Jieshi and ridiculed his claim to the Chinese mainland. The 1955 crisis ended when China seized a few minor islands in the Taiwan Strait but abandoned efforts to capture Quemoy. Tensions resumed in 1958 when China renewed its shelling of Quemoy and

Eisenhower ordered the American navy to resupply nationalist troops on the island. After some tense moments, the Chinese declined to shoot at the American ships, and the Americans convinced Jiang to stop provoking China.

Eisenhower used the CIA to deal with a variety of threats in both the Middle East and Central America. The agency played an especially important role in deposing regimes outside the Soviet sphere that challenged American or Western domination of raw materials, including regimes in Iran, Guatemala, and Cuba.

In 1951 Iran's nationalistic (but non-Communist) prime minister, Mohammed Mossadeq, seized the holdings of the Anglo-Iranian Oil Company without compensating its British owners. In retaliation, major European and American oil companies organized a boycott, refusing to purchase, transport, or refine Iranian petroleum. In May 1953, as the boycott was causing economic havoc in Iran, Mossadeq informed Eisenhower that unless the boycott was ended, he might seek Soviet assistance. Eisenhower rebuffed Iran's request for U.S. support and endorsed the British position.

Shah Mohammed Reza Pahlavi, Iran's monarch, had played only a minor role in the nation's politics since succeeding his father during the Second World War. The young shah resented Mossadeq's influence and saw the crisis as an opportunity to regain real power by playing up the Soviet threat. His interests coincided with those of American diplomats and oil companies who hoped to pre-empt Britain's dominant role in the Iranian oil industry. To prevent any Soviet role in Iran and to preserve access to the region's petroleum, Eisenhower authorized a CIA coup to topple Mossadeq and put the shah in control.

Kermit Roosevelt, the grandson of Theodore Roosevelt and a veteran spy, played a key role in the coup. Arriving in Teheran in August 1953, he made contact with the shah and with a general in the Iranian army, Fazollah Zahedi. Roosevelt financed demonstrations against Mossadeq that were joined by army and police personnel. The shah fled briefly to Rome as the army restored order. Zahedi's forces stormed the parliament and arrested Mossadeq, and the general became prime minister. The shah, backed by U.S. aid, returned to power. Americans also arranged a petroleum deal that kept prices low and granted American companies a substantial stake in Iranian oil fields.

The Middle East remained in turmoil throughout the 1950s. Arabs felt humiliated by Israel's creation and military victory in 1948 and the continued ability of the tiny Jewish state to defeat its far more numerous neighbors. Although at the time Britain and France, rather than the United States, provided most of Israel's weapons, American Jews made substantial private contributions to Israel.

Such was the situation when Gamal Abdel Nasser, an Egyptian army officer, toppled the inept pro-British King Farouk in 1952. Nasser emerged as a popular and ambitious leader who envisioned Egypt as the center of a revived Arab world. He bought arms from the Soviet bloc, but he also sought economic assistance from the West to finance construction of the immense

Aswan Dam across the Nile. Dulles initially favored American financing for the project but canceled aid in July 1956 when Nasser extended diplomatic recognition to Communist China. Eisenhower feared that Nasser's appeal to Arabs would destabilize the oil-rich region—even though Egypt had little oil of its own—boosting Soviet influence or endangering the supply of cheap petroleum.

Nasser retaliated for the withdrawal of American aid by nationalizing the British-owned Suez Canal, through which much of Europe's oil supply passed. Britain and France decided to send forces to recover the canal and, they hoped, topple Nasser. They coordinated their plan with Israel, which also feared Nasser. In accordance with the joint plan, on October 29, 1956, the Israeli army attacked and defeated the Egyptian army on the Sinai Peninsula and camped just east of the canal. Britain and France then sent troops with the stated goal of protecting the Suez Canal from destruction. The European powers demanded that both the Egyptian and Israeli armies withdraw from either side of the waterway and return it to European control.

These actions infuriated Dulles and Eisenhower. Despite their own dislike of Nasser, they feared that European meddling in Egypt would strengthen Arab radicals and distract world attention from the crisis in Hungary, where Soviet forces were crushing an uprising. The fact that America's two closest allies, England and France, had acted in secret embarrassed the American leaders. The United States joined the Soviet Union in condemning the Suez attack, and the otherwise dueling superpowers supported a UN-mandated cease-fire. Dulles, taking advantage of the halt in the region's oil trade (vessels sunk by the Egyptians were blocking shipments through the canal) pressed Latin American exporters to embargo petroleum sales to Britain and France until their forces left Egypt. Washington also threatened to block private American aid to Israel. By December 1956 the invaders had left Egypt, Nasser had claimed a victory over imperialism, and British prime minister Anthony Eden had resigned in disgrace.

In January 1957 Eisenhower persuaded Congress to approve a resolution empowering him in advance to use force to "block Communist aggression" in the Middle East. With this so-called Eisenhower Doctrine Washington hoped to reassure conservative Arab rulers in Saudi Arabia, Jordan, and Iraq by posing as their protector against both Soviet influence and Nasser.

During 1957 a series of coups swept Syria, Jordan, and Iraq. In 1958 Nasser forged an alliance among Egypt, Syria, and Yemen, creating the United Arab Republic. In July a pro-Nasser officer, General Abdel Karim Kassim, toppled the pro-Western Iraqi king, Faisal, and considered allying his new government with Egypt. American officials feared that Nasser and his followers throughout the region would block Western access to Middle Eastern oil.

Eisenhower decided to make a show of strength in tiny Lebanon, where for months a political crisis had shaken the government. Much of the trouble stemmed from the resentment among the Muslim majority at the dominant political role played by the Maronite Catholic minority. In July 1958 Lebanese president Camille Chamoun, a Maronite, outraged Muslims by suggesting he might stay in office when his term expired a few months later. When Egypt encouraged Muslims to depose the Christian-dominated government in Beirut, Chamoun appealed for American assistance.

In a move intended to scare Nasser and stiffen the spine of conservative Arabs, on July 14, 1958, Eisenhower ordered fourteen thousand Marines, with tactical nuclear capability and backed by a large fleet, to suppress what he called a Communist-inspired threat to Lebanon. Actually, by the time the Marines landed in Beirut, most of the rioting had ended. Sunbathers gaped as landing craft disgorged troops onto Beirut's posh beach front.

The operation achieved its basic aim of limiting Nasser's influence over Middle Eastern oil supplies. The Lebanese factions patched together a compromise, Iraq dropped plans to ally with Egypt and promised to protect Western-owned oil facilities, and Khrushchev informed Nasser that the Soviet Union would not assist him in any direct challenge to the United States. Although the Middle East remained chronically unstable and the Arabs and Israelis would fight several more wars, Eisenhower's show of force held the line through the end of the decade.

The Eisenhower administration tried to block Communist influence in Latin America as well. Aside from military aid, Washington provided very little assistance to Latin America. It paid lip service to democracy but allied itself with the region's often repressive armed forces. In 1953 Eisenhower and Dulles identified a major crisis in Latin America, the "Communist infection" of Guatemala, one of the region's poorest nations.

Guatemala's Spanish-descended elite exercised nearly feudal control over the large Indian population. Some 2 percent of the population controlled 70 percent of the land. In addition, the American-owned United Fruit Company, a banana grower, held vast tracts of Guatemala's farmland, much of which remained uncultivated. United Fruit also controlled much of the country's rail, port, and communications systems. United Fruit was not the most exploitative employer in Guatemala, but its American employees lived in luxury while its peasant workers made a dollar a day.

Some modest economic and social reform began in Guatemala in the late 1940s. In 1951 President Jacobo Arbenz Guzman ordered the redistribution to the poor of large uncultivated land holdings and sponsored new labor and wage reforms. For Guatemala, these actions were revolutionary. Arbenz drafted plans to build new roads and ports that would break United Fruit's transportation monopoly. He also expropriated four hundred thousand acres of uncultivated company land, offering $3 per acre compensation, a figure based on the declared tax value of the property. United Fruit demanded $75 per acre and persuaded the Eisenhower administration to intercede on its behalf. State Department officials, several of whom had past business associations with United Fruit, claimed that the company and country were under a Communist assault that threatened the entire hemisphere.

In the summer of 1953 Eisenhower authorized the CIA to stage a coup in Guatemala. From bases in Honduras and Nicaragua, the CIA organized a small force of Guatemalan exiles under Carlos Castillo Armas. In June a thousand CIA-directed exiles entered Guatemala and set up a base camp. CIA radio stations broadcast reports of a massive invasion. A few small planes dropped anti-Arbenz leaflets in the capital while the pilots threw sticks of dynamite out of their cockpits. In a panic, Arbenz tried to arm a peasant militia. The regular army, worried over being caught between American forces and angry peasants, forced Arbenz to resign on June 27. Castillo Armas and his comrades took over.

Eisenhower considered the Guatemalan coup a model Cold War triumph. The new Guatemalan rulers restored United Fruit's lands and rolled back most other reforms. Over the next four decades a succession of military governments slaughtered more than one hundred thousand Indians, labor organizers, students, intellectuals, and guerrillas who challenged the ruling elite.

Despite this success in Guatemala, chronic poverty in Latin America led to instability elsewhere in the region. The Cuban Revolution of 1959 proved especially frightening to Americans. Washington had tolerated Cuba's longtime dictator, Fulgencio Batista, because he protected foreign investments and supported the United States in the Cold War. As a reward, Cuban sugar enjoyed privileged access to the American market. This profited wealthy landowners—among them many Americans—but few benefits trickled down to the plantation workers.

Batista's regime collapsed on New Year's Day 1959 when Fidel Castro led a small guerrilla army into Havana. The son of a well-to-do family who had lived for a time in New York, Castro had once dreamed of pitching for the New York Yankees. Trained as a lawyer, he led a failed rebellion in the early 1950s, spent time in a Cuban prison, and launched a second revolt in 1956. Castro called for socialist reforms but had no specific Marxist program or links with the Soviet Union when he took power.

At first Washington took a wait-and-see attitude. Castro legalized the country's small Communist Party, made anti-American speeches, ousted moderates from his movement, canceled promised elections, and executed about five hundred of Batista's henchmen. During a visit to Washington in April 1959, Castro insisted he wanted good relations with America. But when he expropriated foreign-owned property and signed a trade deal with Moscow, Eisenhower decided the Cuban leader was a dangerous pro-Soviet puppet.

Although Castro lost popularity among the Cuban elite, many ordinary Cubans admired his bold challenge to Uncle Sam. Castro's spunk in standing up to the United States also made him something of a hero in the rest of Latin America. After cutting trade and diplomatic ties with Cuba, in mid-1960 Eisenhower decided to eliminate Castro. He authorized the CIA to covertly undermine Castro's regime and to train an army of exiled Cubans to invade the island. Mindful of the fate of Guatemala's Arbenz, Castro organized a popular militia armed with Soviet weapons. A year later the CIA plan led to the disastrous Bay of Pigs invasion, for which the next president, John F. Kennedy, took the blame.

The Eisenhower administration proved far more cautious about intervening in areas where the Soviet Union had direct interests. This fact was emphasized by the 1956 uprising in Hungary. In the autumn of that year, inspired by Khrushchev's recent speech denouncing Stalin, ordinary citizens as well as local Communist officials in Hungary revolted against Soviet domination. Reformers among the Hungarian Communists gained control of the party and began to dismantle the country's secret police apparatus. Moscow held back at first, but it intervened brutally when Communist leader Imre Nagy declared that Hungary would quit the Warsaw Pact. Early in November, in the middle of the Suez crisis, Khrushchev sent Russian tanks into Budapest to crush this heresy. Although CIA-supported Radio Free Europe had urged Eastern Europeans to revolt against the Soviet Union, when the Hungarians acted Washington refused to help or to provide any military assistance.

The Cuban revolution and the uprising in Hungary created a major refugee problem for the United States. Even though the 1952 McCarran-Walter Act had barred most immigration from Eastern Europe, the Eisenhower administration invoked special provisions to allow about 38,000 Hungarians and 125,000 Cubans to enter the country as refugees from Communist tyranny. During this same period, however, the American government implemented "Operation Wetback," the mass deportation of 1 million undocumented Mexican migrants. Unlike those fleeing Hungary and Cuba, the Mexicans were considered economic rather than political refugees.

The Space Race and the Arms Race

In October 1957 the Soviet Union captured world attention by launching a basketball-sized earth-orbiting satellite, *Sputnik I.* A month later the Russians launched the thousand-pound *Sputnik II,* which carried a dog into orbit. Many journalists and public figures shared the sentiments of Senator Lyndon Johnson of Texas, chair of the Armed Services Committee's Preparedness Subcommittee, when he expressed astonishment that another nation might achieve technological superiority over the United States.

Despite the impression of U.S. tardiness left by the Soviets' success, nearly all of the rocket boosters and missile systems deployed by the United States up through the 1980s were developed during the late 1950s. When *Sputnik I* went aloft, Eisenhower assured his cabinet that the Soviet achievement posed no great threat. He explained that American rockets would soon be operational and hinted at a closely guarded secret: pictures taken from the U-2, a high-flying American spy plane, revealed that despite the success with *Sputnik,* the Soviets had only a modest rocket arsenal.

Administration efforts to belittle the Soviets' achievement did little to quell public anxiety. Democratic politicians, educators, journalists, and military contractors charged that the Soviets had humiliated the United States and that their satellite threatened national security. Each of these groups used *Sputnik* as leverage to achieve its own agenda: to embarrass the administra-

Elementary school children in a "duck and cover" drill. Such exercises were often held in classrooms during the 1950s. *Corbis-Bettmann*

tion, to secure more aid for education, or to force an increase in defense spending.

Under pressure, Eisenhower advanced the date for launching an American satellite. In December 1957, in the middle of Senate hearings on *Sputnik,* a hastily prepared Vanguard rocket exploded on takeoff. Critics promptly dubbed it "Flopnik." Several months elapsed before the United States successfully launched a satellite.

As the Senate hearings concluded, Johnson warned of widening gaps between the United States and the Soviet Union in aircraft, missiles, submarines, and high technology. Because the United States stood on the verge of losing the "battle of brainpower," he called for increases in space and military spending as well as massive federal aid to education. Eisenhower responded by appointing a White House science adviser and increasing funding for the National Science Foundation. He worked with Congress to create the National Aeronautics and Space Administration, with an initial budget of $340 million.

He also supported passage of the National Defense Education Act, a billion-dollar package of federal aid for schools and universities.

Despite charges by several leading Democrats that the Soviets had opened up a perilous "missile gap," Eisenhower tried hard to resist unwarranted increases in defense spending. U-2 reconnaissance revealed that the Russians had not put their rockets into full production. As with their long-range bombers, they had deployed a few prototype rockets as a bluff—to impress the Third World and to cover up their comparative weakness. In reality, the military balance strongly favored the United States. But by reinforcing the widespread overestimation of Soviet rocket technology, Khrushchev's sometimes bellicose rhetoric actually helped the cause of Americans who wanted to accelerate the arms race.

The First Stirrings of Détente

Even as the space race and the arms race were fueling public anxiety over the Soviets, a countervailing trend began to emerge. Eisenhower and Khrushchev took some careful initial steps toward détente, talking with each other at summit meetings and establishing a temporary moratorium on nuclear tests. Although these efforts produced no lasting agreements, they did set a precedent for future negotiations.

Prodded by the NATO allies and his own desire to lessen the nuclear threat, Eisenhower agreed in July 1955 to meet the Soviet leadership at a summit in Geneva. Eisenhower stunned the Soviets by calling for an "open skies" policy, under which each side would be free to conduct aerial reconnaissance of the other's military facilities. The United States had little to lose and much to gain from such an arrangement. The Russians dismissed the proposal as a "bald espionage plot," and it went nowhere. Despite the lack of any formal agreement, both sides left the summit praising the "spirit of Geneva," a willingness to talk among opposing blocs.

In July 1959 Eisenhower sent Vice President Richard Nixon on a good-will trip to the Soviet Union. During an impromptu debate with Khrushchev held in a model American kitchen at a Moscow trade fair, Nixon proposed shifting the terms of East-West competition. During what journalists dubbed the "kitchen debate," the vice president boasted that most Americans owned houses stocked with appliances that made life easier. Confident that America had the edge in the appliance race, Nixon asked, "Would it not be better to compete in the relative merits of washing machines than in the strength of rockets?"

In the fall of 1959 the Soviet leader visited the United States and conferred with Eisenhower at Camp David, the presidential retreat in Maryland. As in the earlier meeting between Eisenhower and Khrushchev, no formal agreements emerged. But the two leaders found it useful to take each other's measure, and both spoke of the "spirit of Camp David," which observers took

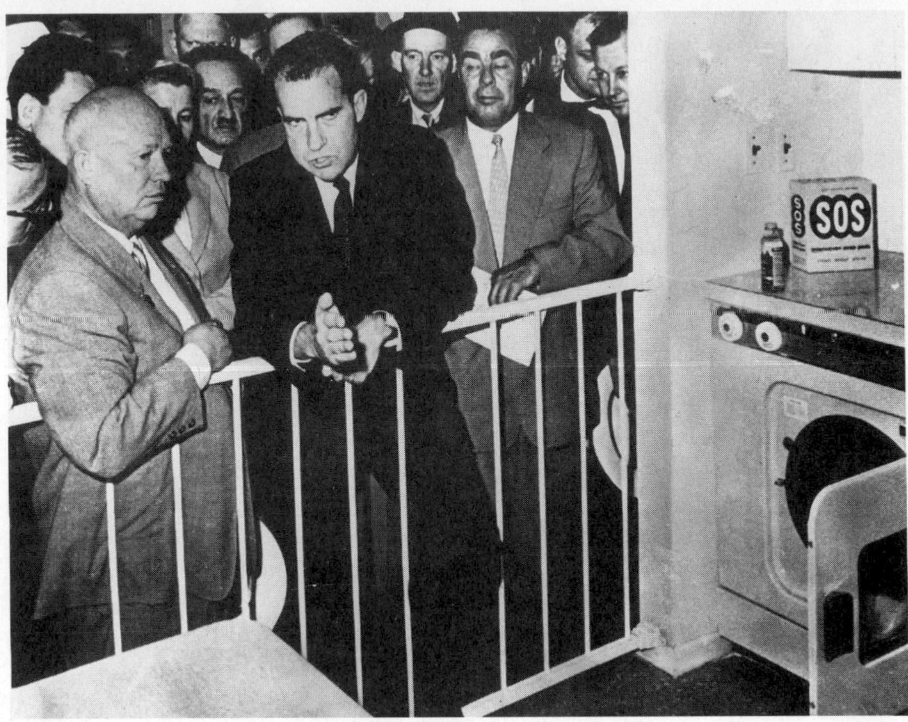

In July 1959, Vice President Nixon and Soviet Premier Nikita Khrushchev debated the merits of capitalism, communism, and American washing machines at a Moscow trade exhibition. *Howard Sochurek/*Life *magazine © Time, Inc.*

to mean an informal reduction in tensions. The Soviet leader traveled throughout the United States and agreed to meet Eisenhower in Paris the following spring.

To Eisenhower, contacts with Khrushchev offered a chance to reduce the danger of nuclear war and to slow the development in America of a garrisoned state obsessed with security. The president believed that massive defense spending had contributed to America's emerging foreign trade deficit and to the economic recession of 1958. For his part, Khrushchev hoped that a reduction in tension would improve his ability to hold off Soviet hawks, who demanded greater missile production. For both Khrushchev and Eisenhower, one of the central issues was an agreement to limit nuclear testing.

During the 1950s both the Soviet Union and the United States added tens of thousands of weapons to their nuclear arsenals. This entailed a frantic effort to expand uranium mining, plutonium production, and weapons testing, mostly in the American West and on Pacific islands. Between 1945 and 1963 atmospheric bomb tests were conducted at sites in Nevada and the South

Pacific. Not until 1997 did the government release data that showed millions of Americans in all areas of the country had been exposed to dangerous levels of radioactive fallout. In the drive to maximize production, the Atomic Energy Commission (AEC) routinely dismissed concerns about radioactive fallout from nuclear facilities and tests. According to the AEC, the best policy was "not to be worried about fallout." Schoolchildren were instructed through cartoons featuring "Bert the Turtle" that in case of nuclear war, they would be safe beneath their desks if they remembered to "duck and cover."

Even in the 1950s, opposition existed to atmospheric testing of nuclear weapons. British author Nevil Shute's best-selling novel *On the Beach* (1957) depicted the end of human life caused by fallout from a nuclear war. Ten thousand scientists from numerous nations signed a petition in favor of a test ban. At congressional hearings scientists reported that even small amounts of radioactive strontium in milk increased the dangers of cancer and genetic injury to fetuses. An antinuclear citizens group, the Committee for a Sane Nuclear Policy (SANE), formed in 1957 and soon boasted twenty-five thousand members. As part of a disarmament program, SANE called for halting weapons tests.

Eisenhower sympathized with some of the concerns voiced by critics of the atomic arms race but would not approve a test ban unless the Soviets allowed extensive on-site inspections of their nuclear weapons facilities. In 1958, however, the president's new science adviser, James Killian, convinced Eisenhower that a global network of seismic stations could detect most nuclear explosions, even those underground. While their subordinates worked on the terms of a treaty, Khrushchev and Eisenhower agreed to an informal test moratorium, to be effective in October. Although the two sides disagreed on many details of a broader test ban, Khrushchev inched toward accepting Eisenhower's calls for inspections. It seemed possible that a test ban treaty might be agreed to at an upcoming summit.

The May 1960 Paris summit proved a fiasco, however. On the eve of the meeting, an American U-2 spy plane crashed inside the Soviet Union, brought down either by a Soviet missile or by engine failure. Eisenhower had approved this risky mission in the hope of gathering photographic evidence confirming that, despite Khrushchev's boasts, the Soviet Union had not deployed many long-range rockets. Such data would allow the Americans to take greater risks in arms control discussions. Sadly, the failed mission proved fatal for this cause.

After American officials released a cover story about a missing weather aircraft, Moscow announced that in fact it had downed a spy plane. When Eisenhower denied this (believing the pilot could not survive a crash), Khrushchev amazed the world by displaying pilot Francis Gary Powers, who confessed to espionage. Eisenhower was so depressed he considered resigning.

When the two world leaders met in Paris, Khrushchev demanded that Eisenhower apologize to the Soviet people for the U-2 mission. Eisenhower refused, the summit broke up, and an opportunity to limit nuclear testing and slow the arms race had slipped away. The informal moratorium on nuclear testing lasted until the fall of 1961, when both sides resumed bomb tests.

✦ Conclusion

By the end of his presidency, Eisenhower sensed the limits of his achievements in foreign policy. He also worried that American society would face increased regimentation if the nation remained shackled to its huge and growing defense budget. His reflections on these matters were evident in his remarkable farewell address of January 1961, which has been quoted repeatedly ever since. Eisenhower warned against the temptation to solve domestic problems through "some spectacular and costly action" abroad. The old general deplored the view that large increases in defense spending would create miraculous solutions to the nation's troubles. The greatest threat to democracy, he observed, came from a new phenomenon, the "conjunction of an immense military establishment and a large arms industry." He warned that Americans needed to guard against the unwarranted influence of this "military-industrial complex."

Eisenhower began his presidency proclaiming the New Look, which emphasized the use of nuclear weapons and the doctrine of massive retaliation. He presided over a dramatic build-up of the nation's nuclear stockpile and the development of ICBMs. He also intervened repeatedly in Third World conflicts, often employing the CIA to undermine governments he considered dangerous. He deepened the American involvement in Vietnam, which would have tragic consequences in the 1960s and 1970s.

Nevertheless, most historians see Eisenhower as a president who basically kept the peace. After ending the Korean War he avoided further direct conflicts with the Soviet Union and China. Although he and Dulles brandished nuclear weapons as the ultimate threat, he never authorized a nuclear attack. In the early years of his administration he made significant efforts to restrain defense spending, and in his second term he took steps toward détente with the Soviet Union.

✦ Further Reading

On the Truman presidency, see: Robert J. Donovan, *Conflict and Crisis: The Presidency of Harry S. Truman, 1945–48* (1977) and *Tumultuous Years: The Presidency of Harry S. Truman, 1949–53* (1982); Alonzo S. Hamby, *Man of the People: A Life of Harry S. Truman* (1995); David McCullough, *Truman* (1992); Norman D. Markowitz, *The Rise and Fall of the People's Century: Henry A. Wallace and American Liberalism, 1941–48* (1973). On the Red Scare and McCarthyism, see: David Caute, *The Great Fear* (1977); Athan Theoharis, *Seeds of Repression: Harry S. Truman and the Origins of McCarthyism* (1971); Richard Gid

Powers, *Secrecy and Power: The Life of J. Edgar Hoover* (1987) and *Not Without Honor: The History of American Anti-Communism* (1995); William L. O'Neill, *A Better World: Stalinism and American Intellectuals* (1983); Richard M. Freeland, *The Truman Doctrine and the Origins of McCarthyism* (1972); David M. Oshinsky, *A Conspiracy So Immense: The World of Joe McCarthy* (1983); Thomas C. Reeves, *The Life and Times of Joe McCarthy* (1982); Ellen W. Schrecker, *No Ivory Tower: McCarthyism in the Universities* (1986); Richard Fried, *Nightmare in Red: The McCarthy Era in Perspective* (1990). On the Cold War, see: H. W. Brands, Jr., *The Cold Warriors* (1988); Robert A. Divine, *Eisenhower and the Cold War* (1981); Richard Immerman, *John Foster Dulles and the Diplomacy of the Cold War* (1990); Melvyn Leffler, *A Preponderance of Power: National Security, The Truman Administration, and the Cold War* (1991); H. W. Brands, *The Devil We Knew: Americans and the Cold War* (1993); Walter Isaacson and Evan Thomas, *The Wise Men: Six Friends and the World They Made* (1986); Michael Hogan, *The Marshall Plan* (1987); Daniel Yergin, *A Shattered Peace* (1977); John Gaddis, *The United States and the Origins of the Cold War, 1941–47* (1972); Gordon Chang, *Enemies and Friends: The United States, China, and the Soviet Union, 1948–1972* (1989); Walter A. McDougall, *The Heavens and the Earth: A Political History of the Space Age* (1985). On Asian developments, see: Robert M. Blum, *Drawing the Line* (1982); Michael Schaller, *The American Occupation of Japan: The Origins of the Cold War in Asia* (1985), *Douglas MacArthur: The Far Eastern General* (1989), and *Altered States: The U.S. and Japan Since the Occupation* (1997); Bruce Cumings, *The Origins of the Korean War* (2 vols., 1981, 1990); Callum A. MacDonald, *Korea* (1987); Burton I. Kauffman, *The Korean War* (1986). On immigration, see: David Reimers, *Still the Golden Door* (2nd ed., 1992); Leonard Dinnerstein, *America and the Survivors of the Holocaust* (1982). On the nuclear arms race, see: Paul Boyer, *By the Bomb's Early Light* (1990); Gregg Herken, *The Winning Weapon* (1981); David Holloway, *Stalin and the Bomb* (1994); Howard Ball, *Justice Downwind: America's Nuclear Testing Program in the 1950s* (1986); Robert A. Divine, *Blowing on the Wind: The Nuclear Test Ban Debate, 1954–60* (1978); Tad Bartimus, *Trinity's Children: Living Along America's Nuclear Highway* (1991); Jonathan Weisgall, *Operation Crossroads: The Atomic Tests at Bikini Atoll* (1994); Carole Gallagher, *American Ground Zero* (1993). On Eisenhower and U.S. foreign policy in the 1950s, see: Stephen E. Ambrose, *Eisenhower: The President* (1984) and *Ike's Spies* (1981); Stephen G. Rabe, *Eisenhower and Latin America* (1988); George McT. Kahin, *Intervention: How America Became Involved in Vietnam* (1986); David L. Anderson, *Trapped by Success: The Eisenhower Administration and Vietnam* (1991); John Gaddis, *The Long Peace* (1987); Michael Beschloss, *Mayday* (1986); Thomas Paterson, *Contesting Castro: The United States and the Triumph of the Cuban Revolution* (1994).

✦✦✦

CHAPTER 9

America at Home, 1945–1960

✦ **A Levittown family, 1957.**

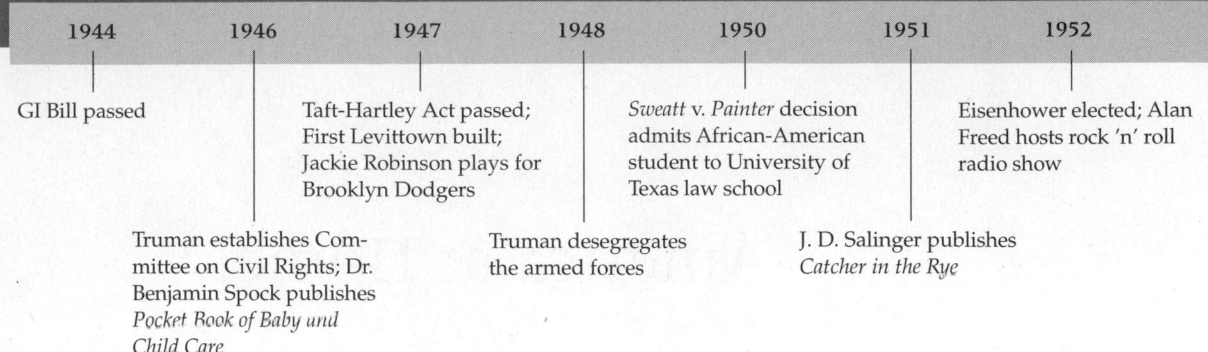

IN 1942 THE flinty actress Katherine Hepburn, known for her portrayals of independent career women, narrated one of the first propaganda films produced by the Office of War Information. Reading from a script written by First Lady Eleanor Roosevelt, Hepburn decried the wartime manpower shortage in scientific and technical fields. She urged American women to meet the emergency by applying for jobs in government and industry. That same year Oscar-winner Greer Garson portrayed Marie Curie, the most famous woman scientist in history. As the war effort heated up, thousands of U.S. women would follow in Curie's footsteps. Unheard-of opportunities for women opened up in engineering, chemistry, and even physics in burgeoning wartime industries, from petroleum and metallurgical firms to rubber and pharmaceuticals manufacturers.

Science and industry continued their partnership after the war. But as male veterans flooded the labor market, trained and experienced women found themselves denied advancement or frozen out of even entry-level technical positions. Experts agreed that women had to get out of the work force and back into the home, for their own good and for the health and well-being of the nation. As sociologist Ferdinand Lundberg and psychiatrist Marynia Farnham explained in their 1947 bestseller *Modern Woman: The Lost Sex,*

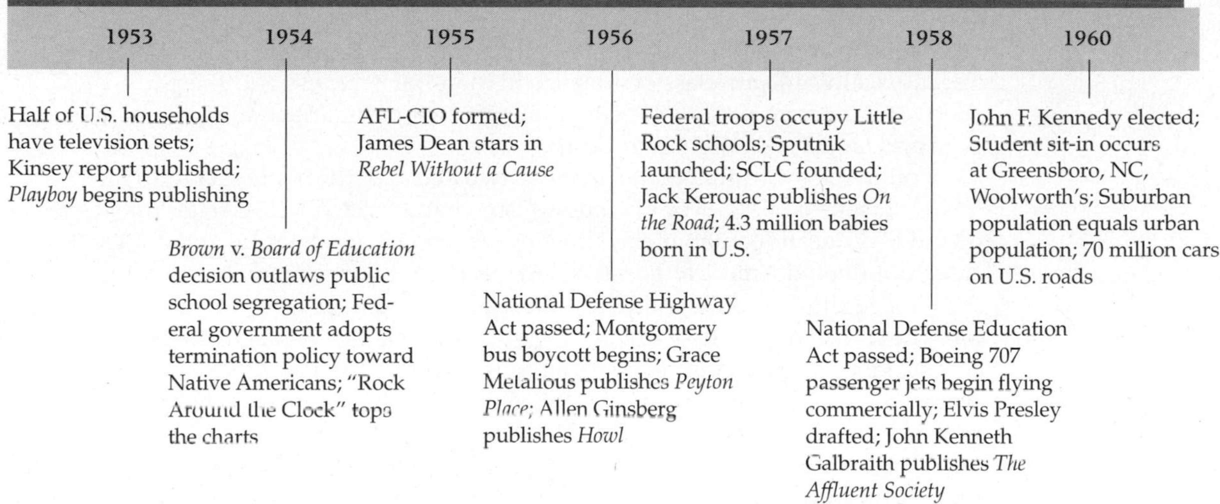

"Women are the pivot around which much of the unhappiness of the day revolves, like a captive planet. To a significant extent they are responsible for it. . . . Women as a whole (with exceptions) are maladjusted, much more so than men. For men have appropriate means to social adjustment: economic and political power, scientific power, and athletic prowess." Women, Farnham and Lundberg insisted, should seek happiness in the domestic realm, pursuing their time-honored roles of homemaker and mother. Their message reached a sympathetic, or at least resigned, audience.

In the immediate aftermath of the war, Americans were glad to turn their attention to domestic matters. Young people were eager to return to peacetime jobs and raise families. With money in their pockets, Americans rushed to new homes in suburbia, started having children in record numbers, and went on a spree of consumer buying, snapping up home appliances, automobiles, and the newfangled electronic gadgets called televisions.

By 1953 most Americans believed they had entered an era of well-deserved stability and prosperity. "The fifties" as a distinct epoch began with the election of President Dwight D. Eisenhower and ended in January, 1961, when John F. Kennedy entered the White House. Early in this period the Korean War and McCarthyism faded, Soviet dictator Joseph Stalin died, and the overwhelmingly popular Eisenhower brought a sense of security to American life. Paradoxically, middle-class confidence in material progress and the perfectibility of American society coexisted alongside fervent anticommunist paranoia and anxiety about nuclear destruction.

Following the tumult of the previous two decades, the home seemed a safe haven. Just as containment of communism characterized U.S. foreign policy, a kind of domestic containment, stressing traditional gender roles and domesticity, dominated American social life. In the ideal suburban family the mother kept house and raised the children while the husband went off to a white-collar job. The children grew up with a strong sense of American values. But beneath this surface stability there were dangerous forces to be contained. The 1950s were years of change and upheaval. Not only did continued population movements, the automobile, television, and advanced technology change the face of American life, but critics began to complain that the apparent consensus on American society was a hollow one. Young people developed their own subculture and proclaimed it in rock-'n'-roll music, to their elders' alarm. Meanwhile, the civil rights struggle erupted in the South, demanding that Americans confront issues that had too long been ignored.

✦ The Affluent Society

Americans hoped that the end of World War II would mean a return to pre-Depression prosperity, that the economic gains brought on by wartime mobilization would endure. The Truman administration unabashedly, and sometimes successfully, followed in FDR's New Deal footsteps. Even the Republican Eisenhower promoted massive government programs and public works, while insisting that government ought to play a more passive role in the marketplace.

With the coming of peace, the first order of business was demobilization. Mustering out the 12 million GIs who had served in the war proved relatively easy. In less than two years the number of Americans in uniform fell by 90 percent. But the demobilized GIs returned to an economy in which the booming production of war goods had ceased. Even before the war ended, mass layoffs had begun in aircraft plants and other key wartime industries. Within a few days of Japan's surrender, nearly 2 million more were out of work. With vivid memories of the Great Depression, many Americans feared a return of widespread unemployment.

Returning servicemen had less difficulty finding jobs than many experts had predicted. A significant number of ex-servicemen replaced women workers, 3 million of whom were eventually laid off. Labor unions and factory owners followed the suggestion of a senator who called on Congress to force "wives and mothers back to the kitchen." Both private employers and the civil service gave veterans preference over other job applicants. Even though 75 percent of women who wished to continue to work eventually found postwar employment, they had to settle for clerical, sales, and light manufacturing work rather than more lucrative skilled factory labor. In 1950 nearly one-third of all women held paying jobs, up from 27 percent before the war. At the same time, wages declined from about $50 to $37 per week for white women, and to half that for black women. Men experienced a far smaller drop in pay.

The American economy performed well during the Truman years. The steep inflation of 1946 to 1947 leveled off, to reappear only briefly early in the Korean War, and the gross domestic product rose an average of 4 percent annually. The number of Americans with jobs increased from the wartime high of 53 million to 60 million in 1948 and 64 million by 1952. Labor unions accepted increasing mechanization in industrial jobs, and management offered in return soaring wages and good benefits, established through regular collective bargaining. Truman's most influential economic advisers believed that the government should create greater demand—and thus more jobs—through increased spending. By 1949 these economists were promoting new defense spending as a key to growth.

Education Expands

The line between defense spending and entitlement programs has not always been clear in the United States. For example, veterans' benefits not only assist a particular group of citizens, they also enable the country to staff its military establishment (by providing incentives for enlistment). Prodded by President Roosevelt and the American Legion, Congress voted in 1944 to establish entitlements for returning soldiers. The Servicemen's Readjustment Act of 1944, or the GI Bill, as nearly everyone called it, benefited millions of veterans and their families. The program provided temporary unemployment benefits for veterans, plus hiring preferences in civil service jobs, new hospitals and health benefits, low-interest loans to start businesses and purchase homes, and tuition and living stipends for college and vocational education. Demobilized soldiers who could not find work received $20 per week—more than the minimum wage of 40 cents per hour—for up to a year. This program alone paid out nearly $4 billion during the postwar years. Those pursuing a college education received $110 a month, plus an allowance for dependents and payment of tuition, fees, and books.

Before 1945 few people of moderate means could afford to attend college. The postwar surge of veterans into both public and private universities created a far more democratic system of higher education—a change that would have far-reaching social consequences. Over 2 million students, or half of the total male enrollment at the nation's institutions of higher learning, attended college on the GI Bill. Nearly half of the veterans were married, which forced colleges to drop their prohibitions against the enrollment of married students. Couples were housed in Quonset huts, trailers, and converted fraternity houses. As the mass demand for higher education grew, state legislatures funded public universities more generously than before the war. Federal and state dollars built new libraries, classrooms, dormitories, and laboratories.

By 1947 the total federal outlay for veterans' education had reached $2.25 billion, and that was just the beginning. When the program ended in 1956, the Veterans Administration (VA) had spent about $14 billion on schooling—compared to nothing before the war. The skills acquired by this generation boosted their job mobility and incomes, allowing the government to recoup much of its outlay in increased tax revenues.

Because a comparatively small number of women had served in uniform, women received few direct educational benefits. Still, more women attended college after the war than before. They were steered away from careers that would place them in competition with men, however. Active sex discrimination and quotas led to a decline in female enrollment in law, business, and medical schools. Harvard Business School, for example, did not admit women until 1963. The writer Fannie Hurst lamented that in the wake of the war, a "sleeping sickness" had spread among the nation's women: "They are retrogressing into . . . that thing known as The Home."

The Suburbs Boom

Many of those homes were located in the nation's burgeoning suburbs. During the Truman years, white Americans flocked to suburbia (blacks and other people of color were often barred from buying homes in suburban enclaves.) Americans had begun leaving the cities in the nineteenth century, but only after 1945 could the United States begin to be called a suburban nation. Between 1940 and 1970 the proportion of suburban dwellers increased from 19.5 to 37.6 percent (see table).

Up until 1945 the housing industry had focused on building custom homes or urban multifamily buildings. But housing prices in these units generally exceeded the $50 or so per month that most veterans could afford. After the war the needs of veterans meshed with a new trend in the construction industry: the increasing dominance of large construction firms, those having over one hundred employees and building over one hundred houses per year.

TABLE 9.1 Geographic Distribution of United States Population, 1930–1970 (in percentages)

Year	Central Cities	Suburbs	Rural Areas and Small Towns
1940	31.6	19.5	48.9
1950	32.3	23.8	43.9
1960	32.6	30.7	36.7
1970	31.4	37.6	31.0

Source: Adapted from U.S. Bureau of the Census, *Decennial Censuses, 1930–1970* (Washington, D.C.: U.S. Government Printing Office).

Meanwhile, the National Association of Home Builders and the National Association of Realtors were lobbying to shape federal housing policy. Following the war the Federal Housing Administration (FHA) began insuring thirty-year bank mortgages with only a 5 to 10 percent down payment. The VA provided additional support under the GI Bill, so qualifying veterans could often take title for a token $1 down. The result of these developments was a housing boom, particularly in suburbia. Housing starts jumped from 114,000 in 1944 to 1.7 million in 1950. By 1950 federal agencies insured more than a third of all mortgages—a figure that surpassed 40 percent by 1955. In addition to FHA and VA loan guarantees, the government's tax policy promoted housing growth by allowing a deduction for mortgage interest.

Levittown, named after builder William Levitt, became a synonym for suburban development. Levitt, a builder of luxury homes before 1941, pioneered prefabrication techniques for navy housing during the war. In 1947 he decided to mass-produce affordable private homes. The first Levittown, a planned community of seventeen thousand homes, sprang from a potato field on Long Island, New York. Even larger projects followed in Pennsylvania and New Jersey.

The Levittown landscape was built for comfort, and for cars. *Joe Scherschel,* Life *magazine © Time Warner, Inc.*

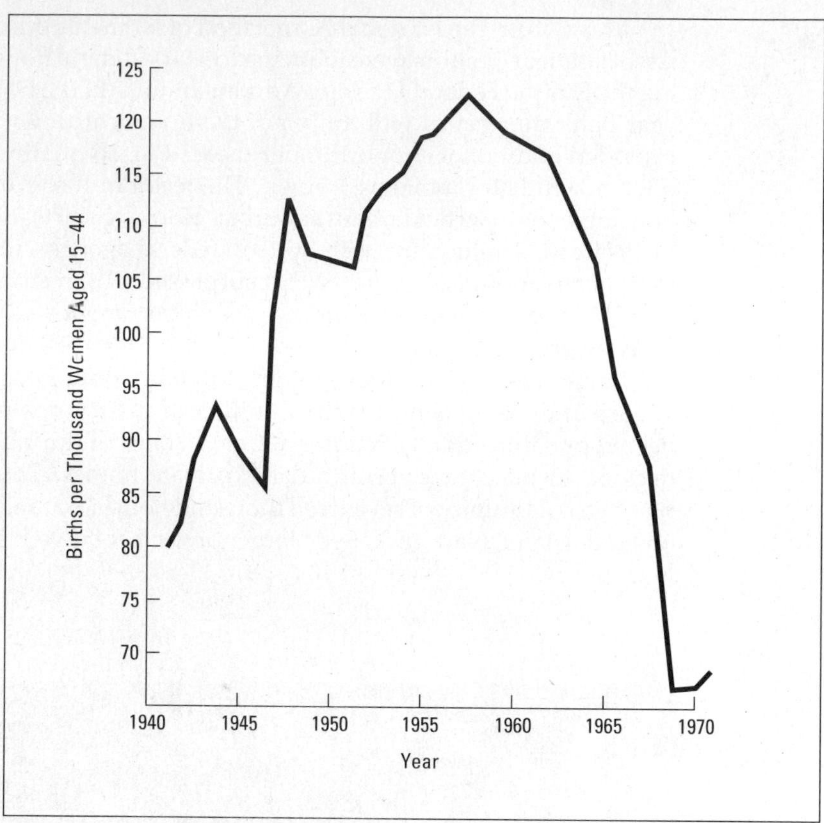

Birthrate, 1940–1970

Levitt did for homes what Henry Ford had done for the automobile. Materials were precut and assembled by teams of semiskilled laborers and moved to lots as needed. Roving crews laid concrete foundations en masse, traveling up one side of a street and down the other. Instead of hiring union painters and carpenters, Levitt trained unskilled workers to do specific isolated tasks, such as spray painting or using power tools, on an assembly-line basis. The company bought its own forests, milled its own lumber, and bought standard kitchen and bathroom appliances in bulk to equip the new houses. At the height of Levittown construction, a house was completed every sixteen minutes. With a VA loan, a veteran could move into a new home for $56 per month, which was often less than the cost of renting an apartment.

Levitt made home ownership a reality for the postwar middle class, as Ford had done for car ownership. But Levittown was only the most conspicuous example of a widespread trend. Across the United States, surrounding the cities, new suburbs composed of similar-looking middle-class houses began to appear. In a chaotic world, the free-standing, single-family, self-contained, all-electric suburban home was presented as a refuge where the homemaker could take charge of housework and child care, but the appliances did all the real work. The necessities of the suburban good life could be purchased in the new, streamlined suburban shopping centers and malls; their number increased from eight thousand to four thousand in the first postwar decade.

Levittown and its successors were designed especially for young and growing families. The birthrate, which had been unusually low during the Great Depression, began a dramatic rise in 1944. By 1946 the nation was experiencing a baby boom that lasted into the 1960s. The average number of children born to an American family increased from 2.4 to 3.2 between 1945 and 1957, when the boom peaked. Annual births rose from 1.2 million in 1945 to 1.8 million in that period. Fueled by the continuing baby boom (see figure), the American population surged by 30 million in the 1950s, reaching 180 million by the end of the decade. When births peaked at 4.3 million in 1957, a third of all Americans were aged 14 or younger. This created exceptional demands for new housing, appliances, toys, and schools. Between 1950 and 1960, total school enrollment in kindergarten through twelfth grade increased from 28 million to 42 million.

Young parents in new houses in new places looked for new ideas on how to raise children. In previous decades child-rearing manuals had warned against the dangers of coddling, indulging, and overstimulating children. Pediatrician Benjamin Spock challenged these assumptions in his 1946 *Pocket Book of Baby and Child Care.* Spock urged parents to have fun with their kids. He encouraged physical contact and emotional nurturing as keys to healthy development. The book sold 20 million copies within ten years and over 40 million by 1990.

Generally speaking, the growth of the nation's suburbs resulted in a decline of its central cities. The FHA gave preference to subsidizing single-family, detached homes in the $7,000 to $10,000 range. Until the 1960s it provided few loans for buying or improving existing multifamily housing in racially mixed neighborhoods. Redlining by lenders and insurance companies restricted African-Americans and other people of color to neighborhoods in older cities and kept them out of the suburbs. In 1950, of 20 million suburban Americans, only 1 million were nonwhite. Levittown barred "members of other than the Caucasian race" from buying homes. A decade after the development opened, not one of Long Island Levittown's eighty-two thousand residents was black.

Except for in the South and the West, where rural-to-urban migration continued, most large U.S. cities either lost population or barely held steady during the 1950s. Increasingly, poor blacks and whites and immigrants from Puerto Rico, Mexico, and Latin America replaced the mobile white middle class in the cities. Public and private discrimination contributed to drawing a "white noose" around the increasingly nonwhite cities. As business firms and white families left the cities in a pattern that came to be known as "white flight," they took with them the jobs and income that had contributed to urban tax revenues and employment. By 1960 the suburban population of 60 million equaled that of all of the nation's urban areas.

At first most suburbanites commuted to jobs in the central cities, but by 1960 most worked closer to home. Suburban employment and manufacturing rose dramatically, while employment in the twenty-five largest cities declined about 7 percent during the decade. Downtown commercial districts lost business to suburban shopping centers surrounded by acres of parking lots.

The American population continued to shift west, with California growing by 50 percent. Florida and Texas also attracted many newcomers. The gains in urban population in the West and in suburban population in the Northeast came partly at the expense of rural America. The number of agricultural workers fell to barely 6 percent of the population, down two-thirds since America entered the Second World War. At the same time, the increased use of chemical fertilizers, herbicides, and pesticides, along with irrigation in the West, produced ever larger farm yields.

The Car Culture

The rise of the suburbs had other lasting effects as well. One was the increased demand for cars and better roads. By 1960 the United States had nearly 70 million vehicles on the road. Two-thirds of the nation's employees drove to work. In Los Angeles County alone, more cars plied the freeways than in all of Asia or South America.

These cars were not the staid models of the 1940s. Detroit built sleeker, bigger, gaudier, and more expensive machines than ever before. The public adored two- and three-tone models, tail fins, and wraparound windshields. Innovations like power steering, automatic transmissions, and air conditioning made cars more comfortable and convenient. Auto tourism became a major form of family leisure. Bobby Troupe's hit song "Get Your Kicks on Route 66" reflected the increasingly common cross-country family trips to national parks and new amusement complexes like Disneyland.

In 1956 a bipartisan movement in Congress pushed to build an interstate highway system. Later that year Congress passed the National Defense Highway Act. This massive building program authorized the construction of forty thousand miles of new highways, with Washington paying 90 percent of the initial $50 billion tab through taxes on tires and fuel. The interstate highway system dwarfed anything built by the New Deal. Justified as a defense measure, the road-building program had important subsidiary effects. By subsidizing the car culture with thousands of miles of city-to-suburb freeways while denying funds for inner-city mass transit, government promoted suburban development at the cost of the cities.

The public's enthusiasm for the automobile allowed manufacturers to ignore their products' poor safety and efficiency records and to disregard rising air pollution. The mounting death toll on the highways (forty thousand in 1959) elicited little concern, although a young Harvard law student, Ralph

Nader, worried enough to begin probing auto safety as early as 1957. The big Detroit automakers either ignored their few critics or dismissed them as malcontents, but concerns about the dangers of the car culture simmered. By the early 1960s many urban planners and ordinary Americans had begun to question the wisdom of dividing cities with smog-producing freeways while permitting mass transit to decay. Still, during the fifties nearly everyone celebrated public road subsidies for private automobiles. Gasoline was cheap, and highways were seemingly free.

The Age of Television

The emerging car culture was only one manifestation of the national search for pleasure and adventure that characterized the period. Leisure and entertainment in general were becoming big business. In 1947 radio still reigned as the nation's major source of electronic information and entertainment. Out of some 38 million households, 34 million had at least one radio. Radio broadcasts brought news, music, comedy, melodrama, and soap operas to an immense audience. Already, however, a newer electronic medium, the television, was poised to upstage radio. In 1946 the Federal Communications Commission (FCC) licensed twenty-six new television stations to serve the public. Sets remained both scarce and expensive for a time, and only a few programs, mostly sports events, were televised each night. Drama and variety shows soon joined the schedule, however, and enough television sets were produced that ordinary families could buy one. By 1949 about 1 million homes, mostly in large cities, received broadcasts, on sixty-nine stations. Ten years later, six hundred stations reached 44 million households with televisions nationwide.

Television's influence on American life was soon manifest in ways both large and small. In 1948 both the Democratic and Republican Parties held their presidential nominating conventions in Philadelphia because the city possessed a coaxial cable hookup that allowed viewing by an audience of 10 million. In cities with television stations, movie ticket sales plummeted, old-time vaudeville revues died, and attendance at live sporting events fell. *The Milton Berle Show,* television's first great hit, attracted such large audiences that water pressure in cities dropped during the show's commercial breaks as viewers rushed to the toilet.

The television industry expanded quickly in the early 1950s as the FCC sped up its licensing procedures. Quality improved as the size of TV sets increased, and prices fell to an average of $200. By the time Eisenhower took office, in 1953, half of all American homes had a set. For the rest of the decade sales ranged between 5 and 7 million units annually. By 1960, fully 90 percent of all homes had at least one television.

At first the comedy shows, crime shows, Westerns, variety shows, quiz shows, and soap operas on television resembled radio programs with scenery added. Some early comedy-variety offerings, like Sid Caesar's *Your Show of*

American viewers loved Lucille Ball, the brilliant comedian whose hare brained escapades mocked the idea of wifely obedience. *Collection of David J. and Janice L. Frent*

Shows (1950–1954), provided quality writing and acting. Sophisticated live drama aired through the mid-1950s on such shows as *Kraft Television Theater, Playhouse 90,* and *Studio One.* But toward the end of the 1950s Hollywood began selling old movies to television and producing low-budget, made-for-TV movies. This effectively removed most original drama from television.

Among the most successful comedy shows of the 1950s was *I Love Lucy,* which ran in several formats from 1951 through 1974 and became a model for many subsequent situation comedies, or sitcoms. Lucille Ball played Lucy Ricardo, the scatterbrained wife of Cuban-born band leader Ricky Ricardo, played by Desi Arnaz, her real-life husband. On the most popular episode of the show, aired on January 19, 1953, Lucy re-enacted the recent birth of her son. Although pregnancy was seldom depicted on television, the scriptwriters had blended fiction and reality by coordinating the season's story development with Lucille Ball's pregnancy. This episode drew a much larger share of the nation's television viewing audience than President Dwight D. Eisenhower's inaugural speech the next day.

Because of the technical difficulty of live remote filming, news coverage was not a staple of television until the early 1960s. Still, Edward R. Murrow, a pioneer radio and TV investigative journalist, produced some exceptionally good work for CBS, including an exposé of Senator Joseph McCarthy on *See It Now.* But most television news came in a fifteen-minute format. Coverage resembled the *March of Time* newsreels shown in theaters—long on emotional images and the pithy narration of human interest stories, short on news content and analysis. As innovations such as the video camera made it possible to follow breaking stories, the television networks expanded their nightly news coverage to half an hour in 1963, promoting the programs heavily to win audience share.

Television producers generally provided entertainment, not enlightenment. *Howdy Doody,* a light-hearted romp among marionettes and caricatured Indians, set the tone for children's programming. Westerns like *Hopalong Cassidy* and *The Lone Ranger* also played to young viewers. Soap operas and quiz shows dominated the daytime airwaves. Inexpensive to produce, they appealed to busy housewives, who could break up their household routine with TV viewing.

In the evening, family-oriented situation comedies proliferated. The decade's big hits included *The Adventures of Ozzie and Harriet, The Danny Thomas Show, The Donna Reed Show, Leave It to Beaver, Father Knows Best,* and *The Honeymooners.* Except for the last—in which bus driver Ralph Kramden (Jackie Gleason) and his sewer-worker buddy Ed Norton (Art Carney) schemed to get rich—these were middle-class fables in which white suburban families with a homemaker mother and a father who worked in a white-collar job lived pleasant lives. On television people of color appeared only as servants. Television's need to attract mass audiences to earn advertising revenue ensured that its content would be bland and relatively conservative

The New Sports Industry

Nowhere was the impact of television on popular culture clearer than in the area of sports. After the Second World War professional and college sports assumed a growing significance in American life. Sporting events became social occasions through which Americans affirmed the superiority of their country and their community. By the late 1940s professional basketball and ice hockey leagues had joined the nation's baseball and football leagues in providing entertainment for an avid public. Sports took on the trappings of a secular religion. In the suburbs, Little League baseball and football, modeled on the professional leagues, enrolled millions of children.

Television was part of this change because it elevated players to unprecedented fame and gave fans a new and often closer look at their idols. By the 1960s sports had become a major part of broadcasting. Television also became the key to sports profits, for TV payments soon exceeded the revenue from ticket sales.

In other ways, however, the economic structure of professional sports seemed a throwback to feudalism. According to a 1922 Supreme Court ruling, reaffirmed in 1972, baseball clubs were exempt from federal antitrust regulations. Football and basketball teams claimed similar rights. As a result, teams could use reserve and option clauses in players' contracts to prevent them from signing with any other team. Similarly, the annual player drafts gave teams exclusive rights to bargain with the players they drafted. These restrictions bound a professional athlete to his original team unless the team decided to trade or sell him. When players dared to question contract restrictions, some club owners accused them of having Communist sympathies.

Desegregation proceeded slowly in professional and college athletics. After Jackie Robinson broke baseball's color line in 1947, professional teams began to hire black athletes, although the pace varied from sport to sport. Some southern college basketball teams refused to recruit African-Americans or play against teams that did. Because the segregated programs gradually became uncompetitive, their fans' frustration helped force them to recruit blacks as well as whites.

As the nation's population shifted toward the West and the Sunbelt, the owners of professional teams began to move their franchises to these areas, often provoking outcries from loyal fans. When baseball owner Walter O'Malley took his Brooklyn Dodgers to Los Angeles in the late 1950s, New Yorkers decried his betrayal and demanded a congressional investigation. But during the next decade many teams relocated. Although the old fans protested, fans in the new cities hastened to the stadiums and arenas or watched the games on television.

✦ The Politics of Moderation

By the fall of 1946 a wave of strikes in the automobile, electrical, coal, and transportation industries, along with price inflation, shortages of consumer goods, and a perception among the electorate that Truman was out of his depth, eroded support for the Democratic Party. In the November election the Republican Party picked up eleven Senate and fifty-six House seats, gaining a majority in both houses of Congress for the first time since 1930. Senator Robert Taft, nicknamed "Mr. Republican," emerged as the informal head of the party in Congress. Long critical of New Deal domestic and foreign programs, Taft denounced the "corrupting idea that we can legislate prosperity, legislate equality, legislate opportunity."

Despite their new control of Congress, the Republicans had only modest success unraveling the New Deal legacy. They did, however, effect significant changes in labor law. Moves to limit the right to strike and to abolish the "closed shop"—an arrangement in which workers were compelled to join unions—had begun during the Second World War. Building on such antilabor sentiment, Senator Taft and New Jersey Republican congressman Fred A. Hartley introduced a law to curb union power. The Taft-Hartley Act of 1947, passed over Truman's veto, outlawed closed shops, barred secondary boycotts, made unions liable for a variety of monetary damages, established procedures for decertification elections, and permitted the president to impose an eighty-day cooling-off period in labor disputes, during which unions could not strike. Taft-Hartley also required union officials to sign an anti-Communist affidavit.

The law bolstered conservative labor leaders and discouraged new organizing drives, especially in the largely nonunion South, but it did not destroy existing unions that followed its provisions. In heavy industries like steel and automobile manufacturing, unions maintained their position, winning good wages and substantial benefits for their members by cooperating with management plans to mechanize more and more jobs. The greatest impact of the Taft-Hartley Act was felt in the Sunbelt states of the South and West, where legislatures responded to business lobbying by passing right-to-work laws that barred making union membership a requirement for employment. To get out of union contracts, many labor-intensive industries, such as textiles, began to relocate to the Sunbelt.

Clearly by the beginning of the 1950s the nation's politics were swinging to the right. The question was, how far right? General Dwight D. Eisenhower, widely known by his nickname, "Ike," chose politics as a second career at age sixty-two. Despite this late beginning he became one of the most popular and successful presidents in the postwar era. During his eight years in the White House, he averaged an approval rating of 64 percent. The public was reassured by his calming, grandfatherly style and seldom questioned his rather disengaged stewardship of domestic policy. Were it not for the provisions of the Twenty-second Amendment, which bars presidents from serving a third term, he might have won reelection in 1960.

Eisenhower's 1952 campaign, an observer remarked, was "a masterpiece of evasion." His vagueness calmed fears that a Republican in the White House would roll back the achievements of the New Deal, and his status as a war hero reassured the public that he could handle foreign threats. When he promised that, if elected, he would "go to Korea," voters interpreted this to mean that the general who had liberated Western Europe had a secret plan to end the Korean stalemate.

In contrast, the Democrats entered the campaign in disarray. No clear candidate emerged before the convention, and few wanted to be associated closely with the unpopular incumbent, Harry S Truman. Governor Adlai Stevenson of Illinois, whose grandfather had served as vice president in the 1890s, received his party's nomination on the third ballot. Considered a liberal northerner, he tried to balance the ticket by choosing Senator John Sparkman of Alabama, a segregationist, as his running mate.

The most exciting moment in the campaign occurred when allegations surfaced that Eisenhower's young running mate, Richard M. Nixon, had pocketed $18,000 in campaign contributions. Eisenhower considered dumping him until Nixon appeared on television with his family to deny any

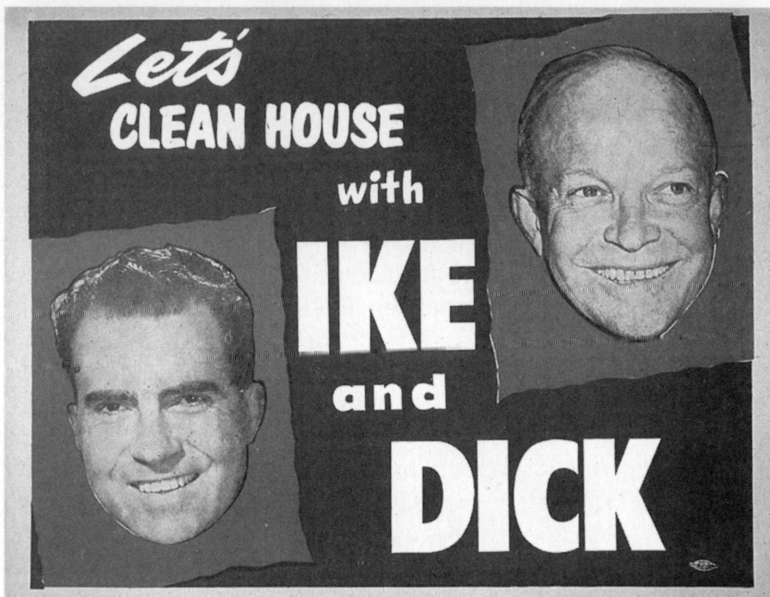

Candidates Eisenhower and Nixon marketed themselves as average, upstanding guys in the 1952 presidential election. *Lester Glasner Collection/Neal Peters*

impropriety. In a maudlin but effective performance known forever after as the "Checkers speech," Nixon admitted accepting one personal gift, a cocker spaniel named Checkers, on behalf of his daughters.

In the November election more Americans—over 61 million—voted than ever before. They opted for change, giving Eisenhower 34 million votes to Stevenson's 27 million. White voters alarmed by the Democrats' support for civil rights gave the Republicans four states in the South, which until then had been solidly Democratic.The Republicans also won narrow majorities of nine seats in the House and one seat in the Senate.

Eisenhower was not intensely partisan. He did not equate the GOP with patriotism or the Democrats with treason, and he expended little energy campaigning for other Republicans. This stance probably contributed to his public popularity, but it did not endear him to the hard-liners within his party. Even more important, Eisenhower had no intention of trying to roll back the New Deal legacy—long a cherished plan of conservative Republicans. In his first term, in fact, he approved the extension of Social Security benefits to 10 million additional workers and signed a law raising the minimum wage from 75 cents to $1.00 per hour. He also reluctantly accepted farm subsidies and created the cabinet-level Department of Health, Education and Welfare.

Eisenhower took a similarly moderate position on communism. He maintained the loyalty program inherited from Truman and approved the firing of many innocent federal employees, but in his public utterances he downplayed the danger of internal subversion. The July 1953 armistice in Korea and the political demise of Senator McCarthy a year later (see Chapter 8) helped to quiet the Red Scare. Eisenhower also attempted to rein in the military budget, which had shot up rapidly during the Korean War.

Overall Eisenhower promoted a moderately conservative movement but recognized a strong role for government in domestic affairs and a permanent global role for America. Beginning in 1955, following the loss of the Republican majorities in Congress, Eisenhower often cooperated with powerful congressional Democrats. At times he even considered forming a new centrist political party that might bring Democrats and Republicans together.

✦ Cracks in the Picture Window

Although Eisenhower exuded an aura of stability, American life was changing in significant ways, powered in part by a booming economy. Economic growth during the 1950s averaged more than 4 percent annually, despite recessions in 1954, 1958, and 1960. Inflation remained below 2 percent and unemployment below 5 percent; a record high employment of 66.5 million was reached in 1960. The GNP nearly doubled between 1950 and 1960, to $500 billion.

With high employment and higher incomes, Americans found more ways to spend their wages. Lenient bank lending policies and the advent of the credit card also stimulated consumer spending. The Diners Club and American Express credit cards were both introduced during the 1950s, followed by oil company, hotel chain, and department store credit cards. As a record number of young families furnished homes and clothed children, private debt climbed from $73 billion to $200 billion between 1950 and 1960.

The New Corporate Economy

The profile of American industry and business also changed during the 1950s. Mergers accelerated, with the result that the two hundred largest U.S. corporations controlled over half of all the nation's business assets by the end of the decade. Some corporations were also beginning to expand across national borders. Heavy industry and manufacturing declined, with new job growth clustered in the service, clerical, and managerial sectors. By 1956 white-collar workers outnumbered blue-collar workers for the first time.

Many of the newer industries invested heavily in research and development. By the middle of the decade some half-million workers were employed in the research divisions of about three thousand U.S. companies. The federal government also increased its investment in science, financing over one-half of all scientific research by universities and corporate laboratories. As a result of this commitment, new technologies such as jet aircraft, new medicines, and new consumer electronics were developed. Antibiotics, tranquilizers, and the polio vaccine revolutionized medicine. The transistor made possible miniaturized radios and an infant computer industry. The Boeing 707, the first regularly scheduled passenger jet, entered commercial service in 1958.

Meanwhile, the labor movement struggled, with only partial success, to hold its own. In 1955 the American Federation of Labor and the Congress of Industrial Organizations overcame their long-time rivalry and merged to form the AFL-CIO. But congressional investigations into union ties to organized crime, along with the federal conviction of Teamsters Union president Dave Beck, a protégé of controversial Teamster founder Jimmy Hoffa, tarnished labor's image and led to new legal restrictions on the labor movement. Although the number of union members remained fairly steady, the unionized proportion of the total work force declined with the loss of jobs in heavy industry. The unions that managed to penetrate the newer white-collar sectors, such as the American Federation of State, County and Municipal Employees (AFSCME), accounted for a growing percentage of union membership.

Throughout the decade business leaders and some economists boasted of creating a "people's capitalism" that ensured the equal distribution of abundance and erased class divisions. While many Americans did enjoy a rising standard of living, wealth remained highly concentrated, as it had throughout the century. In 1960 a mere 1 percent of the population possessed one-third of the nation's wealth, and the top 5 percent controlled over half of it. Half of all families had no savings account, and 40 million Americans, almost one-fourth of the population, lived near or below the poverty line, then figured as an income of $3,000 per year for a family of four. The poverty rate was especially high among the elderly, racial minorities, and rural Americans.

1950s Family Values

On the surface Americans seemed a content lot during the fifties. They also became increasingly devout. By the end of the decade, two-thirds of the population claimed formal church membership and regular attendance at houses of worship, up from 48 percent before the Second World War. Ninety-seven percent professed belief in God. President Eisenhower encouraged this trend, hosting White House prayer breakfasts. Congress added "under God" to the Pledge of Allegiance and put the motto "In God We Trust" on paper money. Religious popularizers like Billy Graham became celebrities, appearing in newspapers, on radio and television, and on best-seller lists. Presbyterian minister Norman Vincent Peale's *The Power of Positive Thinking* (1952) was on the best-seller list for three years. Christianity, like parenthood and the suburban nuclear family, became a measure of Americanism and a rejection of atheistic communism.

On one issue both religious and secular opinion leaders agreed emphatically—the need for a strong American family founded on traditional values. But the fifties family was nothing if not innovative. During the decade, American women reversed a hundred-year trend by marrying younger and having more babies. Advice columns, television shows, and schools emphasized traditional gender roles, with husbands going to work and wives remaining in the home. A fear of sexual chaos brought on by the Cold War emerged as a common theme. Wartime mobility had unleashed the sexual energy of those who had left their hometowns in search of jobs or to serve in the armed forces. Both women and men found new opportunities for sexual expression, and some found ways to act on their homosexual desires. After the war a reaction against sexual nonconformity set in with a vengeance. Popular literature discussed the dangers posed by "loose women" and "sex perverts" who might be in league with the Soviet Union. Senator Joseph McCarthy, whose close aide Roy Cohn was a closeted homosexual, warned that "sexual perverts [had] infiltrated our government" and were "perhaps as dangerous as real Communists."

The dominant domestic ideology of the period, which Betty Friedan labeled "the feminine mystique" in her 1963 book of that title, defined women as wives and mothers. But in fact a third of all women worked for wages, and total female employment grew in the 1950s from 16.5 million to 23 million, representing a third of the work force. Nevertheless, in popular thinking women belonged at home, raising children and keeping house. A growing number of women did attend college, however, despite these cultural norms. Adlai Stevenson exhorted women at Smith College not to feel frustrated by their distance from the "great issues and stirring debate" for which their education was preparing them. A woman could be a good citizen, he claimed, by helping her husband find value in his work and by teaching her children the uniqueness of each individual. Prodded by such assertions from civic leaders and the media, it is not surprising that the average mother in the 1950s had between three and four children, usually by age thirty, and the birth rate continued to rise until 1957.

In spite of the formal sexual orthodoxy of the era, there were portents of a more emancipated future. Contraception, accepted by all the major faiths except the Roman Catholic Church, became common as a means of spacing pregnancies and limiting births. Sex was more openly discussed and displayed during the 1950s than in most earlier periods. Popular science became a vehicle for sexual openness in 1953 when Dr. Alfred C. Kinsey published his best-selling *Sexual Behavior in the Human Female,* a sequel to his 1948 work on male sexuality. Kinsey's six thousand case histories revealed that women, like men, engaged in a wide variety of sexual acts both before and after marriage.

Artistic representations of sex became more open in the 1950s. In the film industry, for example, the Hollywood Production Code had long barred use of words like *virgin* and *seduction* and restricted the sexual content of films. Even married couples were shown sleeping in separate beds. By the mid-1950s the code was relaxed, however, and screen sex became more graphic than before.

During the same years, the Supreme Court overturned several state laws restricting publication of serious erotic literature like D. H. Lawrence's *Lady Chatterley's Lover.* Such books became more widely available, and writers of less renown also offered some steamy reading. The decade's most popular novel, *Peyton Place* (1956), sold almost 10 million copies. The book jacket promised that author Grace Metalious, a young housewife, lifted "the lid off a small New England town," exposing lust, rape, incest, alcoholism, murder, and hypocrisy.

Playboy magazine was surely the most influential erotic publication of the decade. Its glossy centerfolds brought bare-breasted women into millions of homes, displaying them like one more new consumer product. When Hugh Hefner first published *Playboy* in December 1953, he featured the rising starlet Marilyn Monroe as "Playmate of the Month." Slick, upscale, and replete with the hedonistic "Playboy philosophy," selections from serious writers, and airbrushed photographs of busty beauties, *Playboy* represented a quantum leap from the grimy "girlie mags" of the prewar years. By 1956 its circulation had reached one-half million per month.

Besides pressuring women into domestic roles, the massive profamily propaganda of the fifties stifled many men, who, fleeing commitment, found *Playboy* a temporary escape. Hefner pitched his magazine to college students and young status-conscious men who wanted to date, not marry, the centerfold models.

The Growth of the Youth Culture

If *Playboy* spoke to the desires of young men, the emerging art form of rock 'n' roll touched a deep chord in American youths of both sexes. As television gave radio increasingly stiff competition, radio stations became less profitable, prompting many of them to change their formats. Before the 1950s mainstream radio had featured fatuous songs like "How Much Is That Doggie in the Window." In contrast, African-American popular music, often called "race music," vibrated with creative energy, but white audiences had little exposure to it. To reach new listeners and to make the distinctive black style more acceptable, some disc jockeys called it rhythm and blues, or R&B.

In 1952 Cleveland disc jockey Alan Freed premiered an R&B radio show called *Moondog's Rock 'n' Roll Party.* The term "rockin' and rollin'" originally referred to sexual intercourse, but Freed toned down the sexual references, connecting the words *rock 'n' roll* to the style of dancing associated with the music. From then on the barriers between white and black music began to tumble. White audiences opened their ears to black music at the same time the civil rights movement was challenging the racism of white society.

In 1954 Bill Haley, a portly, nearly middle-aged white band leader, recorded "Rock Around the Clock," an exuberant tune that became the theme song of the popular film *Blackboard Jungle* (1955). The movie chronicled the struggle of a young teacher in a run-down inner-city high school who tried to motivate alienated, poor youth. The film's message—crime does not pay, and middle-class values are a salvation—is scarcely remembered. But "Rock Around the Clock," critics and audiences agreed, gave *Blackboard Jungle* its "insurrectionary power." The music brought white middle-class youth to their feet. Theater owners reported spontaneous dancing in the aisles.

The record industry was especially eager to appeal to white youth, because they represented an enormous market. "Teenagers," a relatively recent term for those who enjoyed a prolonged adolescence before entering the labor force, formed an expanding group during the 1950s. Early in the decade they purchased some 40 percent of all records, radios, and cameras and over half of all movie tickets. By 1959 the teenage market—including money spent by parents on teenagers and by teenagers on themselves—topped $10 billion per year. With so much at stake, record producers hustled to find more white recording artists who employed the black sound in a form acceptable to white teenagers.

The biggest find was a nineteen-year-old part-time truck driver from Tupelo, Mississippi—Elvis Presley. Born poor, he had taught himself the guitar and learned the R&B style. In live performances he aroused his fans, both female and male, by undulating his body and thrusting his hips in a style he attributed to revivalist preachers. Presley virtually created the image of the hypersexed male rock star, replete with long hair, leather jacket, a sneering expression, and a sultry demeanor.

By 1956 Elvis had become a national sensation. He released a series of hits, including "Heartbreak Hotel," "Don't Be Cruel," "Love Me Tender," and "I'm All Shook Up," and sold over 14 million records that year. He appeared on Ed Sullivan's popular TV variety show, where the cameras focused above the waist to conceal the young man's suggestive thrusts. Over 80 percent of all American viewers watched this performance. Between early 1956 and March 1958, when the army drafted him, Presley released fourteen consecutive million-seller records. Presley's success not only set a standard for other white rock singers but also spurred white acceptance of African-American artists such as Ray Charles, Chuck Berry, Little Richard, and Fats Domino.

While the young went wild over rock 'n' roll, parents recoiled at its influence. *Life* magazine contrasted Elvis's "bump and grind routine" to the more respectable performances of all-American crooner Frank Sinatra. Sinatra himself called rock 'n' roll the "martial music of every sideburned delinquent on the face of the earth." Some clergy condemned Presley's music as satanic, and many cities refused to permit rock concerts at their public facilities.

In fact, some rock lyrics did make fun of middle-class values. Besides its generally sensual, even sexual emphasis, rock music ridiculed work ("Get a Job"), downplayed school ("Don't Know Much About History"), mixed religion with sex ("Teen Angel"), scoffed at authority ("Charlie Brown, He's a Clown"), and celebrated irresponsibility ("Rock Around the Clock"). Popular music had never before so blatantly defied social mores or so distinguished youth from older generations. Thus for many adults "rock 'n' roll" became a convenient shorthand for explaining the problem with the country's young people.

Such fears, and the discontented youth that gave rise to them, were forcefully depicted in films like *The Wild Ones* (1953), *Rebel Without a Cause* (1955), and *Blackboard Jungle* (1955). These three movies featured actors Marlon Brando, James Dean, and Sidney Poitier as young toughs who oozed anger, sexuality, and contempt for their elders. They presented an even stronger challenge to the order of things than did Holden Caufield, the alienated teenage hero of J. D. Salinger's exceedingly popular novel *Catcher in the Rye* (1951). Despite the films' overt messages that violence and immorality were wrong, most teenagers who flocked to see Brando, Dean, and Poitier cheered the unrepentant rebels, not those characters who accepted their elders' advice.

Among parents who had just experienced war, peace and quiet seemed a good bargain. Young people, however, wanted something more. A youth subculture was beginning to emerge, and many parents worried about it. They blamed the music, movies, books, and comics of the day, and even the television programs that to later generations would seem so innocent. Some people invoked the Communist specter. Early in the decade, Justice Department officials helped one Hollywood studio produce a film warning that "throughout the United States today, indeed throughout the free world, a deadly war is being waged." The "Communist enemy," the film declared, was trying to subvert American youth by spreading drugs and encouraging obscenity in the mass media.

Fear of an epidemic of juvenile crime grew especially intense in the mid-1950s. Parents, journalists, police, and politicians warned that juvenile delinquency among all classes threatened the foundations of society. Some blamed working mothers for slighting family discipline. Others argued that the popular culture glamorized crime. Once delinquency became a hot topic, police tended to report offenses they had previously overlooked as trivial.

A dramatic increase in violent crime and drug use, mostly of heroin, did occur among minorities in the festering urban ghettos. Youth gangs flourished in the ethnic ghettos of New York, Chicago, Los Angeles, and a few other large cities. But the majority of African-American and Hispanic gangs in the low-income housing projects were not violent. Despite scare stories, youth gangs outside these enclaves had only tiny memberships. Complaints about gangs often served as code language for criticism of people of color.

Growth of Education

Many political liberals and professional educators attributed juvenile delinquency and a host of other social ills to the lack of federal aid to public schools. Without more money for buildings, equipment, and libraries, they argued, teachers could not cope with surging enrollments and the constant accumulation of new information. Only higher salaries, paid for by taxes, would lure talented college graduates into teaching.

Conservatives, on the other hand, blamed the educational establishment itself for poor student performance. The right wing believed that John Dewey's popular ideas of "progressive education," with their emphasis on social relevance, democratic ideals, and pragmatism, had undermined respect for the acquisition of basic skills, traditional values, and culture. They called for a return to basics, more classroom discipline, and the teaching of religious values.

The debate over education took on a life of its own, with few participants managing to show that educational quality had actually declined. Neither liberal nor conservative critics fully acknowledged that part of the problem lay in the changing nature of mass education. Before the Second World War relatively few students had finished high school, and even fewer had gone to college. Public primary schools had sought to instill some basic discipline and to teach rudimentary reading and arithmetic skills. The wealthy attended private schools, and talented students of modest means benefited from special college preparatory courses in public high schools.

Postwar prosperity resulted in many more working-class youths attending high school. As blacks and Hispanics migrated to urban areas, they became a major presence in public schools, increasing the cultural and social diversity in the schools as well as the proportion of working-class students. Tensions within this newly varied population, combined with the baby boom and the rapid expansion of the suburbs, strained the nation's educational system. Moreover, a growing number of parents now expected the schools to play a more comprehensive role than ever before. Schools were expected to teach job skills, citizenship, driver's education, and a sophisticated science, math, and literature curriculum to a broader cross section of students than in earlier decades. To complicate the problem, by tradition American schools were locally funded and controlled, making it difficult to promote change at the national level.

The debate reached new heights after October 1957, when the Soviet Union launched the first artificial satellite, *Sputnik I.* Journalists and politicians described the Soviet Union's system as a model of successful mass education. Communism, it seemed, had won the space race by winning the education race. What would Moscow win next?

Senator Lyndon B. Johnson of Texas, a former schoolteacher, the Democratic majority leader, and a presidential aspirant, chaired a committee investigating the impact of Moscow's space coup. Long an advocate of federal support for education, he now called for creating a "reservoir of trained and educated minds" through federal aid to the nation's schools. Congress and President Eisenhower cooperated in September 1958, passing the National Defense Education Act (NDEA), a billion-dollar package, supplemented by state grants, that provided aid to schools and universities. It granted funds for school construction, student loans and scholarships, and the teaching of

"The only ones for me are the mad ones," wrote Jack Kerouac, whose novels celebrated mobility, spontaneity, spirituality, cheap wine, poetry, and sex. *F. DeWitt*

science, mathematics, and foreign languages. In the following two decades the NDEA and successor programs had a huge impact on American education at all levels, from the primary grades through graduate and professional schools. As with the GI Bill of a decade earlier, loans and fellowships allowed many more students to pursue advanced degrees. By 1960 U.S. universities were granting ten thousand doctorates annually, three times the pre-World War II number. With NDEA assistance, a record number of students enrolled in college during the 1960s. As never before, Americans assumed that a bright student, whatever his or her social background, should and would go to college.

Social Critics

The fifties role models for college rebels were the Beats, a group of iconoclastic writers who captured public attention late in the decade. Their defiance of social and literary conventions, as well as their embrace of drugs, Eastern mysticism, and homosexuality, outraged the middle class and excited many teenagers and young adults. Beatniks, as they became known, disparaged Christianity, work, materialism, family life, patriotism, and interest in winning the Cold War. The poet Allen Ginsberg gained national attention in 1956 when San Francisco police charged him with obscenity for publishing his poem *Howl,* a highly personal cry against American materialism and mass culture. At his trial, prominent writers and critics defended the poem, which discussed madness, drugs, travel, ecstasy, and various forms of sexuality. The Beats achieved further fame in 1957 with the appearance of novelist Jack Kerouac's best seller *On the Road,* a raucous, thinly fictionalized account of the author's cross-country travel with his unconventional friends.

Despite such rumblings of rebellion, most social commentators agreed that the United States had solved the major material problems afflicting society. The persisting pockets of poverty, such as those among African-Americans, were seen as minor embarrassments rather than as major problems. An influential analysis published by Daniel Bell near the end of the decade, *The End of Ideology,* argued that the passionate ideological crusades of earlier years no longer had relevance. The United States had mastered the production of abundance and now had only to decide how to allocate the wealth.

Nevertheless, some critics began to question the social mores and culture that arose from the decade of calm prosperity. This general theme appeared in such books as David Riesman's *The Lonely Crowd* (1950), Sloan Wilson's *The Man in the Gray Flannel Suit* (1955), William H. Whyte, Jr.'s *The Organization Man* (1955), John Keats's *The Crack in the Picture Window* (1957), and Richard Gordon's *The Split Level Trap* (1960). Riesman and Whyte discussed the eclipse of the "inner-directed" personality. Instead of relying on internal drives and values, they charged, Americans had become "other-directed," little more than sheep who sought approval and rewards from peers.

Critics also attacked the all-pervasive consumer culture. In a trilogy of best sellers criticizing the advertising industry—*The Hidden Persuaders* (1957), *The Status Seekers* (1959), and *The Waste Makers* (1959)—journalist Vance Packard blamed mass marketing and the concept of "planned obsolescence" for turning citizens into insatiable consumers who pursued the accumulation of appliances and gadgets as life's highest purpose. Other exposés of American life portrayed shoddily built subdivisions full of haggard men, tense and anxious women, and spoiled children.

In a widely read critique, *The Affluent Society* (1958), economist John Kenneth Galbraith noted the triumphs of liberal capitalism since 1945. Yet public services were in terrible shape, Galbraith pointed out, and many groups still experienced poverty. Galbraith called for government intervention to ameliorate the misery that persisted in the midst of luxury. Only a few of the social critics of the period claimed to find basic structural flaws in American society. One of these was sociologist C. Wright Mills, whose book *The Power Elite* (1956) asserted that a small group of military, business, and political leaders controlled the country and left the majority of Americans powerless. Herbert Marcuse, a German émigré philosopher, blended Freudian psychology and Marxism in his *Eros and Civilization* (1956), which argued that a tiny minority manipulated the lives of most people and perpetuated unique forms of psychological repression. In 1960, in *Growing Up Absurd,* Paul Goodman criticized U.S. schools and other institutions for stifling creativity and individualism. These critics offered evidence that America's problems had not disappeared or been forgotten. Their dissent foreshadowed the radical challenges to the status quo that emerged during the 1960s.

✦ Continuing Struggles: Civil Rights and Civil Liberties

At a time when so many Americans enjoyed abundance, African-Americans were still denied basic human rights. Blacks emerged from the New Deal and the Second World War with higher aspirations and expectations; they were less willing to settle for a second-class position in American society. Like much of the population, African-Americans were highly mobile after the Second World War, continuing the migration patterns that began during the war years (see map). In the rural South, federal agricultural subsidies dating from the 1930s limited the production of cotton and other crops and helped finance farm mechanization. One effect was to push black sharecroppers off the land. Some went to southern cities like Atlanta and Birmingham. More went north and west.

The migrants did not find residential integration in their new communities. Just as the newcomers arrived, white Americans were leaving the cities for the suburbs. During the 1950s the nation's twelve largest central cities lost 3.6 million whites while they gained 4.5 million nonwhites. By 1960 over half of all African-Americans lived in the largely poor and mostly black central cities. The new suburban communities remained nearly all white.

While de facto segregation in housing and education plagued the North, the South had extended its Jim Crow laws to the point that separate public facilities—including rest rooms, bus station waiting rooms, drinking fountains, even courtroom bibles—were legally required for each race. With such daily humiliations and ubiquitous reminders of blacks' second-class status, segregation first came under fire in the South. As a result, racism wore a more violent face south of the Mason-Dixon line. Led in many cases by war veterans, African-Americans organized voter-registration drives in the South, encountering white hostility and sometimes violence. After hearing reports of blacks who were killed or blinded for daring to assert their voting rights, President Truman acted. In late 1946 he established the President's Committee on Civil Rights to recommend steps for the federal government to take. This panel urged government action to ensure that all Americans enjoyed equal opportunity in education, housing, and employment. It called for federal laws against lynching and poll taxes, creation of the Fair Employment Practices Commission, and a strong Civil Rights Division within the Justice Department.

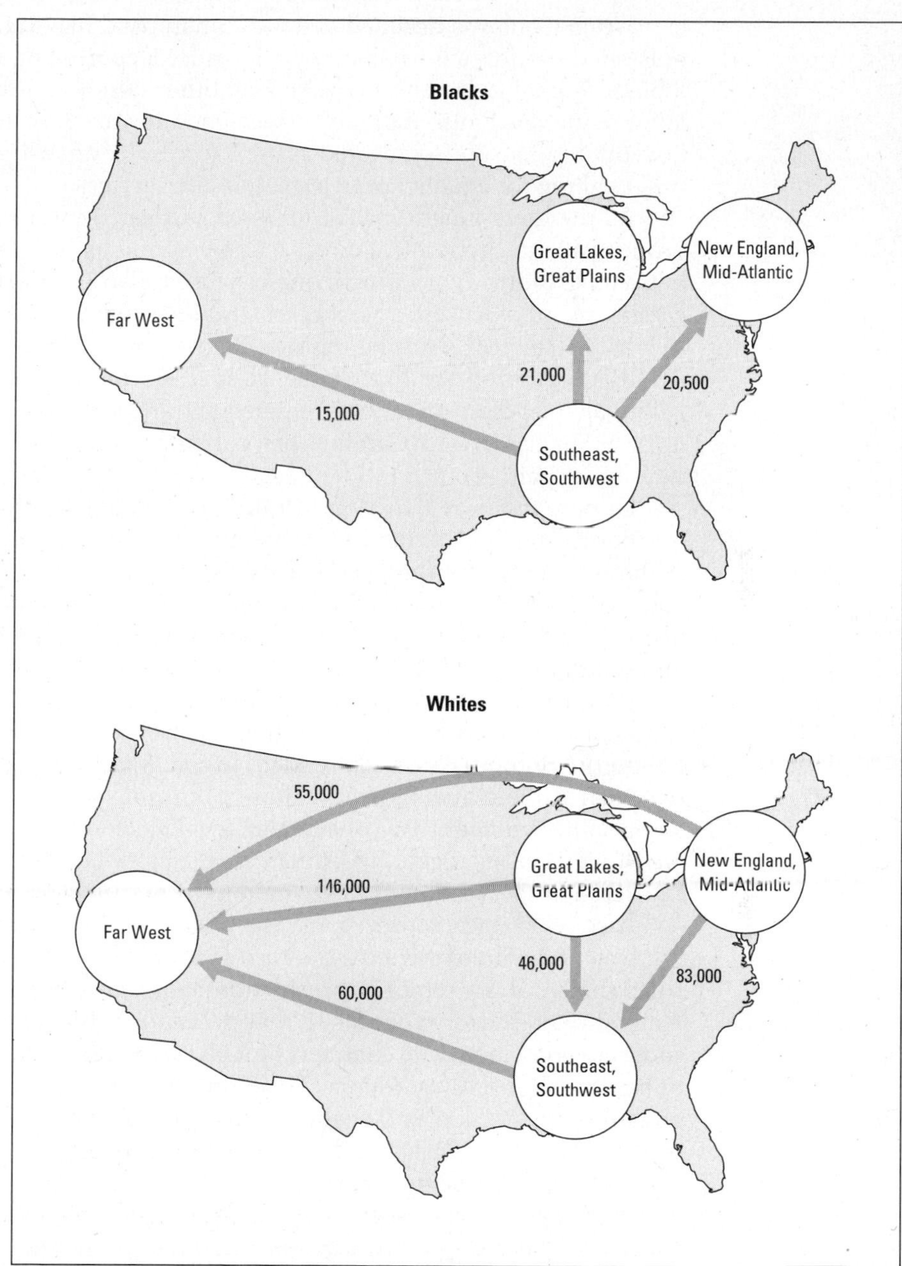

Average Annual Regional Migration, 1947–1960

When Congress declined to act, Truman used his executive authority to bolster civil rights enforcement by the Justice Department. He also appointed a black federal judge and made several other minority appointments. When labor leader A. Philip Randolph threatened in July 1948 to organize a draft boycott against the segregated armed forces, Truman issued an executive order calling for equality of treatment in the services.

As the government inched forward, African-American individuals and groups pursued nonviolent direct action inspired by India's Mohandas ("Mahatma") Gandhi. Two women, one of whom, Patricia Harris, later became a cabinet member in the Carter administration, staged the first civil rights sit-in in Washington, D.C., during the war. In 1947 the Congress of Racial Equality (CORE) organized the first "freedom ride" to test a recent Supreme Court ruling against discrimination in interstate transportation. The group made it as far as Durham, North Carolina, before being arrested and sentenced to thirty days on a chain gang.

During the next two years CORE carried out lunch counter sit-ins in northern cities and organized a swim-in at Palisades Park in New Jersey. Although mobs beat the participants, the amusement park and many lunch counters were desegregated. These small and hard-won victories convinced activists of the importance of direct action for mobilizing their communities and maintaining political pressure on the white establishment.

Progress was being made in the legal realm too. The Supreme Court gradually extended judicial protection for the civil rights of minorities. Even before the Second World War ended, in *Smith* v. *Allwright* (1944), the Court overturned the segregationist whites-only primary system that prevailed in some southern states. Two years later, in *Morgan* v. *Virginia* (1946), the Court held that racial segregation on interstate buses violated federal law. (This was the decision the freedom riders set out to test in 1947.)

A series of judicial decisions also began to chip away at segregation in housing and employment. At the turn of the century the Supreme Court had ruled that local laws enforcing residential segregation violated the Fourteenth Amendment. It had undermined that decision, however, by permitting state courts to enforce private contracts that barred minorities from specific developments. But in *Shelly* v. *Kraemer* (1948) the justices decided that this ruse gave government sanction to illegal discrimination and ordered that state courts could not enforce restrictive clauses in private contracts.

Nothing represented more powerfully the unequal status of African-Americans than school segregation. The decision in *Plessy* v. *Ferguson* (1896) permitted states to provide schools and other public services for blacks that were "separate but equal." By 1938 Chief Justice Hughes had suggested that southern states wishing to continue separate-but-equal education ought to make black-only schools truly equal. In 1948 the Court took up the case of Ada Sipuel, who had graduated with a strong record from the State College for Negroes in Langston, Oklahoma. She was refused admission to the University of Oklahoma Law School (the only one in the state) on racial grounds but was told that a separate school for blacks with "substantially equal" facilities would soon open. Represented by Thurgood Marshall, chief counsel of the National Association for the Advancement of Colored People (NAACP), she sued for admission to the existing school. In *Sipuel* v. *Board of Regents of the University of Oklahoma,* the justices ruled unanimously that Oklahoma must provide Sipuel with a legal education "in conformity with the equal protection clause of the Fourteenth Amendment and . . . provide it as soon as it does for applicants of any other group." The university regents then created a sham law school by roping off a tiny area within the state capitol building and assigning three teachers to Sipuel. Marshall challenged this ruse, but the Court declined further action.

Two years later the University of Oklahoma admitted, under pressure, a sixty-eight-year-old African-American, George W. McLaurin, to its graduate program in education. The university ordered McLaurin to sit in a doorway outside the classroom, to use a special desk in a segregated section of the library, and to eat alone in a cafeteria annex. When the NAACP challenged these rules, McLaurin was permitted to sit inside the classroom so long as his seat was encircled by a railing with a sign that read "Reserved for Colored." A unanimous Supreme Court, in *McLaurin* v. *Oklahoma State Regents* (1950), struck down these rules.

That same year the Court decided in *Sweatt* v. *Painter* (1950) that Texas had not provided a black law student with equal facilities by building a makeshift classroom, without a library or a real faculty, at segregated Prairie View A&M College. The Court ordered that Herman Marion Sweatt be admitted to the University of Texas Law School at Austin. This was the first Supreme Court–ordered admission of a black student to an all-white school on the ground that the state had failed in its duty to provide equal segregated facilities.

In these various decisions the U.S. Supreme Court did not outlaw segregation or overturn the separate-but-equal ruling from 1896. However, its findings did encourage civil rights advocates to escalate the attack on school segregation, placing the system under constant judicial siege. By 1952 the NAACP was pressing five suits against public school segregation. A majority of justices seemed willing to force states to honor the "equal" part of the "separate but equal" doctrine of the *Plessy* decision.

The five new suits before the high court in 1952 were eventually combined under the heading of one key case, which involved Linda Brown of Topeka, Kansas. Each morning she had to walk past a nearby "whites only" school to a bus stop where she would be transported to a "coloreds only" school. NAACP chief attorney Thurgood Marshall abandoned the piecemeal strategy he had followed to that point and likened the "separate but equal" rule to the black codes established to restrict African-American rights after the Civil War. Insisting that segregation violated the Fourteenth Amendment, Marshall also submitted research by psychologist Kenneth Clark suggesting that African-American children educated in single-race schools suffered lasting emotional and intellectual damage.

The Supreme Court heard arguments in *Brown* v. *Board of Education* late in 1952 but delayed ruling. In September 1953, in the midst of their deliberations, Chief Justice Fred Vinson died. A year before, presidential candidate Eisenhower had secured support from Governor Earl Warren of California by promising him the first opening on the Supreme Court. Eisenhower had some qualms about appointing Warren to the most influential seat on the court, but he honored his promise.

Neither Eisenhower nor most other Americans imagined how fateful this appointment would become. Warren had scant interest in legal scholarship or precedent; he viewed the Supreme Court as a unique force for protecting the weak, the oppressed, and the disadvantaged, who had little political influence, locally or nationally. Warren persuaded all eight associate justices to join him in a unanimous opinion, issued in May 1954, that struck down the *Plessy* decision of 1896 and outlawed segregation in public education. For Warren the issue was simple justice. In education, he declared, "separate but equal has no place. Separate educational facilities are inherently unequal."

In practice the *Brown* decision affected only public schools, not the comprehensive web of segregation laws that prevailed in twenty-four states as well as the District of Columbia. Moreover, the Supreme Court delayed implementing its ruling and called for consultation between local authorities and judges. During 1954 and 1955 the High Court heard the NAACP demand "integration now," while southern states requested delays and demagogues called for "segregation forever." During this interim period the Court's delays and President Eisenhower's uneasiness over the desegregation ruling helped fuel a massive resistance movement.

Warren again spoke for a unanimous Court in May 1955, ruling in a case called *Brown II* that school segregation must be ended everywhere in the nation. However, because local conditions varied, school districts were permitted to make a "prompt and reasonable start towards full compliance" under the oversight of federal district courts. Although desegregation should begin with "all deliberate speed," the court issued no timetable for its accomplishment.

Southern officials hoped that federal district judges would wink at delays and, as a Georgia official remarked, define a "reasonable time as one or two hundred years." When district judges insisted on prompt action, however, segregationists dug in their heels. In several southern states "white citizens' councils" sprang up to intimidate parents and school boards attempting to integrate the schools. Over one hundred members of Congress signed a "southern manifesto" opposing the *Brown* decision. Senator Harry F. Byrd, a Democrat from Virginia, called for massive resistance, and several state legislatures in the South declared they would defy the supposedly unconstitutional Supreme Court rulings.

Several southern states curtailed or abolished public schools, turning over the buildings to all-white private academies. At one point Mississippi and South Carolina actually amended their constitutions to abolish public education, and Virginia closed its public schools for several months. Because of resistance and hostility to integration, in 1960 most schools in the South and many in the North remained as segregated as before. Far from being resolved, the issue would become the focus of public debate again and again in later decades.

President Eisenhower did little to promote the Supreme Court rulings. As army chief of staff in 1948 he had defended military segregation, arguing that "if we attempt to force someone to like someone else, we are just going to get into trouble." Pressed by the contending factions to endorse or denounce the *Brown* ruling, Eisenhower privately blamed Earl Warren for the crisis and called his appointment of the judge the "biggest damn fool mistake I ever made."

Eisenhower's greatest effort on behalf of change came in response to a direct challenge to federal authority in Little Rock, Arkansas. In 1957 the relatively moderate Little Rock school board accepted a court order to allow nine African-American students to enroll in the city's Central High School. But Governor Orval Faubus called out the National Guard to block them. When a federal court ordered the troops to withdraw, a white mob surrounded the school, taunting and threatening the blacks attempting to enroll. Faced with massive local defiance of a federal court order—and embarrassed by Soviet propaganda publicizing American racism, which found a wide audience in the Third World—Eisenhower felt compelled to send a thousand army troops and ten thousand National Guardsmen to protect the students, maintain safety, and enforce the court order.

The troops stayed a year. In 1958 Governor Faubus closed the Little Rock schools, which reopened as white academies, in an effort to prevent integration. A year later a federal court disallowed this move. The whole episode, including vivid pictures of the howling mob and the frightened but dignified African-American students, became an international embarrassment to the United States.

The administration tried to mollify critics by introducing a civil rights bill to Congress in 1957. Attorney General Herbert Brownell had expressed outrage when a Mississippi registrar disqualified an African-American voter for failing to answer the question "How many bubbles are in a bar of soap?" But Brownell also had political motives for pressing a civil rights bill: he hoped that a debate on the question would divide the northern and southern wings of the Democratic Party and curb the influence of presidential hopeful Lyndon Johnson. The ploy failed when Johnson used his persuasive talents to convince a majority of Democrats to support the Civil Rights Act of 1957, an amended version of an earlier bill that declared support for black voting rights but offered no means of enforcement. To make matters worse for the Republicans, when Eisenhower signed the bill he criticized it for going too far, too fast. This helped solidify the Democratic hold on African-American voters.

In passing the Civil Rights Act, Congress was responding in part to a rising tide of grassroots activism on the part of African-Americans. Perhaps the most

✦ ✦ ✦

Biographical Profile

Martin Luther King, Jr., 1929–1968

Martin Luther King, Jr., a twenty-seven-year-old preacher new to the city of Montgomery, Alabama, came from a prominent family in Atlanta. His father, Martin Luther King, Sr., ministered to a large congregation and encouraged his son to pursue a broad education, including a doctorate in theology from Boston University. The younger King gradually emerged as a leader of the 1955–1956 Montgomery bus boycott because of his talents and passionate oratory. He told local and national audiences that the time had come for his people to cease tolerating "anything less than freedom and justice." Influenced by the philosophies of Henry David Thoreau and Mohandas Gandhi, King applied the principle of nonviolent civil disobedience to the boycott. He emerged from the Montgomery ordeal totally committed to the fight against segregation, and by then he had become the nation's most prominent African-American leader.

> *"There comes a time when people get tired of being trampled over by the iron feet of oppression. There comes a time, my friends, when people get tired of being thrown across the abyss of humiliation, where they experience the bleakness of nagging despair. . . . We are here—we are here because we are tired now.*
>
> *"Now let us say that we are not here advocating violence. We have overcome that. I want it to be known throughout Montgomery and throughout this nation that we are Christian people. The only weapon that we have in our hands this evening is the weapon of protest. . . . The great glory of American democracy is the right to protest for right."*
>
> —Martin Luther King, Jr., in a speech to a mass meeting, Montgomery, 1955

---

famous example of this activism was the resistance of a woman named Rosa Parks. Shortly before Christmas 1955, Parks, secretary of the Montgomery, Alabama, branch of the NAACP, boarded a bus to ride home. She sat near the front of the bus. When ordered to vacate her seat and move to the rear so that a white passenger might sit, she refused. Parks declared that she had decided to discover "once and for all what rights I had as a human being and a citizen." She was arrested for violating the law requiring separate seating for whites and blacks on public buses.

The Women's Political Council, a group of African-American professional women, knew of Parks's stature in the community and her support for civil rights causes, and they considered her case an ideal test case. The council conferred with other community leaders and decided to mobilize grassroots support for a challenge to the law by enlisting the help of Baptist ministers, including Ralph Abernathy and Martin Luther King, Jr., in a black boycott of Montgomery buses.

For an entire year some fifty thousand African-Americans walked or rode in car-pools rather than ride the segregated buses of Montgomery. Organizer JoAnn Gibson Robinson compared the immense car-pool operation to a military campaign. Boycott leaders did not insist on full integration; they asked only that passengers be seated on a first-come, first-served basis, with blacks seating themselves from the rear to the front and whites from the front to the rear. City officials responded to this modest request by indicting protest leaders for violating state antiboycott laws and by banning car-pools as a public nuisance. Terrorists bombed black churches and the homes of black activists, including King's. By November 1956 these pressures had nearly broken the movement. But then the Supreme Court overturned Alabama's bus segregation law, under which Parks had been arrested. This left the city and the bus company no legal recourse against the boycott and a financial disincentive to continue resisting integration. Thus the combination of grassroots and judicial activism achieved victory.

African-American women sparked, organized, and staffed the Montgomery campaign, but the boycott also illustrates the critical role that black churches and ministers played in the early civil rights crusade. Because segregation had excluded blacks from most forms of political activity in the South, churches were the one permissible setting for community organizing among African-Americans. They provided a base of support, local leadership, some financial resources, a common language and culture, and a sense of empowerment that could be turned toward political goals. Ministers such as King and Abernathy molded religion into a political weapon by portraying heroes like Moses and Jesus as social revolutionaries. Soon after the Montgomery boycott, local ministers organized the Southern Christian Leadership Conference (SCLC). Established in 1957, the SCLC brought together community leaders with a mass base of church membership to protest segregation.

Many other African-Americans challenged segregation by the end of the decade. College students in the South took the boldest initiative. In February 1960 four students from the North Carolina Agricultural and Technical College, after shopping in a Greensboro, North Carolina, Woolworth's store, sat down at the lunch counter and ordered coffee. When the manager refused to serve them, they stayed there until the store closed, when they were arrested.

Rosa Parks symbolized the Montgomery Bus Boycott, the watershed battle against segregation of public transportation in the South. *Corbis-Bettmann*

Over the next several weeks this tactic spread quickly. Lunch counter sit-ins occurred in over thirty cities. Many of the protesters were arrested, and some were beaten. Most of them stuck to King's strategy of nonviolence, even in the face of direct assaults. The effort yielded notable successes, with many national chain stores integrating their lunch counters. In 1960, led by organizer Ella Baker, student activists created the Student Non-Violent Coordinating Committee (SNCC). Over the next few years the SNCC would play a major role in challenging segregation.

Despite important achievements, at the close of the 1950s most African-Americans still attended predominantly segregated schools and lived in all-black neighborhoods. Few in the South could vote. Many more personal sacrifices by civil rights activists, and the intervention of a sympathetic federal government, would be necessary to affect real change.

The civil rights movement brought together diverse Americans who had fought long and hard against discrimination. Mexican-Americans also organized on their own behalf in the postwar period. Such groups as the League of United Latin American Citizens and the GI Forum resisted discrimination and segregation in the West, mounting legal challenges that overturned school segregation in California and banned the exclusion of Mexican-Americans from Texas juries.

In the West many Mexican-Americans, Indians, and other people of color resisted Anglo reformers' calls for cultural assimilation. They sought to maintain the languages and traditions that made their groups distinctive. Even as the federal government and courts began extending new support to African-Americans, the Eisenhower administration and Congress imposed several well-intentioned but ultimately calamitous policies on Native Americans. Reversing New Deal efforts to expand assistance to Indian tribes, the federal government adopted a policy of "termination" that entailed the gradual liquidation of many Indian reservations and social services. The government justified these measures as a way to reduce costs and expand states' rights and the rights of individual Native Americans.

Between 1954 and 1960 the federal government withdrew benefits from sixty-one tribes. Many reservations were absorbed by the states in which they were located, becoming new counties. The tribes now had to pay state taxes and conform to state regulations. To raise the cash required to pay those taxes, many tribes and individual Native Americans had to sell their land or mineral rights to outside interests. For example, the Klamaths of Oregon, enticed by offers from lumber companies, sold off most of their ponderosa pine forests. The Menominees of Wisconsin sold much of their reservation land to wealthy Chicagoans who built vacation cabins on former tribal holdings.

The financial gains from these deals proved fleeting. Within a few years the tribes were far worse off than before, with social problems such as unemployment, alcoholism, and suicide taking a growing toll. Thereafter, an increasing number of Indians abandoned their ancestral lands altogether. By the end of the 1960s, half the Native American population had relocated to urban areas.

As the Warren Court took on segregation, it also moved to expand the civil liberties of all Americans. Starting in 1956 the Supreme Court began to unravel the restraints on free speech and political action that had been imposed during the Red Scare. Although Eisenhower complained bitterly about Warren's liberal activism, he appointed as associate justice William J. Brennan (1956–1990), who became an even more forceful exponent of civil rights and civil liberties. Three other Eisenhower appointees, John Marshall Harlan (1955–1971), Charles E. Whittaker (1957–1962), and Potter Stewart (1958–1981), were moderates. Hugo Black and William O. Douglas, Roosevelt's appointees, joined Warren and Brennan in a solid four-vote liberal block. On occasion they won support from Justice Frankfurter or one of the three other Eisenhower appointees. In 1962 President Kennedy's appointment of Arthur Goldberg as associate justice solidified the liberal direction of the Warren Court.

The Court nullified antisubversion statutes in forty-two states with its decision in the 1956 case *Pennsylvania* v. *Nelson*. In 1957, in *Jencks* v. *United States*, the Court dealt a blow to government witch hunts by insisting that accused persons have the right to examine the evidence gathered against them. That same year, in *Yates* v. *United States,* the Supreme Court overturned the conviction of fourteen midlevel Communist Party officials sentenced for violating the Smith Act. The justices ruled that verbal calls for toppling the government did not constitute a crime.

In subsequent decisions, Warren and Brennan led the Supreme Court to impose severe restrictions on the use of the Smith and McCarran Acts. The Court also forbade the government to deny passports to accused Communists or to bar them from certain jobs. And so even as the nation's elected officials embraced social and political conservatism, a Supreme Court composed of men appointed to lifetime terms committed itself to liberal goals.

✦ Eisenhower's Second-Term Blues

As Eisenhower entered the final year of his first term, the public seemed at ease with his casual style of leadership. The Korean War had ended, Senator McCarthy was a spent force, Stalin's successors called for peaceful coexistence, and the economy was robust. Only Eisenhower's health worried voters. He suffered a serious heart attack in September 1955 and a disabling attack of ileitis, an intestinal disorder, the next June. His speedy recovery quieted most fears, however. Eisenhower decided to run again.

The Democrats renominated Adlai Stevenson. Stevenson raised serious questions about poverty, the lack of a national health program, and the administration's reluctance to fund public schools. A decade later, Lyndon Johnson would revive these ideas in his Great Society programs. Stevenson also favored ending the draft and halting the open-air testing of atomic weapons, even as he condemned Eisenhower for losing half of Indochina to communism and for not building as many long-range bombers as the Soviets.

The outbreak of an anti-Soviet uprising in Hungary and the Anglo-French-Israeli invasion of Egypt just days before the election made it seem imperative to return the tried and tested general and statesman to the White House. On election day in November 1956, Eisenhower gathered 58 percent of the popular vote, over 35 million votes to Stevenson's 26 million. The public liked Ike far more than it liked his party, however. The Democrats held a four-seat majority in the Senate and a twenty-nine seat majority in the House. Their majority was widened further by the congressional elections of 1958, which came in the midst of a recession.

In November 1957 Eisenhower suffered a mild stroke. Although his mental powers were intact, his slurred speech made his public communication even less effective than before. That autumn several foreign and domestic events called his leadership into question. After his dispatch of troops to Little Rock to protect the black students at Central High School, various critics called his actions either too great or too modest a response. The clamor over *Sputnik* prompted Democrats to ridicule Eisenhower for starving education and spending too little on space and defense projects. The new Soviet leader, Nikita Khrushchev, began making whirlwind tours of the Third World, offering aid and winning praise for his country's support of emerging nations. In 1958 Eisenhower's powerful chief of staff, Sherman Adams, resigned amid allegations that he had accepted expensive fur coats from a contractor. In Congress, the Democrats took the lead in funding the NDEA and space research.

By 1960 political discontent was percolating just beneath the surface. The third economic recession since Eisenhower took office, along with new challenges from Moscow, a Communist revolution in Cuba, and a sense that America needed younger, more dynamic leadership, gave the Eisenhower administration a tired, somewhat shabby appearance. Yet Eisenhower remained a hero to most Americans. They credited him with ending the Korean War and delivering peace and prosperity. Now they were ready for the future.

✦ Conclusion

The early postwar years were a time of consolidation for the New Deal's social reforms. Neither President Truman nor more radical reformers succeeded in winning large-scale expansions of social services. In most cases, however, neither did conservatives succeed in turning back the clock. The Roosevelt legacy of a large, active federal government was preserved.

Because of the GI Bill of 1944, which eventually financed a college education for more than 2 million students, higher education took on a more democratic character. At the same time, liberal FHA and VA loan guarantee policies helped start a postwar building boom, a key contributor to postwar prosperity. Important characteristics of postwar America were emerging: higher education for greater numbers; a middle-class population shift from the cities to the suburbs; a growing concentration of minorities in the central cities; surging interest in consumer products, such as home appliances and televisions; and a baby boom that by the 1950s and 1960s would lead to an increasingly youth-oriented culture.

For women, the heroic wartime days of Rosie the Riveter were gone. Women were turned out of industrial jobs and encouraged to stay home with their families. Although many managed to return to work, they generally had to settle for lower-paying jobs. More women attended college than before the war, but they were barred from professional advancement in science and technology, law, medicine, and business.

For ethnic minorities these years brought similarly mixed results. Native Americans faced difficulties brought on by the policy of termination. Mexicans continued to migrate to the United States, but like Mexican-Americans they faced persistent discrimination in their new country. Mexican-Americans and Indians grappled with the problem of seeking equality while maintaining their cultural distinctiveness. African-Americans made significant progress toward civil rights through voter registration drives, legal challenges to segregation, and the new tactics of the sit-in and the freedom ride. Sometimes black activists encountered violent resistance, and the legislative and executive branches took only small and slow steps to help. Yet crucial court victories set the scene for the major civil rights challenges of the 1960s.

In retrospect the fifties seem a curiously contradictory period in American life. Working-class Americans made gains as their unions cooperated with management, even as they accepted the inevitability of automation. Middle-class suburban families embraced the trappings of prosperity—the automobile, home appliances, television, sports, jet travel, and other new miracles of consumerism. But young people, inspired by their own emerging subculture, entered a period of ferment. Despite the emphasis on happy families, sex outside of marriage was discussed more openly. Women were going to work in greater numbers, not quite fulfilling their idealized roles as housewives and mothers. Intellectual critics challenged the era's conformity and consumerism, and the Beat writers dared to suggest that drugs, sex, and ecstatic religious experiences might be more rewarding than patriotism.

In spite of the country's overall prosperity, one in four Americans lived near or below the poverty line at the end of the decade, and some economists had begun to pay serious attention to this problem. By then, too, the civil rights revolution was well under way; the African-American struggle to end segregation and claim equal rights was in the process of transforming the social landscape.

✦ Further Reading

On Eisenhower and the politics of the 1950s, see: Charles Alexander, *Holding the Line* (1975); Stephen E. Ambrose, *Eisenhower: The President* (1984); Barbara B. Clowse, *Brainpower for the Cold War: The Sputnik Crisis and the National Defense Education Act of 1958* (1981); Fred I. Greenstein, *The Hidden Hand Presidency* (1982). On social change, see: Keith W. Olson, *The G.I. Bill, the Veterans, and the Colleges* (1974); Alan Berube, *Coming Out Under Fire: The History of Gay Men and Women in World War II* (1991); Elaine T. May, *Homeward Bound: American Families in the Cold War Era* (1988); Kenneth Jackson, *Crabgrass Frontier: The Suburbanization of the United States* (1985); Herbert J. Gans, *The Levittowners* (1967); Erik Barnouw, *Tube of Plenty* (1982); George Lipsitz, *Time Passages* (1990); Mark H. Rose, *Interstate: Express Highway Politics, 1941–56* (1979). On civil rights, see: Nicholas Lemann, *The Promised Land: The Great Black Migration and How It Changed America* (1991); Mark V. Tushnet, *The NAACP's Legal Strategy Against Segregated Education* (1987); Taylor Branch, *Parting the Waters: America in the King Years, 1954–63* (1988); David J. Garrow, *Bearing the Cross: Martin Luther King, Jr., and the Southern Christian Leadership Conference* (1986); Richard Kluger, *Simple Justice* (1975); Mario Garcia, *Mexican Americans: Leadership, Ideology, and Identity, 1930–1960.*

✦✦✦
CHAPTER 10

The Triumph and Tragedy of Liberalism, 1960–1968

✦ A poster urging African-Americans to register to vote.

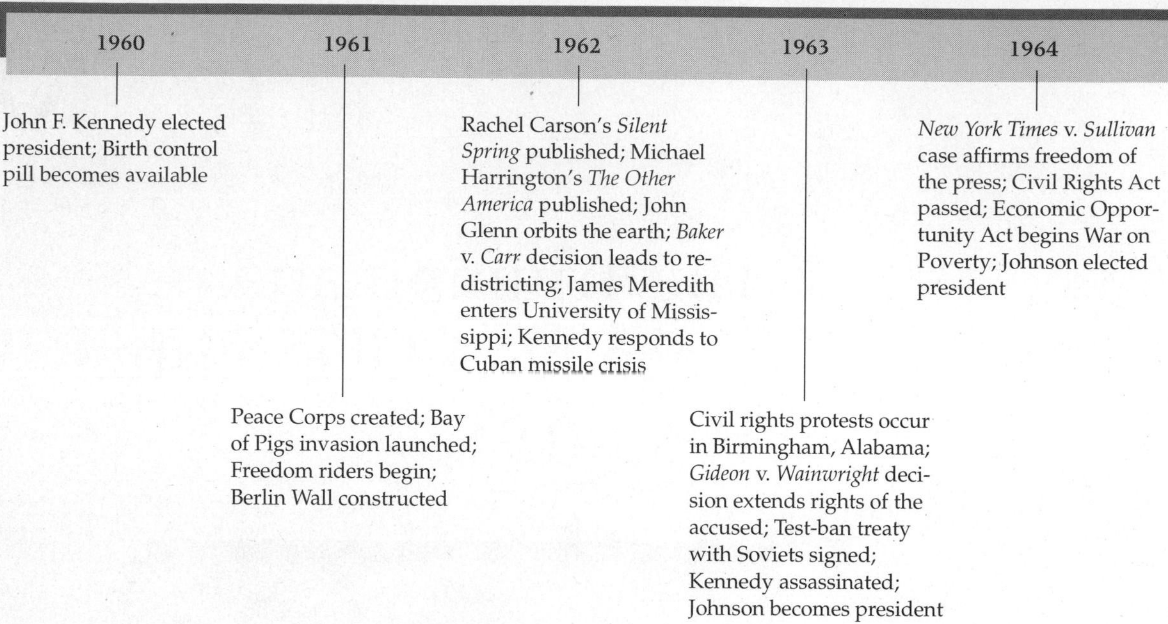

THE SECOND WORLD War stimulated the development of new chemicals and synthetics that were generally hailed as miracle products. But miracles sometimes come with hidden price tags. While other scientists perfected plastics, Rachel Carson, a marine biologist with a Ph.D. from Johns Hopkins University, spent the war years working for the U.S. Bureau of Fisheries, writing conservation bulletins. In the decades after 1945 she became increasingly worried that the very chemicals that had helped America's farmers become the most productive on earth were also spoiling the nation's fields, wilderness, and wetlands and killing the wildlife she loved so much. After writing several award-winning nature books, including *The Sea Around Us* (1951) and *The Edge of the Sea* (1955), Carson wrote a book that helped change the way Americans thought about their relationship with the world around them. She had long been concerned about the indiscriminate use of one purported miracle product, the lethal, long-lasting insecticide DDT. When a friend's private bird sanctuary was sprayed with DDT under a state mosquito-control program,

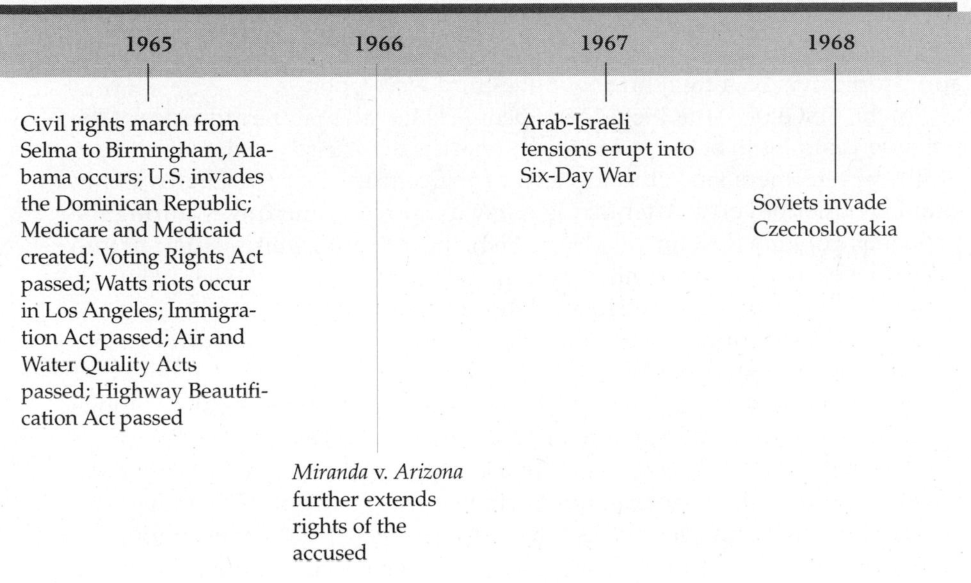

Carson was shocked by the resulting mass death of the sanctuary's birds and insects. In 1962 she published *Silent Spring,* an indictment of DDT and numerous other chemicals that were poisoning the earth, air, and water.

Silent Spring helped give birth to the modern environmental movement, one element of a dramatic re-evaluation of American society that gained force during the 1960s. The hopes and fears of the postwar generation reached a peak in the decade following the Eisenhower years. Never before had the American middle class felt more prosperous. Most owned cars, televisions, and suburban detached houses. Education was more widespread than ever: over half of all eighteen-year-olds graduated from high school, and a quarter went on to college. Yet rarely had there been as acute an awareness of the number of poor people living in the United States. A quarter of all Americans—as many as 40 or 50 million people—lived desperate lives marked by hunger, disease, poor housing, and sparse educational or employment opportunities. Conditions were worst for African-Americans, of whom more than half lived below the poverty line; female-headed families, of which about half were poor; and people over 65, of whom about one-third were poor.

In the first half of the 1960s many people believed that the affluence of the postwar years could be extended to all Americans, to finally realize the dream of liberal reformers since the the turn of the century that the United States could conquer poverty. After taking a few antipoverty initiatives during the presidency of John F. Kennedy (1961–1963), the federal government went into overdrive early in the administration of Lyndon B. Johnson (1963–1969). Six months after he became president, Johnson proclaimed that "we have the opportunity to not only move toward the rich society and the powerful society but upward to the Great Society." Over the next two years Congress, at Johnson's urging, breathed life into the Great Society with the most ambitious program of domestic reform legislation since the New Deal.

The gap between the limitless promise and the grim realities of American life intensified demands to expand the rights of many people. The movement to guarantee civil rights for blacks achieved the passage of the most important protective laws in a century. These successes encouraged others—women, students, and members of other racial or ethnic groups—to demand their legal rights. The Supreme Court became a major instrument in enlarging the legal protection enjoyed by Americans.

At mid-decade many Americans believed Johnson's Great Society lay within their grasp. It would be a place, the president proclaimed, "where the city of man serves not only the needs of the body and the demands of commerce but the desire for beauty and the hunger for community." Americans expressed similar optimism about their foreign policy. Containment of the Soviet Union and its allies continued to be the central focus of American relations with the rest of the world. John F. Kennedy won the presidency in 1960 with a promise to do more than his predecessor had done to vanquish communism. The Johnson administration intensified this assertiveness. Until the war in Vietnam escalated in 1965, most Americans thought they could have it all—both at home and abroad.

But such aspirations proved short-lived and absurdly exaggerated. By 1967 widespread public resistance stalled domestic reform. A backlash against the civil rights and student movements, combined with growing frustration over the bloody war in Vietnam, nearly destroyed political liberalism and the belief that government action could make the United States prosperous and harmonious. Instead of finding a spirit of community and boundless optimism, in 1968 Americans faced a deeply polarized society and dark prospects for the future.

✦ Kennedy and the New Frontier

Americans voted for change in the election of 1960. Massachusetts Democratic senator John F. Kennedy defeated Republican vice president Richard M. Nixon with a call to shake off the torpor of the Eisenhower years and get the

John F. Kennedy and Richard M. Nixon exchange small talk after one of their televised debates. *Ed Clark,* Life *magazine* © *Time, Inc.*

country moving again with a more assertive foreign policy and greater use of federal power at home. Only forty-two years old when he announced his candidacy in January 1960, Kennedy believed that his moderate stance on the controversial issues of the 1950s would distinguish him favorably in voters' minds from the party's liberal and conservative wings. He astutely concluded that voters would respond best to a candidate who projected energy and managerial competence and promised to lead his fellow citizens to a New Frontier. Kennedy won seven presidential primaries and took the nomination on the first ballot. He then selected Texas senator Lyndon B. Johnson as his running mate, with the hope that Johnson would help him carry Texas and as much of the South as possible.

A key element in Kennedy's campaign against Nixon was a series of four face-to-face televised debates. The first Kennedy-Nixon debate proved crucial, because most voters had never seen Kennedy before, whereas Nixon had been a familiar figure for the last eight years. Kennedy appeared not as an inexperienced youth but as a knowledgeable, self-assured, handsome candidate. His crisp, fact-filled delivery made him seem Nixon's equal and erased "experience" as an edge for the incumbent vice president.

During the campaign each man tried to convince the voters that he would confront "the Communist threat" with more determination than his opponent, and each indicated that he would oppose the Soviet Union more vigorously than the Eisenhower administration had. Kennedy deftly turned the still-controversial issue of his Catholicism to his advantage, neutralizing anti-Catholic sentiments and winning the hearts of his fellow Catholics. In a brilliant performance before the Houston Ministerial Association, he declared that, "I am not the Catholic candidate for president, I am the Democratic candidate, who happens to be Catholic."

Another gesture helped him secure the votes of blacks. African-Americans were cool to Kennedy because of his lukewarm support for civil rights legislation during his years in Congress. John and his brother Robert melted the animosity with two telephone calls in late October 1960. The candidate made a sympathetic call to the wife of civil rights leader Martin Luther King, Jr., who was incarcerated in a rural Georgia jail on trumped-up charges. Robert telephoned the judge who had jailed King, urging him to release the minister. News of the Kennedy brothers' efforts helped produce a massive turnout for Kennedy among African-Americans, who perceived greater potential in the young Massachusetts senator than in Vice President Nixon. In the November election Kennedy won a razor-thin plurality of 118,574 votes out of the total of 68,334,888 votes cast. Kennedy won 80 percent of the Catholic vote, up from the approximately 63 percent of Catholics who had voted for Democratic candidates since Roosevelt, and this gain proved important in the electoral college. African-Americans, too, helped Kennedy win key northern industrial states. Although most blacks still could not vote in the South, those who did provided crucial victory margins in North and South Carolina and Texas.

Kennedy's inauguration took place on January 20, 1961, a bitterly cold day with a blinding sun reflecting from the newly fallen snow. The new president delivered one of the most polished speeches of his life, promising to "pay any price, bear any burden, meet any hardship, support any friend, oppose any foe, to assure the survival and success of liberty." He stirred listeners with the proclamation that "the torch has been passed to a new generation of Americans—born in this century, tempered by war, disciplined by a hard and bitter peace." Most of his language challenged the Soviet Union; he insisted, for example, that "only when our arms are sufficient beyond doubt can we be certain beyond doubt that they will never be used." He called for sacrifices from his compatriots: "And so my fellow Americans, ask not what your country can do for you—ask what you can do for your country."

The brilliant inauguration set the tone of the following thousand days of the Kennedy administration. He and his family projected an image of energy, fitness, cultural refinement, and even sexual excitement. In choosing his advisers and key administrators, Kennedy appointed a group that writer David Halberstam would later call "the best and the brightest." They were young and educated mostly at Ivy League universities; many boasted impressive accomplishments in business or academia. These new stars in Washington added to the Kennedy aura. Kennedy assembled a cabinet of men who shared his view that managerial competence, not commitment to any particular program, mattered most in the conduct of public affairs.

Foreign Policy: The Quest for Victory

Like its predecessors, the Kennedy administration pursued the policy of containing the Soviet Union and opposing revolutionary change in the Third World. Discarding Eisenhower's doctrine of massive retaliation, Kennedy substituted the principle of "flexible response," designed to increase the administration's options for dealing with both the Soviet Union and leftist movements elsewhere. In 1961 and 1962 the United States confronted the Soviet Union and its Third World clients as assertively as ever before, hoping for a decisive victory in the Cold War. In the aftermath of the Cuban missile crisis of October 1962, ordinary citizens and policy planners paid more attention to the danger of nuclear war with the Soviets. Cold War tensions began to ease in 1963 as authorities in both countries looked for alternatives to their permanent competition.

The new president worried about Fidel Castro like a man with a toothache: the pain would not get better, and Kennedy could not take his mind off it. Castro began supporting revolutionaries throughout Latin America in 1960. In response, during the last months of the Eisenhower administration the Central Intelligence Agency (CIA) began planning a U.S.-sponsored invasion of Cuba by anti-Castro Cuban exiles (see map). The newly inaugurated Kennedy endorsed the invasion, with minor adjustments designed to allow the U.S. government to deny its involvement.

The invasion began at first light on April 17, 1961, when a brigade of CIA-trained Cuban exiles hit the beaches at the Bay of Pigs in southern Cuba. Despite CIA predictions of a friendly reception, they encountered furious resistance. The Cuban defenders sank many of the invaders' landing craft. Attackers who made it ashore became easy targets for Castro's tanks and fighter planes. By the evening of the first day, officials in Washington knew that the operation had failed. Within seventy-two hours the Cuban army had captured 1,189 invaders and killed 114; only about 150 escaped death or capture.

In the aftermath of the Bay of Pigs debacle, Kennedy set about restoring the image he had tried to craft of a decisive, successful, active leader. He embarked on a public relations offensive against Castro, implying that the United States would look for other ways to end Castro's regime. In the summer of 1961 the CIA proceeded with a plan, code-named Operation Mongoose, to discredit, overthrow, or kill Castro and drafted plans to invade the island once more. After a series of fantastic schemes to harass the Cuban leader by slipping him LSD or beard removers or to kill him with exploding darts went nowhere, the CIA turned to the Mafia for help. Mafia chiefs had helped the Eisenhower administration in its efforts to kill Castro, hoping to regain control of their

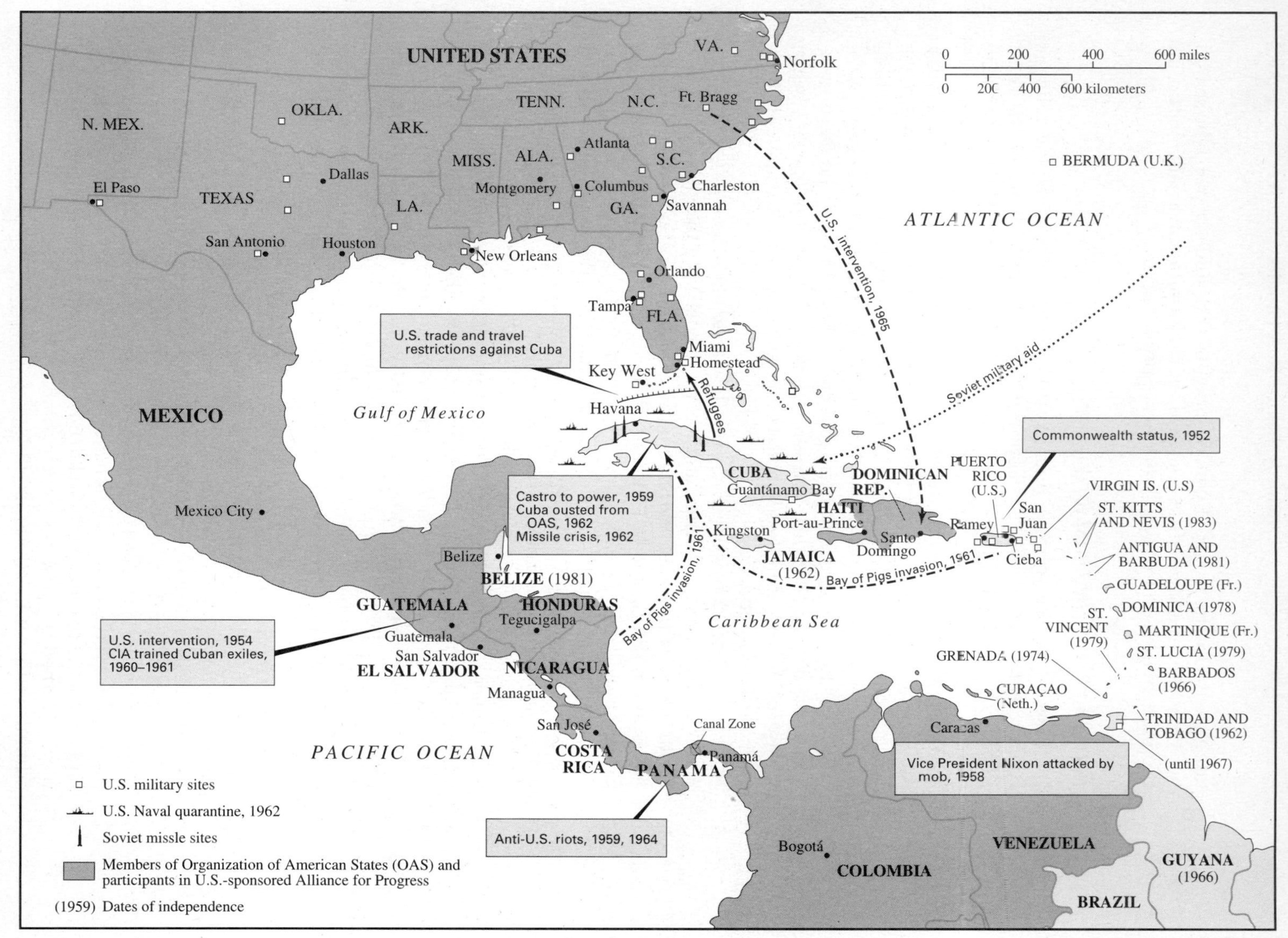

The United States in the Caribbean and Latin America During the Cold War, the United States exerted powerful influence over the political and economic life of its Western Hemisphere neighbors.

casinos, which had been closed by the revolutionaries. Eventually the connection between the administration and the criminals became too hot for top officials, and the matter was dropped. Still, Kennedy kept up the pressure in the hopes of unseating Castro.

Elsewhere in the developing world, the Kennedy administration used a variety of methods to encourage people and governments to support the United States in its global competition with the Soviet Union. During the election campaign of 1960 Kennedy had accused the Eisenhower administration of indifference to poverty in Latin America and lack of support for independence movements in Africa and Asia. The new administration sought to restore America's prestige among the poor or newly independent states of Latin America, Africa, and Asia by helping them build modern societies.

The Kennedy administration developed a foreign assistance program for the Western Hemisphere called the Alliance for Progress. Over the next eight years the United States provided about $10 billion in assistance to Western Hemisphere nations; an additional $8 billion came from private agencies. Kennedy also promised to advance political and social reform in Latin America by pressuring the region's political leaders to revise tax and land laws that favored the rich. The hopes raised by the Alliance for Progress made disappointment almost inevitable. Creating just and prosperous societies in the Western Hemisphere proved far harder than restoring modern, industrial European countries to the prosperity they had enjoyed before the Second World War.

Another program enjoyed better success. The Peace Corps, a volunteer program that reflected Kennedy's desire to encourage active commitment among America's young people, became one of the most popular government programs in recent history. Like other Kennedy initiatives, the Peace Corps originated from a sense that Eisenhower had done too little to oppose communism abroad. During the campaign Kennedy proposed that "our young men and women, dedicated to freedom, are fully capable of overcoming the efforts of Mr. Khrushchev's missionaries who are dedicated to undermining that freedom."

President Kennedy appointed his brother-in-law, Sargent Shriver, to organize the Peace Corps. By the end of 1963 about seven thousand Peace Corps volunteers, mostly recent college graduates under the age of twenty-five, went to work in forty-four countries in Asia, Africa, and Latin America. More than half worked in education, fighting adult illiteracy and teaching children. The rest helped with community development, public works, health care, and agricultural programs. The personal impact of their service lasted for generations. Some Americans learned from the exchange of ideas the Peace Corps promoted. The more sophisticated volunteers returned home with a heightened appreciation of other cultures. Instead of seeing the problems of poorer lands in terms of the competition between the United States and the Soviet Union, many returning volunteers believed that the United States must learn to understand Third World countries' own culture and history.

Peace Corps volunteer in Honduras helping a child learn to read. *Bob Daemmrick*

The Kennedy administration also intensified direct American opposition to the Soviet Union. Hoping to demonstrate his mastery of foreign affairs, Kennedy met with Nikita Khrushchev, the general secretary of the Soviet Communist Party, at a hastily arranged summit in Vienna in June 1961. Instead of the get-acquainted session he had expected to have with Khrushchev, the president found himself caught up in a dangerous crisis involving the future of Berlin.

The four victorious Allies (the United States, the Soviet Union, Great Britain, and France) had occupied Berlin since 1945. Emerging Cold War tensions had blocked progress on a formal peace settlement, leaving the future of Berlin unresolved. The city was divided into Eastern and Western sectors, and the entire municipality was completely surrounded by the German Democratic Republic (East Germany). The Western powers, however, refused to recognize the sovereignty of the German Democratic Republic or its control over East Berlin. The Federal Republic of Germany (West Germany) insisted that the two Germanies must eventually be reunited and that East Germany was a puppet of the Soviet Union. For their part, the Western powers had retained their right to supervise the affairs of West Berlin.

At the Vienna summit Khrushchev raised the issue of Berlin as a way of bolstering the sagging legitimacy of East Germany. He insisted that the victorious Allies finally resolve the German problem by signing a peace treaty recognizing the legitimacy of the Democratic Republic. If no progress occurred soon, he threatened, he would sign a separate peace treaty with East Germany, ceding to that government control over land and air access to Berlin. The Western powers had been strongly committed to West Berlin's existence ever since they had airlifted supplies to the city in 1948. The loss of West Berlin, many feared, would erode faith in Washington's ability to defend other friendly areas challenged by the Soviet Union. In addition to his tough stance on Berlin, Khrushchev surprised Kennedy by affirming Soviet support for what he called "wars of national liberation" in Southeast Asia and Latin America.

In the aftermath of the summit the United States came close to war with the Soviet Union over Berlin. Within hours after returning to the United States, Kennedy explained to the U.S. public that the Soviet leader believed that "the tide of history was moving his way, that the revolution of rising people would eventually be a Communist revolution, and that the so-called wars of national revolution supported by the Kremlin would replace the old method of direct aggression and invasion." Behind the scenes Kennedy prepared U.S. military forces for a showdown with the Soviets over Berlin. To prevent the Soviets from making good their threat to limit access to Berlin, Kennedy let them know that Washington no longer felt bound by its earlier pledge not to unloose a pre emptive nuclear strike. On July 25 Kennedy further defied the Soviets with a bellicose speech. "If we do not meet our commitments to Berlin, where will we later stand?" he asked the American public. He reactivated some reserve units, sending them immediately to Germany, and increased the armed forces by over two hundred thousand troops by doubling draft calls and dropping the exemption for married men.

While American anxieties grew, in early August events in Germany changed the course of the crisis. The constant stream of refugees from East to West Germany became a flood in July. Thirty thousand East Germans left their dreary police state for the robust economic opportunities of the West. The East German government responded to the exodus on the night of August 13 by beginning construction of a concrete and barbed-wire fence between East and West Berlin. Within three days what became known as the Berlin Wall became an almost impenetrable barrier preventing East Germans from fleeing to West Berlin. The wall would stand for almost three decades, and hundreds of East Germans would be shot trying to escape through it or over it. Yet despite the moral outrage it sparked in the West, the construction of the Berlin Wall actually defused the crisis in 1961. It allowed the Soviets and the East Germans to stop the flow of refugees with brutal simplicity and thereby avoid a diplomatic showdown with the West.

The Kennedy administration adopted a more complex mixture of military threats and diplomatic bargaining during the Cuban missile crisis of October 1962, one of the most pivotal and dangerous episodes of the Cold War. In the summer of 1962 the Cubans accurately believed that another American-sponsored invasion of their island might be launched at any time. Thus in July Raul Castro, Fidel's brother, visited Moscow and pleaded for Soviet help against the CIA's Operation Mongoose. It was in response to this plea that Khrushchev supplied Cuba with intermediate-range nuclear missiles (IRBMs) and technicians to operate them. The missiles were capable of firing nuclear warheads at targets in the eastern third of the United States.

The missiles offered little effective protection against the small-scale harassment of Operation Mongoose, but from the Kremlin's perspective the weapons served Soviet interests in several ways. They matched the IRBMs the United States had stationed in Turkey and aimed at the Soviet Union. The weapons probably would make Castro feel safer and more grateful than ever for Moscow's help. Most of all, Khrushchev believed that sending the missiles to Cuba had little cost. Since it did not matter where missiles were fired from, they really had not increased the threat to the United States, so Khrushchev did not expect the United States to risk war to force the missiles out.

Khrushchev did not reckon with America's obsession with Cuba and with the emphasis that would be placed on the Cuba issue as the fall congressional campaigns approached their climax. On the night of October 15 the CIA developed photographs taken by a U-2 spy plane that showed construction of a launch site for missiles with a range of about two thousand miles. The president saw the pictures and exploded that he had been "taken" by the Soviets, who had assured him in September that only defensive antiaircraft missiles would be situated in Cuba. The missiles had to be removed, he told his aides. Otherwise the United States would be vulnerable to attack, the public would be terrified, and "Ken Keating," a New York Republican senator who had been warning for weeks about Soviet missile construction in Cuba, "will probably be the next president of the United States."

An executive committee made up of the administration's principal foreign and defense policy officials met secretly over the next twelve days to fashion a response that would force the Soviets to back down but avoid igniting a world war. From the beginning the participants agreed that the missiles presented an unacceptable threat. Allowing them to stay in Cuba would represent a humiliating retreat for an administration committed to waging the Cold War more aggressively than the apparently cautious Eisenhower had. A majority of the executive committee endorsed the idea of a blockade of Cuba as a way of forcing the Soviets to remove the missiles.

On Monday, October 22, the blockade began. One hundred and eight U.S. Navy ships patrolled the Atlantic and Caribbean under orders to intercept and inspect any vessel bound for Cuba to make certain it was not carrying more offensive weapons. At 7 P.M. that evening Kennedy went on television to deliver one of the most somber speeches any president had ever given. He claimed that the Soviet Union had transformed Cuba into a strategic base that threatened the United States and the rest of the Western Hemisphere. The United States had to force the removal of the missiles, he said, "if our courage and our commitments are ever to be trusted again by either friend or foe."

Americans anxiously waited out the next several days. The blockade succeeded in preventing the movement of further weapons to Cuba, because neither the Americans nor the Soviets wanted the situation to deteriorate into war. The quarantine did not, however, settle the matter of the missile sites already under construction. Kennedy insisted that the Soviet leader demolish the sites and remove the missiles already in Cuba. Khrushchev offered to remove the missiles and the manned bombers, but he also proposed a swap: he would act only if the United States removed its IRBMs from Turkey. Kennedy ignored the offer of an exchange and instead repeated that the Soviet missiles had to be eliminated. Faced with the overwhelming military might of the United States and astonished that the young American president would actually risk a nuclear war over a largely symbolic issue, Khrushchev capitulated. It appeared to the relieved American public that Kennedy had won a great victory. In the aftermath of the crisis, however, the United States quietly implemented an exchange of missiles in Turkey for those in Cuba. Washington removed its IRBMs from Turkey and promised not to invade Cuba. In return the Soviets took their manned bombers out of Cuba and pledged they would never again install offensive weapons on the island.

During the crisis and for generations afterward, Kennedy won high praise for his grace under pressure and the way he had sifted conflicting advice to make his decisions. By means of skillful diplomatic initiatives that allowed Khrushchev room to maneuver, he forced the Soviet Union to retreat without a fight. The eventual removal of American missiles from Turkey offered the Soviets a small measure of satisfaction. Yet Kennedy had risked nuclear war simply to show his toughness toward Khrushchev and Castro; the missiles in Cuba never threatened the security of the United States in the way the president indicated at the time.

The extraordinary dangers brought to the fore by the Cuban missile crisis sobered both Americans and Soviets, encouraging officials and ordinary citizens in both countries to look for ways to avoid future confrontations. In the aftermath of the showdown, relations between the superpowers began to improve. In the next six months the two governments agreed to install a direct communications link, a teletype hot line, connecting the Kremlin with the White House. Kennedy abandoned some of his harsh anti-Communist rhetoric and urged other Americans to do the same. Americans and Soviets had a mutual interest in ending the arms race, the president declared: "We all breathe the same air. We all cherish our children's future." In 1963 the United States and the Soviet Union signed the Limited Test Ban Treaty, ending the above-ground nuclear tests that had resumed in 1961. The two sides promised to work on a more comprehensive treaty banning underground nuclear explosions as well. In another three months, however, Kennedy was dead. Whether he would have made further progress on détente had he lived is impossible to know.

New Frontiers at Home

In domestic affairs the Kennedy administration tried to shake the torpor of the Eisenhower years by promoting increased economic growth. When Kennedy promised in 1960 to get the country moving again, to a large extent he was pledging to engineer an economic recovery. Economic growth had averaged about 3 percent per year from 1953 to 1960, but that average masked wild yearly swings. Furthermore, the country had suffered sharp recessions in 1954, 1958, and 1960.

Efforts to bolster economic growth worked slowly, but eventually the economy expanded robustly. The Kennedy administration proposed adjusting federal tax laws to encourage private investment. In April 1961 Kennedy sent Congress a message urging the elimination of "preferential treatment of various groups," referring to the complicated system of tax deductions, or "loopholes," that had arisen since 1945. He also pushed Congress to enact tax credits for business investment, to encourage businesses to modernize their plants and equipment. At first the proposed legislation received little attention, and when Congress resumed work on the tax issue in the summer of 1963, it preserved most of the tax loopholes and gave greater preferences to corporations than Kennedy had originally requested. The revised bill finally passed in the early months of the Johnson administration.

Overall the economy began to improve in the Kennedy years. In contrast to the fluctuations of the 1950s, economic growth held to a steady 3 percent per year. Unemployment began to decline from 6 percent to under 5 percent. In 1961 and 1962 inflation also fell to the nearly negligible rate of 1 percent per year. Business leaders felt reassured by the Kennedy administration's resistance to calls for policies designed to redistribute wealth. The administration's commitment to tax reduction as a means of stimulating economic growth cheered businesses, and the enactment of Kennedy's tax bill early in the Johnson administration helped spark a major economic boom.

Although the movement of the white middle class to the suburbs continued throughout the 1960s, by the time of Kennedy's inauguration the mood had begun to change. More Americans became impatient with the ideal of the cozy suburban family home with its shining appliances, late-model car, and breadwinning father and housewife mother. Not until later in the decade would this shift in attitude become great enough to spawn a full-scale counterculture, but the trend became apparent in the early sixties.

Many Americans showed a heightened awareness of those who had been left out of postwar prosperity. Public concern grew about the plight of the fifth of the American population, approximately 25 million people, living in poverty. Largely forgotten since the end of the Second World War, the poorest Americans lived in decaying cities and remote rural areas. In 1962 Michael

Harrington, a former social worker, challenged this indifference in his book *The Other America*. Harrington decried a vicious cycle in which "there are people in the affluent society who are poor because they are poor; and who stay poor because they are poor." He spoke directly to the country's leaders, explaining to them that "the fate of the poor hangs on the decisions of the better off."

The Other America made a deep impression on intellectuals and opinion makers. Kennedy found Harrington's book a troubling critique of his own timid efforts to revitalize the American economy and make the excitement of the New Frontier reach everyone in the country. He asked the chairman of the Council of Economic Advisers to develop plans for a more vigorous assault on poverty.

The Push for Civil Rights

At the same time, the movement to end legal discrimination based on race approached its peak. African-Americans had mobilized against segregation for years, and by the 1960s their efforts commanded the attention of most white Americans, provoking a mixture of support and resistance. As public officials gradually realized how important it was to end legally sanctioned segregation, the Kennedy administration began to take steps to aid grassroots efforts. In 1961, fully six years after the Supreme Court had ruled that segregation in public schools had to end "with all deliberate speed," separation of the races remained a fact of life across the nation, especially in southern and border regions. Not only were many public schools and universities closed to blacks—so were many public transportation systems, bathroom facilities, parks, and privately owned restaurants, motels and hotels, and lunch counters. The National Association for the Advancement of Colored People (NAACP), the most prominent of the black civil rights organizations, had sought to build on the victory in the landmark *Brown* v. *Board of Education* case by persuading the courts to order quicker desegregation and encouraging Congress to pass civil rights legislation protecting black voters. The NAACP's pressure had led to the desegregation of some school districts and the passage of a civil rights law in the late 1950s, but progress remained painfully slow. After the sit-in at the Greensboro, North Carolina, Woolworth's in 1960 the sit-in movement spread, along with marches, demonstrations, and other protests against legally sanctioned discrimination.

Many ordinary citizens believed that the government would not act on civil rights unless pressured from below. By the spring of 1961 blacks and whites had joined together in a campaign of civil disobedience to force the Kennedy administration to take a more aggressive stand. In early May two busloads of blacks and whites left Washington, D.C., for a trip across the segregated South. Calling themselves freedom riders, the travelers challenged state laws prohibiting mixed seating on interstate buses and requiring public accommodations along the way to maintain "whites only" and "colored only" facilities. When the travelers reached Alabama, hate-filled opponents threatened their lives. In Anniston, Alabama, a white mob attacked one bus with pipes, slashed the tires, and demanded that the freedom riders leave the bus. The mob surrounded the disabled bus, and someone threw a bomb through the window. When the freedom riders ran from the vehicle, the mob beat them. One man was punched in the face while others stomped on his chest until he lost consciousness. Even more brutal assaults occurred later in Birmingham. The governor urged the freedom riders to "get out of Alabama as soon as possible."

The inexcusable refusal by local authorities to protect U.S. citizens goaded Kennedy into action. The violence had been photographed and shown in newspapers and on television, shocking many Americans. The president, sickened by the sight of the violence, ordered U.S. marshals to Alabama to protect the freedom riders, and the Justice Department enjoined racist organizations from interfering further with the buses.

John and Robert Kennedy expressed their greatest commitment to civil rights in September 1962, during a confrontation with Mississippi governor Ross Barnett over the enrollment of James Meredith, a black man, at the state's university in Oxford. Meredith had applied for admission to the University of Mississippi in January 1961. The university refused, but Supreme Court Justice Hugo Black ordered officials to let him in. Playing to strong racist sentiments throughout the state, the governor vowed not to surrender to "the evil and illegal forces of tyranny." He promised that Meredith would never register.

The president and his brother (whom JFK had made his attorney general) spoke several times on the telephone to the governor, but they could not reach an agreement. Hundreds of whites converged on the college town, intent on chasing Meredith away. When Meredith finally reached the campus (escorted by federal marshals), over a thousand white demonstrators blocked his path, screaming "Go to Cuba, nigger lovers, go to Cuba!" They threw rocks and bottles at the line of marshals. Then some members of the mob, now numbering over two thousand, opened fire with shotguns and rifles, killing a British journalist and injuring two other people. In the midst of the violence, Kennedy ordered twenty-three thousand army troops to Oxford to quell the rioting and ensure that Meredith could enroll for classes and study in relative peace.

In 1963 Martin Luther King, Jr., sought to increase the momentum of the movement for civil rights. In May he helped organize demonstrations for an end to segregation in Birmingham, Alabama. Police used clubs, dogs, and fire hoses to chase and arrest the demonstrators. Kennedy watched the police dogs in action on television with the rest of the country and confessed that the brutality made him sick. On June 10, during a national address focusing on civil rights, Kennedy rejected the notion that the United States could be the land of the free "except for the Negroes." He announced that he would send Congress a major civil rights bill. The law would guarantee service to all Americans regardless of race in public accommodations—hotels, restaurants,

Martin Luther King, Jr., addresses about three hundred thousand people gathered at the Lincoln Memorial to demand passage of civil rights legislation. *Francis Miller,* Life *magazine © Time, Inc.*

theaters, retail stores, and similar establishments. Moreover, it would grant the federal government greater authority to pursue lawsuits against segregation in public education and increase the Justice Department's powers to protect the voting rights of racial minorities.

To maintain pressure on Congress, several civil rights leaders revived the idea, first presented in 1941, of a march on Washington to promote civil rights. On August 28, 1963, a crowd of about three hundred thousand people, mostly black but including people of all races, filled the mall facing the Lincoln Memorial. Led by folk singer Joan Baez, they sang the spiritual "We Shall Overcome," which had become the unofficial anthem of the civil rights movement. The climax came when Martin Luther King, Jr., offered to the watching world an inspiring vision of the future: "I have a dream that one day *all* God's children, black men and white men, Jews and Gentiles, Protestants and Catholics, will be able to join hands and sing in the words of the old Negro spiritual, 'Free at last! Free at last! Thank God Almighty, we are free at last!'"

Technology: Hope and Fear

Americans' appreciation of the benefits of technology reached its zenith in the early 1960s. Yet by the time Kennedy was murdered in November 1963 fears about the potential negative impact of modern science and engineering on everyday life had grown. In April 1961 Soviet cosmonaut Yuri Gagarin

✦ ✦ ✦

Biographical Profile

Robert F. Kennedy, 1925–1968

No one embodied the restless energy of the New Frontier better than Robert F. Kennedy. President John F. Kennedy wanted his brother Robert to be part of his administration, so he made him attorney general. Robert moved like a whirlwind through the Justice Department. He cracked down on the Mafia and relentlessly pursued James Hoffa, the corrupt president of the Teamsters Union.

Robert was as intellectually curious as his older brother, but he realized more quickly that the problems of racial discrimination and poverty demanded a moral response. The mistreatment of black freedom riders in the segregated South appalled the attorney general, and he urged his brother to take action against the injustice of discrimination. He also encouraged the president to use the vast resources of the federal government to improve conditions for the poorest Americans.

Robert Kennedy seemed to die a little when his brother was slain. In 1964 Robert moved to New York and won election to the Senate. A breach soon opened between Kennedy and President Lyndon B. Johnson. He supported the Great Society program of domestic social reform, but he came to despise the president. By 1966 Kennedy had joined a handful of Senate doves who opposed the war in Vietnam. Kennedy's reputation as a

---

became the first man to orbit the earth. Americans felt ashamed and frightened. The Kennedy administration wanted to act quickly to lift the nation's flagging spirits. The president told a press conference that he was tired of seeing the United States come in second. In late May the president went before Congress to announce his goal of "landing a man on the moon, and returning him safely to earth, . . . before the decade is out."

To fulfill this mission Congress encouraged NASA to create the Apollo program, which had the ultimate goal of sending an American to the moon. In the summer of 1961 two U.S. astronauts made space flights lasting about fifteen minutes in capsules launched by Atlas rockets. Then, in February 1962, liberal hero circled the globe. A South African newspaper characterized his visit in 1966 as "the best thing that has happened to South Africa for years. It is as if a window has been flung open and a gust of fresh air has swept into a room."

After Senator Eugene McCarthy of Minnesota won a stunning upset victory in the New Hampshire primary in March 1967, Kennedy challenged Johnson for the Democratic Party's presidential nomination. Unlike Johnson, he promised voters that he would end the unpopular war in Vietnam. Within weeks Johnson announced that he would not run again, and Kennedy's popularity seemed undefeatable. But two and a half months later Robert Kennedy was gunned down by Sirhan Sirhan, a Palestinian immigrant angry at the senator's support of Israel as he celebrated his victory in the California Democratic presidential primary.

"Let no one be discouraged by the belief that there is nothing one man or one woman can do against the enormous array of the world's ills—against misery and ignorance and violence. Few will have the greatness to bend history itself; but each of us can work to change a small portion of events, and in the total of all those acts will be written the history of this generation.

"Each time a man stands up for an ideal, or acts to improve the lot of others, or strikes out against injustice, he sends a tiny ripple of hope, and crossing each other from a million different centers of energy and daring those ripples build a current which can sweep down the mightiest walls of oppression and injustice."

—Robert Kennedy speaking in Capetown, South Africa, June 11, 1966.

---

ten months after Gagarin's orbit, Marine Lieutenant Colonel John Glenn was strapped into *Friendship 7* and blasted into orbit. His success buoyed Americans, who had seen too many events that seemed to point to a decline in U.S. power, influence, and scientific pre-eminence. Glenn was a guest at the White House and enjoyed a ticker tape parade down Manhattan's Broadway, the likes of which had not been seen since Charles Lindbergh returned in triumph after his solo flight from New York to Paris in 1927. A decade later Glenn was elected a Democratic senator from Ohio.

Although Americans relished their country's technological accomplishments, they began to worry about a concern that would become increasingly important in later years: the quality of the natural environment. Some would come to believe that scientific and technological developments had actually made life worse. In 1962 science writer Rachel Carson published *Silent Spring.* Carson's work alarmed the public. Kennedy ordered a study of the pesticide problem. In May 1963 his science advisers reported that chemical pesticides had done extensive damage to the country's fish, birds, and other wildlife and that traces of toxic chemicals had been found in humans. They urged elimination of the use of toxic pesticides. Seven years later the newly formed Environmental Protection Agency banned the use of DDT, the most harmful pesticide, in the United States.

Assassination

Kennedy's endorsement of civil rights during the fall of 1963 complicated his bid for reelection in the South. As in 1960, a key state was Texas. Seeking to bolster his own standing in his home state, Vice President Lyndon B. Johnson persuaded the president to visit Texas in the fall. At noon on Friday, November 22, the president landed in Dallas. He and Mrs. Kennedy then joined Governor John Connally and his wife, Nellie, in an open-air limousine for a trip downtown, where Kennedy was scheduled to speak. The motorcade route had been published days before to ensure the largest crowd possible. Noticing the thousands of cheering people lining the motorcade route, Mrs. Connally told the president, "You can't say Dallas doesn't love you." Kennedy replied, "That's obvious." Seconds later, at 12:33 P.M., three shots rang out. Two bullets hit the president; one passed through his throat, and the other exploded through the back of his head. The motorcade raced to nearby Parkland Hospital, where Kennedy was pronounced dead at 1:00 P.M.

Later that afternoon police arrested twenty-four-year-old Lee Harvey Oswald and charged him with the shooting. A Marine Corps veteran and a lonely drifter, Oswald had recently returned from a long stay in the Soviet Union. He worked in the Texas Book Depository, the building from which the shots had been fired. Oswald had flitted among various political causes on both the Left and the Right, making it difficult for investigators to determine his motives. The likelihood of ever discovering Oswald's true allegiances disappeared two days after the Kennedy assassination. That Sunday most Americans sat glued to their television sets, watching hundreds of thousands of grief-stricken mourners file past a closed casket in the Capitol rotunda. When the networks cut away to the basement of the Dallas police station to show Oswald being escorted to another jail, millions of viewers saw nightclub owner Jack Ruby step out of a crowd and kill Oswald with a bullet to the abdomen.

In December President Johnson appointed a special commission, chaired by Chief Justice Earl Warren, to investigate the assassination. Less than a year later the Warren Commission filed a report concluding that Oswald had killed

Kennedy himself, acting alone. Despite the report, numerous people—especially among the many Americans who became increasingly frustrated with and alienated from their government during the sixties—believed that a conspiracy had been behind Kennedy's murder. But in the decades after the Warren Report, little tangible evidence has come to light to demonstrate that its conclusions were flawed.

The belief that Kennedy had died at the hands of conspirators reflected an effort on the part of many Americans to make sense out of a violent act that had deeply shaken their faith in the country's institutions. Within five years of that fateful November afternoon, Americans came to see their society as violent and dangerous. Those who followed Kennedy seemed to lack his ability to inspire the nation. Many traced the beginning of their sense that America "wasn't working right anymore" to the day Kennedy died.

The Kennedy Record

After Kennedy's death Americans quickly elevated him to the status of a martyr. His optimism, wit, intelligence, and charm—all of which had encouraged the feeling that American society could accomplish anything—were snuffed out in an instant. He was only forty-six years old when he died. Within six months of his murder journalist Theodore White had bestowed on his administration the name "Camelot." Popularized by the 1962 Broadway musical of that title, the term referred to the mythical kingdom of Arthur and the Knights of the Round Table. In this view Kennedy's 1,037-day administration represented a brief, shining moment during which the nation's political leaders had spoken to the finest aspirations of Americans.

The reality was more complicated. Kennedy and his advisers had been molded by the experiences of the postwar world. They represented a new generation nurtured by the Cold War, an activist federal government, and the military-industrial complex. Skeptical of ideology and serenely self-confident, Kennedy's officials and their circle of friends believed the nation's problems could be mastered and managed. That was their strength, because it encouraged their curiosity about different people, trends, and ideas. They learned from their setbacks and mistakes, and by 1963 their skepticism even extended to the belief expressed by Kennedy in 1960 that the United States could vanquish the Soviet Union through sheer will power. Their self-confidence offered Americans hope.

Yet the style of cool self-reliance favored by Kennedy and his advisers also entailed certain weaknesses. Their reluctance to display emotion or passion in public stunted their ability to empathize with groups that had been excluded from the bounty of American society. Although the Kennedy administration did more for civil rights than its predecessor had done, this support was largely the result of intense pressure and dramatic events that could not be ignored. On the questions of poverty and the environment, Kennedy took important first steps; historians can only speculate whether his administration would have accomplished significantly more had he lived longer. Overall his domestic program reflected a politics of consensus, much like Eisenhower's had.

In foreign affairs he also continued an earlier trend, the reflexive anticommunism of the Cold War, but with a particularly aggressive twist. His propensity for taking a tough, confrontational stance with the Soviets led the world to the brink of nuclear holocaust. Only after the near disaster of the Cuban missile crisis did he begin to move toward détente.

✦ Johnson and the Great Society

Lyndon Johnson perceived the widespread desire among Americans to distribute the benefits of postwar affluence more evenly. He had witnessed deprivation firsthand during the Great Depression, and he was strongly motivated to erase it. But Johnson was a man of many contradictions. He came to political maturity in the 1930s as a New Dealer; but he was also a veteran of rough Texas politics, which had taught him to shape his positions to the currents of the times. Thus he had often shelved his commitment to the poor to serve the interests of the richest and most reactionary factions in the Lone Star State. In his thirty years of public life, Johnson, a huge man, six feet four inches tall, big-handed, with an enormous face and an overbearing presence, had charmed, flattered, and bullied his way to the top. Rivals and political foes feared, resented, and eventually hated his abusive manner and the twists and turns of his political positions.

A Texas senator since 1949, Johnson toyed with the idea of a presidential run in 1960, but he hesitated. By the time he declared his candidacy, the week before the Democratic convention, it was too late. Eventually Johnson, reviled by many of Kennedy's most ardent backers as a southwestern political fixer and manipulator, became the Democratic vice-presidential candidate.

Johnson helped Kennedy carry Texas and much of the lower South and New Mexico. But Johnson never won the hearts of Kennedy's staff, many of whom ridiculed him as "Uncle Corn Pone." By the fall of 1963 he had seriously considered leaving the ticket in 1964. Release came through the tragedy of assassination. Johnson took the oath of office aboard Air Force One with a stricken Mrs. Kennedy looking on, her clothes splattered with the blood of the slain president. Unlike Harry Truman, who became president following the death of Roosevelt in 1945, Johnson asked his predecessor's staff to stay, but it was nearly impossible to forge harmony between Kennedy's circle and the assistants who had served Johnson when he was vice president.

Immediately after Kennedy's funeral he addressed Congress, calling for unity, consensus, and a continuation of the slain hero's vision. In January 1964 he pledged to continue Kennedy's program, but with even more of an activist stamp. Along with civil rights—the basic moral issue of the day—he emphasized the need to eliminate the blight of poverty. "This administration today, here and now, declares unconditional war on poverty in America," he pledged. "It will not be a short or easy struggle, but we shall not rest until that war is won."

Johnson plunged immediately into the effort to pass the landmark civil rights bill advocated by the demonstrators in Washington in August 1963. Despite the thrilling rhetoric of the marchers at the Lincoln Memorial, the bill languished in the Senate. Early in 1964 the House of Representatives, with the assistance of the Johnson administration, added two additional titles to the bill. One empowered the Justice Department to intervene and file suit whenever a person's civil rights had been violated. The other created the Fair Employment Practices Commission, giving it the power to outlaw racially based discrimination in hiring and promotion in firms employing more than one hundred people. The House also added provisions in Title VII forbidding discrimination based on sex as well as race; these later had a dramatic impact on reducing discrimination against women. The bill sailed through the House on February 10 by a vote of 290 to 130.

Things were more difficult in the Senate, however, where southerners and other opponents of the law threatened to defeat it with a filibuster. Johnson went to work with his legendary "treatment" to force senators to end debate and bring the legislation to a vote on the floor. With the aid of Minnesota Democratic senator Hubert Humphrey, he wooed Senator Everett Dirksen of Illinois, the Republican minority leader. Dirksen became convinced that the party of Abraham Lincoln could not afford to be responsible for the defeat of civil rights legislation. Finally, after a two-and-a-half-month filibuster, the Senate passed the law on July 2, 1964, by a vote of 73 to 27.

Johnson yearned to be elected president in his own right. He hoped not just to win but to demolish the Republican nominee. As "president of all the people," he could preside successfully over a legislative program as rich as the New Deal.

It appeared that Johnson's task would be made easier by recent changes within the Republican party. Conservative Republicans had had enough of their party's acceptance of the basic tenets of the New Deal. Senator Barry Goldwater of Arizona, the standard-bearer for the new conservatives, was a product of the newly powerful Sunbelt. Goldwater sealed the nomination with a victory over New York governor Nelson Rockefeller in the June California primary. At the Republican national convention he virtually read the moderates out of the Republican party with his famous pronouncement, "Extremism in the defense of liberty is no vice! . . . Moderation in the pursuit of justice is no virtue!"

In Goldwater, Lyndon Johnson found the perfect opponent. Choosing Senator Hubert Humphrey of Minnesota as his running mate, Johnson campaigned as a unifier and a builder of consensus. In contrast to Goldwater, who seemed sharp, divisive, and ultimately frightening to the public, Johnson looked conciliatory. The Arizona senator alarmed voters with talk of permitting battlefield commanders to have control over nuclear weapons. His proposals to make Social Security private and to sell the Tennessee Valley Authority confirmed suspicions that he was a radical "kook" who wanted to dismantle the most popular programs of the New Deal.

Johnson's victory on election day represented the greatest presidential landslide since the previous century. He carried forty-four states and 60.7 percent of the popular vote. Nevertheless, there were some ominous signs in the vote distribution. Throughout the South—the base of the Democrats' success in presidential elections since 1932—Johnson received only 51 percent of the white vote, a signal that his party's control of that region had slipped. In fact, this would be the last time that a Democratic presidential candidate would win a majority of the southern white vote. In the Deep South Goldwater's conservative appeal was especially effective. In addition to his native Arizona, Goldwater carried South Carolina, Georgia, Alabama, Mississippi, and Louisiana. White voters there were enraged by the Civil Rights Act, and grave fissures had appeared in the New Deal coalition.

The Great Society: Successes and Disappointments

Spurred by Lyndon Johnson, Congress in 1965 and 1966 enacted the most significant social reform legislation since the New Deal. Designed to win Johnson's "War on Poverty" and create the "Great Society" he had promised, these programs enhanced the role of the federal government in promoting health, economic welfare, education, urban renewal, and civil rights. Great Society programs drew on a long tradition of scientific philanthropy dating back to the turn of the century. Since that time progressive social reformers in the United States had believed that the poor were mostly immigrants whose culture did not conform to that of the dominant white Protestant majority. The poor could be helped to achieve a stable position in American society, they believed, by extending down to them the hands of the well-to-do and of intellectuals who had studied their problems. In the 1960s the federal government revived this approach, seeking out solutions to the problems of poverty from intellectuals who had studied the conditions of poor Americans. Consultants came to Washington to help draft into law the ideas social scientists had created over the past twenty years.

The Great Society was not limited to programs designed to eliminate poverty, however. Great Society legislation also served the needs of middle-class and wealthy Americans. Creators of the Great Society hoped to give everyone a stake in the legislation's success. They wanted to avoid policies that appeared to take resources from one group and give them to another.

Extending federally funded health care benefits to the elderly was one of the first and most popular of the Great Society initiatives. In 1965, heeding the president's call to improve access to health care for elderly Americans, Congress enacted the ambitious program known as Medicare. The legislation created compulsory hospital insurance for Americans over 65 who were covered by Social Security. Congress also included voluntary insurance to cover doctors' fees. A complementary program, known as Medicaid, was enacted in 1966; it provided participating states with matching federal grants to pay the medical bills of welfare recipients or the indigent of all ages.

Medicare and Medicaid gained wide popularity because they covered nearly everyone at one time or another in their lives. The programs substantially reduced the gap in medical treatment between the poor and the rich. By 1970 the proportion of Americans who had never visited a physician fell from 19 percent to 8 percent. Prenatal visits by pregnant women increased, helping to lower the infant mortality rate by 33 percent. Among African-Americans the change in infant mortality was especially noticeable, declining from 40 deaths per one thousand births in 1965 to 30.9 in 1970 and 24.2 in 1975.

In 1965 Congress also passed a spectacular array of measures directly aimed at reducing poverty. It created the Office of Economic Opportunity (OEO) to supervise the War on Poverty. Johnson appointed Sargent Shriver, who had successfully headed the Peace Corps, as the OEO's first director. Congress created the food stamp program, providing food assistance to people whose incomes fell below a certain level. The program worked well. Ten years after its enactment, research indicated that government efforts had been "almost fully effective in reducing flagrant malnutrition."

Because experts on social deprivation considered education a key means of helping young people climb out of poverty, Congress created the Head Start program to assist the preschool children of impoverished families. This too was successful. Later studies revealed that Head Start children had substantial advantages over poor children who did not enroll. They gained an average of seven points on IQ tests and were half as likely as nonparticipants to repeat grades in school or to be assigned to special education classes. Long-term studies suggested that as they entered their teenage and young adult years, "Head Starters" completed more years of school, worked more steadily, and engaged in less criminal behavior. Congress also provided aid to secondary and higher education through grants to school districts with large numbers of poor children and through scholarships and loans to college students.

To aid urban renewal, Congress created the Model Cities program, but this was less successful. As it was first conceived, Model Cities was intended to work with only six communities. But by the time it got under way in 1966, the number of cities had grown to over one hundred, while the amount of money appropriated remained the same. Powerful members of Congress channeled the lion's share of the benefits to their own districts. As one urban affairs expert put it, "the law provided too little money for too many cities" and so could not even approach the vision of its founders.

To oversee the distribution of grants for Great Society programs, Congress established the cabinet-level Department of Housing and Urban Development and Department of Transportation. Federal money made a start in reducing the grinding poverty in urban centers, but Congress did not fund the new departments fully in the 1965–1967 period. By the time the Johnson administration asked for a new housing act in 1968, much of the enthusiasm for the Great Society had ebbed. The costs of the Vietnam War made Congress reluctant to fund programs designed to replace the dilapidated tenements housing the urban poor.

Despite the many flaws of the antipoverty programs and the resistance they elicited, they had some real successes. They helped reduce the number of people living in poverty by about 50 percent in a decade. The standards of medical care improved dramatically. Education reached impoverished rural and urban children in ways that had never before seemed possible. Job training provided a means of breaking out of the cycle of poverty. If the Johnson administration did not vanquish poverty in the United States, it at least gave many Americans an opportunity for a better life.

The issue of poverty became inextricably bound up with race. Some of the most far-reaching changes created by the Great Society involved expanding the right to vote to people who had previously been excluded from the polls because of their race. Demonstrations in Alabama helped set the stage for congressional action on voting rights. For six weeks in early 1965, Martin Luther King, Jr., and the Student Non-Violent Coordinating Committee organized demonstrations in Selma for the right to vote. When marching demonstrators were clubbed and tear-gassed by Alabama state troopers, the scenes of violence appeared on national television news. For the culminating march to Montgomery, thousands of people flew in.

Johnson seized the opportunity presented by the Selma-to-Montgomery march to deliver a moving speech before Congress, calling for a voting rights act. If African-Americans did not gain equal voting rights, Johnson declared, "we will have failed as a people and a nation." He asked his fellow citizens to "overcome the crippling legacy of bigotry and injustice." Adopting the slogan of the civil rights movement, he insisted that "we *shall* overcome."

Congress obliged with the Voting Rights Act of 1965, a measure that empowered the Justice Department to register voters directly in localities where discrimination appeared to exist. Over the next three years the law resulted in the registration of an additional 740,000 black voters. The overall rate of African-American registration rose from 31 percent to 57 percent. The law eventually produced an increase in black officeholders as well. The number of blacks in the House of Representatives rose from five to seventeen in the next twenty years, and the total number of black public officials increased from 103 to 3,503.

The Great Society also sponsored programs that appealed directly to the American middle class. In 1965 Congress established the National Endowment for the Arts (NEA) and the National Endowment for the Humanities (NEH). Each endowment offered grants, both directly and through state councils, to individuals and to institutions such as universities, museums, ballet companies, and local arts centers. The NEA and NEH sponsored conferences, produced films, offered fellowships for scholars and creative writers, and funded university courses and new curricula. Together the NEA and NEH had a vast effect on the arts and humanities throughout the nation. The proliferation of local theater and dance companies, the development of many young artists and writers, the expansion of scholarly research—all of these were aided by NEA and NEH programs.

Television, too, came under the aegis of the Great Society. To improve the nation's programming, Congress in 1967 provided direct federal subsidies for public programming with the creation of the Corporation for Public Broadcasting (CPB). The CPB distributed grants to produce TV shows and helped with the operating budgets of local public TV stations. Programs such as *Sesame Street* for preschoolers and *Nova,* a highly regarded series on science, received support from the CPB. Five years later, in 1972, Congress added National Public Radio, a network of noncommercial radio stations. Those stations, and some programs aired on them, received some support from the CPB.

The Great Society also demonstrated a concern for the natural environment. Congress enacted legislation mandating improvement in air and water quality. Moreover, the president's wife, Lady Bird Johnson, took the lead in fostering a more beautiful environment along the nation's roads. She pressed her husband to endorse the Highway Beautification Act, which was passed in 1965.

In addition to its efforts to improve the lives of American citizens, Johnson's Great Society had a profound influence on immigration from other countries. In the 1960s the immigration quota system dating from the 1920s was still in effect. Its rigid quotas reflected deep-rooted racial and ethnic biases. President Kennedy had presented Congress with an immigration reform package that would have abolished discrimination against immigrants based on national origin. The bill languished until Kennedy's death, but Johnson resubmitted it to the reform-minded Congress in 1965. When it passed that year, few predicted the dramatic impact it would have on later immigration patterns. It phased out the national quota system over the next three years. In place of quotas based on immigrants' national origins, Congress substituted a system of priorities: the highest priorities went to applicants holding desirable job skills and those with close relatives (parents and siblings) already in the United States.

Because the law gave first preference to family members, Congress expected that the new mix of immigrants would closely resemble the old one. Such speculation made sense in the context of the times, but it proved profoundly wrong in predicting the contours of the next wave of immigration to the United States. Over the next twenty years immigration from Asia, the Caribbean countries, and South America shot up. Residents of these lands found the American economy extraordinarily attractive compared with the meager opportunities in their own countries. By 1979 the seven leading sources of immigrants to the United States were all non-European:

Mexico	52,000
Philippines	41,300
China, Taiwan, Hong Kong	30,180
Korea	29,348
Jamaica	19,714
India	19,708
Dominican Republic	17,519

Changes in the National Economy

In the early years of his administration, when the Great Society programs were springing into bloom, Johnson's domestic reforms were bolstered by the greatest peacetime economic boom since the end of the Second World War. Unemployment fell to 3.7 percent, its lowest level since the Korean War. The gross national product grew by over 4 percent per year from 1964 to 1966. Moreover, government expenditures and receipts were in rough balance during these years.

The boom hastened the rise of the Sunbelt. Spending for the military and for space exploration continued to flow to the states of the South, Southwest, and West. California consolidated its position as the premier defense contracting state, and Texas surpassed New York as the second. By the end of the 1960s the federal payroll in the ten states of the Sunbelt amounted to $10 billion per year, double the amount in all the other states combined.

Other businesses grew most rapidly in the Sunbelt. The oil industry, long headquartered in the Northeast, began to relocate to Texas, Oklahoma, and California. Banking also boomed in the Sunbelt. San Francisco's Bank of America became the largest in the country, with hundreds of branches serving retail customers. Alert to consumer trends, it promoted its credit card, BankAmericard, among the middle class. In 1965 four big Chicago banks started MasterCard; two years later four California banks created Master Charge. Ads urged participants to use their plastic cards to purchase everyday items—gasoline, clothing, meals—as well as larger items like television sets and lawn mowers. Eventually Bank of America sold shares of its credit card business to a consortium of other banks and changed the name of the card to VISA, and Master Charge merged with MasterCard, retaining the latter name. Wall Street also surged. The New York Stock Exchange enjoyed its greatest growth since the 1920s in the period from 1963 to 1966, with prices more than doubling in those years. But celebrations of the economic boom proved premature. By 1966 the growing war in Vietnam (see Chapter 11) had unleashed unexpected inflation. The inflation rate began to fluctuate between 2.5 percent and 4 percent per year. For people accustomed to the many years of price stability since the Korean War, this was a frightening prospect.

In 1966 and 1967 prices rose by more than 4 percent each year; in 1968 inflation hit 6 percent. Inflation hurt pensioners living on fixed incomes. It also hurt small savers, because interest rates were kept low by government regulations. At first it actually helped some poor people, because wages for unskilled labor rose faster than those for skilled workers. What seemed worst about inflation was its persistence and its tendency to keep rising. A 3 percent rate of inflation might be tolerable if it went no higher. In the last years of the Johnson administration, however, the annual rate of inflation rose steadily, discouraging savings, making long-term investment difficult, and souring the public on further costly programs to aid the poor.

The Supreme Court and Civil Liberties

While Lyndon Johnson promoted his Great Society, the Supreme Court was engaged in other sorts of liberal reforms. Still led by Chief Justice Earl Warren, the Court expanded on its work of the 1950s, enlarging the rights of individuals, altering criminal law, and regulating national and state voting systems.

Together, Presidents Johnson and Kennedy appointed four justices to the Supreme Court. Byron White, named by Kennedy, became one of the more conservative members. But Arthur Goldberg (1962–1965), Abe Fortas (1965–1969), and Thurgood Marshall (1967–1991) joined with Warren, Hugo Black, William O. Douglas, and William Brennan to consolidate the Court's liberal majority.

The Court's liberal majority required that the government show a compelling need if it were to restrict liberty. If it could not, citizens' freedoms could not be abridged. In several decisions the Court protected citizens' rights to protest the war in Vietnam. It also broadened the protection for new media to write or broadcast information or opinions about public figures or government officials. In *New York Times* v. *Sullivan* (1964) the Court ruled that the Police and Fire Commissioner of Montgomery, Alabama had not been libeled when the newspaper printed an ad signed by dozens of civil rights advocates claiming that the police had "unleashed an unprecedented wave of terror" against black civil rights demonstrators. The Court decided that public figures could claim to have been libeled only if statements about them were recklessly false and made with "actual malice."

The Warren Court won praise from civil libertarians and stirred opposition from traditionalists with a series of decisions interpreting the First Amendment's ban on the establishment of a state religion. In 1962 the Court banned states and localities from allowing prayer in public schools. Conservatives denounced the decisions as examples of judicial lawmaking, and to a substantial minority of Christians the Court's rulings were highly offensive. From 1963 through the mid-1980s, opponents of the rulings tried repeatedly to pass constitutional amendments permitting prayers or Bible reading in public schools. Although these efforts failed, they were a key element in the conservative tide that rose in the 1970s.

The Court also expanded the rights of persons accused of crimes and mandated new procedures for law enforcement officers investigating crimes and making arrests. In a landmark case, *Gideon* v. *Wainwright* (1963), the Court affirmed that the right to a fair trial included the right to qualified legal counsel. Thus if a defendant could not afford an attorney, the state would have to provide one. In *Miranda* v. *Arizona* (1966), with a more controversial, 5–4 ruling, the Warren Court gave new meaning to the Fifth Amendment's protection against self-incrimination. The Court set standards for police to follow when arresting suspects. Accused persons had to be informed in clear language (later called the Miranda warnings) that they had a right to remain silent and that anything they said could be used against them in court. Police officers had to tell suspects that they had a right to a lawyer and that if they could not afford to hire one, legal counsel would be provided free by the state.

The Court also enlarged the right to privacy. In 1965 the Court struck down an 1879 Connecticut law prohibiting the use of contraceptive devices—even by married couples—and penalizing anyone who gave advice on birth control. In *Griswold* v. *Connecticut* Justice Douglas held that the state's ban on contraception violated a long-established right of privacy. Although such a right was not specified in the Constitution, Douglas inferred it from other rights (notably, the protection of freedom of expression and limitations on the government's powers to search and seize property) that were specified. One of the Court's liberals, Hugo Black, dissented. Black considered himself a strict constructionist, and he could find no specific right of privacy among the Constitution's provisions. Black's reservations made an impression on some legal scholars, but the popular reaction to the *Griswold* decision was highly favorable, because few people wanted the state intruding into their bedrooms.

The Court also helped set rules for elections, making them more representative and democratic. In *Baker* v. *Carr* (1962) the Court declared that the size of state legislative districts had to reflect their population density. After this decision, underrepresented urban and suburban voters had a wedge with which to sue to have district lines redrawn. They based their appeals on the simple rule of "one person, one vote," and the Court agreed with them.

By 1968 the seventy-seven-year-old Earl Warren had been chief justice for fifteen years and had presided over some of the most far-reaching decisions in the Court's history. Because Warren wanted Johnson to have the opportunity to appoint a chief justice, he told the president that he intended to resign as soon as his successor could be confirmed. The president had a candidate in mind—Abe Fortas. An associate justice since 1965, Fortas was a long-time friend who, in violation of tradition, had continued to give Johnson political advice after his appointment to the Court in 1965. During those three years Fortas had become a stalwart member of Warren's liberal majority. Fortas's nomination faced immediate difficulties in the Senate, however. Democrats still held the majority, but Republicans used a number of delaying tactics throughout the summer. They expected Richard Nixon to win the upcoming presidential election, and they wanted him, not Johnson, to appoint a new chief justice. Faced with charges of cronyism, Fortas asked Johnson to withdraw his nomination in October. Warren remained chief justice until 1969, when President Nixon named Warren Burger, a conservative federal judge from Minneapolis, to replace him.

The end of the Warren Court marked the conclusion of a sixteen-year epoch in which the rights of individuals had been expanded and arbitrary government power curtailed. At the beginning of this period the Court had outlawed segregation in public schools; by the end it had expanded First Amendment rights in ways that affected the daily lives of most Americans. It had validated the growing pluralism in American life. Yet its endorsement of social change came at a substantial cost to the Court's authority in subsequent years. Traditionalists who bemoaned the pluralism the Court had affirmed attacked the justices' work. Over the next twenty years conservatives derided what they called the social engineering and judicial activism of the Warren Court, using it as a wedge issue to gain political advantage. While the subsequent Burger and Rehnquist Courts did not reverse many of the decisions of the Warren years, they curtailed many of their practical applications.

Decline of the Great Society

Despite the high hopes raised in 1964 and the amazing spate of Great Society legislation passed in 1965 and 1966, the good feelings lasted barely eighteen months. By late 1966 the impetus behind the Great Society had dwindled. Among the principal reasons for this decline were the war in Vietnam and a white backlash against the extension of civil rights.

Johnson's efforts to secure equality for all races reached their high point with the Voting Rights Act of 1965. Many observers realized that ending social and economic inequality between the races would require more than the removal of legal barriers. In the summer of 1965 Johnson spoke on the vicious circle of "despair and deprivation" among African-Americans. He explained that the voting rights law was "the beginning of freedom . . . but freedom is not enough." The reasons for the increasing economic gap between whites and blacks were complex, he explained, deriving mainly from "ancient brutality, past injustice, and present prejudice." But Johnson also placed some of the responsibility for black poverty on the cultural conditions of African-Americans. Drawing on the work of Assistant Secretary of Labor Daniel Patrick Moynihan, he emphasized the dreadful effects of "the breakdown of the Negro family structure." "When the family collapses," Johnson said, "it is the children that are usually damaged. When it happens on a massive scale, the community itself is crippled."

Johnson's speech, supplemented by Moynihan's fuller exposition of the roots of black poverty in a report called *The Negro Family: The Case for National Action,* was supposed to set the agenda for further government action to reduce poverty. Moynihan had expected that an investigation into the cultural reasons why many African-Americans and their communities remained impoverished would lead to better antipoverty programs. But that was not to be. A White House conference that met in November with the goal of expanding earlier civil rights legislation broke up in acrimony over the Moynihan report. Some African-Americans, expressing new feelings of racial pride and resentment over what they perceived as condescending meddling by white liberals, denounced Moynihan's conclusions as racist. A number of critics concluded that the report blamed the victims of discrimination for their plight. Analysts found flaws in Moynihan's methods and described ongoing strengths in the African-American family structure.

Despite its apparently condescending tone, the Moynihan report represented a serious attempt to address a complex problem. But the early criticism undermined support for it. At the same time, Johnson was being distracted by the growing problem in Vietnam. In July 1965 he committed U.S. ground forces to the war, and over the next few years, as the war consumed ever more of the government's resources and the administration's attention, the problems of poverty and racial inequality became less of a priority.

Another factor intervened as well. Already, in the summer of 1964, race riots had struck New York City and several other cities in New York and New Jersey. These proved to be only preludes of what was to come. In August 1965 a major riot erupted in Watts, a predominantly African-American section of Los Angeles. The insurrection sprang from black economic frustration and from rage at the brutality of the city's all-white police force. Nevertheless, the events in Watts shocked moderate whites, who only five months before had been moved by the nonviolence and moral force of the demonstrators at Selma. White support for racial equality began to erode.

Many whites resented the efforts during the next year of Martin Luther King, Jr., and other civil rights leaders to desegregate housing in northern cities. Suspicion was also aroused by the Supreme Court's strengthening of the rights of people accused of crimes. Moreover, the race riots spread from one city to another after 1965; by 1968, Detroit, Newark, Washington, Cincinnati, and many other cities across the country had experienced major rioting. Whites were further alienated by the militancy of a newer generation of black leaders. By the time of the congressional elections of 1966, white anger at blacks had become a key political force. The white backlash, along with voter dissatisfaction with the Johnson administration's handling of the Vietnam War, propelled the Republicans to a gain of forty-seven seats in the House of

Malcolm X, a prominent advocate of African-American militancy. By 1965 many African-Americans became disillusioned with the slow pace of progress on civil rights and, like Malcolm X, abandoned nonviolence. *Michael Ochs Archives*

Representatives and three in the Senate. The backlash had an effect at the state level as well.

Over the next two years white distrust of social reform grew. Working-class whites, many descended from eastern or southern European immigrants, came to despise the Johnson administration. As prices rose and the government seemed powerless to stop inflation, these white ethnics believed that their needs had been overlooked in the effort to end poverty and forge the Great Society. The urban riots and the Supreme Court's extension of the protections afforded criminal defendants infuriated white ethnic groups. Johnson seemed bereft of ideas to reconstruct his shattered consensus. One day after the U.S. Army had quelled the July 1967 Detroit riot, at a cost of forty-four lives, the president called for a day of prayer for "order and reconciliation among men." He created a presidential commission to study the causes of urban violence. Yet when the commission submitted its report in

1968, describing the emergence of "two nations, separate but unequal, white and black," Johnson refused to receive it.

Thereafter the Great Society ground down. The flood of legislation of 1965 slowed to a trickle after the new Congress assembled in 1967. The only major law passed was a housing bill, submitted in 1968, aimed at replacing the dilapidated dwellings of northern cities devastated by riots. This law also banned racial or religious discrimination in the sale or rental of housing. Other Great Society programs withered at the end of the Johnson administration. Unwilling to fund both the Vietnam War and the War on Poverty, Congress cut back on the latter. The president gradually lost heart too, as he saw support for the poor become a liability among whites.

Johnson's Foreign Policy

The excitement and controversies created by the Great Society and the dramatic escalation of the war in Vietnam left the Johnson administration with neither the time nor the inclination to think deeply about relations with the rest of the world. Essentially the administration continued the efforts begun earlier in the Cold War to project American power around the globe. Not comfortable with foreign affairs himself, the president relied on advice from the national security experts he had inherited from Kennedy. The United States became involved in a series of regional disputes in Latin America, the Middle East, and Europe, but these attempts to influence world affairs met with little success. By 1968 U.S. foreign affairs experts were calling for a new direction in foreign policy. Johnson attempted to relax tensions with the Soviet Union, but his efforts at détente (discussed later) came up short.

The Johnson administration reversed Kennedy's halting efforts to foster social reform in the Western Hemisphere. In March 1964 the director of the Alliance for Progress announced that the organization would change its emphasis; instead of focusing on land reform and reducing the gap between rich and poor, the alliance would try to spark economic growth in developing nations. Henceforth, he said, the United States should be neutral on social reform and protect its private investments. The United States would no longer require Latin American governments receiving U.S. support to adopt democracy when faced with a Communist or other revolutionary movement. This policy provided an excuse for allowing military regimes to protect U.S. interests in Latin America.

Besides its suspicion of social reform in Latin America, the Johnson administration also displayed an insensitivity to issues of national pride and identity in the region. Early in 1964, for example, the administration had to confront Panamanians demanding an end to U.S. control over the Panama Canal. Riots left twenty-four Panamanians and four American soldiers dead. Johnson promised Panama's president that the United States would discuss revisions to the Panama Canal treaty, but the ensuing talks made little progress.

President Lyndon B. Johnson relied heavily on Secretary of Defense Robert McNamara for advice on foreign policy. *Corbis/Bettmann*

In 1965, faced with a potential leftist government in the Dominican Republic, the Johnson administration reverted to direct military intervention. In December 1962 the Dominicans elected as their president Juan Bosch, a leftist but not a Communist. He soon ran afoul of the Dominican military, which overthrew him in the fall of 1963. In April 1965 young army officers sympathetic to Bosch ousted the military-backed government. Their more conservative seniors panicked and appealed to the American ambassador for help. Shooting broke out on the streets of Santo Domingo, and the U.S. envoy wired Washington that a Communist revolution was at hand. President Johnson decided to send the Marines and the army to quell the uprising and install another conservative government. The U.S. forces trounced the leftists and eventually helped put a conservative, Joaquin Balaguer, in power. But the intervention produced a furious reaction. At home, liberals were dismayed that the United States had resorted to using force and intervening in a way repugnant to most Latin Americans.

In June 1967 the Six-Day War between Israel and the Arab states of Egypt, Syria, and Jordan further strained America's foreign relations and created a bitter legacy. Egypt's President Gamal Abdel Nasser, yearning to recover from the humiliating defeat his country had suffered in the Suez war of 1956, looked for ways to threaten Israel in the spring of 1967. He demanded that the United Nations remove its buffer forces from the Sinai Peninsula, which separated Israel and Egypt. He sent his forces to Sharm el Sheik, at the tip of the Sinai

Peninsula, and closed the Strait of Tiran to ships bound for Israel's important southern port of Eilat.

At this point the United States stepped in to head off a war. Johnson begged the Israelis not to respond to Nasser until the United States could organize an international flotilla to break the blockade. But Europeans declined to join the effort. Perceiving only a halfhearted American effort on their behalf, the Israelis took matters into their own hands on the morning of June 5. Their planes destroyed most of Egypt's air force on the ground, while their tanks knifed across the Sinai Peninsula. The Israelis also moved against Jordan, which had been shelling the western section of Jerusalem, and two days later attacked Syria as well. Within six days Israel had taken the Sinai from Egypt; the West Bank of the Jordan River, including the eastern part of Jerusalem, from Jordan; and the Golan Heights from Syria. After the war the United Nations called for Israeli withdrawal from the captured territories in return for Arab recognition of Israel's right to exist. The United Nations also asked for a settlement to the problem of Palestinian Arabs, hundreds of thousands of whom had been made homeless by Israel's conquest of the West Bank and Gaza. Neither Israel nor the Arabs responded to these resolutions, and the dispute between Israel, the Arab states, and the Palestinians, who wanted a state of their own, became more bitter than ever.

Two weeks after the Six-Day War ended in 1967, Soviet prime minister Alexei Kosygin visited New York for a special UN General Assembly session to discuss peace in the Middle East. Kosygin also met Johnson in New Jersey. The president sought the Soviet leader's help in arranging an end to the war in Vietnam. Kosygin refused, because he wanted to show the North Vietnamese that the Soviet Union could do more for them than Moscow's Communist rival, the People's Republic of China. The two men made more progress in addressing the competition in nuclear arms. They promised to begin negotiations to limit the number of bombs each side had aimed at the other and to meet regularly to defuse tensions.

Steps toward détente went no further in the remaining eighteen months of the Johnson administration. On August 20, 1967, Soviet tanks rumbled into Prague, Czechoslovakia, to crush the Czechs' experiment with liberalized socialism. Moscow feared that Czech leader Alexander Dubcek secretly wanted to dismantle the one-party state. In the climate of hostility evoked by the crushing of Czechoslovakian freedom, Johnson decided he could not afford the political risk of meeting with Soviet leaders to discuss arms control. As in previous administrations, genuine détente with the Soviet Union remained only a tantalizing possibility.

✦ Conclusion

By the end of 1968 it appeared that the hopes of the beginning of the decade had been dashed. The excitement of John Kennedy's inauguration gave way to the bitterness of his assassination. The New Frontier had promised the country new youth and vigor in the White House, and the Kennedy administration provided these qualities in abundance. The burden of acting on the many unsolved problems Kennedy left behind, however, fell on Lyndon Johnson, a very different man. President Johnson had done more than any other president since Franklin Roosevelt to spur Americans to reform their society. The Civil Rights Act of 1964 and the Voting Rights Act of 1965 had helped remove the legal barriers facing African-Americans. The War on Poverty had reduced hunger and suffering, and Medicare had improved access to health care. Meanwhile, Johnson's appointees to the Supreme Court had bolstered the liberal group of justices committed to expanding civil liberties and ensuring fair representation in Congress. Yet by the end of Johnson's presidency, most of the early enthusiasm had lapsed. The Vietnam War was draining the government's funds and energy. Too many Great Society programs were underfunded or mired in administrative red tape. Race riots had erupted across the country, and a white backlash had arisen, blocking further attempts at social reform.

But it was his foreign policy, not domestic affairs, that ultimately led to Lyndon Johnson's downfall. As demonstrated by his administration's intervention in the Dominican Republic, Johnson believed in the usefulness of military power for suppressing leftists and Communists in the Third World. In this he was fundamentally no different from his predecessors. Yet as the next chapter explains, it was Johnson who dramatically raised the stakes in Vietnam and who took most of the blame for the American failure there.

✦ Further Reading

On politics and policies in the Kennedy administration, see: James N. Giglio, *The Presidency of John F. Kennedy* (1991); Allan Matusow, *The Unraveling of America: A History of Liberalism in the 1960s* (1984); Herbert Parmet, *JFK: The Presidency of John F. Kennedy* (1983); Richard Reeves, *President Kennedy: Profile in Power* (1993); Thomas C. Reeves, *A Question of Character: A Life of John F. Kennedy* (1991); Theodore Sorensen, *Kennedy* (1965); Arthur M. Schlesinger, Jr., *A Thousand Days* (1966) and *Robert F. Kennedy and His Times* (1978); Theodore H. White, *The Making of the President, 1960* (1961); David Knapp and Kenneth Polk, *Scouting the War on Poverty: Social Reform Politics in the Kennedy Administration* (1971). On the assassination, see: Gerald Posner, *Case Closed: Lee Harvey Oswald and the Assassination of JFK* (1993). On space policy, see: Walter A. McDougall, . . . *The Heavens and the Earth: A Political History of the Space Age* (1985). On civil rights, see: Taylor Branch, *Parting the Waters: America in the King Years, 1954–1963* (1988); David Garrow, *Bearing the Cross: Martin Luther King, Jr. and the Southern Christian Leadership Conference* (1986). On environmentalism, see: Samuel P. Hays, *Beauty, Health, and Permanence: Environmental Politics in the United States, 1955–85* (1987); Marc Reisner, *Cadillac Desert: The American West and Its Disappearing Water*. On foreign policy, see: Thomas Paterson, ed., *Kennedy's Quest for Victory: American Foreign Policy, 1961–1963*

(1989); Thomas Paterson, *Contesting Castro: The United States and the Triumph of the Cuban Revolution* (1994); Michael Beschloss, *The Crisis Years: Kennedy and Khrushchev 1960–1963* (1991); Montague Kern, Patricia W. Levering, and Ralph B. Levering, *The Kennedy Crises: The Press, the Presidency and Foreign Policy* (1983); Richard Walton, *Cold War and Counter-revolution* (1972); John Lewis Gaddis, *Strategies of Containment* (1981); Thomas Schoenbaum, *Waging Peace and War: Dean Rusk in the Truman, Kennedy and Johnson Years* (1988); Trumbull Higgins, *The Perfect Failure: Kennedy, Eisenhower and the Bay of Pigs* (1987); Richard D. Mahoney, *JFK: Ordeal in Africa* (1983). On the personalities and policies of the Johnson administration, see: Robert Caro, *The Path to Power* (1983) and *Means of Ascent* (1989); Robert Dallek, *Lone Star Rising: Lyndon Johnson, 1908–1960* (1991); Doris Kearns, *Lyndon Johnson and the American Dream* (1977); Merle Miller, *Lyndon: An Oral Biography* (1980); Allan M. Matusow, *The Unraveling of America: A History of Liberalism in the 1960s* (1984). On Great Society programs, see: Daniel P. Moynihan, *Maximum Feasible Misunderstanding* (1970); David Reimers, *Still the Golden Door: The Third World Comes to America*, 2d ed. (1992); John E. Schwarz, *America's Hidden Success: A Reassessment of Public Policy from Kennedy to Reagan* (1988); Irwin Unger, *The Best of Intentions: The Triumph and Failure of the Great Society Under Kennedy, Johnson, and Nixon* (1996); Michael Katz, *The Undeserving Poor: From the War on Poverty to the War on Welfare* (1989); Nicholas Lemann, *The Promised Land: The Great Black Migration and How It Changed America* (1991); Henry Hampton and Steve Fayer, *Voices of Freedom: An Oral History of the Civil Rights Movement* (1991). On the Supreme Court, see: Melvin Urofsky, *The Continuity of Change: The Supreme Court and Individual Liberties, 1953–1986* (1991); Bernard Schwartz, *Super Chief: Earl Warren and His Supreme Court* (1983); Fred Graham, *The Due Process Revolution: The Warren Court's Impact on Criminal Law* (1977). On foreign affairs, see: Warren Cohen and Nancy Bernkopf Tucker, eds., *Lyndon Johnson Confronts the World: American Foreign Policy, 1963–1968* (1994); Diane B. Kunz, ed., *The Diplomacy of The Crucial Decade: American Foreign Relations During the 1960s* (1994); Thomas Schoenbaum, *Waging Peace and War: Dean Rusk in the Truman, Kennedy and Johnson Years* (1988).

✦✦✦
CHAPTER 11

The Vietnam Quagmire, 1961–1968

✦ **An antiwar demonstration protesting U.S. involvement in Vietnam.**

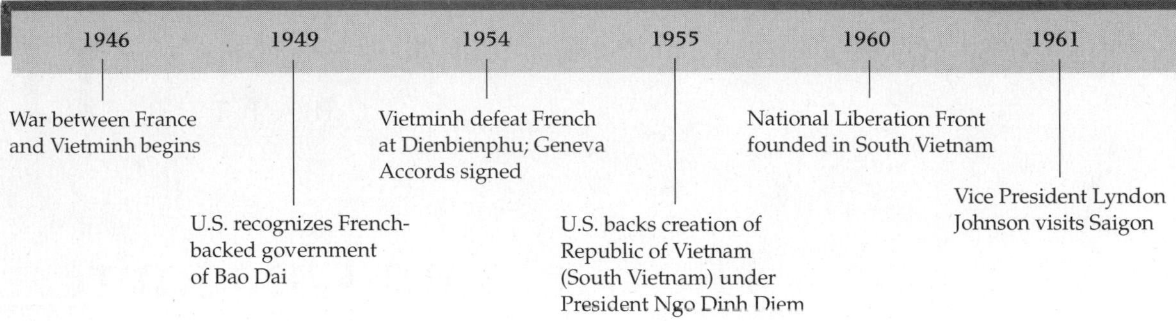

THERE WERE 540,000 U.S. troops in Vietnam in 1968; most of them were conscripts, drafted under Selective Service. That summer Paul Milligan, a young man from Des Moines, received an induction notice. He dutifully reported for service to his local draft board, but there was no military transport available that day to take him to Fort Polk for basic training. Instead he was given the job of filing case histories at the draft office. The work was light and the day was hot, so Milligan began reading the files to ease his boredom. In case after case, he discovered, other men of his same age, physical condition, and educational and marital or parental status had avoided the draft through a variety of stratagems and deceptions. Initially Milligan thought that what those others had done was wrong, but as he read on he began to feel like a fool for having allowed himself to be drafted. He telephoned his mother that night, telling her, "The whole setup is corrupt. I don't need to *be* here! I don't need to *be* here! I don't need to *be* here! I simply didn't *need* to be drafted!" But two months later Milligan went to Vietnam, where he became one of the more than fifty thousand American soldiers killed.

In the 1960s American involvement in the war in Vietnam grew from a minor issue of little interest to most people into a frightening nightmare affecting nearly every aspect of American life. Popular anguish over the

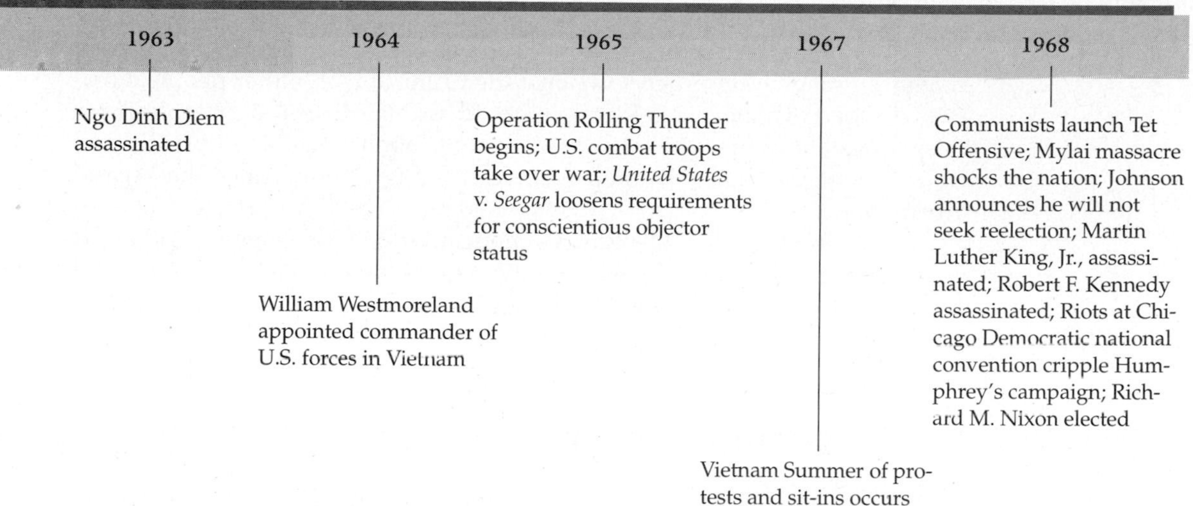

seemingly endless war opened deep fissures in many enduring political, social, cultural, and religious institutions. Chapter 12 explores the culture of protest that the Vietnam War helped to foster; this chapter focuses on the war itself and its meaning for American politics and foreign policy.

From the beginning of American involvement in Southeast Asia in the late 1940s until Lyndon Johnson decided that because of the war he could not win reelection in 1968, U.S. politicians, diplomats, and military leaders consistently misunderstood the rapidly changing conditions in Vietnam. Their failure to grasp the intensity of the revolutionary nationalism in Southeast Asia led to futile attempts to create a non-Communist regime in the southern half of Vietnam. In the devastating war that ensued, American bombs, guns, and money ruined Vietnam physically, economically, and socially. The seemingly endless conflict also took a profound toll on many of the American soldiers who fought it.

As the war dragged on, Americans at home became sick of the brutal and inconclusive fighting. Their revulsion at the war gradually led to a widespread loss of faith in government and authority. Public frustration eroded the general consensus on foreign policy developed in earlier decades. Many Americans continued to believe that the United States should oppose communism and revolution abroad, but they became disillusioned with the war in Vietnam because it made little progress against the Communists. Other people, however, decided that the war in Vietnam should not have been fought at all. These misgivings about Vietnam spread into doubts about the overall principle of containment that had governed American foreign policy since the Second World War.

In the 1968 presidential election Americans voted for change, hoping that a new administration could extricate them from the Vietnamese morass. But more than four years—and another presidential election—would pass before a cease-fire agreement was signed.

✦ The Growth of American Commitment in Vietnam, 1945–1964

Like most other Americans in the years after 1945, Kennedy believed that containment of communism should be the principal goal of American foreign policy. But precisely because the involvement in Vietnam represented only a small part of that larger strategy, Americans never thought deeply about events in Vietnam until the United States was deeply involved in the war. From Truman through Kennedy, each administration gradually enlarged the U.S. commitment in Vietnam, setting the stage for a dramatic escalation under Lyndon Johnson.

The United States had backed alternatives to the Communist Democratic Republic of Vietnam (North Vietnam) ever since its inception on September 2, 1945, the day the Second World War ended in Asia. The Truman administration, preoccupied with more pressing issues in Europe and other parts of Asia, paid little attention to North Vietnam's charismatic leader, Ho Chi Minh, and his government in Hanoi. The United States spurned North Vietnam's pleas for diplomatic recognition. During 1946 war broke out between Ho's Vietminh nationalist-Communist guerrillas and French troops, who were trying to re-establish France's colonial power in Indochina. Despite some uneasiness about supporting colonial rule, the Truman administration backed France and its puppet Vietnamese regime. By the end of 1952 Washington was paying 40 percent of the cost of the war.

During the Eisenhower administration the French required even more American aid. Despite the confident assertion of Secretary of State John Foster Dulles that an additional infusion of $400 million would help France "break the organized body of Communist aggression by the end of the 1955 fighting season," the Vietminh gained strength. By March 1954 the United States was paying 70 percent of the cost of the war, yet the French military position at Dienbienphu became desperate. As noted in Chapter 8, Eisenhower toyed with the idea of launching a U.S. air strike or ground invasion but ultimately held off, and the Vietminh overran Dienbienphu on May 7, 1954.

Although Dienbienphu was a catastrophe for France, Washington almost welcomed the defeat, for it provided a high-profile opportunity to demon-

Ho Chi Minh, the leader of the Democratic Republic of Vietnam (North Vietnam), whose forces defeated first the French and then the Americans. *Howard Sochurek,* Life *magazine © Time, Inc.*

strate American anti-Communist resolve. Unlike France, which was tainted in the region as a colonial power, the United States could sponsor a so-called third force composed of Vietnamese nationalists who opposed both the Communists and the French. This was the approach Eisenhower had in mind when a peace conference between France and the Vietminh convened at Geneva, Switzerland. Although the United States sent representatives to the conference, it was not a signatory to the Geneva Accords. Indeed, it soon helped to undermine them.

Nation Building in South Vietnam, 1954–1960

The Geneva Accords temporarily partitioned Vietnam along the seventeenth parallel. Following the conference the United States became more deeply involved in Southeast Asia than ever. In late 1954 the Eisenhower administration sponsored the creation of the Southeast Asia Treaty Organiza-

The United States supported Ngo Dinh Diem, President of the Republic of Vietnam (South Vietnam), from 1954 until 1963. *Corbis/Bettmann*

tion (SEATO), a military alliance roughly patterned on NATO. Although the Republic of Vietnam (South Vietnam) never formally joined SEATO, the United States based its involvement in Vietnamese politics partly on the South's having accepted protection from the alliance. Washington helped install Ngo Dinh Diem as prime minister of the state of Vietnam. Diem then proclaimed the creation of the new nation of the Republic of Vietnam in the South, with Saigon as its capital and himself as its president. In 1956 the United States supported Diem when he refused to allow the nationwide unification elections promised by the Geneva agreements. The United States further assisted Diem in creating the Army of the Republic of Vietnam (ARVN) and a South Vietnamese police force.

Eisenhower publicly advanced what came to be known as the domino theory: if Vietnam fell to communism, he said, the rest of Indochina and then Southeast Asia would topple like a row of dominoes. General J. Lawton Collins, the special U.S. representative to Vietnam, recommended in 1955 that Washington withdraw its support from the haughty, unpopular Diem, a Catholic in a predominantly Buddhist land; but Secretary of State Dulles declared that "the decision to back Diem has gone to the point of no return."

Vowing to exterminate vestiges of the popular Vietminh in the South, Diem had his army and police arrest twenty thousand former members of the movement and kill over a thousand in a span of three years. These bald actions won praise from American lawmakers looking for effective anti-Communist action in Southeast Asia. Senator John F. Kennedy, for example, glorified the new South Vietnam as "the cornerstone of the Free World in Southeast Asia, the keystone to the arch, the finger in the dike."

Despite such backing for Diem in the United States, the remnants of the Vietminh, assisted by North Vietnam, managed to challenge his regime. On December 20, 1960, they founded the National Front for the Liberation of Vietnam (NLF) and began guerrilla attacks against the South. By mid-1961 NLF forces, referred to as the Vietcong by the South Vietnamese, had succeeded in gaining control of 58 percent of the territory of South Vietnam.

The Kennedy Administration and Vietnam, 1961–1963

When he became president, Kennedy decided that the Eisenhower administration had not done enough to help Diem. The new American president saw the conflict in Vietnam as a pivotal part of the global struggle between the United States and the Soviet Union. After the catastrophic Bay of Pigs invasion and the chilly 1961 summit with Nikita Khrushchev in Vienna, he especially desired some measure of success against the Communists in Vietnam. Some of his staff suggested using the army's Special Forces, or Green Berets, against the Vietminh. Walt Rostow, a member of the National Security Council and formerly an economist at the Massachusetts Institute of Technology, recommended making South Vietnam a showcase of Third World capitalist development by helping it industrialize.

Kennedy responded with an additional $42 million beyond the $220 million already being spent annually to aid South Vietnam. He sent hundreds more troops to advise the ARVN on how to fight, and he ordered four hundred Green Berets to lead nine thousand mountain tribesmen in an effort to stop Vietcong infiltration from North Vietnam. He also directed the CIA to conduct commando raids against North Vietnam. The United States provided heavy weapons to South Vietnamese provincial civil guards (local militias) to use against the Vietcong in rural areas. By late 1961 there were 3,205 American advisers in South Vietnam, and that number rose to 9,000 the next year. The American advisers, who did not limit their activities to advising, helped the ARVN move hundreds of thousands of peasants from their homes to "strategic hamlets."

Massing peasants into strategic hamlets made it easier for the South Vietnamese government to hunt for NLF fighters, but it also gave the NLF a weapon in its propaganda war against Saigon. Once the rural people were installed in the hamlets, separating them from land their families had tilled for generations, South Vietnamese forces bombed and napalmed the countryside to terrify and exterminate the NLF. Despite the use of strategic hamlets,

The ritual suicide of Buddhist monks protesting the authoritarian regime of South Vietnam stunned the world and diminished American support for President Ngo Dinh Diem. *Corbis/Bettmann*

thousands of civilians, including women and children, lost their lives. The NLF used the destruction of the countryside to its own advantage by telling peasants that the Saigon government was bombing and burning its own citizens. Yet General Paul D. Harkins, in charge of the American advisory forces, dismissed complaints that indiscriminate bombing only alienated the population from the Saigon government. Napalm, he said, "really puts the fear of God into the Vietcong, and that is what counts."

While Harkins kept up a stream of optimistic reports on progress against the NLF, American field advisers grew disgusted with what they considered the cowardice and corruption of the ARVN and the South Vietnamese government. ARVN officers showed more interest in stealing their subordinates' pay than in engaging the NLF. On January 2, 1963, the NLF scored a huge triumph against the ARVN at the battle of Ap Bac, twenty miles from Saigon. By mid-1963 the Kennedy administration, once so supportive of Ngo Dinh Diem, viewed him and his family as obstacles to success against the NLF. The Vietnamese peasantry disdained the strategic hamlets and hated Diem's connections to the old landlord class. Leaders of the Buddhist sects, who composed over two-thirds of the population of the South, condemned his pro-Catholic policies and demanded Diem's resignation. Buddhists and students led street demonstrations against the government in June; the police responded with clubs and tear gas. On June 11 a seventy-three-year-old Buddhist monk, Thich Quang Duc, turned the Buddhist uprising from a local affair into an international crisis by immolating himself in the middle of a busy Saigon intersection. His ritual suicide was captured on film and broadcast around the world. Americans reacted with horror. Senator Frank Church, an Idaho Democrat, told the Senate that "such grisly scenes have not been witnessed since the Christian martyrs marched hand-in-hand into the Roman arenas." President Diem's sister-in-law, Madame Ngo Dinh Nhu, provoked further outrage against Diem and his family when she told American journalists that she would be "happy to provide the mustard for the monks' next barbecue."

By August 1963 the Kennedy administration had decided that General Collins had been right eight years before: Diem's family, known as the Ngo family, must either change its ways and broaden its government to include nonfamily members and non-Catholics or be removed from office. That summer, to secure Republican support for his policies, the president appointed an old Republican rival, Henry Cabot Lodge, as the new ambassador to South Vietnam. The day after his arrival in Saigon, Lodge encouraged a plot by some of the ARVN's top generals to oust the Ngos, but the generals aborted their plans in fear that Diem had discovered the plot.

Diem dug in his heels and turned on the Americans. His brother Nhu hinted darkly at a deal with North Vietnam that would leave the Ngo family in charge of a neutralized South Vietnam. At this point Ambassador Lodge, in Saigon, along with Secretary of Defense Robert McNamara and Assistant Secretary of State for Far Eastern Affairs Roger Hilsman, the officials in Washington most concerned with Vietnam policy, decided to encourage the dissident ARVN generals to reactivate their plans for a coup. On November 1, 1963, the plotters seized control of the presidential palace and captured Diem and Nhu. Informed in advance of the coup, Ambassador Lodge did little to offer the Ngos safe conduct out of the country. Instead they were murdered by the plotters early on the morning of November 2, and a new government, headed by General Duong Van Minh, took over.

Despite later claims by some of Kennedy's political advisers that Kennedy would have reduced the American military commitment in Vietnam after the election of 1964, the president remained dedicated to achieving victory over the Communists up to the date of his assassination, three weeks after Diem's death. All in all, the Kennedy administration bequeathed Lyndon Johnson a terrible burden with its policies in South Vietnam. Sixteen thousand U.S. Army, Navy, and Marine Corps "advisers" were conducting daily operations against the NLF, who nevertheless continued to increase their control over the countryside. Increased American efforts produced diminishing returns. The more fighting American soldiers did, the less the ARVN and its officers seemed willing to do. The government of South Vietnam enjoyed little support, except from a coterie of ARVN generals who preferred ease in Saigon to fighting in the field. In the countryside, where over 80 percent of the population resided, the national government had become at best a nuisance and more often the enemy. Many Vietnamese peasants had lost patience and perhaps hope. Despite Kennedy's pleas for Americans not to weary of the war, his successor would have a difficult time pursuing the vision of a victorious Republic of Vietnam.

The Tonkin Gulf Resolution

Soon the new South Vietnamese government of Duong Van Minh proved no more amenable to American advice than had Ngo Dinh Diem and his family. The resistance of the Saigon government to American suggestions for waging the war presented the new Johnson administration with an exquisite dilemma, one it never resolved. The South Vietnamese authorities seemed incapable of winning the war by themselves, so they needed American assistance. Yet the more the Americans helped, the less the South Vietnamese did for themselves, thereby encouraging the Americans to get more deeply involved. The growing U.S. presence, in turn, helped validate the propaganda claims of the NLF and the North Vietnamese that the South Vietnamese authorities were American puppets. New to the presidency and trying to follow Kennedy's policies, Lyndon Johnson relied on the advice of his predecessor's foreign policy experts. Almost to a man they believed that the United States needed to increase its presence in South Vietnam, pursue the war more vigorously, and, if necessary, replace General Minh with someone more compliant with Washington's desires. Early in 1964 Walt Rostow, the head of the State Department's policy planning staff, urged "a direct political-military showdown with Hanoi" before the end of the year. The president, facing an election campaign, favored delay, hoping to keep Vietnam off the front pages and the evening news. The president was not willing to turn away from the militant course his subordinates favored, but neither did he want to disrupt the consensus among the voters that he expected would carry him to victory in the fall.

As Johnson procrastinated, U.S. military and diplomatic planners moved to alter the military situation in South Vietnam. In late January 1964 the Pentagon helped engineer another coup in Saigon, one that replaced General Minh with General Nguyen Khanh, who the Americans thought would aggressively fight the North Vietnamese. In June 1964 some of the president's principal advisers floated the idea of pursuing a congressional resolution supporting American air or ground action against North Vietnam. Six weeks later, after the raucous Republican convention had nominated Senator Barry Goldwater for president, two controversial incidents off the coast of North Vietnam justified the introduction of just such a resolution and provided an excuse for air strikes by U.S. forces against North Vietnamese naval bases and oil storage facilities. Two U.S. destroyers, the *Maddox* and the *C. Turner Joy,* had been conducting patrols supporting South Vietnamese naval operations along the North Vietnamese coast, bordering the Gulf of Tonkin (see map). The patrols provoked the North Vietnamese navy to attack the *Maddox* on the night of August 2, 1964. Two nights later, in heavy seas, the commander of the *C. Turner Joy* thought his ship was under attack and ordered his crew to return fire. They did so but hit nothing, probably because no North Vietnamese patrol boats were in the area and there had been no hostile fire. As Johnson later acknowledged, "For all I know, our navy may have been shooting at whales out there." The assault on the *Maddox* did occur, although Secretary of Defense McNamara was not telling the truth when he asserted that "the *Maddox* was operating in international waters and was carrying out a routine patrol of the type we carry out all over the world at all times."

Despite the falsehoods, McNamara's claims carried the day in Congress, which passed the Tonkin Gulf Resolution on August 7. The House voted unanimously in favor of this legislation, and in the Senate only two members, Oregon Democrat Wayne Morse and Alaska Democrat Ernest Gruening, voted against it. The resolution authorized the president to "take all necessary measures to repel any armed attack against the forces of the United States and to prevent further aggression." The resolution also permitted "all necessary steps, including the use of armed force," to assist any member of SEATO that asked for American military aid. Although South Vietnam was not in fact a member of SEATO, the alliance had agreed to extend its protection to South Vietnam.

The resolution's extraordinarily broad grant of authority to the nation's chief executive had no time limit. Later Johnson would use it to justify greatly enlarged American participation in the war. Senator Morse predicted that the other lawmakers would eventually regret having approved such a blank check for Vietnam. One who did was J. William Fulbright, an Arkansas Democrat and chairman of the Senate Foreign Relations Committee, who presented the resolution on the Senate floor. Within a year he opposed further U.S. participation in the war. He later lamented that he was "hoodwinked and taken in by the president of the United States, the Secretary of State and the Chief of Staff and the Secretary of Defense," who had lied to him about what had happened in the Gulf of Tonkin. Had he known the truth, he suggested, he would not have supported the resolution.

The Tonkin Gulf Resolution removed Vietnam from the political debate during the 1964 election campaign. Goldwater, who had earlier berated Johnson for being timid in Vietnam and had even suggested possibly using nuclear weapons against North Vietnam, fully supported the Tonkin Gulf Resolution and the limited air raid Johnson ordered against North Vietnam. For his part, Johnson stood serenely in the middle of the road on Vietnam. Most Americans believed he wanted to keep the United States out of a full-scale shooting war but still prevent a Communist victory. His major campaign speech on Vietnam sounded moderate, but it left considerable room for greater American involvement at a later date. He said that "only as a last resort" would he "start dropping bombs around that are likely to involve

American boys in a war in Asia with 700 million Chinese." He could not guarantee the future, he said, but "we are not going [to go] north and drop bombs at this stage of the game, and we are not going [to go] south and run out and leave it for the Communists to take over."

✦ Escalation of the War

The year 1965 marked the point of no return for the United States in Vietnam. By July Johnson had made a series of fateful decisions that transformed the fighting in Vietnam into an American war. Nevertheless, throughout the period of gradually increasing American military involvement in Vietnam (or "escalation," as it was called), the Johnson administration attempted to wage a "limited war." Johnson wanted to break the will of the North Vietnamese without provoking a military response from the Soviet Union or China (see map). Administration officials believed that limiting the extent of the war would lessen the impact on the American public, making it easier to sustain political support for the war. It proved nearly impossible, however, to wage a limited war effectively. Every step up the ladder of escalation alarmed potential adversaries abroad and created new anxieties at home. And efforts to restrict the scope of the war relieved pressure on North Vietnam and generated opposition from those Americans who wanted to defeat North Vietnam quickly with the use of massive military power.

The Americanization of the War, 1965

In February 1965 Johnson authorized a sustained bombing campaign against the North. That summer he took the final steps toward committing one hundred thousand U.S. ground troops to the war. No longer would the fiction be maintained that American soldiers acted only as advisers to the ARVN; U.S. forces would be conducting wide-scale operations on their own, without accompanying ARVN units. Undersecretary of State George Ball, one of the few high officials skeptical of the importance of Vietnam and doubtful that the United States could prevail, said the United States was "on the tiger's back" in Vietnam. It would prove difficult, he warned, to decide "where to dismount."

Facing perpetual weakness and change in the South Vietnamese government, Pentagon planners concluded that bombing the North would help to save the South. General Maxwell Taylor, now ambassador to South Vietnam, told Johnson early in 1965 that air raids against the North would "inject some life into the dejected spirits" of the South Vietnamese. Taylor thought bombing would "bring pressure on the will of the chiefs of the DRV [Ho Chi Minh and his advisers]. As practical men, they cannot wish to see the fruits of ten years of labor destroyed by slowly escalating air attacks."

Vietnam During the War Vietnamese nationalists and revolutionaries fought a thirty-year war, first against the French and then against the Americans.

On February 7, 1965, a company of Vietcong soldiers attacked the barracks of the American advisers at Pleiku in the central highlands of South Vietnam, killing 8 Americans, wounding 126, and destroying ten planes. The Pleiku attack provided the justification for sustained bombing of the North. Johnson first ordered a single retaliatory mission similar to the one undertaken after the Gulf of Tonkin incident the previous August, but this did not stop calls for harsher action. On February 13 Johnson authorized Operation Rolling Thunder, and sustained bombing of the North began. In April American and South Vietnamese pilots flew 3,600 sorties against targets in the North—fuel depots, railroad yards, bridges, power plants, and munitions factories.

For the remainder of his term Johnson worried about provoking Chinese intervention in the war, with a repeat of the disastrous consequences the United States had suffered in Korea. To minimize the risk of Chinese interference, Johnson avoided bombing close to China's border with Vietnam. For the same reason, he denied repeated military requests to invade North Vietnam with ground troops. Such precautions worked, and China and the Soviet Union did not go beyond supplying North Vietnam with weapons. Yet air war advocates within the U.S. military believed that Johnson acted too cautiously. They doubted that the Chinese or Soviets intended to enter the war, and they believed the restrictions on bombing targets limited the effectiveness of the air campaign.

Rolling Thunder delivered little more than temporary relief from Vietcong success, so the American commander in South Vietnam, General William Westmoreland, called for direct American ground action throughout the South. But Johnson still resisted a full Americanization of the war, and at a speech at Johns Hopkins University in April 1965 he offered to have "unconditional discussions" with North Vietnam to end the war.

By June 1965 Westmoreland wanted another 150,000 troops deployed to fight the ground war throughout the South. Throughout July Johnson consulted with his principal advisers on the best course to take in Vietnam. Johnson was skeptical of the usefulness of supplying additional American troops, but he was unwilling to accept an NLF victory. The only course he could tolerate, therefore, was continued gradual increases in the American commitment—the very policy that had failed over the previous year. He hoped to keep the build-up as quiet as possible to avoid a raucous debate in the press or in Congress and to prevent public disillusionment of the sort that had wrecked the Truman administration during the Korean War. He also worried that a congressional debate on Vietnam would ruin his plans for the Great Society.

During the July meetings the president said to General Earle Wheeler, chairman of the Joint Chiefs of Staff, "Tell me this. What will happen if we put in one hundred thousand more men and then two, three years later, you tell me you need five hundred thousand more? How would you expect me to respond to that? And what makes you think Ho Chi Minh won't put in another one hundred thousand and match us every bit of the way?" Wheeler responded, "This means greater bodies of men from North Vietnam, which will allow us to cream them." Johnson's fear proved prophetic, and Wheeler's reply foretold some of the folly of the commanders' later efforts to win the war by killing more and more Vietnamese fighters.

Undersecretary of State George Ball offered the most spirited dissent, explaining that the United States could not win in Vietnam. He predicted that the struggle would be a protracted one, as in the Korean War, and that once again public opinion would turn against an inconclusive war. The United States would lose prestige around the world, he warned, when it became obvious that its vast military could not defeat a guerrilla force.

Eventually, though, all of the rest of the president's advisers concurred that adding one hundred thousand Americans to the ninety thousand troops already in Vietnam would help stabilize the situation without causing a backlash against the war in Congress or among the public. Most agreed to reject the request from the Joint Chiefs of Staff to call up the army reserves. Such a move would dramatically raise the stakes at home and abroad, perhaps necessitating a presidential declaration of a state of emergency and a request for several billion dollars. In that event, Johnson worried, the Great Society would die, and worse, Hanoi would likely ask the Chinese and the Soviets for more aid.

At the end of July Johnson decided to inform congressional leaders that he intended to send another one hundred thousand men by the end of the year, without calling up reserve units. With few exceptions, Republican and Democratic leaders in Congress supported the move. Speaker of the House John McCormack thought there was no alternative. "The lesson of Hitler and Mussolini is clear," he reflected. Senator Russell Long, a conservative Democrat from Louisiana, wondered, "If a nation with 14 million can make Uncle Sam run, what will China think?" Only Senator Mike Mansfield of Montana, Johnson's successor as majority leader and an early supporter of Diem, doubted the wisdom of Americanizing the war: "Whatever pledge we had was to *assist* [South Vietnam] in its own defense. Since then there has been no government of legitimacy. . . . We owe this government nothing." Mansfield also pointed out the limited American stakes in Vietnam. Even if the United States won the war, Mansfield said, "what have you achieved? It is by no means a 'vital' area of U.S. concern." Johnson was unpersuaded by Mansfield, and at a low-key midday press conference on July 28, 1965, he announced the deployment of the additional troops.

Fighting the War, 1966–1967

During 1966 and 1967 the number of U.S. troops in South Vietnam rose from 190,000 to 535,000 (see figure). Yet even this force could not prevail against the NLF, and it actually contributed to the deterioration of the government and armed forces of South Vietnam. The Americans were trying to apply lessons learned in conventional wars—particularly the Second World War and

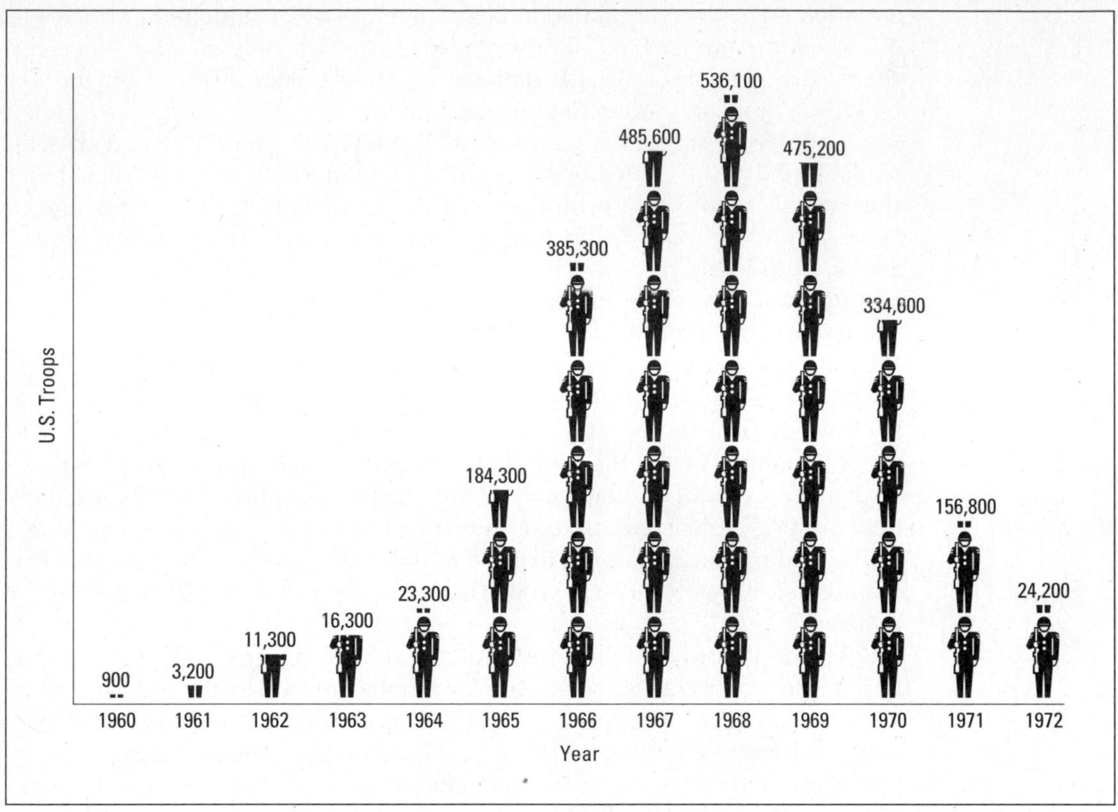

Levels of U.S. Forces in Vietnam at Year's End By 1968 the United States had stationed more than 500,000 soldiers in Vietnam.

Korea—to a very different kind of struggle. The course that Pentagon strategists pursued made sense to them as members of a productive, industrial society. Substitute machines for soldiers, they reasoned, and casualties will decline and public support continue. But the advocates of a high-tech war misunderstood the realities of the conflict in Vietnam. The methods they followed removed the American forces from direct contact with the people they ostensibly were helping and ultimately contributed to the loss of the war.

General Westmoreland tried to perfect a strategy of attrition—that is, a gradual wearing down of the enemy—against the Vietcong and North Vietnamese. He used helicopters to send troops into the countryside on search-and-destroy missions to root out and kill enemy soldiers. Americans would fly out in the morning, pursue the Vietcong in firefights, count the dead, and return to their bases in the evening. The measure of success became the "body count" of enemy soldiers killed, rather than the territory captured, the standard in earlier wars. The procedure encouraged abuses. Local commanders, hoping to please their superiors in Saigon, inflated the death figures. Moreover, reliance on the body count offered an incentive to shoot first and ask no questions. The army developed strict rules of engagement designed to prevent indiscriminate shooting of noncombatants. But the confusion engendered by a war without clearly defined front lines, enemy forces who looked like civilians, and the presence of civilians on the battlefield—together with the demands of the body count policy—led to some atrocities.

Before U.S. troops descended from their helicopters, giant B-52 bombers and smaller fighter jets would pound the countryside. The United States dropped more bombs each month in Vietnam than fell on all of Europe during the entire Second World War. But the B-52 raids, code-named Arc Light, merely alerted the Vietcong and North Vietnamese forces that the Americans were on their way, giving them time to withdraw or dive into hundreds of miles of tunnels to protect themselves. The Vietcong also learned to use unexploded U.S. bombs and artillery shells against the Americans. About 2 percent of the artillery shells and 5 percent of the bombs from the B-52s did not explode on impact. The enemy developed shrewd booby traps using these unexploded bombs, killing or wounding thousands of inexperienced American troops. In 1966 over one thousand American soldiers died of wounds caused by booby traps, and in the first six months of 1967, a total of 17 percent of all American casualties resulted from mines or booby traps. The dollar cost of the bombing also mounted quickly, to about $2.5 billion per year.

The NLF forces kept gaining strength on the ground with guerrilla tactics developed earlier by the Vietminh. They avoided firefights where they could, forcing the Americans to waste enormous energy and materiel for meager gains. They continued their political organization in the countryside even as American bombers flew overhead. One American correspondent, alarmed at the apparent inability of U.S. commanders to acknowledge the strengths of the NLF, complained to a general, "How do you expect our forces to win the hearts and minds of the people when all they do is take off from one army base and fly overhead at 1,500 feet while Charlie [one of many nicknames for the NLF] is sitting down there and he's got 'em by the testicles jerking, and every time he jerks their hearts and mind follow?"

Despite such complaints, the U.S. Army continued to rely on search-and-destroy operations. The largest occurred in late 1966 and early 1967. In one such mission, which lasted from September to November 1966, twenty-two thousand U.S. and ARVN troops, supported by B-52 bombers and massive artillery fire, pursued the NLF northwest of Saigon. In another search-and-destroy operation from February through May 1967, American soldiers followed raids by B-52s that reduced the lush Vietnamese landscape to the eerie bleakness of the moon, making hundreds of square miles uninhabitable by the very peasants the Americans were supposedly helping. Americans entering villages to root out the Vietcong sometimes carried out so-called Zippo raids (named for a brand of cigarette lighter), igniting the peasants' thatched huts

North Vietnam's commander Vo Nguyen Giap, who organized the Vietnam People's Army to fight the Americans. *Corbis/Bettmann*

with tracer bullets, flame throwers, and lighters to deny sanctuary to the enemy.

Such actions not only enraged the peasantry but also shocked Americans who saw film footage on the evening news. And the enormous firepower failed to eradicate the Vietcong, who simply melted away until the assaults stopped. One reporter likened each blow to "a sledgehammer on a floating cork; somehow the cork refused to stay down." An American general later acknowledged that it was physically impossible to keep the enemy from slipping away.

All the while, North Vietnamese commander General Nguyen Vo Giap, the victor at Dienbienphu, thought the Americans were playing into his hands as he waged a protracted guerrilla war. The search-and-destroy operations took Americans away from the heavily populated coastal plain, where the NLF and the North gained strength among the population. As the Americans engaged in inconclusive battles in the interior, they paid less attention to "pacification," the effort to bind the peasantry to the Saigon government.

If anything, the Saigon government lost even more of its people's affection as the American war devastated the countryside. As part of their effort to deny sanctuary to the enemy, American forces used giant transport planes to spray trees with defoliants. Between 1962 and 1972 the Americans dropped over 1 million pounds of chemicals such as Agent Orange on the forests of South Vietnam, destroying more than half of them. Some of the crews jokingly adopted the motto "Only You Can Prevent Forests," but many crew members later suffered serious health problems that probably derived from the toxins they dropped.

The effects on the crops of South Vietnamese farmers—the ostensible beneficiaries of the war effort—were immediate and devastating. Deadly defoliants dropped from planes on a suspected Vietcong area in the afternoon would soon drift over friendly villages; by the next morning fruit would fall from nearby trees and leaves on rubber plants would turn brown and break off. South Vietnamese farmers blamed the Americans for the loss of their crops, and they feared the defoliants harmed animal and human life as well. The birth of a physically or mentally impaired infant was often blamed on the defoliation campaigns. American forces also used poisons to destroy rice crops grown in Vietcong areas, expecting the hungry enemy to emerge and fight. This strategy overlooked the NLF's practice of buying or taking rice from the peasants, and the Americans ruined ten pounds of rice grown by friendly farmers for every pound of Vietcong rice they destroyed. South Vietnam, once an exporter of rice, began importing it from neighboring countries and even the United States as the war ground on.

The havoc in the countryside forced hundreds of thousands of peasants to flee their homes. Between 1964 and 1969 more than 4 million South Vietnamese, one-fourth of the population, were refugees at one time or another. Those who remained on their land often did so only because they feared that the Vietcong would redistribute it if they left. Many of those who fled the terror from the skies, the defoliants, the artillery barrages, or the Zippo raids swarmed to cities that had neither room nor facilities for them; others languished in squalid refugee camps.

The population of Saigon, under 500,000 in the 1950s, swelled to 1.5 million by the mid-1960s. The capital and other cities near American installations-Danang, Camranh Bay, Hue, to name a few—changed from Asian commercial centers conducting business in traditional ways to army boom towns. Seedy bars and brothels sprang up near American bases, with women and girls as young as thirteen prostituting themselves for the GIs. Senator J. William Fulbright complained that the United States had transformed South Vietnam "into a gigantic whorehouse." Over one hundred thousand Amerasian children were born of liaisons between American soldiers and Vietnamese women. These children of mixed race were scorned by other Vietnamese, and after the Americans departed they suffered terrible privations.

The presence of over five hundred thousand Americans transformed the Vietnamese economy. Emphasis shifted from producing food and rubber to servicing the influx of newcomers. At first the GIs paid cash in U.S. dollars for the goods they wanted. Because of sharply increased demand, prices zoomed 170 percent in 1966 and 1967, and many Vietnamese, who lacked the kind of income the GIs enjoyed, could no longer afford the basic necessities of life. To halt the price rises, the army started paying its soldiers in scrip good only on U.S. bases. Vietnamese entrepreneurs responded by importing watches, tape recorders, motorcycles, radios, and numerous other goods to sell to local people who worked for the Americans and were paid in South Vietnamese currency.

Corruption, already a problem before the Americans arrived en masse, vastly increased in 1966. The South Vietnamese government rented space to the Americans at exorbitant prices. South Vietnamese officials took bribes from contractors wishing to do business with U.S. agencies, including military bases and rural development organizations. Others demanded payment for licenses, permits, visas, and passports. Some Saigon officials traded in opium, and many engaged in the flourishing black market. Everything was for sale—U.S. government scrip, South Vietnamese piasters, Scotch whiskey, watches, hand grenades, rifles.

Despite the rapid escalation that began in 1966, by late 1967 the war seemed interminable. McNamara's prediction of late 1966 that he could "see the light at the end of the tunnel in Vietnam" provoked the rueful rejoinder that what he had glimpsed was the headlight of another train engineered by Ho Chi Minh. Thirteen thousand U.S. servicemen had been killed. Only the lowliest goal—denying a victory to the NLF—had been realized, and even that success might not last. Other American war aims—creating a stable South Vietnamese government capable of waging the war on its own, winning the affection of the South Vietnamese people, and forcing the North to quit—had become more elusive than ever. As American involvement intensified, South Vietnamese society dissolved. People either became dependents of the United States or went underground to join the NLF. The South Vietnamese government, once the object of Washington's confidence-building measures, slipped into dependence or obstructionism.

Military Service and the Draft

Although the fighting took place far from the United States, the war deeply affected the way many Americans lived their lives. Military service became an important, life-changing experience for over 2 million American men. Combat soldiers encountered racial tensions, battled stifling boredom punctuated by periods of intense fear (many turned to drugs to relieve the pressure), and witnessed or participated in savage brutality against the Vietnamese. Most soldiers accepted these conditions as part of the hardships of military service, but many bore psychological and emotional scars for years after their return from Vietnam. Nearly 80 percent of the U.S. troops in Vietnam served as support personnel, not combat troops, however, and their service was far less traumatic. But even those Americans who did not fight were changed by the war. Millions of young men spent a substantial part of their late adolescence and young adulthood wondering whether they would be drafted or seeking ways to avoid it. Far more men did not go to Vietnam than went, but still the war created deep divisions among an entire generation. Those who fought in the war often resented those who did not, and people who did not go to Vietnam sometimes treated those who did with scorn, pity, or condescension.

Unlike the Second World War, when the armed forces needed nearly every able-bodied American man, the military effort in Vietnam required less than half the eligible population. Of the 27 million available men between the ages of nineteen and twenty-six, 16 million never served in the armed forces. Of the 11 million who did, 9 million enlisted and 2.2 million were drafted under the terms of the Selective Service Act of 1947. A total of approximately 2.8 million men, along with 6,400 women, actually saw service in Vietnam between 1961 and 1973.

Although the draft took only about 10 percent of the men subject to its call, Selective Service affected the lives of nearly everybody. A major study of the draft conducted after the war concluded that it "cast the entire generation into a contest for survival." The draft, "through an elaborate structure of deferments, exemptions, legal technicalities, and noncombat military alternatives . . . rewarded those who manipulated the system to their advantage." As the war became more dangerous and American casualties rose to three hundred dead per week, many young men looked for ways to avoid the fighting. A number of options were available: draft deferments for marriage (dropped in 1965), fatherhood, or student status; enlistment in the National Guard or the army reserves; voluntary enlistment with the stipulation that they serve in places other than Vietnam; and service in noncombat zones in Vietnam.

The wealthy and educated, those most aware of the intricacies of the system, knew best how to avoid the most dangerous duty. As a result, only 24 percent of eligible men from high-income families entered the military, only 9 percent served in Vietnam, and only 7 percent saw combat, mostly as officers. Of the eligible men from middle-income families, 30 percent served in the military, 12 percent served in Vietnam, and 7 percent served in combat. For low-income men, 40 percent entered military service, 19 percent went to Vietnam, and 15 percent saw combat. Such discrepancies produced distressing inequities in the make-up of the forces bearing the brunt of the heaviest fighting.

The Selective Service system appeared corrupt and demeaning to many of those who faced conscription. Three-quarters of the 16 million men who did not serve in Vietnam admitted that they had changed their life plans to stay away from Vietnam, and a majority (55 percent) said they actively took steps to avoid the draft. Because of the draft, male college enrollments were about 6 to 7 percent higher than they otherwise would have been. Until 1968 graduate students earned deferments, so graduate school applications shot up in 1966 and 1967.

Other options remained for those without deferments. Even if drafted, a man had to be physically fit before he could be inducted. Some young men used family doctors to document phony conditions that would keep them out of the service. One physician commented that "the traditional doctor-patient relationship is one of preserving life. I save lives by keeping people out of the Army."

A network of draft counselors, initially sponsored by pacifist churches and organizations, arose to advise young men of their rights under the Selective Service Act and of legal ways to avoid induction. After a 1965 Supreme Court ruling in *United States* v. *Seegar,* conscientious objector status was available to anyone with a "sincerely founded reason" for opposing war. Before that time only members of recognized pacifist sects—for example, Mennonites, Quakers, Jehovah's Witnesses, Brethren of God—had been entitled to register as conscientious objectors. After *Seegar,* draft counselors advised young men on how to present their antiwar beliefs in a persuasive way. Not surprisingly, the educated and articulate fared better than the poor and the less well connected at obtaining conscientious objector status.

For the men who went to Vietnam, life in the armed forces bore little resemblance to the experiences of their fathers or older brothers in the Second World War and the Korean War—and no likeness at all to the idealized versions of those wars presented in movies and television programs. For combat soldiers Vietnam was sometimes a brutal and demoralizing experience. One day a young man would be in the relatively familiar surroundings of his stateside military base; the next day, after a twenty-hour flight, he would land at Camranh Bay, Danang, or Saigon and be hit with a blast of hot, humid air. Newcomers to Vietnam could often see artillery or smoke from bombs as they approached the airport. A nurse remembered a deadly quiet settling over the passenger cabin of her plane as soon as the coast of Vietnam came into view. The captain announced that the Vietcong were shelling the airfield. "He said he was going to drop us off and get right back into the air. The plane made a steep landing into the airfield. They opened the door. We ran out and the troops going home ran onto the plane." A frightened young conscript felt moments before landing that "they're gonna just be standing there and they're gonna blow our ass away." The enemy, often indistinguishable from the local population, could materialize suddenly from the jungle and attack with horrible efficiency. On patrol, a soldier might be blown apart at any moment by a booby trap. Conventional precautions and tactics often seemed irrelevant. It was especially difficult to maintain the troops' morale when they saw more and more lives lost for little or no gain.

Between 7,500 and 11,000 American women, mostly military nurses, also served in Vietnam. All were volunteers over twenty years of age, and most were officers. These women saw a different sort of war. As a tiny minority, military women saw their special needs ignored by their commanders. When women got sick, they shared wards and bathrooms with men. Helmets did not

A medic tends to a wounded American soldier in Vietnam. *Catherine Leroy/SIPA Press*

accommodate women's smaller heads or longer hair styles. Most women adapted to this overwhelmingly male environment and followed what one sociologist characterized as the unwritten rule of gender relations in Vietnam: "Men protected women; women, in turn, comforted the men."

The nurses saw firsthand the destruction wrought by the war. They served twelve-hour shifts, six days a week, in evacuation hospital trauma units. The ready availability of helicopters profoundly changed the nature of wartime medicine in Vietnam. Men who would have died from their wounds had they been fighting in World War II or Korea were saved by being quickly evacuated to forward field hospitals. One nurse recalled looking at a wounded man's wristwatch as she prepared him for surgery: it had stopped seventeen minutes earlier. For those who reached a forward hospital, the mortality rate was low, about 3 percent. The wounded spent an average of four days in a field hospital before being flown to more fully equipped facilities in Japan, Hawaii, or the mainland United States. Many of the women found their initial exposures to

✦ ✦ ✦

Biographical Profile

William C. Westmoreland, 1914–

William C. Westmoreland grew up wanting to be a soldier. Born in 1914 in a South Carolina cotton-mill town, he thrilled to stories of his ancestors' heroics during the Civil War. After attending West Point he rose swiftly through the army ranks during the Second World War and Korea. By age forty-two he was the army's youngest major general. In 1960 he returned to his beloved West Point as superintendent.

Greater responsibility was thrust on Westmoreland in June 1964 when President Johnson named him commander of the American forces in Vietnam. Like most successful officers who had fought in Europe during the Second World War, Westmoreland believed that American military technology could overwhelm any adversary; he therefore followed a strategy of attrition against the North Vietnamese. At first the new commander seemed a welcome relief from his ineffectual predecessor, General Paul D. Harkins. Handsome and friendly, Westmoreland got along well with his soldiers, and *Time* magazine named him Man of the Year in 1966.

But Vietnam was not Europe, and Westmoreland never grasped that the United States was engaged in a political struggle more than a military engagement. Over the years his faith

the badly wounded men shocking. "I quickly learned," one recalled, "that I was not in a John Wayne movie. The devastating injuries just came in and came in." Many of the wounded were very young, averaging nineteen years of age, whereas the nurses were in their mid-twenties. The nurses thought the soldiers looked like their high school classmates, and they sometimes wept over the tragedy of youths crippled before they could enjoy the fullness of life. But the hard work, the companionship in the trauma units, and the sense of helping very needy people strengthened the nurses. Unlike many combat soldiers, who grew ever more disillusioned as their tour of duty went on, many nurses developed a strong sense of accomplishment in Vietnam. Many served multiin a military solution to the Vietnam conflict became less persuasive to administration officials and the American public. After the Tet Offensive of early 1968 (see page 421), his optimistic promises to Congress the previous November seemed almost foolish, and President Johnson denied his request for more troops. In June 1968 Westmoreland was recalled from Vietnam to serve as army chief of staff for the next four years.

After his retirement he became bitter about the eventual Communist victory in Vietnam and his own falling reputation at home. By then military experts had derided his strategy of attrition as ill-informed and unimaginative. From 1982 to 1985 Westmoreland pressed a libel suit against CBS News for claiming that he had deliberately misled Johnson by underestimating the number of enemy soldiers. Finally he dropped the suit, and CBS stated that it had not intended to cast doubt on his truthfulness. This awkward legal resolution served only to emphasize the blight that Vietnam had cast on the general's career.

"I recommended continuation of the one-year tour that had been set for advisers. It was my belief that lengthy involuntary tours would more likely bring about a hue and cry to 'bring the boys home' than a tour in which the 'boys would come home' after one year unless they volunteered to stay longer. Also in anticipation of a long war, it seemed to me that the burden of service should be shared by a cross-section of American youth. I did not anticipate that a number of our young men would be allowed by national policy to defer service by going to a college campus.

"I hoped, perhaps with folly, that an emerging sense of South Vietnamese nationalism and a revitalized will in South Vietnam—manifested in a viable government and a proficient fighting force—would in the long run compensate for the inevitable waning of public support in the United States for a difficult war."

—from Westmoreland's book *The Lessons of Vietnam,* edited by W. Scott Thompson and Donaldson D. Frizzell (New York: Taylor and Francis/Crane Russak and Co., 1977)

---

ple tours of duty, and they often married men whom they had met in Vietnam, sharing unique memories of stress under fire. "I cannot imagine life without him," one nurse remarked about her husband fifteen years after the war. "We understand each other the way few people could."

The difficulties faced by soldiers in Vietnam were compounded by the military's personnel policies. Unlike earlier wars, in which soldiers had served "for the duration," soldiers had a one-year tour of duty in Vietnam, spread over thirteen months, with thirty days' leave for "rest and recreation." A combination of demographics, politics, and military management needs prompted this arrangement. Because the pool of available soldiers far exceeded the number needed, keeping five hundred thousand men at the front while allowing *all* others to steer free of battle would cause resentment among those who fought, and it would erode public support for the war. Therefore the military limited the time of service and continually rotated the forces.

According to General Westmoreland, fixing the date when each GI would leave Vietnam helped to boost morale and give each soldier a goal. In fact, however, the goal often became self-preservation: men approaching the end of their tour became reluctant to fight. No one wanted to be killed or wounded, but risking death or injury a few weeks before mustering out appeared especially pointless. One commander called the twelve-month tour "the worst personnel policy in history." To make matters worse, units did not stay together throughout their tours, increasing soldiers' and officers' sense of isolation. Napoleon once observed that "soldiers have to eat soup together for a long time before they are ready to fight," but Americans discarded that lesson in Vietnam. Troops killed or wounded were replaced by newcomers, whose tour of duty expired later than those of other men in the unit. Combat soldiers relied on the support of friends who entered Vietnam with them and found it difficult to bond with others. Mostly men relied on themselves.

Officers, too, never remained with units throughout their terms, because the armed forces rotated commanders, down to the level of platoon lieutenants, every six months. Disgruntled commanders complained that the same war was fought over again every six months. The policy arose because it allowed officers to experience a variety of command positions, a sure way of gaining promotion in the professional force developed after the Second World War. Such résumé enhancement—"ticketpunching," as it came to be known—eliminated the possibility of strong bonds forming between officers and their men. In many cases the young lieutenants who served as platoon commanders never even learned the basic combat skills that would inspire confidence in the soldiers under their command.

The lack of rapport between commanders and soldiers sometimes made personal hostilities difficult to control. The murder of officers by enlisted men—often with a fragmentation grenade or other anonymous weapon—became frequent enough, especially late in the war, to earn its own slang term, "fragging." Moreover, the armed forces reflected the racial tensions of American society as a whole. As animosity between blacks and whites grew back home during the late sixties, racial divisions deepened inside the armed forces as well. Many black soldiers had no white friends in the ostensibly integrated units. Inevitably, some of the violence among GIs took on a racial tone.

News of atrocities against the Vietnamese, whom some GIs referred to as "gooks," undermined support for the soldiers back home in the United States. In a long war against an enemy that could strike without warning and then instantly melt away, soldiers sometimes disregarded the so-called Rules of Engagement that regulated behavior toward the enemy. Once the body count became the principal means of measuring success in the war, some soldiers became brutal. A few men chopped off the ears of dead Vietnamese for trophies. Some GIs gave up the nearly impossible task of distinguishing the Vietcong from uninvolved civilians; besides burning peasants' houses, they began shooting any Vietnamese they saw. "If it moves, it's VC [Vietcong]" became a common slogan for American soldiers. The most dramatic atrocity of the war occurred in March 1968, when American soldiers massacred more than five hundred unarmed Vietnamese villagers, mostly women and children, at the hamlet of Mylai; the military managed to keep the incident secret until the next year, but it eventually became a symbol of the war's brutality and the deepening divisions among the American public over the war. Many people at home expressed sympathy for the young American soldiers who they believed had succumbed to the stress of combat. A smaller but significant group of people considered such atrocities a compelling reason for the United States to quit Vietnam.

To escape the fear and absurdity of a war without front lines, leadership, or clear goals, some soldiers turned to drugs. Marijuana, opium, and heroin were freely available and inexpensive in the cities, because officials of the South Vietnamese government engaged in the drug trade. So did the CIA, which used profits from drugs to finance a secret counterinsurgency in the highlands and along the Laotian border. Because soldiers conducting search-and-destroy patrols returned often to bases near the cities, they could obtain drugs for use while fighting.

Overall, soldiers who experienced combat in Vietnam developed greater psychological and emotional difficulties than did the 80 percent of servicemen and servicewomen who served in support roles. The latter group readjusted relatively readily to their previous roles in society once they returned home. Surveys taken ten and twenty years after the war indicated that the subsequent life and careers of noncombat soldiers had developed similarly to those of men of the same race and social and economic status who had not gone to Vietnam. The picture was darker and much more complex for combat veterans, however. They experienced significantly higher levels of symptoms associated with posttraumatic stress disorder, including drug and alcohol abuse, difficulties sustaining family relationships, trouble finding and maintaining employment, violence, and suicide. A larger proportion of Vietnam War veterans experienced these problems than did veterans of the Second World War. Their Vietnam experience alone does not explain the increase, however. The rates of all of the disorders associated with posttraumatic stress disorder increased for society at large following World War II, up through the post-Vietnam era. Moreover, there were significant differences in the experiences of combat veterans of different social backgrounds and race. White combat veterans, many of whom had come from less privileged backgrounds than men who stayed home, did more poorly in life than did white nonveterans. The post-Vietnam experience of people of color reflected just the opposite trend. For many African-Americans, Hispanics, and Native Americans military service proved a means of social advancement. Their post-Vietnam experiences tended to be more fortunate than those of nonwhite men of similar economic status who had not gone into the military and served in Vietnam.

✦ The Rise of Dissent and the Collapse of the Cold War Consensus

In addition to the soldiers in Vietnam, at least one man in Washington approached nervous exhaustion as the war expanded: President Johnson. The war had gone on longer than his military advisers had predicted, and still there was no clear end in sight. The continuation of the war threatened to wreck his cherished Great Society legislation, and it put into doubt his chances for reelection in 1968.

Johnson's personal crisis was deepened by mounting criticism of the war from former supporters. Arkansas senator J. William Fulbright, chairman of the Senate Foreign Relations Committee and an old friend from Johnson's days as majority leader, was among the first moderate public figures to dissent from the build-up in Vietnam. In September 1965 Fulbright told the Senate that "U.S. policy in the Dominican crisis [the previous April] has been characterized by a lack of candor." The same problem plagued Johnson's explanations for his actions in Vietnam, the senator said.

The following February Fulbright's committee opened televised hearings on Vietnam policy. Numerous foreign policy experts told the committee that the administration had headed down the wrong road in Vietnam. George F. Kennan, one of the architects of containment, worried that the "unbalanced concentration of resources and attention" in Vietnam was diverting Washington from what he believed should be the true focus of U.S. foreign policy—Europe. General James Gavin, a Second World War air combat hero, urged that the United States stop the bombing, send no more troops, retreat to enclaves in Vietnam, and look for a negotiated settlement. Fulbright expressed disbelief at Secretary of State Dean Rusk's repeated assertions that "this is a clear case of international Communist aggression." The chairman thought that most of the world viewed the conflict in Vietnam as "a civil war in which outside parties have become involved." Two months later Fulbright observed that the war had damaged the Great Society and hurt the nation's relations with the Soviet Union and Europe. He lamented "the arrogance of power," which he defined as a "psychological need that nations seem to have to prove that they are bigger, stronger, better than other nations."

While Fulbright and about a dozen other senators were dissenting from the policy of escalation in 1966, more potent opposition to the war arose in the form of a citizens' peace movement. Opposition to the war in Vietnam brought together distinct groups of people—political liberals opposed to the war (known as "doves"), nonviolent pacifists, and social revolutionaries and radical pacifists. Beginning in 1965 they organized "teach-ins," in which opponents of the war lectured college audiences on the evils of the war. The peace movement also sponsored demonstrations against the administration, a "Vietnam Summer" of protests against the war in 1967, and an effort to "dump Johnson" in 1968 and replace him with someone who would extricate the United States from the endless war.

Public antiwar activism surged in the spring of 1967. Martin Luther King, Jr., who previously had expressed quiet misgivings about the war, openly broke with the Johnson administration. He endorsed the Vietnam Summer, called for de-escalation, and helped organize a new protest group called Negotiation Now! On April 15 crowds of one hundred thousand in New York and fifty thousand in San Francisco heard speakers from both the antiwar and the civil rights movements call for an end to the war and a recommitment to the goal of racial equality at home. Johnson grew alarmed at the possibility that King and pediatrician Benjamin Spock, now an antiwar activist, might run for president and vice president, respectively, in 1968. The White House was so worried about it that Press Secretary George Christian leaked to columnists friendly to the administration FBI files purporting to show King's connections to the Communist Party.

Federal agencies constantly observed, infiltrated, and harassed dissident and antiwar groups. The FBI compared Senator Fulbright's position during his 1966 Vietnam hearing to those taken by the Communist Party. The CIA infiltrated such antiwar groups as Women Strike for Peace, the Washington Peace Center, SANE, the Congress on Racial Equality (which had begun sponsoring antiwar measures), the War Resisters League, and the National Mobilization Committee Against the War. In August 1967 the CIA initiated Operation Chaos, designed to disrupt and confuse the antiwar movement. Agents sent phony letters defaming antiwar leaders to editors of publications; other agents infiltrated antiwar groups and called for bombings or violent confrontation with police. Eventually the CIA opened files on over seven thousand Americans opposed to the war—in violation of its charter, which stipulated that it would not operate inside the United States.

The president became frantic as plans developed for a massive march on Washington in October 1967 to demand a halt to the bombing and immediate negotiations to end the war. To discredit the peace movement, Johnson asked his attorney general, Ramsey Clark, to leak information about the left-wing and Communist affiliations of some of its leaders. Nevertheless, on October 21 a crowd estimated at one hundred thousand assembled on the Mall in front of the Lincoln Memorial to hear speeches opposing the war. Later a group of about fifty thousand marched to the Pentagon, where scores crossed police lines and were arrested.

Just as important in changing public attitudes toward the war were the nightly televised newscasts that brought the fighting and the devastation of Vietnamese society into American living rooms. Reporters and camera crews traveled with platoons to the helicopter landing zones and recorded the firefights in Vietnamese villages. They captured on film the flames of the Zippo raids, the moans of wounded soldiers, the terror in the eyes of children left homeless by the fighting. What they could not show, because it did not happen, was the sort of scene in which GIs liberated a village to the cheers of grateful residents. For a public brought up on the heroic newsreels of the Second World War, when such images had brought tears of pride to those on the home front, the sharp contrast between the "good war" of 1941–1945 and the quagmire of Vietnam proved particularly disillusioning.

As this "living room war" ground on without progress, Americans at home, like the soldiers in the field, had trouble distinguishing friendly Vietnamese from the enemy, and they wanted no part of either. The fighting appeared pointless, and the public longed for relief from a war it had not approved. Distrust of the government rose sharply in 1967 as observers noted a yawning "credibility gap" between the optimism of the president and his advisers and the continuing violence shown on TV every evening.

Antiwar activities, the failure to achieve victory, and press coverage of the horrors of the fighting altered the way the public viewed the war. Throughout the country there was a sharp division between "hawks," who supported the American war effort, and "doves," who opposed it. In the beginning of 1967 most Americans were still hawks, willing to escalate the war if only it could be won decisively. Fewer than a third of the public told a Gallup poll that they believed the war had been a mistake. By July that figure had risen to 41 percent, and by the time of the Washington march in October, 46 percent thought the United States should never have entered the war. Yet the number calling for an immediate American withdrawal remained low. A mere 6 percent wanted withdrawal in February, and by December that proportion had risen only to 10 percent. Nevertheless, in the fall only 28 percent of the public approved of President Johnson's handling of the war. Most Americans found themselves neither hawks nor doves on Vietnam; they simply wanted relief.

By the end of 1967 doubts over further escalation of the war assailed even some of the war's most ardent backers. The president wondered about the usefulness of bombing North Vietnam. Secretary of Defense McNamara became morose at the lack of progress. The effort to secure the countryside had, "if anything, gone backward," he admitted. At one point he recommended an unconditional halt to the bombing to get serious negotiations started, but Johnson refused after learning that the Joint Chiefs of Staff had threatened to resign, en masse, if the bombing was stopped. As he began to despair of winning the war through advanced technology, McNamara wanted out. In the fall of 1967 Johnson accepted McNamara's resignation from the Defense Department, replacing him with long-time Democratic Party adviser Clark Clifford in February 1968.

In the fall of 1967 the president hoped that an optimistic assessment of the war from the battlefield commander might buy time with the restless public. In November General Westmoreland returned to Washington and explained to reporters that he was "very, very encouraged" because "we are making real progress." He told Congress that the North Vietnamese and Vietcong could not hold out much longer. He thought that U.S. forces had reached a point where the end of the war was in view.

Westmoreland's rosy scenario made headlines, but Johnson's civilian advisers worried about the effect of the war on the domestic tranquility and the position of the United States in the rest of the world. Johnson then assembled a group of so-called Wise Men, foreign policy officials who had served various administrations since 1940, to chart a future path in Vietnam. They supported Johnson's course to that point but warned that "endless inconclusive fighting" had become "the most serious cause of domestic disquiet." At the end of 1967 Johnson agreed to review the ground war to find a way to reduce American casualties and turn over more of the fighting to the ARVN.

At 2:45 A.M. on January 30, 1968—the first day of Tet, the Vietnamese New Year—a squad of nineteen Vietcong commandos blasted a hole in the wall protecting the U.S. embassy in Saigon, ran into the courtyard, and engaged the Marine guards inside for the next six hours. All nineteen commandos were killed, but the damage they did to Washington's position in Vietnam could not be repaired. The assault on the embassy was the most dramatic part of a coordinated offensive by the North Vietnamese and NLF forces against the population centers of South Vietnam over the Tet holidays. They attacked the Saigon airport, the presidential palace, and the headquarters of the ARVN's general staff. With the benefit of complete surprise, the North Vietnamese and NLF battled with the Americans and ARVN for control of thirty-six of forty-four provincial capitals, five of six major cities, and sixty-four district capitals.

In most areas the Americans and the ARVN repulsed the Communists, killing perhaps 40,000 while losing 3,400 of their own. The cost to Vietnamese civilians ran much higher, with 1 million refugees swelling the already teeming camps in two weeks. One of the most grisly scenes occurred in the old imperial capital of Hue, once noted for its serene beauty. The Vietcong succeeded in controlling the city for six weeks. When the battle ended and the Americans and the ARVN recaptured Hue, their bombs and artillery had left it, according to one soldier, a "shattered, stinking hulk, its streets choked with rubble and rotting bodies." The ARVN uncovered a mass grave containing the bodies of 2,800 South Vietnamese officeholders who had been executed by the Vietcong.

On the American side the principal casualty was the cheery scenario of progress in the war. After Tet, Westmoreland's assurances of the previous fall that an American victory could be achieved within two years sounded hopelessly unrealistic. His claims in the midst of the battle that the United States had defeated the enemy provoked derision. CBS News anchor Walter Cronkite, until this point supportive of the Johnson administration, growled, "What the hell is going on? I thought we were winning the war." Cronkite publicly denounced "the optimists who have been wrong in the past." One of the most famous photographs of the war, showing the commander of the

Saigon police shooting a Vietcong suspect in the head in the middle of a busy street, outraged opinion at home.

In Washington, Johnson, already discouraged by the lack of progress and by McNamara's defection, grappled with Westmoreland's request for an additional 206,000 men. Failure to provide them, the general implied, would mean losing the war. For Johnson, however, sending that many troops seemed a major escalation; it would risk Chinese or Soviet intervention and would further inflame public opinion at home. Before even considering Westmoreland's request, the president asked the new secretary of defense, Clark Clifford, to undertake a complete review of the administration's Vietnam policy.

Like McNamara before him, Clifford, once a hawk, now doubted whether more troops would produce any progress. "I see more and more fighting with more and more casualties on the U.S. side and no end in sight to the action," he told the president. Civilian experts in the Defense Department revived a 1967 proposal by McNamara to change from the search-and-destroy strategy to one of "population security." American forces would protect the bulk of the South's civilian population but encourage the ARVN to bear more of the burden of fighting the enemy. American casualties probably would decline, reducing public unhappiness at home, but the hope of military victory would vanish. Clifford therefore pressed for a negotiated settlement. In early March Johnson rejected Westmoreland's request for another 206,000 men.

Before deciding on future commitments, Johnson held another series of White House debates in mid-March. On one side stood Clifford, who now argued that the public demanded an end to the war, noting the "tremendous erosion of support" among the nation's business and legal elite. Clifford and like-minded policy analysts thought it foolish for the United States to go deeper into the "hopeless bog" of Vietnam. He pointed to European displeasure over the American preoccupation with Vietnam, noting in particular that the French were demanding gold payment for their dollar holdings. On the other side of the debate were Secretary of State Rusk and National Security Adviser Walt Rostow. Rusk advocated a public announcement of a partial bombing halt, expecting that the North Vietnamese would reject it. Rostow told the president to "hang in there" in the face of a restless and fickle public. He likened Johnson's position to that of Abraham Lincoln's during the darkest days of the Civil War, when the public had reviled him.

Johnson could no longer ignore the mounting pressure to reverse course in Vietnam. Working with a trusted speech writer, he prepared an address to be broadcast nationwide on the evening of March 31, 1968. In it he promised a partial bombing halt that would limit American attacks to the region immediately north of the demilitarized zone at the seventeenth parallel. He promised to expand this partial bombing halt to a complete one "if our restraint is matched by restraint in Hanoi." He named Averell Harriman, a long-time presidential adviser, as head of an American delegation that would try to open peace talks with North Vietnam. Then, in a passage he wrote himself and kept secret from everyone but his wife, he withdrew from the 1968 presidential race.

In order to devote himself fully to the negotiations he had just promised, he pledged, "I shall not seek, and I will not accept, the nomination of my party for another term as your president."

✦ The Election of 1968

Lyndon Johnson had another reason for not seeking the nomination: he might not have received it. Anguish over the war had turned the Democrats against one another. For several years many liberals and partisans of the Kennedy family had stifled their misgivings about Johnson because they supported his domestic reform agenda; now, however, they revolted and looked for someone to challenge him for the nomination. After numerous prominent Democrats resisted calls to get into the race, an obscure Midwestern senator, Eugene McCarthy of Minnesota, allowed himself to be drafted into running in the March 12, 1968, New Hampshire presidential primary.

McCarthy's campaign seemed laughable at first. He had few assistants, little money, and virtually no press coverage. Everything changed in February, however, as the public reeled from the shock of the Tet Offensive. Thousands of college-age volunteers hurried to New Hampshire to help the campaign. McCarthy made Vietnam his issue, demanding a bombing halt and negotiations. Johnson's supporters took the bait. They ran TV ads in which an announcer warned that "the Communists in Vietnam are watching the New Hampshire primary." They denounced McCarthy as "a champion of appeasement and surrender" and predicted that he would receive less than a third of the vote. On election day McCarthy won 42.2 percent of the vote—coming within a few hundred votes of defeating Johnson—and twenty of the state's twenty-four convention delegates.

McCarthy's showing rattled the president and shook Robert Kennedy, who reconsidered his earlier refusal to enter the race now that it appeared a challenge to Johnson might succeed. After consulting old supporters and trying unsuccessfully to persuade McCarthy to withdraw in his favor, Kennedy announced his candidacy for the Democratic nomination on March 16. Johnson's worst nightmare had come to life. As he explained to a biographer, "the thing I had feared from the first day of my presidency was actually coming true. Robert Kennedy had openly announced his intention to reclaim the throne in the memory of his brother. And the American people, swayed by the magic of the name, were dancing in the streets." Two weeks later Johnson announced his withdrawal.

Aftershocks from Johnson's speech still rumbled when, four days later, on April 4, James Earl Ray killed Martin Luther King, Jr., as King stood on the balcony of the Lorraine Motel in Memphis, Tennessee. The assassination ignited another spurt of black rage. Riots erupted in more than a hundred cities; within a week, police, the army, and the National Guard had killed thirty-seven people. Several blocks of downtown Washington were burned and looted. In Chicago, Mayor Richard J. Daley ordered his police to "shoot to kill arsonists, and shoot to maim looters." Spiro T. Agnew, the Republican governor of Maryland (elected in 1966 as a moderate on race relations), summoned the leaders of his state's NAACP and Urban League chapters to Annapolis and warned them that he held them personally responsible for the devastation of Baltimore.

Two months later came Robert Kennedy's rendezvous with an assassin's bullet. Early in the morning on Wednesday, June 6, hours after he had eked out a narrow victory over Eugene McCarthy in the California Democratic primary, Kennedy was shot by Sirhan Sirhan, a Palestinian immigrant angry at the New York senator's support for Israel. Once more the country suffered through a funeral for one of the Kennedy brothers: a Requiem mass in New York's St. Patrick's Cathedral, followed by a sad train ride south to Washington. Hundreds of thousands of mourners lined the tracks under a blazing sun. One senator on the train recalled that as he looked into their faces, "I saw sorrow, bewilderment. I saw fury and I saw fright." Robert Kennedy was buried next to his brother John in Arlington National Cemetery.

With Kennedy dead McCarthy continued as the standard-bearer for some of the antiwar Democrats, who hoped to deny the nomination to Vice President Hubert Humphrey, the prowar faction's choice. Despite the antiwar group's efforts, however, Humphrey gained the nomination at the party's tumultuous August convention in Chicago. Inside the convention hall the McCarthy and Kennedy forces now backing Senator George McGovern who entered the race after Kennedy's murder, lost a narrow vote on a "peace plank" in the platform, repudiating the Johnson administration's handling of the Vietnam War. Humphrey won the nomination by a two-to-one margin. On that same sultry night, the Chicago police force went mad, clubbing and tear-gassing a crowd of ten thousand demonstrators who had come to the city to protest the war. The police chased demonstrators into McCarthy's suite in a downtown hotel, beating several bloody and unconscious. Television cameras caught it all.

After such chaos, the Democratic nomination appeared worthless for Humphrey. Polls put him 16 percentage points behind the Republican nominee, former vice president Richard Nixon. After losing the 1962 race for governor of California, Nixon had resurrected his political career by traveling the country, supporting local Republican candidates. A third candidate also ran, Alabama governor George Wallace, who had broken with the Democrats over civil rights. Some polls showed Wallace gaining 20 percent of the vote, much of it from formerly Democratic working-class whites, largely but not exclusively in the South.

Both Nixon and Wallace fed the public's disgust with Vietnam. The Republican nominee, a hawk when escalation had begun in 1965, condemned the present stalemate. While presenting no specific way to end the war, Nixon promised an early "peace with honor" and hinted at a plan to reduce U.S. participation. Nixon also pursued a "southern strategy," seeking the votes of

Demonstrators protesting President Lyndon B. Johnson's policies in Vietnam during the Democratic National Convention in Chicago in August 1968. *Wide World Photos*

white Democrats who were enraged at blacks. Promising to restore respect for law and order, he decried the riots that Johnson and Humphrey had not stopped. His vice-presidential nominee, Spiro Agnew, helped this cause by recalling the angry lecture he had delivered to African-American leaders after the April riots in Baltimore and on Maryland's eastern shore. Wallace also intimated that he could end the war faster than Humphrey. He named retired Air Force general Curtis LeMay, an undisguised hawk, as his running mate, hoping to capitalize on nationalistic feelings. But LeMay's inflammatory remark that he would "bomb North Vietnam into the Stone Age" alarmed voters, and Wallace's campaign began to fade in late September.

Humphrey's campaign languished for six weeks after the Democratic convention. Liberals wanted nothing to do with him, even though he was running against Nixon, their old adversary. Johnson refused to release Humphrey from the obligation of supporting the administration's Vietnam policy. Desperate for a way to distance himself from the stalemate in Vietnam, Humphrey announced on September 30 that he favored a total halt to the bombing "as an acceptable risk for peace, because I believe that it could lead to a success in negotiations and a shorter war." Suddenly Humphrey began to close the gap with Nixon, as many antiwar Democrats decided they preferred him to a man they despised.

Talks in Paris between the United States, North Vietnam, South Vietnam, and the NLF began in the summer but stalled over the issue of who could participate. The North Vietnamese refused to grant the Saigon government a separate place at the table, and the United States denied recognition to the NLF. The delegations wrangled for months over this problem, and the seemingly endless "talks about the talks" came to symbolize in the American public's mind their frustration with the interminable war. The conversations finally progressed in the days before the November election, since the Communists preferred a Humphrey victory to a win by the more hawkish Nixon. The Nixon camp worried that a breakthrough in the Paris talks might give the election to Humphrey. Working for Nixon, Anna Chennault, a conservative supporter of President Nguyen Van Thieu of South Vietnam, encouraged him to resist reaching an agreement until after the election, in the hope of boosting Nixon. Nevertheless, the weekend before the election Johnson announced a total bombing halt along the lines Humphrey had promised. The parties at Paris scheduled serious discussions on ending the war to begin immediately after election day, November 5.

Nixon won by a scant 510,000 votes, taking only 43.6 percent of the total (see map). Humphrey drew 42.9 percent and Wallace 13.5 percent. Humphrey's supporters believed that given another four days he would have won, since he had gained 7 percentage points in Gallup polls in the five days before the voting. That may have been wishful thinking: the drop in the Democratic portion of the vote from 1964, when Johnson took nearly 61 percent, represented a striking decline.

The story of the events in Vietnam resumes in Chapter 13. Although Nixon took office with an apparent mandate for change, American troops continued to fight in Vietnam for another four years.

✦ Conclusion

By the time of the 1968 election most Americans wanted to end the Vietnam War, but they still disagreed about how to do so. The American involvement that had begun quietly under President Truman had been gradually increased by Presidents Eisenhower and Kennedy until Lyndon Johnson took the fateful step of committing the United States to a massive air and ground war. And the more the United States contributed to the war effort, the more the corrupt government of South Vietnam grew dependent on American support. The result was a cycle of continual frustration.

The war devastated Vietnam—its land, its people, its society. It also proved tragic for many of the Americans who fought there. By the end of 1968 the war had already cost about thirty-seven thousand American lives, a number that would rise to over fifty-eight thousand by the time the United States withdrew its forces in 1973. A significant number of American troops who returned physically unscathed suffered long-term psychological and emotional dis-

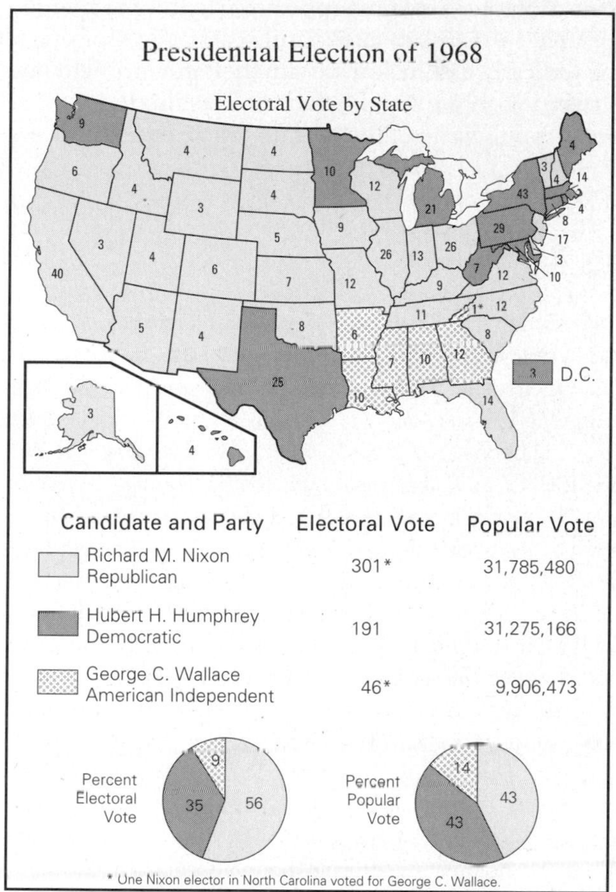

The Election of 1968 In the election of 1968, Republican Richard M. Nixon narrowly defeated Democrat Hubert H. Humphrey.

abilities. Most showed no overt symptoms of distress but believed that their efforts in Vietnam had been futile and were unappreciated at home. The disillusionment of many veterans contributed to a larger sense in the United States that the country's public institutions had failed.

At home, opposition to the war became widespread and bitter, ruining Johnson's chance for reelection in 1968 and throwing the Democratic Party into turmoil. Because the war raised doubts about the power of American technology and weapons to mold events around the world, some Americans even began to question the basic idea of containment that had guided U.S. foreign policy since the late 1940s.

By dividing the American public, the Vietnam War also helped open the deep chasms in American society that became the principal legacy of the 1960s.

As the next chapter explains, opposition to the war merged with other political and social movements to form a full-scale culture of protest. Many Americans became radically disillusioned with their government and society. They came to distrust not only the politicians in Washington but also all other forms of authority, and their rebellion stimulated an equally strong conservative backlash.

✦ Further Reading

For overviews of the war, see: George C. Herring, *America's Longest War: The United States and Vietnam, 1950–1975,* (1996); Stanley Karnow, *Vietnam: A History* (1991); Robert D. Schulzinger, *A Time for War: The United States and Vietnam, 1941–1975* (1997); Marilyn B. Young, *The Vietnam Wars* (1990). On the politics and diplomacy of the war, see: William C. Gibbons, *The U.S. Government and the Vietnam War* (4 vols., 1986–1994); George McT. Kahin, *Intervention: How America Became Involved in Vietnam* (1986); Larry Berman, *Planning a Tragedy* (1983) and *Lyndon Johnson's War* (1989); George Herring, *LBJ and Vietnam* (1994); Robert McNamara, *In Retrospect: The Tragedy and Lessons of Vietnam* (1995); Edwin Moise, *Tonkin Gulf and the Escalation of the Vietnam War* (1996); Brian VanDerMark, *Into the Quagmire: Lyndon Johnson and the Escalation of the Vietnam War* (1991). On fighting the war, see: Neil Sheehan, *A Bright Shining Lie: John Paul Vann and America in Vietnam* (1988); Andrew Krepenevich, *The Army and Vietnam* (1989); Peter G. McDonald, *Giap: The Victor in Vietnam* (1993); Kathryn Marshall, *In the Combat Zone: An Oral History of American Women in Vietnam, 1966–1975* (1987); Elizabeth Norman, *Women at War: The Story of Fifty Combat Nurses in Vietnam* (1990); Wallace Berry, *Bloods: An Oral History of the War by Black Veterans* (1984); Mark Baker, *Nam* (1982); Don Oberdorfer, *Tet* (1979); Ronald Spector, *After Tet: The Bloodiest Year of the Vietnam War* (1993). On the home front during the war, see: Christian Appy, *Working Class War: American Combat Soldiers and Vietnam* (1993); Terry Anderson, *The Movement and the Sixties* (1995); Lawrence Baskir and William Strauss, *Chance and Circumstance: The War, the Draft and the Vietnam Generation* (1978); Charles DeBenedetti with Charles Chatfield, *An American Ordeal: The Antiwar Movement of the Vietnam Era* (1990); Melvin Small and William C. Hoover, eds., *Give Peace a Chance: Exploring the Vietnam Antiwar Movement* (1992); Tom Wells, *The War Within: America's Battle Over Vietnam* (1994). On the political upheavals of 1968, see: Lewis Chester, Godfrey Hodgson, and Bruce Paige, *An American Melodrama* (1970); James Miller, *"Democracy Is in the Streets"* (1987); Todd Gitlin, *The Sixties* (1987); David Farber, *Chicago '68* (1988); David Caute, *The Year of the Barricades* (1988).

✦✦✦ CHAPTER 12

Cultural Revolutions, 1960–1980

✦ **A hippie wedding.**

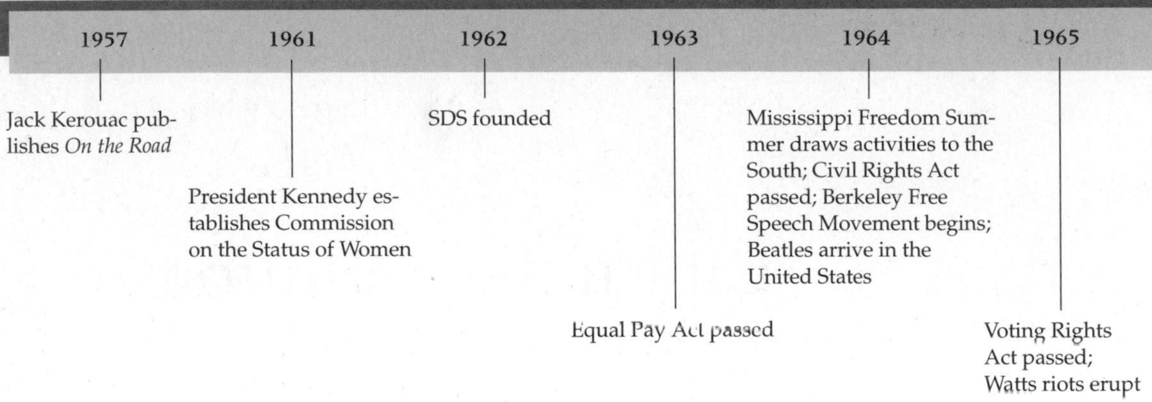

YOUNG BEN BRADDOCK, antihero of Mike Nichols's 1967 hit movie *The Graduate,* wasn't feeling so great when he arrived home in Los Angeles after graduating from college. His rich parents showered him with gifts—a red Italian sports car, a scuba diving outfit—but Ben was somehow embarrassed by their lavishness. His father asked him what was wrong, and he replied, "It's about my future. I want it to be . . . different." At his graduation party, his parents' wealthy friends overwhelmed him with phony praise and pressing counsel. One man, Mr. McGuire, cornered Ben and offered one of the most memorable pieces of advice in the history of American cinema. "I just want to say one word to you. . . . Just one word," he told the captive Ben. "Are you listening?"

"Yes I am," Ben replied with comically stoic desperation.

"*Plastics,*" exclaimed Mr. McGuire.

"Exactly how do you mean that?" Ben inquired.

"There's a great future in plastics. Think about it. Will you think about it?" Mr. McGuire asked.

"Yes I will," Ben nodded, hardly reassured.

By the mid-1960s psychologists and sociologists had documented a growing alienation among America's young. Even the children of privilege felt dissatisfied with the American dream of riches and stability. Paul Goodman's

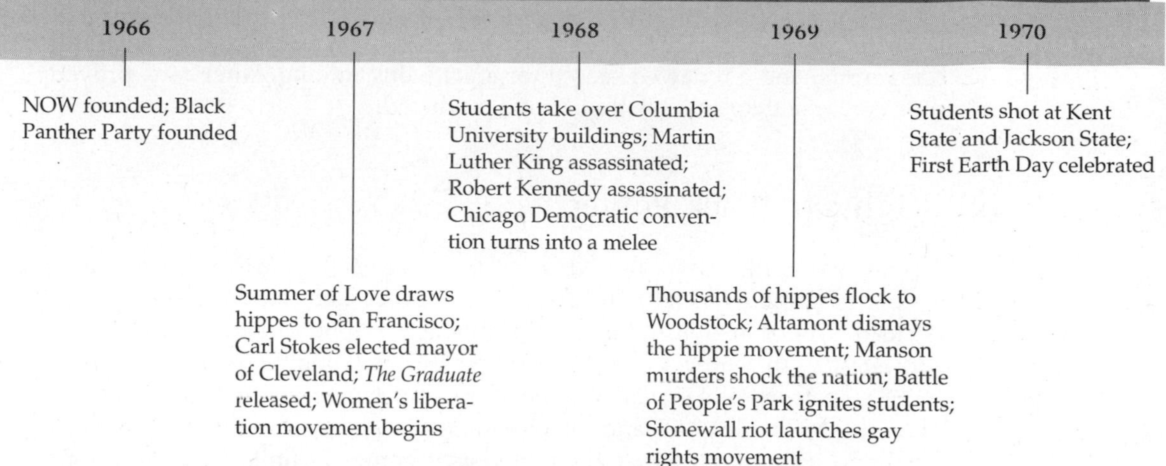

Growing Up Absurd, Kenneth Keniston's *The Uncommitted,* and Philip Slater's *The Pursuit of Loneliness* depicted a generation at loose ends, disconnected from meaningful relations with other people and lacking a sense of purpose in life. Social critics and therapists alike wondered where this vast, free-floating group might end up and whether it would drag society down with its lethargy, lose itself in narcissism, or maybe find something meaningful to do.

Others had more reason to feel disaffected, and they began to raise their voices in increasingly angry protest. African-American writer Richard Wright had sounded a forceful note of black rage as early as 1940 with his novel *Native Son,* and in the 1960s black writers from Black Panther leader Eldridge Cleaver to poet June Jordan took up Wright's legacy. Women began to find words to defy the restrictions society had placed on them. From these very diverse, sometimes contradictory threads the sixties wove a new politics and culture of protest.

By the early 1970s the political and cultural upheavals of the sixties had generated multiple, often unintended consequences. The civil rights and feminist movements had inspired calls for the liberation not only of blacks and women but also of all other people of color, gays and lesbians, people with disabilities, and the elderly. The New Left's antiwar crusade gave rise to a deep mistrust of authority that, ironically, fed a resurgence of conservatives' opposition to "big government." The sexual revolution bore fruit both delicious and dangerous, and a renewed search for spirituality among Americans proved more volatile than anyone might have predicted.

✦ From Civil Rights to Black Power

For some fifty years the National Association for the Advancement of Colored People (NAACP) and the Urban League had led the campaign for African-American civil rights. Civil rights activists believed their cause was consistent with democratic and Christian principles, and they saw their movement as instrumental in realizing the promise of America. They used a variety of methods. The NAACP and the Urban League directed their efforts toward legal and judicial reforms. Other activists organized public demonstrations against segregation. By the early 1960s sit-ins, boycotts, and protest marches had become widespread, but the decade would soon see the emergence of more radical approaches.

By 1964 the civil rights movement had begun to focus on community organization and voter registration as its primary tactics in the fight against racism. These methods were used primarily in the South, where racial hatred and a race-based caste system were particularly open and entrenched. Rank-and-file civil rights workers in organizations like the Congress of Racial Equality (CORE), the Southern Christian Leadership Conference (SCLC), and the Student Non-Violent Coordinating Committee (SNCC) faced potential and actual white violence on a daily basis.

While Congress debated the Civil Rights Act of 1964, the SCLC's Martin Luther King, Jr., courted a national television audience, eloquently preaching restraint and the use of nonviolent direct action, including boycotts, sit-ins, and demonstrations, to press for change. King was a pivotal figure in the civil rights movement. He retained the support of white liberals, who provided much of the movement's financial backing, while bolstering the increasingly frustrated younger African-Americans who held the front line in the battle for equality. Confronting white violence with dignity and leading peaceful protest marches in the face of brutal resistance, King had dazzled the nation. His "I Have a Dream" speech at the massive 1963 march on Washington had a particularly strong impact on the public. Many rank-and-file organizers, however, found King aloof and abstract.

During the summer of 1964 thousands of black and white students spent their college vacations in Mississippi, where white resistance to integration was deep and militant. These young activists sought to break the white monopoly on political power, using a weapon dear to the American political system: the vote. The SNCC's Mississippi Freedom Summer project attracted more than a thousand students, mostly white, to help veteran black and white southern workers register African-American voters for the newly created, racially integrated Mississippi Freedom Democratic Party (MFDP). Volunteers also walked picket lines, attended innumerable meetings, and organized education projects and community centers.

The Mississippi state legislature reacted to the challenge by doubling the state police force, planning riot control measures, and introducing an "anti-invasion" bill intended to keep civil rights workers out of the state. White vigilante groups mounted a campaign of intimidation, ranging from harassment to bombings and killings. In June civil rights workers Andrew Goodman, Michael Schwerner, and James Chaney—two northern whites and a southern black—were murdered. Yet the volunteers kept coming, sleeping in shifts on bare mattresses, living on peanut butter, cranking mimeograph machines, and tramping the hot streets. Sustained by idealism, SNCC workers wanted not only to end segregation and the political repression of African-Americans but also to live out their own vision of a racially integrated "beloved community" based on respect, affection, and social justice. African-American women and men like Fanny Lou Hamer and Bob Moses inspired younger white college students from the North with their bravery and their tirelessness.

The beloved community was riddled with tension, however. Living in fear of "nightriders" who fired shots through their windows at night and telephoned bomb threats, civil rights workers also had to cope with racial friction within their own ranks. Long-time black workers worried that whites, who did not face the risks blacks encountered daily because of their race, were trying to take over the movement. Interracial sexual relations caused conflict between black and white women and between women and men of both races.

The SNCC succeeded in mobilizing enough voters to enable the MFDP to mount a challenge to the whites-only delegation the regular state party sent to the 1964 Democratic national convention in Atlantic City in August. MFDP delegation leader Fanny Lou Hamer electrified a national television audience as she testified to the Democratic Party's Credentials Committee that she had been denied the right to vote, jailed, and beaten. "We are asking the American people," she said, "is *this* the land of the free and the home of the brave?" The MFDP demanded that its delegation be seated in place of the official state delegation. But at President Johnson's insistence white liberals like Senator Hubert Humphrey of Minnesota and southern conservatives in the party leadership worked out what they termed a compromise: the white delegation was seated, after promising not to bolt the Democratic Party later on, and two MFDP representatives received delegate-at-large status. To SNCC members the arrangement seemed a betrayal, a triumph of political expediency over morality. Two disillusioned African-American activists, Stokely Carmichael and Charles Hamilton, wrote that the lesson of Atlantic City was clear: "Black people . . . could not rely on their so-called allies."

By the time of the Atlantic City convention African-Americans throughout the country were revealing their frustration at the limited success of nonviolent tactics. Martin Luther King, Jr., framed his endorsement of civil disobedience in the language and spirit of Christian forbearance: "One who breaks an unjust law must do so openly, lovingly, and with a willingness to accept the penalty." But patience was running low. Although the 1964 Civil Rights Act had nominally established racial equality in the eyes of the law, black civil rights workers had learned through experience that white lawlessness seldom brought penalties. If nonviolent civil disobedience failed to gain justice, King warned, "millions of Negroes will, out of frustration and despair, seek solace and security in black nationalist ideologies."

King's expectations were fulfilled. Many blacks began to reject Christian forbearance altogether. Some sought new meaning in a black separatist Islamic faith. Malcolm X, the nation's most prominent and eloquent Black Muslim, spoke out for black nationalism, explicitly rejected integration, and advocated meeting violence with violence. On the secular front, rioting broke out in Harlem in the summer of 1964.

By the early months of 1965 the concept of "black and white together" in the civil rights movement was being eclipsed. Malcolm X had begun to tone down his antiwhite message and to seek some new solution to the problem of racism, but he was gunned down in February, probably murdered by followers of Black Muslim leader Elijah Muhammad. Other civil rights leaders persisted in trying to channel the movement's energies into integrated, nonviolent action, but their protests seemed inadequate in the face of white brutality. In March a national television audience watched as Selma, Alabama, sheriff Jim Clark ordered his men to meet civil rights marchers with clubs and tear gas. Martin Luther King, Jr., and Ralph Bunche led a group of 3,200 people on a fifty-mile march from Selma to the heavily fortified state capitol at Montgomery, where they were joined by 25,000 supporters. In the course of the Selma campaign three activists were killed. Many Americans were struck by the contrast between the violence of the Selma police and the peaceful nature of the marchers. The Voting Rights Act of 1965, signed in early August, passed partly as a legacy of the Selma march and President Johnson's revulsion at the violent police response to it. But the costs of peaceful tactics were becoming unbearable to movement veterans.

Around the nation, African-Americans responded to the slow pace of change with increasing fury. In August 1965 five days of looting and rioting broke out in Watts, a black ghetto in Los Angeles. Residents of Watts had reason to be frustrated: although Los Angeles as a whole was booming, the city's blacks were worse off than ever. Median income in Watts had dropped 8 percent between 1959 and 1965. Thirty percent of the adult men in the neighborhood were unemployed. Los Angeles police, mostly white and sometimes openly racist, did little to win the community's trust. By the time the riot subsided, thirty-four people had died, four thousand had been arrested, and much of the area had been leveled. The Los Angeles police chief blamed civil rights workers; the city's mayor blamed Communists. From the ashes arose a cry of revolutionary despair—"burn, baby, burn"—that would fuel both the rhetoric of the Black Power movement and the white backlash against African-American rights.

The cover of a 1967 SNCC pamphlet put a new ideology in stark black and white. *Wide World Photos*

The revolutionary movement crystallized during a march through Mississippi in the summer of 1966. Some civil rights activists, like Floyd McKissick of CORE and John Lewis, former chairman of the SNCC, still supported the goal of integration and the tactics of nonviolence. But for most, patience was wearing thin. The SNCC's Stokely Carmichael announced the formation of a new organization, the Black Panther Party, with a new goal: Black Power. To his African-American listeners he declared, "It's time we stand up and take over." To society at large he issued a warning: "Move on over, or we'll move on over you."

Within a year weary veterans of the civil rights movement had been displaced in the public eye by young militants. The SNCC became the organizing center of the Black Power movement. Carmichael and the new chairman of the organization, H. Rap Brown, viewed the increasingly common ghetto disturbances as a dress rehearsal for revolution. Meanwhile the federal government offered only a weak response to black rage. The following year President Johnson appointed Illinois governor Otto Kerner to head a commission to study the situation. When the Kerner Commission delivered a report concluding that the United States was rapidly becoming two nations, one black and poor, the other white and rich, Johnson did nothing. He was too preoccupied with the Vietnam War to pursue his promised Great Society.

Urging students at black colleges to "fight for liberation by any means necessary," Carmichael declared, "To hell with the laws of the United States." At a Black Power conference in Newark, held on the heels of a riot in which police killed twenty-five African-Americans, a thousand participants approved resolutions affirming the right of black people to revolt and calling for a separate black nation and black militia. In 1968 Carmichael, Brown, and the SNCC were replaced by the Black Panthers as the most visible militant group. Wearing leather jackets and carrying weapons, the Panthers often resembled an elite paramilitary unit, and they conveyed a radical message. As the Panthers provoked considerable uneasiness among the white middle class, they became the objects of heavy surveillance by the FBI. They had frequent confrontations with local police, including shoot-outs that left some Panthers dead and others under arrest.

✦ SDS and the Rise of the New Left

As African-American groups became more militant, so did other, predominantly white organizations that arose to challenge the structure of American politics and society. Collectively these groups came to be called the New Left, to distinguish them from the Old Left of the 1930s through the 1950s.

Those who came of age in the early sixties were beneficiaries of American affluence and the huge expansion of the nation's colleges and universities. Between 1945 and 1965 public spending on higher education rose from $742.1 million to $6.9 billion per year. The booming universities provided the chance for a small but growing group of students to imagine things as they ought to be, rather than as they were. Uneasy in the presence of the world's growing atomic arsenal and ignited by the civil rights movement, they were less wedded to traditional political affiliations than their predecessors in the Old Left and more optimistic about the prospects for sweeping social change.

In 1962 young, mostly white activists founded the most influential and best-known New Left group, Students for a Democratic Society (SDS). At the 1962 SDS meeting in Port Huron, Michigan, Tom Hayden articulated the organization's concerns and goals in the "Port Huron Statement." Hayden criticized college students' apathy toward politics. The presence of widespread poverty in the country and the unchallenged power of the military-industrial complex, he said, threatened the nation's best traditions. Hayden called for a restoration of participatory democracy to make the country's political parties, corporations, and government more responsive to ordinary people. Embracing Hayden's hopeful message, thousands of white students flocked into civil rights work in the early 1960s. Some SDS members went south. Others, in 1964, went to work in northern ghettos, attempting to organize an interracial movement of the poor.

Soon their involvement in the civil rights movement inspired student activists to take up other issues in other places. Mario Savio and Jack Weinberg, two veterans of the Mississippi Freedom Summer, returned to the University of California at Berkeley in the fall of 1964, planning to continue recruitment for the movement. When administrators forbade them to speak and recruit on campus, students took over the administration building, declared a strike, and enlisted faculty support for the removal of restrictions on free expression on campus. Calling themselves the Berkeley Free Speech Movement, activists expressed both their joy and their anger in words once thought unacceptable in polite company, and conservative Americans began to see in Berkeley a symbol of lawlessness and sin.

Campus protests quickly spread. By 1965 there were disturbances at Yale, Ohio State, the University of Kansas, Brooklyn College, Michigan State, and St. John's University. Disputes often arose over issues of personal conduct rather than national politics. College students of the fifties had accepted (or secretly violated) the time-honored doctrine of *in loco parentis,* according to which the institution had the right and the obligation to stand in for students' parents and regulate their behavior. But by the mid-1960s the campus regulations—particularly those that attempted to preserve the conservative dating rituals of the fifties—seemed quaint, artificial, and restrictive. Students began to oppose all kinds of limitations on their behavior, from rules governing where they could live, what hours they could be out, and who might visit their rooms to dress codes and smoking regulations. Students at single-sex institutions agitated for coeducation.

Even without these personal lifestyle issues, national politics provided more than enough cause for dissent, particularly as President Johnson escalated the American war in Vietnam. As nightly television news broadcasts brought American television watchers pictures of the bloodiness and futility of the nation's policy, government officials' pronouncements seemed patently false. Berkeley's Jack Weinberg admonished his fellow students not to trust anyone over thirty, and enterprising American journalists began to believe that there was no point in trusting *anyone* in power. On campuses, in cities, and on military bases, "underground" newspapers sprang up to offer a more radical alternative to the conventional news sources.

Even the mainstream press began to mistrust the information released by "official sources." Investigative reporters like Seymour Hersh of the *New York Times* began to look beyond government press releases to get at the truth of national policy. In 1969 Hersh broke the story of the Mylai massacre in Vietnam. Hersh and other journalists accepted the professional risks of upsetting their previously cozy relationships with government sources, and as a result they managed to uncover important stories that government officials were attempting to suppress.

The Vietnam War soon became the main focus of student protest. Because male students were directly threatened by the rising draft calls, opposition to the draft mobilized a huge new constituency for the protest movement. When

SDS endorsed draft resistance, its membership swelled. Draft counseling centers sprang up across the country. And by the late 1960s many parents of draft-age men had also changed their views on Vietnam.

Local SDS chapters and other draft resistance groups pretty much determined their own tactics. Some sponsored draft card burnings. Others held sit-ins at Selective Service induction centers, opposed university Reserve Officers' Training Corps (ROTC) programs, protested military recruiters' visits to campus, or demonstrated against corporations involved in defense work. Between January 1 and June 15, 1968, according to the National Student Association, there were about 221 major antiwar demonstrations at over one hundred colleges and universities, involving some forty thousand students.

Tactics varied widely from campus to campus and from one demonstration to another. Across the country, many college professors and even high school teachers initiated "teach-ins" to educate curious students about Vietnamese history and politics. There were notable efforts to join student groups with other organizations to orchestrate national protests against the war. In the summer of 1967 twenty thousand people participated in the Vietnam Summer, an effort modeled on the Mississippi Freedom Summer. Stop the Draft Week, in October 1967, culminated in a march on the Pentagon in which fifty thousand people crossed the Arlington Memorial Bridge, some to picket, some to pray, others to attempt to storm the premier bastion of the nation's military-industrial complex. Brilliantly (if egocentrically) recounted in Norman Mailer's *Armies of the Night*—a prime example of the developing "New Journalism" style of writing, which aimed to probe beneath the surface of events—the march on the Pentagon included not only student groups but also many others opposed to the war. Among those present were Berkeley Free Speech activist Jerry Rubin, child care expert Dr. Benjamin Spock, linguistics theorist Noam Chomsky, and poet Robert Lowell. The event even had its comic aspects: Ed Sanders, leader of a rock band called the Fugs, proposed a "grope for peace," and radical leader Abbie Hoffman coordinated an attempt to levitate the Pentagon.

Sociologist Todd Gitlin, an early president of SDS, noted that as the war became more violent, the antiwar movement became more militant. Antiwar demonstrators had often stressed the contrast between their own peace-loving outlook and the brutality of their government's policy, carrying signs reading "Make Love, Not War" and putting flowers in the barrels of guns pointed at them by police and troops charged with keeping order at demonstrations. By 1967, however, antiwar activists were preaching a harder line, and demonstrators had adopted a tougher posture. In Oakland, California, protests during Stop the Draft Week turned into bloody confrontations with the police.

By 1967 SDS was embracing a new, confrontational stance; its publications began referring to the authorities as "pigs." Some New Leftists declared free speech a sham and shouted down progovernment speakers. National Liberation Front flags began to appear at antiwar rallies, alienating many middle-of-the-road Americans. Many Americans opposed the war and sympathized with

The clenched fist of militance and the peace sign mingled at antiwar demonstrations in the late 1960s. *Roger Malloch/Magnum*

the demands of the radicals but found it hard to accept tactics that included violating property rights.

Nowhere was campus conflict more spectacular than at Columbia University in New York. Columbia embodied what campus radicals condemned. A bastion of Ivy League privilege on the edge of the Harlem ghetto, the university owned slum properties and held major defense research contracts. On April 23, 1968, the Columbia SDS chapter joined with black militants in taking over university buildings, including the university president's office. Columbia students held the buildings for eight days, after which New York City police moved in with billy clubs and arrested 692 people, three-quarters of them students. A student strike forced the university to close early for the year.

The American student protests were part of an international drive toward student militance. The Columbia uprising had its counterpart in Paris, where angry protesters erected barricades in the streets and battled police. But not all students—and certainly not all young people—joined the protests. Some opposed only the war and the draft; some sympathized but stayed out of the streets. Many young people—political conservatives, white southerners, working-class youths who did not go to college, graduate students who had invested time and money pursuing professional careers—were either unaffected by the protests or opposed to them. Nevertheless, the campus conflicts of the sixties reflected more than differences over government and university policies; they revealed a deep gulf between the "straight" social standards of the older generation and the new beliefs of those who came of age in the sixties.

✦ The Counterculture

At the same time that young people were becoming more radical politically, they also began to experiment with new ways of living, inspired in many cases by the Beat writers who had emerged in the 1950s. "The only ones for me," novelist Jack Kerouac wrote in his 1957 epic *On the Road*, "are the mad ones, the ones who are mad to live, mad to talk, mad to be saved, desirous of everything at the same time, the ones who never yawn or say a commonplace thing, but burn, burn, burn like fabulous yellow roman candles." Along with other writers of the Beat Generation, Kerouac came to symbolize the rejection of bourgeois comfort and the embrace of a life of sensation seeking, adventure, and personal authenticity.

Some of the Beat literati, notably poet Allen Ginsberg, became political dissidents in the sixties. Others, like Kerouac, rejected politics as corrupt. All were involved in a protest against mainstream American culture. "Squares" pursued their American dream in suburban comfort, drinking martinis and surreptitiously breaking their marriage vows, their aesthetic tastes defined by the likes of television's *Hit Parade*. Beats, or Hipsters, as they were also called, had another set of standards for their American dream. They lived in bare apartments in urban enclaves like New York's Greenwich Village and San Francisco's North Beach, expanded the range of recreational drugs from sweet wine to marijuana and heroin, and listened to the incendiary, experimental jazz of Charlie "Yardbird" Parker, Dizzy Gillespie, and Miles Davis. Willing to die early and, they hoped, leave pretty corpses, the young Beat poets foreshadowed a movement that widened by the later 1960s into the counterculture, a loosely defined phenomenon that involved new types of music, drugs, religious experimentation, and sexual freedom.

The popular culture the Beats despised was undergoing its own transformation. A revival of folk music, identified with the Old Left since the 1930s, meant commercial success in the sixties for protest singers like Joan Baez and Bob Dylan. Their folk music helped harness the energies of political protest and the yearning among young Americans for social change. But it was rock 'n' roll that served as the primary musical catalyst for the counterculture.

For millions of American girls, the arrival of the Beatles in the United States in 1964 was a watershed. No musicians had ever achieved the mass popularity and cultural influence of these four young Englishmen, John Lennon, Paul McCartney, George Harrison, and Ringo Starr. Their live performances were scenes of mass female hysteria—"Beatlemania," it was called—replete with shrieking, crying, fainting teenage girls. As they had during the Elvis Presley phenomenon of the late 1950s, parents began to worry that their children were getting out of control. But the transformation of rock music and the youth culture it represented was only beginning. By the mid-1960s the sentimental love songs of the Beatles' early years gave way to the overt sexual come-ons of other groups, such as the Rolling Stones and the Doors. The innocence of Lennon and McCartney's "I Wanna Hold Your Hand" became Mick Jagger's easy invitation in "Let's Spend the Night Together" and the urgency of Jim Morrison's plea to "Touch Me."

Many girls relished the prospect of sexual freedom. In Los Angeles, Hollywood clubs and the Sunset Strip attracted thousands of teenage girls, parading in miniskirts and seeking fun and vicarious fame by having sex with members of male rock bands. These "groupies" were complicit in their own sexual exploitation and subjected themselves to grave health risks, but they also represented a new, open, and defiant insistence on the right to sexual pleasure, for women as well as men. The birth control pill, first marketed in 1960, made pleasure without procreation more possible and accelerated the gradual repeal of state "blue laws" restricting the dispensing of contraceptives.

Though groupies were only a small segment of the youth population, the ideal of sexual freedom was spreading rapidly, galvanized by the rock music that expressed the desires and demands of young people. As the counterculture developed, the music continued to evolve. Soon a "psychedelic" rock music, often known as acid rock, was celebrating the use of mind-altering drugs. Groups like the Grateful Dead and Jefferson Airplane turned their sets into dizzying, deafening swirls of sound. A young white woman named Janis Joplin sang a steamy, screeching, tortured, blues-driven rock that gave her almost legendary status as a prodigy of the counterculture.

Like Joplin, most of the avant-garde performers were white. Ironically, at a time when many black political leaders were turning from civil rights to Black Power, African-American musicians succeeded in reaching a broad commercial audience by taking a fairly cautious approach. The best-known black recording artists were associated with Motown, the Detroit music company masterminded by black songwriter-entrepreneur Berry Gordy, Jr. Motown singers like Stevie Wonder and groups like the Temptations and the Supremes combined musical virtuosity with lush production, precise choreography, glittering costumes, and a bland message. One exception to this trend was James Brown, the "godfather of soul," who marked out the frontiers of raw sex appeal. Another black innovator was guitarist Jimi Hendrix, whose incendiary playing was in the vanguard of the psychedelic style.

Along with sex and rock 'n' roll, the counterculture featured the abundant use of drugs. The Beatles took lysergic acid diethylamide (LSD), a chemical

Janis Joplin, who died of a drug overdose in 1970, was one of the top rock singers of the 1960s. Here she is performing at the Festival for Peace held in New York just before her death. *Corbis/Bettmann*

better known as "acid," and in their path-breaking album *Sergeant Pepper's Lonely Hearts Club Band* declared, "I'd love to turn you on." Many in the stoned world stuck to milder forms of intoxication, like marijuana, which was said to impair short-term memory but had limited long-term effects. Some, like rock idols Janis Joplin, Jim Morrison, and Jimi Hendrix, combined alcohol with substances such as barbiturates, amphetamines, cocaine, and heroin until their dependencies killed them.

The term *psychedelic,* when it first came into wide use in the counterculture, referred to the altered perceptions brought on by hallucinogenic drugs. Counterculture adherents used these drugs to expand their minds and reach a higher level of understanding. Drug use was also a way of expressing the antimaterialist, antiauthoritarian ethos of the era. For many, the use of such perception-altering substances as marijuana and LSD became akin to religious sacraments. LSD had first been introduced into the United States as part of a CIA program to develop substances for use in chemical warfare. Harvard professors Timothy Leary and Richard Alpert conducted psychological experiments with LSD, and by 1960 they were enthusiastic advocates of hallucinogenic drugs. When Harvard fired them for using students as subjects in their research, they became outlaw heroes. Leary advised the nation's youth to "Turn on, tune in, and drop out." Alpert embraced Eastern spirituality and reincarnated himself as guru Baba Ram Dass.

Still others celebrated the recreational dimension of opening up what British writer Aldous Huxley had called "the doors of perception." Novelist Ken Kesey, who participated in CIA-sponsored drug experiments at Stanford, founded a mobile commune called the Merry Pranksters, which traveled in a wildly painted bus called "Furthur." In cities up and down the West Coast, the Pranksters held "acid tests"—parties incorporating avant-garde rock 'n' roll, multimedia spectacles, and the mass distribution of free LSD. In San Francisco the Pranksters joined forces with master businessman Bill Graham to produce the Tripps Festival, an event at the Fillmore Auditorium starring the city's premier acid rock bands.

Soon new forms of popular behavior and expression grew up around the music and drug scenes. Adopting the Beat Generation's notion that a posture of "hipness" constituted a form of social protest, counterculture adherents called themselves "hippies." The hippie style, with its flowing hair and bell-bottom jeans, transformed the appearance of American young people. Devotees of the psychedelic culture adopted some of the trappings of Eastern mysticism, sporting bells, beads, flowing robes, and sandals, lighting incense, and festooning their households with Indian-print bedspreads. They wove flowers into their hair. They changed their diet, demanding more "natural" foods to enhance their spiritual health.

By the summer of 1967 there were hippie neighborhoods in most American cities and college towns. In particular, San Francisco's Haight-Ashbury district became a magnet for people preaching the virtues of love, dope, music, sex, and "flower power." While radical politicos proclaimed that the summer of 1967 would be the Vietnam Summer, hippies announced the Summer of Love. This hedonistic interlude was supposed to transform society, not by agitating for wide-scale social change or an end to the war but by encouraging individuals to drop out of the rat race and sample the pleasures of the senses. Networks and news magazines predicted a migration of thousands of young people to "the Haight" that summer to "crash" in communal pads, "groove" at concerts, and shower each other and apprehensive local authorities with peace, love, and flowers. "If you're going to San Francisco," one popular song advised, "be sure to wear some flowers in your hair."

There was plenty of good music, considerable good feeling, and a profusion of flowers in the Haight that summer. Serious politics also made an appearance in the street dramas and free feeds. But there was also blight. Most hippies stayed home, but thousands did come. Though many observers of the time believed that the hippie influx into San Francisco represented a revolt against affluence, it was instead a sign that the ideal of the happy American family often papered over serious family conflicts. Class was no distinguishing factor among the migrants to San Francisco during the Summer of Love; the young people came from poor, working-class, middle-class, and wealthy backgrounds. Rather, those who ran off to the Haight were disproportionately children from severely troubled homes. They were as often throwaways as runaways; many were victims of parental abuse or neglect.

Few migrants to the Haight had the skills to sustain themselves in a city suddenly flooded with their kind. Thus Haight hippies often turned to panhandling or prostitution and drug dealing to earn their keep. Drugs traded included marijuana and acid and also such addictive substances as amphetamines, cocaine, and heroin, which led to overdoses and outbreaks of hepatitis from dirty needles. The cutthroat drug business kept Haight residents vulnerable to exploitation and physical violence.

Like dope, free love turned out to have a high price. Hippie girls, presumed to be sexually liberated, sometimes found they were expected to exchange sex for food and shelter; some concluded that prostitution for cash was a better bargain than sexual barter. The assumption that all young women sought sexual liaisons left Haight women particularly exposed to sexual assault. Sexual promiscuity, whether chosen, forced, or economically necessary, led to an epidemic of venereal disease. Free medical clinics as well as soup kitchens were overwhelmed by demand.

Despite its outward rejection of convention, the counterculture exhibited many of the social problems and prejudices of American society in general. Crash pads, though hospitable, often re-created conventional household hierarchies. One young woman who went with a girlfriend to the Haight for a weekend reported with some disgust that her friend "moved into the first commune we entered and became a 'housemother,' which means she did all the cooking and cleaning. Very communal." Racial tensions, like gender roles, persisted among the hip as well as the square. Relations between the predominantly white hippies in the Haight and the nearby black community in the Fillmore were terrible.

Even as the Haight-Ashbury experience revealed contradictions in the counterculture, the music persisted, helping to keep the spirit of the cultural revolution alive. Promoters had begun to stage large-scale, open-air rock festivals to attract the faithful. These reached a high point with the Woodstock Music Festival of August 1969, a rain- and mud-soaked gathering of four hundred thousand rock fans in upstate New York. The unexpectedly huge crowd posed many serious problems for the organizers, particularly in providing sanitation, food, and water. The audience had difficulty actually hearing the music and seeing the stage. Traffic was so bad that state authorities closed down the New York State Thruway. In spite of these troubles, however, many members of the audience would look back on Woodstock as the grandest experience of the sixties, a demonstration that hundreds of thousands could come together for "three days of peace and music." The festival developed an almost mythological aura as the high point of the counterculture movement.

At the opposite extreme was the festival at Altamont Speedway in California the following winter. In the spirit of drug fellowship, the headlining Rolling Stones made the common counterculture mistake of assuming that anyone who uses illegal drugs must have humane values. The Stones had invited the Hell's Angels motorcycle gang to provide festival security. The Angels, who resembled flower children only in their taste for dope, stabbed one person to death in front of the stage as Mick Jagger looked on aghast. Before the day was out four people were dead, and many others had been severely injured.

Events like Altamont and news of the unloving side of the Haight-Ashbury experience led many cultural rebels to conclude that the only salvation for the counterculture lay in cultivating their own garden. Across the country, disaffected hippies sought spiritual salvation and physical health by returning to the land. College students moved out of dormitories and into rural farmhouses, bought sacks of brown rice, and planted organic gardens. Most communes were short-lived, falling apart when faced with such issues as how to share expenses, whom to include or exclude, and how to divide up work. The communes that lasted tended to be very hierarchical, such as The Farm in Tennessee, and many others devoted to Eastern religious practices.

Of course, authoritarianism did not guarantee stability or virtue. The most infamous of the communes, the murderous Manson Family, left Haight-Ashbury to settle, finally, in the dry Santa Susana Mountains of southern California. Charles Manson held his mostly female followers so completely spellbound that by December of 1969 they willingly committed multiple murders on his orders. Hippie communes embodied a fundamental tension in American society, the tension between a longing for connectedness and a desire for personal liberty. If most lasted but a short time and seemed more dedicated to escapism than to solving the problems of postindustrial society, they nevertheless represented a desire for a way of life dedicated less to the pursuit of consumer goods than to a vision of a meaningful existence. As often as not, those who experimented with communal living pondered not only human relations but also the complicated connections between people and the natural world. Some who began by raising organic vegetables became pioneers of the environmental movement.

While communards sought a place apart from the crass materialism of mainstream America, the counterculture spread to younger groups as well, becoming part of the everyday world of high school students from the mid-1960s to the mid-1970s. And as it spread there were many people ready to capitalize on its economic potential. Bill Graham grew fabulously wealthy promoting rock concerts. Psychedelic artist Peter Max eventually marketed his talents to some fifty companies, including Sears and General Electric. The counterculture spawned new business opportunities for purveyors of dietary and spiritual nostrums, record store operators, and proprietors of "head shops," T-shirt stores, health food operations, and hip clothing boutiques.

✦ 1968: A Year of Cataclysm and Its Aftermath

To some extent the three movements this chapter has traced—Black Power, the New Left, and the counterculture—represented separate strands of antiestablishment protest during the sixties. Often they differed from one another in both their goals and their methods. For instance, the Black Panthers had no intention of wearing flowers in their hair; hippies were frequently indifferent to politics, believing that salvation lay in altering the mind and spirit; and some political radicals of the New Left could not fathom how anyone could lie around smoking marijuana when there was a rally to attend. But the membership of the three movements overlapped, and they generally shared a basic opposition to racism, social injustice, bourgeois consumerism, and the Vietnam War. As the climate of protest intensified in the late 1960s there were more and more occasions when the various strands came together. This was particularly true in 1968, a cataclysmic year for American society and politics.

On December 31, 1967, some important members of the counterculture and the New Left joined forces. Radical leaders Abbie Hoffman and Jerry Rubin; black activist-comedian Dick Gregory; Beat poet Allen Ginsberg; counterculture writer Paul Krassner of *The Realist*, the nation's oldest underground newspaper; and several others founded the Youth International Party, better known as the Yippies. Applying a combination of militant tactics, freakish pranks, and humor, Yippies worked hard at making headlines. They planned to turn the Democratic national convention in Chicago the following summer into a "Festival of Life," featuring rock music and elaborate practical jokes—a kind of revolutionary dance party.

The Yippies were not the only set of protesters on the political stage, nor by any means were they the most representative of dissident youth. When Senator Eugene McCarthy, a liberal opponent of the Vietnam War, decided to challenge Lyndon Johnson in the 1968 New Hampshire presidential primary, thousands of students turned out for his campaign. Aware that their hippie style would alienate middle-of-the-road and middle-aged voters, they cut their hair, put aside their bell-bottoms, and donned coats and ties or skirts and sweaters, becoming "Clean for Gene." In a paroxysm of political idealism they took the McCarthy campaign across the nation, converting flower power to grassroots organization, their Volkswagen Beetles sprouting the distinctive blue-and-white daisy-shaped McCarthy bumper stickers. When McCarthy nearly defeated Johnson in the New Hampshire presidential primary, they tasted victory and redoubled their envelope-stuffing and precinct-walking efforts. Johnson's announcement on March 31 that he would not run for reelection was their great moment of triumph.

This well-scrubbed foray into electoral politics fell victim to an increasing national climate of violence and confrontation, however. The first great shock came on April 4, 1968, when Martin Luther King, Jr., was assassinated by white supremacist James Earl Ray in Memphis, Tennessee. King had gone to the city on behalf of striking sanitation workers, almost all of whom were black and who represented the abused, overworked, yet politically mobilized people he hoped to reach in his attempts to launch an interracial Poor People's Campaign.

Despite King's own optimism, many African-Americans could find no way to understand his murder except as proof of the futility of the nonviolent strategy he had advocated. "When white America killed Dr. King," said Stokely Carmichael, "she declared war." The riots that broke out in more than a hundred cities lasted more than a week. More than sixty-five thousand federal troops were called out to try to restore order.

Yet, almost miraculously, thousands of activists clung to King's nonviolent vision. Two months after his murder, supporters of the Poor People's Campaign, led now by the SCLC's Reverend Ralph David Abernathy, built a makeshift settlement of tents and plywood shacks in the shadow of the Washington Monument. King's widow, Coretta Scott King, spoke often during the month-long existence of Resurrection City, as the protesters called their shantytown, stressing nonviolence and reminding her audience that "starving a child is violence, suppressing a culture is violence, contempt for poverty is violence."

Unfortunately these words could not stem the tide of violence. After New York Democratic senator Robert Kennedy announced his candidacy for the Democratic presidential nomination, offering antiwar voters another choice, some of McCarthy's student supporters went over to the Kennedy camp. More significantly, Kennedy became the overwhelming choice of black and Mexican-American voters, who considered him the strongest candidate on civil rights. Minority voters were impressed by Kennedy's support for Cesar Chávez and the United Farm Workers, a predominantly Mexican-American union trying to win rudimentary concessions in wages and working conditions from California grape growers. On the strength of minority support, Kennedy won the California primary on June 5, 1968, getting enough delegates to raise the possibility of a deadlocked Democratic convention. But his shooting by Sirhan Sirhan, a Palestinian angry at Kennedy's support for Israel, came only a few hours after the polls closed. When Kennedy died the next morning, many Americans believed that he took with him the sense that electoral politics offered real possibilities for change.

Expecting strong antiwar protests at the Democratic national convention in August, Chicago authorities turned the city into an armed camp. Barbed wire enclosed the convention center, twelve thousand Chicago police were

Robert Kennedy owed his victory in the 1968 California Democratic primary to minority workers who endorsed his support for the United Farm Workers. *Michael Rougier,* Life *magazine © Time, Inc.*

deployed on twelve-hour shifts, and some six thousand troops of the Illinois National Guard were called out, along with about as many army troops. A significant number of undercover FBI agents attended. The overwhelming majority of antiwar activists stayed away. On most days during the convention there were perhaps four thousand demonstrators, with crowds peaking at possibly ten thousand on August 28. Thus, police generally outnumbered demonstrators by a factor of three or four to one, and federal records suggest that the ranks of the protesters were extensively infiltrated by government agents.

Those who did come to protest were hardly a representative cross section of the antiwar movement. Male demonstrators at Chicago outnumbered females by eight or ten to one, imparting a particularly macho flavor to the action. The Yippies came prepared to make a farce out of the convention: "Our concept of revolution," said Abbie Hoffman, "is that it's fun." Paul Krassner terrified city residents by suggesting that demonstrators might attempt to alter people's consciousness by putting LSD into the city's water supply. An infuriated Mayor Richard J. Daley refused to let demonstrators camp in city parks, a move guaranteeing that there would be plenty of restless people looking for conflict. A small minority of demonstrators representing the extreme Left, perhaps as many as three hundred, came to Chicago hoping to provoke violence.

The police obliged them, acting without strategy or discipline in a week-long melee observers would come to call a police riot. Over the course of the convention they repeatedly cleared Lincoln Park with tear gas and clubs. Police and demonstrators clashed in Grant Park, across from presumptive nominee Hubert Humphrey's headquarters in the Hilton. Television cameras recorded the head bashing, and some antiwar convention delegates went into the streets to support the demonstrators. Candidate Humphrey could smell tear gas from his hotel room. Reporters, bystanders, and demonstrators alike were beaten and gassed. A total of 668 people were arrested.

Meanwhile, inside the convention center, Mayor Daley retained control, loading the galleries with supporters waving banners that read "We Love Mayor Daley." Most Americans seemed to believe that the mayor and the police had responded appropriately. Less than 20 percent of those contacted in a national telephone poll thought the police had used too much force in putting down the demonstrations. Hubert Humphrey said the Chicago police had done "nothing wrong." To the strains of "Happy Days Are Here Again," he accepted the presidential nomination, his party in ruins around him.

No matter what Humphrey did later to placate voters who despised hippies and protesters, the Democrats were firmly linked in the public mind, ironically, with those who had come to demonstrate against them. As a result the protests in Chicago aided the November victory of Republican candidate Richard Nixon, who had been nominated at a carefully orchestrated meeting in Miami that looked like a love feast compared to the mayhem at Chicago. Nixon seemed a reassuring presence to those he would come to call "the silent majority" of Americans.

Although the Right gained momentum after Chicago, spurred on by the inflammatory rhetoric of independent presidential candidate George Wallace and Republican vice-presidential contender Spiro Agnew, the Left was transformed but not dead. SDS boomed. Some movement leaders, increasingly seduced by the romance of violent revolution, considered the convention a triumph. Tom Hayden and seven others, including Hoffman and Rubin, were indicted for conspiring to incite a riot at the convention.

Campus confrontation became the rule of the day. In May 1969 police and demonstrators clashed in Berkeley at the battle of People's Park. The park, which belonged to the University of California, had once been a weedy meeting place for dope dealers and their customers but had since been turned into a community garden. The university, claiming it wanted to build a soccer field on the spot, asked police to seal off the area while bulldozers razed the gardens. When marchers moved in to take back the park, the police opened up with birdshot, buckshot, and tear gas. Governor Ronald Reagan sent in three thousand National Guardsmen, who occupied the park for seventeen days. People's Park became a symbol of radical struggle and of the communal

Antiwar leader Tom Hayden returned to Lincoln Park in Chicago for a demonstration in 1969. *Corbis/Bettmann*

alternative to private property; it also underlined the emerging importance of ecological issues, pitting organic gardeners against bulldozers, tomatoes against tear gas.

Disturbances that spring at Cornell, Harvard, Stanford, and nearly three hundred other campuses included more than a hundred incidents involving arson and attempted or actual bombings. The voices of the counterculture grew more militant. Jefferson Airplane, a San Francisco rock group that had risen to fame by combining powerful vocal and instrumental performances with odes to the mind-expanding power of LSD, turned to celebrating insurrection, crowing, "Look what's happenin' out in the streets/Got to Revolution!"

All the while, some activists worked hard to repair the damaged credibility of the antiwar movement with the public at large. The New Mobilization, a coalition of moderate antiwar advocates, organized massive peace demonstrations in the fall of 1969, calling for a Vietnam War Moratorium. Across the nation, millions of people responded, holding rallies, teach-ins, marches, and meetings. On the day of the demonstrations, October 15, one hundred thousand people gathered on Boston Common; in New York City, a series of mass meetings even included one on Wall Street. Nationwide crowd estimates ranged from 2 million to 15 million. The following month, more than half a million people gathered in Washington, D.C., for a follow-up protest in the largest demonstration ever held in that city.

The escalating climate of violence claimed more and more lives. On December 4, 1969, Chicago police raided the local Black Panther headquarters, killing Panther leaders Fred Hampton and Mark Clark in their beds. SDS splintered and soon became dominated by a faction calling itself the Weathermen, after a line in a Bob Dylan song: "You don't need a weatherman to know which way the wind blows." They announced a new goal: "the destruction of U.S. imperialism and the achievement of a classless world." Rejecting coalition politics of any kind, the Weathermen embraced a worldwide Communist revolution.

A week before the October demonstrations, two or three hundred Weathermen street fighters battled Chicago police in a confrontation that came to be known as the Days of Rage. In the next year the message of the antiwar movement became ever more conflicted. While thousands assembled to light candles and sing "Give Peace a Chance," a relatively few shock troops fantasized about violence, trained for street fighting, and built bombs. Between September 1969 and May 1970 there were at least 250 bombings of draft boards, ROTC buildings, federal offices, and corporate headquarters. In March 1970 three bombers from the Weather Underground, as the Weathermen now called themselves, died when they blew themselves up in a New York townhouse. The following August a bomb exploded in the University of Wisconsin mathematics building, killing a graduate student who was working on a research project in a facility thought to be empty.

In 1970 there were more than 9,400 incidents of protest; over 700 involved arrests, more than 400 involved damage to property, and over 200 involved violence to persons. The confrontations peaked in May, when President Nixon revealed that U.S. troops had invaded neutral Cambodia, a state neighboring Vietnam. The announcement set off a wave of student strikes; at least seventy-five campuses shut down for the rest of the academic year, and students at Northwestern University announced that their institution had seceded from the United States. Some thirty ROTC buildings were burned or bombed in the first week of May, including the one at Kent State University, in Kent, Ohio. Governor James Rhodes called in National Guard troops to restore order on campus; on May 4 nervous guardsmen opened fire on student demonstrators and passers-by, killing four and wounding nine. Ten days later police killed two more students and wounded nine at Jackson State, a predominantly black campus in Mississippi. Torn and bloody, the country seemed to be consuming its young—a cannibalism some deplored, others embraced.

As the decade's radical and antiwar protests culminated in these violent confrontations, another protest movement was developing—more quietly at

This classic photograph of the 1970 Kent State killings became the visual icon for the idea that the Vietnam War had torn the country apart. *John Filo*

first, but possessing the potential for even greater long-term impact. This was the movement for women's liberation, a product of a new feminist consciousness.

✦ The Rise of the New Feminism

Even in the relatively quiescent 1950s there had been some organized and articulate attempts to come to grips with women's issues. A few unions had sought to organize service and clerical workers and women factory employees, like those in California's canneries, in the immediate postwar period. Sometimes organizing across ethnic lines, working-class women had pushed for equal pay for equal work and had begun to consider economic and social questions that would not be fully articulated until the 1980s. The idea that women belonged at home because they were nurturing, timid creatures entirely different from competitive, capable men did not go unquestioned, even in its heyday. Even in the 1950s some magazines, including *Ladies' Home Journal* and *Good Housekeeping*, published articles celebrating the benefits of paid work for women and featuring profiles of successful career women.

By 1960 women's issues had begun to receive attention in the federal government. In 1961 President Kennedy established the Commission on the Status of Women (CSW), headed by Eleanor Roosevelt. Congress also began to discuss discrimination against working women and passed the Equal Pay Act of 1963, making it illegal to pay women less than men for the same job. However, the decade's most significant piece of legislation in the area of women's rights became law almost serendipitously. As Congress debated the 1964 Civil Rights Act, a reactionary Virginia congressman, Democrat Howard W. Smith, attempted to kill the bill by introducing an amendment that he believed would reduce the whole matter of civil rights to an absurdity. Title VII prohibited discrimination on the basis of sex. Encouraged by business and professional women, a group of liberal northerners, led by Democratic representative Martha Griffith of Michigan, pushed the amendment through, and it became law along with the rest of the bill. The Equal Employment Opportunity Commission (EEOC), charged with enforcing the bans on occupational discrimination mandated in the Civil Rights Act, did not at first take sex discrimination complaints seriously, but under pressure it ultimately began to enforce the law.

Meanwhile, discontent had been brewing in the tranquil suburbs. In 1960, when *Redbook* magazine ran an article titled "Why Young Mothers Feel Trapped" and invited readers to respond, the editors received an astonishing twenty-four thousand replies. In 1963 came the publication of Betty Friedan's *The Feminine Mystique,* which blasted the social waste of isolating educated, talented women in the household. The home was no haven in a heartless world, Friedan explained, but a "comfortable concentration camp." Middle-class American women felt depressed, useless, and assailed by, in Friedan's memorable words, "the problem that has no name." Speaking for this group (but not, for example, for African-American mothers, whose families' survival had long depended on their ability to find paid work of any kind), Friedan believed that the solution lay in giving women meaningful jobs outside the home. In 1966 Friedan was among the founders of the National Organization for Women (NOW), the first national lobby for women's rights since the suffrage era, dedicated to the liberal goals of achieving for women political and economic opportunities equal to those enjoyed by men.

The women's movement gained momentum because it was rooted in widespread, long-term social change. Among other factors, more and more women were becoming educated. Between 1950 and 1974 college enrollment for men increased by 234 percent; for women the increase was 456 percent. Even more important, both married and single women were entering the paid work force (see figure). During the Second World War female employment had increased from 27 percent of adult women (in 1940) to 36 percent (in 1945). Female employment dropped off temporarily immediately after the war, but by 1960 it had bounced back: 37.7 percent of women aged sixteen and over were employed, constituting 33 percent of the total work force. A decade later 43 percent of women aged sixteen and over were in the work force, and the

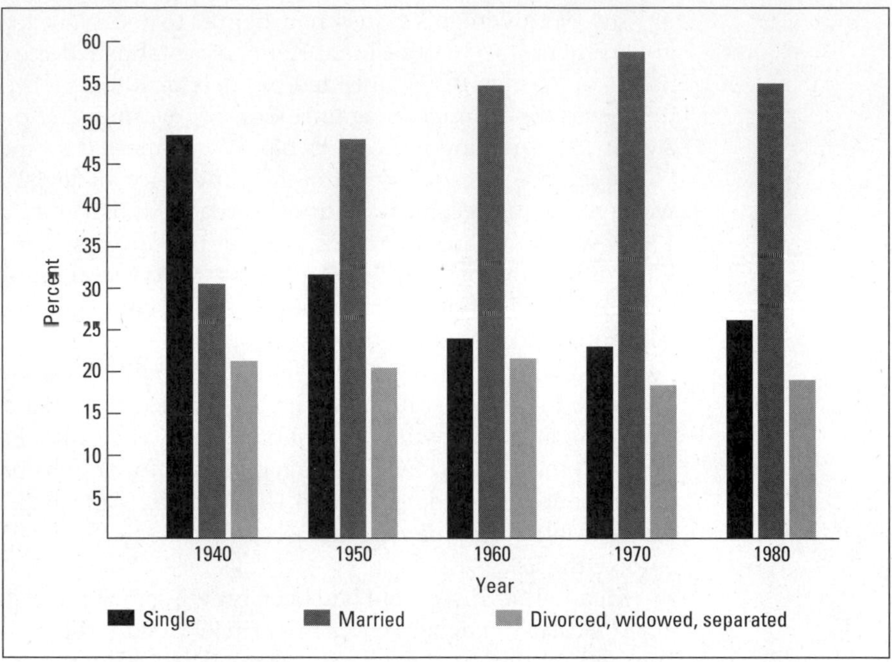

Women in the Workforce, 1930–1990 After World War II, more and more married women went to work for pay.

numbers continued to rise steadily. Also, more and more working women were married: by 1962 they accounted for 60 percent of the female work force. Many were mothers as well: as early as 1970, one-third of women with children under six years of age held or sought jobs.

Despite these gains, women workers still had fewer job options than their male counterparts. They generally crowded into female-dominated occupations, including nursing, clerical work, teaching, and domestic work, that paid less than men's jobs. In 1955 the median compensation for women in full-time, year-round employment was 64 percent of men's earnings. By 1960 the figure had dropped to 61 percent, and by 1975 full-time women workers were earning only 58.8 percent of what men earned. Even when they did the same work as men, they were paid less. The EEOC was understaffed and often reluctant to pursue complaints about infringements of the Equal Pay Act. Moreover, employers could skirt the whole issue by writing slightly different job descriptions and giving different titles to men and women employed in substantially the same activities.

Even though more and more women held full-time, paying jobs, most Americans still assumed that women would continue to do most of the housework. According to figures that changed very little between 1955 and the early 1970s, full-time housewives spent between 52 and 56 hours per week doing housework. Wives who worked full time outside the home still reported spending about 26 hours per week in housekeeping. And whether or not their wives worked, husbands spent about 1.6 hours per day, or 11.2 hours per week, doing household tasks, including yard work.

Perhaps most important of all, the myth of the happy nuclear family was crumbling. There was a greater acknowledgment of the tensions within families: women could not count on the family as a protected haven; they would have to find ways of making their own way in the world. A rising divorce rate, concern about women who had been widowed or abandoned, and growing alarm over family violence and abuse all heralded an urgent need to re-evaluate women's place in American society.

The dramatic changes in women's roles in society were bound to have political consequences, particularly since civil rights activists were bringing racial injustice to the nation's attention, liberal politicians were embracing social reform, and radical dissidents were questioning the distribution of power in American society. The civil rights effort and the New Left fell short of their immediate political goals, but both proved to be seedbeds for a feminist movement of lasting impact and immense scope.

In the fall of 1964 several SNCC women, including Ruby Doris Smith Robinson, Casey Hayden, Mary King, and Maria Varela, drafted a paper on women's position in the organization. Robinson recognized that as a woman she shared some common ground with Mary King and Casey Hayden, who were both white, but as an African-American she believed that the organization should be black-led and black-dominated. King and Hayden recognized that a turn toward Black Power within the SNCC would leave no place for them in a movement to which they had devoted years of their lives. But if the ideology of Black Power left them out of the SNCC, its focus on difference inspired them to begin distinguishing how American women's social status differed from men's. A year later, in the fall of 1965, King and Hayden anonymously composed "a kind of memo" to women in the peace and freedom movements, arguing that women and blacks both "seem to be caught up in a common-law caste system . . . which, at its worst, uses and exploits women." When they raised the problem of male dominance among their fellow activists, men generally responded by laughing at them. Several months earlier, at a SNCC meeting where the position of women in the movement had been raised, Stokely Carmichael had quipped, "The position of women in SNCC is prone!" Those who heard the remark, including Mary King, "collapsed with hilarity," but when the laughter faded, the serious question remained.

By June 1967 women had found a language to express their grievances. They named the problem—sexism (sometimes called "male chauvinism"). They also named the solution—women's liberation. Liberal NOW activists focused on eliminating discriminatory wage rates and fighting for legal equality for women, pushing hard for a constitutional amendment to guarantee equal rights. The radical feminists, who sometimes began as NOW members but more often came out of the civil rights movement and the New Left, identified a new set of political issues, including child care, abortion, birth control, sexuality, family violence, and the sharing of housework. Soon, meeting in small groups to discuss not only war or racism but also problems that seemed intensely individual and private, they developed a new organizing tool: "consciousness raising." Identifying common grievances, they found that what appeared to be individual problems of different women involved much larger questions of social power. Feminist writer Robin Morgan turned this insight into the slogan "The personal is political."

From the start the New Feminism, often called "the second wave" to distinguish it from the women's rights movement of the late nineteenth and early twentieth centuries, faced formidable obstacles. All kinds of people felt threatened by the prospect of women's liberation: conservative men, who stood to lose the privileges of their sex; middle-class women, especially housewives, who worried that men would simply abandon their breadwinner role and women would lose whatever protections they had; fundamentalist Christians, who believed that women's traditional role in the family was biblically ordained; and even leftist men, many of whom were accustomed to treating women as assistant radicals and sex objects. The mainstream press, moreover, tended to treat the women's movement as a joke and to ridicule feminist activists.

The task of building a movement based on women's common problems, interests, and objectives was also deeply complicated by the very diversity of the women the movement hoped to mobilize. Certainly race made a difference in women's lives. Even in the early days of the SNCC, differences between black and white women had raised tensions, with black women articulating grievances and goals that diverged from those of their white sisters in the "beloved community." Class, age, sexual preference, and occupational status also divided women. Middle-class housewives who had expected that their husbands would protect them were far less equipped to face the challenges of economic independence than were college-age women battling sex quotas in law school admissions. Lesbian activists saw their interests as diverging in significant ways from those of heterosexual women. Mexican-American mothers who made their living as migrant farm laborers or domestic workers had different needs from the affluent women who bought the produce they picked or hired them to clean their homes.

A few feminist activists took a page out of the Yippies' book and sought to create splashy media events to gain a national audience. A week after the 1968 Chicago convention, Morgan and almost two hundred other protesters at the Miss America Pageant in Atlantic City crowned a live sheep "Miss America." But although both radical and moderate feminists hoped to use television and newspapers to popularize their cause, print and broadcast media inevitably played up conflicts among women and demeaned feminist actions and goals.

A group of feminist activists gathered at the New York home of Betty Friedan in 1973. Those pictured include Betty Friedan and Yoko Ono. *Corbis/Bettmann*

Because of the enormous diversity of the issues affecting women, feminists had different views on both long- and short-term goals for the movement. Some argued that the first order of business was to dismantle the capitalist system, which particularly oppressed women. Others believed that the movement should concentrate first on eradicating male domination. Some believed men could be reformed and that women had an obligation to maintain relations with men. Shulamith Firestone declared that "a revolutionary in every bedroom cannot fail to shake up the status quo." Others rejected heterosexuality, some for political reasons, some because women's liberation allowed them to reveal a long-hidden lesbian identity. As different visions of the women's movement proliferated, so did the movement's tactics, victories, failures, and institutions.

By the mid-1970s women had made inroads into male-dominated professions, mounted successful challenges to legal and economic discrimination, founded new enterprises, and claimed new rights. Yet much remained to be done. While the privileges of race and class enabled a few American women to "have it all," many more were highly vulnerable. The wage gap between men and women persisted. As some women made strides in professional circles, many others fell deeper into poverty.

✦ Legacies of Cultural and Political Dissent

Although the women's movement has continued, with various shifts in emphasis, to the present day, the other protest movements of the sixties gradually faded or evolved into new, less sensational forms. The New Left never recovered from the cataclysmic spring of 1970, when the killings at Kent State capped a surge of bombings and confrontations. After that, some self-proclaimed revolutionaries went underground. Moderate dissidents seemed dazed by the escalating climate of hatred. Some, declaring themselves burned out, retreated from politics altogether. Many left the movement to pursue other political goals. Eventually the peace settlement in Vietnam removed the principal issue that had united the many threads of the New Left. But the legacy of 1960s political protest was not forgotten. Most obviously, future administrations knew that an unpopular war abroad might provoke widespread rebellion at home.

The counterculture, once it gained massive publicity in the late 1960s, saw many of its distinctive attributes absorbed by the mainstream culture. Hippie styles in hair and clothing and psychedelic music became popular enough to lose some of their revolutionary impact. More important, society at large became more sexually permissive; indeed, the "sexual revolution" was a prominent legacy of the sixties. Recreational drug use spread far beyond hippie enclaves, winning converts in many segments of American society. Meanwhile some erstwhile hippies drifted into more conventional lives—or at least their habits no longer seemed extraordinary. Others continued to pursue spiritual fulfillment in religious and therapeutic groups that identified themselves as part of a "New Age" of expanded consciousness. Rooting out one's inner demons, whether through meditation, confrontation, long soaks in seaside hot springs, or hard labor in religious communes, occupied some inheritors of the counterculture tradition. Tofu, yogurt, herb tea, and bulk grains showed up on supermarket shelves. And searching to "free their minds instead," as John Lennon had advised, millions of Americans took part in a burgeoning "self-help" movement, buying books to help them "get in touch" with their inner essences, watching television shows that featured empathetic therapists, and joining support groups to overcome habits that were more and more often referred to as addictions.

In a sense the nation reversed Robin Morgan's slogan of the 1960s: the political became personal. Millions of Americans expressed renewed interest in religion. In contrast to the earlier revival of the 1950s, when millions had crowded churches and synagogues that avoided dogma and ritual, the most popular sects of the 1970s promised structure, authority, orthodoxy, and a return to lost moral values. On the one hand, the "mainline" Protestant churches—Episcopalian, Presbyterian, Methodist, Congregationalist, and some of the Baptist groups—lost members and influence in the 1970s; so did modern Catholicism and Conservative and Reform Judaism. On the other hand, interest in fundamentalist, evangelical, and Pentecostal Protestant denominations; Mormonism; traditional Catholicism; Orthodox Judaism; and a rich variety of Eastern practices such as Zen, Hinduism, yoga, and Tibetan Buddhism surged. Much of the gain in religious observance was among young people, including members of the sixties counterculture, who looked for meaning and connections in their lives. California governor Jerry Brown explained that young people yearned to re-establish "neighborhood and community responsibility," and churches promised a way to achieve that goal. Renewed interest in religion and traditional morality affirmed peoples' sense of their own identity in a changing and often inexplicable world.

For some the search for a new spiritual anchor meant a turn to the Right. Committed to overturning liberalism and restoring old values, fundamentalist Christian religious leaders gave a strong impetus to the conservative movement. Many of them took to the airwaves as television preachers, and a huge "electronic church" developed, with a weekly audience of millions of viewers. Their popularity further eroded attendance at mainline Protestant churches, which could not offer the same flashy showmanship. The TV preachers of the New Right damned liberalism, feminism, sex education, divorce, cohabitation, homosexuality, and the teaching of evolution in the schools. The most successful televangelists, as they were called—including Jerry Falwell, Pat Robertson, Jim and Tammy Bakker, and Oral Roberts—raised millions of dollars in contributions from their viewers. More and more they connected religion with politics. "We have enough votes to run the country," Robertson declared. In 1979 Falwell formed the Moral Majority, an organization dedicated to "pro-God, pro-family policies in government." He urged other fundamentalist ministers to abandon Jimmy Carter and help raise converts for the Moral Majority and the Republican Party.

A few dramatic instances suggested that some spiritually searching Americans had become so alienated from ordinary institutions that they put their lives at the disposal of their religious institutions. The Reverend Sun Myung Moon, a Korean evangelist with close ties to South Korea's intelligence agency, recruited thousands of mostly young Americans into his Unification Church. Known as Moonies, the church members gave their possessions to the church, lived communally, worked in proliferating church-owned businesses, and recruited others on college campuses, in airports, and on public streets. Moon structured every moment in the lives of his followers. Once he officiated at a mass wedding of thousands of couples who had been paired together by church officials. Conviction on tax evasion charges eventually put Moon in prison, though his organization remained profitable and influential; he was later released.

The most chilling episode came in November 1978, when Jim Jones and the People's Temple became household words. Jones's People's Temple attracted thousands of members, mostly poor and black, in California in the 1970s. Jones promised a racially integrated community in which people of all colors would share everything. He became prominent in the San Francisco Bay Area, but growing public opposition persuaded him to lead about a thousand of his entranced followers to the jungles of the South American country of Guyana, where they established a supposedly utopian community, Jonestown. When a U.S. congressman visited the settlement in November 1978 to investigate claims that members were being held against their will, Jones's followers murdered him. Soon thereafter, Jones and 915 People's Temple members drank cyanide-laced Kool-Aid and died. A tape recorder captured an appalling record of Jones's crazed voice encouraging believers to force poison down their children's throats and commit "revolutionary suicide protesting against the conditions of an inhumane world."

The nation reacted with horror to the news of Jonestown. By this time some anguished parents whose adult children had joined "cults" were hiring strongmen to seize the young people and "deprogram" them. Cultural observers decried the proliferation of nonrational and antirational approaches to spirituality. Historian Christopher Lasch assailed the "hedonism, narcissism and cult of the self" characteristic of several new religious movements. Writer Tom Wolfe went further, putting a label on the entire culture of the 1970s: the Me Decade.

But idealism and the struggle for social justice had not entirely succumbed to the allures of narcissism. The civil rights movement, transformed by Black Power, had fragmented, but it had multiplied, not died. While some leaders were in exile and others were dead, still others began to move into the political mainstream. SCLC workers Andrew Young and Jesse Jackson, who had stood with Martin Luther King, Jr., when he was shot in Memphis, led the next generation of activists and became powers to be reckoned with in the Democratic Party. Blacks and women held more and more local and national political offices. Beginning with Carl Stokes of Cleveland, who in 1967 became the first African-American mayor of a major American city, blacks moved into positions of power in the nation's urban centers. By 1990 former SNCC president John Lewis would win election to the U.S. Congress.

The push for African-American rights also spawned a new, multicultural politics of difference. By the late 1960s Native Americans had organized to raise public awareness of the history of their oppression, adopting both militant and moderate tactics. Members of the American Indian Movement occupied Alcatraz Island in San Francisco Bay and staged a mass protest at Wounded Knee, South Dakota, the site of a notorious massacre of Lakota (Sioux) Indians in 1890. Other Indian advocates formed such organizations as the Native American Rights Fund to pursue legal change. By 1980 Native Americans succeeded in forcing the federal government to return some important tribal lands and to provide compensation for other lands that had been confiscated by whites.

Mexican-Americans, galvanized by Cesar Chávez's charismatic leadership and his success in organizing the United Farm Workers, pressed for reform in the treatment of Latinos. Although U.S. Latinos shared a common language and culture, they or their families had come from places as diverse as Mexico, Chile, Nicaragua, Cuba, and Puerto Rico, under enormously divergent circumstances. As they struggled to articulate common goals in organizations like the League of United Latin American Citizens and to come to grips with differences among themselves, they became an increasingly important part of the American political and economic picture, especially in the Sunbelt. Latino students, particularly Mexican-Americans, organized campus groups that continue to play a prominent role at universities across the country.

Just as the protest movements of the sixties had mobilized people to eradicate racial, ethnic, and gender discrimination, they also created the possibility of a civil rights movement based on sexuality. On June 29, 1969, police raided the Stonewall Inn, a gay bar in Greenwich Village. Instead of accepting arrest, patrons fought back with rocks and bottles, a confrontation heralded as the beginning of the gay liberation movement. Gay and lesbian activists moved quickly to redefine homosexuality not as a perversion but as a legitimate sexual identity. Though they did not reach a consensus as to whether sexual preference was inborn or chosen, they enabled millions of homosexuals to come out of the closet, redrew the boundaries of sexuality, and organized to claim a share of political power in many American cities. The gay community would face its greatest crisis in the 1980s, when it became the first American group to suffer the devastating epidemic of acquired immune deficiency syndrome, or AIDS.

For others who carried on the political legacy of the sixties, the fate of the earth seemed the most pressing issue. Hippies who had experienced the majesty and endangerment of nature during LSD trips in California redwood groves became advocates of environmentalism. Others took a more political road to the ecology movement: peace advocates worried about the environmental threat of nuclear weapons, and critics of large corporations focused on those that sold shoddy and dangerous products in the United States and the Third World. In 1970 environmental activists held the first Earth Day—part teach-in, part demonstration—designed to promote awareness of humans' impact on the natural environment. Books like Rachel Carson's *Silent Spring,* an indictment of modern pesticides; Paul Ehrlich's *The Population Bomb,* a vision of demographic doom; Barry Commoner's *Science and Society,* a critique of the nuclear power industry; and Ralph Nader's *Unsafe at Any Speed,* an exposé of the automobile business, inspired a new awareness of the connections between technology, politics, personal freedom, and environmental dangers.

✦✦✦

Biographical Profile

Rachel Carson, 1907–1964

The Second World War stimulated the development of new chemicals and synthetics that were generally hailed as miracle products. But miracles do not come free. While other scientists pursued the perfection of plastics, biologist Rachel Carson spent the war years working for the U.S. Bureau of Fisheries, writing conservation bulletins. In the years following, Rachel Carson would turn her talents to exposing the ecological hazards of new industries spawned by wartime economic mobilization.

Unlike most government writers, Carson combined the insight of a scientist with the grace of a poet. As a child growing up in Pennsylvania she had aspired to a literary career, publishing her first story at the age of ten. But in college she was inspired to study biology, and she earned a master's degree in zoology at Johns Hopkins University. During summers in graduate school she worked at the Marine Biology Laboratory in Woods Hole, Massachusetts, where she developed a lifelong passion for the sea.

After writing award-winning nature books, including *The Sea Around Us* (1951) and *The Edge of the Sea* (1955), Carson wrote the book that would change the way Americans thought about the world around them. She had long been concerned about the indiscriminate use of one purported miracle product, the insecticide DDT, a substance both lethal and long-lasting. When a friend's private bird sanctuary was sprayed with DDT under a state-mandated mosquito-control program, Carson was horrified by the resulting mass death of its birds and insects. In 1962 she published *Silent Spring*, an indictment not only of DDT but also of numerous other materials with which humans were poisoning the earth, air, and water. Despite vicious attempts by the chemical industry to discredit the book, *Silent Spring* spawned a worldwide outcry and gave birth to the modern environmental movement.

> *"The 'control of nature' is a phrase conceived in arrogance, born of the Neanderthal age of biology and philosophy, when it was supposed that nature exists for the convenience of man. . . . It is our alarming misfortune that so primitive a science has armed itself with the most modern and terrible weapons, and that in turning them against the insects it has also turned them against the earth."*
>
> —from *Silent Spring*

A huge and diverse array of organizations would in ensuing years press and expand the environmentalist agenda. Through lobbying and letter-writing campaigns, middle-of-the-road, predominately white organizations like the Sierra Club, the Nature Conservancy, and the Audubon Society mobilized nature lovers on behalf of endangered animals and plants and against development in wilderness areas. More militant groups like Earth First! engaged in what they called "monkey-wrenching," after the title of a novel by environmentalist writer Edward Abbey. Their tactics included sabotaging construction equipment and driving metal spikes into trees to destroy loggers' chain saws. Other groups, like the Southwest Organizing Project, headquartered in New Mexico, made the connection between racism and environmental degradation and coined the term *environmental justice.* Activists noted developers' and policymakers' predilection for locating toxic waste dumps in minority communities and pointed out the seeming indifference of many white environmentalists to the disproportionate ecological dangers minority communities routinely faced. In time environmental groups would become a formidable national political force, and Congress would respond to their concerns by establishing the federal Environmental Protection Agency.

✦ Conclusion

In the 1960s and early 1970s millions of Americans launched a full frontal assault on conventional behavior, smashing the barriers between public and private life and legitimizing new ideas and new forms of behavior. They exposed the depth of racial oppression in the United States, catalyzed the American withdrawal from Vietnam, began a sexual revolution, helped found a lasting feminist movement and widen opportunities for American women, promoted recognition of the pluralism of American society, and sparked new concern for the environment.

But these changes brought controversy and, sometimes, troubling consequences. Young radicals contributed to the climate of violence that engulfed American society by the 1970s. Moreover, by justifying their sometimes outrageous behavior in the name of personal freedom, they paved the way for what historian Christopher Lasch would call "the culture of narcissism"—the retreat of many Americans into the pursuit of personal pleasure. Although social observers would later contrast the inwardly focused Me Decade with the more socially focused sixties, the cultivation of the self was to some extent a legacy of those radical years, an outgrowth of the Yippies and the hippies, the rock festivals and the drugs and the Summer of Love. It seemed in the 1970s that the values characteristic of a commitment to social justice were just as applicable to a philosophy of individualism.

The culture of protest demanded a great deal of those who took part in it, and there were casualties. Drugs ended too many musical careers too soon.

Charismatic Black Panther leader Huey Newton would die in a shoot-out as he tried to make a drug deal. Some simply wanted to retire from dangerous advocacy and live a quiet life.

However, many sixties activists persisted in their commitment to social justice. The SNCC's John Lewis took his commitment to racial justice to Congress. Another SNCC veteran, Maria Varela, moved to northern New Mexico to create institutions promoting economic self-sufficiency for Hispanic villagers. SDS's Tom Hayden campaigned for economic democracy from the halls of the California state legislature. In 1993 feminist lawyer Ruth Bader Ginsburg was appointed to the U.S. Supreme Court. Grateful Dead member Bob Weir became a committed environmentalist, urging fans at Dead concerts to help save the Brazilian rain forest.

Despite the 1970s' reputation as a narcissistic decade, many Americans continued to exhibit a deep dedication to social justice. Disdain for politicians, and lingering sentiments against the Vietnam War, led people to take politics into their own hands. On the Left they joined feminist, environmental, gay rights, and civil rights organizations. A significant number continued to participate in political protests which, though generally smaller and more polite than those of the sixties, were no less earnest. Groups like the United Farm Workers; the American Federation of State, County, and Municipal Employees; and Friends of the Earth raised new issues and made steady gains. Reform-minded people trained to be teachers, at all levels, inspired by an idealistic view of education as a path to social betterment. Others worked in a wide variety of socially responsible businesses, from child care centers, health collectives, and food co-ops to land trusts, muckraking magazines, and ethical investment firms.

The unruly, diverse, sometimes shimmeringly beautiful, sometimes corrosively ugly political and cultural energies unleashed in the sixties took many directions, and almost inevitably they prompted a counterrevolution. President Nixon's attorney general, John Mitchell, looked at the turmoil of the late 1960s and predicted that "this country's going to go so far right, you won't believe it." That old enemy of the Left, Ronald Reagan, ultimately led the Right on a triumphal march to power, and even some former hippies and leftists moved to the opposite end of the political spectrum. Jerry Rubin, who had helped lead the Yippie protest at the 1968 Democratic convention, put on a suit and became a Wall Street wizard; Black Panther Eldridge Cleaver repudiated revolutionary politics and in the 1980s ran for public office in California as a Republican. The Religious Right of the 1980s and 1990s would adopt, with immense success, grassroots organizing techniques first developed by radicals of the 1960s and 1970s.

But even though the Right marshaled its forces and made a successful run for the White House, capitalizing on widespread reaction against the cultural turmoil of the sixties, they could not turn back the clock. Race- and gender-based hierarchies that had once seemed natural appeared, by 1980, unjust and unacceptable. Sexual freedoms once unthinkable were now commonplace.

Popular culture and the fine arts alike vibrated with a new spirit of openness and experimentation. To the horror of some and the delight of others, nothing would ever be the same.

✦ Further Reading

For an overview of the 1960s, see: David Farber, *The Age of Great Dreams: America in the 1960s* (1994). On civil rights and Black Power, see: Clayborn Carson, *In Struggle: SNCC and the Black Awakening of the 1960s* (1981); William H. Chafe, *Civilities and Civil Rights: Greensboro, North Carolina, and the Black Struggle for Freedom* (1980); David J. Garrow, *Bearing the Cross: Martin Luther King, Jr., and the Southern Christian Leadership Conference* (1986); Harvard Sitkoff, *The Struggle for Black Equality, 1954–1981.* On the New Left and the antiwar movement, see: Wini Breines, *The Great Refusal: Community and Organization in the New Left* (1983); Todd Gitlin, *The Sixties: Years of Hope, Days of Rage* (1987); James Miller, *"Democracy Is in the Streets": From Port Huron to the Siege of Chicago* (1987); W. J. Rorabaugh, *Berkeley at War* (1989); Kirkpatrick Sale, *SDS* (1973). On the counterculture, see: Charles Perry, *The Haight-Ashbury* (1984); Theodore Roszak, *The Making of a Counterculture* (1969); Nicholas Von Hoffman, *We Are the People Our Parents Warned Us Against* (1968); Warren J. Belasco, *Appetite for Change: How the Counterculture Took on the Food Industry, 1966–1988* (1989). On women's changing lives and the women's movement, see: William H. Chafe, *The American Woman: Her Changing Social, Economic, and Political Role, 1920–1970* (1972); Flora Davis, *Moving the Mountain: The Women's Movement in America Since 1960* (1991); Susan J. Douglas, *Where the Girls Are: Growing Up Female with the Mass Media* (1994); Alice Echols, *Daring to Be Bad: Radical Feminism in America, 1967–1975* (1989); Barbara Ehrenreich et al., *Re-making Love: The Feminization of Sex* (1987); Sara Evans, *Personal Politics* (1978); Flora Davis, *Moving the Mountain: The Women's Movement in America since 1960* (1991); Vicki L. Ruiz, *Cannery Women, Cannery Lives* (1987); Winnifrid D. Wandersee, *On the Move: American Women in the 1970s* (1988). On the emerging gay community, see: John D'Emilio, *Sexual Politics, Sexual Communities: The Making of a Homosexual Minority in the United States, 1940–1970* (1983). General accounts of society and politics in the 1970s include: Peter N. Carroll, *It Seemed Like Nothing Happened* (1982); Christopher Lasch, *The Culture of Narcissism* (1979); Steve Fraser and Gary Gerstle, eds., *The Rise and Fall of the New Deal Order, 1930–1980* (1989); Michael Barone, *Our Country* (1990); Theodore H. White, *America in Search of Itself, 1956–1980* (1982).

✦✦✦ CHAPTER 13

A Crisis of Confidence and Some New Opportunities, 1969–1980

✦ *Washington Post* reporters Bob Woodward (left) and Carl Bernstein, 1973.

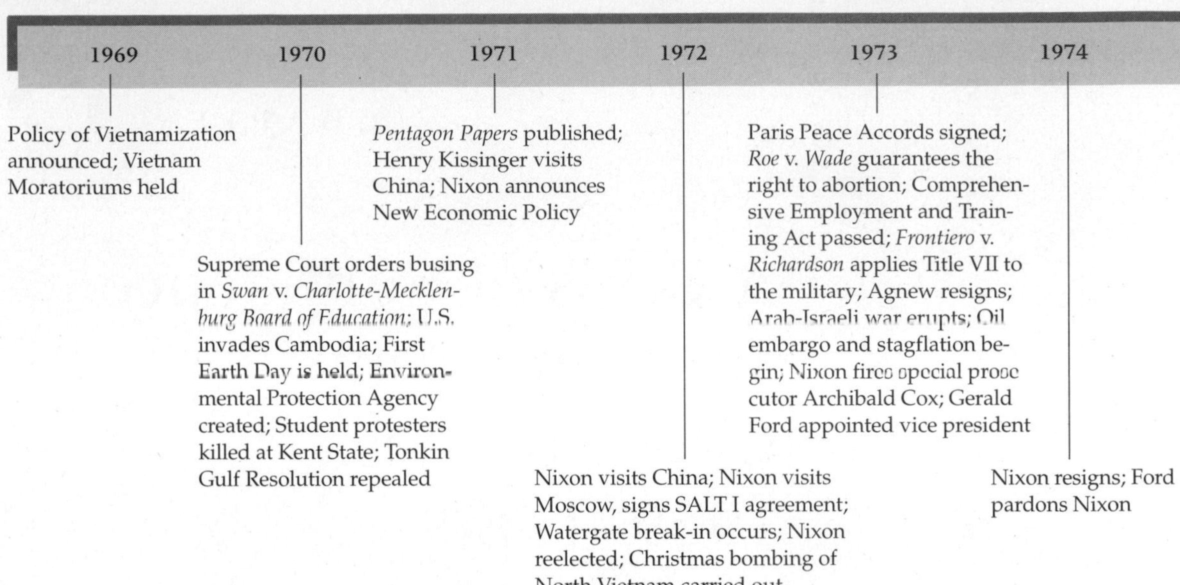

WHEN LARRY HAYNES returned from his tour of duty in Vietnam to the Robert Taylor Homes on the South Side of Chicago in 1971, he discovered that the vast, nearly all black housing project had changed in the year he had been gone. There were more guns, more drugs, and fewer families. "I wasn't going to come back and get into a society that was really going down," he recalled. "I wanted to go *up*. I couldn't see staying in the projects." Haynes came home with a piece of shrapnel in his back. He had tried heroin a couple of times in Vietnam, but he hadn't gotten addicted. He believed that the discipline of military life and the exposure to a wider world he had received had been good for him. He soon got a job as a security guard at a hospital in Evanston, a suburb just north of Chicago. Despite the fact that he was regularly harassed by the police when he got off the train at night and went to work, Haynes kept at it. Within a few years he had a job as a mechanic at the post office in Evanston. He moved from the public housing project to a middle-class black neighborhood in Evanston, where he married, had two children, and stayed on at the post office. But Larry Haynes left behind at the Taylor Homes a sister

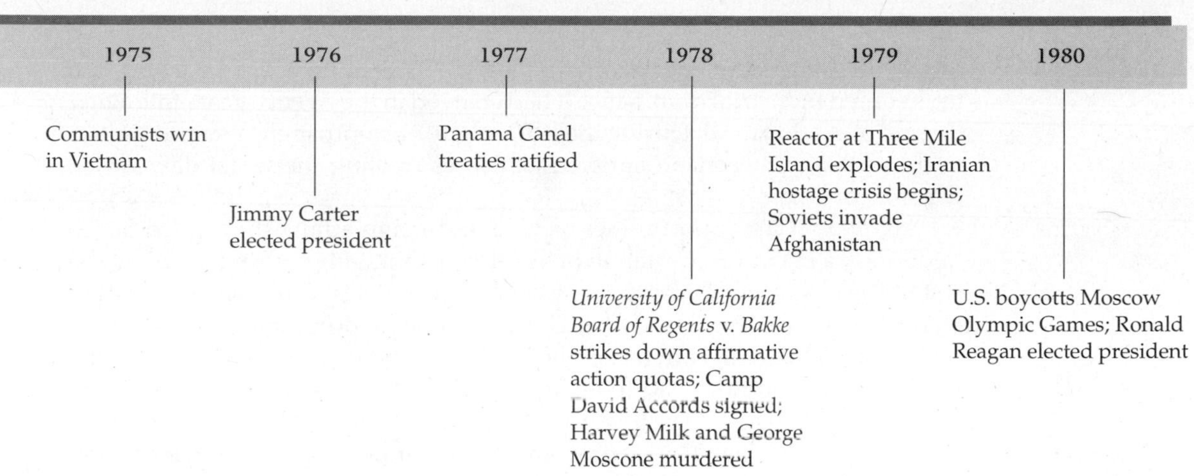

and four brothers, who were without jobs, dependent on welfare, and in trouble with the law. They had little hope of ever making it to the relative affluence and stability of Evanston.

Many Americans, including many whose circumstances differed profoundly from those of the Haynes family, found the twelve years from 1969 to 1980 a time of turmoil and trouble. Confidence in the nation's public institutions, already badly battered by the social chaos brought on by the war in Vietnam and by the backlash against the civil rights movement, plunged further in the midst of the gravest constitutional crisis of the century—the abuse of public power by President Nixon in the scandal that came to be known as Watergate. As the scandal unfolded, and in the years immediately following it, many Americans came to distrust officials of all sorts. They doubted that any of the country's large institutions—including its government, its businesses, its schools and universities, and its religious institutions—really met their needs. For the first time in decades, public opinion polls reported that most Americans expected the future to be worse than the past.

Much of the anxiety was economic, as the United States was losing the undisputed industrial dominance it had enjoyed in the twenty years following the end of World War II. During the 1970s many once-prosperous communities in the industrial heartland suffered job losses rivaling the worst days of the Great Depression.

Yet there were opportunities as well. In foreign affairs the United States undertook a major re-evaluation of its relationship with the Soviet Union, the rest of the Communist world, its own Western allies, and nations outside the arena of the Cold War. The end of U.S. economic predominance and the onus of the war in Vietnam convinced many officials and ordinary citizens that the burden of containment had to be lightened. Consequently the United States undertook promising steps toward détente with the Soviet Union and unfroze relations with China. The improvement in relations with the Soviet Union faded by the end of the 1970s, but it prepared the ground for the end of the Cold War a decade later.

The 1970s were years of profound change. The devastation of old industries cleared the way for new economic development. The United States underwent a wrenching transition from an economy based mostly on manufacturing to a more robust one based more on services, information, and technological innovation. Much of the exuberant expansion of rights and opportunities for women and minorities that began in the 1960s continued in the 1970s. Men and women, black and white, straight and gay—all explored new ways of living. Ironically, the administration of Richard M. Nixon, who was elected in 1968 with the support of people angered by the reforms of the Great Society, consolidated and in some cases expanded these efforts. Nixon's successors, Republican Gerald R. Ford (1974–1977) and Democrat Jimmy Carter (1977–1981), both continued this consolidation.

✦ Foreign Policy During the Nixon Administration

Richard Nixon won the presidency in 1968 in part by tapping the public's deep dismay over the costs of global intervention. He assailed "the policies and mistakes of the past," focusing the voters' attention on the endless fighting in Southeast Asia. His own plans for solving the Vietnam riddle remained murky, however: his campaign speeches promised only "peace with honor."

Aware of the war's increasing unpopularity, Nixon also considered Vietnam a drain on American resources and a diversion from what he felt should be the principal focus of U.S. foreign policy—managing the dangerous competition with the Soviet Union. Reducing the attention on Vietnam and restoring American freedom of action in the rest of the world became the new administration's first foreign policy goal.

Within a month of the election Nixon began what *Time* magazine later called an "improbable partnership" with Henry Kissinger, a forty-five-year-old, German-born Harvard professor whom Nixon selected as his national security adviser. From 1969 to 1974 Nixon and Kissinger orchestrated some of the greatest reversals in U.S. foreign policy since the beginning of the Cold War. Working secretly, contemptuous of the foreign affairs bureaucracy, they produced dramatic meetings with old adversaries, altered the course of the war in Vietnam, reduced tensions with the Soviet Union, opened relations with China, and thrust the United States into the Middle East as the principal foreign mediator in the region. The public cheered these accomplishments, but by the time the president resigned in disgrace over the Watergate scandal in August 1974, détente had soured, and a settlement in Vietnam had remained illusory.

The Retreat from Vietnam

Nixon and Kissinger knew that the public would not long stand for a continued stalemate in Vietnam. "I'm not going to end up like [Lyndon Johnson]," Nixon promised, "holed up in the White House, afraid to show my face on the street. I'm going to stop that war. Fast." Ultimately the Nixon administration pursued three somewhat conflicted goals at once: reducing public attention on Vietnam, negotiating a face-saving arrangement with Hanoi, and bolstering the military capacity of Saigon.

In June 1969 Nixon met with South Vietnam's president, Nguyen Van Thieu, on Midway Island to explain his policy of "Vietnamization," a scheme for turning more of the fighting over to the ARVN. Nixon then publicly announced the withdrawal of twenty-five thousand American troops from the war zone. Fewer American troops would mean lower monthly draft calls, which Nixon hoped would in turn reduce young people's anger about the war. In 1969 he also replaced the aging, abrasive General Lewis Hershey as head of the Selective Service System with Curtis Tarr, who promised to make the draft fairer by introducing a lottery in which men were selected randomly on the basis of their birth dates.

All the while, U.S. planes were expanding the air war to Vietnam's neighbor Cambodia with a series of secret bombing raids. The bombing was meant to stop the North Vietnamese from using Cambodian trails to infiltrate South Vietnam with soldiers and supplies. Over the next fifteen months U.S. B-52s flew more than 3,600 raids, dropping over one hundred thousand tons of bombs inside Cambodia's borders.

Conditions in the American army in Vietnam deteriorated as Vietnamization proceeded. Formerly, individual soldiers had been reluctant to fight as they neared the end of their tour of duty; now whole platoons resisted orders to proceed with the few search-and-destroy operations that remained. No one wanted to be among the last killed or wounded in a war that had become the responsibility of the Vietnamese. American commanders saw the army disintegrating before their eyes. Drug use rose. In 1970 the command estimated that sixty-five thousand soldiers were using narcotics. More frightening were the more than two thousand reports in 1970 of "fragging," as soldiers attacked unpopular officers with fragmentation bombs or rifles.

To retain public support for Vietnamization the administration tried to neutralize the appeal of opponents of the war, who had regrouped after the climactic events of the 1968 presidential campaign. The two Vietnam War Moratoriums, in October and November 1969 (see Chapter 12), attracted millions of people to demonstrations in city squares and on college campuses across the country. After the first Moratorium Nixon delivered a nationally televised speech in which he appealed to the "silent majority" of Americans to reject the antiwar movement. "North Vietnam cannot humiliate the United States," he warned. "Only Americans can do that." To make sure of his support, Nixon encouraged Vice President Spiro Agnew to deliver a stinging rebuke to the press. Agnew assailed journalists as "an effete corps of impudent snobs" who sympathized with the antiwar demonstrations. Attorney General John Mitchell authorized the FBI to tap the telephones of the organizers of the Moratoriums. Six months later Nixon approved a plan to infiltrate, burglarize, wiretap, trick, and provoke into violence a variety of antiwar and liberal groups "who pose a threat to our national security."

In the spring of 1970 Nixon decided on a series of dramatic military gestures to demonstrate his commitment to supporting the South Vietnamese government, even as the United States was drawing back its troops in Vietnam. In March he announced plans to remove an additional 150,000 troops by the end of the year. At the same time, Cambodia's chief of staff, General Lon Nol, overthrew the government of Prince Norodom Sihanouk. Unlike Sihanouk, Lon Nol sided clearly with the Americans and South Vietnamese and wanted them to rid neutral Cambodia of the North Vietnamese, who used Cambodia's border region to support insurgents in South Vietnam. In late April Nixon decided to invade Cambodia. On the evening of April 30 he went before the American public to plead for support. "If when the chips are down," he said, "the world's most powerful nation acts like a pitiful, helpless giant, the forces of totalitarianism and anarchy will threaten free nations and free institutions throughout the world." The invasion yielded modest military gains, killing two thousand enemy troops and destroying eight thousand bunkers, and it may have bought some time for additional Vietnamization. It failed completely, however, in its larger goal of reversing the military trend toward victory for the North. The ARVN forces fought poorly, and their incompetence and unwillingness to fight were clearly evident on evening news programs. The U.S. and ARVN forces also failed to find the headquarters of the North Vietnamese operations, a supposed "nerve center" located in Cambodia.

Worst of all from Nixon's point of view, the Cambodian operation provoked some of the most furious antiwar demonstrations of the Vietnam era. After National Guard troops killed four protesters at Kent State University, news of the slaughter further inflamed antiwar passions. Over one hundred thousand young people spontaneously converged on Washington to petition Congress to end the war. Congress responded to the public concern over the Cambodian invasion by repealing the 1964 Tonkin Gulf Resolution, used by Presidents Johnson and Nixon to justify continued American participation in the fighting.

By the middle of 1970 Nixon's honeymoon with the public over Vietnam had ended. The expansion of the war into Cambodia had revived the domestic turmoil of 1968. Antiwar outbursts following the Cambodian invasion further polarized the nation, with hawkish Americans becoming ever more committed to Nixon. A few days after the National Guardsmen killed the Kent State protesters, New York construction workers rampaged through the city's financial district. They beat up antiwar demonstrators, forced officials at City Hall to raise the American flag (which had been lowered in mourning after the Kent State killings), and smashed windows at nearby Pace College. Two weeks later the head of the New York Labor Council led an estimated sixty thousand to one hundred thousand flag-waving union members in a march supporting the invasion of Cambodia and opposing the antiwar demonstrations. Nixon received them warmly at the White House.

A year later, on Sunday, June 13, 1971, the *New York Times* began a series of stories on the origins of U.S. involvement in the war in Vietnam. "My God, there it is!" said former Defense Department official Leslie Gelb when he opened his newspaper that morning. "It" was the forty-seven-volume *History of the U.S. Decision-Making Process on Vietnam, 1945–1967,* popularly known as the *Pentagon Papers.* Gelb had compiled the history at Secretary of Defense Robert McNamara's request in 1968. Daniel Ellsberg, a former Defense Department official who had grown disillusioned with the war, had leaked copies of the *Pentagon Papers* to the paper. The secret history cast a dark shadow over the foreign policy of every administration from Truman through Johnson. The documents revealed that American officials had ignored international agreements, manipulated the Saigon government, and deliberately misinformed Congress and the public about the true conditions in Vietnam. The *Pentagon Papers* convinced some people who had previously remained undecided about the war that the government had long known that the original commitment to Vietnam was a mistake.

The Nixon administration sought to block further publication of the *Pentagon Papers,* but the *Times* appealed in federal court. On June 30 the Supreme Court issued a decision in favor of the newspaper's right to publish. In the aftermath of this judicial rebuff, Nixon aide John Ehrlichman created the White House "plumbers unit," so-called because it was charged with stopping further leaks from government officials. The plumbers' operations were far more sinister than their playful name suggested. In the summer of 1971 E. Howard Hunt, a former CIA agent working for Ehrlichman, led a squad of plumbers consisting of several anti-Castro Cuban exiles with ties to the CIA in a burglary of the office of Daniel Ellsberg's psychiatrist, looking for discrediting information to leak to the press.

Meanwhile the Paris peace talks stalled in 1971, as neither the United States nor the North Vietnamese would make any concessions. For example, Washington would not stop supporting the Thieu government, and the Communist negotiators refused even to acknowledge that they had troops in the South. For the remainder of the year the United States combined negotiations in Paris with threats to the Saigon government and ferocious bombing of North Vietnam. American officials believed that détente with the Soviet Union and the growing warmth between the United States and China (discussed later in the chapter) would force Hanoi to offer concessions. These hopes proved futile: North Vietnam remained firmly committed to forcing the United States out.

In March 1972 a force of 120,000 North Vietnamese troops launched a full-scale invasion of the South. Only six thousand of the ninety-five thousand American troops remaining in the South were combat soldiers, so the North Vietnamese met little resistance, approaching to within sixty miles of Saigon. The ARVN threw all its reserves into meeting the assault from the North, allowing Vietcong guerrillas in the South to attack and overrun villages in the heavily populated Mekong Delta, near the capital. In response, on May 8 Nixon ordered the largest escalation of the war since 1968. U.S. forces mined Haiphong harbor, blockaded other North Vietnamese harbors, and engaged in the heaviest bombing of the North since the war began.

In late summer the Paris negotiations between Kissinger and the North Vietnamese representative, Le Duc Tho, finally moved forward. The national security adviser pointed to public opinion polls that showed Nixon had a 30 percent lead over Senator George McGovern, who had been nominated by a divided Democratic Party to oppose Nixon in the November presidential election. Nixon would surely win a second term, Kissinger told the North Vietnamese, and they would receive the best possible offer from the president if they reached an agreement *before* the election. His strategy seemed to work: in October the two sides agreed on the outline of a settlement. The United States would remove its troops within sixty days of a cease-fire agreement, and the North would release all American prisoners of war (POWs). The United States would limit its military aid to the South to the replacement of lost weaponry and the training of new Vietnamese troops. Kissinger also held out the possibility of reconstruction assistance for North Vietnam. In a reversal of policy, the United States agreed that North Vietnamese and Vietcong forces in the South could stay in place and administer the areas under their control. Hanoi backed off from its demand that the United States depose the Saigon regime. The Thieu government would remain in power, but it would be expected to make a good-faith effort to include other factions, including the NLF.

Less than two weeks before the election, Kissinger made public the major features of his agreement with Le Duc Tho, announcing that "peace is at hand." Work remained, he acknowledged, but he anticipated a quick settlement.

Although Kissinger's announcement virtually ensured Nixon's reelection, it proved inaccurate. The South Vietnamese government panicked. Fearing abandonment by the United States and realizing that his regime had no more popular support than earlier South Vietnamese governments, President Thieu balked at signing an agreement that permitted any North Vietnamese forces to remain in the South.

Once he was safely reelected, Nixon tried to persuade Thieu to drop his objections to the October agreement. Kissinger's deputy, General Alexander Haig, traveled to Saigon to make bribes and threats. On the one hand, if Thieu would agree to the accords, the United States would provide economic and military aid; also, hints were dropped that the United States would resume bombing if the North violated the accords. On the other hand, if Thieu rejected the Paris agreement, the United States would sign it anyway and leave South Vietnam to fend for itself. Kissinger authorized Haig to tell the South Vietnamese leader that the president had committed himself to ending the war and would proceed regardless of what Saigon chose to do. But still Thieu would not sign the accord.

The North Vietnamese refused to consider significant modifications to the agreement to break the impasse, so Nixon decided to bludgeon the North into reopening the talks. On December 22 the United States unleashed the heaviest bombing campaign of the war against the North. Over the next twelve days B-52s dropped thirty-six thousand tons of explosives, more than had been unleashed in the entire period from 1969 to 1971. Approximately 1,600 civilians were killed in Hanoi and Haiphong. Critics at home and abroad expressed outrage at Nixon's behavior. Several characterized him as a madman. The president's approval rating in public opinion polls dropped to 39 percent.

The bombing and Nixon's eagerness to end the war restarted the stalled negotiations. Talks between Kissinger and Le Duc Tho resumed in Paris in early January. They made a few cosmetic changes to the October agreement but kept the major provisions of the earlier draft, and on January 27, 1973, they signed a cease-fire. The United States promised to withdraw its remaining troops within sixty days in return for the release of U.S. POWs. The North promised not to raise the number of its troops in the South. The Thieu government would remain in power, while plans for "political reconciliation" would go forward in the South. The Saigon government did not sign the Paris accords, but this time Thieu indicated his approval, provided that the United States promised to protect South Vietnam from future North Vietnamese attacks.

Americans felt great relief at the apparent end of the war and the imminent return of the POWs. Yet the peace Nixon had promised in 1968 had been a long time in the making. The four years of the Nixon administration had seen some of the heaviest fighting and worst suffering of the war. Officials estimated that 107,000 South Vietnamese soldiers and approximately half a million North Vietnamese and NLF fighters lost their lives in the period. Another 20,553

American troops were killed during those four years, bringing the total number of American deaths to over 58,000. The number of civilians killed was estimated at over 1 million.

There was considerable doubt whether the cease-fire truly represented "peace with honor," as Nixon claimed. The agreement left the government of South Vietnam in place but did not resolve the fundamental issue of the war: was Vietnam one country or two? The official recognition of the NLF and of the North's right to keep troops in the South ensured that the struggle would continue. For the Communists, the Paris agreement merely represented another pause in their thirty-year effort to unify the country under their leadership. Certain that history was on their side, they waited for the opportune moment to complete their revolution.

Détente with the Soviet Union

Even before the settlement in Vietnam, the Nixon administration had taken major steps in other foreign policy arenas. One of the most significant was an attempt to resurrect détente with the Soviet Union. Relations between Washington and Moscow had been strained since the August 1968 Soviet invasion of Czechoslovakia. But a reduction of tensions with the Soviet Union would benefit both sides.

For three years the Nixon administration conducted a series of highly complicated negotiations, known as the Strategic Arms Limitation Talks (SALT), with the Soviet Union. The talks culminated in a summit between Nixon and Soviet Communist Party general secretary Leonid Brezhnev in May 1972. The two men worked out three agreements. First was an antiballistic missile (ABM) treaty limiting each power to only two ABM sites. Second was the SALT-I treaty, or Interim Agreement on Limitations of Strategic Armaments, which included a pledge to limit land-based missiles for five years to the number contemplated under the U.S. arms program (reducing planned Soviet arms construction by approximately 33 percent). Finally, a document called the "Basic Principles of U.S.-Soviet Relations" was drafted, in which each country promised to base subsequent relations on "the principle of equality." Together the three agreements formed the basis of détente between the superpowers for the next two years.

Arms control talks made little progress for the remainder of the Nixon administration. As the Watergate scandal grew in 1973 and engulfed the president in 1974, Nixon attempted to regain his public standing through two more summits with Brezhnev. The Soviet leader visited Nixon in Washington in June 1973, and Nixon returned the favor with a trip to Moscow and the Crimea in late June and early July 1974, barely six weeks before his forced resignation. Neither meeting produced major breakthroughs, although subsidiary pacts were signed to help prevent nuclear war and to limit the power of nuclear test explosions.

President Richard M. Nixon and his wife Pat atop the Great Wall of China, February 1972.
Nixon Presidential Library

The Opening to China

On July 15, 1971, President Nixon announced that National Security Adviser Kissinger had just returned from Beijing, where he had conferred with the Chinese and prepared for a presidential visit to China in 1972. Nixon and Kissinger had engineered one of the most dramatic diplomatic turnarounds of the twentieth century in nearly complete secrecy.

Both China and the United States had much to gain by resuming diplomatic contact, which had been severed at the beginning of the Korean War. China wanted ties to the United States to help deter Soviet aggression. Washington saw improved relations with China as a way of reasserting influence in Asia lost in the Vietnam War. Closer relations with China could also put pressure on the Soviet Union in arms control talks or regional disputes.

Kissinger discussed all these issues with Zhou Enlai during his whirlwind forty-nine-hour visit. They agreed that Soviet domination of much of Europe

✦ ✦ ✦

Biographical Profile

Henry Kissinger, 1923–

The German-born Henry Kissinger became the principal architect of U.S. foreign policy from 1969 to 1976. Richard Nixon appointed Kissinger, a Harvard professor of international relations who had previously advised presidents and presidential candidates of both parties, as his national security adviser in 1969.

Kissinger and Nixon concentrated foreign policy authority in the White House, excluding the secretary of state and the professionals in the foreign affairs bureaucracy. Kissinger helped divert public attention away from the catastrophic war in Vietnam. He fostered détente with the Soviet Union and secretly began to unfreeze relations between the United States and the People's Republic of China. After he flew to Beijing in July 1971 to arrange a visit by President Nixon to China the next year, he became one of the most admired people in the United States. His stature rose even further when he won the 1973 Nobel Peace Prize for his role in arranging the cease-fire in Vietnam. By that time he was secretary of state as well as national security adviser. In 1974 he arranged the disengagement of the Israeli, Egyptian, and

---

and Asia threatened world stability; they noted that the United States, the world's leading conservative power, could preserve that stability. Kissinger observed that continuing American ties to Taiwan should not prevent Washington and Beijing from working together. The two countries agreed to discuss their mutual interests over the next several months as they prepared for Nixon's visit.

Nixon began a spectacular five-day visit to China on February 21, 1972. Nixon and Kissinger received a well-photographed audience with Chairman Mao Zedong. Nixon and his wife, Pat, walked along the Great Wall, and Pat visited the Beijing Zoo to acknowledge the gift to the United States of two cuddly giant pandas. A communiqué issued at Shanghai at the end of the trip announced that each country would open an "interest section"—an informal embassy—in the other's capital. The two powers agreed to disagree over Taiwan, with the United States planning to maintain its formal Chinese

Syrian forces that had clashed in October 1973. When Nixon resigned in disgrace in 1974, Kissinger appeared more indispensable than ever.

Kissinger remained secretary of state in the administration of Gerald R. Ford. By that time, however, his reputation had suffered a sharp decline. The cease-fire in Vietnam disintegrated, and some critics began to consider détente with the Soviet Union to be much more advantageous to Soviet than to U.S. interests. Kissinger's handling of foreign relations became a major issue in the 1976 presidential campaign. Republican challenger Ronald Reagan derided détente as a bad bargain that gave the Soviets military superiority. Democrat Jimmy Carter, the eventual winner, criticized Kissinger for ignoring other countries' human rights records in conducting American foreign policy.

After he left office in 1977, Kissinger commented publicly on foreign affairs and advised presidents privately. He also became wealthy as a foreign affairs consultant.

"What extraordinary vehicles destiny selects to accomplish its designs. This man [Richard Nixon], so lonely in his hour of triumph, so ungenerous in some of his motivations, had navigated our nation through one of the most anguishing periods of its history. Not by nature courageous, he had steeled himself to conspicuous acts of rare courage. Not normally outgoing, he had forced himself to rally his people to its challenge. He had striven for a revolution in American foreign policy so that it would overcome the disastrous oscillations between overcommitment and isolation. Despised by the establishment, ambiguous in his human perceptions, he had yet held fast to a sense of national responsibility, determined to prove that the strongest free country had no right to abdicate."

—from Kissinger's book *White House Years* (Boston: Little, Brown, 1979), pp. 1475–1476.

---

embassy there. The communiqué observed that both the Peoples' Republic of China and the United States agreed that China was a single country. Although it warned the Soviet Union that the United States and China mutually opposed Soviet hegemony, the communiqué promised that their new relationship threatened no one. Although Nixon and Mao each expressed support for his own favorite in the Vietnam War, the Shanghai communiqué, by its very existence, demonstrated that the United States had moved beyond a preoccupation with Vietnam.

American Diplomacy in the Middle East

In October 1973 war broke out again in the Middle East. Ever since the Six-Day War of 1967, little progress had been made in bringing Israel and its neighbors to the peace table. The United States had become the principal arms supplier to Israel and Jordan, while the Soviet Union replenished the losses incurred by Egypt and Syria in the 1967 fighting. The Arab states refused to meet Israel face to face, and the Jewish state vowed not to consider relinquishing the territories it had taken in the Six-Day War—East Jerusalem, the West Bank of the Jordan River, the Golan Heights, and the Sinai Peninsula—unless its neighbors agreed to recognize its right to exist and make peace with it. Egypt's President Gamal Abdel Nasser launched a war of attrition against Israel's forces along the Suez Canal and the eastern Sinai in 1969 and 1970. These events formed the background to the Middle East crisis of 1973.

Nasser died in 1970. By 1973 Anwar Sadat, his successor, found the situation of "no war, no peace" intolerable. Despairing that the United States or the United Nations would ever persuade Israel to withdraw from the captured territories, he agreed with Syria to coordinate an attack on Israeli positions in the Sinai Peninsula and the Golan Heights. On October 6—Yom Kippur, the holiest day of the Jewish religious calendar—Egyptian and Syrian forces struck. The attackers achieved more in the first three days of the conflict than Arab armies had gained in three previous wars with Israel. Egyptian troops crossed the Suez Canal and captured hundreds of stunned Israelis. In the north, Syria reclaimed a large portion of the Golan Heights and threatened to slice Israel in two. Within a week Israel's military position appeared desperate, and Prime Minister Golda Meir begged Washington for a resupply of planes, tanks, and ammunition.

Nixon agreed to the largest airlift of equipment and armaments since the Second World War. Assured of receiving new arms, Israel counterattacked, driving the Syrians off the Golan Heights and threatening the Syrian capital, Damascus. In the south, Israel's tanks turned back the advancing Egyptians. Now well-supplied by the United States, Israel resisted a joint U.S.-Soviet call for an immediate end to the fighting. Its tanks crossed the Suez Canal and threatened to destroy Egypt's army and enter Cairo. The Soviets responded with a threat to enter the fighting on Egypt's side, and the United States countered by putting its forces in the Mediterranean on high alert. At this point a cease-fire was finally cemented. Israeli forces occupied the east bank of the canal, Egyptian troops stood on the west bank, and Israel was in control of more Syrian territory than it had held at the beginning of the fighting.

In November 1973 Kissinger conducted several rounds of negotiations between the combatants, moving between the capitals of Israel, Egypt, and Syria in an effort that was quickly labeled "shuttle diplomacy." Over the next eighteen months he arranged the disengagement of the three countries' military forces in the Sinai and the Golan Heights. Israel's armies withdrew from the banks of the Suez Canal, permitting the reopening of that waterway. Kissinger also redrew the cease-fire line between Israel and Syria, but the hostility between Israel and its neighbors continued.

An Assessment of Foreign Policy in the Nixon Years

Immediately after Richard Nixon resigned the presidency in disgrace in 1974, analysts looking for something praiseworthy in his record focused on his foreign policy. Many observers believed that he had turned away from the sterile divisions of the Cold War, in which Americans saw a Soviet plot behind every world problem. The result was a more flexible and intelligent foreign policy than most would have expected from a visceral anti-Communist like Nixon. His collaboration with Kissinger re-established White House control over the fractured apparatus of foreign policy. Kissinger's travels to China, the Soviet Union, and the Middle East represented a triumph for U.S. foreign policy, and his shuttle diplomacy among the capitals of the Arab states and Israel appeared to prepare the ground for an eventual settlement of the Arab-Israeli conflict. In the years following Nixon's departure, other analysts recapitulated the view that Nixon had conducted foreign policy well, whatever his failings in the Watergate scandal.

Many of Nixon's and Kissinger's apparent successes proved transitory, however, breaking down by 1976. The peace agreement in Indochina—for which more than twenty thousand additional American lives had been sacrificed after Nixon took office—collapsed in 1975. The much-heralded détente with the Soviet Union, already weakened in 1974, did not survive the Ford administration. The opening to China progressed in the late 1970s; but curiously it was Carter, who was often criticized for being naive about international relations, who actually accomplished more, by resuming formal diplomatic relations with China. The high hopes for peace in the Middle East had also diminished by 1974. The Carter administration exceeded Kissinger's efforts by brokering a peace treaty between Israel and Egypt in 1978 and 1979. When the Cold War ended, however, it was clear that Nixon and Kissinger had understood how both the United States and the Soviet Union had needed to end their wasteful competition.

✦ Domestic Policy During the Nixon Administration

At home the Nixon administration tried to continue the process of undermining support for Lyndon Johnson's Great Society. During the campaign of 1968 Nixon endorsed the goals of reducing economic inequality, conquering poverty, and ending racial discrimination, but he complained that the Great Society programs of President Johnson had failed to meet these goals. Nixon claimed that the War on Poverty had been lost because of mismanagement by incompetent bureaucrats. He spoke for the principles of better management and of helping the poor and underprivileged help themselves. But the overall tendency of the Nixon administration was to de-emphasize social programs and oppose further efforts at racial equality.

Recasting the Welfare State

Following the tenets of many conservative thinkers, Nixon wanted to transfer much of the responsibility for social programs from the large federal bureaucracy to states and municipalities. The aim was to increase efficiency, make the programs more responsive to local interests, and reduce federal interference.

To accomplish this shift of responsibility, Nixon sponsored a system known as revenue sharing, which lasted for ten years. Revenue sharing divided up the funds from federal programs and made the money available to states and municipalities for use in education, urban development, transportation, job training, rural development, and law enforcement. The program did help states and cities pay for new buildings, parks, police cars, and jails. However, when times were hard and resources scarce, cities used the revenue sharing funds to meet their daily expenses. Rarely did local governments volunteer to use the federal grants directly to aid the poor. To make certain that some funds were applied to job training, in 1973 Congress passed the Comprehensive Employment and Training Act (CETA), designed to educate poor people for jobs. Over the next ten years some six hundred thousand CETA graduates found work through the training programs.

Reforming the welfare system presented Nixon with an opportunity to surpass the accomplishments of the Great Society while also pursuing "welfare cheats"—a theme he had sounded during the 1968 presidential campaign. The largest welfare program, known as Aid for Families with Dependent Children (AFDC), had provided welfare assistance to generations of Americans. Many poor people and their children seemed unable to break out of an apparently endless cycle of poverty. Every dollar earned by a working welfare parent was deducted from his or her welfare check. Nixon proposed replacing AFDC with the Family Assistance Program (FAP), which would include a negative income tax. Under this system poor people would receive money from the government instead of paying taxes. But an unusual alignment of liberals opposed to the FAP's requirement that recipients work and conservatives opposed to any monetary grants for the poor killed the program.

In 1972 Congress finally passed a new welfare bill, without any provision for a guaranteed income for poor families with children. It did, however, include a new program, Supplemental Security Income, that provided a guaranteed income for the elderly (many of whom were not poor) and for the blind and disabled. At the same time, Congress authorized automatic cost-of-living increases, tied to the consumer price index, for all Social Security recipients. Such payments went to rich and poor alike. Over the next twenty years the annual cost-of-living adjustments to Social Security payments proved to be an enormously popular entitlement, but one that contributed substantially to large budget deficits. The attempt to find a better system for helping the poor went no further during the Nixon administration.

On the first Earth Day, April 21, 1970, Americans across the country rallied in support of government action to clean up the environment. *Leonard Freed/ Magnum*

The government made more substantial progress toward protecting the environment under Nixon. In the early 1970s Washington began to respond to public demands that the government regulate businesses whose activities were deemed environmentally destructive, harmful to consumers, or dangerous to worker safety. During the 1970s the EPA brought hundreds of suits against industrial polluters of the nation's water and air. The agency required environmental impact studies for all new construction receiving federal funds; these studies had to clearly delineate the effects of the projects on traffic congestion, pollution, housing, wildlife, and a host of other concerns. The EPA set fuel efficiency standards for cars and required automobile manufacturers to reduce the carbon monoxide emissions from the vehicles they sold. In studies on the effect of power plants on the atmosphere, the EPA determined that the burning of high-sulfur coal had created "acid rain" in the Northeast and neighboring Canada, harming that region's forests and fisheries. Although such reports alerted the public to environmental dangers, they also contributed to a growing sense that some problems exceeded the government's capacity to provide solutions. During the Nixon years Congress also created the Consumer Products Safety Commission (CPSC) and the Occupational Safety and Health Administration (OSHA). Both agencies were supposed to make daily life safer and healthier.

The environmental and consumer protection agencies created in the early 1970s reflected the public concerns of the time. The Nixon administration enforced these laws, although with less enthusiasm than the laws' sponsors in the Democratic-controlled Congress. Overall the government did more to address environmental and safety concerns in the early 1970s than at any time in the next twenty years.

Even as the Nixon administration tried but failed to help the poorest Americans significantly, it energetically opposed further progress on civil rights for African-Americans. The Nixon approach to civil rights came to be governed more and more by the so-called southern strategy—the attempt by the Republican Party to woo traditionally Democratic white southern voters. During the 1968 campaign Nixon took a stand against the busing of schoolchildren to achieve racial integration. In many areas in the northern states the public schools reflected de facto segregation—resulting not from law but from the fact that whites and blacks lived in different neighborhoods. By the time of Nixon's presidency, federal courts were increasingly ordering the use of busing to end de facto segregation in northern as well as southern school districts. This led to considerable white protest. After contributing to the public outcry against busing, the Nixon administration sponsored a 1974 law demanding that federal courts and government agencies use busing only as a last resort.

In August 1969 the Department of Health, Education and Welfare (HEW) petitioned the Fifth District Court for a three-month delay in the desegregation of twenty-three Mississippi school districts. This was the first time since 1954 that the federal government had intervened to *slow* the pace of desegregation. The Supreme Court reversed the delay unanimously in *Alexander* v. *Holmes County Board of Education* (1969). Legally mandated segregation ended in the South in the subsequent two years. By 1971 a total of 44 percent of black children in the South attended schools where white students constituted the majority. In the North and West, by comparison, only 28 percent of black schoolchildren studied in schools with a majority of white students.

Although the Nixon administration resisted further progress on civil rights for people of color, the government under Nixon did advance the legal rights of women. A revitalized women's movement (see Chapter 12) had brought women's issues to national prominence. In response Congress passed the Equal Rights Amendment (ERA) to the Constitution and submitted it to the states for ratification in early 1972. The ERA was soon ratified by thirty-five of the thirty-eight states necessary for it to take effect. Though the ERA eventually fell short of adoption, the widespread activism of its supporters helped to focus attention on women's issues.

Crime and drug use became major issues during the Nixon years. During the 1968 campaign Nixon had blamed the "permissiveness" of Johnson's attorney general, Ramsey Clark, for a rise in street crime in the nation. Nixon soon realized, however, that the federal government had few direct law enforcement powers to combat crime in the streets. Faced with a local problem

about which the federal government could do little, the Nixon administration tried several tactics: it tried to shift the blame for drugs and crime to its opponents, it manipulated statistics to magnify both the original problem and the effect of the administration's own remedies, and finally, it engaged in drug raids that violated the civil liberties of the accused and possibly the Constitution as well. Although the drug war undermined civil liberties, it improved Nixon's public image. Several celebrities joined the antidrug effort. Singer Sammy Davis, Jr., who later admitted to his own alcohol and drug abuse, and TV personality Art Linkletter, whose daughter had died while under the influence of LSD, lectured against the dangers of heroin. Elvis Presley came to the White House to tell Nixon, "I really believe in what you're doing."

The Burger Court

A major element in Nixon's appeals to southerners, whites, and conservatives during the 1968 campaign lay in his promise to reverse the direction taken by the Supreme Court under Chief Justice Earl Warren by appointing conservative justices to the Court. He expected that his appointees would revise the Warren Court's decisions expanding civil rights for racial minorities, civil liberties for individuals, and the rights of criminal defendants. Nixon appointed a new chief justice, Warren Burger, and three new associate justices, Harry Blackmun, Lewis Powell, and William Rehnquist. But the new members surprised both their supporters and their detractors with their rulings. Instead of reversing the Warren Court's emphasis on enlarging the rights of individuals and curtailing the powers of government officials, the Court in the early seventies consolidated the earlier decisions.

The Burger Court's decisions built on the civil rights gains of the Warren years. For example, the Court concluded that discriminatory *effects* as well as intentions had been outlawed by the Civil Rights Act of 1964. By far the most controversial civil rights issue to reach the Court during the Nixon years was the use of school busing to achieve racial desegregation. In two important cases, *Swann* v. *Charlotte-Mecklenburg Board of Education* (1971) and *Keyes* v. *Denver School District No. 1* (1973), the Supreme Court mandated busing of schoolchildren to achieve racial balance in the schools.

Overall the Supreme Court's support for busing helped the cause of school desegregation, but it also contributed to a decline in white middle-class trust in the public schools. In urban districts that faced desegregation orders, many parents removed their children from the public school system, either by enrolling them in private or religious schools or by moving to the suburbs. Over the next decade, as this so-called white flight undermined support for public education, most school bond issues brought before voters were defeated. By stimulating white exodus, the busing conflict also hastened the transformation of northern and midwestern urban centers into predominantly poor, black, and Hispanic areas. The less stake the white middle class had in the fate of the cities, the less support it gave to government programs to revitalize urban life. By reinforcing this trend with its decisions on busing, the Supreme Court unintentionally spurred the ongoing crisis in the nation's cities.

In the atmosphere of increasing awareness of discrimination against women, the Supreme Court decided a number of cases that prohibited discrimination on the basis of sex, an issue mostly neglected by the generally more liberal Warren Court. In *Reed* v. *Reed* (1971) the Court held that legislation differentiating between the sexes "must be reasonable, not arbitrary." The same year the Court ruled in *Phillips* v. *Martin Marietta* that Title VII of the Civil Rights Act forbade corporate hiring practices that discriminated against mothers with small children. In *Frontiero* v. *Richardson* (1973) the Court applied Title VII to the military, requiring the armed services to provide the same fringe benefits and pensions to both men and women.

The Court went beyond issues of pay equity and job rights when it overturned all state laws restricting abortions in *Roe* v. *Wade* (1973). Feminists and civil liberties lawyers had challenged a Texas law that made any abortion a felony. The test case involved a poor single woman who believed she could not afford to raise a child. Justice Harry Blackmun, writing for the seven-member majority, opened a new era in reproductive law by ruling that the right of privacy established by *Griswold* v. *Connecticut* (1965) was "broad enough to encompass a woman's decision whether or not to terminate her pregnancy." The decision provided an absolute right to abortion during the first trimester of pregnancy, when, experts agreed, the fetus is not "viable"—that is, cannot live outside the mother's body. During the second trimester, when viability becomes more possible, states could regulate, but not outlaw, abortions. Only for the last thirteen weeks of pregnancy, according to the *Roe* decision, could state laws prohibit abortion.

Roe made abortion readily available, and many women soon took for granted their right to a safe, legal abortion. However, the *Roe* decision produced more public dissent than any other Court ruling since *Brown* v. *Board of Education* struck down school segregation in 1954. The justices who wrote the *Roe* opinion and the women's rights advocates who supported it probably underestimated the anger it would cause. Since 1869 Catholic doctrine had held that life begins at the moment of conception, and many Catholics and other traditionalists assailed *Roe* as judicial sanction of murder. Over the next decade opposition to *Roe* became even more of a rallying point for conservatives than did the Warren Court's protection of the rights of criminal suspects.

Managing the Economy

The behavior of the U.S. economy in the early 1970s defied the expectations of nearly all conventional economists. Prior to that time prices generally remained steady or fell in slow times and rose only in boom periods. But in the Nixon years the United States experienced both inflation and slow or nonexistent growth. Nixon confronted this so-called stagflation by abandoning his long-held economic positions; in fact, he adopted some policies of political rivals that he had once derided. Inflation, the scourge of the Great Society, stubbornly hovered at around 6 percent. Still worse, unemployment rose steadily from 3.8 percent in 1968 to over 6 percent in 1971. In later years economists would identify some of the reasons for this change: the population bulge of baby boomers, who had reached maturity and had begun to spend more money on consumer goods; an increased proportion in the work force of entry-level workers, whose skill levels were less than that of more experienced employees; the competition posed by the revived economies of Japan and Germany; and the inflationary effects of the Vietnam War.

Nixon wanted the country to emerge from the doldrums of stagflation before the 1972 election. Early in 1971 he acknowledged that government wage and price controls might be necessary. Conditions worsened later that year. Although the United States continued to export more than it imported, overseas spending by the government (mostly for the maintenance of hundreds of military bases) and by private citizens meant that the number of dollars going abroad exceeded the value of foreign currency coming into the United States. (Such an economic situation is known as a balance-of-payments deficit.) The problem had worsened during the Vietnam War years, as the central banks of France and West Germany began converting some of their dollars to gold. After a further slide in U.S. exports in mid-1971, international investors began worrying about the dollar's strength, and many bought West German marks instead. In August the Bank of England, previously supportive of U.S. economic policy, demanded that its holdings in American dollars be redeemed in gold.

Over the weekend of August 14–15, economic advisers huddled with the president at Camp David to devise a plan to save the dollar and halt inflation. Nixon and his advisers believed that wage and price controls would stop inflation before the 1972 election. On Sunday evening, August 15, 1971, the president presented a program called the New Economic Policy. He proclaimed a ninety-day freeze on wages and prices. Thereafter a government wage and price commission would monitor price increases and employee contracts, rescinding excessive increases. Over the next year the United States and the major trading nations ended the system, created in 1944, of fixed exchange rates among the world's currencies. By 1972 the value of the world's currencies were "floated," to be determined daily in currency exchange markets around the world.

The New Economic Policy tried to slow the escalating trade deficit with a temporary 10 percent surtax on imports. Nixon also cut government social spending by $4.7 billion and reduced business taxes. The New Economic Policy seemed another example of pragmatic action by an administration willing to break with old orthodoxy. In a Gallup poll taken a week after Nixon's August 15 speech, 73 percent of respondents approved of the new policy.

Although Nixon's policy resulted in some limited economic improvements, nothing could halt inflation after the 1973 Arab-Israeli war and the subsequent oil embargo by the Arab oil-producing states. The price of oil rose 400 percent, from $2 to $4 per barrel, and the effects of that increase caused other costs to shoot up throughout the economies of the industrial world. American prices rose by more than 7 percent in 1974 and 1975.

The New Economic Policy demonstrated both the potential and the limits of Nixon's flexible approach to economic management in a time of rapid change. By endorsing Keynesian techniques to reduce inflation and foster growth, Nixon followed the practices of his predecessors since the Second World War. But fine-tuning the economy proved far more difficult than Nixon's economists had hoped. The long-term ineffectiveness of wage and price controls contributed to the growing sense that the nation's public institutions did not work.

The Election of 1972

With the economy in the doldrums, the Democrats originally had high hopes for the 1972 election. Nixon's southern strategy had failed during the 1970 congressional election, with only one Democratic southern seat falling to a Republican. On the eve of election day Edmund Muskie, the vice-presidential candidate in 1968, had persuasively derided Nixon's "politics of fear" in a televised address. In 1971 Muskie emerged as the favorite for the Democratic presidential nomination. With his rugged good looks and moderate views, Muskie appeared able to unite the Democrats, and early 1972 opinion polls showed him tied with Nixon at 42 percent.

Alarmed by Muskie's popularity rating, functionaries of Nixon's Committee to Re-Elect the President (CREEP) made plans to discredit him, hoping to encourage the nomination of the weakest possible Democratic candidate to oppose Nixon in 1972. That turned out to be South Dakota senator George McGovern. Unlike Muskie, McGovern had clearly articulated liberal views. McGovern attracted an army of fervent volunteers opposed to the war in Vietnam, alarmed by Nixon's hostility to civil rights, and dismayed by the administration's resistance to expanding Great Society programs. Over the next four months McGovern won close to a majority of the delegates to the Democratic national convention through his primary victories over a crowded field of opponents.

Although McGovern won the nomination, many old-line Democrats refused to support him. McGovern's chances declined further when he chose Missouri senator Thomas Eagleton as his running mate. McGovern had hoped that Eagleton's Catholicism and moderate views would appeal to traditional Democrats uncomfortable with the antiwar youth backing him. The day after the nomination, news surfaced that Eagleton had been hospitalized three times in the 1960s for depression and exhaustion. Initially McGovern said he was "1,000 percent for Tom Eagleton" and that he did not intend to drop him from the ticket. But Eagleton then admitted that he had received electroshock treatment while hospitalized and that he still took tranquilizers. Pressure from the media and his campaign staff convinced McGovern to drop Eagleton. Coming so soon after his "1,000 percent" endorsement of Eagleton, McGovern's abrupt reversal made him look unpredictable, weak, and possibly foolish. The process of finding a replacement became a fiasco. McGovern finally selected Sargent Shriver, the Kennedy relative who had formerly directed the Peace Corps and the Office of Economic Opportunity.

In November Nixon won in a massive landslide, gaining 61 percent of the popular vote and carrying 49 states (see map). Only Massachusetts and the District of Columbia went for McGovern. A number of social and political issues contributed to the size of Nixon's victory. His foreign policy triumphs had broad appeal. McGovern's support from antiwar activists and political newcomers had alarmed traditional voters. Voter turnout declined in 1972, and the election was decided by the same segments of the electorate that typically went to the polls. Eighteen- to twenty-year-olds, allowed to vote for the first time under the Twenty-sixth Amendment (adopted in 1971), turned out in fewer numbers than any other group—and half of them voted for Nixon, because he had promised to end the draft in 1973. White working-class Democrats deserted McGovern in droves. The southern strategy finally worked: three-quarters of those who had voted for Wallace in 1968 supported Nixon in 1972.

Watergate and the Abuse of Power

Unknown to nearly everyone but a handful of trusted CREEP operatives and the White House, an astonishing abuse of government power had begun as early as 1969. Ever since he had gone to Washington as a new congressman in 1947, Nixon had considered himself a victim who was never given proper respect by his political adversaries. Even the praise heaped on his foreign policy did not eliminate his feeling that he and his administration were embattled. Feeling isolated and victimized and taking little satisfaction in good news, Nixon lashed out at those he considered his domestic enemies, setting in motion a series of illegal, unconstitutional abuses of presidential power. The scope of the illegalities was unprecedented, ranging from unfair campaign practices—sometimes trivialized as "dirty tricks"—to using the Internal Revenue Service (IRS) to harass opponents, engaging in domestic espionage, and obstructing investigation of these illegalities by law enforcement agencies.

During the 1972 presidential campaign George McGovern had tried but failed to arouse public interest in a curious incident: a break-in at Democratic National Committee headquarters at the Watergate office complex in Washington, D.C., on the night of June 17, 1972, by five men employed by CREEP. When the Washington police apprehended the five CREEP employees on June 17, they stumbled into a complicated web of abuse of presidential power.

President Richard M. Nixon (second from right) with his principal aides, Henry Kissinger (far left), John Ehrlichman, and H. R. "Bob" Haldeman (far right) in the Oval Office of the White House. *Nixon Presidential Library*

In early 1972 John Mitchell, Nixon's campaign manager, approved a plan developed by G. Gordon Liddy, a former FBI agent working for CREEP, to use millions of dollars raised illegally from private donors to disrupt the Democratic Party during the election. Operatives hired by Liddy planted bugging devices in Democratic Committee chairman Lawrence O'Brien's office at the Watergate complex. Two weeks later one of the bugs malfunctioned; the burglars returned to repair it on the night of June 16. At 1:50 A.M. on June 17 a night watchman noticed tape on the door of the Democrats' office and called the District of Columbia police, who arrested five men, one of whom had Liddy's White House telephone number in his address book.

Immediately after the arrests the White House began a cover-up. Over the next three months Nixon and his principal aides successfully obstructed the Watergate investigation. On June 23 Nixon outlined to H. R. Haldeman, his chief of staff, a plan for the CIA to warn the FBI to "stay the hell out of this." Nixon's conversations with Haldeman on June 23 were recorded on tape and eventually came to light in August 1974, providing proof of the president's efforts to obstruct justice.

In mid-September it appeared that the cover-up had succeeded. A federal grand jury indicted Liddy and the men arrested at the Democratic headquarters. A Justice Department spokesman claimed that "we have absolutely no evidence that anyone else should be charged." Relieved, Nixon called John Dean, his counsel and the man in charge of covering up White House involvement in Watergate, into his office late that afternoon and congratulated him: "The way you handled [the cover-up], it seems to me has been very skillful—putting your fingers in the dikes every time that leaks have sprung here and sprung there." Nixon went on to ruminate about his plans for a second administration. He was pleased that Dean had been keeping notes on "a lot of people who are less than our friends." Those people "are asking for it," Nixon said, "and they are going to get it."

Watergate faded but did not die in the winter of 1972 and 1973. Early in 1973 the Senate decided to create a select seven-member committee (four Democrats and three Republicans), chaired by the conservative constitutional expert Sam Ervin of North Carolina, to investigate the break-in and sabotage against the Democrats in the 1972 campaign. The trial of the Watergate burglars revealed little at first, because they all pleaded guilty and denied White House involvement. But Judge John Sirica, who clearly did not believe the story that no one had directed their operation, squeezed the burglars for information about who had employed them. All the while, Nixon instructed aides called to testify before the Ervin committee or the grand jury investigating Watergate to avoid perjury by saying, "I don't remember."

On May 17 the Senate Watergate Committee began televised hearings that continued throughout the summer of 1973. At hairdressing salons, muffler shops, bars, and business offices across the country, Americans interrupted their daily routines to stare at TV sets tuned to the Watergate hearings. In late June, granted immunity from prosecution for what he might reveal, fired presidential counsel John Dean took the stand. For two days he read in a monotone a 245-page statement describing the details of the cover-up. He characterized Watergate as emerging from "a climate of excessive concern over the political impact of demonstrators, excessive concern over leaks, an insatiable appetite for political intelligence."

The hearings reached their climax in mid-July, when Alexander Butterfield, an aide in charge of office management at the White House, revealed that Nixon had been tape-recording his own conversations in the Oval Office ever since 1970. Tapes existed that could show whether Dean was telling the truth. Immediately a variety of government agencies investigating Watergate tried to acquire the tapes, but Nixon refused to release them.

Another scandal hit the White House in late August when federal prosecutors in Baltimore said they were investigating Vice President Spiro Agnew for bribery, extortion, and tax fraud connected with his term as governor of Maryland. After first denying all wrongdoing, Agnew pleaded no contest to a single count of tax evasion and resigned in October.

Agnew's resignation left a vacancy in the vice presidency, and under the terms of the Twenty-fifth Amendment, adopted in the aftermath of John Kennedy's assassination, the president could name a successor, to be confirmed by a majority vote of Congress. Nixon selected Republican minority leader Gerald R. Ford of Michigan, a Republican stalwart who was well-liked by his peers. He had little knowledge of or experience with foreign affairs. He was best known for his unswerving loyalty to Nixon through the many dizzying turns of the administration's foreign and domestic policy.

By October 1973 the full dimensions of the cover-up began to emerge. Nixon, mindful of his conversations with Haldeman and Dean plotting the cover-up, realized that releasing complete tapes to Archibald Cox, the special prosecutor he had appointed to investigate Watergate, would doom him. On Saturday night, October 20, Nixon fired Cox and several high ranking Justice Department officials. Nixon also abolished the special prosecutor's office and sent FBI agents to prevent Cox's subordinates from gaining access to his files.

A firestorm of protest engulfed Capitol Hill over the next forty-eight hours. Over 1 million telephone calls and telegrams flooded senators' and representatives' offices protesting the "Saturday Night Massacre." People who earlier had given Nixon the benefit of the doubt and believed that he would cooperate with investigators changed their minds and thought that he wanted to hide his involvement in lawbreaking. The next week eight impeachment resolutions were referred to the House Judiciary Committee, chaired by New Jersey's Peter Rodino. The eruption of public anger over Nixon's stonewalling on the tapes forced another White House surrender. The president's lawyer announced Nixon's willingness to release subpoenaed tapes to Judge Sirica. A new independent prosecutor, Houston lawyer Leon Jaworski, resumed the investigations.

As public distrust of Nixon increased in 1974, the staff of the House Judiciary Committee carefully prepared a case for impeachment. Continual requests for tapes and documents were met by White House delays and halfhearted compliance. In late July 1974 the committee had impeachment articles ready. On July 27, in a nationally televised session, six Republicans joined all twenty-one Democrats on the committee, forming a majority of twenty-seven to eleven, to adopt the first article, which charged Nixon with obstruction of justice for his involvement in the cover-up of the Watergate break-in. Over the next two days the committee adopted two more articles of impeachment. If the full House of Representatives concurred, Nixon would become only the second president in U.S. history to be impeached (the first having been Andrew Johnson in 1868). He would then be brought to trial before the Senate, which would decide whether to remove the president from office.

The Supreme Court quickly delivered another blow to Nixon. In *United States* v. *Nixon,* by an 8-to-0 ruling, the Court demanded that he turn over to Sirica tapes of sixty-four conversations deemed essential evidence in the cover-up trials of six former aides. Nixon's lawyer agreed to turn over the tapes by the August 7 deadline set by Sirica. On August 5 Nixon released transcripts of his June 23, 1972, conversations with Haldeman. The transcripts revealed how the two men had planned to use the CIA to throw the FBI off the scent of the Watergate investigation. Here was the "smoking gun" his defenders had insisted did not exist, for the conversations showed Nixon's early knowledge of and participation in the cover-up. Nixon conceded in a written statement that the tapes were "at variance with certain of my previous statements" and acknowledged that impeachment by the full House was "virtually a foregone conclusion." Nixon's impending resignation became public the evening of August 8; in a televised address he told the nation that he intended to leave office at noon the next day. On the morning of August 9 he said farewell to his staff in a tearful speech. He climbed into a helicopter on the White House lawn, flew to Andrews Air Force Base, and boarded *Air Force One* for a flight to California, becoming the first American president ever to resign from the nation's highest office. While Nixon was en route to the West Coast, Gerald Ford took the oath of office as the new president. Ford proclaimed that "the long national nightmare" of Watergate was over.

Nixon's Domestic Record and the Implications of Watergate

Richard Nixon's defenders at the time of his resignation and in subsequent years tended to focus on his achievements in foreign policy, particularly the steps he took toward cooperating with the Soviet Union and China. In some ways, however, his domestic record showed a similar creativity, particularly his early plan for welfare reform and his willingness to scrap his conservative economic approach in favor of wage and price controls. Unfortunately he was most creative at devising ways to undercut his political opponents. His presidency became dominated by his obsession with his supposed enemies and his determination to "get" them before they could "get" him. President Nixon did more to divide the nation than to unite it. In the end, most of the substantive changes in domestic affairs during his administration came from Congress and the Supreme Court rather than from the executive branch. As the Court extended its civil rights rulings into the controversial areas of busing and abortion rights, Congress passed key legislation to protect the environment and promote public health and safety.

Ironically it was Nixon's resignation that finally unified the country. No other event since John Kennedy's assassination had done more to bring Americans together. A president who had tried to exploit his power in illegal and unethical ways had failed to dominate the government and intimidate his opposition into silence. As his cynical manipulations of people and events became known during the Watergate investigations, Americans asserted their sense of justice and fair play. Besides agreeing that justice had been done, Americans breathed a collective sigh of relief that the country's government had withstood the strain of the Watergate crisis.

The overall implications of Watergate are difficult to assess. Nixon's abuses of power were finally checked, but perhaps only as a result of fortunate circumstances. Will the system work again if another president tries to subvert the country's laws and institutions?

✦ Social and Economic Changes During the 1970s

Even as many Americans spent hours sitting transfixed before their television sets watching the Watergate drama, they went about their daily lives. By 1974 long-term changes in gender roles, family patterns, and personal desires had become so apparent that many Americans believed the time had come to develop new ways to deal with their transformed lives. Fewer and fewer households conformed to the picture of the once-idealized nuclear family, headed by a father who worked outside the home to support a mother who cared for the children. The proportion of women who worked outside the home continued to grow. By 1970 one-third of mothers with children under six years of age held or sought jobs; by 1984 a total of 52 percent had joined the work force. In 1975 the Labor Department reported that only 7 percent of American families fit the category of a "typical" four-person household—a married couple living together with their two minor children.

Changing Roles for Men and Women

The growing numbers of divorced men and women, never-married individuals, unmarried couples living together, working women, single mothers, and openly gay men and women made American diversity visible at a time when Americans were speaking more openly about the emotional issues of sexuality and gender. Yet in many cases those whose way of life diverged from earlier norms continued to encounter economic hardship and persistent hostility. At the same time, some traditionalists feared for their cherished values, and they joined a growing conservative movement to reverse threatening social trends.

Divorce became more commonplace in the 1970s, continuing a trend begun early in the twentieth century. For those marrying for the first time, 44 percent would dissolve their union in divorce; for second or subsequent marriages the figure was predicted to reach 60 percent. Couples divorced for many reasons: they no longer cared for each other; one of them found the other physically or mentally abusive; they believed they could make it economically outside of marriage; they considered it difficult to repair their deteriorating relationship; or they no longer feared the disapproval of family, friends, their religious congregation, or their community. Divorce had lost the stigma once attached to it.

These changing attitudes coincided with the enactment of "no-fault" divorce laws. These statutes permitted either party to divorce when he or she believed that "irreconcilable differences" had caused the breakdown of their marriage. Advocates of the new family relations laws believed they would allow people in unsatisfactory marriages to find a legal way out and still retain their dignity. It was also hoped that reduced acrimony would make it easier for divorced parents to cooperate in the future rearing of their children. The new laws tried to treat men and women equally, recognize a wife's contribution to a marital partnership, and end old assumptions that women's roles were subordinate to those of men.

No-fault divorce laws achieved many of their goals, but they also brought some unintended negative consequences for women and children. The divorce revolution hurt at least two classes of women: older women who had not worked outside the home during their marriage and mothers of young children. The laws supposedly treated men and women equally, but they defined equality strictly in dollar terms. Older women who had been homemakers for years found they had few assets and limited job opportunities after their divorce. Instead of compensating them for their long periods as mothers and homemakers, the new laws expected them to be as capable of supporting themselves as men. Alimony, once a staple of divorce settlements, was awarded rarely under the new system. The economic burden of divorce fell even more heavily on women with young children. Judges divided marital property equally, and in most cases the largest single asset was a family's house, which the court ordered sold. A mother with minor children, possessing only half the proceeds from the sale of a home, found herself looking for new shelter at a time of rising housing costs. Judges ordered child support, but fewer than half of the fathers paid the full amount assessed by the courts.

In taking on these issues, women's groups confronted a social problem that would become more and more critical as the century neared an end. Sociologist Diana Peace coined the phrase "the feminization of poverty" to describe the fastest-growing segment of poor people in America. Of course, the economic problems affected children as well as their mothers. From 1970 to 1982 the proportion of children living in poverty grew from 15 percent to 21 percent. Most of this growth was accounted for by children living in female-headed households.

At the same time, childbirth among unmarried women and teenagers began to rise, placing further burdens on both mothers and children. Unskilled, uneducated, poor young single mothers faced serious hardships. Good-paying jobs were scarce, especially in depressed cities. Even when they found work, these mothers often discovered that their paychecks barely covered the cost of child care, if they could even find it. Some of these women, unable to get work or adequate child care, relied on public assistance, which fostered dependency and did little to help them out of their situation.

Higher divorce rates were only one indication of profound changes in American families. Throughout the 1970s Americans adopted a variety of alternatives to the traditional nuclear family. The number of adults living alone increased 60 percent in the seventies, constituting 23 percent of all households by 1980. Some of the increase was accounted for by older, widowed people who were living longer, but most of the rise reflected an increase in the number of single people under the age of thirty-five living alone. At the same time, the number of unmarried couples living together tripled to 1.6 million, and one-third of them had children.

Rates of divorce and living together rose, but so did the marriage rate. Eighty percent of separated or divorced people remarried within three years. Sociologists described "blended families" in which children lived with step-parents, step-siblings, and half-siblings. Experts projected that more than half of all children born in the seventies would spend part of their childhood living in arrangements other than a household headed by their own biological mother and father and with only their biological brothers or sisters. Forty percent would spend time in a single-parent household, almost always headed by a woman. On the positive side, the best of these blended families offered webs of nurture and affection. When successful, the new living arrangements re-created in different form the warmth of the old-fashioned extended family of grandparents, aunts, uncles, and cousins that many thought had been lost.

Changes in family and sexual relationships frightened and angered traditionalists, who considered their own way of life threatened. Opposition to the growing assertiveness of women crystallized in a movement to prevent ratification of the Equal Rights Amendment. Passed by Congress and sent to the states in 1972, the ERA needed ratification by thirty-eight state legislatures before March 1979 or it would die. After quickly gaining passage in thirty-five states, supporters were stymied in the three more they needed. In July 1978 Congress extended the deadline for three more years, but the proposed amendment was never ratified.

Another sign of trouble in the American family came from horrifying reports of physical, sexual, and emotional abuse of children and spouses. Modern families may not have been more violent than earlier ones, but once feminists and child advocates insisted that the issues of wife battering and child abuse be taken seriously, behavior once considered acceptable was no longer tolerated. Most abusive acts went unreported, so documented cases represented only the tip of the iceberg. Although hard figures were difficult to obtain, experts estimated that between 1.5 and 2.3 million of the 46 million children living with both parents between the ages of three and seventeen had been battered by one or both parents in their lifetime. Similar figures were reported for domestic partners—almost always women beaten by their mates. Sexual abuse of children also seemed to climb.

Greater openness about sexuality encouraged gay Americans to seek validation from straight society and the end of ingrained prejudices and stereotypes. The campaign for gay rights achieved notable gains in the seventies. For instance, the American Psychiatric Association dropped its classification of homosexuality as a mental disorder and joined a growing call for the extension of civil rights protection to homosexuals.

In their daily lives, gays and lesbians found new self-confidence and visibility in the 1970s. Gay men established well-defined, separate neighborhoods in many large and middle-sized American cities. Lesbians, though less geographically concentrated, nonetheless created communities for themselves in various ways, claiming a culture of their own through music, art, and literature and founding successful entertainment businesses. Gays and lesbians spoke openly of the love and caring they experienced together. They publicly acknowledged their sexual orientation, formed organizations to advance their interests, and published newspapers, newsletters, and magazines addressing their concerns. Gays and lesbians lobbied municipalities, states, and the federal government to eliminate restrictions against homosexuals in employment, housing, and various government programs. Some laws changed, but Congress did not act to alter procedures on the national level.

Opponents of gay rights soon mounted a counterattack. After the Miami City Council banned discrimination against homosexuals, singer Anita Bryant began a campaign to repeal the new law. In June 1977 Bryant's Save Our Children movement organized a referendum that repealed the law by a two-to-one majority. The size of the vote shook gays and advocates of civil liberties across the country. San Francisco mayor George Moscone, elected with the support of the city's sizable gay community, condemned the repeal as "terribly wrong." In November 1978 Moscone and Harvey Milk, the first openly gay member of the San Francisco Board of Supervisors, the city council, were gunned down by a former colleague on the Board, Dan White, who had voted against San Francisco's gay rights law. Although police arrested White with the smoking gun in his hand, he won acquittal by a local jury on murder charges. After the verdict about ten thousand supporters of Milk and Moscone rioted, chanting, "He got away with murder."

Economic Problems and Social Divisions

Had the nation's economy boomed as it had during the early 1960s, prosperity might have assuaged some of the social tensions and uncertainties of the 1970s. However, the manufacturing sector of the economy began to decline in the mid-1970s. Inflation took a heavy toll on Americans, making many worry about the future. Stagflation remained a serious problem. Prices rose because the growth in American productivity had slowed and because a fourfold increase in petroleum prices produced an "oil shock" that rippled through the economy. After September 1978, as the revolution in Iran sent oil prices soaring again, inflation became rampant. The annual rate of increase in the consumer price index climbed steadily from an already high 7 percent in May 1978 to 11.3 percent in July 1979. The cost of goods that people bought and used everyday rose even faster. The pump price of gasoline went up 52 percent from September 1978 to September 1979. Americans panicked, fearing they could not get gas no matter what they paid. By the summer of 1979 cars were lining up five hundred deep at some service stations.

An unemployed steelworker leaves the plant of the Bethlehem Steel Corporation where he has been laid off after sixteen years of work. Such layoffs signaled the decline of American heavy industry. *Wide World Photos*

Fear of shortages and high prices extended beyond motor fuel. As prices on home heating oil, used mostly in the Northeast and Midwest, shot up during 1979, people in those regions glumly contemplated a cold, expensive winter. Food prices also took off. Consumers felt the pinch every time they went to the supermarket, and TV news broadcasts did not let them forget it when they returned home.

Inflation made it harder for businesses to modernize. One secretary of the treasury lamented that "you can't figure your rate of return, so you postpone investments." Competitors in Japan and Germany, where inflation remained below 3 percent, spent two to three times more than American firms on upgrading their manufacturing facilities.

American manufacturing experienced a devastating decline because of foreign competition, mismanagement, and aging equipment. Observers called the industrial East and Midwest the "Rustbelt," a dispiriting characterization of the decline of American technology, engineering, and wealth. The automobile industry, once the proud symbol of American affluence and engineering pre-eminence, suffered a real depression. U.S. automakers sold 9.3 million cars in 1978 but only 6.6 million in 1980. Over two hundred thousand well-paid, skilled workers lost their jobs in Michigan, Ohio, and Indiana, the heart of the auto industry. Feeling the pinch at the fuel pump, people paid less attention to Detroit's slick ads and switched to less powerful but more sensible vehicles manufactured in Germany and Japan. Consumers understood that imports cost less to operate, ran better, and required fewer repairs than U.S.-made cars.

Throughout the country other kinds of manufacturing jobs declined as well, especially in the large cities. The shrinking job market for unskilled workers had a severe effect on the urban poor. In earlier decades American cities had been a magnet for unskilled European immigrants and rural blacks from the South; many of these migrants had found blue-collar work that improved their economic condition. With the loss of industrial employment, however, poverty worsened in many American cities. In northern cities, especially, deindustrialization, a declining tax base, and increased poverty nearly overwhelmed municipal services.

✦ The Ford and Carter Administrations

From the start of his presidency, Gerald Ford tried to put the memory of Watergate to rest. His homey style contrasted with Nixon's awkward defensiveness. The new president, the adored and adoring father of four happy young adults, seemed at peace with himself, his family, and his country. In contrast to Nixon, who had cheated on his income taxes, Ford paid his fair share. He was often photographed playing golf like a Midwestern small businessman. At first Ford relished his role as a regular guy. "I don't want a honeymoon," he told Congress three days after taking office, "I want a good marriage." He could take a joke, too. He laughed when photographers snapped pictures of his awkward moments—for instance, when his errant golf balls hit surprised spectators or when he stumbled on the gangway and banged his head on the doorway of *Air Force One*.

"Gerald Ford is an awfully nice man who isn't up to the presidency," wrote John Osborne in *The New Republic*. Osborne shared the feeling of millions of Americans who first welcomed Ford's assumption of the presidency in August 1974 as a breath of fresh air but who soon saw Ford as inept. Ford alienated potential supporters with his pardon of Richard Nixon one month after he took office. Ford believed that a protracted trial of the former president would only rivet the public eye on the misdeeds of Watergate, diverting attention from what Ford was trying to accomplish and hurting Republican chances in the upcoming congressional elections. On Sunday morning, September 8, 1974, Ford announced that he had provided a "full, free, and absolute pardon" to the former president. Nixon formally accepted the pardon, an act equivalent to acknowledging guilt, but he claimed only to have made "mistakes" in the Watergate affair. The public felt betrayed by Ford and dissatisfied that Nixon would not admit he had broken the law. The new president's approval rating dropped from 72 percent to 49 percent.

Voters, angry at the pardon and stagflation, took out their frustrations during the 1974 congressional elections. Democrats overwhelmed Republicans with gains of forty-six House seats, giving them a majority of 290 to the

A U.S. helicopter evacuates frantic South Vietnamese from the roof of a Saigon apartment building in the chaotic last days of the Vietnam War. *Corbis/Bettmann*

Republicans' 145—enough to override a presidential veto without any Republican votes. They picked up an additional four seats in the Senate. They also won almost all of the governorships in major states. After the election of 1974 there were more Democratic officeholders than at any time since the early New Deal.

Troubles abroad contributed to the gnawing fear that events had slipped out of control, the country's fortunes had plunged, and its leaders had lost their sense of direction. In early 1975 the Communist Party leadership in Hanoi decided that the moment had arrived for a decisive victory in the Vietnam War. North Vietnamese forces captured an important outpost in the central highlands in March. When Thieu ordered his troops to withdraw, they fled in terror, leaving their weapons behind; the troops fought hundreds of thousands of panicked refugees for space in the clogged roads and on planes leaving for the South.

As the rout of South Vietnam's armed forces quickened in April, Americans fled Vietnam. The high point of Ford's young presidency came when he announced on April 23 at Tulane University that "the war in Vietnam is over as far as the United States is concerned." On April 29 the last American helicopters lifted off from the roof of the embassy in Saigon. The next day the remnant of the government of the Republic of Vietnam surrendered, and North Vietnamese and Vietcong troops renamed Saigon as Ho Chi Minh City. The Americans evacuated about 150,000 Vietnamese employees and supporters, but they left hundreds of thousands more behind. TV viewers at home were disgusted by images of U.S. Marines clubbing screaming, terrified Vietnamese to keep them away from the American embassy and of terrified people clinging to the runners of departing helicopters. Scenes of ARVN soldiers shoving and shooting the weak, the elderly, and women with small children to secure a place on the few evacuation planes represented to many the horror, chaos, and futility of the war in Vietnam.

That war had lasted so long that most Americans preferred to forget it, or at least not to speak publicly about it. They temporarily followed Secretary of State Kissinger's urging "to put Vietnam behind us." On May 12 Ford tried to take some of the sting out of the defeat in Vietnam by ordering Marines to attack Cambodian Communist forces that had captured the *S.S. Mayaguez,* a civilian freighter that had strayed into Cambodian waters. The Marines destroyed a Cambodian port and lost thirty-eight men before locating the crew of the *Mayaguez,* whom the Cambodians had already released.

Détente with the Soviet Union, already strained in the aftermath of the October 1973 Mideast war, declined further in the Ford administration. Calls to push the Soviets on human rights intensified. Conservatives complained when Ford would not meet Aleksandr Solzhenitsyn, an exiled Russian novelist who had been stripped of his Soviet citizenship after winning the Nobel Prize for literature for his books describing the Soviet police state. The president's standing slipped further in August 1975 when he attended the Conference on Security and Cooperation in Europe, convened in Helsinki. There, thirty-five European and North American nations recognized the borders created in Europe at the end of the Second World War. The Helsinki Conference produced a declaration of human rights that supported freedom of migration, expression, and religion. Conservatives and Cold Warriors in the United States ignored that part of the proceedings and criticized American acknowledgment of the legitimacy of Communist rule in Eastern Europe.

In the fall of 1975 Ford appeared more vulnerable than ever. Ronald Reagan, a former governor of California and a champion of conservatives, announced his candidacy for the Republican presidential nomination in November. He complained that "our nation's capital has become the seat of a buddy system that functions for its own benefit." Using themes that he had developed over the previous twenty years, Reagan stressed his opposition to a wide variety of institutions and trends: the federal government, Social Security, busing for integration, student radicalism, sexual promiscuity, abortion, the ERA, détente, and accommodation with the Third World. He advocated lower taxes, prayer in public schools, and an assertive foreign policy designed to erase the stain of the defeat in Vietnam. Reagan defeated Ford in a series of southern and western primaries after criticizing the Nixon-Ford-

Kissinger policy of détente and demanding an end to negotiations over relinquishing U.S. control of the Panama Canal.

Ford eked out a narrow victory over Reagan at the Republican convention in Kansas City, pleading with party regulars not to humiliate a sitting Republican president. He capitulated to the conservatives by dropping his vice president, Nelson Rockefeller, and replacing him with sharp-tongued Kansas senator Robert Dole. The president toughened the American stand on arms control with the Soviet Union, thereby blocking completion of the SALT-II treaty before the election, and suspended work on the Panama Canal treaty. Ford also accepted a conservative platform that adopted many of Reagan's positions—"less government, less spending, less inflation."

Democratic primary voters chose Jimmy Carter, former governor of Georgia, to oppose Ford in the fall election. A graduate of the Naval Academy at Annapolis, Carter had served in a nuclear submarine before leaving the navy in 1953 to take over his family's peanut warehouse in the southern Georgia town of Plains. He won election to the Georgia state legislature and ran for governor in 1966 but lost to segregationist Lester Maddox. He won the governorship in 1970. As governor Carter became a model advocate of the New South, too busy attracting modern industry to the burgeoning Sunbelt to dwell on the sour racial divisions of the past. He declared in his inaugural address that "the time for racial segregation is over," and he ordered a portrait of Martin Luther King, Jr., hung in the state capitol. His governorship drew business to Georgia and healed many racial wounds of the previous decade.

A deeply religious man, Carter stressed old Protestant virtues in his campaign for the presidency. He liked to quote a sentence from the theologian Reinhold Niebuhr: "The sad duty of politics is to establish justice in a sinful world." Virtually unknown at the beginning of 1976, he followed the advice of political professionals who grasped what the public wanted in the wake of Watergate and Vietnam. Specific programs mattered less than confidence in the rectitude and competence of the country's leaders. At a time when nearly all Washington politicians were under suspicion, Carter effectively used his status as an outsider untouched by the failures and scandals of the federal government. "I'm not a lawyer, I'm not a member of Congress, and I've never served in Washington," Carter told responsive audiences as he traveled the country in the winter of 1975–1976 looking for support in caucuses and primaries.

If voters did not know where he stood on specific issues, they admired his honesty. He guaranteed "a government as good as the American people." When forced to take a stand on specifics—abortion, busing, amnesty for draft evaders—Carter tried to occupy the middle ground. Although Carter won no primaries outside the South after April, he continued to accumulate delegates. He wrapped up the nomination in June. A month later the Democrats met in optimism and harmony, in sharp contrast to their two previous gatherings. To appease traditional liberals Carter chose one of them, Minnesota senator Walter Mondale, as his vice-presidential nominee.

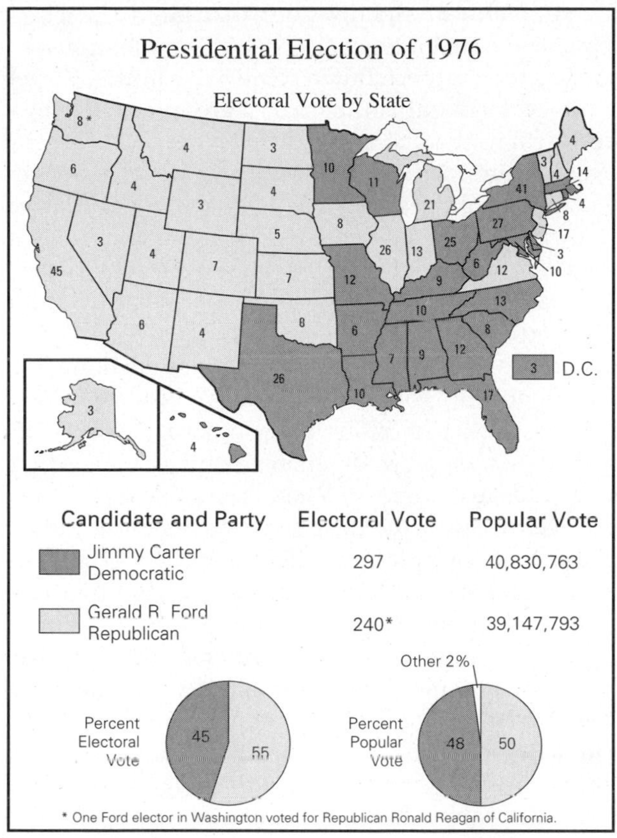

The Election of 1976 Democrat Jimmy Carter defeated Gerald Ford in the election of 1976 with a promise to restore Americans' faith in their leaders and public institutions.

On election day Carter defeated Ford by taking 50.1 percent of the popular vote, compared to Ford's 48 percent (see map). Carter won 297 electoral votes to Ford's 241. Anger at the Nixon pardon, unhappiness with the sluggish economy, and doubts about Ford's ability to lead persuaded a majority to cast their lot with Carter. His backers admired his sincerity and morality and believed him to be more intelligent than Ford. That was enough to make them suspend doubts about the direction of his policies and concerns that he had gone too far in stressing his lack of ties to official Washington. Could such an outsider follow through on a program even if he had one? Only time would tell.

As president, Jimmy Carter emphasized his outsider status and kept at arm's length the Democrats who dominated Congress. Perhaps no politician could have overcome the divisions that faced Carter—in the country as a whole and even in his own party—in a contentious era in which leaders commanded little respect. But in some ways Jimmy Carter was at a particular disadvantage. His rural, southern background and his moderate-to-conservative predilections distanced him from many of the other leaders in his party. Moreover, as president he emphasized skillful management rather than a clearly stated set of principles, and even when he did articulate his beliefs, he tended to be inconsistent in implementing them. When the government programs he inherited or initiated did not work, he also lost his reputation as a manager, and by the end of his term in office he had little authority over the nation he had tried to lead.

Some of Carter's early policy initiatives encountered congressional hostility. He offended important Democrats in February 1977 by abruptly canceling nineteen water projects in the southern, Rocky Mountain, and western states. These dams, river diversions, and irrigation systems had dubious economic value relative to their cost. They also represented tangible evidence of the wastefulness of the despised "Washington buddy system," in which legislators spent years building alliances by agreeing to support one another's pet construction projects. For a president committed to reducing waste and judging each government program on its economic and social merits rather than its popularity among powerful interest groups or prominent politicians, the cancellation seemed logical. Politically, however, the decision angered many Democrats, whose local support hinged on their ability to deliver public works to their districts.

Carter's proposals succeeded with Congress only when it appeared that they would not require higher taxes or add to the federal deficit. For example, pursuing his campaign's distrust of the federal government, he obtained congressional support for plans to end federal controls over transportation. In 1978 the Civil Aeronautics Board began the process of deregulating the airline industry, allowing carriers to set their own prices and determine their own routes. The immediate results were dramatically lower fares, more airlines, and a tripling of airline traffic. Airline deregulation also had a downside, as numerous smaller communities saw their airline service decline or even disappear.

Carter's effort to compromise on divisive social issues dissatisfied important groups within his party and left an impression of a confused president who did not know where he wanted to lead the country. He sought a middle ground on abortion where none existed. When the Supreme Court upheld a congressional measure forbidding the use of Medicaid funds for abortion except in cases where the mother's life was threatened, supporters of reproductive choice complained that the decision unfairly penalized poor women. Carter responded that "there are many things in life that are unfair, that wealthy people can afford that poor people can't."

The Carter administration also failed to resolve the nation's deep divisions on the question of affirmative action programs. To guarantee fairer, more

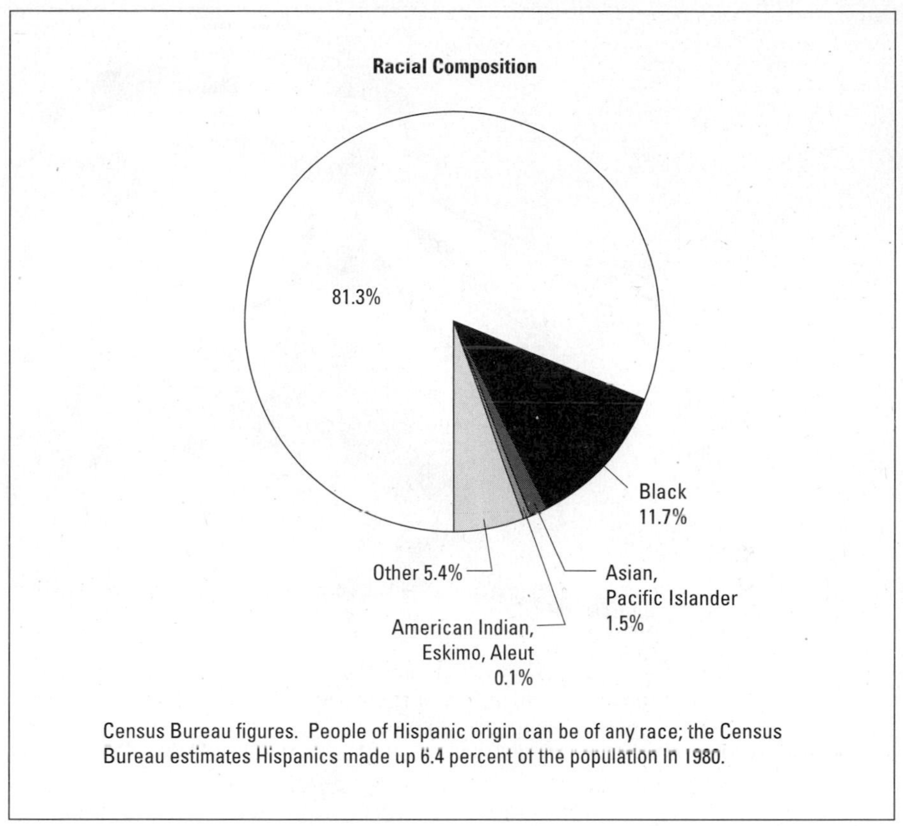

The U.S. Population Profile, 1970–1980 During the 1980s, nonwhites made up a greater proportion of the U.S. population.

proportional representation of minority groups in jobs and schools, many such programs had established minimum quotas for minorities and for women, but this arrangement began to provoke strong resentment among those who did not benefit from such quotas (see figure). Carter supported the Supreme Court's effort to solve the dilemma in *University of California Board of Regents* v. *Bakke* (1978). A majority of the justices allowed affirmative action programs based on race but invalidated rigid quota systems. The Court's sharply divided ruling failed to still the controversy about the steps that institutions should take to redress previous discrimination.

As politicians squabbled in Washington and the president's popularity fell, backlash grew against government at all levels. Officeholders in both parties lost primaries to conservative insurgents who accused incumbents of supporting higher taxes. In the next two years the idea of a substantial cut in income taxes grew from an eccentric theory into the centerpiece of conserva-

In the mid-1970s Americans feared that their thirst for imported gasoline would lead to the destruction of their cherished lifestyle based on cheap fuel powering huge, inefficient cars. *Don Wright,* Miami News, *1976, Tribune Media Services*

tive Republicans' program for the 1980s presidential campaign. Ronald Reagan, preparing for another run at the White House, told supporters that opposition to taxes was "a little bit like dumping those cases of tea off the boat in Boston Harbor."

By July 1979 President Carter's approval rating had fallen to a dismal 29 percent. The president knew he had to do something, but what? Carter listened to pollster Patrick Caddell, who noted a "national malaise" characterized by voters' alienation from traditional institutions. Carter decided to apologize for his administration's shortcomings. He acknowledged merit in the complaint that he had "been managing, not leading" the country, and he begged citizens to "have faith in our country—not only in the government, but in our own ability to solve great problems." The next day he fired or accepted the resignation of five cabinet members.

Carter's reappraisal failed to restore faith in his leadership. During the cabinet shakeup the president appointed Paul Volcker, a twenty-year veteran of the Treasury Department and the New York Federal Reserve Bank, to chair the Federal Reserve Board. Volcker confronted an economic crisis of high prices, slowed production, and mounting unemployment. As inflation continued throughout the summer of 1979, the stock market fell, and economists predicted an economic slump for the following winter. Volcker responded by driving interest rates above 15 percent to stop inflation; but by the beginning of 1980 prices were still rising, and 8 million Americans were out of work. In April 1980 the economy entered its sharpest recession since 1974. Americans wondered if people could buy a house with mortgage rates at 18 percent. Could they fill up their cars to drive to work? Would there be a job to drive to?

Despite rising public skepticism, the Carter administration made serious attempts to confront long-term challenges. Carter's major legislative initiative promised a national policy for energy. Since the Arab oil boycott in the winter of 1973 and 1974, Americans had spent long hours in gasoline lines, seen oil prices rise fourfold, groaned under the weight of inflation, and worried that half of their oil came from foreign sources.

In April 1977 Carter unveiled a series of measures to reverse these trends. Like Carter's other programs, his energy policy sought to satisfy a variety of competing and antagonistic regional and economic interests. In the process it offended more people than it pleased. He asked for the creation of a Department of Energy. He called for tax incentives and penalties to encourage consumers to conserve energy and producers to drill more oil and gas wells. Critics quickly pounced on the contradictory nature of the program. Speaking for conservatives, Ronald Reagan complained that "our problem isn't a shortage of oil, it's a surplus of government." Liberals objected that too much had been offered to oil companies and too little to the poor.

Congress finally passed a greatly modified version of his energy program in November 1978, about the time oil prices began another sharp rise in response to the revolution in Iran. The final law gave more benefits both to oil companies and to their opponents. Appealing to advocates of alternative fuels, many of whom despised the huge multinational oil companies, the law created the Solar Energy Research Institute. At the federal, state, and local levels, governments sponsored research on a multiplicity of alternative energy sources and conservation programs, from wind power and geothermal energy to new plans for mass transit and efficient building designs. The federal government made environmental responsibility attractive to the public by, for example, giving homeowners tax breaks for insulating. But there was also something for corporate America. Congress authorized investment in a giant synthetic fuels corporation, controlled by the giant oil firms, to extract petroleum from rocks in Colorado, Utah, and Wyoming. Lawmakers further assisted the major oil producers with plans to spend over $10 billion to fill the "strategic petroleum reserve," a vast supply of government-purchased oil, first authorized in 1975, to be stored in deep Louisiana and Texas caverns.

As Congress struggled to craft an energy policy acceptable to different regions and economic interests, Americans became increasingly skeptical about the ability of technology and engineering to improve their lives. Instead they feared that modern technologies might not be safe. By the early 1970s, for example, residents of the Love Canal neighborhood in Niagara Falls, New

York, had noticed foul air, blackened trees, a high incidence of cancer, numerous miscarriages, and babies born with birth defects. Experts eventually traced the problems to hazardous materials buried thirty years before by the Hooker Chemical Company. The federal government declared an emergency in the area and ordered the people living there to move out.

Fears about the safety of nuclear power, heavily promoted in the 1950s as the cleanest, cheapest form of electricity available, expanded in March 1979 when a reactor at Three Mile Island near Harrisburg, Pennsylvania, badly malfunctioned. One hundred thousand residents fled their homes, and many did not believe officials who told them two weeks later that it was safe to return. As public fears mounted, electric companies responded by canceling over thirty proposed new nuclear power plants.

The near catastrophe at Three Mile Island also fed more general fears about degradation of the environment. Washington created a $1.6 billion "Superfund," paid for by taxes on polluting industries, to clean up toxic waste sites. The Carter administration also placed over 100 million acres of Alaskan land under federal protection, barring mining or petroleum development there. Yet such actions could not reverse concern about the spoiling of the nation's land, air, and water. The environmental movement grew, and many environmentalists expressed increasing skepticism about the benefits of unrestrained economic growth.

Foreign Affairs in the Carter Years

Despite Jimmy Carter's troubles on the domestic front, his administration initially succeeded in restoring the reversal of American foreign policy away from the Cold War and military confrontation with the Soviet Union. Carter was also a strong advocate of human rights abroad and of sensitivity to the needs of poor nations. But the administration lost its foreign policy momentum in 1979, and its last eighteen months saw a series of foreign policy rebuffs and catastrophes.

Carter began by tackling difficult problems that had defied earlier presidents. In 1976 Gerald Ford had stopped negotiations with Panama on the future of the Panama Canal. Carter resumed those negotiations, expressing a desire to "get away permanently from an attitude of paternalism" in dealing with Latin America. In September 1977 the United States and Panama signed two treaties granting ownership of the canal to Panama on December 31, 1999, and giving the United States the right to defend the waterway thereafter. The treaties were popular in Panama and throughout Latin America, where people hoped that the American government seriously wanted to treat its neighbors as equals. But U.S. ownership of the canal touched a patriotic chord, and it took hard lobbying by Carter to achieve ratification of the treaties by a narrow margin in March 1978.

Carter achieved his greatest triumph in foreign affairs by arranging the first peace treaty between Israel and one of its Arab neighbors, Egypt. As in the case of the canal treaties, the Carter administration went beyond the steps taken by its predecessors and initially won praise for its actions, but ultimately provoked a political backlash. Carter believed that Egyptian president Anwar Sadat had become a "man who would change history" when he courageously flew to Jerusalem in November 1977 to address Israel's parliament and offer an end to the thirty-year state of war between the Jewish state and its neighbors. Israelis were euphoric in the aftermath of Sadat's trip, but the Palestinians and most of the Arab states damned him as a traitor. The excitement faded in 1978, as Egypt and Israel had made little progress in their talks. It was then that President Carter became personally involved as a mediator.

Carter invited Sadat and Israel's Prime Minister Menachem Begin to a series of conversations in Washington, and in September 1978 he arranged a joint meeting with them at Camp David, the presidential retreat in the Maryland mountains. Carter dropped all other work to concentrate on bridging the gap between Egypt and Israel. His determination paid off with the signing of the "Framework for Peace in the Middle East," which promised a treaty between Egypt and Israel, a five-year transitional authority of Israelis and Palestinians in the West Bank and Gaza, and negotiations on the final status of the occupied territories.

The initial congratulations gave way to suspicions and recriminations, however. It took six months, not the promised three, plus another round of personal diplomacy from Carter before an Israeli-Egyptian treaty was signed in Washington in March 1979. The other Arab states and the Palestine Liberation Organization (PLO) refused to join the Camp David peace process and ostracized Egypt. Israel did not offer real autonomy to the Palestinians and continued its policy of not dealing with the PLO. American supporters of Israel sensed that Carter admired Sadat but distrusted Begin.

Carter believed that the United States had for too long ignored the fate of ordinary people in foreign countries who suffered mistreatment at the hands of their own government. He promised to pay far greater attention to the promotion of human rights abroad, hoping thereby to restore America's moral image, which had been badly tarnished by the war in Vietnam. The administration made significant progress in promoting human rights in its first two years. Congress created a new position, assistant secretary of state for human rights. But the administration soon encountered difficulty applying standards of human rights strictly and impartially. The State Department criticized some old friends of the United States in Latin America, but political expediency caused the administration to temper its criticism of other long-term partners in important areas of the world.

The decline of détente that began in the Nixon administration continued, for the most part, in the Carter years. At first Carter tried to reduce tensions with the Soviet Union. The new administration attempted to demonstrate that it could conclude a better arms control agreement than the SALT-II treaty, which the Ford administration had abandoned in 1976. In 1977 the United States offered the Soviets an arms control treaty with far deeper cuts than those proposed by Ford, but Moscow rejected the proposal. Two years later, in June 1979, Carter and Soviet leader Leonid Brezhnev signed the SALT-II treaty, limiting each side to 2,400 nuclear launchers, about what the Ford administration had sought in 1976.

Had the SALT-II treaty been ready earlier in Carter's term, the Senate might have ratified it. By 1979, however, Carter was a weak president, unpopular even among Democrats. Opponents complained that the treaty gave the Soviets advantages in land-based missiles and criticized Moscow's encouragement of revolutionaries in Africa. As Carter mobilized support for the treaty, he also tried to demonstrate his concern about threatening Soviet behavior by advocating the construction of new, more destructive weapons. He accepted West German requests to station mid-range U.S. missiles in Europe to counter similar Soviet weapons, and he recommended that all NATO countries increase their defense spending by 3 percent above inflation. Congress and the public found such moves confusing, and in the fall of 1979 the Senate Armed Services Committee voted against ratification of the SALT-II treaty. Facing certain defeat in the full Senate, Carter withdrew the treaty from consideration in January 1980.

Carter justified shelving the treaty on the grounds that the Soviets' invasion of Afghanistan in late December 1979 represented the "gravest threat to peace" since the end of the Second World War. To punish Moscow he refused to send athletes to the upcoming Moscow Olympics, a decision that upset hundreds of would-be American participants; he also embargoed grain shipments to the Soviets, infuriating thousands of American farmers; and he revived registration for the draft, alarming millions of young men.

Americans would likely have tolerated these foreign affairs difficulties had it not been for the rage and impotent frustration generated by the capture of the U.S. embassy and its staff in Teheran, Iran, on November 4, 1979. The revolution in Iran had simmered beneath the surface for decades. In 1953 the United States had restored Shah Mohammed Reza Pahlavi to power in a CIA-sponsored coup that toppled the government that had forced the shah into exile. The monarch had then embarked on an expensive effort to modernize his country. With this development came fifty thousand American technicians and military advisers. The shah's revolution from above elevated a new class of merchants and technicians, who adopted Western mores and lifestyles. Many of them also resented the shah's iron-fisted rule, however. The shah's secret police jailed and tortured thousands of dissenters. Among those most hostile to the rapid social changes were followers of traditional Islam. One of the men most eager to sweep out Western influences, depose the shah, and create a society based on the Koran was an elderly ayatollah, or religious leader, Ruholla Khomeini. A long-time opponent of the shah, the exiled Khomeini had fervently encouraged a revolution. By February 1979 Khomeini's followers had triumphed, evicting the shah and greeting the returning ayatollah as their savior.

The Iranian revolution affected Americans' lives directly in the spring of 1979 when the new Islamic government raised the price of oil and indirectly caused gasoline lines in the United States. Throughout the summer of 1979 the United States tried to maintain an acceptable relationship with the new Islamic

As Iranian militants hold dozens of U.S. diplomats hostage inside, a huge gathering outside the American embassy taunts the United States. *Wide World Photos*

leadership in Teheran. But when President Carter admitted the deposed shah to New York for medical treatment in October, he infuriated the Iranian revolutionaries. Khomeini told his followers that the admission of the shah represented a plot by "the Great Satan"—the United States—in collaboration with "American-loving rotten brains" in Teheran to restore the shah to power in Iran. A week later revolutionary students seized the American embassy.

The initial reaction in the United States to the capture of about seventy Americans temporarily revived Carter's flagging standing. Showing his dogged energy, he froze Iran's assets in the United States, growled that American "honor" had been besmirched by the militants, and vowed not to travel out of Washington until the hostages came home. But public patience eventually wore out. Relatives and friends of the hostages tied yellow ribbons around trees, mailboxes, and telephone poles to keep the plight of the captives firmly in the public mind. Ronald Reagan, running for the Republican nomination, implied that "our friend" the shah would not have lost his throne if the Carter administration had not betrayed him by criticizing his secret police for torturing political opponents. Reagan also suggested that Carter's inability to free the prisoners reflected his general lack of competence.

In April Carter authorized a military mission to rescue the hostages. On April 24 eight helicopters took off from an aircraft carrier in the Persian Gulf, en route to a desert rendezvous with transport planes. One chopper malfunctioned, and the remaining seven flew into a dust storm. Two more were abandoned, and the site commander decided that the five remaining helicopters were not enough to mount a successful rescue operation. As the remaining choppers prepared to withdraw, another helicopter collided with a refueling plane, killing eight servicemen. The White House announced the failure of the mission, and some Americans believed the aborted mission was yet another demonstration of the limits of U.S. technology and government incompetence.

After the failure of the rescue attempt, public concern about the fate of the hostages diminished slightly. Carter finally left the White House to campaign actively for the presidency. Diplomacy proceeded behind the scenes, and the administration tried to arrange a deal with Iran for release of the captives before election day, November 4, 1980. Unfortunately for Carter's reelection chances, these efforts did not bear fruit until early 1981. The hostages finally flew to freedom on January 20, half an hour after Ronald Reagan took the oath of office as president.

The Election of 1980

The failure to gain the release of the hostages sealed Carter's fate with the electorate. Carter's advisers believed he could overcome Reagan, the Republican candidate, by picturing him as a dangerous reactionary, but that strategy backfired. Carter and Reagan debated head to head in late October. Carter believed that his greater intelligence and command of the facts would make his conservative challenger appear untrustworthy, but the president badly miscalculated. Carter recalled the limits of the last few years: "We have demanded that the American people sacrifice, and they have done that very well." Reagan, on the other hand, reminded voters how much austerity hurt: "We do not have to go on sharing in sacrifice," he said. Reagan's training as an actor carried the day. Simply by standing next to Carter and not appearing confused or saying something foolish, Reagan became acceptable to people who wanted something, anything, different from what they had experienced in the recent past. In his summary remarks he looked directly at the camera with his cheerful blue eyes and told Americans to "ask yourself, are you better off than you were four years ago?"

A week later, voters answered with a sharp "No!" Surveys showed Carter's support collapsing in the weekend before polling day, as it became clear that the hostages would not be on their way home. Voters believed that whatever Reagan did would be an improvement over Carter's hand-wringing, sermons, and demands for sacrifice. Reagan won 51 percent of the popular vote, and Carter won 41 percent (see map). John Anderson, a former Repub-

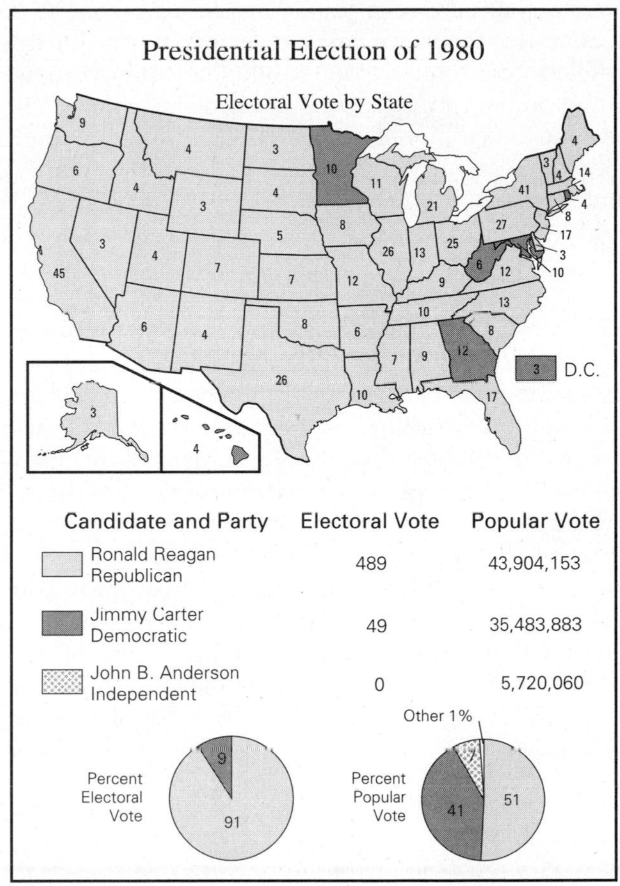

The Election of 1980 Republican Ronald Reagan's victory in the election of 1980 began a conservative era in American politics.

lican representative running as an independent, who promised greater fiscal restraint than Carter and more respect for civil rights and individual liberty than Reagan, won 7 percent. For the first time since 1954 the Republicans carried the Senate, and they gained thirty-three seats in the House as well. Americans wanted change, and Reagan would deliver more than many expected.

✦ Conclusion

In the midst of Watergate, the Vietnam War, and the upheavals of the 1960s and 1970s, Americans confronted changes in their way of life that demanded creativity and perseverance on an everyday basis. They longed for inspiring leaders and more effective public institutions. Yet the disillusionment and disorientation of the recent past ran so deep that politicians found it virtually impossible to create or restore public faith in government. Richard Nixon, brilliant, brooding, angry and vengeful, achieved much in foreign affairs. Yet he also contributed more than any single individual to the widespread disillusionment and cynicism of the 1970s. Gerald Ford and Jimmy Carter both confronted problems that exceeded their capabilities. Ford, an unelected leader, lacked both a base of popular support and a clearly articulated view of how to restore public confidence. Carter had some advantages over his predecessor, because he could credibly claim to be an outsider who, like most ordinary Americans, was not responsible for the disappointments of the Johnson and Nixon years. By 1980 it became apparent, however, that Carter's good intentions, intelligence, and firmly rooted moral values were not enough.

Although many ordinary Americans continued to work hard to consolidate and extend the gains of the social justice movements of the 1960s, the economic and social problems of the times frustrated both the nation's leaders and the public at large. Soaring inflation and a decline in manufacturing industries put the country's economic future in doubt. Americans became more aware of the environmental costs of industrial and nuclear development. The cultural changes of the 1960s had brought a new sense of freedom to personal relationships, but the growing diversity of American households presented new and sometimes bewildering challenges. Gay men and lesbians achieved greater legitimacy, but the New Right targeted homosexuals for special criticism.

Crystallizing many of the public's frustrations, a revived conservative movement elected candidates across the country. When President Carter failed to resolve the Iranian hostage crisis before the 1980 election, the public found a final reason to reject him and turn instead to Ronald Reagan, a conservative champion who promised Americans that the future could still be bright and free from the limitations and malaise of the 1970s.

✦ Further Reading

For general accounts of the policies and personalities of the period, see: Stephen E. Ambrose, *Nixon* (vols. 2 and 3, 1989, 1991); Peter N. Carroll, *It Seemed Like Nothing Happened* (1982); Jimmy Carter, *Keeping Faith: Memoirs of a President* (1981); Steve Fraser and Gary Gerstle (eds.) *The Rise and Fall of the New Deal Order, 1930–1980,* (1989); Gerald Greene, *The Presidency of Gerald Ford* (1995); Kim McQuaid, *The Anxious Years: America in the Vietnam and Watergate Era* (1989). For foreign policy from 1969 to 1980, see: Raymond L. Garthoff, *Détente and Confrontation: American-Soviet Relations from Nixon to Reagan* (1994); Henry Kissinger, *White House Years* (1979), *Years of Upheaval* (1982), and *Diplomacy* (1994); Walter Isaacson, *Kissinger: A Biography* (1992); Robert D. Schulzinger, *Henry Kissinger: Doctor of Diplomacy* (1989); Gaddis Smith, *Morality, Reason and Power: American Diplomacy in the Carter Years* (1986); Zbigniew Brzezinski, *Power and Principle:*

Memoirs of the National Security Adviser (1983); Cyrus Vance, *Hard Choices: Critical Years in American Foreign Policy* (1983). For the last years of the Vietnam War, see: Robert D. Schulzinger, *A Time for War: The United States and Vietnam, 1941–1975,* (1997). For domestic policy, see: Joan Hoff, *Nixon Reconsidered* (1994); Nicholas Lemann, *The Promised Land: The Great Black Migration and How It Changed America* (1991); A. James Reichley, *Conservatives in an Era of Change* (1981); Irwin Unger, *The Best of Intentions: The Triumph and Failure of the Great Society Under Kennedy, Johnson and Nixon* (1996). For the Supreme Court, see: Melvin Urofsky, *The Continuity of Change: The Supreme Court and Civil Liberties, 1953–1986* (1991); Harvey Wilkerson, *From Brown to Bakke* (1979). For Watergate, see: Stanley I. Kutler, *The Wars of Watergate* (1990); H. R. Haldeman, *The Haldeman Diaries* (1994). For issues concerning gender, the family, and sexuality, see: Flora Davis, *Moving the Mountain: The Women's Movement in America Since 1960* (1991); John D'Emilio, *Sexual Politics, Sexual Communities: The Making of a Homosexual Minority in the United States, 1940–1970* (1983); Judith Stacey, *Brave New Families: Stories of Domestic Upheaval in Late Twentieth-Century America* (1990). For economic upheavals, see: Barry Bluestone and Bennett Harrison, *The Deindustrialization of America* (1982); David Halberstam, *The Reckoning* (1986); Daniel Yergin, *The Prize* (1991).

✦✦✦
CHAPTER **14**

Illusion and Renewal: Conservatism Ascendant, 1980–1992

✦ **Jubilant Germans tear down the Berlin Wall, 1989.**

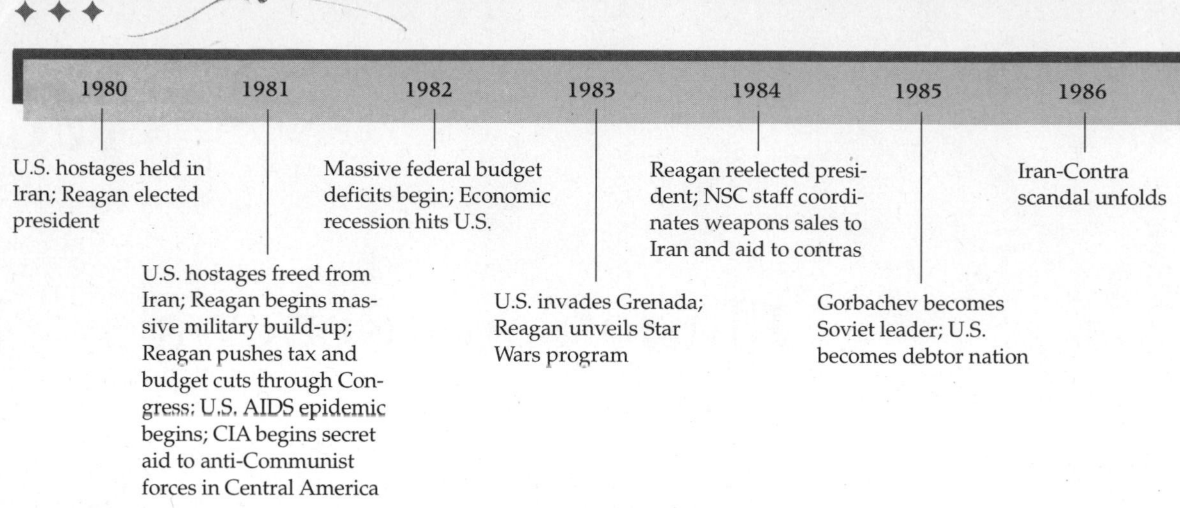

ON MARCH 30, 1981, nine weeks into his first term, a crazed gunman shot President Ronald Reagan. The attacker, John Hinkley, suffered from the delusion that attacking Reagan would win him the affections of actress Jodie Foster. Foster had starred in a film, *Taxi Driver,* that depicted the attempted murder of a politician. Firing a cheap handgun, Hinkley hit Reagan just an inch from his heart and gravely wounded presidential press secretary James Brady.

In the hospital operating room the injured president told his wife, "Honey, I forgot to duck." Older Americans may have recalled these as the words spoken by boxer Jack Dempsey after losing a bout to Gene Tunney fifty years earlier. As he went under the surgeon's knife, Reagan jokingly asked if the medical staff were Republicans. "We're all Republicans today," came the good-natured reply.

After nearly twenty years of political and social turmoil—a presidential assassination, an unpopular war, a president forced from office, economic decline, and humiliation in the Middle East—Reagan's humor and charm, as well as his survival and rapid recovery after Hinkley's attack, made most Americans feel good about themselves and helped restore their faith in the presidency. During the next eight years Reagan enjoyed a broad base of support that allowed him to dominate national politics.

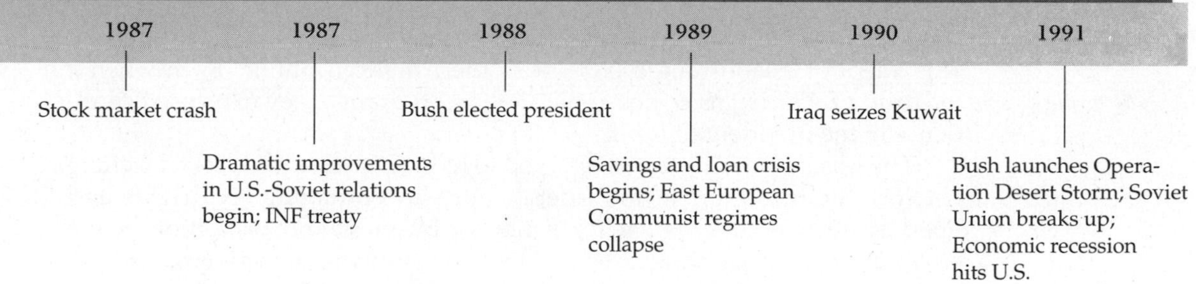

By 1980 the collapse of détente with the Soviet Union, combined with stagflation and the prolonged captivity of Americans in Iran, had doomed the Carter administration, pulled a pall over liberalism, and energized a conservative movement that found its voice in Ronald Reagan. Without providing much detail about what he planned to do if elected, the Republican presidential nominee called for a restoration of national strength and pride. "This is the greatest country in the world," he declared. "We have the talent, we have the drive, we have the imagination. Now all we need is the leadership." A large number of working-class, southern, and Catholic Democrats, uncomfortable with their party leaders' stands on issues such as abortion, affirmative action, school busing, welfare, and crime, deserted the party of Roosevelt to vote for Reagan.

At his inauguration on January 20, 1981, President Reagan scoffed at Carter's talk of a "national malaise." Americans were not people to dream "small dreams," he said. Reversing the central tenet of U.S. national politics since the New Deal, Reagan declared that "in the present crisis . . . government is not the solution to our problem; government *is* the problem." Over the next twelve years Reagan and his successor, George Bush, through recession and recovery, Cold War and détente, promoted policies designed to halt or even roll back many of the New Deal's accomplishments. Like Roosevelt, Reagan was adept at establishing a bond with the American public. Even when a majority of Americans opposed his specific programs, they expressed confidence in the president himself.

The Reagan administration worked to reduce the country's social welfare network, limit the role of the federal courts in promoting civil rights and liberties, reduce government regulation of business and protection of the environment, slash income taxes, and foster a conservative social ethic around such issues as abortion rights and the role of religion in public life. Rather than supporting government efforts to foster greater equality, Reagan insisted that market forces would create new wealth and ensure its equitable distribution.

✦ The Reagan Era

Born in Tampico, Illinois, in 1911, Ronald Reagan grew up in a series of small towns along the Mississippi River. Although he spoke with nostalgia about his childhood, he experienced many hardships as a child. His alcoholic father had trouble keeping a job, and the family moved frequently, often just ahead of the bill collector.

In spite of these problems, Reagan made the most of his life. Encouraged by his fervently religious mother, he attended college. After graduation he found work as a sports announcer at an Iowa radio station. During the 1930s the future president's father went to work for a New Deal relief agency. Reagan became an avid Roosevelt supporter; he especially admired FDR's optimism. Long after he became a conservative Republican, Reagan continued to borrow lines originally spoken by Roosevelt.

While visiting Hollywood in 1937 Reagan took a screen test and won a contract with the Warner Brothers film studio. During the Second World War he served in the Army Air Corps in a Hollywood unit that made morale-boosting films. After 1945 Reagan's film career declined, but he became increasingly active in the Screen Actors Guild, serving as union president from 1947 to 1952. After his first marriage ended in divorce in 1949, he married actress Nancy Davis in 1952. During this period fear of communism transformed his political outlook, as it did for many other Americans. He committed himself to the fight against what he called "the Communist plan to take over the motion picture business." In 1954 Reagan began working as a spokesman for the General Electric company. Over an eight-year period he visited GE plants, speaking to executives, workers, and local chambers of commerce about the threat to "traditional values" posed by big government and communism.

The Emergence of Ronald Reagan

Reagan gained notoriety in 1964 when he campaigned actively for Republican presidential nominee Barry Goldwater. In 1966 he ran successfully for governor in California, defeating incumbent Edmund G. "Pat" Brown. Although Brown had presided over a period of prosperity, many middle-class citizens resented rising taxes, the violent Watts race riots of 1965, the Berkeley Free Speech Movement, and antiwar demonstrations at the state's public colleges and universities. Reagan governed more moderately during his two terms in office (1966–1974) than many expected.

In 1976 Reagan unsuccessfully challenged President Gerald Ford for the Republican nomination. Four years later Reagan secured the GOP nomination, chose his chief rival George Bush as his running mate, and waged a spirited campaign against the Democratic incumbent, Jimmy Carter. In the general election campaign Reagan downplayed his more extreme beliefs, such as his long-time dislike of Social Security, focusing instead on the themes of renewal, strength, and national pride. Reagan projected common sense, spoke of past heroes, and offered simple, reassuring answers to complex questions.

The generalities paid off in his victory over Carter in the November election. Not only did Republicans take control of the Senate for the first time in nearly three decades, they also picked up some three dozen additional House seats. In an astute move Reagan reached outside his conservative circle to appoint James A. Baker III, a close friend of Vice President George Bush, as White House chief of staff. Baker insisted that key legislation be passed during the first few months of the new administration, while the Democrats were in disarray. He persuaded Reagan to emphasize two things: tax cuts and a defense build-up. "If we can do that," Baker predicted, "the rest will take care of itself."

A critic of the progressive income tax, Reagan believed that people should be rewarded for achieving wealth, not taxed at higher rates for doing so. He was impressed by the ideas of conservative economists—sometimes called "supply-siders"—who argued that a policy of cutting tax rates would pay for itself by stimulating business activity: freed from the burden of higher taxes and given extra capital to work with, the nation's entrepreneurs would unleash market forces that would spur rapid economic growth.

Reagan also criticized deficit spending by the government. The Democrats, he complained, had "mortgaged our future and our children's future for the temporary convenience of the present." With the national debt approaching $1 trillion, disaster loomed. The new president argued that lower social spending would both save money and encourage people to help themselves.

In January 1981 Reagan asked Congress to cut most federal income and business tax rates by 25 percent over three years, lower the top income tax rate from 70 percent to 50 percent, and enact various other tax incentives for business. He proposed to shift many social programs from the federal government to the states, to eliminate others, to trim Social Security benefits, and to cut back federal regulation of business, the environment, and public health. Reagan proved effective in pushing his program. Organized labor feared opposing him after he summarily fired several thousand air traffic controllers who had violated their contract by going on strike. The Democrats, reduced in number and shell-shocked, were reluctant to stand in the way of politically popular tax cuts. By the fall of 1981 Congress had approved most of the tax cuts. However, since the public still favored many federal programs, Congress cut government spending only modestly.

The nation experienced a steep economic recession during 1982 and 1983. The recession was caused partly by the decision of Paul Volcker, chairman of the Federal Reserve Board and a Carter appointee, to raise interest rates to stifle inflation. Unemployment rose to over 10 percent, while business failures, farm foreclosures, and homelessness increased dramatically. Reagan's approval rating declined, and the Democrats made substantial gains in the 1982 congressional elections. Nevertheless, Reagan refused to alter his priorities and predicted recovery before 1984.

Reagan's forecast of better times proved correct. High interest rates gradually squeezed inflation out of the economy. Changes in world markets drove down oil prices and reduced the cost of imported fuel. Massive defense spending created a boom in the high-technology and aerospace industries of New England, the Southwest, and the West Coast. The economic expansion that began at the end of 1983 lasted into the early 1990s.

Realities of the Reagan Era

Reagan's high public approval rating, along with his success at communicating his ideas and his faith in America, often gave the impression that the nation's problems were vanishing before the onslaught of new pride and optimism. In many cases, however, the reality did not match the administration's upbeat rhetoric.

At Reagan's urging, Congress cut taxes deeply. However, at their constituents' urging, legislators cut spending on social programs only modestly. This pleased a public eager to pay less and still receive government services. The results were massive budget deficits during the Reagan and Bush administrations. The national debt tripled from $1 trillion in 1981 to almost $3 trillion in 1989. Under Bush the deficit climbed to $4 trillion (see figures). The money the federal government borrowed at home and abroad to fund the budget deficit meant fewer dollars were available for investment in research, new plants, and machinery.

The economic expansion of the 1980s was highly selective. Prosperity tended to flow to both coasts, partly because of defense spending. Although the Northeast and California boomed, the upper Midwest experienced a loss of high-paying industrial jobs, continuing the decline begun in the 1970s.

Even in nationwide terms the long economic expansion of the later Reagan and early Bush years was less impressive than it looked. Compared to the stagflation of the late 1970s it was a marked improvement, but if the base of comparison is extended to the entire period from 1945 to 1980, the recovery appears more modest. Unemployment remained higher than in most years between 1947 and 1973. Wages continued to stagnate, although the impact was

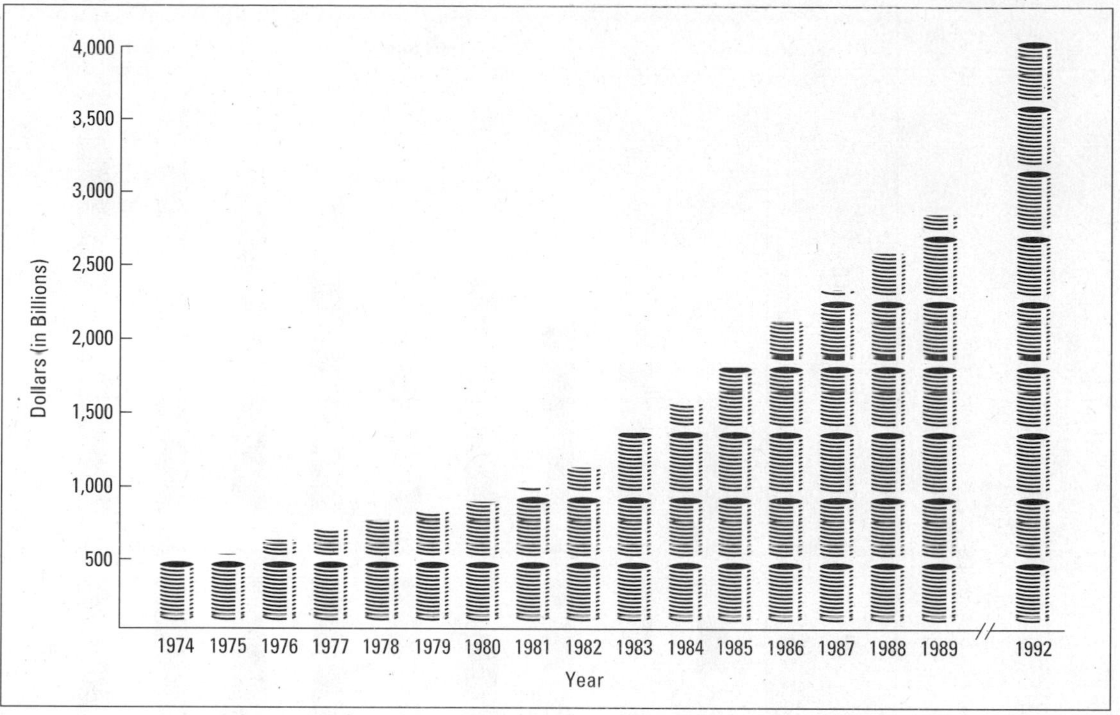

America's Rising National Debt, 1974–1992 America's national debt, which rose sporadically throughout the 1970s, soared to record heights during the 1980s and early 1990s. Under Presidents Reagan and Bush, large defense expenditures and tax cuts caused the national debt to grow by $3 trillion.

masked by an increase in the number of working wives and mothers, whose earnings boosted total family income. Despite the supply-siders' predictions, the economy grew no faster in the 1980s than it had during previous postwar decades.

Richer Americans did especially well in the 1980s. Reagan's policies nearly doubled the share of the national income that went to the wealthiest 1 percent of Americans, from 8.1 percent to about 15 percent. By the end of the 1980s the top 1 percent of Americans, some 834,000 households, were worth more than the bottom 90 percent combined, or 84 million households. Between the early 1980s and the early 1990s the gap between rich, middle class, and poor in the United States was bigger than at any time since the end of the Second World War (see figure).

Increasingly poverty became the lot of women and children. The feminization of poverty grew more severe during the 1980s, partly because of the rising numbers of children born to single mothers. The number of children living with a never-married mother soared by 70 percent between 1983 and

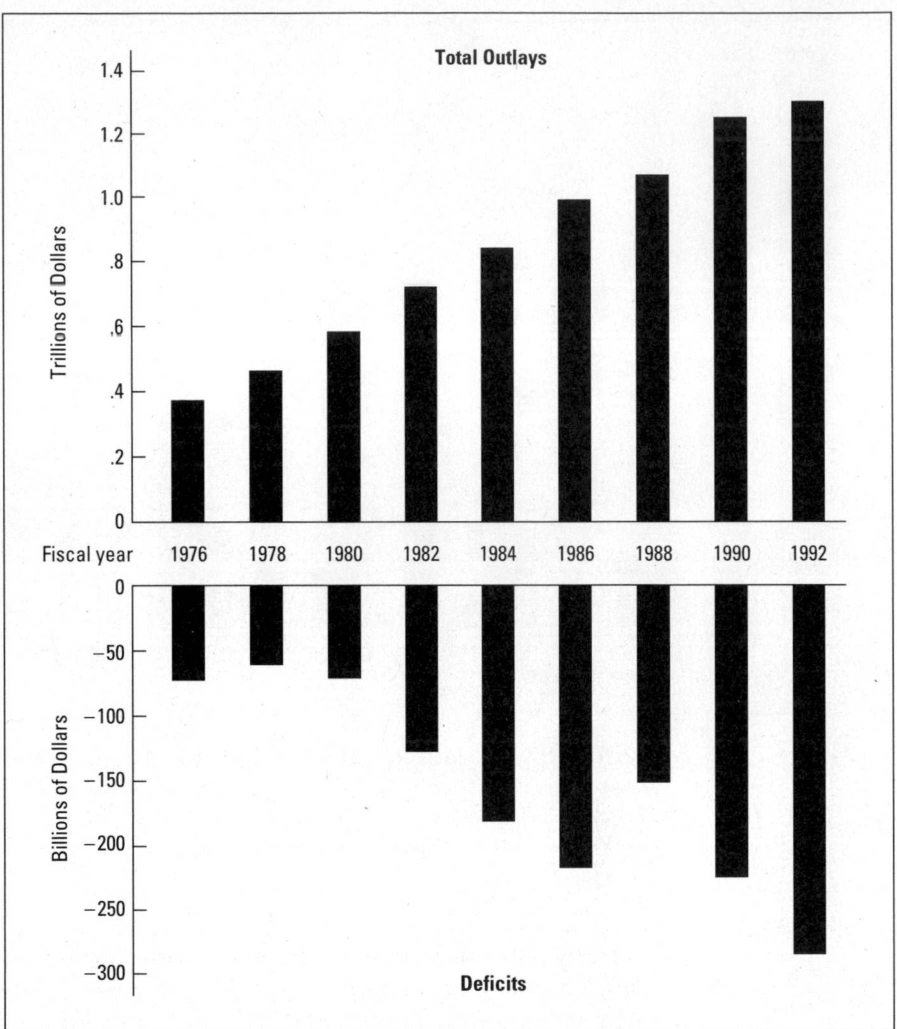

Annual Federal Budget Expenditures and Deficits, 1976–1992 Despite talk of balanced budgets and lower spending, both spending and red ink grew during the Reagan and Bush administrations.

1993. By the early 1990s one-fourth of all U.S. births were to unwed mothers. The rate for African-American and Hispanic women was about 50 percent and 33 per cent, respectively. Compared to married women, unwed mothers were less likely to receive prenatal care, finish high school, or hold a paying job. The Reagan administration worsened the crisis by cutting funds for the Women-Infants-Children (WIC) program, which provided prenatal and postnatal care to poor women.

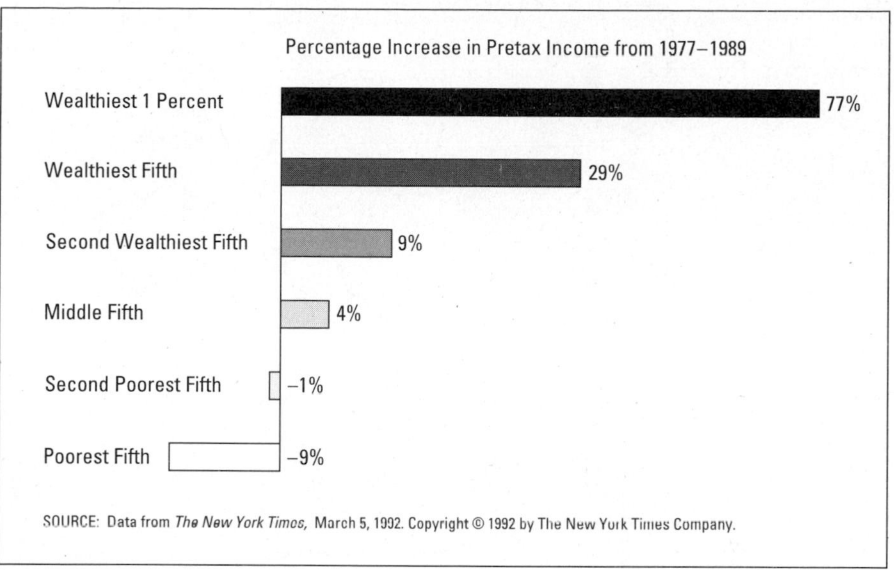

Distribution of Wealth, 1977–1989 Between 1977 and 1989, the richest 1 percent of American families reaped most of the gains from economic growth. The trend continued until 1993.

In the early 1980s the poverty rate for all Americans stood at about 13 percent, about where it was when Lyndon Johnson left office. However, the nature of poverty had changed (see figure). Before passage of the Great Society programs, the elderly and the disabled made up a larger share of the poor. Increased spending on Social Security and Medicare after 1965 had dramatically improved their lot. For the bulk of the poor in the 1980s—single mothers, young children, and young men with few job skills—total federal welfare spending had not grown significantly, and with inflation the value of welfare payments had actually decreased.

Government and the Private Sector

Government regulation of business, the environment, and banking was one of the most important innovations of the New Deal and had long been criticized by conservatives. The Carter administration eliminated some regulations that limited competition in the airline, railroad, and trucking industries. Generally consumers benefited from these changes.

Under Reagan federal agencies went much further. They abolished many rules, ranging from requirements for stronger car bumpers to restraints on offshore oil drilling. The budgets for government watchdogs like the Environmental Protection Agency, the Occupational Health and Safety Administration, and the Securities and Exchange Commission were slashed. Staff

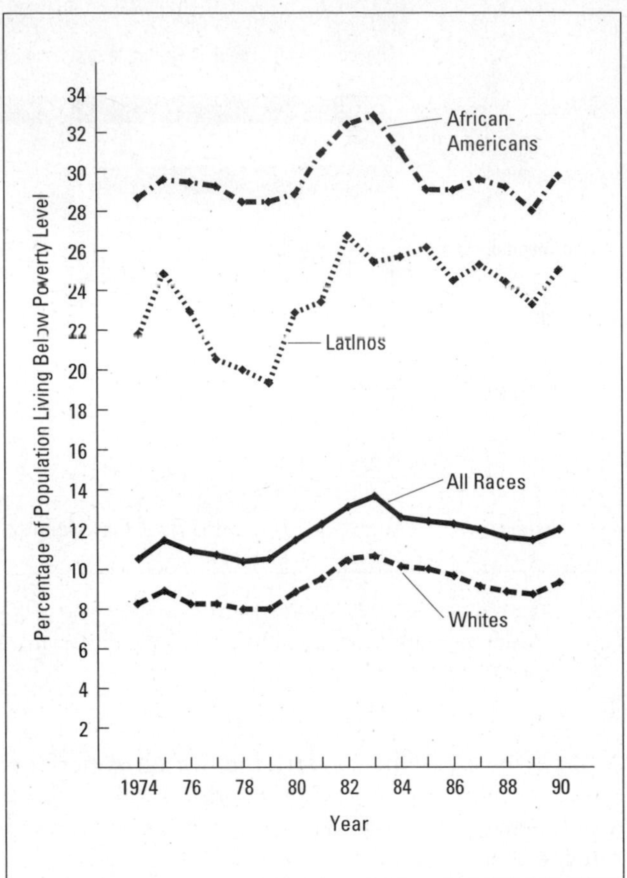

Poverty in America by Race, 1974–1989 Poverty in America rose in the early 1980s, but subsided afterwards. Note that the percentage of African-Americans and Hispanics living below the poverty level was much higher than that for whites.

shortages made it difficult for these agencies to enforce what rules remained. One example of how the Reagan administration twisted the original purpose of a government program took place in the Department of Housing and Urban Development (HUD). Over several years the administration cut HUD's budget by nearly 75 percent. In 1989 investigators discovered that billions of public dollars intended for low-income housing had been invested instead in luxury apartments, golf courses, and swimming pools.

The misuse of HUD funds paled in comparison to the debacle that overwhelmed the savings and loan industry. For many years savings and loan institutions (also called S&Ls or "thrifts") had lost depositors because unregulated money-market funds paid a higher rate of interest. To make banks and

S&Ls more competitive, Congress agreed in 1980 to raise the level of federal deposit insurance for individual bank and S&L accounts to $100,000 and to allow the institutions to pay any interest rate they chose. In 1982 Reagan prodded Congress to go further and deregulate most S&L operations. Previously S&Ls had been limited to extending low-risk mortgage loans for single-family homes. After 1982 they were permitted to invest depositors' funds in undeveloped land, commercial real estate, shopping malls, artwork, junk bonds, and virtually anything else. Profits from these ventures benefited the S&L owners directly, and federal deposit insurance protected depositors from potential losses. If an S&L failed, its depositors were insured for up to $100,000 per account.

These relaxed rules fueled both a construction boom and massive fraud. Lenders such as Charles Keating, head of the Lincoln Savings and Loan in California, found it easy and profitable to collude with builders to drive up the cost of projects, yielding bigger fees for all the principals and almost certain failure for overpriced properties. Some S&L officers made dubious loans to business partners or paid themselves exorbitant salaries, with little fear of exposure. Properties were often "flipped" (sold back and forth) several times for ever-higher prices.

Intervention by federal regulators might have limited the cost of the eventual debacle. But the Reagan administration and the industry used various loopholes to keep wobbling S&Ls afloat. By 1989 hundreds of S&Ls had failed, and few of those still in operation remained profitable. The federal government created the Resolution Trust Corporation to take over a huge inventory of vacant buildings and obligations from the failed thrifts. The final cost to taxpayers of the bailout was about $150 billion in direct costs and another $100 billion in interest. By any measure this was the biggest bank heist in the nation's history.

Civil Rights and Conservative Justice

Like many conservatives, President Reagan objected to many of the decisions the Supreme Court had made since it outlawed segregation in 1954. He believed that liberal judges and their rulings were responsible for a decline in morals, a rise in premarital sex, and the banishment of religion from public school classrooms. The president was particularly anxious to change the direction the country had taken in the areas of civil rights and civil liberties.

Reagan opposed most civil rights laws and supported a constitutional amendment to outlaw school busing. As president he opposed the ultimately successful effort to establish a federal holiday honoring Martin Luther King, Jr. He also tried to restore tax benefits to segregated private schools and colleges. When the 1965 Voting Rights Act came up for renewal, Reagan unsuccessfully urged Congress to kill it.

In 1988 members of Congress took the initiative in redressing the massive violation of the rights of Japanese-Americans that occurred during World War II. The president signed, but said little about, the Japanese-American Redress and Reparations Act, which offered a belated apology to the 112,000 internees and payment of $20,000 each to the 60,000 of them who were still alive.

Reagan believed that the court system favored the rights of accused criminals, to the detriment of government power and victims' rights. During the 1980s legislators at both the state and national level responded to public fears about crime with laws that mandated longer, compulsory prison sentences for many offenses. Jail populations doubled, and prison construction accounted for the fastest-growing outlays in state budgets. The combined federal, state, and local prison population increased over 8 percent each year from 1985 to 1995, rising from 744,000 to 1,585,000. In the mid-1990s one out of every 167 Americans was in prison or jail, the highest rate among the world's democracies.

President Reagan's principal contribution to the campaign for conservative justice lay in his judicial appointments. During his two terms he appointed about four hundred federal judges—a majority of all those sitting in 1988—as well as a chief justice of the Supreme Court and three associate justices. Nearly all were fairly young, white males of a markedly conservative bent.

The president's first three Supreme Court appointments were confirmed rather easily by the Senate. Sandra Day O'Connor—the first female justice—and Antonin Scalia joined the Court as associate justices, and William Rehnquist was promoted to chief justice. But the Senate, which had a Democratic majority after 1986, rejected the 1987 nomination of Robert Bork, an outspoken conservative. Many senators were offended by Bork's abrasive personality. Moreover, Bork's contention that the Constitution offered little protection for privacy, free speech, women, and minorities aroused anger in the Senate. Undeterred by Bork's rejection, Reagan then nominated Anthony Kennedy, who also held conservative legal views but did not antagonize people in the same way as Bork. Kennedy was easily confirmed in 1988.

Gradually the Reagan appointees changed the tenor of the Supreme Court's rulings. After 1984 the Court whittled away at previous decisions that had made police responsible for advising suspects of their rights. The Court approved limitations on bail, affirmed most state death penalty laws, and allowed the introduction in court of some types of illegally seized evidence. The conservative majority also made it harder for women, minorities, the elderly, and the disabled to sue private employers for job discrimination.

Society and Culture in the 1980s

The 1980s were marked by a re-emergence of conservative values. Many of Reagan's supporters stressed family values, clean living, religion, attention to the basics in education, and cultural unity. At the same time, the nation experienced a renewed drug crisis, a decline in the reputation of public education, a series of scandals among right-wing television evangelists, the beginning of the acquired immune deficiency syndrome (AIDS) epidemic, and rising rates of immigration from the Third World.

During the 1980s and early 1990s illegal drug use continued to be commonplace. Marijuana, the most common drug among the young, had been tried at least once by a majority of adults. Public worry about drug use grew rapidly during the second half of the 1980s. Changed attitudes stemmed in part from the appearance of "crack," an inexpensive cocaine derivative that became widely available by the middle of the decade. Although accurate numbers are hard to come by, many experts believe that drug use among whites and the middle class had peaked by the early 1980s. When crack became popular some users were middle class, but a large concentration of users was found among poor, urban, minority youth. Even though annual deaths from tobacco (four hundred thousand) and alcohol (two hundred thousand) far outweighed the five thousand to ten thousand deaths caused by narcotics, President and Mrs. Reagan urged the public to fight back. "Just say no" was the widely circulated slogan of Nancy Reagan's antidrug campaign. Like most citizens, however, the Reagans seemed more concerned about the escalation of drug-related violence than about the question of why youths used drugs or how to rehabilitate users. The administration focused its antidrug efforts on a dramatic but largely futile campaign to interdict supplies, arrest dealers, and throw users into jail. By 1989 the federal government and the states were spending almost $15 billion annually on the war on drugs, mostly on police, courts, and new prison space. Much less money and effort went into education and rehabilitation.

Upon taking office in 1989 President George Bush declared a new offensive in the war on drugs. With the Defense Department freed from many of its Cold War duties, the president assigned the military to work with Latin American governments to suppress cocaine production and exports. Bush appointed a "drug czar" to coordinate the campaign, and Congress enacted laws mandating long sentences for drug-related felonies.

Drug czar William Bennett promised a quick victory in the war on drugs but spent most of his energy exchanging insults with other government officials and members of Congress. Unable to show any results beyond a slight decline in middle-class drug use that probably had little to do with government efforts, Bennett resigned after less than two years on the job, and the war on drugs soon lost the attention of both Bush and the American public. It resurfaced now and then, usually at election time, when candidates blamed one another for the ongoing drug problem.

A related, if less dramatic, debate raged over public education. Japanese "super students" sparked the 1980s counterpart to the 1950s panic over the perceived superiority of Soviet education. The Department of Education's 1983 study *A Nation at Risk* reported that "if an unfriendly foreign power had attempted to impose on America the mediocre educational performance that exists today, we might well have viewed it as an act of war." Most Americans shared these doubts about the public schools, but few agreed on a remedy. Conservatives blamed teachers' unions and a permissive educational system that neglected Western cultural traditions and "the three R's." Liberals argued that public schools were underfunded and hard put to teach both traditional subjects and the new skills needed in a competitive world. Reagan praised the report but ignored its call for government action. Once he was reelected he fired Secretary of Education Terrel Bell, who had issued the report.

Jimmy Carter had been the first to link Evangelical Christianity with presidential politics, but Ronald Reagan captured the movement and delivered it to the Republican Party. Evangelical Christianity experienced a dramatic growth during the 1970s. Although there were many varieties of Evangelical and fundamentalist Christians, they all tended to be angered by social permissiveness and Supreme Court rulings permitting abortion and prohibiting school-sponsored prayer.

Republican officials capitalized on the ability of television-based ministers to mobilize an audience of millions on behalf of the Republican cause. Preachers like Jim Bakker, Jimmy Swaggart, Oral Roberts, and Pat Robertson, who represented a variety of Protestant sects and traditions, saw themselves as potential king makers. Jerry Falwell, founder of the Moral Majority, boasted that he hoped to "bring about a moral and conservative revolution" by electing sympathetic politicians. By 1985 the electronic ministries were raising well over $1 billion annually.

Successful "televangelists" like Jimmy Swaggart and Jim Bakker fulminated against the threat posed to America by immorality, communism, abortion, and "secular humanism"—the belief that humans, not God, are the source of morality. They also celebrated a gospel of wealth, arguing that money and nice possessions were a sign of divine grace. Salvation was readily available to those who showed their faith through generous donations.

Many televangelists were honest and sincere, less inclined to flamboyant theatrics and flagrant fund-raising than Swaggart and the Bakkers. The Reverend Billy Graham, for example, had preached the gospel on television since the 1950s. Although conservative politically, he generally avoided partisan politics and any hint of financial impropriety.

Television ministries experienced a major setback in 1987 when several of the most outrageous televangelists suffered scandal and humiliation. Federal prosecutors indicted Jim Bakker on numerous counts of fraud and conspiracy for bilking his followers of $158 million that was supposed to have been invested in a combined hotel and religious theme park called Heritage USA. A jury convicted Bakker of cheating his investors, and he received a stiff jail term. Several other televangelists soon fell from grace. Jimmy Swaggart admitted that he had bought sex from prostitutes. Pat Robertson's 1988 crusade for the Republican presidential nomination collapsed amid public ridicule after he announced he would use prayer to divert a hurricane from Virginia to New York. In the wake of these embarrassments, many televangelists assumed a lower profile, although religious conservatives remained an important political force.

Ronald Reagan and the Religious Right celebrated the "traditional" family, consisting of a breadwinning husband and a wife who served as mother

The AIDS memorial quilt displayed here at the Washington Memorial commemorates the many victims of this terrible disease. *Smithsonian Institution*

and homemaker. Yet the so-called traditional household continued to decline in the 1980s. By the mid-1980s the proportion of adult women with jobs outside the home surpassed 50 percent for the first time in the country's history, and it continued to rise.

The issue of abortion remained controversial. Reagan persuaded Congress to bar Medicaid-funded abortions for poor women and to limit funding for other forms of birth control. Instead he advocated "chastity clinics," in which counselors would advise teenage girls and unmarried women to avoid pregnancy by avoiding sex. The role played by young males was largely ignored. The president also encouraged right-to-life (antiabortion) groups to support politicians opposed to abortion and to work against candidates who favored a woman's right to choose.

Many commentators proclaimed that the 1980s were witnessing the end of the sexual revolution that had begun during the 1960s. The outbreak of the AIDS epidemic in the early 1980s did indeed make Americans more cautious about sexual relations. The deadly human immunodeficiency virus (HIV), which causes AIDS, destroys the body's immune system, leaving its victims vulnerable to opportunistic infections. The virus is transmitted from person to person through the exchange of bodily fluids, particularly blood and semen.

In the early years of the epidemic, sexual transmission of HIV was especially prevalent among gay men. Intravenous drug users who shared needles were also at grave risk, as were their sex partners. Before tests were developed to screen the nation's blood supply, many hemophiliacs caught the virus through transfusions. By the mid-1990s, 250,000 Americans had died of AIDS, and 1 million others were infected with HIV.

Because many of the first people with AIDS were gay men or drug abusers, Reagan and his conservative backers at first opposed spending much federal money on AIDS research or preventive education. In October 1985 the death from AIDS of Rock Hudson, a popular film star and a personal friend of the Reagans, helped to humanize the disease, both for the president and for the public at large. The president appointed an AIDS commission, which recommended higher funding for AIDS research, education programs, and treatment. Reagan urged compassion for people with AIDS, but he refused to endorse his own surgeon general's call for publicity to encourage the use of condoms.

Changes in U.S. immigration law after 1965 led to increasing numbers of Asians and Hispanics coming to the United States. By the 1980s almost 45 percent of documented immigrants came from Asia and the Middle East, and about as many came from Latin America and the Caribbean; just over 10 percent came from Europe. The increase in Asian immigration was especially dramatic during the 1980s (see figure).

Immigration aroused mixed feelings among the general public. The large number of undocumented Mexicans living in the United States—a number estimated at anywhere between 3 million and 15 million—aroused special concern. Some whites feared the erosion of English as the national language as new cultures and tongues proliferated. Voters in California, Arizona, and Florida passed laws declaring English the official state language.

After years of debate about how to control immigration, in 1986 Congress passed the Simpson-Rodino Act. It offered legal status to several million undocumented aliens living in the United States but imposed fines on employers who hired new undocumented workers. The law appeared to have little impact on undocumented immigrants or on those who employed them. During the 1990s about 1 million people immigrated legally to this country each year, historically a very high number.

Reelection and the Second Administration

By 1984, as the economy climbed out of recession and into a long expansion, Ronald Reagan had become a formidable opponent for any Democratic challenger. Most voters enjoyed a few more dollars in their pockets from the tax cut, inflation had practically disappeared, and abstract difficulties such as the rapidly growing budget deficit had little immediate impact on individual Americans. The public felt comforted by an assertive foreign policy. Reagan even managed to share the glory of the American athletes at the Los Angeles

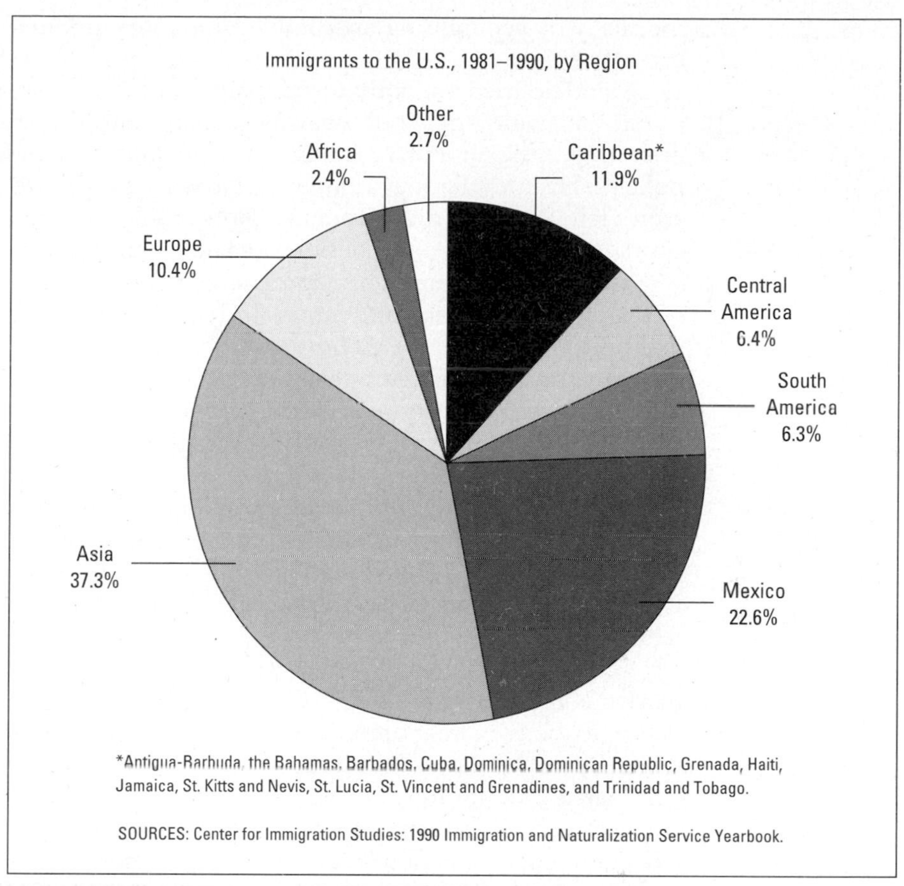

Moving to America Since the 1980s, most immigrants have come from Latin America and Asia.

Summer Olympics, who won an unusually large number of gold medals partly because of a Soviet boycott of the games.

The president's Democratic challenger, former vice president Walter Mondale, emphasized his many years of government experience and his endorsements by organized labor, ethnic organizations, women's groups, teachers, environmentalists, and other liberal elements in the Democratic Party. Critics dismissed Mondale's celebration of the glory days of the Democrats and his search for endorsements as pandering to "special interests."

After a slow and highly visible search for an appropriate running mate, Mondale selected New York congresswoman Geraldine Ferraro. As the first woman nominated for the national ticket by a major party, Ferraro excited millions of Americans. She proved a smart, articulate candidate who held her own in debates with Vice President George Bush. Republicans attacked her indirectly by spotlighting tax complications surrounding her husband's real estate business.

Mondale tried valiantly to campaign on the issues. He bombarded the public with warnings about runaway government spending, an out-of-control arms race, environmental disasters, and the unfairness of Reagan's economic policies. His most famous campaign line was "He'll raise taxes; so will I. He won't tell you; I just did." Commentators briefly praised Mondale's political courage but within a week decided he had committed political suicide.

The president's speeches and commercials emphasized the themes of redemption, patriotism, and family. In 1980 Reagan had run against government; in 1984 he *was* the government—but it made no difference. His campaign theme, summarized by a newspaper as "don't worry, be happy," carried him to a sweep of forty-nine states. Nevertheless, Democrats retained their majority in the House and pecked away at the slim Republican majority in the Senate.

During his second administration several internal staff changes as well as external policy reverses diminished Reagan's luster. James Baker and Edwin Meese left the White House staff to serve in the cabinet, and Michael Deaver went into private business. Without their close guidance, Reagan seemed to falter.

The president had recovered his poise by the summer of 1986. As the stock market surged to record highs, Congress passed a major income tax reform package, the economic centerpiece of Reagan's second term. The law closed many loopholes and reduced the system's multiple tax brackets to three. It eliminated taxes for the poorest Americans.

However, despite the president's popularity, he failed to achieve a definitive realignment in national politics. In the congressional elections of November 1986, even as Reagan rode high in the polls, the Democrats regained control of the Senate and increased their majority in the House. The Democratic majority blocked administration proposals to cut social programs further, expand defense spending, and intervene more directly in Central America. Congress also rejected proposed constitutional amendments banning abortion and permitting school prayer.

By late 1986 the Iran-contra affair (discussed later in the chapter) had become public, and during the next year it proved a profound embarrassment to the administration. Then, in October 1987, a collapse in stock prices jolted the confident economic mood that had prevailed since 1983. In mid-October the Dow Jones stock index fell 600 points in a few days, losing almost a fourth of its value and reviving memories of the 1929 stock market crash that had ushered in the Great Depression. Wall Street recovered within a year, but the minicrash created anxieties about the economy that proved impossible to shake.

The combined impact of the Iran-contra scandal and Wall Street's jitters in 1987 might have become Reagan's epitaph. But the president proved surprisingly able to adjust to circumstances. During 1988 relations between the United States and the Soviet Union improved dramatically, creating the possibility for an end to the Cold War. Reagan left office with an overall 68 percent approval rating, higher than that of any president since Franklin D. Roosevelt.

✦ From the New Cold War to the New World Order

As a presidential candidate Reagan had insisted that "there *are* simple answers" to complex questions. He complained that the United States suffered from a "Vietnam syndrome," a guilt complex that rendered it unwilling to use force to resist Soviet pressure and defend American friends and interests abroad. Reagan pledged to restore America's military superiority, defend its allies, and assist anti-Communist movements throughout the world.

Beneath the rhetoric, however, the president simply pursued old policies more vigorously, as opposed to initiating new ones. Reagan's talk of restraining Moscow's "evil empire" harked back to the Truman Doctrine, the policy of containment, and the birth of NATO. His interventions in Central America and the Caribbean echoed the policies of Dwight Eisenhower, John Kennedy, and Lyndon Johnson. Yet, despite his anti-Soviet posturing, by the end of his administration Reagan presided over the most dramatic thawing in relations with the Soviet Union since the collapse of the Grand Alliance in 1945.

On assuming the presidency George Bush reaped continued benefits from the break in superpower hostility. Peaceful uprisings toppled the Communist governments in Eastern Europe, culminating in the dramatic demolition of the Berlin Wall and the reunification of Germany. By the end of 1991 the Soviet Union had ceased to exist, replaced by a Russian government with an elected president, and a host of ethnic successor states, mostly in central Asia.

A yawning gap separated the rhetoric and the reality of Reagan's foreign policy. It is uncertain whether Reagan even thought in terms of a coherent strategy before 1983; accumulation of military hardware and covert paramilitary operations passed for a foreign policy. Convinced that "negotiating from strength" would yield results, Reagan relied on an arms build-up to wring concessions from Moscow and a rollback of Soviet influence.

Throughout his first term Reagan tried to cast the Soviet Union as evil incarnate. The Soviet Union, he remarked with much oversimplification, "underlies all the unrest that is going on. If they weren't engaged in this game of dominoes, there wouldn't be any hot spots in the world." Encouraging the CIA to conduct paramilitary operations in the Third World emerged as a central feature of Reagan's foreign policy. He appointed his friend and campaign manager, William Casey, to head the intelligence agency. Casey made the CIA an active player in the battle against Soviet influence in the Third World. After convincing Congress to abandon Carter-era restraints on covert operations, the CIA funded anti-Communist guerrillas in Angola, Mozambique, Afghanistan, and Central America. Covert warfare minimized the risk of direct confrontation with the Soviets and gave the administration the freedom to act with minimal congressional oversight and media attention.

Most foreign aid under Reagan and Bush went to a handful of countries, mostly for military purposes. Israel and Egypt each received several billion dollars, and the Philippines, Turkey, Pakistan, and El Salvador also received large amounts. America devoted less than one-third of 1 percent of its GNP to helping other nations, a lower rate than any other industrialized democracy.

Despite Reagan's general dislike of Communist governments, he managed to find common ground with the People's Republic of China. In 1981 China threatened to downgrade its relations with the United States when Reagan sold weapons to Taiwan. But Reagan was counting on Chinese help to support anti-Soviet guerrillas in Afghanistan, and China desired American technology and trade. As a result, both sides compromised. In August 1982 they agreed that the United States could continue to sell weapons to Taiwan if it promised to reduce its sales over time. President Reagan visited China in 1984 and dropped all critical references to the Communist government.

The real pillar of Reagan's foreign policy was his staggering arms buildup. To achieve its announced goal of "peace through strength," the administration developed an ambitious scheme to boost annual defense spending by more than $100 billion, to a total of just above $300 billion a year. The Department of Defense spent lavishly on advanced weapons—especially nuclear-tipped missiles and long-range bombers—intended for a war with the Soviet Union.

These weapons systems were immensely powerful, expensive, and controversial. Critics charged that MX missiles were so powerful and accurate that in a crisis the Soviets would be tempted to strike first, to destroy the missiles before they could be launched, and consequently American commanders would feel pressured to use the weapons in a pre-emptive strike. Thus instead of enhancing deterrence by preserving a reserve force to retaliate against a Soviet first strike, the new weapons created a hair-trigger, "use-it-or-lose-it" situation in which nervous strategists on both sides might feel impelled to act first.

Congress appropriated most of the defense funds Reagan asked for. This lack of congressional opposition stemmed in part from the fact that two decades of arms limitation talks with the Soviets had borne meager fruit. Many Democrats appreciated Reagan's tough rhetoric and favored a more assertive foreign policy, even though they feared that the administration might provoke a war.

On the question of arms control the administration adopted a contradictory policy. Reagan denounced the unratified SALT II treaty put together by Carter, claiming that it locked in a Soviet advantage. But the Joint Chiefs of Staff convinced Reagan to stay within the SALT II guidelines, because they restrained the Soviets as much as the Americans. In 1982 Reagan called for renewed arms control talks with Moscow. But these negotiations—the Strategic Arms Reduction Talks (START) on long-range missiles and the Intermediate Nuclear Forces (INF) talks on medium-range weapons—quickly foundered. In December 1983 the United States began deployment of cruise and Pershing II missiles in Western Europe, prompting the Soviets to cancel talks on arms control.

Reagan, who like many people wished for a way to defend U.S. civilians against missiles, embraced the idea of a high-technology fix that would neutralize Soviet weapons without the pitfalls of negotiation. In March 1983 Reagan presented a startling vision of a peaceful future in which his Strategic Defense Initiative (SDI), as he called it, would render nuclear weapons "impotent and obsolete." Reagan proposed a vast research and development project to perfect a space-based antimissile system using nuclear-powered lasers. Critics promptly dubbed the concept "Star Wars," after the popular fantasy movie of that name. Most scientists ridiculed the project as both unworkable and a dangerous escalation of the arms race. Others speculated that the program was a ploy to bankrupt the Soviet Union. Presidents Reagan and Bush spent nearly $20 billion on the project over the next decade. In 1993 the Pentagon shelved most SDI research.

Although the Soviet government denounced Reagan as a warmonger, until 1985 it mounted no effective response to the American military build-up. Old and ailing Leonid Brezhnev, in power since 1964, presided over a lethargic, corrupt administration during his last years in power. Upon his death in 1982 the Communist oligarchy selected Yuri Andropov, the government's security chief, as general secretary. Although he was considered something of a reformer, Andropov was deathly ill for most of his brief tenure in office. Following Andropov's death in 1984 party elders tapped a lackluster timeserver, Konstantin Chernenko, to be their new leader. Ill with emphysema, Chernenko lived only one year. When asked why he refused to convene a summit with his Soviet counterpart, Reagan quipped, "They keep dying on me." Only in 1985, when the fifty-four-year-old Mikhail Gorbachev emerged as general secretary, did the Soviet Union have an effective leader.

Various events in the 1980s gave Reagan opportunities to sharpen his anti-Communist rhetoric. In December 1981 Moscow pressured the Polish army to impose martial law and to suppress the Solidarity labor movement, which organized workers to challenge Communist rule. Reagan denounced Moscow for unleashing the "forces of tyranny" against its neighbor. The president also provided secret financial aid to Solidarity. In September 1983 a tragic Soviet error outraged Americans. A series of navigational mistakes led Korean Air Lines Flight 007 to stray far off course en route from Alaska to Seoul. After flying over Soviet territory the 747 airliner was attacked by a Soviet fighter pilot; all 269 people on board were killed. Although Reagan soon learned through intelligence intercepts that Soviet air defense personnel really had thought that the airliner was a spy plane, he branded the plane's downing a barbaric "crime against humanity."

America and the Middle East

As it confronted the Soviet Union with its massive arms build-up, the Reagan administration also tried to address some of the thornier problems of the Middle East. Like his predecessors, however, President Reagan found it difficult to impose American solutions in the region. The Arab-Israeli conflict continued to resist peaceful settlement. Prolonged strife in Lebanon and Afghanistan remained unresolved, and a bloody war between Iran and Iraq set the stage for further Persian Gulf problems in the 1990s. Making these issues more urgent was the rise in terrorist attacks around the world, many of them against American targets.

In the early 1980s armed religious and political factions within Lebanon were embroiled in civil conflict. At the same time, Israel was bombing areas in Lebanon controlled by the Palestine Liberation Organization (PLO), a group held responsible for guerrilla and terrorist attacks on Israeli targets. The PLO was the largest of the political organizations that claimed to represent ethnic Palestinians who had been displaced from their homeland following the creation of Israel.

In June 1982 Secretary of State Alexander Haig approved Israel's invasion of Lebanon to destroy the PLO's forces. In August, as Israeli forces surrounded Beirut, the United States arranged for the evacuation of the PLO forces it had earlier sought to eradicate. Meanwhile the assassination of Christian Lebanese leader Bashir Gemayel on September 14 sparked Christian massacres of Palestinians living in Beirut's refugee camps.

As Lebanon devolved into anarchy, the United States, France, and Italy sent peace-keeping forces to Beirut, hoping to shore up Christian Lebanese forces and balance the other military units in the area, including Syrian troops. Each of these forces dominated parts of the fragile country. But Lebanese Muslims bitterly resented Western aid to the Christian minority. On April 18, 1983, a suicide squad attacked the American embassy in Beirut, killing sixty-three people, and on October 23 an Islamic terrorist drove a truck filled with explosives into the U.S. Marine barracks near Beirut's airport, killing 241 Marines. French troops were also attacked.

President Reagan offered a moving tribute to the slaughtered young men, but he could not explain what they had died for. In his 1984 State of the Union address he declared that keeping the Marines in Lebanon was "central to our credibility on a global scale." But two weeks later the president ordered American troops out of Beirut, and the warring Lebanese factions resumed their communal slaughter.

Like the conflict in Lebanon, the problem of the Palestinians—who lived under Israeli occupation or in refugee camps—defied an American solution. In 1987 Palestinians living in territory that Israel had occupied since 1967 began an *intifadah,* or civilian uprising, against Israeli authorities. Israeli troops and police responded harshly, killing some seven hundred Palestinians over the next three years.

In 1988 PLO leader Yasir Arafat declared that his organization had accepted Israel's right to exist—an important concession that prompted Washington to begin diplomatic contacts with the PLO. It was not until 1993, however, that Israeli and Palestinian officials were able to reach even tentative agreement on terms for partial self-government in areas such as the West Bank and Gaza Strip, which Israel had occupied since 1967. Even then, making progress toward settling the Palestinian refugee issue and the Arab-Israeli conflict as a whole proved extremely difficult.

The Reagan administration focused much of its antiterrorist sentiment on Libya's demagogic strongman, Muammar Qaddafi. Flush with cash from the sale of oil, Qaddafi bought Soviet military hardware and bankrolled a number of terrorist groups operating in the Middle East and Europe. The Libyan leader's flamboyant, aggressive style and his fondness for insulting American leaders outraged President Reagan. Washington deployed a large naval flotilla in the Gulf of Sidra, on Libya's northern coast. Qaddafi, who claimed the gulf as territorial waters, clashed several times with the Americans as he dared them to cross his "line of death." U.S. and Libyan jets fought air duels over the gulf in 1981 and again in 1988, with the loss of several Libyan planes.

In April 1986 Libyan agents were implicated in the bombing of a Berlin nightclub frequented by American soldiers. Reagan, calling Qaddafi the "mad dog of the Middle East," sent planes to attack Tripoli. Thereafter Qaddafi remained a bitter critic of the United States but tempered his activities against American allies and interests.

A bloody nine-year-war between Iraq and Iran, fought for regional influence, took the lives of nearly 2 million people between 1980 and 1988. Washington distrusted both Iraqi leader Saddam Hussein and Iran's Ayatollah Khomeini. A victory by either side, American experts feared, would lead one of the two countries to dominate the oil-rich Middle East. To prevent this Washington played a balancing act, providing secret military aid and intelligence to whichever side appeared to be losing at the time. From 1981 to 1986 this generally meant helping Iran, whereas after 1986 Washington often assisted Iraq.

Finally exhausted by their vast mutual bloodletting, Iran and Iraq signed a cease-fire in August 1988, but they maintained their territorial claims. During the conflict, Iraq had developed and used poison gas against Iran and had pushed ahead with work on developing an atomic bomb. Despite these threats the Reagan and Bush administrations considered Iraq a useful counterforce to Iran and quietly provided financial support to Saddam Hussein. The expansion of Iraqi power had grave consequences, however, for it encouraged Iraq's later invasion of Kuwait, sparking the Persian Gulf War of 1991.

When Soviet forces invaded Afghanistan in December 1979, they and the puppet government in Kabul began a brutal struggle to suppress Afghanistan's anti-Communist guerrillas, or *mujahidin*. Several thousand *mujahidin* sympathizers entered Afghanistan from other Muslim countries; many were Islamic fundamentalists who admired the Ayatollah Khomeini's regime in Iran. Anxious to impede Soviet domination of Afghanistan, the Reagan administration ignored the risks of sponsoring such groups and provided them with advanced weapons. The war continued until 1988, when Soviet leader Mikhail Gorbachev blamed the bloody struggle on his dead predecessors and withdrew Soviet forces. Fighting among the Afghans continued despite the end of foreign intervention.

As with the secret U.S. support for Iraq, the policy of aiding Afghan guerrillas came back to haunt the United States. During the 1990s some Islamic guerrillas used their American training and weapons to attack various "enemies" of Islam, including the Egyptian government, moderate Arab regimes, U.S. military personnel in Saudi Arabia, American airliners, and New York's World Trade Center, which was bombed in 1993.

Adventures South of the Border

Throughout the twentieth century the United States had intervened frequently in the affairs of its neighbors in Central America and the Caribbean. The Reagan administration, obsessed by what it perceived to be the Communist threat to the Western Hemisphere from a "Moscow-Havana" axis and hoping to erase the memory of Vietnam with some old-fashioned muscle-flexing, revived this tradition. During the Reagan years the United States invaded Grenada, financed civil wars in El Salvador and Nicaragua, and used economic pressure in an effort to topple the government in Panama.

Despite his success in generating public support for other initiatives, Reagan failed to arouse enthusiasm for intervention in Central America. Few members of Congress or ordinary Americans believed that the future of the free world depended on what regime held power in Managua or Tegucigalpa. Opinion polls taken throughout the 1980s revealed that three-fourths of the public did not know or care what groups the United States favored or opposed in the region. They certainly opposed sending troops there.

Unable to build congressional or popular support for direct intervention, the Reagan administration relied on a combination of military aid and covert warfare in Central America. Between 1981 and 1988 Washington sent at least $4 billion in military and economic aid to El Salvador. A terribly poor country in which 2 percent of the people controlled nearly all the wealth, El Salvador had been racked by rural rebellion since the 1920s. Although the country had nominally been ruled since 1979 by a moderate reformer, Christian Democrat José Napoleon Duarte, El Salvador's right-wing military held the real power.

American aid slowed but did not end the leftist offensive in El Salvador. The Salvadorian military squandered much of the money and waged a fierce campaign of repression against civilians suspected of sympathizing with the rebels or agitating for social change. Army death squads killed as many as seventy thousand peasants, teachers, union organizers, and church workers. When the Reagan administration learned that Salvadorian military units trained by Americans had massacred hundreds of unarmed villagers in contested areas, Washington kept the information secret and called American journalists who reported on the atrocities left-wing dupes.

After eight years of bloodshed Duarte's government had neither defeated the guerrillas nor carried out promised reforms. In 1988 Duarte and his followers lost an election to the ultra-right-wing ARENA party. The war and the civilian deaths continued until 1992, when both sides wore themselves out. A truce was declared, and the former guerrilla fighters participated in new elections. International observers questioned the fairness of the election, which ARENA won, but the leftists accepted the outcome. The large-scale killing ceased, but El Salvador remained impoverished and violent.

In contrast to its prolonged and less-than-successful intervention in El Salvador's affairs, the Reagan administration achieved a quick victory through direct military action in Grenada. A tiny Caribbean island and former British colony that relied on nutmeg exports for its livelihood, Grenada had been ruled by a Marxist, Maurice Bishop, since 1979 and was all but ignored by Washington. The main American presence consisted of five hundred medical students enrolled in St. George's University School of Medicine. A contingent of armed Cuban construction workers also labored on the island, building a new airport that Prime Minister Bishop called a project to boost tourism but Washington saw as a potential Cuban or Soviet air base.

On October 12, 1983, General Hudson Austin overthrew Bishop, who had recently softened his anti-Yankee rhetoric. Austin murdered his rival, imposed martial law, and announced a strict curfew. On October 23 the terrorist attack on the Marine barracks in Beirut, in which 241 Americans lost their lives, took place. Frustrated by their inability to prevent or extract revenge for this outrage in Lebanon, the president's advisers remembered the medical students in Grenada. Although none were known to face danger, administration officials considered their fate sufficiently in doubt to warrant military intervention. A rescue mission, moreover, might divert attention from the carnage in Beirut. After consulting with the leaders of a few tiny Caribbean islands whom Washington had otherwise ignored, on October 25 Reagan ordered thousands of Marines and army troops to storm ashore and liberate Grenada from what he called a "brutal gang of thugs."

The American forces met little resistance from Grenada's army, and most islanders welcomed the invaders. Free elections soon restored representative government, but Washington rapidly lost interest in helping the island. Grenada returned to its normal poverty and obscurity, searching for a benefactor to complete its airport.

The Iran-Contra Affair

During Reagan's eight years as president nothing tarnished his reputation so profoundly as his decision to illegally sell weapons to Iran as part of a plan to ransom hostages in Beirut and fund anti-Communist guerrillas in Central America. As the main force behind a complicated scheme that both violated the law and defied common sense, Reagan came close to destroying his own administration.

In 1980 presidential candidate Reagan denounced Jimmy Carter for abandoning a long-time American client, Nicaraguan dictator Anastasio Somoza.

Somoza had been overthrown by the Sandinistas in 1979. On taking office Reagan accused the Sandinista leadership of turning Nicaragua into a "Soviet ally on the American mainland." The Sandinistas were Marxists; they disliked the United States, and they sought aid from the Soviet Union. They also broke their promise to restore full democracy. But Sandinista human rights abuses paled before the gory record of neighboring El Salvador and Guatemala—regimes Reagan strongly supported. Since fewer people lived in all Nicaragua than in some neighborhoods of Mexico City, talk of a Sandinista threat to the hemisphere was grossly exaggerated.

In 1981 Reagan ordered CIA director William Casey to organize an anti-Sandinista force among Nicaraguan exiles. The contras—or, as Reagan called them, freedom fighters—survived almost entirely on American aid. By 1985 their ranks had swelled to between ten and twenty thousand men. Some contra political leaders were genuine democrats who had opposed Somoza, but most of the military commanders, who held the real power in the movement, were veterans of Somoza's army.

CIA director Casey lied to Congress when he told them that the CIA and the contras did not seek to topple the Sandinista regime but merely sought to block Sandinista aid to left-wing groups in the region. Congress grew restive when it learned that the contras had killed thousands of civilians in an effort to seize power in Nicaragua. Representative Edward P. Boland, a Democrat from Massachusetts, sponsored a congressional resolution in 1982 that barred the CIA from funding or aiding the contra effort to topple the Nicaraguan government.

To get around this legislative ban on aid to the contras, officials in the CIA, the State Department, and the National Security Council (NSC) induced several foreign governments to aid the guerrillas in return for American goodwill or repayment through indirect means. Casey and Lieutenant Colonel Oliver North, an NSC staff member, also raised money from private Americans to support the contras. Soon these activities began to overlap with other questionable actions in the Middle East.

During the early 1980s Shiite militias linked to Iran had kidnapped several private American citizens (and one CIA agent) living in Beirut. Reagan was deeply moved by the plight of these victims, even though they had ignored State Department advice to leave Lebanon. When the grieving families of seven American citizens held hostage pleaded with the president to win their loved ones' release, he allowed his natural sympathy to supersede the national interest. Reagan ordered that everything possible be done to win their freedom.

Starting in July 1985, in an effort to win the hostages' release, Reagan's aides entered into a deal with Iran. Operating through an Iranian businessman living in the United States, National Security Adviser Robert McFarlane arranged (with Reagan's approval) to sell antitank and antiaircraft missiles and military spare parts to the Iranian armed forces, which needed the equipment to fight Iraq. Over the next eighteen months North and McFarlane brokered the sale of several thousand missiles to Iran. This action violated U.S.

law, since Iran was classified as a "terrorist state." It was a crime to sell weapons to such a nation unless the president formally notified Congress that he intended to do so.

After the first arms sales the pro-Iranian Lebanese released only one American. Some of Reagan's advisers, such as Secretary of State George Shultz and Defense Secretary Caspar Weinberger, urged the president to cease all contact with Iran. Instead Reagan told North and McFarlane to keep trying. When Admiral John Poindexter replaced McFarlane as head of the NSC early in 1986, the president urged him to continue on the same path.

Over the course of the secret arms sales, three American hostages were released from Beirut, but they were replaced by new kidnapping victims. However, the scheme paid a dividend. North and McFarlane overcharged the Iranians for the several thousand missiles sold to them, resulting in a $20 million profit. Instead of returning this money to the Treasury as required by law, North used the funds to covertly support the contras fighting the Nicaraguan government. He jested that the Ayatollah had made a "*contra*bution" to the cause.

The bizarre scheme began to unravel on October 5, 1986, when Sandinista gunners shot down a CIA-chartered plane ferrying weapons to the contras. One crew member survived the crash and confessed to being part of a secret American aid program. The Iranian connection came to light at the beginning of November, three days before the midterm congressional elections, when a Lebanese magazine printed an account of the arms-for-hostages deal. Iranian officials confirmed the story and added that the alleged moderates with whom North, McFarlane, and Poindexter had dealt were actually agents of the Ayatollah Khomeini.

As the Iran-contra scandal unfolded during the final months of 1986, President Reagan insisted he knew nothing about any arms-for-hostages deal or the diversion of profits to the contras. But the public no longer believed him, by a wide margin. Reagan's overall approval rating plummeted to below 50 percent. Anxious to shift responsibility, the president telephoned North, called him a "national hero" whose work would make a great movie someday, and fired him and Poindexter.

To stop the clamor of criticism, Reagan appointed a special three-member review board, chaired by a former senator from Texas, John Tower. The Tower Commission report in February 1987 began to flesh out the details, showing how the arms deal had devolved into a ransom scheme designed, in part, to raise illegal funds for the contras. The president's actions, the group concluded, "ran directly counter" to his public promise to punish terrorism. The report portrayed Reagan as remote, disengaged, uninformed, and easily manipulated.

On March 4, 1987, the president accepted the conclusions of the Tower report while still denying responsibility. Whatever the facts suggested, he claimed that in his heart he never meant to trade arms for hostages. In the wake of the Tower Report congressional committees began investigating the Iran-contra incident. Much of the testimony during the summer of 1987 focused on Oliver North. The telegenic officer vigorously defended his own actions and his president. He chided Congress for ignoring the Sandinista threat and declared that he and Reagan had the right to protect national security even if their actions broke the law.

Congress conducted the hearings at a rapid pace, even though administration stonewalling blocked access to crucial documents. North, Poindexter, and other key players lied about their roles, but evidence of their untruthfulness surfaced only later. CIA director Casey died before his involvement could be probed.

In March 1988 a special prosecutor indicted North, Poindexter, and eventually numerous other State Department and CIA officials. Most were convicted or pleaded guilty. The Supreme Court later overturned the convictions of North and Poindexter for technical reasons. Although they had sidestepped questions about the president's involvement during their congressional testimony, both North and Poindexter later stated that Reagan knew and approved of everything they had done.

Although it first seemed possible that the scandal might topple the Reagan administration, a number of factors mitigated its impact. Members of the House and Senate were reluctant to link Reagan directly to illegal acts. They feared popular retribution if Congress were blamed for bringing down another chief executive, as they had Nixon in 1974. The public grew confused by the complicated story of arms sales and hostage releases and guessed that Reagan, too, might have been more befuddled than cunning.

Most Americans cared little about the diversion of funds to the contras. Although many people resented the selling of U.S. arms to the hated ayatollah, the congressional hearings did not concentrate on this part of the drama. Moreover, by the summer of 1987 improved relations with the Soviet Union were distracting the public's attention away from the shabby episode. The Democrats, who again controlled both houses of Congress, favored a relaxation of Cold War tensions. With Reagan showing renewed interest in negotiating with the Soviets, they had a strong incentive to mute criticism of his past lapses.

As for Nicaragua, the problem solved itself shortly after Reagan left office. In February 1990 the Sandinistas held free elections. They lost to a moderately conservative coalition and went into political opposition. This peaceful transition occurred only after the United States terminated its military aid to the contras.

Summit Politics

Dramatic changes inside the Soviet Union helped salvage the Reagan presidency. Mikhail Gorbachev, who became general secretary of the Soviet Communist Party in March 1985, was the best-educated, most worldly, and least dogmatic man to lead his country since Lenin. He blamed his three predecessors for presiding over a twenty-year period of stagnation. Gor-

By 1987 Soviet and American policies finally became synchronized. Reagan and Gorbachev are pictured here during their Reykjavík summit meeting held in Iceland in 1986. *Reagan Presidential Library*

bachev recognized that the Soviet Union had fallen far behind most Western and many Asian nations in economic and technological progress. Soviet industry produced shoddy goods. The old methods of central planning and authoritarian control yielded diminishing returns and were ill suited for international competition in the age of high technology. Corruption and despair permeated all aspects of Soviet society. This internal crisis made it nearly impossible for the Soviet Union to continue along the path it had followed for seventy years.

Gorbachev proclaimed new policies of *perestroika* (social and economic restructuring) and *glasnost* (openness and democracy). The Soviet leadership slowly moved toward accepting the principles of representative government and market economics. Pulling the Soviet Union out of its torpor, Gorbachev and his colleagues concluded, would require cooperation with the capitalist community as well as domestic liberalization. The Soviet leader traveled around the globe, assuring foreign governments that he represented a new type of communism. Britain's conservative prime minister, Margaret Thatcher, whom Reagan admired, called Gorbachev "charming" and someone with whom the West could do business.

Reagan and Gorbachev held a get-acquainted meeting in Geneva in November 1985 that produced few results. They met again at Reykjavik, Iceland, in October 1986. This time they engaged in far-reaching discussions about eliminating nuclear missiles and weapons. The talks broke down, however, when Gorbachev balked at accepting U.S. deployment of the SDI antimissile system.

Despite this setback Soviet-American relations improved rapidly. During 1987, in the wake of the Iran-contra scandal, Reagan replaced many of his hard-line, anti-Soviet advisers. Reagan's new group of foreign policy advisers were pragmatic professionals who supported arms control negotiations with the Soviets. Equally important, Nancy Reagan encouraged her husband to pursue an agreement with Gorbachev. A fierce defender of her husband's image, the first lady hoped that an arms control agreement, not the Iran-contra affair, would become the president's legacy.

In the autumn of 1987 Soviet and American arms negotiators agreed on a treaty to remove all INF missiles—that is, intermediate-range nuclear missiles—from Europe. The agreement to destroy them represented the first time the two superpowers had agreed to abolish an entire category of weapons. Gorbachev even accepted a long-standing American demand for mutual on-site inspection to ensure compliance. In December 1987 the Soviet leader visited Washington to sign the INF treaty.

Both Reagan and Gorbachev enjoyed a boost in their domestic popularity from the improved superpower relations. In a sense the waning of the Cold War rescued both Reagan and Gorbachev from a host of domestic problems. The two leaders agreed to meet again in Moscow in June 1988. Simply by appearing in the heart of what he had frequently called "the evil empire" and by embracing Gorbachev in front of Lenin's tomb, Reagan further blunted the Cold War. Asked if he still considered the Soviets the "focus of evil in the modern world," he answered, "they've changed." Although the United States and Soviet Union still had thirty thousand nuclear weapons aimed at each other, in the new spirit of the time few people worried. During 1988 the Soviets withdrew their troops from Afghanistan and supported efforts to end civil conflicts in Africa and Southeast Asia.

The administration's success in burying the Iran-contra scandal and improving ties with the Soviets dealt Vice President Bush a winning hand in the 1988 election. Coasting on a wave of domestic prosperity and foreign stability, Bush parlayed his own foreign policy expertise into an electoral triumph in November.

✦ The 1988 Election

As Ronald Reagan approached the end of his second term, Democrats hoped to win back the White House by restoring the New Deal coalition that had splintered during the previous two decades. But the Democratic Party's divisions had not healed. Seven of the eight men seeking the Democratic nomination tried to steer discussion away from the contentious issues of race, social policy, and foreign affairs. They insisted that Democrats were competent managers who could adjust more rapidly to a changing world. Only Jesse Jackson, the first African-American to win a substantial political following at the presidential level, championed traditional liberal causes, criticizing his fellow Democrats for "moving their policies to the right like Ronald Reagan."

By the spring of 1988 only two major Democratic candidates remained: Jesse Jackson and Massachusetts governor Michael Dukakis. Although Dukakis was a relative unknown, he easily outpolled his opponent in party primaries, in which Jackson's image as a radical dogged him. To secure the nomination Dukakis shunned the unpopular label of "liberal," promised not to raise taxes, and claimed that he could achieve for the nation the rapid economic growth his state had experienced during his term as governor.

In his pursuit of the Republican nomination Vice President George Bush had to fend off primary challenges from Reagan aide Patrick Buchanan and Kansas senator Robert Dole. Both accused him of being an inauthentic conservative, posing as a Reaganite to hide his "Eastern Establishment, liberal Republicanism." Although Bush secured his party's nomination, these accusations haunted him. Early campaign gaffes and accusations that he was merely Reagan's "lap dog" belied Bush's competitiveness and accomplishments. The son of a wealthy Republican senator from Connecticut, Bush had left college during World War II to become the youngest fighter pilot in the U.S. Navy. Late in the war he had been shot down in combat and rescued from the Pacific. A navy photographer filmed him being pulled to safety from the sea, and a clip of the incident, showing a smiling, boyish Bush waving his thanks to his rescuers, became one of the most effective TV spots of the 1988 campaign. After graduating from Yale Bush moved from Connecticut to Texas, made a fortune in the oil business, and served two terms in the U.S. House of Representatives from 1967 to 1971. Defeated in his 1970 bid for a Senate seat, Bush became chairman of the Republican National Committee, the U.S. representative in China, and then the head of the Central Intelligence Agency.

In the most famous statement of the 1988 campaign Bush paraphrased a line from movie hero Clint Eastwood: "Read my lips: no new taxes." Although some critics thought a Washington insider like Bush could not possibly assume Reagan's antigovernment mantle or ignore the need to raise taxes to relieve the mounting deficit, he carried off the act quite easily.

Bush and his advisers focused their campaign on Dukakis's veto of a law requiring schoolteachers to lead their students in the pledge of allegiance, as well as his granting of a prison furlough to a murderer named Willie Horton, who raped a woman while he was out of prison. The fact that Horton was black added to the emotional nature of the incident and allowed Bush to arouse whites' fears that Dukakis was "soft on crime." Dukakis became so bogged down defending himself against these charges that he failed to articulate a program for voters to identify with.

The campaign was widely perceived as being utterly devoid of substance. The title of one book about the election, *The Trivial Pursuit of the Presidency,* neatly summed up the voters' view of the campaign. Bush won with 53 percent of the popular vote and majorities in forty states, running especially strong among white men and in the South. Once again, however, voters returned a majority of Democrats to the House and Senate, resulting in divided government.

✦ The Bush Presidency at Home

In accepting the Republican nomination for president, George Bush pledged to preside over a "kinder, gentler America." Without directly saying so, Bush promised to create an administration more concerned with governing and meeting people's needs than had been true under his predecessor. This outlook helped him win the election, but it put him on a collision course with the more extreme conservative elements that dominated the Republican Party.

A number of trends helped make Bush popular and sustain good feelings about his administration through mid-1991. The economic expansion that had begun under Reagan continued well into 1990. The changes sweeping the Communist world, as well as military successes in Panama and the Persian Gulf, made Bush appear both active and successful in the area of foreign policy. The public's low opinion of Congress also boosted the president's popularity.

The Republican president and the Democratic majority in Congress cooperated in pushing through some important pieces of legislation in 1990 and 1991. The Americans with Disabilities Act was designed to ensure that government, business, and educational institutions provided equal access to the physically handicapped. The act required that most buildings, walkways, elevators, classrooms, work stations, and rest rooms be reconfigured so that the disabled could use them easily. The Clean Water Act expanded a law first enacted in the 1970s that set federal and state standards for water purity and provided funds for sewage systems and for cleaning up pollution, and an overhauled version of the Clean Air Act set stricter standards for automobile and industrial emissions. The Radiation Exposure Compensation Act provided payments for victims of Cold War uranium mining and atomic testing projects. The Native American Graves Repatriation Act forced museums to return certain bones and cultural artifacts to Indian tribes.

Bush's relative moderation angered some Republicans. In 1991 he signed a civil rights bill that permitted racial and gender quotas in hiring. Aspiring to the title of "the education president," Bush showed interest in improving the performance of the public schools. During 1989 and 1990 he met with governors to outline a series of educational goals. These included improved literacy and high school graduation rates and improved test scores in subjects like science and mathematics. The agenda of the so-called Goals 2000 project was coordinated by the then little-known governor of Arkansas, Bill Clinton. The president endorsed the plan, which involved little new federal funding.

Economic realities forced Bush to retreat from another pillar of the Reagan revolution, the commitment to lower taxes. Faced with a growing deficit and complaints from foreign creditors worried about the value of the U.S. dollar, the president and congressional Democrats agreed to a budget formula in the fall of 1990 that provided for modest tax hikes and modest spending cuts in social programs. Conservative Republicans were enraged at Bush for breaking his "no new taxes" pledge. When an economic recession began at the end of 1990, conservatives attributed it to the president's reversal of Reagan's policy. By the end of 1991 that year's federal deficit had neared a record $300 billion. Meanwhile, liberal Democrats charged that Bush's waffling on both taxes and spending proved that he was ineffective and uncommitted to principle. Reagan's successor found that the middle ground of American politics had disappeared.

Controversies over individual rights continued to strike discordant notes. Two Supreme Court decisions reminded people of issues that had recently divided them. In 1989 the Court affirmed that the First Amendment, through its guarantee of free speech, permitted citizens to burn the flag as an act of political protest. That same year a decision regarding abortion produced longer-lasting ramifications. In *Webster* v. *Reproductive Services of Missouri* the Court ruled by a 5–4 margin that abortion rights could be limited by state law. For example, states could bar abortions in public hospitals or establish waiting periods before the procedure could be legally performed. In the wake of the *Webster* case several states, including Louisiana, Pennsylvania, and Utah, passed laws stopping just short of outright bans on abortion. Physicians, women's groups, and organizations such as Planned Parenthood filed suits to overturn these laws. In a 1992 Pennsylvania case, *Planned Parenthood* v. *Casey*, the Supreme Court narrowly upheld the right to have an abortion but allowed states to impose a broad range of restrictions on them.

Abortion and related issues came to the fore in 1990 and 1991 when justices William Brennan and Thurgood Marshall retired from the Supreme Court. The departure of two of its most liberal justices gave Bush an opportunity to decisively alter the ideological complexion of the Court. To replace Brennan he nominated the virtually unknown David Souter, a judge from New Hampshire who had served for a few months on the federal bench. Souter had never publicly expressed his views on such controversial issues as abortion, the right to privacy, and the death penalty. During his confirmation hearings he maintained his silence on nearly every controversial question. Souter easily won confirmation and emerged as a moderate voice on abortion and most other issues.

To fill the vacancy left by Thurgood Marshall—the Court's first African-American justice—Bush took a different tack. Already in trouble with the Republican right wing for breaking his no-new-taxes pledge and for other signs of "moderation," the president hoped to mend fences by appointing a high-profile conservative. Bush nominated Clarence Thomas, a forty-three-year-old African-American federal appeals court judge who had criticized many of the Supreme Court's past rulings on abortion, school prayer, privacy rights, and the death penalty.

✦ ✦ ✦

Biographical Profile

Clarence Thomas, 1948– and Anita Hill, 1956–

When Supreme Court Justice Thurgood Marshall retired in 1991, President Bush nominated Clarence Thomas to replace the civil rights crusader. Thomas, an African-American conservative, had achieved many impressive goals, including graduating from Yale Law School, in a life that began in poverty. Although he flirted with radical black nationalism while he was a student, he drifted toward conservative politics after graduation. Under Reagan Thomas worked in the Department of Education and, beginning in 1982, as head of the Equal Employment Opportunity Commission (EEOC). Reagan later appointed him to the federal court of appeals. Even though he opposed most positions advocated by civil rights organizations, groups like the NAACP backed his nomination to the Supreme Court, and he appeared headed for quick Senate confirmation.

The process derailed when Anita Hill, a former colleague of Thomas, accused him of sexually harassing her. Like Thomas, Hill had been born to a poor rural family, received a law degree from Yale, and had gone on to work at the EEOC. The Senate Judiciary Committee initially dismissed Hill's allegations but was forced to hold televised hearings on the matter when a journalist leaked the story and the public demanded to know more.

The New World Order

The years 1989 through 1991 witnessed some of the most dramatic changes in global politics since 1945. The world order envisioned by Franklin Roosevelt seemed to finally emerge as the Cold War waned and the United Nations began to function as a forum for global cooperation. As the United States and the Soviet Union ended their rivalry, communism collapsed throughout Eastern Europe. The United States and its allies provided billions of dollars in aid to promote economic reform in the Soviet Union and its former satellites.

At the hearings Hill described how Thomas had harassed her with vivid descriptions of porn flicks, bestiality, and his own sexual prowess. Many members of the all-male committee condescended to Hill and implied that she was unstable. Thomas denied all wrongdoing and denounced the inquiry as a "high-tech lynching." Other women were prepared to back up Hill's accounts, but they were not called to testify.

Although Thomas won confirmation, the episode played an important role in galvanizing women against President Bush and brought discussion of sexual harassment into the mainstream.

"I have been wracking my brains and eating my insides out trying to think of what I could have said or done to Anita Hill to lead her to allege that I was interested in her in more than a professional way, and that I talked with her about . . . X-rated films. . . . I categorically deny all of the allegations. I will not provide the rope for my own lynching."

—Clarence Thomas, from his testimony before the Senate Judiciary Committee, October 11–12, 1991.

"After . . . three months of working at the EEOC he [Thomas] asked me to go out socially with him. What happened next, and telling the world about it, are the two most difficult . . . experiences of my life. I thought that by saying no and explaining my reasons [he] would abandon his social suggestions. He pressed me to justify my reasons for saying no to him. . . . Thomas began to use work situations to discuss sex. His conversations were very vivid. He spoke about acts he has seen in pornographic films [such as] women having sex with animals and films showing group sex and rape scenes. I told him I did not want to talk about these subjects. . . . My efforts to change the subject were rarely successful."

—Anita Hill, from her testimony before the committee.

Bush assembled an experienced group of policymakers to guide his administration. National Security Adviser Brent Scowcroft, Secretary of Defense Richard Cheney, Secretary of State James Baker III, and General Colin Powell, chairman of the Joint Chiefs of Staff, had all held senior positions in the Ford and Reagan administrations.

Bush's greatest accomplishments in foreign policy were more passive than active. He had the good luck to preside over the peaceful collapse of the Soviet empire and the demise of communism as a global force. Not surprisingly, he claimed credit for the good things that happened on his watch. In some ways he resembled his Soviet counterpart, Mikhail Gorbachev. Both recognized the need to move their countries beyond the limits of the Cold War. Like Bush, Gorbachev called for reforms in domestic and foreign policy but often proved unable to harness the forces he unleashed. Shortly after Bush took office Gorbachev permitted free elections to the Soviet parliament. This transformed Soviet politics. In July 1989 Gorbachev stunned the members of the Warsaw Pact alliance by announcing that Moscow no longer cared how the Eastern European states ran their internal affairs. They were free to follow their own road without Soviet interference. Popular demonstrations quickly challenged Communist regimes throughout the region. Gorbachev refused to send troops to prop up the former Soviet puppets.

In November 1989, after several months of street demonstrations, the East German regime opened the Berlin Wall. Soon after, wrecking balls began battering down the Cold War symbol, and street vendors began a thriving trade selling chunks of the hated barrier as gifts to tourists. In October 1990 Germany was reunited. During the same period peaceful democratic revolutions brought down the Communist governments of Poland, Hungary, and Czechoslovakia, replacing them with elected parliaments. Only Rumania and Bulgaria experienced bloodshed or major resistance from officials of the old order. But even in those countries change occurred (see map).

Political ferment inevitably spread into the Soviet heartland. Like Bush, who had spoken of modifying Reagan's policies, Gorbachev advocated a "kinder, gentler" version of communism. He hoped that reform would salvage the decrepit economy and convince the nearly twenty ethnic republics that made up the Soviet Union to remain under Moscow's control. But events overwhelmed him. The Baltic states of Lithuania, Latvia, and Estonia, annexed by the Soviet Union in 1940, asserted their independence in 1990. Soon the residents of Armenia, Azerbaijan, Georgia, Moldavia, and the Ukraine, among others, agitated for independence. Old-line Communists blamed Gorbachev for wrecking the country, and advocates of faster economic and political reforms, such as Boris Yeltsin, criticized him for not moving forward more rapidly. Yeltsin, a former Communist bureaucrat turned reformer, won election as president of the Russian republic in June 1991 and immediately began challenging Gorbachev.

After some hesitation Bush endorsed Gorbachev's gradual approach and held his first of six meetings with the Soviet leader. In November 1990 the two issued a joint message declaring an end to the Cold War. Fearing chaos if America's old adversary collapsed, Bush tried to stem the disintegration of the Soviet Union by criticizing Yeltsin and urging the Soviet republics to remain under Moscow's authority.

Despite support from Washington, Gorbachev's hold on power grew shakier. The Soviet military and bureaucracy demanded restoration of order,

The End of the Cold War in Europe After fifty years of Soviet domination, Mikhail Gorbachev relaxed Moscow's grip on Eastern Europe and ethnic minorities living within the Soviet Union's borders.

while the dozens of ethnic groups in the Soviet Union demanded independence. During the summer of 1991 Gorbachev further outraged the old guard by disbanding the Warsaw Pact, signing a wide-ranging missile-reduction agreement with the United States, and preparing to grant the non-Russian republics greater autonomy under the Soviet umbrella. Hard-line Communist Party officials struck back on August 18, arresting Gorbachev at his villa in the Crimea and proclaiming a new government. The coup failed when Boris Yeltsin and hundreds of thousands of Muscovites took to the streets in defense of Gorbachev. After three days the coup leaders released Gorbachev and surrendered.

Nevertheless, the botched coup brought an end to the Soviet era. After his release Gorbachev led a government with little authority. Fifteen republics declared their independence from Moscow, and Boris Yeltsin emerged as the de facto ruler of Russia. On December 25, 1991, Gorbachev issued a decree dissolving the Soviet Union. He then resigned and turned power in Russia, consisting of about 75 percent of the territory of the former Soviet Union, over to Yeltsin.

China, the other Communist giant, followed a different path from the Soviet Union. It changed too, by stressing free-market economic reform, but it maintained its strict authoritarian rule. Dissatisfied with these half steps, in the spring of 1989 Chinese university students in many cities began to demonstrate in favor of genuine democracy. The biggest gathering occurred in Beijing's Tiananmen Square, where tens of thousands of students built a "goddess of democracy" (modeled on the Statue of Liberty) and defied orders to disperse. On June 4 Chinese leader Deng Xiaoping ordered troops and tanks to scatter the demonstrators. Some soldiers took his instructions literally, running down students with tanks and shooting as many as several thousand in the streets. Americans who saw television pictures of this repression were appalled. But the Bush administration concluded that China's influence in Asia and its surging economic power were so important that the United States should not impose stiff sanctions as punishment for China's mistreatment of its own citizens. American leaders hoped that the passing of the aging old guard and the development of a vibrant free economy would encourage greater political pluralism within China.

Post–Cold War Interventions

The end of the Cold War did not eliminate global instability or challenges to U.S. interests. The Bush administration advanced new rationales for its use of force, including defense of human rights, protection of energy supplies, and suppression of the drug trade.

The first foreign military intervention by the Bush administration took place in Panama. Manuel Noriega, a military officer and long-time CIA informant, assumed power in Panama in 1983. At various times he cooperated

George and Barbara Bush visited American soldiers after the Gulf War. Bush's popularity soared with victory, but soon faded. *Diana Walker/Gamma Liaison*

with or gave assistance to Colombian drug lords, the contras, Fidel Castro, drug smugglers seeking a safe haven for dirty money, and anyone else willing to pay his price. In return for Noriega's allowing the CIA to use Panama as a conduit for aid to the Nicaraguan contras, Reagan ignored his ties to the Colombian cocaine cartels.

When the Nicaraguan conflict wound down in 1988, the Reagan administration applied financial pressure on Panama to ease Noriega out of power. The Bush administration's high-profile war on drugs made Noriega's open involvement with narcotics traffickers an embarrassment to Washington. Resisting American economic and political pressure to resign and go into exile, Noriega voided the results of a May 1989 election his opponents had won and sent his thugs to beat his critics, and some American residents, in the streets.

Fed up with the Panamanian strongman, President Bush dispatched an invasion force of twelve thousand American soldiers on December 20, 1989. They were ordered to arrest Noriega and install the winner of the aborted May election as president. During three days of sporadic fighting fifty-five members of the Panamanian National Guard and twenty-three Americans lost their lives. Several hundred Panamanian civilians may have died when bombs from U.S. planes accidentally fell on their houses. On January 3, 1990, a dazed Noriega emerged from his hiding place in the Vatican embassy. He was arrested and taken to Miami, where a federal jury convicted him of drug trafficking. The American public overwhelmingly approved Bush's intervention in Panama.

U.S. military power faced a far greater challenge after August 2, 1990, when Iraq seized the tiny, oil-rich sheikdom of Kuwait in the Persian Gulf region. Iraqi leader Saddam Hussein had long coveted his oil-rich neighbor, claiming that Kuwait was really a "lost province" of Iraq. By annexing Kuwait he hoped to boost Iraq's ailing economy and play a major role in setting global petroleum prices. The Iraqi leader may have expected Washington to tolerate this land grab, since both Reagan and Bush had authorized generous loans to Iraq, provided Saddam Hussein aid during his war with Iran, and turned a blind eye while Iraq used chemical weapons and began to acquire atomic and biological weapons.

Although Kuwait was no democracy, it was a sovereign state and a member of the United Nations. The United States and its allies feared that if the Iraqi seizure of Kuwait went unchallenged, Saddam Hussein would either invade the neighboring Saudi oil fields or intimidate the Saudis into following his leadership. This might allow Iraq to dominate Middle East oil reserves and destabilize the economies of the entire industrialized world. To prevent this President Bush got the United Nations to impose a tight economic embargo on Iraq and sent some five hundred thousand American troops (including thirty thousand women) to Saudi Arabia as part of a twenty-eight-nation coalition force. Even the Soviet Union, Iraq's former patron and arms supplier, supported the sanctions. By January 15, 1991, diplomatic efforts to get Iraq to withdraw from Kuwait had failed. Congress debated the president's request to authorize military retaliation and approved it by a narrow margin.

On January 17 Bush ordered American planes to begin bombing Iraqi targets and troops. In launching the so-called Desert Storm attack, the president paraphrased the words of President Woodrow Wilson in declaring, "We have before us the opportunity to forge for ourselves a new world order." American and allied planes pounded targets in Iraq and Kuwait for five weeks. On February 23 U.S. ground forces and those of several coalition members launched a ground offensive that liberated Kuwait and drove halfway toward the Iraqi capital of Baghdad in less than one hundred hours. When President Bush accepted Saddam's plea for a cease-fire on February 27 only 223 allied troops had been killed, compared to tens of thousands of Iraqis. The American commander of Desert Storm, General H. Norman Schwartzkopf, became a media star and then a best-selling author. A Gallup poll reported that 90 percent of Americans, an historic high, approved of Bush as president.

Although Kuwaiti sovereignty was restored (democracy was never an issue) and Saudi Arabia defended, Saddam Hussein remained in power. Fearing a vacuum in the region or the triumph of Islamic fundamentalism should the Iraqi dictator be toppled, Bush called off the attack before Saddam was driven from power.

The war had at least one major unintended consequence. PLO chief Yasir Arafat had supported Iraq, prompting the Saudis and other Arab leaders to stop subsidizing the PLO. Bereft of patrons, Arafat soon entered into peace talks with Israel.

Triumph in the Cold War, along with easy victories in Panama and Iraq, lifted George Bush to unprecedented levels of popularity, but only for a short period. Just eight months after Desert Storm, polls revealed that only 39 percent of Americans approved of the direction in which Bush had led the country. The collapse of communism reduced the danger of nuclear war but allowed simmering ethnic and political conflicts to resurface in the former Soviet Union, Yugoslavia, the Middle East, and Africa. As a real and symbolic enemy, the Soviet Union unified America's will to intervene in regional conflicts and play the role of world policeman. Absent a unifying symbol, U.S. politicians and the public were less willing to send peace-keeping forces into harm's way.

After the Soviet specter had evaporated and victory was achieved in the Gulf War, Bush's stature quickly diminished. The president's apathy toward domestic issues, his breaking of his 1990 "Read my lips: no new taxes" campaign pledge, and the deterioration of the American economy during 1991 and 1992 led over 80 percent of U.S. citizens in the spring of 1992 to tell the Gallup poll that they were unhappy with his performance. Bush's proud use of the phrase "new world order" became an object of popular derision.

Bush won his party's nomination in 1992, but he found it difficult to energize his campaign without a foreign enemy. Instead he unleashed a relentless attack on Democratic nominee Bill Clinton's avoidance of the draft and his opposition to the war in Vietnam as a student. But these accusations fell flat. Whereas Reagan's charm and political magic had overwhelmed most nay-sayers (earning him the nickname of "the Teflon president," since it seemed nothing negative would ever "stick" to him), Bush proved a weak second act to the Reagan revolution. Where Reagan had denounced government as the cause of most problems, Bush valued public service and hesitated to crusade against established institutions. Trying to occupy the middle ground between the New Right and the New Deal, he found no place to stand. Officeholders in the 1990s discovered that the American people's patience with their elected leaders—like the very "sound bites" those leaders used to get elected—had become increasingly short.

As memories of the Cold War and Desert Storm faded, Americans worried more about lost jobs and factory closings than about Clinton's lack of previous military service. Although the United States had won its contest with the Soviet Union, it appeared that the real winners in the 1990s—an era in which economic innovation counted more than the power of nuclear warheads—were Japan and Germany.

✦ Conclusion

In his farewell address of January 1953, President Harry Truman voiced a question on the minds of millions of Americans: "Some of you . . . may ask when and how will the Cold War end? I think I can answer that simply. The Communist world has great resources, and it looks strong. But there is a fatal flaw in their society. Theirs is a godless system, a system of slavery; there is no freedom in it, no consent." Truman predicted that as "the free world grows stronger, more united, more attractive to men on both sides of the Iron Curtain—and as the Soviet hopes for easy expansion are blocked—then there will have to come a time of change in the Soviet world. Nobody can say for sure when that is going to be, or exactly how it will come about, whether by revolution, or trouble in the satellite states, or by a change inside the Kremlin." But the president whose term of office coincided with the emergence of the Cold War had no doubt that change would eventually come. "I have a deep and abiding faith in the destiny of free men," Truman concluded. "With patience and courage, we shall some day move on into a new era."

In light of the events of the late 1980s and early 1990s, Truman's words were prescient. In the long run the growing economic strength of the United States, Western Europe, and Japan, as well as the allure of democracy, overwhelmed the rigidity of Soviet totalitarianism. The U.S. policies of promoting world trade and guaranteeing the security of its major allies created the context for this triumph.

Domestically, the 1980s and early 1990s left an ambiguous legacy. Reagan's lofty rhetoric restored a sense of pride that had faltered in the wake of the Vietnam war and economic decline. His policies challenged, if they did not always reverse, the liberalism that underlay government policy since the New Deal. But the conservative movement given voice by Reagan had many contradictory facets. When his successor, George Bush, tried to reconcile the views of social and economic conservatives, he lost the respect of both. The recession of the early 1990s led many Americans to question whether they really wanted a smaller, less responsive government.

Ultimately, determining the national interest at home and abroad fell to a generation of leaders who had to look beyond the simple truths of the Cold War.

✦ Further Reading

On the Reagan-Bush era, see: Garry Wills, *Reagan's America* (1988); Lou Cannon, *President Reagan: The Role of a Lifetime* (1991); Michael Rogin, *Ronald Reagan: The Movie* (1987); Haynes Johnson, *Sleepwalking Through History* (1991); Michael Schaller, *Reckoning with Reagan: America and Its President in the 1980s* (1992); Donald T. Regan, *For the Record* (1988); David Stockman, *The Triumph of Politics* (1986); Benjamin Friedman, *Day of Reckoning: The Consequences of American Economic Policy Under Reagan and After* (1988);

Herman Schwartz, *Packing the Courts* (1988); Jane Mayer and Jill Abramson, *Strange Justice: The Selling of Clarence Thomas* (1994); Kevin Phillips, *The Politics of Rich and Poor* (1990); Randy Shilts, *And the Band Played On: Politics, People, and the AIDS Epidemic* (1987); William Julius Wilson, *The Truly Disadvantaged: The Inner City, the Underclass and Public Policy* (1987); Barbara Ehrenreich, *The Worst Years of Our Lives* (1990); Nicolaus Mills, ed., *Culture in an Age of Money* (1991); Mark Hertsgaard, *On Bended Knee* (1988); Susan Faludi, *Backlash: The Undeclared War Against American Women* (1991); Sidney Blumenthal, *Pledging Allegiance: The Last Campaign of the Cold War* (1990); Jack Germond and Jules Witcover, *Whose Broad Stripes and Bright Stars? The Trivial Pursuit of the Presidency, 1988* (1989); James D. Hunter, *Culture Wars: The Struggle to Define America* (1991); William C. Brennan, *America's Right Turn: From Nixon to Bush* (1994); E. J. Dionne, *Why Americans Hate Politics* (1992); Thomas B. and Mary D. Edsall, *Chain Reaction: The Impact of Race, Rights, and Taxes on American Politics* (1991); Michael Katz, *The Undeserving Poor: From the War on Poverty to the War on Welfare* (1989). On foreign policy, see: Alexander Haig, *Caveat: Reagan, Realism and Foreign Policy* (1984); Caspar Weinberger, *Fighting for Peace* (1990); George P. Shultz, *Turmoil and Triumph* (1993); William Broad, *The Star Warriors* (1985) and *Teller's War: The Top-Secret Story Behind the Star Wars Deception* (1992); Michael Mandelbaum and Strobe Talbott, *Reagan and Gorbachev* (1987); Theodore Draper, *A Very Thin Line: The Iran-Contra Affairs* (1991); Bob Woodward, *Veil* (1987); Jonathan Kwitny, *The Crimes of Patriots: A True Tale of Dope, Dirty Money and the CIA* (1987); Raymond Bonner, *Weakness and Deceit: U.S. Policy and El Salvador* (1984); Mark Danner, *The Massacre at El Mozote: A Parable of the Cold War* (1994); Jane Mayer and Doyle McManus, *Landslide: The Unmaking of the President, 1984–88* (1988); Roy Gutman, *Banana Diplomacy* (1988); Dan Oberdorfer, *The Turn: From the Cold War to the New Era: The U.S. and the Soviet Union, 1983–1990* (1991); Michael R. Beschloss and Strobe Talbott, *At the Highest Levels: The Inside Story of the End of the Cold War* (1993); John L. Gaddis, *The United States and the End of the Cold War* (1992); Alan Friedman, *Spider's Web: The Secret History of How the White House Illegally Armed Iraq* (1993); Rick Atkinson, *Crusade: The Untold Story of the Persian Gulf War* (1993); Stephen R. Graubard, *Mr. Bush's War: Adventures in the Politics of Illusion* (1992); Gale Stokes, *The Walls Came Tumbling Down: The Collapse of Communism in Eastern Europe* (1993); James Baker, *The Politics of Diplomacy: Revolution, War and Peace, 1989–92* (1995); Robert Gates, *From the Shadows: The Ultimate Insider's Story of Five Presidents and How They Won the Cold War* (1996).

♦♦♦

CHAPTER 15

Rumblings of the Future

♦ **An American classroom, late twentieth century.**

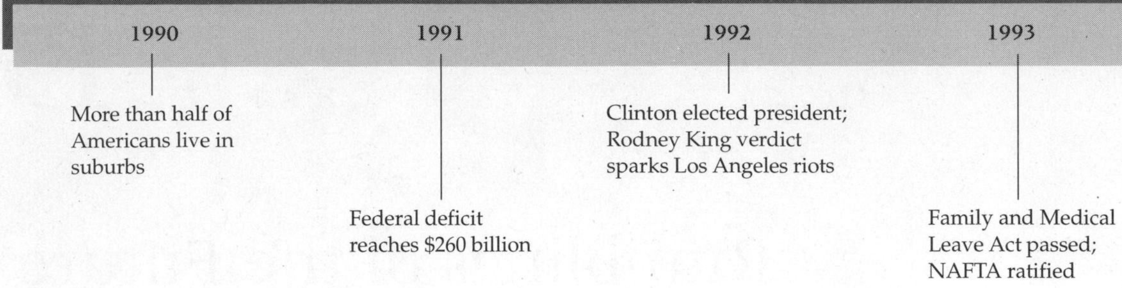

ON THE DAY the future American icon Michael Jeffrey Jordan was born in February 1963, John F. Kennedy was still president, University of Mississippi senior James Meredeth attended classes supported by five hundred federal troops, and the Reverend Martin Luther King, Jr., had not yet told the nation that he had a dream. Scarcely fifteen years had passed since Jackie Robinson had shattered the color barrier in professional sports, and in most of the nation African-American citizens could not enter most hotels, restaurants, retail stores, and movie theaters.

But the freedom struggle was under way and would bear fruit soon, creating a world of new possibilities for children like Jordan. When his father, James, got out of the air force he took a job in a General Electric plant in Wilmington, North Carolina, rising to the rank of supervisor. Michael's mother, Deloris, was a customer service supervisor at a bank. Michael, the fourth of five children, grew up in a big house adjoining twelve acres of fields, across the street from a Baptist church. He played one-on-one under his family's back-yard hoop with his older brother Larry, who teased him about his big ears and dunked on him. He attended integrated schools, counting both blacks and whites among his closest friends. At Wilmington's Laney High School he loved baseball and excelled at basketball, and when he was offered a basketball scholarship at the University of North Carolina (UNC) it was a dream come true.

The rest, of course, is the stuff of sports legend. As a freshman he hit the game-winning jump shot against Georgetown in the NCAA finals. The next year he was chosen College Player of the Year by *Sporting News.* His

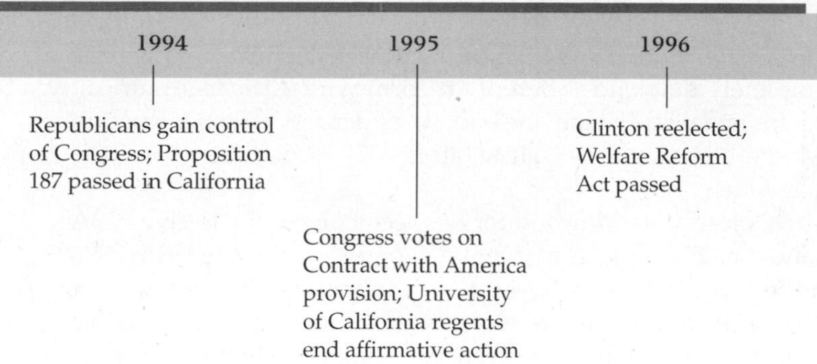

combination of dazzling skill and a friendly, wholesome personality held enormous appeal for his fans. He joked with stadium vendors, signed endless autographs, and had a warm word for everyone. A *New York Times* reporter declared that "there are times when he seems too good to be real." He was a major force on the American amateur team that won an Olympic gold medal in 1984, and he decided to forsake his senior year at UNC to turn professional. He was drafted by the woebegone Chicago Bulls, a team described by more than one commentator as "the dullest in the National Basketball League."

Jordan transformed the Bulls, himself, and the world of sports-related marketing. By the time he was named NBA Rookie of the Year in 1985, Michael Jordan's metamorphis from a self-described "Carolina country boy" to an international symbol was well under way. He had already signed an enormously lucrative contract with Nike, the sporting goods manufacturer that made the unprecedented decision to market a line of sneakers named after the athlete himself. Nike expected to sell perhaps $10 million worth of Air Jordan basketball shoes. As satellites beamed his acrobatic feats around the planet, he brought new attention to the game of basketball and to his own stellar play. Within the year, Air Jordan sales topped $130 million. Playing one-on-one with his brother Larry, he told him to "remember whose name is on your shoes."

Michael Jordan was an African-American hero who seemed to defy, even transcend, American racism. He was the embodiment of wealth, grace, and style—seeming proof that the stunted promise of American life was capable of sending up new shoots. Novelist John Edgar Wideman called him "the black

DiMaggio." Writer David Halberstam told Jordan that he had invented "sports as ballet"—a completely new and different art form with African-American roots. After all, Halberstam added, no one had ever guarded the great Russian émigré dancer Mikhail Baryshnikov. "How tall is he?" Jordan asked Halberstam with a small smile.

During the 1990s Jordan led the suddenly spectacular Bulls to five NBA championships and a record-breaking seventy-two victories in the 1995–1996 season. He won the Most Valuable Player award four times. But he was far more than a gifted athlete; he was the world's most successful and visible pitchman. Television stations played and replayed ads showing Jordan guzzling Gatorade while children sang "I want to be like Mike." He told Americans that they had "better eat their Wheaties." In a McDonald's commercial Jordan and fellow superstar Larry Bird challenged each other to shoot a basket over the Grand Canyon, for the prize of a Big Mac. (Bird had once wondered whether Jordan might not be "God disguised as Michael Jordan.") And Jordan virtually turned himself into a logo for Nike sportswear.

But his charmed life seemed to come unglued after the 1993 championship. Global fame had turned him into a hermit who would check into hotels under an assumed name to avoid being mobbed by fans, wear headphones every time he went out in public to discourage people from talking to him, and not even go out for an evening with his family. Allegations of a gambling problem brought him unwanted personal scrutiny. His father, with whom he maintained a very close relationship, was murdered by teenage thieves when he pulled off the highway into a North Carolina rest area to recover from driving fatigue. Heralded as the greatest athlete ever to play basketball, Jordan announced that he would retire from the game and try his hand at baseball instead. He spent a season and a half in the minor leagues, where his batting average never topped .250.

Jordan returned to basketball in the winter of 1995, slightly out of shape and too late to help the Bulls capture a championship. Some observers wondered if he had, in the hackneyed sports-speak phrase, "lost a step." He had not. By the summer of 1996 the Bulls had been proclaimed the greatest team in basketball history, led by the indisputably greatest player. His guts, hard work, and genius inspired his teammates and won him the admiration, sometimes grudging, of his adversaries. His endorsements multiplied. His worldwide fame matched the earlier global repute of boxer Muhammed Ali, who at the height of his fame was said to have had the most widely recognized name on the planet.

For Americans in the 1990s, traditional sources of security and identity had fragmented or disappeared. Many Americans hoped moving someplace new would solve their problems; others moved because they had to. By 1990 the United States had become a nation always in motion. City dwellers moved to the suburbs, Texans moved to Florida and California, New Yorkers and Michiganders moved to California and Florida and Texas. Chicago, Philadelphia, and Detroit lost hundreds of thousands of people. Los Angeles gained more than a half million residents. Nearly three-quarters of Americans over age sixteen got up every working morning, got in their cars, and drove to work— by themselves—averaging 22.4 minutes in transit. At this most mobile of times in the most mobile country on earth, hometowns, extended families, religious traditions, and political parties no longer served to tell people who they were, how to behave, or where they belonged.

If anything defined community for late-twentieth-century Americans, it was consumption. People determined who they were, in no small measure, according to what they bought. And to a stunning degree, they bought what they saw advertised on television. Celebrity endorsers put an appealing human face on everything from deodorants to Chicken McNuggets. Those who appeared again and again in close-up on television seemed more familiar to viewers than their next-door neighbors. And near the century's end no one was more familiar, more eagerly watched and sought after and admired, than Michael Jordan, the man who could fly. He propelled himself, his team, his sport, and his profession to unrivaled fortune and fame. His fans adored him; they could never get enough of him. Millions of people all around the world wore Chicago Bulls caps and jerseys and jackets, though they could not have located the team's mighty hometown on a map. Michael Jordan, meanwhile, timidly wondered whether the day might soon come when he could take his wife and kids to the movies.

In many ways the closing decade of the twentieth century has echoed the end of the previous century, opening to the strains of economic volatility and fear but moving, cautiously, toward greater prosperity and rising hopes. Both the 1890s and the 1990s ushered in huge economic and political transformations. Between 1890 and 1900 the United States moved decisively into the ranks of the world's industrial societies and great political powers. The country began to acknowledge the presence of widespread poverty in the land of plenty, even as it legalized racial segregation and wholesale discrimination against African-Americans. Between 1990 and the end of the twentieth century the United States has had to come to grips with the promises and perils of postindustrial society, a global economy, the information revolution, and a new political order around the world, while continuing to grapple with the legacy of racism. By the time of the presidential election of 1996 the U.S. economy was growing fast, unemployment was declining, inflation seemed to have been conquered, and the stock market was breaking records. But will prosperity continue, or will the unpredictable eddies of economic life turn out to mask hidden whirlpools? In 1990 one in seven Americans lived below the poverty line. One-quarter of American children between the ages of three and twelve received public assistance. Nearly two-thirds of poor families were "working poor," whose meager wages could not make ends meet. Will the evident health of the American economy translate into a better life for the nation's least fortunate? Will the boom in the consumer economy prove a fragile bubble, blown large and shiny on the breath of staggering credit card debt? Or is it possible that the sense of returning good times is based on some more enduring improvement in Americans' ability to tend the national fortune?

✦ The Economy

Ever since the New Deal U.S. policymakers have believed that it is sometimes appropriate for the federal government to spend more money than it takes in, making up the difference through borrowing. But the Reagan administration's policy of simultaneously cutting taxes and initiating a massive defense build-up sent the deficit spiraling out of control in the 1980s. The government's debt had reached $260 billion by 1991. Critics believed that the rising debt would erode capital formation and render American firms unable to compete around the world. Some commentators and politicians predicted that unless the government made the unpopular decision to raise taxes and cut benefits for the middle class, the American economy would fall behind the economies of Japan and Germany.

In the spring of 1990, facing widespread fear of an impending recession, President Bush finally dropped his 1988 "no new taxes" promise. Bush and congressional leaders hammered out a package of income and excise tax increases and cuts in such popular programs as Medicare and unemployment insurance. In October Congress passed a law raising taxes on the top 2 percent of earners by cutting their deductions, and boosting taxes on gasoline, alcohol, and big-ticket luxury items. Congress expected these measures to reduce the deficit by $40 billion in the next year, with even greater savings in the five years following.

Bush's successor, Bill Clinton, would make deficit cutting a priority. In 1993, at Clinton's urging, Congress once again combined budget cuts with tax increases, focusing new taxes on the wealthiest Americans. As a consequence the deficit fell from an all-time high of $290 billion in 1992 to $107 billion in 1997. The economy improved immensely during that four-year period. Unemployment fell to a twenty-year low, and more than 10 million new jobs were created. However, a variety of problems remained.

If the government was spending so much money, Americans wondered, what were they getting for their tax dollars? It was evident to anyone who drove, flew, took a train, or got sick that the nation's infrastructure was in disrepair and that fundamental social services weren't serving. Estimates for repair of the nation's decaying highways and bridges ranged from $50 billion to $200 billion. Until the 1995 opening of the new Denver International Airport, no new airport had been constructed in the United States since 1974. Not surprisingly, the air transportation system suffered from bottlenecks, delays, and occasional tragic collisions.

The nation's expensive and chaotic medical system also prompted concern. Twelve percent of the U.S. gross national product went toward health care in the 1990s, compared to 6 to 8 percent in the other industrialized nations of the world. Those with full medical insurance received the best care in the world, but 37 million people, most of whom worked, had little or no insurance coverage. Excluded from the benefits of prohibitively expensive high-tech medicine, the overall health of the uninsured working poor lagged far behind that of more fortunate Americans. Moreover, the lack of health insurance for the poor drove up costs for those who were insured, because the uninsured often waited to go to the doctor until they were really sick or else visited expensive emergency rooms for the treatment of relatively minor ailments because they had no access to a personal physician. Drug companies also contributed to the spiraling costs of health care, charging arbitrarily inflated prices for high-demand medications.

American jobs moved from the manufacturing to the service sector as the nation's economy shifted from powerhouse production of cars and steel to a postindustrial mode focused on serving consumers and managing information. To be sure, some jobs in the service sector paid well. For example, most lawyers and doctors earned handsome livings, and the boom in such upscale professions meant rising incomes for certain segments of society. The number of lawyers in the United States increased by nearly 50 percent in the 1980s; by 1990 the country had 756,000 lawyers, more than the total in the rest of the world. The number of medical doctors also rose, from 279,000 in 1970 to 554,000 in 1988. An even greater increase occurred among real estate agents, a group that grew from one hundred thousand to eight hundred thousand in the twenty years after 1970.

Perhaps the greatest force for economic and cultural transformation came from new ways of disseminating information. With the advent of the Internet, the so-called information superhighway that carried a potentially infinite amount of data over telephone lines and fiber optic networks, entrepreneurs found themselves in a position to exploit a new global marketplace. Hundreds of thousands of consumers, advertisers, and just plain curious people browsed the 1990s version of the supermarket, the World Wide Web. The Internet made more information available to more people—and faster—than ever before, but those without computer access lost more and more ground in the struggle to succeed.

Although the increase during the 1990s in upscale service positions in fields like the computer industry was impressive, the vast majority of new jobholders did not find work as professionals. Those without a college education earned less in the new service jobs than their parents or elder siblings had in manufacturing. Also, service employers tended to hire in good times and lay off employees in downturns. A so-called K-Mart economy developed in many of the booming regions of the Sunbelt, where young, uneducated, unskilled workers found work paying only $4 to $6 per hour in discount stores,

✦ ✦ ✦

Biographical Profile

Bill Gates, 1955–

In the mid-1960s few Americans envisioned the ways in which computers would revolutionize American life. Even those most familiar with the machines did not foresee the time when millions of American families would assume the necessity of owning, and using daily, a personal computer. Being interested in computers then, recalled William H. Gates, III, was "not a mainstream thing. I couldn't imagine spending the rest of my life at it." Yet by the 1990s Bill Gates would be America's richest man, an inventor and entrepreneurial genius who built a vast fortune on the world's insatiable appetite for computer technology.

The son of a well-to-do Seattle family, Gates first became fascinated with computers in 1967. By the time he was fourteen Gates was president of his own company, Traf-o-Data. The firm earned $20,000 selling traffic-counting systems to municipalities before its customers even found out that the company was run by high school students. Gates interrupted this thriving career to enroll at Har-

supermarkets, fast-food stores, auto repair shops, hair salons, or banks. Few of these jobs offered benefits such as health insurance.

Dreams and Dread

During the 1980s younger workers found it harder to make ends meet. The purchasing power of households in which the principal wage earner was less than twenty-five years old fell 19 percent from the beginning of the decade to the end. Households whose major wage earner was twenty-five to thirty-four years old also saw their purchasing power erode in the 1980s. Only people over sixty-five, whose Social Security and other pension payments were linked to changes in the cost of living, saw their incomes rise significantly. The sense that the younger generation was losing ground helped revive the fears of the late 1970s. By 1990 public opinion polls once more reflected worries that the future would be grimmer than the past and that children would have a harder time achieving economic security than their parents had.

vard University in 1973, planning to become a lawyer. At the end of his sophomore year he dropped out, however, and moved to Albuquerque, New Mexico, where with his friend Paul Allen he founded Microsoft. Securing a contract with the Tandy Corporation to develop software for Radio Shack computers, Microsoft grew quickly and moved to Seattle. Then the company hit the big time when IBM contacted Gates about creating an operating system for the personal computer the company was developing. The result, MS-DOS, was licensed to more than one hundred companies producing IBM-compatible computers, and by 1981 Microsoft was earning $16 million a year.

Like Thomas Edison, Gates was one of those rare inventors who can master the marketplace as well as the laboratory. In the late 1980s Microsoft introduced its Windows operating system, which allows users to run IBM-compatible computers by clicking on-screen symbols with a hand-held mouse. With Windows Microsoft provided a system as simple and user-friendly as the one pioneered by archrival Apple Computer, but at a fraction of the cost. Soon Windows dominated the marketplace, and Gates, at the age of thirty-two, became a billionaire.

> *"The future is what matters, which is why I don't look back too often. It's just the way I am—even at the ripe old age of 40."*
>
> —from a column on "PC Empowerment," October 10, 1995, republished on Bill Gates's Web page, "The Billboard," in 1997.

The last decade of the twentieth century opened on a note of uncertainty for millions and for some a feeling of dread. Golden California, the symbol and setting of the American dream, was fast becoming an emblem of all that was tense, puzzling, and frightening about America in the 1990s. As the decade wore on Americans watched one news story after another flash out of the seemingly crazy culture on the fault line; many worried that what Los Angeles was today, the whole country would be tomorrow. By 1990 the West Coast version of the postwar suburban ideal had reshaped the nation, now composed primarily of suburbanites, but the view from the picture window was far less tranquil than Americans had expected it to be.

And yet, as the nineties got under way the California Dream persisted—and even went global. During the 1980s as many immigrants entered California as had entered New York in the first decade of the century, mostly from Latin America and Asia. New immigrants energized the nation's cities with their ways and their work. The African-American middle class grew, as did black enrollment in colleges and universities. But most African-Americans felt increasingly isolated and abandoned. A new president, the first Democrat in twelve years, spoke glowingly of a promising future, but more and more Americans took the cynical—and reasonable—view that their leaders were often shortsighted and unwilling to take actions that might offend politically important groups or individuals. More and more Americans abandoned their traditional political loyalties, as the mainstream parties seemed to have less and less to say. Despite the fact that the federal government still represented the largest institution in the nation's life, government seemed to many Americans less and less relevant to their daily experience.

✦ A Nation of Suburbs

In 1990, for the first time, more than half of all Americans lived in urban areas with populations of 1 million or more. Nearly one in four Americans lived in one of five metropolitan areas—New York, Los Angeles, Chicago, San Francisco-Oakland-San Jose, or Philadelphia. Suburban expansion powered metropolitan growth. For example, between 1989 and 1990 net migration to the nation's metropolitan areas reached 1.5 million, but the central cities *lost* 2 million residents. The suburbs gained more than 3.5 million. Indeed, nearly half of all Americans lived in the suburbs. "The suburbs," said geographer Peter Muller, "are no longer *sub* to the *urb*."

The most urbanized and fastest-growing region of the nation was the West (see map). Six of the nation's ten largest cities in 1990 were west of the Mississippi. Cities like Phoenix grew rapidly—24 percent in the 1980s—but their suburbs, like Tempe, Mesa, and Scottsdale, grew even faster, by 40 percent. No American city grew faster in the 1980s than Mesa, Arizona, with a population that topped 288,000, growing by a whopping 89 percent, in the course of the decade. Demographers identified a new urban phenomenon, the "edge city," a former suburb or small town (or a brand new massive development) that had grown to city status, with its own commercial and industrial base, and formed one node in a cluster of such communities composing a multinucleated metropolis.

Some cities, like Colorado Springs and Albuquerque, tried to maintain a single focus by annexing their borderlands, thereby becoming cities without suburbs. But these medium-sized metropolises simply spawned new suburbs of their own. By 1994 Rio Rancho, New Mexico, a bedroom community just northwest of Albuquerque, had used a combination of low housing prices, corporate tax breaks, and generous water rights to lure high-tech corporations, including Intel, the world's largest manufacturer of microchips, to build plants there. Amid a climate of economic uncertainty, with the memory of the oil bust and the Bush recession fresh in politicians' minds, Western states vied with one another for such economic development.

The urban landscape in the 1990s was a product of the almost universal predominance of the private automobile as a form of transportation. Los

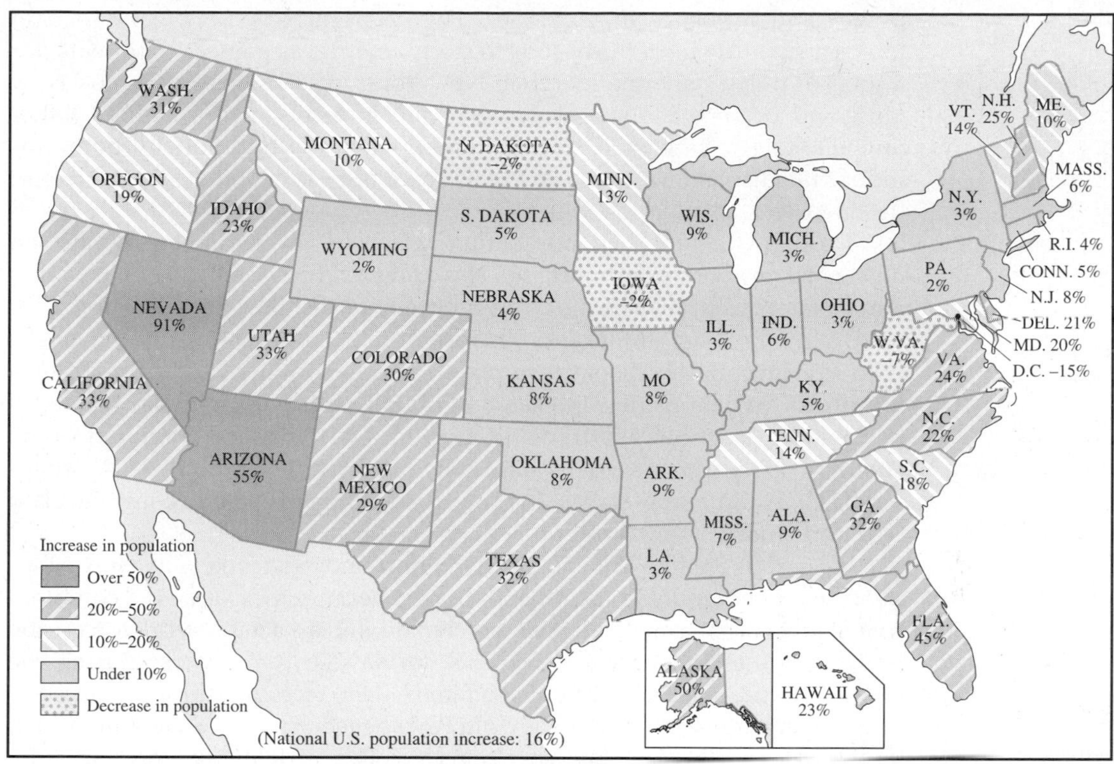

Shift to the Sunbelt, 1980–1995 The nation's fastest growing states were in the West and the South, drawing both immigrants from abroad and immigrants from the Midwest and the Northeast.

Angeles, of course, was considered the epitome of the car culture city, but the same spreading, sprawling urban form had captured the rest of the country as well, from Boston to Houston. And the more freeways Americans built to carry their cars, the more cars arrived to create congestion. Planners and policymakers did what they could to keep their cities moving. Employers in Houston subsidized van pools, and the city set aside car pool lanes on the main freeways. Portland, Oregon, worked to coordinate "intermodal" transportation, so that commuters could mix public buses, cars, bicycles, and feet as means of getting around. Even Los Angeles sought alternatives to the car, opening in 1993 the first section of a twenty-three-mile Wilshire Boulevard subway running west from downtown.

As Americans moved to the Sunbelt the regional balance of power in the House of Representatives shifted. After the 1990 census California gained seven seats, for a total of fifty-two. No state had had such a large share of the representatives in Washington since New York had exercised similar power and influence in the 1880s. For its part, New York continued to lose seats, falling from thirty-four to thirty-one. Texas gained three seats, for a total of thirty, only one less than New York; in 1993 Texas overtook New York and become the second-largest state in terms of population. Other Sunbelt states also gained representation, while the traditionally populous industrial East and Midwest saw their share of representatives in the House decline.

Though the suburban population remained predominately white, an increasing proportion of working-class and middle-class blacks, Hispanics, and Asian-Americans left the cities for the suburbs. Between 1980 and 1990 the black population in the suburbs rose from 5.9 million to 8 million, a 34.4 percent increase. The Hispanic suburban population increased from 5.1 million to 8.7 million during the same period. The Asian-American suburban population also increased dramatically, from 1.5 million to 3.5 million. Some suburban areas were predominately nonwhite by 1994. In cities like Washington, D.C., Atlanta, and Dallas, the suburbanization of the black middle class was particularly noteworthy.

Western cities like Phoenix, Denver, Portland, Salt Lake City, and Albuquerque grew rapidly in the nineties in part because they offered a combination of low taxes, cheap land, pleasant climate, and a tractable work force—the conditions that had been southern California's keys to success during the eighties. In the nineties California suffered a deep recession unprecedented in its postwar history. The end of the Cold War spelled trouble for the state, which had grown utterly dependent on billions of dollars in defense contracts. As the federal government cut programs like the B-1 bomber, defense contractors instituted a series of "reorganizations" and "restructurings," which led to mass layoffs. White-collar employees were no safer than line workers. McDonnell Douglas asked five thousand managers to resign, then offered them the chance to compete against one another for 2,900 jobs. Plants closed or relocated to Sunbelt cities that had aggressively courted them with tax breaks and other incentives. The layoffs and closures had a ripple effect, slowing and stalling business in the state's malls, restaurants, and office complexes. Commercial and residential real estate values spiraled down. California lost eight hundred thousand jobs between 1989 and 1994, more than half of them in Los Angeles County, and economic forecasters gloomily predicted continuing job losses in the hundreds of thousands.

✦ The Globalization of America

As American corporations thought about moving some of their operations out of the United States—eagerly eyeing the cheap labor, minimal environmental regulation, and friendly government officials in Mexico, Asia, and the Caribbean—immigrants flocked into the United States in search of their own American dreams. They came from countries all over the globe, not only

Mexico (though it was still the leading source of immigrants by a wide margin) but also Thailand and Guatemala, Nigeria and Poland, Ireland and India.

The New Immigrants

The shift during the 1980s and 1990s toward nonwhite minorities was the sharpest of the twentieth century. Whites in general represented about 80 percent of the total population, and whites of European background made up only about 76 percent. The remainder were primarily African-American, Latino, Asian, and Native American. Much of the growth in the minority population came from an additional 7.6 million Latinos, half of whom were immigrants. Seven million people immigrated legally to the United States during the 1980s, the vast majority of them of non-European origin. A majority of the public schoolchildren in California were nonwhite or Latino, and these groups accounted for 42 percent of the entire population of the state. Forty percent of the students in New York's schools were nonwhite. In the telephone book for San Jose, California, there were more people with the surname Nguyen, a common Vietnamese name, than Jones. Two hundred thousand people of Middle Eastern ancestry lived in the Detroit area. Nearly 1 million people from Southeast Asia or their children lived in cities across the country. By 1990 four in ten New Yorkers over the age of five spoke a language other than English at home. Around Los Angeles more people in the suburbs than in the central city did not speak English at home. The immigration trends, combined with the high birth rates among African-Americans, Latinos, and Asians, led some experts to predict that by the year 2050 a majority of the American population would trace its roots to a non-European culture.

The 1980s saw one of the largest influxes of immigrants in American history. Even more important, the changing pattern of national origins became pronounced: about 45 percent of the newcomers came from Asia and the Middle East, and another 45 percent came from nations in the Western Hemisphere. No European country was among the top ten places of origin. Countries with extensive cultural, military, or economic contacts with the United States—for example, the Philippines, Korea, and Mexico—provided the lion's share of the immigrants.

The diversity of the newcomers makes it difficult to generalize about them. Some Asian immigrants were highly educated doctors and nurses who joined the staffs of big-city hospitals; some were engineers who pursued careers with high-technology firms. Other Asians from urban backgrounds pooled their resources to establish small retail businesses. Many Vietnamese, Filipinos, and other Asians from rural backgrounds found low-paying employment in service industries or manufacturing. Immigrants from Mexico and the rest of the Western Hemisphere often came to escape poverty and had little education and few financial resources when they arrived. They settled in the urban centers of the West, Southwest, and Midwest, where they worked in unskilled service and manufacturing positions.

Southeast Asian immigrants have transformed American communities nationwide. These Hmong women and their children live in Providence, Rhode Island. *Ira Wyman/Sygma*

As in earlier periods of high immigration, nativists proposed severe restrictions on immigration on the grounds that immigrants would undermine American culture and values. Especially during economic downturns, immigrants became the targets of people who felt their own status and well-being threatened. In 1994 Pete Wilson, the governor of California, supported Proposition 187, a victorious ballot measure that aimed to solve the state's economic woes by refusing medical care for undocumented immigrants and barring their children from the public schools.

Yet most economists and many thoughtful social observers believed that the arrival of the new immigrants enriched the United States. Immigrant workers undeniably provided the labor power for the continued expansion of the American economy, and they brought with them cultural variety that injected fresh energy into American cities. New York Telephone announced that it would offer repair service to customers in 140 languages, including Fiji, French, Russian, Sioux, Swahili, Twi, and Yiddish. A California company provided the interpreters. In Houston the immigrant presence enlivened the barren stretches of eight-lane boulevards, supermarkets, and strip malls. Along one road on the west side of town, Korean, Thai, Vietnamese, and Chinese businesses and professionals leased mall space and erected bilingual and trilingual roadside signs.

Tension and Division

The allure of the United States for immigrants demonstrated the robustness of American society. But divisions between races and economic classes led to a bleaker picture: a sizable proportion of the American population was trapped in poverty and assailed by racial or ethnic hatred. The number of Americans living in poverty declined slightly at the end of the eighties, to 12.8 percent of the population, but the poverty rate remained higher than it had been at any time in the 1970s. Vast differences existed among ethnic groups. Ten percent of whites were considered poor, versus 26 percent of Latinos and 30 percent of blacks. Deprivation continued to fall most heavily on single mothers and children. Despite gains made since the 1960s, many elderly were also poor. Half of the people classified as poor were less than eighteen years old or over sixty-five. Half of black children under the age of six were poor (see figure).

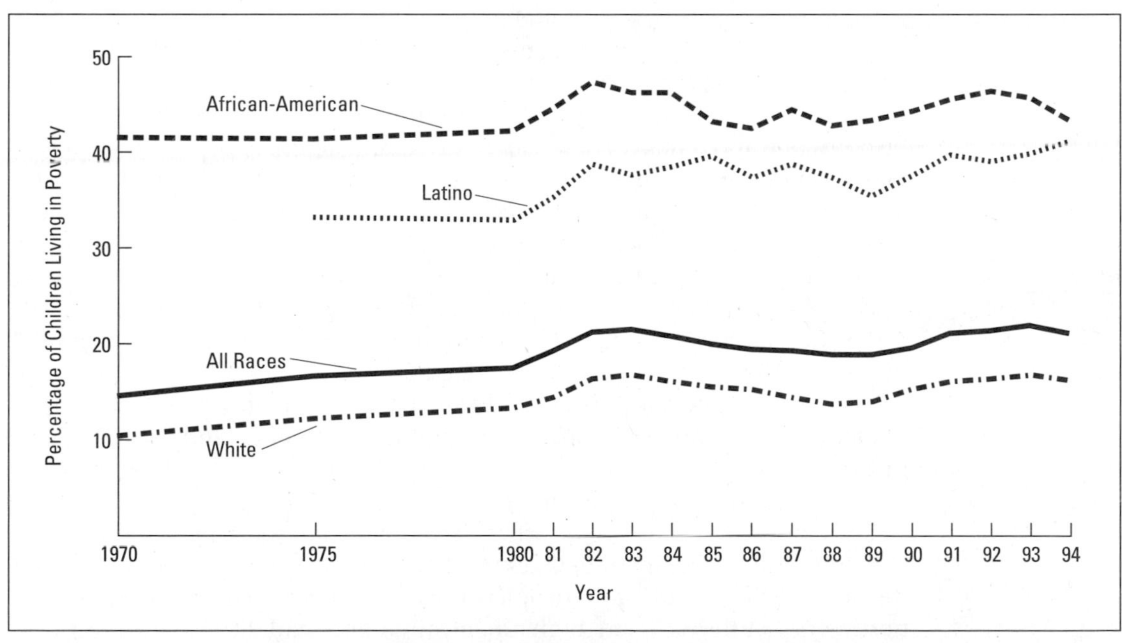

Percentage of American Children Living in Poverty, by Ethnicity, 1970–1994 Poverty rates for African-American and Latino children reached alarming proportions near century's end.

The plight of the poorest African-Americans also contrasted sharply with the conditions of other people of color. *Time* magazine, which devoted a cover story to the growing ethnic diversity in the United States, reported uneasiness among blacks about the growing size of other nonwhite ethnic groups. Latinos stood to surpass African-Americans as the largest "nonwhite" group early in the twenty-first century. Asians and Latinos fared better than blacks economically, and African-Americans feared that their needs would increasingly be ignored by the larger society.

People of all ethnic backgrounds struggled to balance one another's needs for recognition and respect. Controversies continued over affirmative action programs designed to redress centuries of racial discrimination. The issue erupted into the political arena in October 1990 when President Bush vetoed a civil rights act that would have permitted nonwhites and women greater leeway to sue businesses for discrimination in employment. The president claimed that the act would lead employers to establish rigid hiring and promotion quotas. A small but vocal group of black and Latino conservatives agreed. But advocates of affirmative action believed that his veto merely pandered to the resentments of white males, who saw their privileged position being eroded in a more pluralistic society.

The issue of ethnic balance caused special strains in colleges and universities, which faced new difficulties in deciding what should be included in the curriculum and what kinds of people should be hired to teach. Trying to recognize the new cultural diversity of the United States, some universities insisted that students learn something about non-European cultures. Moreover, college administrators—sometimes acting on their own initiative, sometimes in response to pressure—demanded that admission and hiring policies be changed so that a greater proportion of the student body and faculty would be nonwhite and female. These moves to expand access to professional power and mobility and to understand the diverse heritage of the United States sometimes produced a backlash. Efforts to broaden the curriculum to include the literature, thought, and art of Asia, Africa, and Latin America provoked complaints from those who believed the cultural legacy of the West was being unjustly subordinated. Hiring practices that appeared to favor women or minorities led to bitter arguments about the nature of the university and the importance of traditional academic credentials. In 1995 the regents of the University of California voted to end affirmative action programs for minority students, faculty, and staff, sparking both furious protests and similar efforts in other states. In 1996 California voters passed Proposition 209, a ballot initiative that outlawed affirmative action programs in the state.

Although the struggle over affirmative action and social justice on campus was certainly important, the stakes were even higher for those who possessed the least. Millions of poor people—mostly urban and disproportionately nonwhite—suffered from high unemployment, had little education, depended on welfare, and often had no legal means of bettering their situation. Disproportionate among the nation's poor were women of various ethnicities who headed households and raised their children alone.

Young black men experienced some of the direst consequences of generations of poverty and deprivation. Nearly one-fourth of African-American men between the ages of eighteen and thirty had criminal records, were serving jail terms, or were on probation. Although most victims of black criminals were themselves black, the media seized on violent crimes committed by young blacks and Latinos against middle-class whites. Nearing the century's end, the murder rate for African-American men under thirty remained the highest of any group, and a young black man had a greater chance of dying from a gunshot wound than from any other cause.

Reports of the dreadful conditions among the poorest urban African-Americans might have awakened a spirit of community crossing class lines. The picture was so bleak, however, that many middle-class and suburban Americans, worried about their own economic and social status and eager to claim some credit for their ability to hang on, came to hold inner-city residents responsible for their own misery. Consequently whites paid less attention to the racism still directed toward African-Americans. Only television, it seemed, had the power to bring racism home to white Americans.

Race Dramas

In the early morning hours of a Los Angeles Sunday in March 1991, amateur photographer George Holliday was trying out his new video camera when across the street from his Lake View Terrace apartment a fleet of police cars stopped a white sedan. Holliday began taping the event, and his eighty-one-second video of what ensued would soon become a sight so familiar to American television audiences that still photographs taken from it would be immediately identifiable.

While Holliday's camera rolled unseen, Los Angeles Police Department officers, who had been called in to assist the California Highway Patrol after a high-speed freeway chase, pulled twenty-five-year-old Rodney G. King from his car, threw him to the ground, tied his hands behind his back, and beat him severely with their police batons. Police officers swung fifty-six times, using their batons like baseball bats, and kicked King repeatedly in the head as other officers looked on. King was then booked for evading the police and possibly violating his parole on a 1989 robbery conviction. No charges were filed.

King went to the hospital with multiple bruises and fractures. Holliday turned the tape over to the authorities. By week's end the video had been played and replayed on local and network television, illustrating in the starkest terms the often-repeated charge that American law enforcement officers, especially in Los Angeles, did not know the difference between maintaining order and perpetrating violence, particularly in dealing with people of color.

Four white officers were ultimately charged with a total of eleven counts of assault on King, who pronounced himself "just glad not to be dead." When defense attorneys argued that the extensive pretrial publicity would prejudice jurors in Los Angeles, a judge granted a change of venue to Simi Valley, an

This videotape of Los Angeles police officers beating motorist Rodney King sparked outrage across the country. *Sipa*

overwhelmingly white, politically conservative suburban enclave. The jury, composed of ten non-Hispanic whites, one Asian, and one Hispanic, sat through seven weeks of detailed testimony and watched the video—in normal time, slow motion, and super slow motion—over and over again.

On April 29, 1992, they acquitted the defendants of all charges. Los Angeles mayor Tom Bradley—who had been the first African-American to head the Los Angeles Police Department— announced that "today, the system failed us," but called for calm and imposed a dusk-to-dawn curfew. But reaction to the acquittals was immediate and explosive. Over the next three days Los Angeles endured widespread arson, looting, shooting, and beatings. In South Central Los Angeles, a predominately black and Hispanic area, fires raged, store windows were smashed, looters reigned, and white motorists were pulled from their cars and beaten.

The disorder in Los Angeles was a lawless riot to some; an uprising against racial tyranny to others. Governor Wilson called in the National Guard to reinforce a police department caught off guard. As looting spread to affluent, heavily white areas like Beverly Hills, Westwood, and Santa Monica and confrontations erupted between blacks and Koreans in Koreatown, President Bush added five thousand federal troops to the 2,400 California National Guardsmen.

More than 3,700 building fires were set during the riots. Some were allowed to rage out of control because the police lacked the personnel to protect firefighters. Thirty-eight people, mostly black and Hispanic, died. Violence also broke out in San Francisco, Atlanta, New York, and even Madison, Wisconsin. Damage was estimated at $500 million. Most victims were minority business owners and neighborhood bystanders.

Soon the residents of the stricken areas emerged with shovels and brooms to begin cleaning up. Several hundred Koreans gathered along Wilshire Boulevard in an apparently spontaneous demonstration calling for interracial unity and an end to the violence. During the disturbances a stunned Rodney King called for calm. King seemed to speak to far larger issues than the immediate emergency when he pleaded, "People, I just want to say, can we all get along? Can we get along?"

The politics of race, class, and gender produced contradictory and troubling circumstances in the 1990s. One bizarre and bloody event involved one of the nation's most recognizable celebrities, the popular African-American football-hero-turned-sportscaster O. J. Simpson. On June 13, 1994, the bodies of Simpson's white ex-wife, Nicole Brown Simpson, and her white friend, Ronald Goldman, were found outside her Brentwood, California, townhouse. The two were victims of a knife-wielding assailant who had stabbed and slashed them repeatedly. As police prepared to arrest Simpson, he fled in his white Ford Bronco, driven by his football buddy A. C. Cowling. Television cameras from the national networks soon recorded a bizarre low-speed chase in which dozens of police vehicles followed Simpson's slow-moving truck along mile after mile of Los Angeles freeway. By the time the chase neared its end, drivers on the other side of the freeway divide, tuned in to the story on their car radios, flocked to the guard rail and got out of their cars to cheer Simpson, shouting "Go O.J.!" much as they would have had he still been a star running back headed for a touchdown.

As Simpson awaited trial his public nice-guy image fell to revelations of his history of violence toward Nicole during their marriage. Nicole Simpson, reports revealed, had called police on several occasions and once told a 911 operator that she feared Simpson would kill her. At one point Simpson had even pled guilty to battering her, for which he was placed on probation. Advocates for battered women sought to use the case to protest continuing judicial indifference to domestic violence. Some blacks believed that Simpson, because he was a black man accused of murdering two white people, could not receive a fair trial in the United States, notwithstanding his fame and fortune and the fact that he had hired the highest-priced defense team in history.

In October 1995, after months of testimony from experts on DNA evidence, revelations of videotaped racist statements by one of the police detectives who had investigated the murders, and passionate closing statements by the prosecution and defense attorneys, the mostly black jury found Simpson innocent of the crime. In a civil suit brought by the victims' families, decided in January 1997, a mostly white jury found Simpson responsible for the deaths and ordered him to pay damages of $25 million. The verdicts revealed the depth of racial polarization in the United States: many blacks cheered the original acquittal and believed that the second verdict represented racist justice; whites by and large seemed shocked that Simpson had gone free.

The Simpson trial revealed the horror of domestic violence in high places and drew attention to racial conflict within the justice system. At the same time, it sparked a new dialogue about how to come to terms with racial and domestic violence.

✦ Environmental Worries

As Americans wrestled with the social tensions that divided them, they also confronted environmental perils. In 1989 the tanker *Exxon Valdez* ran aground in Alaska's Prince William Sound, causing the largest oil spill in American history. The Coast Guard demanded that Exxon spend $2 billion to wash the crude oil from the sound's beaches and try to clean the feathers and fur of thousands of marine birds and animals befouled by the spill. The Justice Department prosecuted the captain of the tanker for operating it under the influence of alcohol. Having an identifiable villain helped focus public attention on the environment, as did the media-inspired celebration of the twentieth anniversary of the first Earth Day, on April 20, 1990. Across the country people promised to conserve energy, recycle their trash, and patronize businesses that demonstrated concern for the environment.

Environmental Policy

The record on actual environmental initiatives was mixed. Voters, put off by the price of cleanups, defeated costly environmental initiatives in California and New York in the 1990 election. Five years after the *Valdez* oil spill the courts had settled some $15 billion in damage claims from fishermen and Alaska natives, and scientists were beginning to think that the cleanup had been, on balance, more ecologically disruptive than the spill itself. In 1980 Congress had passed the Comprehensive Environmental Response, Compensation, and Liability Act, establishing a "Superfund" to pay for cleaning up toxic waste sites. The EPA-administered cleanup program continued, but some property owners fought designation of their land as a Superfund site, preferring to live with pollution rather than lose all they had invested.

Fearful of officially recognizing a potentially expensive problem, federal officials responded slowly, even scornfully, to scientific concerns about global warming. Many scientists believed that modern agriculture and industry, particularly the burning of fossil fuels, was causing a build-up of carbon dioxide and other "greenhouse gases" in the earth's atmosphere. Some climatologists feared that as a result the earth's temperature would rise over the next hundred years—like a giant greenhouse—melting the polar ice caps, drowning coastal cities, and turning fertile farmland into deserts. Not all scientists agreed, however, and the Bush administration, reluctant to regulate industrial emissions, sided with the skeptics, demanding more studies on the likelihood of global warming. Scientists and environmentalists called for conservation measures and research on alternative energy sources, but Bush administration officials displayed little inclination to revive the discarded energy policies of the 1970s, which had been designed to reduce gasoline use.

Although the Bush administration shied away from a general attack on environmental problems, fearful of costs and of opposition from special interest groups, it did support some environmental laws. Congress approved the first overhaul of the Clean Air Act in thirteen years, setting stricter standards for automobile emissions and requiring municipalities to reduce smog. The measure also addressed for the first time the issue of acid rain: the increasing amount of sulfuric acid in rainfall throughout the Midwest and Northeast, caused by the burning of high-sulfur coal. In addition Congress increased the liability of shipping companies for oil spills and agreed to preserve large coastal areas from Alaska to New England from further development by oil companies. But the Clean Air Act disappointed environmentalists, who pointed out that it included a provision awarding pollution "credits" to companies that complied with emissions standards. Those companies could then sell the credits to corporations that violated the law, bringing polluters into nominal compliance. Conservatives saw pollution credits as a means of injecting marketplace forces into environmental measures. Critics pointed out, however, that the ability to buy pollution credits amounted to a license to continue spewing out toxins and that the air over credit-purchasing factories, and downwind of them, remained dirty.

The Public Responds

Once the public began to understand that industrial pollution included poisonous substances people could neither see nor smell, environmental concerns spawned grassroots organizing, particularly among poor people and people of color, whose neighborhoods most often played host to polluting industrial sites. In East Los Angeles, poor Chicana mothers asserting their right to protect their children from harm organized a group called Mothers of East L.A. to fight a city-sponsored toxic waste incinerator. An investigative reporter in Tucson, Jane Kay, looked into abnormally high rates of cancer in the overwhelmingly Chicano municipality of South Tucson and published a series of articles about groundwater pollution from the use of the solvent trichloral ethylene at the city's airport. Although Kay won a Pulitzer Prize for her stories, the local branch of the Sierra Club was slow to identify South Tucson's plight as an environmental problem.

On the one hand, the 1990s saw a surge in environmental activism among people of color. On the other hand, some Native American leaders sought to turn environmental problems into community development opportunities. Wendell Chino, tribal chairman of the Mescalero Apaches, declared his intention to seek a permit to open a nuclear waste storage facility on Mescalero land, a project Chino claimed would bring wealth and jobs to the community. Another tribal chairman, Jacob Viarrial of the Pojoaque pueblo, decided to put a little pressure on Bruce King, the Democratic governor of New Mexico, who was opposing a casino gaming license for the pueblo. Viarrial went on television to announce that in light of the state's intransigence about gambling, the pueblo, a mere ten miles from Santa Fe, had "no alternative" but to seek a license for a nuclear waste repository. The governor could have his choice, Viarrial implied, between bingo and plutonium on the outskirts of the state's tourist mecca. Within a year the tribes had joined Republicans in a successful effort to oust King, and the new governor signed a gaming pact that at last brought casino gambling to Pojoaque.

Atomic Legacies

Nowhere was the link between government policy and environmental problems clearer than in the case of nuclear waste. The Reagan defense build-up had included a crash program to process plutonium and produce more nuclear weapons. Even before the Cold War ended, scientists, policymakers, and activists began to worry about mounting evidence of safety lapses in the production of nuclear weapons and extensive air, soil, and water contamination around nuclear facilities like the Hanford Reservation in Washington State, the Savannah River facility in South Carolina, and the Rocky Flats installation on a mesa sixteen miles northwest of Denver.

In 1951 the federal government began looking for a place to mass-produce nuclear weapons. Planners settled on the Rocky Flats site because it was close to the bomb laboratory at Los Alamos and near what was then a small city. Additionally, the land was cheap, and air conditioning was not needed. Even then scientists recognized the hazards such a plant might pose to people who lived downwind, but government officials reasoned that the site was "well removed from any residential area." Unfortunately the meteorologists who had reported to the government on wind conditions in the area used bad data. Winds sometimes clocked at one hundred miles per hour swept off the mesa every year, blowing southeast, right over Denver.

From the start Rocky Flats managers put production first, safety second. Releases of radioactive substances occurred regularly. So did fires. A 1969 fire forced a six-month shutdown in weapons production and produced $50 million in damage. Firefighters equipped with radiation detection equipment found plutonium on the ground around the plant, but officials claimed there was "no evidence that plutonium was carried beyond plant boundaries."

In 1974 the Environmental Protection Agency released a study that indicated that cattle in a pasture east of Rocky Flats had more plutonium contamination than cattle that had been set out to graze on the admittedly highly contaminated federal nuclear test site in Nevada. The government began purchasing thousands of acres of land around the Rocky Flats plant. Antinuclear activists and concerned physicians began to document increased rates of

Demonstrators outside Rocky Flats, fall 1990, protested both the production of weapons and the legacy of nuclear waste at the ill-fated bomb factory. *Howard Ruffner/Black Star*

leukemia and cancers of the lymph, lung, thyroid, testes, and breast, paralleling patterns seen at Hiroshima and Nagasaki.

By the late 1980s the Rocky Flats complex had become home to a dangerous assortment of toxic holding ponds, waste dumps, and open-air incineration spots. Contaminated materials, often thrown haphazardly into thousands of fifty-five-gallon drums (one scientist called them "barrels of bubbling yuck"), ranged from plutonium-contaminated oil to Kim Wipes that had been used to cleanse contaminated instruments. Some of the drums were leaking, threatening the entire Denver water supply. In the fall of 1989 Admiral James Watkins, the secretary of energy, declared the plant temporarily closed for "safety improvements." Some scientists suggested that the government simply put a fence around the installation and call it a "national sacrifice zone."

Others, noting the immediate peril of further contamination, addressed the problem of the long-range storage of nuclear waste. In an effort to store a tiny fraction of the nation's radioactive refuse, the government planned to open a repository deep underground outside Carlsbad, New Mexico, in 1988. The plan, known as the Waste Isolation Pilot Project (WIPP), addressed only so-called low-level nuclear waste, the miscellaneous by-products of nuclear manufacturing, rather than high-level trash like spent reactor fuel rods. Engineers dug an immense mine two thousand feet underground in the salt beds around Carlsbad. The WIPP was perpetually mired in controversy, however, as scientists and policymakers tried to allay the concerns of citizens determined not to have a nuclear waste dump in their back yards. The opening of the facility, first slated for 1985, was put off again and again. By the late-1990s scientists had identified thousands more contaminated areas at the nation's nuclear weapons sites, barrels of radioactive garbage continued to pile up around the country, and the United States still had no facility to handle its ever-mounting inventory of nuclear waste.

✦ The Election of 1992

In the spring of 1991, on the heels of victory in the Persian Gulf, President Bush rode a wave of popularity. At that point the pundits were calling Bush unbeatable in 1992, and this assessment was not lost on Democratic Party heavyweights who would have had to begin raising money and organizing their campaigns if they were to challenge Bush in 1992. The task seemed completely hopeless, even for Democratic favorites such as Governor Mario Cuomo of New York, Senator Sam Nunn of Georgia, Senator Bill Bradley of New Jersey, and Senator Al Gore of Tennessee. Each of these men decided not to run.

By the winter of 1991 the field of Democratic candidates looked to many observers like a horse race without a thoroughbred. The press set off to cover the New Hampshire primary campaign in January 1992 in a cynical mood, deeming that the voters were equally turned off to all politicians. To the surprise of many reporters, however, New Hampshire voters flocked to candidates' debates and town meetings, asked sophisticated questions, and appeared to be, amazingly, engaged and even optimistic. At first Governor Bill Clinton of Arkansas, billing himself as a "New Democrat" who favored change, appeared the front-runner. Clinton was thought to have some liabilities, however, including his wife, Hillary Rodham Clinton, a nationally prominent attorney and child welfare advocate. Mrs. Clinton had alienated many housewives when she said that she could have followed the advice of country singer Tammy Wynette, "staying home and baking cookies and standing by my man," but she had made different choices. Still, polls indicated that Hillary, and consequently her husband, had substantial support among working women. In some polls Clinton appeared to be ahead by as many as twenty points.

Then, on January 23, a tabloid newspaper, the *National Star,* ran a story featuring a woman named Gennifer Flowers who claimed that she had had a twelve-year affair with Bill Clinton. Ever since 1988, when the *Miami Herald* had sent a reporter to Washington D.C. to try to catch candidate Gary Hart cheating on his wife, the press had deemed candidates' private conduct fair game and had created what was commonly referred to as "the character issue," a question that required reporting on such things as candidates' sex lives. Another bombshell was soon to come, when allegations surfaced that Clinton had been a Vietnam War draft dodger. Clinton's support in New Hampshire went from 33 percent to 17 percent. Massachusetts senator Paul Tsongas, running as a deficit hawk, won the battle in New Hampshire, but Clinton, refusing to be beaten, would rise again to pronounce himself "The Comeback Kid."

The character issue, it seemed, cut both ways. Many voters sympathized with his marital difficulties or thought such things irrelevant to his qualifications for the presidency. Although his opposition to the Vietnam War alienated some veterans, it struck a chord with members of the baby boom generation. When he later admitted to having tried marijuana (but claiming that he "didn't inhale"), few voters under fifty were shocked.

Clinton was a tireless politician who knew how to appeal to crowds, and his campaign soon gathered steam again. Once his hold on the nomination was secure he ignored the tradition of choosing a running mate who would balance the ticket ideologically and geographically. Instead he chose Al Gore, a man remarkably like himself. Both Clinton and Gore were moderate southerners in their mid-forties. Both were Ivy League–educated intellectuals (Clinton a graduate of Yale Law School, Gore a Harvard alumnus) who loved the details of government. But Gore brought significant strengths of his own to the ticket. He was a Vietnam veteran, and his homemaker wife, Tipper, had made a name for herself campaigning for warning labels on rock records with graphic lyrics. Gore was also an avid environmentalist. Veterans, housewives, and environmentalists were reassured by Clinton's choice of Gore. The Democratic convention, remarkably harmonious, pushed the Clinton ticket nearly twenty points ahead of Bush in the polls.

Bill Clinton's early troubles in the primaries could have dealt George Bush a lucky hand in the general election, but Bush was having problems of his own. His 1988 campaign, in which he had tried to appease "red-meat Republicans" by baiting liberals, opposing abortion, and fulminating against Dukakis for coddling criminals had never really earned him the trust of his party's right wing. Furthermore, by this strategy Bush had lent the power and credibility of the chief executive to rhetoric, policies, and people he couldn't control, from Pat Robertson's Christian Coalition to extreme-right ideologues like former Nixon speechwriter and political columnist Pat Buchanan. Buchanan decided to run against Bush; not many expected him to make much of a difference. But many voters found Bush insensitive to the lives of ordinary people. When Buchanan polled 41 percent to Bush's 57 percent in the New Hampshire primary, Bush determined to meet the challenge from the Right by co-opting it.

The wild card in the deck was the independent candidacy of Texas multibillionaire H. Ross Perot. Running as a "populist," the feisty, plainspoken Perot was willing and able to finance his campaign out of his own pocket. Some people found his claim to be "the people's candidate" far-fetched, but paradoxically his immense wealth lent credibility to his claim that he was beholden to no special interests. Also, he appealed to the millions of voters disillusioned with the two main parties. Democrats concerned about the deficit liked the way Perot stressed the need to tighten the nation's belt and launch austerity measures in government. Republicans worried about the party's turn to the right on social issues were attracted to his position in favor of abortion rights.

By July Perot's support had reached 20 percent among voters, and strategists in both parties were looking over their shoulders. Perot lacked the stomach for the grind of traditional campaigning, however. When he addressed an audience at an NAACP convention as "you people," he was accused of racial insensitivity, a charge that clearly stung him. He claimed the media had misinterpreted his remarks, and he grew increasingly impatient with his inability to control press coverage of his campaign. In the midst of the Democratic convention Perot dropped out of the race, explaining that he was doing so for personal reasons.

The Republican convention, televised from Houston in August, showcased the evangelical Christians and right-wing ideologues who had captured the rank and file of the party, if not the nomination. Most speakers at the convention emphasized what they called "family values," a theme first voiced by Vice President Dan Quayle. In a vitriolic tirade Buchanan bashed gays, accused Hillary Clinton of telling children to sue their parents, and declared that the time had come for "a religious war for the soul of America."

Many who watched the convention, including some lifelong Republicans, found the speakers frighteningly narrow-minded and mean-spirited. Pollsters, moderate party professionals, and many observers warned that the Republicans were not winning much support by campaigning on moral values in a time of economic uncertainty. President Bush insisted that he would do "whatever it takes" to win, and he was determined to push "the character issue" and "family values" all the way to reelection.

Clinton strategists, having already survived a bruising fight for the nomination, understood that the voters in 1992 were far more concerned about the state of the economy than about whether the candidate's wife was too pushy or his libido too strong. Determined to keep the race focused tightly on the need for change and on economic matters, they daily urged Clinton, Gore, and their various spokespeople to "stay on message." Lest anyone forget what the message was, Clinton strategist James Carville posted a sign in Clinton headquarters: "It's the economy, stupid."

The Republicans never recovered from the bad press generated by the convention. Bush and Quayle continued to insist that the economy, which a majority of American people saw as not so good, was just fine and that the real issue was Clinton's character. But the character issue cut both ways. Voters knew that Bush himself had come down on both sides of major issues, from abortion to taxes to balancing the federal budget. Quayle had managed to avoid the draft and Vietnam service by using family connections to get into a National Guard unit. Given the extraordinary changes in people's beliefs and in standards of behavior over the preceding decades, many Americans may have wondered whether their own lives would have stood up to the scrutiny of the press or the rigid codes trumpeted by the Republicans. Unemployment remained above 7 percent, and the deficit had ballooned to $290 billion.

Republicans and Democrats both shuddered when Perot re-entered the race, little more than a month before election day, claiming that his volunteers had convinced him to return. But many who had previously considered him a viable option now wondered whether he was really cut out to be president. Showing a goofy, paranoid streak that his critics had warned about, Perot told a *60 Minutes* reporter about a Republican conspiracy to disrupt his daughter's wedding and about having been the target of assassination attempts in 1970 or 1971 by a commando unit of Black Panthers hired by the North Vietnamese government. Perot insisted that "people try to kill me every year." Despite such outbursts, enough voters were disillusioned with the major parties that Perot continued to rise in the polls. He did well in debates with Bush and Clinton, once again using his pugnacious personality to his advantage.

As election day approached, the president's campaign was clearly in trouble. Even nature seemed to be conspiring against Bush when the most costly natural disaster in the nation's history, Hurricane Andrew, slammed into the Florida coast, leveling huge swaths of the Miami Beach area and leaving nearly a quarter of a million people homeless. As if that were not sufficient, Hurricane Andrew spun out to sea and returned to hammer away at the Louisiana lowlands, narrowly missing New Orleans. The Federal Emergency Management Agency, the government bureau charged with handling such matters, responded sluggishly and inefficiently. Looters roamed through posh Miami neighborhoods, and victims took the law into their own hands, defending their possessions with shotguns. The president went to visit the stricken areas; when reporters asked him why, he replied defensively, "I think it shows that I care."

Trailing in the polls, Bush grew increasingly shrill. He railed at Gore for his environmentalism, telling a crowd that Gore was the "Ozone Man. . . . He's crazy, way out, far out, man." In contrast, Clinton and Gore pounded away at their message stressing change and economic responsibility, while their increasingly optimistic supporters sang along with the campaign's baby boomer theme song, Fleetwood Mac's "Don't Stop (Thinking About Tomorrow)." When it was all over Clinton had achieved an impressive victory in the electoral college. The popular vote was more mixed, however, with Clinton polling 43 percent to Bush's 38 percent and Perot's 9 percent. The president-elect asserted that the voters had sent Washington a message—that they wanted change. As if to drive the point home, the voters gave the Democrats an increased majority in the Senate and elected four women senators, including Carol Mosely Braun of Illinois, the first African-American woman to serve in the Senate.

Senate minority leader Robert Dole promised no honeymoon for the new president, however. With Bush's concession speech barely over, Dole was

Inauguration Day, 1993, on the steps of the Lincoln Memorial. Left to right: Tipper Gore, Vice President Al Gore, President Bill Clinton, Hillary Rodham Clinton. *Corbis/Bettmann*

already pointing out that the Democrats had won the White House with only a minority of all the votes cast. The Republicans, Dole insisted, were determined to represent the majority who had not voted for Clinton.

✦ Clinton's First Term

When the Democrats took office in January 1993, promising sweeping change and a new spirit of hope, many Americans anticipated that partisan bickering and gridlock in Washington were at least on the wane, if not yet completely dead. Clinton laid out an ambitious agenda, beginning with economic recovery and including a national service plan to fund college students' tuition and rebuild the country's infrastructure, welfare reform, one hundred thousand more police on the nation's streets, and a restructuring of the nation's health care system.

To assist him with these tasks and to gratify the millions of Hispanics, blacks, and working women who had given him his victory, Clinton pledged to appoint a cabinet that "looked like America." Clinton named more African-Americans, Latinos, and women to cabinet positions than any of his predecessors. Some of Clinton's appointees started out with ambitious plans. Housing and Urban Development secretary Henry Cisneros, formerly mayor of San Antonio, vowed to clean up the mess left behind by his predecessors, a formidable job. Energy Secretary Hazel O'Leary, the first African-American woman to head a major cabinet department, quietly took the government out of the bomb-making business and opened millions of classified documents about nuclear experiments and other secret projects to public scrutiny.

But the novelty of women and minority appointments soon wore off. Increasing press scrutiny of political appointees' personal lives made meeting the test of acceptability as an officeholder difficult if not impossible. Clinton's first choice for attorney general was forced to withdraw when it was revealed that she had employed an illegal immigrant as a domestic worker. The woman finally confirmed as attorney general, Miami district attorney Janet Reno, was initially enormously popular. Reno was soon criticized, however, for her handling of a stand-off between followers of cult leader David Koresh and agents of the Bureau of Alcohol, Tobacco, and Firearms, which ended in a fiery conflagration at the cult's Waco, Texas, compound. Two African-American appointees, Commerce Secretary Ron Brown and Agriculture Secretary Mike Espy, were investigated for trading on insider connections and taking corporate favors. Cisneros was urged to resign amid disclosures that he had been making cash payments to a former mistress, and O'Leary drew fire for spending too much money on travel. Comedians joked that appointees to the Clinton cabinet could expect many fringe benefits, including their own special prosecutors.

When President Clinton put Mrs. Clinton in charge of developing a plan for reforming the nation's health care system, conservative pundits complained that the First Lady had been granted too much influence for someone the voters had not even elected. Hillary Rodham Clinton aroused strong feelings among both supporters and detractors, but her husband was determined to give her a pivotal role in the administration. Many criticized her health care task force for holding secret meetings and excluding key players like insurance companies and the American Medical Association. Mrs. Clinton's task force ultimately issued an immensely complicated plan, running into the thousands of pages, that called for a system of government-directed "managed competition" among health care providers and insurers. And, in addition to its complexity, delays and equivocations doomed the Clinton plan. Congress whittled away at reform provisions and balked at the idea of universal coverage—of giving the government the power to ensure that every

American would have health insurance. The insurance industry spent millions on a publicity campaign to bury the plan. The Republicans in Congress stalled, sensing that the public wanted lower costs and better benefits but believing that if nothing were done, 1994 voters would blame the Democrats. And, indeed, the failure of the Clinton health care plan would prove disastrous for the administration and for the Democratic Party.

With the Cold War paradigm no longer dominating American foreign policy, Clinton had to formulate new rules for American engagement overseas. The American public expressed two deeply held, valid, but often inconsistent principles regarding U.S. involvement in the world's troubles. They believed that as the world's only remaining superpower, the United States had a unique responsibility in the global arena. Instantaneous televised pictures of human suffering in some of the most remote regions of the world tugged at Americans' heartstrings. At the same time, however, Americans wanted foreign engagements to be brief and cheap, virtually without cost in terms of American lives. The Clinton administration had a hard time reconciling these often incompatible aims.

The administration scored its biggest initial successes in managing old problems left over from the Cold War. Clinton's secretary of state, Warren Christopher, a veteran of the Johnson and Carter administrations, facilitated agreements between Israel and its many foes. In the summer of 1993 Israel and the Palestine Liberation Organization (PLO) reached an agreement calling for mutual recognition and the creation of Palestinian self-rule in Gaza and the West Bank. On September 13, 1993, Israeli prime minister Yitzhak Rabin and PLO chairman Yassir Arafat shook hands at a moving ceremony on the south lawn of the White House. Over the next year Christopher spent a lot of time in the Middle East trying to arrange a comprehensive peace. These efforts bore fruit in the fall of 1994 when Israel and Jordan signed a treaty and pledged cooperation. The Clinton administration also successfully managed the U.S. relationship with Russia, the most powerful of the successor states of the Soviet Union. Clinton formed a quick personal bond with Boris Yeltsin, the Russian president, helping him survive an attempted coup mounted by ultranationalists and Communists in October 1993. But the successes in the Middle East and the warming relations with Russia proved fragile. A right-wing Jew opposed to the peace initiative assassinated Rabin in 1995. Six months later Israel elected a new nationalist prime minister, Benjamin Netanyahu, who pledged to roll back the policy of trading land for peace. Yeltsin was in poor health, and the political future of his country was a day-to-day matter.

The Clinton administration had limited success in navigating those world disorders that did not seem to be continuations of the problems of the Cold War era. Without the Cold War as a framing principle, the administration and the public at large struggled to decide when U.S. interests warranted foreign involvement. During the campaign of 1992 Clinton had faulted the Bush administration for its apparent disregard of the suffering of Bosnian victims of Serb aggression in the civil war in the former Yugoslavia. At that time Clinton had suggested that as president he would lift the U.S. arms embargo against the mostly Muslim Bosnian government and order air strikes against Serb militias. As president he followed a much more cautious approach, however, authorizing a few intermittent and ineffectual air strikes and not lifting the arms embargo until November 1994.

For the first eight months of his administration Clinton continued Bush's policy of using tens of thousands of U.S. soldiers to supply food to starving Somalis. The famine relief seemed so successful that U.S. and other UN forces expanded their mission in Somalia in an effort to create a viable government there. This peacemaking effort quickly brought U.S. forces into conflict with the many armed factions in the country, however. In the summer of 1993 Somali guerrillas began attacking U.S. soldiers, and in October twelve American GIs died in a firefight with Somalis. Clinton ordered American troops out by March 1994.

The bad experience in Somalia made the Clinton administration shy about deploying U.S. forces elsewhere, but media coverage of human suffering overseas made it impossible for the United States to remain disengaged. In the summer of 1994 the administration sent four thousand troops to central Africa to help save nearly 1 million refugees from a hideous civil war in Rwanda from famine and disease. This time the U.S. forces refused to get involved in Rwandan politics, limiting their mission strictly to providing humanitarian aid. The Clinton administration sponsored similarly modest efforts to relieve suffering in Zaire late in 1996.

In the summer of 1994 Cuba once more became a problem for the United States. The Cuban economy suffered severely after the collapse of the Soviet Union, because Moscow no longer provided billions in food and fuel. Thousands of desperate Cubans took to boats and rafts to flee the island for Florida. Mindful that a similar 1980 exodus of 120,000 Cubans had embarrassed Jimmy Carter and contributed to his 1980 defeat, Clinton reversed the traditional U.S. policy of granting asylum to any Cuban who could reach the United States. Instead of allowing the Cubans entry into Florida, the U.S. Coast Guard and Navy rescued the boat people and deposited them at the U.S. navy base in Guantanamo Bay, Cuba. There they shared a makeshift camp with twenty thousand Haitians also denied entry, while the U.S. government made plans to accommodate as many as sixty thousand people at the base. This arrangement assuredly could not last forever.

One notable foreign policy success came in Haiti, where the president had pledged to restore a democratically elected government. Haitian army officers had ousted President Jean Bertrand Aristide in September 1991 and resumed the brutal repression that had plagued Haiti for generations. Tens of thousands of refugees fled the island, but like Bush had done before him, Clinton refused to allow them to enter the United States. The administration tightened an economic embargo on Haiti and obtained UN authorization for a multilateral invasion to restore Aristide, but neither a majority of the public nor the country's top military leadership wanted to invade. The Haitian junta remained defiant, so in October 1994 U.S. forces prepared for an invasion—which the president clearly hoped he could still avoid. At the eleventh hour Clinton sent a special delegation to Port-au-Prince to negotiate an end to the stand-off. American troops were deployed as part of a "transition" force to ensure that Aristide would be allowed to take power, and Clinton avoided a full-scale invasion while still achieving the goal of restoring Haiti's democratically elected leader.

The Republicans in Congress permitted Clinton no honeymoon. His early successes—passage of the Family and Medical Leave Act, ratification of the North American Free Trade Agreement (NAFTA) with Mexico and Canada, and a budget that reduced the deficit for the first time in twelve years—were hard won. Clinton's two moderate appointments to the Supreme Court, Justice Ruth Bader Ginsberg and Justice Stephen Breyer, sailed to confirmation, seemingly the president's only easy victories. A Clinton-backed ban on assault weapons passed narrowly, but the gun lobby promised to win a repeal of the measure. Clinton's critics were growing increasingly vocal. His most ambitious proposals—health care reform in particular—faced opposition from such heavily endowed interests as the insurance industry and the American Medical Association and ultimately failed to win passage. And the character issue continued to plague him. By 1994 a special prosecutor and a congressional committee had begun investigating the Clintons' investment in an Arkansas real estate development called Whitewater that had ties to a failed savings and loan. A former employee of the Arkansas state government was beginning the process of suing the president for sexual harassment.

The 1994 midterm elections provided plenty of evidence that the voters felt that the federal government, particularly the Democrats in Congress, had lost touch with their concerns. House minority leader Newt Gingrich crafted a "Contract with America," signed by most Republican candidates, that called for scaling back the welfare state, balancing the budget, and reforming the government. Republican strategists de-emphasized the social agenda of the Christian Right, focusing instead on the economic issues that had worked so well for the Democrats in 1992. In race after race the voters delivered a stinging rebuke to the Democrats, electing Republicans to governorships and helping them seize control of both houses of Congress. Dubbed by some "the revolt of the angry white men," the election swept in a new generation of conservative leaders, some of whom seemed determined to dismantle the federal government. The 39 percent of Americans who went to the polls represented a far more affluent and conservative constituency than the eligible voting public. And although those who did vote had seemed to say that they wanted less government, whether the election was a mandate for a conservative social agenda was less clear. Voters elected Republican candidates who avowed opposition to abortion and gay rights, but they also defeated measures designed to restrict access to abortion and to bar gay rights laws.

When Congress convened in 1995 the Republicans were in control of both houses for the first time since 1946. Robert Dole, the new Senate majority leader, promised change in Washington, but he expressed less hostility to the Democratic administration than Newt Gingrich, who became Speaker of the House. Gingrich vowed no compromise with the White House. The new Republican leadership announced plans to enact a legislative program ranging from a constitutional amendment requiring a balanced federal budget to a "war on welfare."

The GOP Congress fell far short of enacting all of the provisions of the Contract with America, in part because President Clinton vetoed or threatened to veto particularly deep cuts in entitlement programs. But just as tellingly, GOP leaders quickly abandoned their promises to push term limits and campaign finance reform. Majority Leader Dole, whose skills lay in cutting deals and engineering compromises, found his hands tied by an unusually large, politically extreme, unruly freshman class of representatives led by the pugnacious, headline-seeking Gingrich. Thus for two years the Democratic president and the Republican legislature deadlocked. By 1995 the stalemate over the federal budget had become so bitter that the Republicans shut down the government twice rather than send the president a budget he would agree to sign.

Gingrich believed that the shutdowns would convince the voters that the Republican Party was serious about its intent to scale back the federal government, but his plan backfired. By 1995 there were too many Americans all across the nation, from scientists and secretaries to security guards, who worked for the government. Millions more relied on federal payments like Social Security benefits. The shutdowns caused real hardships for some and inconveniences for many others, and nearly everyone blamed the Republicans.

Ultimately the Republicans learned that the public did not really want to roll back the federal government. Voters had said that they wanted the poor to work for a living—and thus they supported welfare cutbacks—but they did not want to lose middle-class entitlements or see environmental protections cut. At the same time, Clinton read the 1994 Democratic debacle as a sign to move to the center, reasoning that the Democrats could force the Republicans far to the right and take on the 1996 campaign as the party of moderation. In his 1996 State of the Union message he announced that "the era of big government is over," infuriating liberals but foreshadowing the positions he would take throughout the race for reelection.

The Republicans proved unable to field a candidate who could give the president a serious challenge. The one potential Republican candidate voters seemed to like was General Colin Powell, a hero of the Gulf War and the first African-American to attain the position of chairman of the Joint Chiefs of Staff. But Powell decided early on not to run, much to the relief of GOP conservatives who disliked his pro-choice, pro–affirmative action beliefs. The Christian Right remained a strong force in the party, but all the GOP candidates, even the bellicose Pat Buchanan, knew that they had to tone down their rhetoric to win votes. After a lackluster primary season, seventy-three-year-old Senate majority leader Bob Dole emerged as the party's nominee. A skillful Washington deal maker known for his sardonic wit and his dedication to public service, Dole nevertheless failed to connect with the electorate. Voters found him stiff, sharp, and inclined to ramble, and by midsummer the polls showed him trailing Clinton by as much as twenty points.

In July, in an effort to pump up his sagging campaign, Dole decided to distance himself from the gridlock in Washington by quitting the Senate. But few voters bought the idea that stepping down after thirty-five years in politics gave Dole license to run against the government. Dole's choice of Jack Kemp, the former congressman, secretary of housing and urban development, and quarterback of the Buffalo Bills professional football team created a ripple of public interest. Kemp added youth and vigor to the campaign, and he had the reputation of being the one Republican who really cared about the poor and disadvantaged. The ticket's biggest asset may have been Dole's wife, Elizabeth, a high-powered lawyer and former cabinet official in both the Reagan and Bush administrations. Appealing to the "angry white men" who had elected the 104th Congress, Dole insisted that *his* high-powered wife would not be making policy if he were elected. But given Elizabeth Dole's political savvy and record of public service, millions of working women doubtless wondered why.

President Clinton and Vice President Gore ran a disciplined campaign based on the idea that the country was going in the right direction and that the president, who was nearly a quarter of a century younger than the Republican candidate, was the right choice to "build a bridge to the twenty-first century." Republicans charged Clinton with being a "tax-and-spend liberal," but the president, quite plausibly in the minds of most liberals, denied the charges. His record as president demonstrated a readiness to compromise with conservatives. For example, after bitter debate between liberals and moderates within his administration, Clinton decided to sign the Republicans' Welfare Reform Act in July 1996. The act ended the six-decade-long federal commitment to provide cash assistance to the nation's poor children, shifted the burden of paying for welfare to states and municipalities without providing compensating funds, and required heads of families on welfare to find jobs within two years. Welfare benefits were restricted to a lifetime total of five years, and stricter eligibility standards excluded a variety of potential recipients, from legal immigrants to disabled children, from receiving government support. In a particularly bizarre effort to "strengthen families," the Republican Congress insisted that a provision be included stating that any woman on welfare who refused to identify the father of her child would lose at least 25 percent of her benefits.

As the president sprinted to the right, the Republicans found themselves bereft of issues to take to the voters, who agreed that the economy was, after all, pretty good. The Dole tax cut proposal made little sense to a public that had learned, partly at the urging of Ross Perot, that the federal government could not reduce taxes and balance the budget at the same time without eviscerating federal programs like Medicare and Social Security. Perot, running a much more low-key campaign than he had in 1992, drew support chiefly from disaffected Republicans, costing Dole dearly.

When the ballots were counted Clinton had won, with just below 50 percent of the vote to Dole's 41 percent and Perot's 9 percent. Exit polls revealed a "gender gap," with women backing Clinton over Dole by a large margin. Clinton became the first Democrat since Franklin Roosevelt to be reelected to the presidency. The Democrats picked up some seats in the House, but not enough to wrest control from the Republicans, who also maintained a solid hold on the Senate. Ironically, a voting public that had expressed anger at federal gridlock voted for at least two more years of divided government.

Nearing the end of the 1990s, policymakers had reason to feel hopeful that they might at least solve some of the nation's pressing problems. The economy had improved immensely during Clinton's first term. By 1996 unemployment was at a twenty-year low, and the federal budget deficit was down by 60 percent. More than 10 million new jobs had been created since 1992. The stock market continued to rise to record levels, and inflation remained under control. Although the 1996 Welfare Reform Act signaled government leaders' intent to reverse federal social welfare policies that had been in place since the New Deal, a course many saw as disastrously inhumane, policymakers insisted that encouraging self-reliance in the context of a growing economy was a wise course of action. The president had signed popular bills prohibiting gold mining near Yellowstone National Park and establishing the huge Escalante Staircase National Monument in Utah. A bipartisan health care reform bill, sponsored by Democratic senator Edward Kennedy of Massachusetts and Republican senator Nancy Kassebaum of Kansas, enabled workers to keep their health insurance when they left or changed jobs.

But future successes depended on the working relationship between the president and Congress. Clinton seemed subdued in victory and vowed to reach out to Republicans in an effort to work together to serve "the vital center" of the American public. With his usual flair for the symbolic he selected Madeline Albright, the widely respected U.S. ambassador to the United Nations, as the country's first woman secretary of state, and he chose a Republican former senator, William Cohen, as his secretary of defense. Both President Clinton and Speaker Gingrich continued to be plagued by accusations of ethics violations involving their campaign fund-raising, a situation that appeared to inspire both to encourage bipartisan cooperation to tend to the nation's business. The country seemed to be moving into a period of rough parity for the two political parties, a circumstance resembling the political situation of a

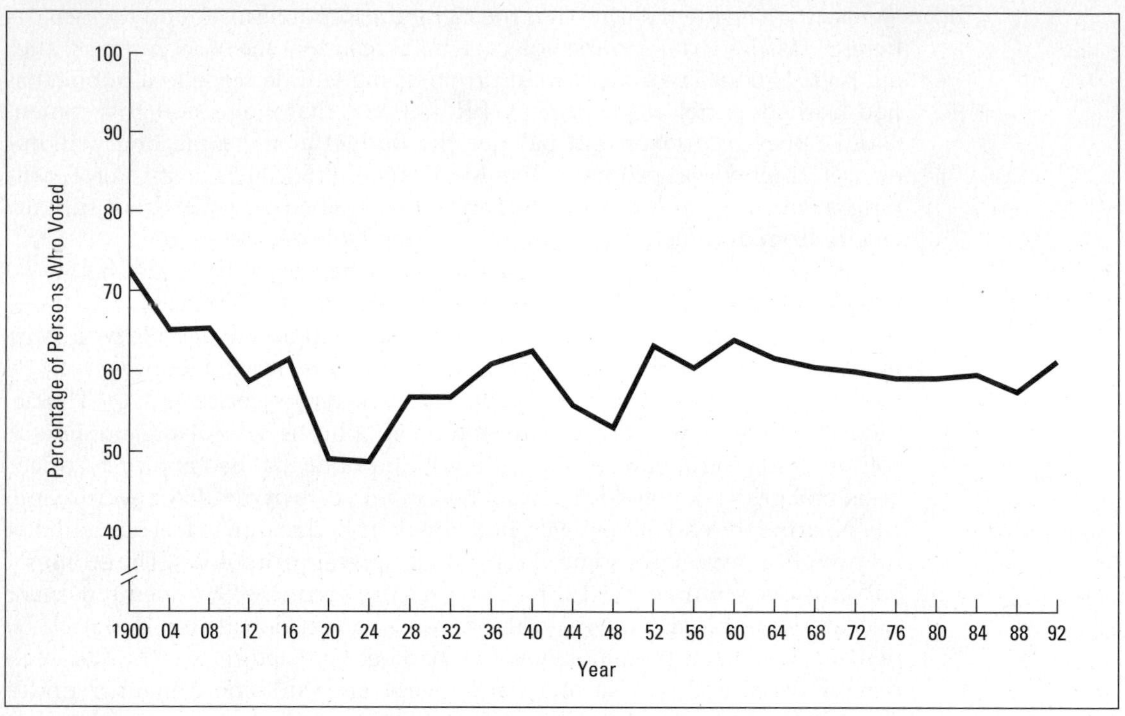

Voter Participation in Presidential Elections, 1900–1992 This figure is based on the percentage of eligible voters. Politicians and pundits have lamented recent voter apathy.

century before. The major difference was that fewer eligible voters bothered to participate in the ritual of electing their leaders. In 1900 a full 77 percent of those eligible cast their ballots for president; voter turnout in the 1996 election was below 50 percent (see figure).

✦ Conclusion

At the end of the splendid, terrifying, revolutionary twentieth century, Americans had a vast, unfinished agenda for their country. Most people believed in the need to foster productivity in the American economy, believing that growing national prosperity would make greater social justice possible. In 1900 more and more influential people began to believe that the government ought to take an active role in ensuring both prosperity and justice, an idea that reached its apogee with the New Deal and shaped American thought and life until the election of 1980. The "Reagan revolution" of the 1980s both reflected and catalyzed a growing belief that the power and influence of the federal government had grown too great. What would arise in its stead was, by century's end, anybody's guess.

As the 1990s drew to a close there was also substantial agreement that such issues as protecting the environment, improving education, reforming the health care system, streamlining government, and restoring the nation's crumbling infrastructure should be given high priority. Little consensus existed about solutions to any of these important problems, however, and attempts to achieve consensus were complicated by continuing social conflicts. Americans had difficulty coming to terms with the wide differences in wealth and power in their diverse society. Racial animosities, differences between ethnic groups, and the ongoing struggle for equality between women and men left a large gap between the social harmony Americans desired and the reality they experienced. Politicians, preoccupied with raising money to finance ever more expensive campaigns, were often afraid of alienating influential supporters by taking on tough questions. As a result, the American public became increasingly disenchanted with politics.

By 1996 a longing for the comforts of community vied with a new spirit of self-absorption in Americans' hearts and minds. Middle-class and working-class people seemed to support the politicians' retreat from the government's commitment to support the nation's poorest people and to turn a blind eye to the continued lucrative tax breaks and subsidies for large corporations. But they cheered their favorite sports teams and sat riveted as national dramas unfolded on television, and millions found new fellowship by joining religious congregations. In a nation founded on immigration, many favored barring entry to new immigrants who might take jobs away from those already here, but immigrants continued to journey to the United States to found new communities in a volatile land. Conservatives like Newt Gingrich argued that in America individuals could and should fend for themselves: whatever severe discrimination some Americans had faced in the past on account of their race, sex, or social class, history was no longer a reason to believe that anyone deserved extra help. President Clinton insisted that education, rather than direct subsidies, would provide the answers to the nation's social problems. What was to come, after the withdrawal of the helping hand, remained to be seen.

Americans knew they were moving into an uncertain future, but the nation seemed to have weathered at least the first stages of the latest global transformation. The economy was robust. The country's leaders insisted that they would put aside partisan bickering and get down to doing the people's business. Over the course of a turbulent, often violent century, human ingenuity had cured diseases once epidemic, made possible instant worldwide communication, and, at least at times, fed the hungry and housed the homeless. Anything, it seemed, might happen, given the will and the imagination. But nothing was guaranteed. The currents of change ran deep and unpredictable at a time when a town could come into being in a year, a person could travel from New Delhi to New York in a day, and a word could go around the world in a heartbeat.

✦ Further Reading

On American society, see: Sam Roberts, *Who We Are: A Portrait of America Based on the Latest U.S. Census* (1993). On cities and suburbanization, see: Carl Abbott, *The Metropolitan Frontier: Cities in the Modern American West* (1994); Mike Davis, *City of Quartz: Excavating the Future in Los Angeles* (1992). On politics, see: Tom Rosenstiel, *Strange Bedfellows: How Television and the Presidential Candidates Changed Politics, 1992* (1994). On the consequences of atomic energy, see: Tad Bartimus and Scott McCartney, *Trinity's Children: Living Along America's Nuclear Highway* (1993). On economic and social policy, see: David Halberstam, *The Next Century* (1991); Robert Reich, *The Work of Nations: Preparing Ourselves for Twenty-first Century Capitalism* (1991); William Julius Wilson, *The Truly Disadvantaged: The Inner City, the Underclass, and Public Policy* (1987). On the Clinton administration's economic policy, see: Bob Woodward, *The Agenda* (1993). On race relations, see: Cornel West, *Race Matters* (1994). Until books on recent events appear, consult the major journals of public affairs: *The Atlantic, Dissent, Harper's, The Nation, The New York Review of Books, The New Republic, The National Review, The Public Interest.* Newsweeklies also contain useful information and interpretations. See *Business Week, The Economist* (London), *Newsweek, Time,* and *U.S. News and World Report.*

INDEX